Geoffrey Phelps

D1547099

DESIGNING TEACHER EVALUATION SYSTEMS

DESIGNING TEACHER EVALUATION SYSTEMS

New Guidance from the Measures of Effective Teaching Project

THOMAS J. KANE
KERRI A. KERR
ROBERT C. PIANTA
EDITORS

JB JOSSEY-BASS™
A Wiley Brand

Cover design by Adrian Morgan
Cover image : © Mehmet Yunas Yeil/Getty
Copyright © 2014 by John Wiley & Sons, Inc. All rights reserved.

Published by Jossey-Bass
A Wiley Brand
One Montgomery Street, Suite 1200, San Francisco, CA 94104-4594—www.josseybass.com

Jossey-Bass books and products are available through most bookstores. To contact Jossey-Bass directly call our Customer Care Department within the U.S. at 800-956-7739, outside the U.S. at 317-572-3986, or fax 317-572-4002.

Wiley publishes in a variety of print and electronic formats and by print-on-demand. Some material included with standard print versions of this book may not be included in e-books or in print-on-demand. If this book refers to media such as a CD or DVD that is not included in the version you purchased, you may download this material at http://booksupport.wiley.com. For more information about Wiley products, visit www.wiley.com.

Library of Congress Cataloging-in-Publication Data has been applied for and is on file with the Library of Congress.

ISBN 978-1-118-83435-0 (cloth);
ISBN 978-1-118-83718-4 (ebk);
ISBN 978-1-118-83722-1(ebk)

Printed in the United States of America
FIRST EDITION

HB Printing   10 9 8 7 6 5 4 3 2 1

CONTENTS

ABOUT THE EDITORS

Thomas Kane is the Walter H. Gale Professor of Education at the Harvard Graduate School of Education and faculty director of Harvard's Center for Education Policy Research. As a deputy director in the K–12 team at the Bill & Melinda Gates Foundation, he directed the Measures of Effective Teaching project. His work has influenced thinking on a range of topics in K–12 and higher education: from measuring teacher effectiveness, to school accountability in the No Child Left Behind Act, to college financial aid, to charter schools, to race-conscious college admissions and measuring the economic payoff to a community from college education. He has been a faculty member at Harvard's Kennedy School of Government and UCLA's School of Public Affairs, as well as serving as a senior economist in President Clinton's Council of Economic Advisers. He has held visiting fellowships at the Brookings Institution and the Hoover Institution at Stanford University.

Kerri A. Kerr is an education research and policy consultant. Her work focuses on managing the implementation of large-scale research projects, as well as advising organizations on successful data, accountability, and evaluation strategies. She joined the Measures of Effective Teaching project team at the project's inception and supported MET's data collection, analysis, and reporting activities throughout the life of the study. Her prior research focused on school leadership, school transitions, and district-wide scaling of education initiatives. Prior to beginning her career as a consultant, she was a researcher at the RAND Corporation and the chief data and accountability officer at New Leaders for New Schools. A former middle school and high school math teacher, Kerr received a Ph.D. in sociology from Johns Hopkins University.

Robert Pianta is the dean of the Curry School of Education, the Novartis US Foundation Professor of Education at the University of Virginia, and founding director of the Center for Advanced Study of Teaching and Learning (CASTL). Pianta's interests focus on the measurement and production of effective teaching in classrooms from preschool to high school. He has published more than three hundred scholarly papers and books on these topics. Pianta is senior developer of the Classroom Assessment Scoring System, a method for observational assessment of teacher-student interaction used in many large-scale applications, and is developer of MyTeachingPartner, a web-based coaching and video professional development program. He consults with foundations and with state and federal agencies.

ABOUT THE CONTRIBUTORS

Jeff Archer is a communications consultant specializing in school improvement issues. Previously he covered the teaching profession and school leadership for *Education Week* and documented school improvement practices for the Effective Practice Incentive Community (EPIC), an online knowledge system created by New Leaders for New Schools. For the MET project, Archer helped direct the project's communication to practitioners.

Courtney A. Bell is a senior research scientist in Educational Testing Service's Understanding Teaching Quality Center. She completed her doctorate at Michigan State University in curriculum, teaching, and educational policy after earning her B.A. in chemistry at Dartmouth College. A former high school science teacher and teacher educator, Bell's work focuses on the measurement of teaching and the intersections of policy and practice.

Lindsay Brown is a Ph.D. candidate in curriculum and teacher education at the Stanford Graduate School of Education. She is also an Institute of Education Sciences (IES) fellow, focusing on issues in teacher quality, teacher performance assessment, and professional development. Before joining the Stanford GSE, she worked as a middle school teacher.

Jing Chen is a research project manager at Educational Testing Service. She received her dual Ph.D. degrees in measurement and quantitative methods and in science education from Michigan State University. Her research interests include human and automated constructed response scoring, test development, test equating, standard setting, and learning progression–based assessments.

Julie Cohen is a post-doctoral fellow at the Center to Support Excellence in Teaching at Stanford University. Beginning in 2014, she will be an assistant professor of curriculum, instruction, and special education at the University of Virginia. Her research focuses on the features of high-quality teaching that cut across content areas and explores how grade level, school settings, and instructional content serve as important contexts for understanding teacher and teaching quality.

Andrew J. Croft is a research associate at the Educational Testing Service. He has provided research support to various projects on teaching quality, educational policy, and the evaluation of teaching. His research interests are teacher preparation, history of education, and teaching and learning in higher education. He received his master's degree in higher and postsecondary education from Teachers College, Columbia University, in 2011.

Charlotte Danielson, a former economist, is an internationally recognized expert in the area of teacher effectiveness, specializing in the design of teacher evaluation systems that, while ensuring teacher quality, also promote professional learning. She advises state education departments and national ministries and departments of education, both in the United States and overseas. She is in demand as a keynote speaker at national and international conferences and as a policy consultant to legislatures and administrative bodies.

John R. Donoghue is a psychometrician and statistical software developer, and co-owner of ClowderConsulting. He has spent more than twenty years in the testing industry, researching statistical models and creating software for practical implementation. Donoghue received his Ph.D. in quantitative psychology from the University of Southern California. His publications range across IRT, cluster analysis, and multiple comparisons.

Ronald F. Ferguson is the creator of the Tripod Project for School Improvement, the faculty co-chair and director of the Achievement Gap Initiative (AGI) at Harvard University, and faculty co-director of the Pathways to Prosperity Project at the Harvard Graduate School of Education. He has taught at Harvard since 1983. His most recent book is *Toward Excellence with Equity: An Emerging Vision for Closing the Achievement Gap*, published by Harvard Education Press.

Drew H. Gitomer is the Rose and Nicholas DeMarzo Chair in the Graduate School of Education at Rutgers University. His research centers on the assessment and evaluation of teaching and related policy issues in teaching and teacher education. Prior to coming to Rutgers, Gitomer was a researcher and senior vice president of research at Educational Testing Service in Princeton, New Jersey, where he led the Understanding Teaching Quality Center.

Pam Grossman is the Nomellini-Olivier Professor of Education at the Stanford University School of Education. She has published broadly in the areas of teacher education and professional education, teacher knowledge, and the teaching of English in secondary schools. She is a member of the National Academy of Education and currently serves as the faculty director of the Center to Support Excellence in Teaching at Stanford.

Christopher A. Hafen is a research scientist at the University of Virginia's Center for Advanced Study of Teaching and Learning and the managing director for the professional development intervention MyTeachingPartner-Secondary. His research interests include understanding the function and development of close relationships in adolescence, with a particular interest in the ways in which contexts drive changes in close relationships over time.

Bridget K. Hamre is an associate research professor and associate director of the University of Virginia's Center for Advanced Study of Teaching and Learning. Hamre's areas of expertise include student-teacher relationships and classroom processes that promote positive academic and social development for children. She has also collaborated in the development and testing of several innovative professional development models to support teachers in improving their classroom practices.

Eric Hirsch is the chief external affairs officer for the New Teacher Center, a non-profit dedicated to improving student learning. Hirsch has served as executive director of the Center for Teaching Quality and as education program manager at the National Conference of State Legislatures. He has led fifty statewide and district teaching conditions initiatives over the past decade, collecting more than 1,000,000 educator surveys. Hirsch has worked with and testified to legislatures and policymakers in thirty-five states; authored more than one hundred articles, reports, book chapters and policy briefs; and presented at numerous conferences about issues of educator quality and effectiveness.

Steven L. Holtzman is a research data analyst in the Data Analysis and Research Technologies group at the Educational Testing Service (ETS). He has served as a research lead on the MET video scoring project as well as several other smaller grants under the MET project. His work at ETS concentrates on the use of a wide variety of data analysis methods to help foster research in many areas of education.

Heather Howell holds a Ph.D. in mathematics education from New York University. She works primarily on research about content knowledge for secondary mathematics teaching. She has taught mathematics in grades 9 through 12 and at the undergraduate level and has worked with pre-service and in-service secondary teachers. Howell is currently a senior research associate in the Understanding Teaching Quality center at Educational Testing Service.

Marshall Jean is a doctoral student in the Department of Sociology at the University of Chicago. As an Institute of Education Sciences Pre-Doctoral Fellow, his research has focused on the application of quantitative analysis to primary and secondary education data. His research interests include homogeneous ability grouping and tracking, the organization of schools, education policy, and how education mediates inequalities in social outcomes.

Jilliam N. Joe is a senior research project manager in the Teaching, Learning, and Cognitive Sciences group at Educational Testing Service. Joe provided psychometric and design support for the MET video scoring project and currently provides research and implementation direction for the Teachscape Focus observer training and certification system. Recently, she co-authored the Gates Foundation's "Foundations of Observation" paper. Joe received her Ph.D. in assessment and measurement from James Madison University.

Dawn Leusner is a research project manager in the Educational Testing Service's (ETS) R&D division, located in Princeton, New Jersey. With more than twenty years of research experience, she holds a master of arts degree in curriculum, instruction, and supervision from Rider University. She also manages the company's institutional review board and is a liaison between ETS and the federal government.

Michael Marder is a professor of physics at The University of Texas at Austin. His research specialty is the physics of brittle fracture. He is executive director of the UTeach Science Program and oversees the preparation of science and mathematics teachers at UT Austin, as well as programs with more than six thousand students at over thirty other universities across the United States that have adopted the UTeach model.

Daniel F. McCaffrey is a principal research scientist at Educational Testing Service. His research focuses on measures of teaching and teacher evaluation, in particular, estimation of teacher value added from student achievement tests. He is also working on methods for conducting causal inference from observational data, with a particular focus on propensity score estimation and weighting when observed covariates are measured with error.

Catherine A. McClellan co-owns Clowder Consulting, providing services in psychometrics, teacher observation, and observer training. On the MET study, she was responsible for the design and implementation of the video scoring of the classroom sessions and the quality of the resulting data. Her research interests include how humans score complex responses; optimal scoring designs; and monitoring data quality. McClellan received her Ph.D. from the University of Florida.

Kata Mihaly is an economist at the RAND Corporation. Her research is focused on the use of multiple measures to evaluate teachers and preparation programs. Mihaly's work examines how value-added model specifications impact the rankings of teacher preparation programs and how statistical methods can be used for combining multiple measures to evaluate teachers. She has been invited to participate in technical panels on teacher and preparation program evaluation.

Yoon Soo Park is an assistant professor at the University of Illinois at Chicago. He holds a Ph.D. in measurement, evaluation, and statistics from Columbia

University. Park's research focuses on the development of psychometric models to study rater behavior in performance-based assessments and diagnosis of skills mastery. He also conducts applied measurement research in medicine and in public health.

Raymond L. Pecheone is a professor of practice at the Graduate School of Education at Stanford University and founder and executive director of the Stanford Center for Assessment, Learning, and Equity (SCALE). Pecheone has been a leader in high stakes educational reform through assessment, spearheading research and policy work that shape district and state policies in curriculum and assessment by building broad-based grassroots support for strategic new approaches.

Geoffrey Phelps is a research scientist in the Understanding Teaching Quality Center at the Educational Testing Service (ETS). Prior to joining ETS in 2010, Phelps was an assistant research scientist at the University of Michigan, where he studied the relation between teaching practice and teacher knowledge in the elementary subjects of mathematics and English language arts. His interests in teaching quality, teacher development, and school improvement stem from his eight years teaching primary grades in Vermont. Phelps received a Ph.D. in teacher education from the University of Michigan.

Morgan S. Polikoff is an assistant professor of education policy at the University of Southern California Rossier School of Education. His research is in two primary areas: (1) the ways content standards are implemented in the classroom and the influence of textbooks and assessments on implementation and (2) improving the design of teacher and school accountability policies.

Yi Qi is a research associate at the Educational Testing Service and holds a master's degree in educational administration. Qi's research interests are policy and evaluation issues related to teacher education and how best to measure teaching practice. She has worked on large scale studies on using classroom observation protocols, along with other measures to evaluate teaching quality.

Stephen W. Raudenbush is the Lewis-Sebring Distinguished Service Professor, Department of Sociology, Harris School of Public Policy, and the college, and chair of the Committee on Education at the University of Chicago. His primary interest is in developing and applying quantitative methods for studying child and youth development within the settings of classrooms, schools, and neighborhoods. He is best known for his work on formulating and applying hierarchical linear models in education and social science. He is a member of the National Academy of Sciences and the American Academy of Arts and Sciences.

Erik A. Ruzek is a postdoctoral researcher at the University of Virginia's Center for Advanced Study of Teaching and Learning. He studies connections between the observed quality of teachers' interactions with students; student perceptions of classroom environments; and student learning and motivation. While primarily investigating middle and high school contexts, Ruzek also conducts research with colleagues on the role of early childhood education on early development and school readiness.

Susan E. Schultz is director of teaching, learning, and assessment at the Stanford Center for Assessment, Learning, and Equity and an instructor in the Stanford Teacher Education Program (STEP). Her current research focuses on teacher education, student learning during groupwork interactions, and designing science performance assessments to evaluate student and teacher knowledge. She developed the Quality Science Teaching (QST) observation instrument and recently received a National Science Foundation grant to modify QST to be used as a formative tool with elementary teachers. She completed her Ph.D. in science curriculum and instruction at Stanford University and is a former high school science teacher.

Douglas O. Staiger is the John French Professor in Economics at Dartmouth College and a research associate at the National Bureau of Economic Research in Cambridge, Massachusetts. He received his B.A. from Williams College and his Ph.D. in economics from MIT. Before joining Dartmouth, he was a faculty member at Stanford and at Harvard. His research interests include the economics of education, economics of healthcare, and statistical methods.

Candace Walkington is an assistant professor of mathematics education in the Simmons School of Education and Human Development at Southern Methodist University. Her research examines ways to engage students in mathematics learning by connecting instruction to their lives, interests, and experiences. She teaches courses for pre-service and in-service teachers that focus on discovery learning and mathematics problem solving.

Barbara H. Weren is a lead research project manager in the Understanding Teaching Quality (UTQ) Center of the Research Division of Educational Testing Service. Her work focuses on teacher knowledge, in particular the development of measures of content knowledge for teaching mathematics, English language arts, and science. Prior to joining the UTQ Center, Weren worked in mathematics and teacher licensure assessment development.

ABOUT THE BILL & MELINDA GATES FOUNDATION

Guided by the belief that every life has equal value, the Bill & Melinda Gates Foundation works to help all people lead healthy, productive lives. In developing countries, it focuses on improving people's health with vaccines and other life-saving tools and giving them the chance to lift themselves out of hunger and extreme poverty. In the United States, it seeks to significantly improve education so that all young people have the opportunity to reach their full potential. Based in Seattle, Washington, the foundation is led by CEO Jeff Raikes and co-chair William H. Gates, Sr., under the direction of Bill and Melinda Gates and Warren Buffett.

BILL *&* MELINDA
GATES *foundation*

DESIGNING TEACHER EVALUATION SYSTEMS

CHAPTER

Why Measure Effective Teaching?

JEFF ARCHER, KERRI A. KERR, AND ROBERT C. PIANTA

Real improvement requires quality measurement. Without stepping on the bathroom scale once or twice a week, we have little hope of knowing whether our efforts at diet and exercise are moving us in the right direction. To be sure, that information alone may not be enough to truly drive different action and, therefore, improved results. We need feedback on our efforts and guidance about what we're doing well and what to do differently. But the number on the scale is a necessary starting place. The same goes for efforts to improve teaching. Teaching and learning will not improve if we fail to give teachers high-quality feedback based on accurate assessments of their instruction as measured against clear standards for what is known to be effective. Without quality measurement of effective teaching, school administrators are left blind when making critical personnel and assignment decisions in an effort to achieve the goal of college readiness for all students. Lacking good data on teaching effectiveness, system leaders are at a loss when assessing the return on professional development dollars.

But measuring teaching is hard. Teaching is a complex interaction among teachers, students, and content that no single measurement tool is likely to capture. The list of things teachers do that may have a significant impact on student learning is extensive. Ensuring accuracy in the face of such complexity poses a major challenge to the design and implementation of tools for measuring effective teaching. Ultimately, real people (teachers, principals, and other evaluators) must be able to make sense of the data to produce actionable improvement plans and to make defensible personnel decisions.

Underlying all these challenges is the fundamental question of validity: To what extent can these measures point toward teaching that leads to the student outcomes we desire? Feedback and evaluation are an exercise in futility if they don't increase the chances that students will learn, grow, and ultimately lead healthy, productive lives.

The research in this book tackles these important and difficult issues through rigorous analysis of an unparalleled collection of data. Between 2009 and 2012, with support from the Bill & Melinda Gates Foundation, the Measures of Effective Teaching (MET) project worked with some three thousand teachers in six urban districts to collect a host of information on the classrooms of roughly 100,000 students. That information included a large array of measures, most notably student survey responses, ratings by trained observers using multiple classroom observation instruments to score lesson videos, and student achievement on state tests and on more cognitively challenging assessments. In one of the most groundbreaking aspects of the project, teachers agreed to have students assigned to them randomly so that analysts could tease out the possible impact of typical student assignment patterns on teachers' effectiveness ratings.

DRIVEN BY THE NEEDS OF PRACTITIONERS

Data collection for the MET project represented a massive engineering feat accomplished by more than two dozen academic and organizational partners, many of whom contributed to this volume. Partners created new instruments, adapted existing ones for large-scale use, and developed new technologies and evaluator training systems. These tools have since informed the design of feedback and evaluation systems in the field to a significant degree. This transfer from research to practice was by design. From the beginning, the intent was to produce evidence-based insights that could be applied in states and districts. The pressing questions of practitioners determined study design:

- How reliable are the measures?

- What does it take to implement them well?

- What is their informational value?

This starting point contrasts with that of typical education studies, which often begin with the questions that can be asked of an existing data set.

In another break from typical large-scale research, the MET project moved fast. Analysis and reporting took months, not years. Analysts released findings on a rolling basis after each major phase of data collection. Pre-publication vetting by academics and practitioners took place at lightning speed, compared with normal peer review processes. The pace was in response to the realities faced by states and districts, not the least of which are the policy requirements for teacher evaluation in the federal Race to the Top initiative and, more recently, those called for among states seeking waivers from certain mandates in the No Child Left Behind Act. While this unprecedented national focus on teaching represents a tremendous opportunity to support better outcomes for students, the lack of evidence-based guidance on teacher evaluation posed a real risk to success if not addressed quickly.

The first wave of findings from the MET project came in a series of reports released between 2010 and 2013. These contributed several key understandings about measuring effective teaching. We found that a well-designed student perception survey can provide reliable feedback on aspects of teaching practice that are predictive of student learning.[1] We discovered that an accurate observation rating requires two or more observations by at least two trained and certified observers.[2] Perhaps most significantly, the MET project's random assignment analysis confirmed that a combination of well-administered measures can, in fact, identify teachers who cause students to learn more.[3] At the same time, a generally balanced set of different measures was seen to produce more stable results and a better indication of student learning on a range of assessments than one that gives a preponderance of weight to a single measure.[4]

SCALING UP RESEARCH CAPACITY

This book represents the second wave of analysis from the MET project and the recognition that the first wave, while groundbreaking, was only the starting point for learning from the rich and complex data set compiled over the course of the project. Thus far, analyses have for the most part been carried out sequentially by a core group of researchers working in consultation with the broader set of MET project partners. But from early on, architects of the MET project intended for a much broader set of questions to be answered by a larger group of research experts. To generate knowledge at a sufficient pace and ensure the collection of data is used to its full potential, multiple teams of researchers must be working on different analyses simultaneously. What binds that work is that it continues to make use of the data collected from the classrooms of the MET project teachers, as well as the commitment to produce findings that can inform the work of states and districts in promoting effective teaching.

No one knows the MET project data better than the experts whose work is presented in these pages. They are the analysts and instrument developers who designed, built, and managed the MET project's extensive data-collection systems. For the research in this book, they organized themselves into teams around questions of mutual interest posed by state and district system leaders, in some cases resulting in cross-fertilization of expertise that might have been unlikely prior to the MET project's emphasis on multiple measures. Teams relied on each other as thought partners and peer reviewers at multiple points as they moved from the definition of research questions to study design to analysis and the presentation of findings. The result of this scaling-up approach is that, instead of producing just one new analysis, the MET project partners have produced fifteen pieces of original analysis for this volume.

This new body of research falls under three broad themes, which provide the book its overarching organization. Chapters in the first section address questions related to the use of data for feedback and evaluation, such as how to interpret volatility of results. In the second section, the researchers examine the interactions between multiple measures and their contexts, including the interplay between measures of teaching practice and measures of student learning. The last section treats individual measures on their own terms, illuminating and testing their underlying frameworks and exploring key design decisions related to their administration. Each chapter was written to include enough quantitative discussion to satisfy researchers and enough description of practice and discussion of implications to help policymakers and practitioners see the relevance of their work.

NEW CHALLENGES, ENDURING OBJECTIVES

The scaling up of research capacity brought to bear on the MET project data enters a third, and particularly exciting, phase as this book goes to press. All of the MET project data have been moved to the Inter-University Consortium for Political and Social Research, housed at the University of Michigan. There, it is being made available to researchers far and wide through a secure, online platform. For the first time, experts not involved in the MET project's design and data collection have access to its thousands of videos, observation scores, student survey responses, student achievement gain measures, and other measures. This longitudinal database maintains teachers' confidentiality by not providing identification information but nonetheless allows for linking all results from the same classroom. The hope is that this book provides inspiration for this new generation of MET project researchers.

As readers ponder where to take the next level of inquiry, they should keep in mind the ultimate objective of closing the gap between teaching as it currently exists in our nation's classrooms and teaching as it needs to be to maximize every student's chances of graduating high school equipped to succeed in college and beyond. To be sure, sizing up that gap is challenging at a time when the field's understanding of college and career readiness is just now coalescing with the implementation of the Common Core State Standards. But the fact of that coalescing only makes quality measurement of teaching more relevant and promising. The habits of inquiry modeled by the MET project are meant to support the best use of measurement to promote effective teaching. Measures will evolve, as does our understanding of student learning needs, but the commitment to quality measurement must endure.

NOTES

1. *Learning about teaching: Initial findings from the measures of effective teaching project.* (2010). Seattle, WA: Bill & Melinda Gates Foundation.

2. Kane, T. J., & Staiger, D. O. (2012). *Gathering feedback for teaching: Combining high-quality observations with student surveys and achievement gains.* Seattle, WA: Bill & Melinda Gates Foundation.

3. Kane, T. J., McCaffrey, D. F., Miller, T., & Staiger, D. O. (2013). *Have we identified effective teachers? Validating measures of effective teaching using random assignment.* Seattle, WA: Bill & Melinda Gates Foundation.

4. Mihaly, K., McCaffrey, D. F., Staiger, D. O., & Lockwood, J. R. (2013). *A composite estimator of effective teaching.* Seattle, WA: Bill & Melinda Gates Foundation.

SECTION

USING DATA FOR FEEDBACK AND EVALUATION

CHAPTER

Grade-Level Variation in Observational Measures of Teacher Effectiveness

KATA MIHALY AND DANIEL F. MCCAFFREY

ABSTRACT

States are rapidly developing new teacher evaluation systems built around measures of student achievement growth and classroom observations using research-based protocol. An important consideration for states and districts is whether equally effective teaching receives the same score on the observation protocol regardless of the classroom context. Of particular concern are potential differences in the functioning of the protocol for teachers at different grade levels, since there are clear differences in expectations for classroom interactions as students mature, and there is evidence that teaching practice differs across grade levels. Using data from the Measure of Effective Teaching (MET) Project, we tested for grade-level differences in the average scores on three research-based observation protocols for grades 4 to 8 math and English language arts (ELA) teachers. We find large differences between scores among teachers in different grade levels that could not be explained by differences in the teacher characteristics, student characteristics, or raters.

INTRODUCTION

In the last three years, states and districts have rapidly developed and adopted new teacher evaluation systems. One key component of these revised evaluation systems is the use of formal observations of teaching practice. According to the National Council on Teacher Quality, thirty-nine states now require annual observations of classroom instruction, and twenty-two of those states require multiple classroom observations each year. The observation instrument scores count for as much as 50 percent of the combined teacher effectiveness ratings in many states (e.g., Pennsylvania, Tennessee, South Dakota). For grades and subjects that are untested, classroom observation accounts for an even larger proportion of the teacher effectiveness score. This focus is justified. Studies have found that observation scores are predictive of student achievement gains (Grossman, Loeb, Cohen, Hammerness, Wyckoff, Boyd, & Lankford, 2010; Jacob & Lefgren, 2008; Kane & Staiger, 2012; Rockoff & Speroni, 2010; Tyler, Taylor, Kane, & Wooten, 2010). Observation scores provide teachers with feedback that can be incorporated into future practice, and teacher performance does improve in response to evaluation (Taylor & Tyler, 2012). Observation scores may be deciding factors in tenure and bonus decisions. For these reasons, it is critical to document and understand whether and how observation scores vary across classrooms, schools, and teachers.

An important consideration for states and districts implementing teacher evaluation systems is whether teachers in different grades can be compared with one another. There is evidence from an earlier generation of observation instruments and teacher surveys that teacher practice differs across grade levels (Vartuli, 1999). It also has been shown that elementary school teachers receive higher ratings from principals than middle school teachers do (Harris & Sass, 2009). However, principal ratings in elementary school are better predictors of student achievement gains than ratings in middle school are (Harris & Sass, 2009; Jacob & Lefgren, 2008), and formal observation ratings of elementary school teachers are better predictors of student achievement gains than ratings of middle school teachers are (Tyler, Taylor, Kane, & Wooten, 2010).

In most states and districts, observation scores are not adjusted for grade-level differences before these scores are used in teacher effectiveness calculations. A tacit assumption underlying the use of unadjusted scores is that observation results are comparable across grade levels and that any difference in observation scores reflects true differences in teaching quality across grades. Moreover, the use of unadjusted scores assumes that the differences in teaching quality that are observed are attributable to teachers alone, rather than the context of the school or classrooms. However, these assumptions have not yet been examined. That examination may have important policy implications. If observation scores reflect true differences in teacher quality, then standardizing observation scores by grade level would not be recommended because it would penalize teachers in lower grades who are objectively better at teaching. However, if contextual factors matter, then the decision to not standardize penalizes middle school teachers and could potentially discourage teachers from teaching these grades.

The purpose of this chapter is to examine grade-level differences in observation scores using data from the Measures of Effective Teaching (MET) study. Among other things, the MET study evaluated video recordings of classroom instruction using multiple observational protocols developed by leading experts in the field. This chapter will focus on the subject-independent scores on Classroom Assessment Scoring System (CLASS) and Framework for Teaching (FfT) protocols, as well as subject-specific scores on the Protocol for Language Arts Teaching Observations (PLATO).[1] Since many of the observational protocols being implemented by states either correspond to one of the MET protocols or contain dimensions and scoring rubrics that have many similarities with the MET protocols, understanding the grade level variation in the MET protocols can inform decisions by districts across the country.

Research Questions

1. *Are there grade-level differences in average observation scores in the MET data?* We document such differences and examine whether they exist in all the participating school districts. We also consider whether grade-level differences show up in all or only some of the dimensions of teaching evaluated by the observation protocols.

2. *Are grade-level differences explained by factors unrelated to teacher quality?* Factors examined include teacher characteristics, classroom composition, rater effects, and school level factors. These factors are further discussed in the following subsection.

3. *Do observation scores predict student achievement gains differently by grade level?* Put another way, are the observation instruments aligned with student test score gains differentially across grades? The differential alignment of observation scores with student test score gains also has implications for how the measures should be used.

We consider the policy implications of our results—specifically, whether observation scores should be standardized by grade level before they are used in teacher effectiveness calculations. By standardizing observation measures, the effectiveness of teachers in the middle grades, as measured in observation scores, will be judged according to a standard different from that for teachers in the lower grades. We discuss the pluses and minuses and consider whether evidence from the analysis supports a particular strategy.

First, however, to furnish some background, we explore in more detail some of the possible explanations for grade-level differences in observation scores. Then we devote some space to our data sources and briefly present our analytic approach.

Potential Explanations for Grade-Level Differences in Observation Scores

The formal observation of teaching practice is a complex process, and observation scores may be influenced by a number of factors. To understand the possible explanations for grade-level differences in observation score, let's consider the formal observation process: a teacher (with certain characteristics, located at a given school) is observed teaching a group of students (with given characteristics) by a rater (with given characteristics) for a period of classroom time and receives a rating on a number of dimensions of their practice. The rater may be located physically in the classroom, or may be watching a video of the classroom interactions.

We consider four potential sources of differences between observation scores of middle school and elementary school teachers.

1. The most straightforward potential explanation is that teachers in elementary and middle school grades are not equally effective.

    a. If differences are related to teacher characteristics that could only affect observation scores through the teacher (e.g., experience, education) or teacher knowledge which are unknown to the rater, this would support the conjecture that teachers are truly differentially effective. Hence, we will test whether differences in observation scores can be accounted for by differences in teacher characteristics.

2. One alternative explanation is that teachers in elementary and middle school grades are equally effective and achieve equal classroom practices and discourse, so their observation scores should be equal, but *rater error or differences in the versions of the protocol yield systematic differences in scores across grade levels*. Rater errors might be related to teacher characteristics, student characteristics, or the raters.

Consequently, we again will test whether differences in observation scores can be explained by differences in teacher or student characteristics between our elementary and middle school samples. We will also test whether the differences can be explained by differences in the raters who conducted the observations of the elementary and middle school teachers. Some protocols use the same version for all grade levels, and others use different versions for elementary and middle school classrooms. If the instrument is the source of any grade-level differences, then they would only occur on the protocol with different instruments at different grade levels.

3. Another alternative explanation is that teachers in middle schools and elementary school grades are equally effective but that the *students differ in ways so that equally effective teachers at different grade levels do not achieve equal classroom practices and discourse*. Scores for the observations would truly be different but they do not represent differences in the effectiveness of teachers. Two possible sources of these grade-level differences in students:

    a. Differences are developmental or environmental and common across all students at different grade levels. For instance, older students are less engaged due to changes in their environment or physiological changes that occur during adolescence, and this is being picked up by observation score differences. We do not have data to explore this source.

    b. Students in the elementary school classrooms in the MET differ from their counterparts in the middle schools participating in the study due to the selection of schools for the study. These differences might manifest in observable differences in student demographics or other factors that we can test by controlling for those differences. The differences in the students might not be observable characteristics. In this case comparing teachers at different grade levels within a school will allow us to explore how much school differences are contributing to any differences we see in scores across grade levels.

4. The final explanation we consider is that teachers in elementary and middle school grades are equally effective, but the *practices and discourse that are effective at different grade levels align differently with the protocol*. For instance, the practices that score high on the protocol might

work well in elementary school grades but not in middle school grades, so teachers in upper grades do not use the practices that lead to high observation scores. Their scores on the protocol would be different, but that does not mean that teachers are differentially effective. If this is true, we might expect the relationship between protocol scores and value-added to be different across grade levels.

WHERE WE FIND OUR DATA

As indicated above, we are concerned with whether observation scores vary across grade levels and, when they do, we are concerned with what explains those variations. We resolve these issues by estimating equations (regressions) relating differences in observation scores to differences in potential explanatory factors. We thus need data on both observation scores and explanatory variables. In this section, we discuss where we find those data.

Observation Scores

We use data from the MET project to understand grade-level differences in observation instrument scores. The MET project is a multi-year study of teaching performance measures supported by the Bill & Melinda Gates Foundation in six large school systems. The study collected information about three thousand teachers in grades 4 through 9 from multiple sources, including student achievement gains, classroom observations, student perceptions of the classroom instructional environment, teacher content knowledge, and surveys of teacher working conditions. The analysis in this chapter is restricted to three of the six districts (New York City; Charlotte, North Carolina; and Hillsborough, Florida). The remaining districts in the MET study (Dallas, Denver, and Memphis) did not have enough teachers participating in every grade to be included in the analysis.

In this chapter we examine teacher observation instrument scores. Teachers in the MET study arranged to have themselves recorded by a panoramic digital video camera four times over the course of a year teaching mathematics or English and language arts (ELA); self-contained classroom teachers were recorded a total of eight times.[2] These videos were then scored by trained raters using a number of observation instruments. In this chapter we focus on three of those instruments: the Classroom Assessment Scoring System (CLASS), developed by Robert Pianta and Bridget Hamre at the University of Virginia; the Framework for Teaching (FfT), developed by Charlotte Danielson (2007); and the Protocol for Language Arts Teaching Observations (PLATO), developed by Pamela Grossman at Stanford University.

These observation instruments share a number of features. Based on literature reviews, expert opinion, and empirical evidence, they divide teaching and learning into discrete aspects of practice (referred to as "dimensions"), and they categorize each dimension into four to seven performance levels. Dimensions can be aggregated into larger categories referred to as "domains." The instruments are designed for making expert inferences about the quality of particular aspects of the teaching observed, as opposed to simply checking for whether certain practices are present. For a more detailed review of the instrument content, please see Kane and Staiger (2011).

CLASS focuses on interactions between students and teachers as the primary mechanism of student learning. The assessment covers all subjects, and it is subdivided into eleven dimensions from three domains of interactions: "emotional support," "classroom organization," and "instructional support," plus a separate domain of "student engagement." The instrument is scored on a 7-point scale.

FfT is grounded in a "constructivist" view of student learning, that is, one with emphasis on intellectual engagement, and it also covers all subjects. The original instrument is divided into four domains, but two of these domains ("planning and preparation" and "professional responsibilities") could not be observed in the videos and were not scored for the MET project. The remaining two domains are subdivided into eight dimensions and are scored on a 4-point scale.

PLATO pertains only to ELA teachers. The instrument emphasizes instructional scaffolding through teacher modeling, explicit teaching of ELA strategies, and guided practice. The MET study implemented a revised version of the original instrument, with six out of the thirteen possible dimensions scored by raters. PLATO is also scored on a 4-point scale.

One of the explanations for grade-level differences in observation scores that was discussed in the previous section relates to the use of the same or different versions of the observation instrument for elementary and middle school teachers. For CLASS, the MET project implemented the "upper elementary" version in grades 4 through 6 and the "secondary" version in grades 7 and 8. MET researchers compared the items on the two versions of the CLASS instrument and found only minimal differences.[3] The same version of the FfT and PLATO were implemented in grades 4 through 8.

For each observation instrument, we construct a "score" by averaging the ratings from the individual dimensions for a particular video recording of a class taught by the teacher.[4] When a video is rated by different raters, we average the scores across the raters. Scores are calculated for FfT and CLASS separately by subject; PLATO pertains only to ELA.[5,6]

Data on Potential Factors Affecting Observation Scores

As mentioned above, classroom composition is a factor that may be a source of differences in observation scores across grade levels, even if there are no differences in teacher quality. Classroom information collected by the MET study includes prior-year state achievement test scores, which are standardized by district, subject, and grade level. Classroom composition also includes data from administrative files on student demographic characteristics—race, ethnicity, gender, eligibility for free or reduced-price lunches, special education status, and age of the student relative to others in the same grade. Finally, we augment these data with more detailed background information collected by the MET study during the administration of the student perception Tripod survey.[7] The surveys collected information about whether the student read a book at home every night, whether the student did homework every night, the presence of a computer in the home, and information about whether the student lives in a single-parent home or is in a nuclear family with more than six people.

Average classroom composition measures are listed in Table 2.1 by subject. About 50 percent of students are male, and a large proportion of students are minorities.[8] Over 40 percent of the student sample was eligible for free or reduced-price lunches. Only approximately 5 percent of students report not owning a computer or not doing homework every night in math classes (with slightly more students not doing homework in ELA classes), and 14 percent of students are in single-parent homes. Because the test scores are standardized, their averages are close to 0, as expected. Similarly, the average relative age is zero because relative age equals the difference between the student's age in years and the average age for all students at his or her grade-level.

TABLE 2.1. **Classroom Composition Summary Statistics**

	MATH	ELA
Male	50.1%	49.9%
Black	24.3%	23.5%
Asian	7.6%	8.3%
Other Race	4.4%	4.3%
Hispanic	26.7%	25.2%
Free or Reduced-Price Lunch	42.3%	42.2%
Special Education	9.4%	8.8%
Don't Read at Home	16.9%	15.3%
Don't Do Homework	5.5%	7.4%
No Computer at Home	5.8%	5.5%
Single-Parent Home	14.0%	13.8%
Large Family	19.3%	18.6%
Prior-Year Test Score	−0.0	0.1
Class Size	23.2	23.2
Relative Age (Years)	0.0	0.0

Note: Standard deviations available upon request.

Teacher characteristics may also be a source of grade-level differences. Our information about teacher characteristics includes gender, race, ethnicity, experience, whether the teacher obtained a master's degree, and the score the teacher received on the content knowledge test (CKT) developed for the MET project.[9] Table 2.2 displays the summary statistics for teacher characteristics by subject.[10] Twenty-four percent of math teachers and 15 percent of ELA teachers were male, and 22 percent (17 percent) of math (ELA) teachers are black. Most teachers have four or more years of experience, and 22 percent (20 percent) of teachers have a master's degree in the subject they teach.[11] The average Content Knowledge score is 46 (47) for math (ELA) teachers, scored out of 100 points.

In some of the analyses, we also used data from student perception surveys and student achievement gains for state tests and for alternative tests administered by the MET project. The confidential student perception surveys were administered in each teacher's class using the Tripod survey instrument. The Tripod questions are gathered under seven headings, or constructs, called the Seven Cs: Care, Control, Clarify, Challenge, Captivate, Confer, and Consolidate. Each of the Cs is measured using multiple survey items.[12] For

TABLE 2.2. Teacher Characteristics Summary Statistics by Subject

	MATH	ELA
Male	23.8%	14.6%
Black	22.4%	17.0%
Hispanic	5.5%	6.4%
Other Race	2.8%	1.5%
0 Years' Experience	1.3%	1.5%
1 Year Experience	5.9%	1.1%
2 Years' Experience	6.2%	6.8%
3 Years' Experience	8.9%	9.6%
Master's Degree	22.3%	19.5%
Content Knowledge	46.1	47.6

Note: Standard deviations available upon request.

the MET project, students in elementary school completed the elementary version of the Tripod survey, and students in middle school completed the middle school version.

The MET project collected data from state test scores and also administered alternative assessments. The alternative assessments included open-ended items and were designed to test higher-order thinking. Students in math classes took the Balanced Assessment in Mathematics, while students in ELA classes took the SAT 9 Open-Ended Reading assessment. The raw test scores were standardized to have a mean of 0 and a standard deviation of 1 (for each district, subject, year, and grade level). For all test scores, we estimated a statistical model of the current year assessment score, controlling for each student's test score in that subject from the prior year and a set of his or her characteristics (a subset of those in Table 2.1), plus the mean prior test score and mean student characteristics in the course section or class the student attends. From the models we obtained an estimate of the teacher's "value added" score for both the state assessment (SVA) and the alternative assessment (AVA).[13]

HOW WE ANALYZED THE DATA

The goals of this chapter are to document whether teacher observation scores on various instruments differ by grade level and to examine the extent to which the grade-level differences are explained by teacher characteristics, classroom composition, rater effects, and differences between schools. We do this by estimating a number of regressions—equations relating the observation score to a set of explanatory variables, where the coefficient estimated for each variable conveys the strength and directionality of the relationship between that variable and observation scores, holding all others in the regression constant. For a detailed technical explanation of the analysis methodology, see Appendix A.

We began with estimating a regression with grade level as the only explanatory variable, to check whether there was a relationship between observation score and grade level. Then we estimated the same regression, adding additional control variables, such as teacher characteristics, classroom composition characteristics, and school identifiers, to determine the extent to which each of these reduced the strength of the relationship between observation score and grade level.

We also estimated regressions that account for differences among raters in their leniency in applying the observation protocol. We estimated these regressions in two steps: first, we estimated a regression relating observation scores to grade level and a rater indicator for each rater (which equals 1 if the rater scored the video, and 0 otherwise). Then we removed the rater effect (as determined by the rater coefficient) from the predicted observation score for each teacher. The adjusted score was what we used as the dependent variable in the second regression, which examines the relationship between observation scores and grade level.[14]

We also explored whether observation scores predict student achievement gains differentially by grade level. In this analysis we predicted value-added scores of state and alternative assessments as a function of grade level, observation scores from the 2009–2010 school year, and interactions of the observation score with grade indicators, as well as classroom composition and teacher characteristics.

ANSWERS TO THE RESEARCH QUESTIONS

Overall, our analysis shows that, in schools participating in the MET project, middle school teachers score lower on all observation instruments than elementary school teachers do. These differences are not the result of differences in such potential explanatory factors as teacher characteristics, classroom composition, instrument effect, rater effects, or school effects. They also do not reflect any grade-level differences in the relationship between observation scores and standardized student achievement test scores. Before we discuss the policy implications of these results, we first show the detailed analyses supporting these conclusions.

Research Question 1: Are There Grade-Level Differences in Observation Scores?

Figure 2.1 presents the grade-level differences in observation scores for FfT, CLASS, and PLATO in math and ELA.[15] The general trend is clear: teachers in grades 4 and 5 score higher than teachers in grade 6, and grade 6 teachers score higher than teachers in grades 7 and 8.[16] Appendix B displays the distribution of the observation scores by grade level for each observation instrument and subject combination. In addition to the higher mean scores in elementary schools, for all observation instruments the scores for teachers in grades 4 and 5 exhibit less variation than the scores of teachers in grades 6, 7, and 8. Put differently, almost all of the lowest scores observed for any instrument are recorded for middle school teachers.

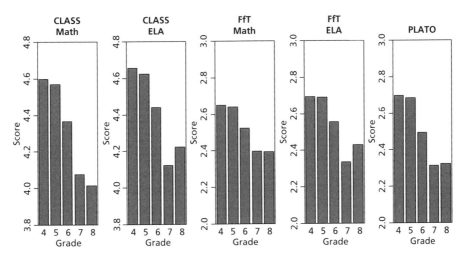

FIGURE 2.1. *MET Observation Scores for Teachers by Grade, All Districts*

The results in Figure 2.1 combine all districts, but combining the sample may mask differences between districts. When we examine the grade-level differences separately for each district in the MET study, the general pattern described above repeats, with higher scores in grades 4 and 5 and the lowest scores in grades 7 and 8. In all districts, the differences between grades tended to be largest for CLASS and smallest for FfT. However, there is some variation in the patterns and, given the small sample of teachers in each district, not all differences are statistically significant. In general, the differences across grades are the largest for teachers in Hillsborough County, Florida, smaller for teachers in New York City and Charlotte, North Carolina.[17]

Most teacher evaluation systems follow the strategy we employ and use the average of dimension scores in creating an overall observation score.[18] A potential problem with averaging is that it may mask differences in how teachers perform on a given dimension. For example, it is possible that students are more difficult to manage in middle school and that the grade-level differences in the average score are being driven by grade-level differences in the dimensions that capture classroom management. We examined the grade-level difference for each dimension score for the five observation instrument–subject combinations in Figure 2.1, and we found that grade-level differences exist in all domains for every instrument, and that these differences are especially large between grades 4 and 7.[19] Thus, it is not the case that middle school teachers are scoring low on a few dimensions of the observation rubric and that this is pulling down the middle school average scores.

Up to this point, we have shown that there are indeed statistically significant grade-level differences in observation instrument scores for all five instrument and subject combinations in the MET data. We also discovered that these differences are observed similarly in every district, and that they are most pronounced in Hillsborough County, Florida. In addition, grade-level differences exist for all dimensions of every instrument we analyzed.

Research Question 2: Do Teacher Characteristics, Classroom Composition, Rater Effects, or Unobserved School Effects Account for Grade-Level Differences?

Here we examine how the results change when potential explanatory variables are added to the analysis. Because the grade-level differences are strongest in Hillsborough County, and because our data for the control variables are the most complete in this district, we restricted the analysis sample to Hillsborough. In Figures 2.2 and 2.3, we display three graphs for math and ELA teachers scored on the CLASS observation rubric. The first shows the observation score difference by grade, unadjusted for any characteristics. The second shows the observation scores by grade, adjusted for the teacher characteristics summarized in Table 2.2. Finally, the last graph shows observation scores by grade level, adjusted with teacher and classroom composition characteristics. The height of the bars shows the average predicted score for a given grade level, and any differences in height indicate that there are differences in the average observation score across grades.

In general, it is apparent that adding teacher or classroom characteristics does not explain grade-level differences in observation scores of math or ELA teachers for the CLASS instrument, because the figures are practically identical across specifications.[20] Now we describe these findings in more detail. Note that while in this section we focus on the CLASS instrument, below we will show that these findings are true for FfT and PLATO as well.

Comparing the first and the second graphs in both figures, there are no noticeable differences between the bars, indicating that adding teacher characteristics to the regression model does not have an impact on grade-level differences in observation scores. To understand these findings we first examined whether there is potential for the teacher characteristics to influence grade-level differences by examining whether teacher characteristics vary by grade.

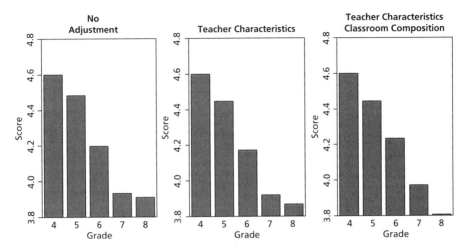

FIGURE 2.2. *Observation Scores by Grade, CLASS Math, Hillsborough County Public Schools*

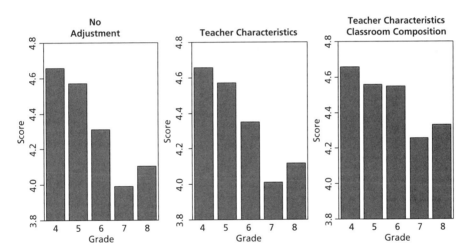

FIGURE 2.3. *Observation Scores by Grade, CLASS ELA, Hillsborough County Public Schools*

We found that in Hillsborough 30 percent of teachers in eighth grade are male, whereas only 13 percent of teachers in fourth grade are male. Similarly, 5 percent of fourth grade teachers in Hillsborough are black, whereas 34 percent of eighth grade teachers are black. There are smaller grade-level differences in experience and master's degree status. Because we found differences in teacher characteristics by grade, there is potential for these characteristics to explain grade-level differences in observation scores.

However, when we included the teacher characteristics in the models, we found that none of the teacher characteristics are systematically associated with observation scores.[21] Among ELA teachers, teachers with three years of experience score higher on CLASS than teachers with four or more years of experience, and a few of the race and ethnicity measures are weakly associated with lower scores. While some of the characteristics are statistically significantly associated with the observation scores, we found no evidence that teachers with particular characteristics receive lower observation scores on every observation rubric, and therefore we have found no evidence that raters are biased against teachers with given characteristics.

Next, we examined whether grade-level differences in observation scores are picking up differences in classroom composition across grades. When we included these measures in the regressions, we found that some classroom composition characteristics are statistically significant and have large effects on the observation score given to the teacher. For example, the prior year test scores of the students in the math classrooms have a strong positive association with observation scores (meaning that teachers with students who score higher on state math achievement tests are rated higher by observers), and the percent of students eligible for free or reduced-price lunches in ELA classrooms is weakly negatively associated with observation scores (so ELA teachers with more low-income students are scored lower by raters). In addition, teachers in classrooms with relatively older students (as compared to the grade-level average) receive higher observation scores. Some of the other characteristics are also statistically significant, but not across multiple observation instruments within a subject or two subjects using the same instrument.[22]

However, when the classroom characteristics are added as controls to our baseline regressions, grade-level differences are unchanged for math teachers, and they are smaller but still statistically significantly different across grades for ELA teachers. While controlling for classroom characteristics accounts for a small portion of grade-level differences, and more so for ELA teachers, it does not explain all of the grade-level differences. At most, the predicted differences in observation scores across grades drop in magnitude by 30 percent.

Next, we turned to the question of whether raters are more lenient for lower grade teachers. To control for this type of leniency bias, we restricted the analysis to those observation protocols in which a rater could rate videos from all five grade levels. FfT and PLATO met this requirement. For these protocols, raters typically observed and rated videos of teachers at all grade levels. Raters scoring CLASS rated either teachers in grades 4 to 6 or grades 7 and 8, but not teachers from both grade ranges. Therefore, we restricted this part of the analysis to observation scores for FfT and PLATO and to ratings that were obtained from raters who provided at least one rating for teachers in every grade level.

In Figures 2.4, 2.5, and 2.6, we display the grade-level differences in observation scores for FfT math, FfT ELA, and PLATO, respectively. These figures include four separate graphs, with the last graph displaying observation score grade-level differences controlling for teacher characteristics, classroom composition, and rater effects.

First we note that the inclusion of teacher characteristics and classroom composition did not impact grade-level differences for FfT or PLATO, similar to the findings discussed above for the CLASS observation rubric. Hence, grade-level differences do not appear to be a result of different versions of the protocol for elementary and middle school classrooms, since the differences appear with all protocols including FfT and PLATO which use a common version of their instrument for all classrooms regardless of grade level.

When we control for rater effects in addition to teacher characteristics and classroom composition we see that the grade-level differences remain relatively unchanged for all three observation instrument and subject combinations. The one exception is FfT ELA ratings, where the height of the bars is closer together, indicating that grade-level differences were reduced (but are still statistically significant). Therefore there is limited evidence of differential rater leniency across grade level in the MET rating scores. Significant differences in scores across grade levels remain, with lower scores for higher-grade classes. Many of the differences are smaller than in models where there are no adjustments, but some remain large relative to the four-point scale and the variance in the scores. The extensive set of controls had little effect on the difference among grade levels for FfT math and PLATO.

In another set of analyses we also considered whether grade-level differences in observation scores were reflecting unobserved differences among schools.[23] These analyses allowed us to control for imbalances across schools in the number of teachers within each grade, and to account for factors such as principal leadership and community environment. To examine whether

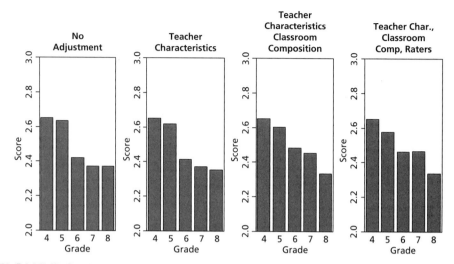

FIGURE 2.4. *Observation Scores by Grade, FfT Math, Hillsborough County Public Schools*

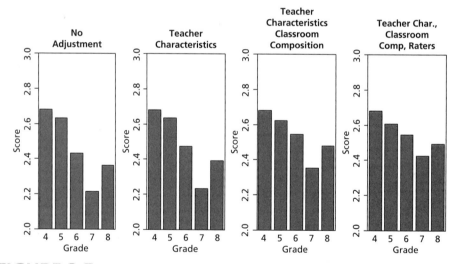

FIGURE 2.5. *Observation Scores by Grade, FfT ELA, Hillsborough County Public Schools*

school factors may be explaining grade-level differences, we estimated regression models that only consider grade-level differences within the same school. Because there were no schools with all five grade levels in the MET sample from Hillsborough, we tested for differences among grades 6, 7, and 8.

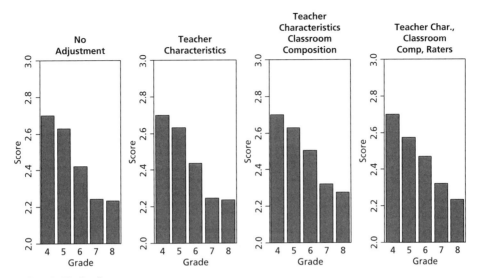

FIGURE 2.6. *Observation Scores by Grade, PLATO, Hillsborough County Public Schools*

We found that significant differences remain between grade 6 and grades 7 and 8, even when we only consider teachers in the same school, especially math teachers.

To summarize, we found that grade-level differences in observation scores are not explained by differences across grades in teacher characteristics, classroom composition, rater leniency, or school factors.

Research Question 3: Do Observation Scores Predict Student Achievement Gains Differently by Grade Level?

Specifically, we wanted to know whether the observation instruments are weaker predictors of student achievement gains in later grades. If teachers in later grades are implementing practices that affect growth on achievement tests, but that are not captured by the instrument, then achievement gains should be more weakly related to observation scores in later grades than in earlier grades.[24]

When we estimated these models, we found no evidence of differences in how well observation scores predict achievement gains across grade levels.[25] These findings hold for predicting both achievement gains on the state-administered test and on the alternative tests administered by the MET study. Therefore, we do not have evidence to support the argument that the instruments are better aligned to measure teacher practice that improves student achievement gains in elementary school than in middle school.

SOME POLICY IMPLICATIONS OF THE RESULTS

We have shown that observation scores for MET teachers differ by grade level. What explains these differences? Not teacher characteristics (experience, education, demographics), classroom composition, or potential rater bias. At most, controlling for these other factors reduces the differences by only about 30 percent. Nor do observation instruments predict achievement test score gains differently in middle school than in elementary. These results are consistent with findings from related studies. Other researchers have found that principal ratings are generally lower for middle school teachers than for elementary teachers, and our analysis of the MET Tripod surveys of students also found lower scores for middle school teachers than for elementary teachers. Given this consistency across contexts and measures, it is unlikely that the results are an artifact of the measurement process. The findings presented here cannot contradict the assertion that teacher and student interactions are of lower quality in middle schools compared to elementary schools.

However, we should not leap to the conclusion that lower observation scores in middle school should be attributed to the teacher. The observation protocols underlying our findings assess classroom activities that involve both teachers and students. Adolescents and elementary school students differ in many ways, and it may be that older students are less engaged due to changes in their environment or physiological changes that occur in the early teenage years. Because the MET study did not collect information on such aspects of student context, we were not able to perform any analyses to examine these questions. All we can say at this point is that either student context or teacher effectiveness appears to be the reason for lower teacher observation scores in middle school. Determining which is the more important factor must await further research.

As we mentioned early in this chapter, finding the reason for lower middle school teacher observation scores has implications for policy—in particular the decision whether to standardize observation scores by grade. If lower scores in middle school are due to teachers, then raw scores would be more appropriate. If the differences are due to other factors, such as student development, then standardized scores would be more appropriate. In the absence of information that would help resolve this conundrum, we cannot recommend either standardizing or not standardizing. Additional data that might be useful are measures of how students contribute to classroom observations. Other helpful data would be scores for teachers who teach classrooms at different grade levels. With such data we could hold the teacher constant and see whether observation scores change with grade level; that would suggest the difference is the student, not the teacher. But teachers who teach classes both in the elementary and middle grades may be very rare, so this type of data may not be available or, if available, it would not be representative of teachers in general.

Ideally, the results presented in this chapter would have provided clear evidence in favor of or against standardizing observation scores by grade. However, they do not. Uncertainty about the source of grade-level differences (students or teachers) creates the potential for risks from both standardizing and not standardizing if observation scores are used in human resource and compensation decisions. On the one hand, if the differences are due to less effective teachers in the middle schools, then a system that standardizes could leave ineffective teachers in place with no incentive to improve. On the other hand, if the differences are due to students, then not standardizing will remove some effective middle school teachers, possibly leave in place ineffective elementary school teachers, and potentially make middle schools less attractive places to work. The job openings created by removing middle school teachers may be difficult to fill, and the people hired might not be as effective as those who were removed.

Even in the face of the uncertainty that remains after our analysis, using observation scores for purposes other than human resource decisions could be productive. Regardless of whether the difference in observation scores across grades is due to students or teachers, our results suggest interactions truly are lower quality in middle schools than in elementary schools. The raw observation scores can direct attention to middle school classrooms where improvement is most needed.

NOTES

1. For more information about the observation instruments used in the MET study, see Kane and Staiger (2012).

2. Over 80 percent of teachers had four or eight video recordings with at least one observation instrument score.

3. Student engagement was defined differently in the two versions, and different examples were used in training across the two versions.

4. Note that for CLASS, the videos were broken into segments, and each segment received a separate rating. Therefore, the CLASS score is calculated by averaging segments to find a video-level score and then averaging dimensions.

5. Elementary teachers created separate video recordings of math and ELA instruction.

6. The scores we use in the analyses are the same scores that were used in the reports produced by the MET project.

7. See below for more information about the Tripod Survey.

8. The excluded category for race is "white."

9. For more details on the content knowledge test, see Kane and Staiger (2012). Note that there is no information available on whether the teacher has a master's degree in New York City, and information about teacher experience in missing in Charlotte, North Carolina.

10. Experience statistics based on 598 observations in math (667 in ELA), master's statistics based on 600 observations in math (677 in ELA), and remaining statistics based on 780 observations in math (859 in ELA). Note that some teachers teach both subjects and are included in the averages of both columns.

11. The excluded category for experience is four or more years.

12. The survey items for each C can be found in Tables 1 and 2 of Kane, McCaffrey, & Staiger (2010).

13. These are the same value-added measures that were used in the final MET report. For more details, see the Technical Appendix of Kane, McCaffrey, & Staiger (2010). The student characteristics varied somewhat by district (depending upon what was available) but typically included student demographics, free or reduced-price lunch, English-language learner status, and special education status.

14. Standard errors are not adjusted for first stage estimation.

15. The figures presented depict the average score on the observation rubric for teachers, separately by grade level. In Figure 2.1, the reported scores are unadjusted for explanatory measures. CLASS scores are on a 7-point scale, while FfT and PLATO scores are on a 4-point scale.

16. For estimates and standard errors, see Appendix Table 2.B.1. Taking into account the precision of the estimates, across all of the observation instruments, grades 4 and 5 scores are not statistically different from one another, grade 6 scores are statistically significantly smaller than grade 4 scores, and scores in grades 7 and 8 are statistically significantly smaller than scores in grade 6. In math, scores in grades 7 and 8 are not significantly different from one another, whereas in ELA, grade 7 scores are lower than grade 8 scores for CLASS and FfT.

17. Regression results available upon request.

18. Note that in some states the average score is calculated by giving some dimension scores higher weight than others. For our calculations, the average was calculated by giving each dimension equal weight.

19. Regression results available upon request.

20. For regression coefficient estimates and standard errors that produced this figure, please see Appendix A.

21. See Appendix Table 2.C.2 for regression coefficients and standard errors.

22. See Tables 2.C.3 and 2.C.4 for the regression coefficients and standard errors from these regressions.

23. See Appendix D for a detailed technical description of the analyses on school effects and the regression results.

24. In technical terms, we should find negative interactions effects between grade level and observation scores in models predicting student achievement gains.

25. See Table 2.E.1 and 2.E.2 for regression coefficients and standard errors. Only four of the twenty interactions are statistically significant, although many of them are positive, indicating stronger, not weaker, relationships between observation scores and achievement gains for higher grade level classes.

REFERENCES AND ADDITIONAL RESOURCES

Fredriksen, K., Rhodes, J., Reddy, R., & Way, N. (2004). Sleepless in Chicago: Tracking the effects of adolescent sleep loss during the middle school years. *Child Development, 75*(1), 84–95.

Grossman, P., Loeb, S., Cohen, J., Hammerness, K., Wyckoff, J. H., Boyd, D. J., & Lankford, H. (2010). *Measure for measure: The relationship between measures of instructional practice in middle school English language arts and teachers' value-added scores* (No. w16015). Washington, DC: National Bureau of Economic Research.

Harris, D. N., & Sass, T. R. (2009, September). *What makes for a good teacher and who can tell?* CALDER Working Paper No. 30.

Jacob, B. A., & Lefgren, L. (2008). Can principals identify effective teachers? Evidence on subjective performance evaluation in education. *Journal of Labor Economics, 26*(1), 101–136.

Jacob, B. A., & Walsh, E. (2011). What's in a rating? *Economics of Education Review, 30*(3), 434–448.

Kane, T. J., McCaffrey, D. F., & Staiger, D.O. (2010). *Learning about teaching: Initial findings from the measures of effective teaching project.* Seattle, WA: Bill & Melinda Gates Foundation.

Kane, T. J., & Staiger, D. O. (2012, March). *Gathering feedback for teachers: Combining high-quality observations with student surveys and achievement gains.* Policy and practice brief prepared for the Bill & Melinda Gates Foundation.

Rockoff, J. E., & Speroni, C. (2010). Subjective and objective evaluations of teacher effectiveness. *American Economic Review, 100*(2), 261–266.

Taylor, E. S., & Tyler, J. H. (2012). The effect of evaluation on teacher performance. *The American Economic Review, 102*(7), 3628–3651.

Tyler, J. H., Taylor, E. S., Kane, T. J., & Wooten, A. L. (2010). Using student performance data to identify effective classroom practices. *American Economic Review, 100*(2), 256–260.

Vartuli, S. (1999). How early childhood teacher beliefs vary across grade level. *Early Childhood Research Quarterly, 14*(4), 489–514.

APPENDIX A. REGRESSION ANALYSIS METHODOLOGY

In our primary data analyses, the dependent variable Y_{ijs} is the observation rating score for teacher i in classroom (or section) j in school s in the 2009–2010 school year. The explanatory variables always include a set of grade-fixed effects for the grade taught by the teacher, γ_i, with grade 4 effects excluded, so that the coefficients for grade effect reflects the difference between the mean for that grade and the mean for fourth grade teachers. A negative coefficient on the fifth grade control variable in this setting indicates that fifth grade teachers are scored lower than fourth grade teachers, all other things held constant. The same holds for the coefficients for grades 6, 7, and 8.

We incrementally add a number of control variables to this baseline specification, including teacher characteristics, X_i, classroom composition characteristics, W_j, and school fixed effects, v_s, to account for unobserved school-level factors that might be correlated with the grade effects. The full specification is given in Equation 1:

$$Y_{ijs} = \mu + \gamma_i + X_i\beta + W_j\delta + v_s + \varepsilon_{ijs} \tag{1}$$

We also estimate specifications that account for unobserved rater factors, to control for any possible biases on the part of raters against middle school teachers that may influence grade-level differences. We use the video-level panel dataset on the observation instruments, where each observation is a video recording of a teacher with scores for each dimension of the observation instrument provided by up to two raters. We remove the rater effect by first estimating a regression model with grade- and rater-fixed effects. For each dimension score, we predict observation score and remove the predicted rater effect. The residual from this estimation is the dimension score with the rater effects removed. We average the rater adjusted dimension scores to obtain the overall observation score for each instrument, and use this as the dependent variable in our analysis.

We also explore whether observation scores predict student achievement gains differentially by grade level. Value-added scores in the 2010–2011 school year, z_{ijs}, are predicted using a combination of grade-fixed effects, γ_i, observation scores from the 2009–2010 school year, Y_{ijs}, interactions of the observation score with grade-fixed effects, θ_{ijs}, as well as classroom composition and teacher characteristics:

$$z_{ijs} = \mu + \gamma_i + Y_{ijs}\alpha + \theta_{ijs} + X_i\beta + W_j\delta + \varepsilon_{ijs}$$

These equations are estimated separately for the state and alternative test by subject (math or ELA).

APPENDIX B. DISTRIBUTION OF OBSERVATION SCORES BY GRADE LEVEL

TABLE 2.B.1. **Grade-Level Differences in Observation Instruments**

	FfT MATH	FfT ELA	CLASS MATH	CLASS ELA	PLATO
Grade 5	−0.0084	−0.0027	−0.0278	−0.0326	−0.0127
	(0.0317)	(0.0287)	(0.0458)	(0.0450)	(0.0285)
Grade 6	−0.1265***	−0.1376***	−0.2302***	−0.2188***	−0.2012***
	(0.0379)	(0.0380)	(0.0562)	(0.0558)	(0.0325)
Grade 7	−0.2511***	−0.3582***	−0.5209***	−0.5338***	−0.3831***
	(0.0392)	(0.0510)	(0.0563)	(0.0679)	(0.0403)
Grade 8	−0.2544***	−0.2643***	−0.5815***	−0.4324***	−0.3733***
	(0.0460)	(0.0468)	(0.0683)	(0.0731)	(0.0399)
Constant	2.6494***	2.6955***	4.5973***	4.6580***	2.6974***
	(0.0227)	(0.0202)	(0.0323)	(0.0317)	(0.0203)
Observations	799	835	797	835	832
R-squared	0.0995	0.1365	0.1936	0.1330	0.2278

Note: Robust standard errors in parentheses; *** $p < 0.01$, ** $p < 0.05$, * $p < 0.1$; grade coefficients are comparisons relative to grade 4. Data are pooled from Hillsborough County, Florida; New York City; and Charlotte, North Carolina.

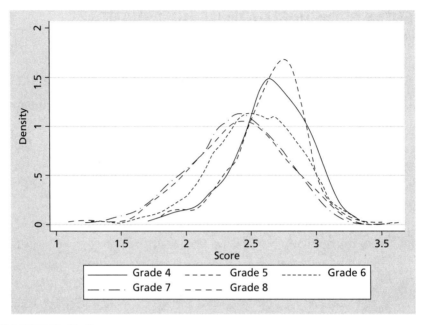

FIGURE 2.B.1. *Distribution of FfT Math Scores by Grade Level*

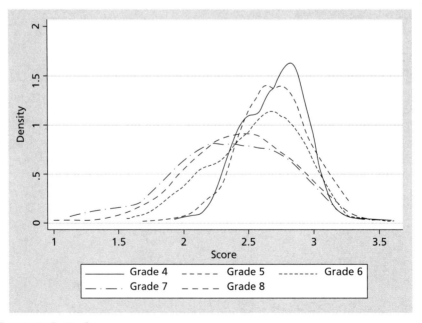

FIGURE 2.B.2. *Distribution of FfT ELA Scores by Grade Level*

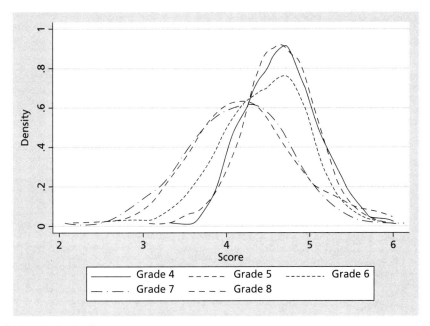

FIGURE 2.B.3. *Distribution of CLASS Math Scores by Grade Level*

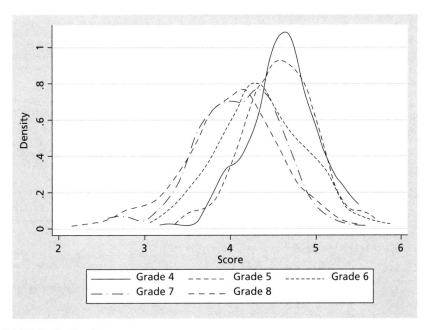

FIGURE 2.B.4. *Distribution of CLASS ELA Scores by Grade Level*

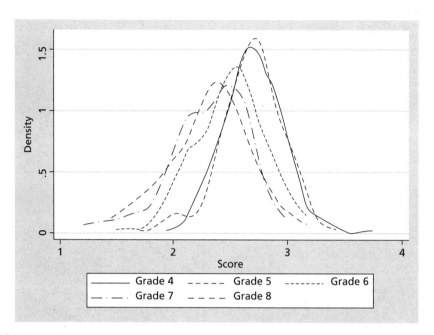

FIGURE 2.B.5. *Distribution of PLATO Scores by Grade Level*

APPENDIX C. DIFFERENCES IN OBSERVATION SCORES BY GRADE LEVEL, HILLSBOROUGH COUNTY PUBLIC SCHOOLS, UNADJUSTED AND ADJUSTED FOR CONTROL MEASURES

TABLE 2.C.1. **Grade-Level Differences in Observation Instruments—Hillsborough**

	FfT MATH	FfT ELA	CLASS MATH	CLASS ELA	PLATO
Grade 5	−0.0147	−0.0497	−0.1158	−0.0876	−0.0702
	(0.0480)	(0.0460)	(0.0756)	(0.0745)	(0.0457)
Grade 6	−0.2296***	−0.2485***	−0.3987***	−0.3476***	−0.2764***
	(0.0461)	(0.0470)	(0.0713)	(0.0742)	(0.0457)
Grade 7	−0.2769***	−0.4647***	−0.6649***	−0.6675***	−0.4546***
	(0.0578)	(0.0731)	(0.0903)	(0.1002)	(0.0586)
Grade 8	−0.2761***	−0.3149***	−0.6866***	−0.5528***	−0.4641***
	(0.0735)	(0.0590)	(0.1151)	(0.0908)	(0.0557)
Constant	2.7700***	2.8079***	4.6979***	4.7554***	2.7910***
	(0.0337)	(0.0314)	(0.0471)	(0.0502)	(0.0336)
Observations	319	358	317	358	357
R-squared	0.1500	0.2052	0.2476	0.2078	0.2994

Note: Robust standard errors in parentheses; *** $p < 0.01$, ** $p < 0.05$, * $p < 0.1$; grade coefficients are comparisons relative to grade 4. Data are pooled from Hillsborough County, Florida; New York City; and Charlotte, North Carolina.

TABLE 2.C.2. Grade-Level Differences in Observation Scores Controlling for Teacher Characteristics—Hillsborough

	FfT MATH	FfT ELA	CLASS MATH	CLASS ELA	PLATO
Grade 5	−0.0309	−0.0439	−0.1501	−0.0878	−0.0662
	(0.0573)	(0.0477)	(0.0958)	(0.0759)	(0.0464)
Grade 6	−0.2352***	−0.2058***	−0.4238***	−0.3089***	−0.2605***
	(0.0555)	(0.0493)	(0.0926)	(0.0757)	(0.0496)
Grade 7	−0.2775***	−0.4468***	−0.6779***	−0.6476***	−0.4511***
	(0.0657)	(0.0717)	(0.0976)	(0.1014)	(0.0589)
Grade 8	−0.2950***	−0.2871***	−0.7274***	−0.5406***	−0.4604***
	(0.0742)	(0.0570)	(0.1486)	(0.0960)	(0.0570)
Male	−0.0526	−0.1129*	−0.0532	−0.0805	−0.0635
	(0.0568)	(0.0584)	(0.0872)	(0.0875)	(0.0498)
Black	−0.0482	−0.1049	−0.1055	−0.1705**	0.0048
	(0.0538)	(0.0671)	(0.0865)	(0.0845)	(0.0537)
Hispanic	0.0156	0.0441	0.0611	−0.1434**	0.0640
	(0.0512)	(0.0543)	(0.1403)	(0.0696)	(0.0512)
Other Race	0.0049	−0.1454	0.1613	−0.1065	−0.2453*
	(0.0933)	(0.1698)	(0.1872)	(0.3110)	(0.1290)
1 Year Exp	−0.2158	−0.1284	0.1157	−0.0782	−0.1407*
	(0.1321)	(0.1192)	(0.1437)	(0.1178)	(0.0839)
2 Years' Exp	−0.0955	−0.1438	−0.0982	0.0346	−0.0595
	(0.0996)	(0.1145)	(0.1408)	(0.1292)	(0.1169)
3 Years' Exp	0.0462	0.1366**	0.0312	0.2576***	0.0449
	(0.0404)	(0.0669)	(0.0831)	(0.0966)	(0.0609)

Master's	−0.0003	−0.0398	−0.0808	0.0572	0.0405
	(0.0436)	(0.0514)	(0.0707)	(0.0882)	(0.0463)
CKT	0.0012	−0.0001	0.0029*	−0.0001	−0.0002
	(0.0008)	(0.0008)	(0.0016)	(0.0011)	(0.0006)
Constant	2.7313***	2.8307***	4.5963***	4.7692***	2.7984***
	(0.0503)	(0.0514)	(0.0790)	(0.0751)	(0.0458)
Observations	319	358	317	358	357
R-squared	0.1761	0.2508	0.2805	0.2428	0.3234

Note: Robust standard errors in parentheses; *** $p < 0.01$, ** $p < 0.05$, * $p < 0.1$; grade coefficients are comparisons relative to grade 4, experience coefficients are comparisons relative to four or more years of experience. There are no teachers with zero years of experience in Hillsborough. CKT is the subject-specific Content Knowledge Test.

TABLE 2.C.3. Grade-Level Differences in Observation Scores Controlling for Classroom Composition—Hillsborough

	FfT MATH	FfT ELA	CLASS MATH	CLASS ELA	PLATO
Grade 5	−0.0336	−0.0665	−0.1257	−0.1050	−0.0741
	(0.0500)	(0.0461)	(0.0815)	(0.0812)	(0.0486)
Grade 6	−0.1550***	−0.1630***	−0.3260***	−0.1481*	−0.2040***
	(0.0518)	(0.0528)	(0.0850)	(0.0791)	(0.0509)
Grade 7	−0.1875**	−0.3413***	−0.6023***	−0.4301***	−0.3782***
	(0.0747)	(0.0915)	(0.1185)	(0.1082)	(0.0639)
Grade 8	−0.3079***	−0.2252***	−0.7658***	−0.3419***	−0.4222***
	(0.0794)	(0.0753)	(0.1224)	(0.1134)	(0.0606)
Prior-Yr Test	0.0739***	0.0100	0.1747***	0.0010	−0.0251
	(0.0255)	(0.0276)	(0.0448)	(0.0412)	(0.0253)

(continued)

(*Table 2.C.3 continued*)

	FfT MATH	FfT ELA	CLASS MATH	CLASS ELA	PLATO
% Male	−0.2318	−0.1292	−0.4352*	−0.5143	−0.3540***
	(0.1406)	(0.1816)	(0.2563)	(0.3306)	(0.1269)
% Sped	0.2346	−0.0862	0.6666***	0.2047	−0.0051
	(0.1695)	(0.1958)	(0.2558)	(0.2988)	(0.2361)
Relative Age	0.0975	0.2937*	−0.0419	0.6794***	0.3013**
	(0.1263)	(0.1674)	(0.2201)	(0.2218)	(0.1372)
% FRL	−0.2466*	−0.2417*	−0.0651	−0.3738*	−0.2845**
	(0.1257)	(0.1254)	(0.2111)	(0.1955)	(0.1176)
% Black	0.0886	−0.2688*	0.2091	−0.0675	−0.0429
	(0.1422)	(0.1533)	(0.2390)	(0.2328)	(0.1337)
% Hispanic	0.0946	−0.1085	0.2592	0.0311	0.0613
	(0.1545)	(0.1675)	(0.2430)	(0.2504)	(0.1380)
% Asian	−0.3838	−0.0615	−0.3160	−0.4781	−0.1161
	(0.3135)	(0.3061)	(0.5585)	(0.4610)	(0.2690)
% Other Race	−0.3564	−0.4954*	−0.2976	−0.3618	−0.3643
	(0.2656)	(0.2781)	(0.3983)	(0.4221)	(0.2689)
Class Size	−0.0045	−0.0140**	0.0067	−0.0084	−0.0073
	(0.0044)	(0.0055)	(0.0070)	(0.0075)	(0.0049)
% Don't Read at Home	−0.1452	−0.3266	0.0119	−0.6478***	−0.2683
	(0.1468)	(0.2062)	(0.2611)	(0.2483)	(0.1691)
% Don't Do Homework	−0.2700	−0.1987	−0.2949	−0.5484**	−0.0803
	(0.2614)	(0.1410)	(0.3066)	(0.2111)	(0.1459)

% No Computer	0.2412	−0.2588	−0.1657	0.0370	−0.0014
	(0.2262)	(0.2497)	(0.3558)	(0.3974)	(0.2173)
% Single Parent Home	−0.0357	0.0704	−0.4196	−0.6463**	0.0656
	(0.1274)	(0.2041)	(0.2700)	(0.3165)	(0.1815)
% Large Family	0.0183	0.3316**	0.2860	0.0286	0.0796
	(0.1330)	(0.1432)	(0.2174)	(0.2563)	(0.1500)
Constant	3.0721***	3.3102***	4.7085***	5.4356***	3.2417***
	(0.1281)	(0.1509)	(0.1872)	(0.2662)	(0.1351)
Observations	318	357	316	357	356
R-squared	0.2605	0.3045	0.3588	0.3086	0.3514

Note: Robust standard errors in parentheses; *** $p < 0.01$, ** $p < 0.05$, * $p < 0.1$; grade coefficients are comparisons relative to grade 4.

TABLE 2.C.4. **Grade-Level Differences in Observation Scores Controlling for Teacher Characteristics and Classroom Composition—Hillsborough**

	FfT MATH	FfT ELA	CLASS MATH	CLASS ELA	PLATO
Grade 5	−0.0464	−0.0579	−0.1545	−0.1017	−0.0700
	(0.0560)	(0.0470)	(0.0938)	(0.0810)	(0.0496)
Grade 6	−0.1665***	−0.1365**	−0.3639***	−0.1120	−0.1924***
	(0.0555)	(0.0557)	(0.0895)	(0.0826)	(0.0568)
Grade 7	−0.1946**	−0.3269***	−0.6240***	−0.4029***	−0.3767***
	(0.0784)	(0.0887)	(0.1145)	(0.1120)	(0.0647)

(continued)

(*Table 2.C.4 continued*)

	FfT MATH	FfT ELA	CLASS MATH	CLASS ELA	PLATO
Grade 8	−0.3171***	−0.1999***	−0.7902***	−0.3268***	−0.4227***
	(0.0805)	(0.0725)	(0.1392)	(0.1191)	(0.0631)
Constant	2.9934***	3.3017***	4.5726***	5.4161***	3.2201***
	(0.1394)	(0.1633)	(0.2123)	(0.2664)	(0.1371)
Teacher Chars	Yes	Yes	Yes	Yes	Yes
Classroom Comp	Yes	Yes	Yes	Yes	Yes
Observations	318	357	316	357	356
R-squared	0.2727	0.3425	0.3803	0.3429	0.3697

Note: Robust standard errors in parentheses; *** $p < 0.01$, ** $p < 0.05$, * $p < 0.1$; grade coefficients are comparisons relative to grade 4; Teacher Characteristics and Classroom Composition from previous tables.

TABLE 2.C.5. Grade-Level Differences in Observation Scores Controlling for Rater Effects—Hillsborough

	FfT MATH	FfT ELA	PLATO
Grade 5	−0.0354	−0.0611	−0.1153**
	(0.0489)	(0.0430)	(0.0468)
Grade 6	−0.2099***	−0.2279***	−0.2896***
	(0.0496)	(0.0421)	(0.0486)
Grade 7	−0.2332***	−0.3865***	−0.4473***
	(0.0576)	(0.0681)	(0.0663)
Grade 8	−0.2868***	−0.2767***	−0.4858***
	(0.0702)	(0.0580)	(0.0599)
Constant	2.7275***	2.7690***	2.7988***
	(0.0360)	(0.0304)	(0.0362)

Observations	303	323	306
R-squared	0.1231	0.1649	0.3007

Note: Robust standard errors in parentheses; *** $p < 0.01$, ** $p < 0.05$, * $p < 0.1$; grade coefficients are comparisons relative to grade 4; CLASS instrument is excluded because raters did not rate it across grade levels.

TABLE 2.C.6. Grade-Level Differences Controlling for Teacher, Classroom, and Rater Effects—Hillsborough

	FfT MATH	FfT ELA	PLATO
Grade 5	−0.0738	−0.0738*	−0.1264**
	(0.0602)	(0.0435)	(0.0496)
Grade 6	−0.1851***	−0.1351**	−0.2271***
	(0.0632)	(0.0568)	(0.0619)
Grade 7	−0.1817**	−0.2543***	−0.3775***
	(0.0705)	(0.0830)	(0.0717)
Grade 8	−0.3139***	−0.1870**	−0.4638***
	(0.0736)	(0.0784)	(0.0739)
Constant	2.9690***	3.2848***	3.0844***
	(0.1462)	(0.1527)	(0.1406)
Teacher Chars	Yes	Yes	Yes
Classroom Chars	Yes	Yes	Yes
Rater Effects	Yes	Yes	Yes
Observations	302	322	305
R-squared	0.2174	0.2885	0.3599

Note: Robust standard errors in parentheses; *** $p < 0.01$, ** $p < 0.05$, * $p < 0.1$; grade coefficients are comparisons relative to grade 4.

TABLE 2.C.7. **Grade-Level Differences in Observations Scores Controlling for Teacher, Classroom, Rater, and School Effects—Hillsborough**

	FfT MATH	FfT ELA	PLATO
Grade 7	0.0154	−0.1242	−0.1615**
	(0.0768)	(0.0780)	(0.0729)
Grade 8	−0.1813**	0.0059	−0.1910**
	(0.0878)	(0.0733)	(0.0804)
Constant	3.2991***	3.1861***	2.9664***
	(0.2995)	(0.2901)	(0.3426)
Teacher Chars	Yes	Yes	Yes
Classroom Chars	Yes	Yes	Yes
Rater Effects	Yes	Yes	Yes
School FE	Yes	Yes	Yes
Observations	186	185	173
R-squared	0.2840	0.4283	0.4962

Note: Robust standard errors in parentheses; *** $p < 0.01$, ** $p < 0.05$, * $p < 0.1$; grade coefficients are comparisons relative to grade 6.

APPENDIX D. SCHOOL FIXED EFFECT ANALYSES

We consider whether grade-level differences in observation scores are picking up unobserved differences among schools. We imposed a number of sample restrictions for this analysis. First, in the MET data there are only a handful of schools where fourth and fifth grade teachers are teaching in the same building as sixth, seventh, and eighth grade teachers. Since we would be including school fixed effects to capture school level differences, we needed to restrict the sample to only middle schools in Hillsborough with teachers in grades 6 through 8. While the largest grade-level differences were observed between fourth grade and seventh grade teachers, there were still significant differences between sixth and seventh grade teachers, so this sample restriction still allowed for informative analyses.

First, as a point of comparison, in Table 2.D.1 we present the results of estimating the grade fixed effects in Hillsborough middle schools relative to the means for grade 6. Then, in Table 2.D.2 we present the same comparisons for the same schools, but accounting for schools and estimating an average within school difference by including school fixed effects in the estimation model. The results from these regressions are quite mixed. While we see that the coefficient on grade-level differences for PLATO drop in magnitude and become insignificant, there are no differences in the coefficients from CLASS math grade effects. It appears that differential sorting of teachers affects scores on some instruments, but this result is not generalizable to all instruments.

TABLE 2.D.1. Grade-Level Differences in Observation Scores—Hillsborough

	FfT MATH	FfT ELA	CLASS MATH	CLASS ELA	PLATO
Grade 7	−0.0711	−0.1982**	−0.2467**	−0.3256***	−0.1757***
	(0.0564)	(0.0777)	(0.0974)	(0.1085)	(0.0593)
Grade 8	−0.0704	−0.0484	−0.2684**	−0.2109**	−0.1852***
	(0.0724)	(0.0645)	(0.1208)	(0.0998)	(0.0565)

(continued)

(Table 2.D.1 continued)

	FfT MATH	FfT ELA	CLASS MATH	CLASS ELA	PLATO
Constant	2.5643***	2.5414***	4.2797***	4.4135***	2.5122***
	(0.0312)	(0.0408)	(0.0594)	(0.0649)	(0.0348)
School FE	No	No	No	No	No
Observations	192	205	190	205	205
R-squared	0.0126	0.0472	0.0617	0.0591	0.0753

Note: Robust standard errors in parentheses; *** $p < 0.01$, ** $p < 0.05$, * $p < 0.1$; grade coefficients are comparisons relative to grade 6.

TABLE 2.D.2. Grade-Level Differences in Observation Scores with School Fixed Effects—Hillsborough

	FfT MATH	FfT ELA	CLASS MATH	CLASS ELA	PLATO
Grade 7	−0.0942	−0.1190	−0.2322**	−0.2563*	−0.0832
	(0.0786)	(0.0906)	(0.1115)	(0.1314)	(0.0715)
Grade 8	−0.0909	−0.0635	−0.2827***	−0.1469	−0.1080*
	(0.0878)	(0.0730)	(0.1024)	(0.1055)	(0.0588)
Constant	2.5768***	2.5263***	4.2780***	4.3705***	2.4580***
	(0.0415)	(0.0464)	(0.0591)	(0.0624)	(0.0390)
School FE	Yes	Yes	Yes	Yes	Yes
Observations	192	205	190	205	205
R-squared	0.1319	0.2878	0.2996	0.3098	0.3301

Note: Robust standard errors in parentheses; *** $p < 0.01$, ** $p < 0.05$, * $p < 0.1$; grade coefficients are comparisons relative to grade 6.

APPENDIX E. PREDICTING ACHIEVEMENT GAINS DIFFERENTIALLY BY GRADE USING OBSERVATION SCORES

TABLE 2.E.1. **Grade-Level Differences in Predicting SVA—Hillsborough**

	FfT MATH	FfT ELA	CLASS MATH	CLASS ELA	PLATO
Observation Score	0.0343 (0.0994)	0.0275 (0.0649)	−0.0228 (0.1170)	0.0148 (0.0653)	−0.0847 (0.0887)
Grade 5	0.1893 (0.5452)	−0.1092 (0.4072)	−0.2881 (0.3873)	0.0513 (0.4189)	−0.2306 (0.3574)
Grade 6	−0.0005 (0.3064)	−0.1097 (0.3499)	−0.0398 (0.3667)	0.4151 (0.3556)	−0.1204 (0.3130)
Grade 7	−0.0914 (0.3093)	−0.2119 (0.3374)	0.0483 (0.3442)	−0.0383 (0.3534)	−0.1726 (0.3038)
Grade 8	−0.3272 (0.3417)	−0.4586 (0.3541)	0.0114 (0.3592)	−0.1520 (0.3462)	−0.2690 (0.2851)
Obs X Grade 5	−0.0418 (0.1916)	0.0395 (0.0869)	0.1119 (0.1388)	−0.0066 (0.0873)	0.0895 (0.1266)
Obs X Grade 6	0.0232 (0.1092)	0.0381 (0.0769)	0.0356 (0.1337)	−0.0815 (0.0741)	0.0613 (0.1125)
Obs X Grade 7	0.0518 (0.1074)	0.0629 (0.0734)	−0.0024 (0.1252)	0.0233 (0.0743)	0.0802 (0.1109)
Obs X Grade 8	0.1599 (0.1200)	0.1333* (0.0802)	0.0159 (0.1315)	0.0512 (0.0727)	0.1235 (0.1019)
Constant	−0.2820 (0.3113)	−0.2900 (0.3109)	0.0571 (0.3444)	−0.0940 (0.3423)	0.2266 (0.2785)

(continued)

(Table 2.E.1 continued)

	FfT MATH	FfT ELA	CLASS MATH	CLASS ELA	PLATO
Teacher Chars	Yes	Yes	Yes	Yes	Yes
Classroom Comp	Yes	Yes	Yes	Yes	Yes
Observations	292	290	313	313	313
R-squared	0.2297	0.2505	0.1405	0.1597	0.1402

Note: Robust standard errors in parentheses; *** $p < 0.01$, ** $p < 0.05$, * $p < 0.1$; grade coefficients are comparisons relative to grade 4.

TABLE 2.E.2. Grade-Level Differences in Predicting AVA—Hillsborough

	FfT MATH	FfT ELA	CLASS MATH	CLASS ELA	PLATO
Observation Score	0.0215	−0.0438	0.2575	0.0727	−0.0294
	(0.1026)	(0.0812)	(0.1707)	(0.0790)	(0.1504)
Grade 5	0.8328**	−0.0527	−0.2841	−0.8897	−0.2892
	(0.3716)	(0.4902)	(0.6243)	(0.6358)	(0.5483)
Grade 6	−0.3351	−0.2489	0.4039	0.2243	0.1556
	(0.3456)	(0.4402)	(0.5597)	(0.5111)	(0.5500)
Grade 7	−0.7390	−1.0228*	0.1813	0.2326	−1.0865**
	(0.5283)	(0.5467)	(0.6041)	(0.5658)	(0.5474)
Grade 8	0.1534	−0.4310	0.9131	0.0965	−0.3613
	(0.4428)	(0.5562)	(0.5659)	(0.5265)	(0.4827)
Obs X Grade 5	−0.2974**	0.0138	0.1214	0.1982	0.1149
	(0.1326)	(0.1022)	(0.2267)	(0.1371)	(0.2035)
Obs X Grade 6	0.1222	0.0486	−0.1048	−0.0312	−0.0348
	(0.1249)	(0.0930)	(0.2081)	(0.1117)	(0.2061)

Obs X Grade 7	0.2644	0.2273*	0.0025	−0.0304	0.4893**
	(0.1996)	(0.1227)	(0.2296)	(0.1317)	(0.2073)
Obs X Grade 8	−0.0769	0.0890	−0.3134	−0.0033	0.1744
	(0.1675)	(0.1299)	(0.2118)	(0.1180)	(0.1847)
Constant	−0.1440	0.1394	−0.9797*	−0.5634	−0.1759
	(0.3090)	(0.4013)	(0.5070)	(0.4240)	(0.4604)
Teacher Chars	Yes	Yes	Yes	Yes	Yes
Classroom Chars	Yes	Yes	Yes	Yes	Yes
Observations	288	286	305	305	305
R-squared	0.2621	0.2442	0.1337	0.1151	0.1216

Note: Robust standard errors in parentheses; *** $p < 0.01$, ** $p < 0.05$, * $p < 0.1$; grade coefficients are comparisons relative to grade 4.

CHAPTER

3

Improving Observational Score Quality

Challenges in Observer Thinking

COURTNEY A. BELL, YI QI, ANDREW J. CROFT, DAWN LEUSNER, DANIEL F. MCCAFFREY, DREW H. GITOMER, AND ROBERT C. PIANTA

ABSTRACT

The use of observation protocols for the evaluation of teaching has become more prevalent in the United States. While several research studies suggest that observers can be trained to score reliably, there is little research on how observers understand and use observation protocols. This chapter expands our understanding of rater thinking and scoring processes by documenting (1) which dimensions of classroom interactions are most challenging and easiest for observers to learn to score accurately and reliably, (2) the dimensions of classroom interactions observers perceive to be the most challenging and easiest to score, and (3) some challenges observers face in learning to score classroom interactions. Bringing together data from two Gates-funded studies, the Measures of Effective Teaching (MET) project and the Understanding Teaching Quality (UTQ) study, we analyze rater agreement statistics from observers in both studies. Then we use think aloud data to describe how observers and master observers assign scores on two general and two subject-specific observation protocols. We found that agreement metrics were lower than desired levels for consequential decisions. Observers had higher levels of agreement and accuracy in the classroom organization and environment domains, as compared to domains that focused on instructional and emotional aspects of classrooms. Observers perceived low-inference dimensions and domains as easier to score than those

(continued)

(*continued*)
that require higher-inference judgments, such as those pertaining to interactions among teachers, students, and subject matter. Observers used four types of scoring strategies: reviewing scoring criteria, using internal or personal criteria, reasoning from memorable videos, and beginning with an assumed score. Master observers and observers used these strategies differently. We conclude the chapter with instrument, training, and policy implications for districts and states to improve the implementation of observation protocols in high-stakes contexts.

INTRODUCTION

As states and districts respond to federal legislation to conduct more publicly accountable teaching evaluations, many localities are including observations as part of their teaching evaluation systems. For the most part, these observations are conducted by individuals already participating in the educational system, such as teachers, principals, curriculum specialists, and coaches. There is, however, little empirical understanding of how educational practitioners understand and score classroom practice using observation protocols. This lack of clarity on the factors that facilitate and constrain educators' learning and use of observation systems makes training and quality control processes at scale more difficult.

Preliminary evidence from a handful of large-scale research studies underway in fourth through tenth grade classrooms suggests that, although observers can be trained to score reliably, there are concerns about initial training, calibration activities designed to keep observers scoring accurately over time, and the use of observation protocols (Bell, Gitomer, McCaffrey, Hamre, Pianta, & Qi, 2012; Bill & Melinda Gates Foundation [BMGF], 2012; Casabianca, McCaffrey, Gitomer, Bell, Hamre, & Pianta, 2013). In early childhood education, where the training and calibration of raters and use of observations at large scale are more common practice (e.g., in national assessments of Head Start quality), concerns also exist, but there is a larger pool of experience, expertise, and knowledge to draw from (e.g., Cash, Hamre, Pianta, & Myers, 2012; Pianta & Hamre, 2009; Pianta, La Paro, & Hamre, 2008). In both early childhood and K–12 contexts, non-trivial proportions of observers struggle to be certified at acceptable levels of agreement, and they may then exhibit undesirable levels of reliability when applying observation tools in the field (e.g., BMGF, 2012; Cash et al., 2012).

Research nominates a wide range of issues that may shape observer reliability. Existing evidence from generalizability studies suggests observers differ in the overall severity of their judgments on specific classrooms (i.e., how lenient or stringent the observer is), their severity on specific lessons, and their consistency and accuracy on specific aspects of classroom practice (e.g., Casabianca, Gitomer, Bell, Hamre, & Pianta, 2013; Mashburn, Downer, Rivers, Brackett, & Martinez, 2011). In two studies, observers scoring lessons in grades 4 through 10 tended to agree with one another on the behavioral aspects of classroom interactions but had more difficulty agreeing on the more complex aspects of classroom interactions (Bell et al., 2012; Bill & Melinda Gates Foundation, 2012). Specifically, the instructional dimensions of observation protocols seemed to be the most challenging dimensions for observers to score reliably (Gitomer, Bell, Qi, McCaffrey, Hamre, & Pianta, 2014). In addition to differences in how observers score classrooms, lessons, and dimensions, in at least one study, researchers noted that observers continue to learn to score in the early days of large-scale scoring, despite robust training, certification, and calibration processes (Casabianca et al., 2013).

It is not clear why particular features of observation protocols are differentially challenging for observers, nor is it completely clear the extent to which some dimensions of teaching are more challenging to score than other dimensions. Moreover, we know from studies of large-scale observational training in early childhood that characteristics of observers, not surprisingly, factor into their judgments of teacher behavior and factor into training outcomes. For example, Cash and colleagues (2012) examined the extent to which observers' attitudes about children were predictive of their scoring reliability for more than seven hundred new trainees. They demonstrated that child-centered versus adult-centered views of adult-child interactions predicted the likelihood of an individual observer passing a certification test, as well as the degree to which a group of observers trained together will vary from master scores. The act of scoring observations of teacher-student interactions is a complex, multi-determined process we are only beginning to understand. The present study is one attempt to deepen that understanding.

Although there is much to be learned about training and observation, we do know the current generation of protocols requires observers to pay careful attention to acts of teaching and learning and to assign a rating to those acts, typically in real time. Such ratings require judgments about interactions and their meaning. Protocols typically require observers to watch for many different aspects of interactions, creating a challenge in parsing the incoming stream of information.

Classroom interactions take place, by definition, in a naturalistic manner, and therefore vary across activities, teachers, and settings. One math lesson might be a review lesson, while another math lesson might be the teaching of a new concept. This may present challenges for observers as they learn to apply scoring criteria to a wide range of lesson topics and formats.

Observers are not blank slates. Most observers are former teachers and, based on that teaching experience, have ideas about what counts as high-quality teaching and learning. For example, in one preK study of observers, researchers found that observers' beliefs about the proper role of the teacher predicted the likelihood of certification on the Classroom Assessment Scoring System (CLASS) instrument (Cash, Hamre, Pianta, & Myers, 2012). Even if observers have never taught, they have spent many years in classrooms as students developing their own ideas about what counts as high-quality teaching and learning (Lortie, 1975).

Amidst the wide range of factors that may shape observer behavior, districts and states must create training procedures and implementation policies that discipline observer judgments in order to produce valid and reliable scores. Assuming that school systems will rely on the observers they already employ (e.g., principals, coaches), policymakers need to better understand the constraints of live observation and how best to assign observers to lessons. They also need to understand how observers process incoming information when observing so that training programs can be strengthened to improve score reliability and accuracy. We believe it is critically important to treat these questions and challenges as opportunities for empirical study, using data and scientific approaches to determine the best possible practical approach. Toward this end, the chapter investigates three questions:

1. What dimensions of classroom interaction are *empirically* most challenging and easiest for observers to learn to score accurately and reliably?

2. What dimensions of classroom interactions do observers *perceive* are most challenging and easiest to learn to score accurately and reliably? Why do they find those the most challenging?

3. What types of challenges do observers face in learning to score those dimensions?

We bring together data from two Gates-funded studies, Measures of Effective Teaching (MET) and Understanding Teaching Quality (UTQ), to describe how observers and master observers process the data from observations and then apply that information in assigning scores. Patterns in observer thinking across four observation protocols are then used to speculate about how observer training could be improved.

The remainder of the chapter is divided into five sections. First, we briefly review research on the nature of rater thinking and observer training. In the second section, we describe the studies, observation protocols, data sets, and our analytic approach. Next, we analyze calibration and certification scores from MET and UTQ to describe features of teaching that have the strongest and weakest levels of rater agreement and accuracy and compare those to rater-identified dimensions of strength and weakness. In order to better understand both objective and self-reported dimensions of strength and weakness, the fourth section draws on think aloud and interview data to identify patterns in observer thinking that are potential causes of scoring inaccuracies. In the final section of the chapter, we offer instrument, training, and policy implications for districts and states.

RESEARCH ON OBSERVER THINKING

Before describing the literature on observer thinking, we specify the nature of an observation protocol. In contrast to the widely held idea that an observation protocol is a sheet of paper with scoring scales or rubrics, observation protocols are comprised of two main elements: scoring criteria and scoring procedures. These two elements may appear in written materials, oral interactions during training, and scored videos of lessons. For example, scoring criteria might include the written scales that describe levels of performance, the verbal or written definitions of the terms, and the video exemplars that codify how classroom interactions should be scored (e.g., basic, proficient, etc.). Similarly, scoring procedures might include written directions about how to take appropriate notes or steps observers are to follow when they are uncertain about what score to assign. Together, scoring criteria and scoring procedures standardize what observers pay attention to and how they do so. Both contribute to the validity and reliability of observations.

Human Scoring of Constructed-Response Questions
There is little empirical research on what observers actually do when they score classroom interactions. Previous validity research on the assignment of scores has almost exclusively been the province of researchers studying

human scoring of open-ended or constructed responses (CR) by test-takers. Although there is research on other CR tests (e.g., medical licensing tests), and certainly in other areas of performance assessment for teachers (Borko, Stecher, Alonzo, Moncure, & McClam, 2005; Moss et al., 2004), much of the work relevant to this analysis has been done by psychometricians in various areas of student testing (e.g., Muckle & Karabatsos, 2009; Raymond, Harik, & Clauser, 2011).

Much of this literature treats raters as information processors. Among other things, the literature investigates established sources of rater error as well as cognitive demand. Established sources of error include how lenient or stringent a rater is, the degree to which a rater's overall perceptions of a response shape his or her specific scores, how raters use the full range of score points, how raters privilege the most recent information they have, and the role of raters' prior knowledge in scoring (e.g., Bernardin, 1978; Borman, 1975; Clauser, Harik, & Margolis, 2006; Engelhard, 2002; Freedman & Calfee, 1983; Wolfe, Kao, & Ranney, 1998). Interestingly, this literature presumes that learning to score is straightforward, and that the instrument and associated training presents little conflict or confusion for observers.

Specifically, the CR literature suggests at least two factors that might influence scoring observations of classroom practice: personal expertise and scoring task demands (Suto, 2012). Teaching experience, content knowledge, scoring experience, and professional training are all background characteristics that may contribute to observers' personal expertise. Specific requirements for observer background are common (e.g., National Board for Professional Teaching Standards [NBPTS] and Connecticut's discontinued BEST program), and researchers frequently recommend such requirements as ways to improve observer reliability (Hakel, Koenig, & Elliott, 2008; Kellor, 2002; Matsumura, Garnier, Pascal, & Valdés, 2002). In the case of observing teaching, scoring task demands might include features such as lesson content and grade level, types of activities, student characteristics, constraints and affordances of video, and applying scoring rubrics. Observers are prepared for scoring task demands through training, certification, and ongoing calibration activities designed to assess their accuracy and consistency over time.

Training Observers to Score Teaching

Training involves multiple days of instructing observers about the instrument, teaching evidence collection, discussions of how scoring criteria apply, and scoring practice. The overall goal of training is for observers to adopt a view of teaching consistent with the instrument and to discipline their judgments about lessons such that they reach an acceptable level of agreement (often 80 percent) with master observers. Observers who meet this level of agreement are then certified and proceed to operational scoring. Some studies require observers to calibrate at regular intervals to ensure scoring accuracy. This usually requires watching some part of a lesson, scoring, and agreeing with master observers' scores at a pre-specified level. Additionally, most studies then assign two observers to score some of the same lessons in order to assess the degree to which observers agree with one another.

Evidence from smaller scale studies demonstrates that observers can be trained to acceptable levels on some observation instruments in the secondary grades (Grossman, Greenberg, Hammerness, Cohen, Alston, & Brown, 2009; Hill, Blunk, Charalambous, Lewis, Phelps, Sleep, & Ball, 2008). Larger scale studies are more mixed about the level of reliability observers obtained given considerable training (BMGF, 2012; Casabianca, Lockwood, & McCaffrey, 2013). While reliabilities of scores in higher grades (i.e., grades 4 through 10) are lower than desired, it is important to note that there is literature in early childhood education suggesting observers can be trained at scale to produce valid and reliable scores (e.g., Early, Barbarin, Bryant, Burchinal, Chang, Clifford et al., 2005; NICHD ECCRN, 2005). It is unclear whether the difference in reliability between studies at different grade levels is a function of the instruments' development (many of the upper grades instruments are relatively new to high-stakes use), the nature of the interactions among teachers and students, subject matter differences between early and later grades, or something else.

Previous performance assessments that made use of observations include two well-known portfolio assessments: Connecticut's discontinued Beginning Educator Support and Training program and the National Board for Professional Teaching Standards certificate program (NBPTS). Both are often widely regarded as meeting acceptable technical standards. They made use of extensive training and quality control procedures, ranging from bias training to extensive double scoring and one-on-one training with raters who do not meet acceptable standards (e.g., Hakel, Koenig, & Elliott, 2008; Ingvarson & Hattie, 2008; Kellor, 2002; Szpara & Wylie, 2005). However, the observation is only one source of evidence that contributed to the overall portfolio score. No specific observation scores were assigned and, thus, no psychometric information specific to the observational component is available.

Important Aspects of Creating Observation Scores

Drawing on the CR and performance assessment literatures, we focus on three aspects of scoring that may contribute to the accuracy and reliability of observational scores:

- The maintenance of an accurate internal representation of the scoring criteria
- Judgments between score points on a rubric
- The collection of evidence to serve as a basis for scoring decisions

Observers can redefine scoring criteria by creating a mental rubric, that is, a version of the scoring criteria that may contain their own biases or construct irrelevant factors (Bejar, 2012). One study indicated that, even when observers of portfolio materials cite the same evidence, they construct different narratives about what is happening and these differences result in divergent scores (Schutz & Moss, 2004). One reason may be that with more experience observers tend to rely more on patterns and automated scoring strategies and less on the scoring criteria (Crisp, 2012).

Even after training, observers may not equally discern differences between score points (Bejar, 2012; Matsumura, Garnier, Pascal, & Valdés, 2002). There are several ways to mitigate this type of error. For example, in the NBPTS assessment observers first assign a whole number value to the response; a plus or a minus can be attached to the whole number value to indicate quarter-point gradations in performance (for example, 3+ converts to a score of 3.25, 3– converts to 2.75, and so on) (Hakel, Koenig, & Elliott, 2008). Another common practice is the use of benchmarks or scoring rationales for each rating level in each criterion for each subject and grade level (Matsumura, Garnier, Slater, & Boston, 2008; Wenzel, Nagaoka, Morris, Billings, & Fendt, 2002). Another common practice is the use of "range finders" or exemplars that sit on the borders of score points. For example, on a 4-point scale, training might deliberately include a low 3 and a high 2 to show raters where the border is between a 2 and a 3. Protocols differ with respect to the types of judgments made across score points. Therefore, each type of assessment brings its own challenges to navigating the space between score points.

Observer efficacy in discerning between score points is contingent on recording evidence to support scoring decisions. While observers commonly take structured notes when observing practice or assessing portfolios (e.g., Kellor, 2002), there is little documentation or guidance about the best ways to record evidence. In addition to such guidance being protocol specific, guidance would also depend on different theoretical views of whether to assess the presence of rubric indicators and then weigh or combine them to make a scoring decision versus observing the whole of the lesson before making reference to specific evidence to support a scoring decision (Crisp, 2012). This chapter reports an investigation of these cognitive processes of collecting and evaluating evidence.

DESCRIPTION OF THE STUDIES, PROTOCOLS, DATA COLLECTION, AND ANALYSES

The analyses draw on data from the MET and UTQ studies to investigate which aspects of classroom interaction are most challenging and easiest for observers to score accurately and reliably. To understand observers' thinking, we used think aloud, stimulated recall, and interviews of observers and master observers from the UTQ study. In what follows, we describe the studies, the protocols investigated, and finally, the analytic methods.

Overview of the MET and UTQ Studies

MET observation data come from nearly three thousand volunteer teachers across six urban school districts located in six states. Four lessons were captured for each teacher in a single year. Four of the five instruments used for observation are included in this analysis: the Classroom Assessment Scoring System (CLASS) protocol (Pianta, La Paro, & Hamre, 2008), the Framework for Teaching (FfT) protocol (Danielson, 2007), the Mathematical Quality of Instruction (MQI) protocol (Hill, Kapitula, & Umland, 2011), and the Protocol for Language Arts Teaching Observation (PLATO) (Grossman et al., 2009). This analysis is limited to grades 6 to 8 mathematics and ELA classrooms to be comparable to the UTQ data. For these grades, two lessons came from one classroom section and two lessons from a second section. The majority of MET observers (50 to 77 percent, depending on protocol) held a master's degree or higher. More than half (52 percent) had ten years or more of classroom teaching experience and four out of ten observers were still teaching at the time of the study. These analyses draw on scores created by sixty-seven MQI, seventy-six PLATO, 125 FfT, and 243 CLASS observers.

The UTQ study collected data in 458 middle school mathematics and ELA classrooms in three county-wide districts in a large southern state. Half of the teachers taught ELA and half taught mathematics. In addition to other data such as student test scores, teacher knowledge tests, and analyses of assignments, each of the 458 teachers was observed four times. The videotaped lessons were scored with two general observation protocols (CLASS and FfT) and one subject-specific observation protocol (MQI or PLATO) by raters who were former teachers. Each teacher was observed in two class sections. Eleven observers contributed video scores on CLASS and FfT. Half of the observers scored PLATO and half scored MQI. UTQ observers had an average of 4.3 years of teaching experience. All were certified in either ELA or mathematics and 50 percent of them held a master's degree or other advanced degree.

While similar in overall design, we include data from both MET and UTQ because the studies differed in the constraints facing observers (e.g., each MET observer scored only one protocol, while UTQ observers scored three; MET observers worked remotely and were not a cohesive group, while UTQ observers saw each other weekly over the two-year project and were all colleagues). By including data from both studies, we can assess the robustness of the reliability findings across constraints and use think aloud data to better understand those reliability findings.

Description of the Observation Protocols

Observation scores were created on the protocols described previously. However, because all four protocols were undergoing revisions during the time of the two studies, there are differences in the specific versions used in MET and UTQ. These are noted in the results section. Each instrument is described briefly below.

CLASS, designed by Robert Pianta, Bridget Hamre, and colleagues at the University of Virginia, is a system of four research-based observation protocols designed to measure preK–12 classroom quality at different grade levels (preK, K–3, upper elementary, and secondary) (Pianta, Hamre, Haynes, Mintz, & La Paro, 2007; Pianta, La Paro, & Hamre, 2008; Rimm-Kaufman, La Paro, Downer, & Pianta, 2005). The protocols measure the Teaching Through Interactions (TTI) model of classroom interactions (Hamre, Pianta, Downer, DeCoster, Jones, Brown et al., 2013). The TTI model conceptualizes teaching and learning from a developmental perspective, focusing on the interactions between teachers and students. CLASS measures general attributes of teaching in three domains: emotional support, classroom organization, and instructional support. Each domain is made up of three to four dimensions (see Table 3.1). Observers score each dimension on a 7-point

TABLE 3.1. **Domains and Dimensions of the General Observation Protocols, CLASS and FfT**

CLASS	FfT
Emotional Support	**Classroom Environment**
Positive climate[a]	Creating an environment of respect and rapport[a]
Teacher sensitivity[a]	Establishing a culture for learning[a]
Regard for adolescent perspective[a]	Managing student behavior[a]
Classroom Organization	Managing classroom procedures[a]
Behavior management[a]	Organizing physical space
Productivity[a]	**Instruction**
Negative climate[a]	Demonstrating knowledge of content and pedagogy
Instructional Support	Using questioning and discussion techniques[a]
Instructional learning formats[a]	Engaging students in learning[a]
Content understanding[a]	Using assessment in instruction[a]
Analysis and problem solving[a]	Communicating with students[a]
Quality of feedback[a]	Demonstrating flexibility and responsiveness
Student Engagement	

Note: In the MET study, one more dimension, Instructional Dialogue, was scored as a part of the instructional support domain for CLASS.

[a]These dimensions were scored in both MET and UTQ.

scale. Each scale is anchored with videos and elaborated descriptions of practice at the low (1, 2), middle (3, 4, 5), and high (6, 7) score bands.

Similar to CLASS, Charlotte Danielson's instrument, FfT, is an observational system that is widely used to support evaluation, mentoring, and professional development (Danielson, 2007). Teachers across grade levels are scored on four domains: preparation, classroom environment, instruction, and professional responsibilities. Unlike CLASS, a single instrument is used at all grade levels. FfT is based on a framework developed from the research literature at Educational Testing Service and used in the Praxis III exam (Dwyer, 1994; Leusner & Ohls, 2008). Although FfT has evolved since its early years, current versions still subdivide each domain into components and elements, and specify performance levels coded on a 4-point scale. In both MET and UTQ, only the classroom environment (domain 2) and instruction (domain 3) domains were scored.

The studies also collected scores on two subject-specific protocols, MQI and PLATO. MQI is a protocol designed specifically to measure the quality of mathematical interactions in mathematics classrooms. MQI was developed by Heather Hill and her colleagues and has been used for a range of purposes. Originally developed as a tool to investigate the validity of assessments of content knowledge for teaching, MQI underwent significant changes over the course of the MET and UTQ studies. MQI Lite was used in the MET study, and a full (though now outdated) version of MQI was used in UTQ (see Table 3.2). Despite these differences, in both studies MQI is organized into five domains, which are then comprised of twenty dimensions, each of which is scored on a 3-point scale. Research on MQI has begun to establish its validity argument (e.g., Hill et al., 2008; Hill, Kapitula, & Umland, 2011).

The fourth protocol, PLATO, was developed by Pam Grossman and her colleagues at Stanford. It was designed to assess the quality of interactions in ELA classrooms. The versions used in MET and UTQ were somewhat different, as an earlier and longer version was used in UTQ (see Table 3.2). However, in both versions, observers assign scores on a 4-point scale, on up to fourteen dimensions that are aggregated into four domains. A description of the dimensions in the current version of the protocol is described online. Research on the protocol has begun to document the relationship of scores on PLATO to value-added measures (e.g., Grossman, Loeb,

TABLE 3.2. **Domains and Dimensions of the Subject-Specific Observation Protocols, MQI and PLATO in UTQ and MET Studies**

MQI	PLATO
Richness of the Mathematics[a]	**Disciplinary Demand of Classroom Talk and Activity**
Use of representation or model	Purpose
Multiple representations or models	Intellectual challenge[a]
Multiple solution strategies for a single problem	Classroom discourse[a]
Explicit links among any combination of symbols, concrete pictures, diagrams, solution strategies, etc.	Text-based Instruction
Mathematical explanations	**Instructional Scaffolding**
Mathematically generalizing statement	Explicit strategy instruction[a]
High cognitive demand task	Models/modeling[a]
Procedural-Computational Work[a]	Guided practice
Teacher describes mathematical steps of a procedural or computation	Accommodations for language learning
Students describe mathematical steps of a procedure or computation	**Representation and Use of Content**
Students practice applying an established procedure	Representation of content
Errors in the Mathematics[a]	Connections to prior knowledge
Major mathematical errors or serious mathematical oversights	Connections to personal and cultural experiences
Errors in notation (mathematical symbols) or mathematical language	**Classroom Environment**
Lack of clarity in presentation of mathematical content	Behavior management[a]
Misunderstands student production	Time management[a]

Positive Mathematical Interactions[a]

Identifies mathematical insight in specific student questions, comments, work

Makes productive mathematical use of student errors

Teacher understands non-standard student solution methods

Student Cognitive Demand[a]

Students provide explanations

Students ask why question or make counter-claim

Student makes a conjecture, draws on evidence to form a conclusion, and/or engages in reasoning about a hypothetical and/or general case

Note: In the MET study, scores on MQI Lite were defined and given on five dimensions: Richness, Student Participation in Meaning Making and Reasoning, Errors and Imprecision, Working with Students and Mathematics, and Explicitness and Thoroughness.

[a]These dimensions were scored in both MET and UTQ.

Cohen, Hammerness, Wyckoff, Boyd, & Lankford, 2010; also see Chapter 10 in this volume by Grossman, Cohen, and Brown).

Data Set 1: Score Creation, Aggregation, and Analysis

Both studies produced two types of scores from videotaped lessons: operational scores and calibration scores. Operational scores are the scores used for all study analyses. For MET, approximately 5 percent of all lessons were double scored for all four protocols. For UTQ, approximately 20 percent of all lessons were double scored for all four protocols. Calibration scores are the scores generated by scoring exercises used to monitor observer performance during the operational scoring period.

In both studies, video-recorded lessons were divided into observation segments and scores were given to the various dimensions at the segment level during operational scoring. The length of each segment varied by protocol, ranging from seven to fifteen minutes. Except for the scoring of the CLASS protocol in the MET study, an observer was assigned to a lesson and would rate all the segments in that lesson in the order in which they occurred. Observers were assigned to segments rather than lessons when scoring CLASS in the MET study.

For all protocols, we calculated a range of descriptive and agreement statistics. For FfT, MQI, and PLATO, we aggregated the segment level data to the lesson level and calculated the intraclass correlation coefficients (ICC), a correlation that assesses the similarity of grouped data. The proportions of exact agreement were calculated with rounded lesson-level data. We also calculated exact plus adjacent agreement for CLASS (i.e., within one score point). Domain statistics were the average of dimension results, except for MQI, for which we used rater assigned domain scores to calculate domain statistics. For CLASS, all inter-rater reliability and descriptive statistics were calculated at the segment level for both studies.

Calibration data were generated from the calibration exercises for both studies. In UTQ calibration activities, all observers scored a lesson that had already been scored by a master observer. Calibration videos were not reused and thirty-three or thirty-four calibration exercises were completed for each of the four protocols. In the MET study, fifteen-minute video clips were used in calibration exercises for CLASS, FfT, and PLATO. For MQI, five clips (two to four minutes long), were scored in each calibration exercise. Due to the scope and timing of the MET project, observers generally saw the same calibration video more than once. Thus, MET calibration analyses are limited to scores that met both of the following criteria: (1) scores were created by observers who calibrated on at least half of the calibration videos for that protocol and (2) scores were the first scores the observer gave to a specific video. These criteria eliminate observers who did not calibrate on a range of videos; they also alleviate concerns that calibration scores reflect observers' consistency and accuracy on previously viewed videos. Using these criteria made the data from the two studies more comparable. For both studies, inter-rater reliability analyses for calibration data were conducted at the segment level.

Data Set 2: Observer Thinking Data Collection and Analyses

In order to understand observers' thinking when they create scores, we examined the behavior and performance of a subgroup of UTQ observers. Six observers and seven master observers completed two video calibration exercises, and we compared the processes they used and thinking they demonstrated while scoring. These exercises were separate from the operational and calibration scoring described above. The calibrations were completed by both sets of observers, and data was collected in two stages.

In the first stage, the first two authors of this chapter collected think aloud and stimulated recall data from thirteen UTQ observers. Observers were asked to complete a calibration exercise as they normally would, thinking out loud when possible. All observers thought aloud during the scoring parts of their work, but only about one-third of observers thought aloud while watching the video and taking notes. After the observer completed all scoring, a stimulated recall session was conducted in which researchers asked specific questions about how the observer was thinking about specific scales (e.g., how she decided on a particular score or why a certain score could not be higher or lower than what the observer assigned). Each of the six observers used one generic and one subject-specific protocol for which they were certified. While some sessions were conducted in person, many were conducted remotely through web videoconferencing technology. All sessions were audio recorded. Each master observer had mastery of just one protocol and completed one calibration exercise on that instrument. Think aloud and stimulated recall sessions were conducted in the same manner described for the other observers. Table 3.3 shows the think aloud data collection details by instrument.

In the second stage, three research team members collected interview data from the thirteen UTQ observers. All semi-structured interviews were conducted over the phone; interviews were audio recorded and transcribed. After transcription, all transcripts were imported into NVivo for coding.

A set of initial codes was developed and applied broadly. Those codes included uncertainty and reasoning. The uncertainty code was meant to broadly cover all of the places in which observers explicitly stated uncertainty in the scoring process or where uncertainty was observed in their speech (i.e., expressions of "I'm not sure about this" or "this is a difficult dimension to score" were evidence of *uncertainty stated*, and instances where

TABLE 3.3. **Think Aloud Observers and Master Observers by Instrument**

Instrument	Observers	Master Observers	Total
CLASS	Ashley Ginger Laurie	Madison Matt	5
FfT	Lee Elizabeth Marie	Christine	4
MQI	Elizabeth Laurie Lee	Holly Sara Michelle	6
PLATO	Ashley Ginger Marie	Juno	4

Note: All observer and master observer names are pseudonyms.

an observer struggled to decide a final score were coded as *uncertainty observed*). In the first iteration of coding, we applied the reasoning codes very broadly to include both processes observers used for scoring and stated reasons for final scores.

The first four authors coded the think aloud and stimulated recall transcripts and then met to discuss the emerging themes. Using the major emergent themes, authors engaged in a process of revising codes, recoding, checking one another's codes, adding additional codes, and repeating the cycle again. There were three cycles of code definition, refinement, recoding, and accuracy checks.

OBSERVER CONSISTENCY, ACCURACY, AND PERCEPTIONS OF DIMENSION DIFFICULTY

In this section, we summarize our findings around observers' consistency and accuracy across dimensions. Then we identify observers' perceptions of the difficulty associated with scoring specific dimensions as well as the factors they identify as contributing to those difficulties.

Observer Consistency and Accuracy

There are at least two aspects of observer consistency and accuracy important to large scale implementation of observation protocols: (1) the *absolute* level of observer performance as measured by generally accepted standards of the field and (2) *relative* levels of performance among scales (i.e., which scales observers perform better or worse on compared to one another). Across the two studies, domain agreement levels varied by protocol, with exact agreement on MQI, FfT, and PLATO ranging from 42 to 90 percent and exact plus adjacent agreement on CLASS ranging from 68 to 92 percent (Tables 3.A.1 through 3.A.8). The intraclass correlation coefficients ranged from −.02 to .75 across protocols and studies. While there were differences by protocol and some domains in some data sets met acceptable levels (using 80 percent agreement and .60 correlation as rough standards (Cicchetti & Sparrow, 1981), generally, all of the protocols' agreement metrics can be characterized as relatively low.

While this describes the general pattern, there were differences across the two data sets (UTQ and MET) in the absolute levels of accuracy and consistency for specific dimensions. Some of these differences were moderate in magnitude. Although our data do not allow us to pinpoint the causes of these differences, we hypothesize some of the differences are the result of interactions among training quality, observer error, and the clarity of the scoring criteria in the instruments themselves. Some differences may also be the result of differences in the underlying variation in the data. The standard deviations of the double scored data show that, in general, MET scores had more variation than did UTQ scores. The UTQ double scored dataset spans two subjects, three grade levels, three districts, and one state, as compared to MET, which spans two subjects, three grade levels, five districts, and five states.

Because calibration videos are like tests for the observer, one might suspect that observers perform differently when scoring for calibration, as compared to scoring operationally. Generally, we did not see this. There were similar levels of consistency and accuracy. Although there were exceptions to this generalization, they were not large, and they were not always in the same direction. Notably, observers do not always perform better on calibration exercises.

Observers' ability to reliably score all dimensions of teaching varied. As Tables 3.1 and 3.2 detail, three of the four protocols require observers to score all aspects of classroom interactions typically seen in a lesson. MQI, the fourth protocol, focuses on mathematical interactions; there are no scales for the emotional or organizational aspects of classroom interactions. Drawing only on data from CLASS, FfT, and PLATO, there was a mixed pattern of observer agreement across domains (Tables 3.A.1 through 3.A.8). The pattern varied by protocol and the particular observer agreement metric.

For all three protocols in both studies, the exact and adjacent agreement percentages suggest that observers had higher levels of agreement and accuracy in the classroom organization and environment domains and lower levels of agreement in the domains that focused on instructional and emotional aspects of classroom interactions. The classroom organization and environment domains tend to have some dimensions that require somewhat lower-inference decisions and fewer judgments that focus on the interactions between teachers, students, and the subject matter being taught. The instructional and emotional aspects of classroom interactions tend to be characterized by somewhat higher-level inferences (e.g., the state of students' understanding, the appropriateness of a particular sequence of events) and complex interactions between and among teachers and students.

Correlational indicators of agreement (ICCs) were less consistent across protocols. For FfT, the ICC data supports the previously described pattern in three of four cases. In the fourth case (MET calibration data), observers' scores were more consistent in the instructional domain than in the environment domain. For CLASS, only the MET double scored data adhered to this pattern. In the three other cases, observers were more consistent on the instructional support or emotional support domains than on the classroom organization domain. PLATO was similar to CLASS. Only the MET double scored data showed observers scoring more consistently in the classroom environment domain; in the other three cases, classroom environment was not the most consistent domain.

Correlations are sensitive to the underlying distribution of scores. In the cases for which the pattern does not hold, the standard deviations of the classroom management or environment domains are smaller than the standard deviations of the other domains. It is possible that this smaller range of scores contributes to the differences between the patterns in the agreement and correlation metrics. Although the literature is somewhat limited, inter-observer reliability data from other studies suggest that observers seem to struggle most with the more complex aspects of classroom interaction (e.g., Bell et al., 2012; Gitomer et al., 2014).

Observer Perceptions of Dimension Difficulty

Although the pattern in these data is mixed with respect to which domains observers were more and less consistent on, when asked which dimensions were harder and easier to score, observers were remarkably consistent. Few dimensions were easy. The dimensions observers listed as easier were all lower inference and concerned with organizational and behavioral aspects of classrooms (Table 3.A.9). Observers found that dimensions requiring higher-level inferences with attention to the interactions among teachers, students, and subject matter were the most challenging to score. These dimensions were generally in the instructional domains.

In interviews, observers nominated two main reasons for why certain dimensions were harder to score than others. They thought the scoring criteria were applied inconsistently by master observers or were applied in ways they did not agree with or understand. Lee [pseudonyms are used for observers] explained this inconsistency in master observers. She said, "I feel like they wavered a lot in what they were teaching us. Like one week a teacher would do something and they [master observers] scored it this way, and the next week a teacher would do the same thing, and they scored another score. And so I felt always confused as to what I was actually really looking for." Lee and other observers who identified this inconsistency perceived certain dimensions' scoring criteria were interpreted variably over the study, and this variability contributed to observers' confusion about how to score those dimensions correctly.

Observers also thought certain dimensions were hard to score because they did not agree with or understand how master observers interpreted the scoring criteria. Marie's comment is representative of the explanations observers offered about this disagreement. Describing why two instructional dimensions were hard for her, Marie said, "It still was never clear even when they [master observers] gave their explanation and justification on why they scored a specific way. I, in my head, could still not wrap my mind around their logic." Whereas Marie's comments suggest confusion over how to apply the scoring criteria, Ashley's comments described a similar issue, but seemed to suggest disagreement with the application of scoring criteria. She explained that she continued over the study's two years to disagree with master observers about how to interpret certain dimensions, therefore struggling to score those dimensions accurately. She said, "Sometimes I think my view of certain strategies and certain things that are going on in the classroom differ from their perspective, and it's always been that way. And I have never been able to get past how they look at certain things in the classroom." All six of the observers had confusion or disagreement with how specific dimensions were implemented in training, certification, and calibration activities on at least one protocol. In the next section, we speculate about the source of this confusion and disagreement.

OBSERVER REASONING, POTENTIAL SOURCES OF ERROR, AND STUDY LIMITATIONS

Two related tasks were involved in learning to score accurately: learning the protocol and learning how to apply the protocol. Learning the protocol involved learning the terms, categorizing classroom interactions, and knowing the scoring criteria in enough depth and with enough frequency that they became internalized. The second learning task required observers to learn how to apply specific scoring criteria to particular instances of teaching and learning. Our findings suggest there were challenges for observers in both of the learning tasks.

The protocol scoring criteria, practices, and procedures taught to observers can be thought of as the tools observers use to standardize their judgments. But tools are used in many ways. The think aloud and stimulated recall data can provide insight into how UTQ observers and master observers used the tools they had. We describe the general reasoning strategies observers used and then explain how observer and master observer thinking differed when they were uncertain about what score to give. These differences identify some potential sources of observer error.

Reasoning Strategies

Observers and master observers used four strategies to arrive at a score. In general, observers used a single strategy for a given dimension; however, occasionally an observer used more than one reasoning strategy.

Reviewing the scoring criteria. A common strategy among both observers and master observers was to determine a score by *reviewing the scoring criteria*. When reasoning in this way, the observer systematically went through the scoring criteria, most often reading aloud or referencing each indicator while reviewing the evidence from the lesson. The text below is a representative example of this way of reasoning. Madison, a master observer, was scoring a CLASS dimension, Analysis and Problem Solving. She said:

> *Analysis and Problem Solving . . . so there, he is giving them an opportunity to think broadly. So the whole question about what the world would be like if there were not legal or illegal drugs does offer them some opportunities to think. But he is not really scaffolding, not in any sort of way. So it's hard to know exactly how students are doing that. He's not really particularly getting them to do any problem solving. There is a little bit of modeling of meta-cognition when he's checking in with the students, their own self-evaluations. So I'm not sure if I wrote it down, but I do remember a couple of times when he was just giving feedback with someone around like, "Why are you doing what I tell you not to do? Why do you think that the paper is getting into. . . . ?" [He does] do a little bit of thinking and putting something around how they would write the paragraph. So again, sort of like Content Understanding. There's not a lot of analysis here, but there is a little. I would say because there's still a little higher-level thinking and some of meta-cognition, I would rate that a three.*

In this example, Madison goes through each of the indicators that comprise Analysis and Problem Solving—opportunities for higher level thinking, problem solving, and meta-cognition—and connects each one to evidence from the video. Using this strategy, she arrives at a score.

Using internal criteria. In contrast to using the scoring criteria, some observers used their *internal criteria* to guide them to a score. When an observer used her internal criteria, she decided a score based on her overall sense of where the performance fell along a continuum of practice. Observers using this strategy did not use a step-by-step process to determine a score. Often observers would state a score and, when asked to further explain their reasoning, would state a relationship between the video viewed and an underlying continuum of practice or would judge the teaching interactions by criteria that were marginally related to the protocol. In Ashley's statement below, she describes her process as going with her feeling, and that feeling is based on her experiences, and where this particular video falls on the underlying continuum she has developed based on those experiences. Ashley explained:

> And like I said, I'll just go with what I feel at first. There's already formulas that I've gone through with everybody else. I already have an idea of where my score is going to land, based on what I've been hearing and what I've been seeing. So I go based on opinions first, and then I go back and take a look at things that I feel I need to read over.

Ashley's example also shows how an observer might combine strategies, first using internal criteria to guide her and then using another strategy (in this case scoring criteria) for the dimensions of which she was unsure. When asked how she knew which dimensions to review, she explained they were dimensions that she was not confident about. While it is possible that observers using an internal criteria strategy are using the observation protocol in appropriate ways, we did not find evidence of this.

Reasoning from memorable videos. A third strategy used less frequently was to *reason from a memorable video* or set of teaching behaviors. Using this strategy, the observer compares some set of behaviors or a numerical score on the lesson she is currently scoring with other videos or behaviors she has seen. Often the comparison is to training or calibration videos/scores. For example, when scoring the behavior management dimension, Ginger explained:

> Behavior management . . . yeah, I think they are on task. You have to like clobber somebody in order to get lower than a 4. [laughter] I think below [a 4], but I just remember that video we did in training. I always think about that video, and it's just total chaos in the classroom and he gets a 4.

Assumed score. The final strategy observers used was reasoning from an *assumed score.* In this strategy, the observer began reasoning with a specific numerical score that was typical for a dimension, given a certain set of behaviors. The observer might then adjust the assumed score after referring back to the evidence or checking the scoring criteria. In contrast to the internal scoring criteria, where the criteria for the decision were not articulated or they were unrelated to the protocol, observers using the assumed score strategy were able to explicitly link the behaviors of the video being scored with previous scores for similar behaviors. The assumed score is based on the observation protocol's scoring criteria, and those criteria are explicitly referenced by the observer.

During her think aloud session, Ashley said, "I rarely take notes for negative climate unless I see like there's a problem in the class. It's usually going to be around a 1 or 2 unless there's a really big issue."

This statement was consistent with Ashley's actions when she scored the negative climate dimension. She did not take notes, and there were very few actions that would have caused the score to move higher than a 1 or a 2.

A master observer, Madison, spoke aloud as she scored the behavior management dimension:

> *Okay, behavior management. So there was a little bit of lack of clarity right at the beginning in terms of what he wanted, but there was also basically no misbehavior. And typically when we see no misbehavior, it's going to score at the high end unless it's a situation in which the teacher is doing a ton of redirection, even though there isn't much misbehavior. Okay, I'm going to read through the indicators. [reads scoring criteria] I would say he's sort of a mix of that. . . . This would be a 7 because the students are generally well-behaved, but the teacher isn't proactive.*

In her thinking, Madison talked through the evidence, linked it to a typical score ("the high end"), and then used another strategy (checking the scoring criteria) to arrive at a more specific score ("a 7").

Potential Sources of Error in Observers' Thinking

If we presume that master observers' reasoning is something observers should emulate so as to achieve greater consistency and accuracy, we found differences in frequency with which master observers and observers used particular reasoning strategies.

Master observers almost always reasoned to a score using the rubric, the language of the rubric, and rules of thumb that were tied to the rubric. They also took notes in ways that made sense of the actions in the classroom, focusing on writing down evidence that would be useful to the scoring criteria later. Master observers did not generally report thinking about what the score for the lesson would be during the observation time; this type of thinking was restricted to the scoring part of their efforts.

Observers often used their rubrics to reason toward scores; however, the language they used when talking out loud and when explaining their rationale after the lesson was scored was more loosely tied to the rubric than that of master observers. They also used the scoring criteria less frequently than master observers did. There was wider variation in how observers took notes, but like master observers, observers recorded evidence aligned to the scoring criteria. Occasionally, observers would reflect on what the lesson scores would be during the note-taking stage of the observations.

Observers used two reasoning strategies that master observers rarely used. Observers relied on internal criteria when they were uncertain about what score to assign, and they used specific, memorable training or calibration videos as a basis for their reasoning. They remembered, for example, that a particular segment of a lesson during training received a 4 for behavior management and used those behaviors and scores as a benchmark for the types of behaviors that could still be scored as a 4. Master observers never used memorable videos in this way.

Because teaching varies by occasion—e.g., one lesson is primarily a small group literature lesson, another is a whole group grammar lesson—there will always be some uncertainty about how to interpret and score evidence. Thus, it is important to know how observers deal with uncertainty when they have it. We found that sometimes observers and master observers dealt with it similarly by going back to the scoring criteria and proceeding through it indicator by indicator. However, there were many instances in which observers used internal criteria when master observers used a careful review of the scoring criteria.

Observers sometimes used internal criteria when they were uncertain about a particular dimension or had ongoing trouble understanding how to apply the rules of a specific dimension's scoring scale. In discussing the scores she assigned for FfT on the content knowledge dimension,

Lee explained that sometimes she used her instincts on lessons when it was not clear how the evidence should be scored:

> *Content knowledge is probably one of my most difficult, and I usually end up kind of just going with a feeling that I have one way or the other—which I know is not the best way to score—because the rubric doesn't make much sense to me. The wording of it is confusing to me. I have a very difficult time with it. My hard part is always deciding between basic and proficient. So I never quite know what bumps it from basic to proficient. There are some lessons that are very clear that it's proficient; and some lessons are very clear that it's basic. But those kind of mid-level ones I usually just kind of end up hoping or having a feeling or taking a guess.*

Lee was uncomfortable with the approach of relying on internal criteria, but in the face of ongoing uncertainty and confusion, this was the process she used. As she described, she only needed to rely on internal criteria for the lessons that fell somewhere in the middle of basic and proficient. It is possible that master observers occasionally used internal criteria when they were uncertain; however, they did not articulate that strategy to us. Instead, they stated their uncertainty and then used the scoring criteria to reason to a score.

Across the think alouds and interviews, master observers used the scoring criteria more consistently, particularly when they were uncertain. In contrast, observers used other strategies in addition to the scoring criteria. When they were uncertain, they relied on these other strategies more than master observers did. Our sample does not allow us to make claims about whether the use of these other strategies caused observers to make errors, although it is certainly possible, perhaps likely, that such strategy use is related to scoring errors.

Study Limitations

There are a number of important limitations of this study. First, the observers who provided the think aloud data are not typical observers. Although research on typical observers is scarce, at least three characteristics make the think aloud observers atypical. They are unusual in the large number of lessons they scored over roughly two years, the amount of feedback they received on their scoring, and their access to instrument developers. Each one of them scored at least 545 lessons, with the average observer scoring 716 lessons. If we imagine principals do three observations a week in a school year with approximately thirty-six weeks, it would take principals more than six years to achieve this level of experience. Thus, it is possible that these highly experienced observers developed thought patterns that may differ from the patterns principals and other non-research staff will develop. Future research on observer thinking should investigate various groups of observers so as to better understand the robustness of our findings.

These observers also did not have relationships with the teachers they scored, nor were the observers responsible for the quality of the teaching they observed. It is possible that observer thinking, accuracy, and even the dimensions that are challenging may differ if observers and teachers have ongoing professional relationships and are also responsible for improving the teaching that is being scored. For example, if observers work in a district that has been engaged in system-wide professional learning about how to ask high-quality questions, perhaps dimensions that require judgments of question quality would have higher, rather than lower, reliability.

The study presumes that the validity of observation scores is improved if regular observers behave more like master observers. This assumption is defensible if master observers create scores that have stronger validity than the scores less skilled observers create. While determining the validity of master observers' scores is outside the scope of this chapter, this is an important issue worth investigating in future research.

Finally, it is important to situate the findings of observer reasoning in context. The think aloud data on how observers and master observers created scores came from a single study, the UTQ study. Observers were well supported, used helpful but specific scoring software, were encouraged to provide feedback to the study PIs as the work evolved, and were given feedback on their performance regularly so they knew what dimensions they were and were not skilled at scoring. The think aloud data contain many references to the language in the protocols, calibration activities, and the training heuristics and procedures taught to the observers. Given this, it is possible that the ways in which these observers thought and the differences between their thinking and master observers' thinking will differ from other observers in other protocol implementations. There might, for example, be different reasoning strategies if observers are taught to take notes in very specific ways, use scoring software that differs from the UTQ software, or are not calibrated weekly. Because the think aloud data are limited to a single study, we cannot know how the findings will generalize to other contexts. However, our findings are similar enough to insights from the CR literature that it is reasonable to use our findings as a starting place for future research as well as for revisions to ongoing training efforts.

IMPLICATIONS FOR TRAINING AND OBSERVATIONAL POLICY DECISIONS

Given the nature of learning to score, the strategies observers use to create scores, and current levels of accuracy and consistency, there are a number of strategies that could improve current implementations of observation protocols. In order to address the finding that scoring can be challenging for observers, we suggest the following recommendations:

1. Approach the training of observers differentially. One size does not fit all. Almost all observers are likely to need help scoring the interactional components of lessons. Spend less training effort on the lower-inference aspects of teaching and learning. Spend more training effort on dimensions with lower levels of accuracy and consistency.

2. Create a professional learning environment that supports observers learning to score, provides opportunities for practice and feedback, and uses a set of master videos that are scored in a consistent and coherent manner.

3. Identify aspects of training materials and scoring scales that contribute to rater disagreement. Revise existing scoring criteria and procedures to improve clarity and decrease the cognitive demand on observers.

We also found that observers who were certified and calibrated regularly paid careful attention to master observers' scores and thinking. Therefore, we suggest:

4. Teach observers to

   ■ Take notes in the same way as master observers take notes

   ■ Attend to interactions, not just teachers' actions, and use evidence of the quality of the interactions when deciding on scores

   ■ Use the language of the protocol when reasoning about, discussing, and scoring instruction

   ■ Use the scoring criteria to reason when they are uncertain

5. On dimensions that are particularly difficult to score reliably, provide as much practice and feedback to observers as possible.

Finally, there were important differences between the research contexts upon which this chapter is based and the world of teacher evaluation. In order for systems to be developed at scale, those systems must be feasible, defensible, and sensitive to local context. We recommend that policymakers

6. Identify cross-dimension learning challenges and develop training modules that can be used to supplement the main training activities, cost little to administer, and can be completed at times that are sensitive to observers' learning needs. These might include

   - Learning to attend to students when scoring

   - Weighing competing evidence within a dimension

   - Understanding how cognitive demand looks in classrooms

   - Understanding what observational evidence of student understanding looks like

7. Build in small amounts of double scoring by skilled observers during operational scoring to document the dimensions that are more challenging for observers and to mitigate the adverse incentive for observers to do whatever it takes to pass the certification test while not disciplining their observational skills in practice.

8. Expect there to be disagreements among master observers and observers that stem from legitimately different interpretations of complex events. Plan for and monitor these conversations. Develop artifacts that document why a specific video clip is evidence of a specific score on some dimensions. This artifact collection will codify and standardize the language of the scoring criteria and provide examples to observers still refining their skills.

9. Acknowledge there is an affective aspect to learning to score, taking certification tests, and operational scoring that must be disciplined through training, co-observing, and monitoring. Plan to support observers as they experience a range of affective reactions to the work of observing.

REFERENCES AND ADDITIONAL RESOURCES

Bejar, I. (2012). Rater cognition: Implications for validity. *Educational Assessment, 31*(3), 2–9. doi: 10.1111/j.1745–3992.2012.00238.x

Bell, C. A., Gitomer, D. H., McCaffrey, D. F., Hamre, B. K., Pianta, R. C., & Qi, Y. (2012). An argument approach to observation protocol validity. *Educational Assessment, 17*(2–3), 62–87. doi: 10.1080/10627197.2012.715014

Bernardin, H. J. (1978). Effects of rater training on leniency and halo errors in student ratings of instructors. *Journal of Applied Psychology, 63*(3), 301–308. doi: 10.1037/00219010.63.3.301

Bill & Melinda Gates Foundation. (2012). *Gathering feedback for teaching: Combining high quality observations with student surveys and achievement gains.* Seattle, WA: Author.

Borko, H., Stecher, B. M., Alonzo, A. C., Moncure, S., & McClam, S. (2005). Artifact packages for characterizing classroom practice: A pilot study. *Educational Assessment, 10*(2), 73–104. doi: 10.1207/s15326977ea1002_1

Borman, W. C. (1975). Effects of instructions to avoid halo error on reliability and validity of performance evaluation ratings. *Journal of Applied Psychology, 60*(5), 556–560. doi: 10.1037/0021–9010.60.5.556

Casabianca, J., McCaffrey, D. F., Gitomer, D. H., Bell, C. A., & Hamre, B. H., & Pianta, R. (2013). Effect of observation mode on measures of secondary mathematics teaching. *Educational and Psychological Measurement.* doi: 10.1177/0013164413486987

Casabianca, J. M, Lockwood, J. R., & McCaffrey, D. F. (2013). Rater drift in classroom observation scores. Unpublished manuscript.

Cash, A. H., Hamre, B. K., Pianta, R. C., & Myers, S. S. (2012). Rater calibration when observational assessment occurs at large scale: Degree of calibration and characteristics of raters associated with calibration. *Early Childhood Research Quarterly, 27*(3), 529–542. doi: 10.1016/j.ecresq.2011.12.006

Cicchetti, D. V., & Sparrow, S. A. (1981). Developing criteria for establishing inter-rater reliability of specific items: Applications to assessment of adaptive behavior. *American Journal of Mental Deficiency, 86*(2), 127–137. Retrieved from http://psycnet.apa.org/psycinfo/1982–00095–001

Clauser, B. E., Harik, P., & Margolis, M. J. (2006). A multivariate generalizability analysis of data from a performance assessment of physicians' clinical skills. *Journal of Educational Measurement, 43,* 173–191. doi: 10.1111/j.1745–3984.2006.00012.x

Crisp, V. (2012). An investigation of rater cognition in the assessment of projects. *Educational Assessment, 31*(3), 10–20. doi: 10.1111/j.1745–3992.2012.00239.x

Danielson, C. (2007). *Enhancing professional practice: A framework for teaching.* Alexandria, VA: Association for Supervision & Curriculum Development.

Dwyer, C. A (1994). *Development of the knowledge base for the PRAXIS III: Classroom performance assessments assessment criteria.* Princeton, NJ: Educational Testing Service.

Early, D., Barbarin, O., Bryant, B., Burchinal, M., Chang, F., Clifford, R., et al. (2005). Pre-kindergarten in eleven states: NCEDL's multi-state study of pre-kindergarten and state-wide early educational programs (SWEEP) study. Retrieved September 30, 2005, from www.ncedl.org

Engelhard, G. (2002). Monitoring raters in performance assessments. In G. Tindal & T. Haladyna (Eds.), *Large-scale assessment programs for all students: Validity, technical accuracy, and implementation* (pp. 261–287). Mahwah, NJ: Lawrence Erlbaum Associates.

Freedman, S. W., & Calfee, R. C. (1983). Holistic assessment of writing: Experimental design and cognitive theory. In P. Mosenthal, L. Taymor, & S. A. Walmsley (Eds.), *Research on writing: Principals and method* (pp. 75–98). New York, NY: Longman.

Gitomer, D. H., Bell, C. A., Qi, Y., McCaffrey, D. F., Hamre, B. K., & Pianta, R. C. (2014). The instructional challenge in improving teaching quality: Lessons from a classroom observation protocol. *Teachers College Record, 116*(6), Retrieved from http://www.tcrecord.org/Content .asp?ContentId=17460

Grossman, P., Greenberg, S., Hammerness, K., Cohen, J., Alston, C., & Brown, M. (2009). *Development of the Protocol for Language Arts Teaching Observation (PLATO).* Paper presented at the annual meeting of the American Educational Research Association, San Diego, California.

Grossman, P., Loeb, S., Cohen, J., Hammerness, K. M., Wyckoff, J., Boyd, D., & Lankford, H. (2010). *Measure for measure: The relationship between measures of instructional practice in middle school English Language Arts and teachers' value-added scores* (NBER Working Paper). Cambridge, MA: The National Bureau of Economic Research.

Hakel, M. D., Koenig, J. A., & Elliott, S. W. (2008). *Assessing accomplished teaching: Advanced-level certification programs.* Washington, DC: National Academy Press.

Hamre, B. K., Pianta, R. C., Downer, J. T., DeCoster, J., Jones, S., Brown, J., . . . & Hakigami, A. (2013). Teaching through interactions: Testing a developmental framework of effective teaching in over 4,000 classrooms. *Elementary School Journal, 113*(4), 461–487.

Hill, H. C., Kapitula, L. R. & Umland, K. L. (2011). A validity argument approach to evaluating value-added scores. *American Educational Research Journal, 48*(3), 794–831. doi: 10.3102/0002831210387916

Hill, H. C., Blunk, M., Charalambous, C., Lewis, J., Phelps, G. C., Sleep, L., & Ball, D. L. (2008). Mathematical knowledge for teaching and the mathematical quality of instruction: An exploratory study. *Cognition and Instruction, 26*, 430–511. doi: 10.1080/07370000802177235

Ingvarson, L., & Hattie, J. (2008). *Assessing teachers for professional certification: The first decade of the National Board for Professional Teaching Standards.* Amsterdam/Boston: Elsevier/JAI.

Kellor, E. M. (2002). *Performance-based licensure in Connecticut* (CPRE-UW Working Paper Series TC-02–10). Madison, WI: Consortium for Policy Research in Education.

Leusner, D., & Ohls, S. (2008, July). *Praxis III™ Research Update Summary.* (ETS Research Memorandum No. RM-08–09). Princeton, NJ: Educational Testing Service.

Lortie, D. C. (1975). *Schoolteacher: A sociological study.* Chicago, IL: University of Chicago Press.

Mashburn, A. J., Downer, J. T., Rivers, S. E., Brackett, M. A., & Martinez, A. (2011, under review). Improving the power of an experimental study of a social and emotional learning program: Application of generalizability theory to the measurement of classroom-level outcomes. *Prevention Science.*

Matsumura, L. C., Garnier, H., Pascal, J., & Valdés, R. (2002). Measuring instructional quality in accountability systems: Classroom assignments and student achievement. *Educational Assessment, 8*(3), 207–229. doi: 10.1207/S15326977EA0803_01

Matsumura, L. C., Garnier, H., Slater, S. C., & Boston, M. (2008). Toward measuring instructional interactions "at-scale." *Educational Assessment, 13*, 267–300. doi: 10.1080/10627190802602541

Moss, P. A., Sutherland, L. M., Haniford, L., Miller, R., Johnson, D., Geist, P. K., . . . & Pecheone, R. L. (2004). Interrogating the generalizability of portfolio assessments of beginning teachers: A qualitative study. *Education Policy Analysis Archives, 12*(32), 1–70. Retrieved from http://epaa. asu.edu/ojs/article/view/187

Muckle, T. J., & Karabatsos, G. (2009). Hierarchical generalized linear models for the analysis of judge ratings. *Journal of Educational Measurement, 46*(2), 198–219. doi: 10.1111/j.1745–3984.2009.00078.x

NICHD ECCRN. (2005). A day in third grade: A large-scale study of classroom quality and teacher and student behavior. *Elementary School Journal, 105*(3), 305–323. doi: 10.1086/428746.

Pianta, R., & Hamre, B. K. (2009). Conceptualization, measurement, and improvement of classroom processes: Standardized observation can leverage capacity. *Educational Researcher, 38*(2), 109–119. doi: 10.3102/0013189X09332374

Pianta, R. C., La Paro, K. M., & Hamre, B. K. (2008). *Classroom Assessment Scoring System.* Baltimore, MD: Paul H. Brookes.

Pianta, R. C., Hamre, B. K., Haynes, N. J., Mintz, S. L., & La Paro, K. M. (2007). *Classroom Assessment Scoring System manual, middle/secondary version.* Charlottesville, NC: University of Virginia Press.

Raymond, M. R., Harik, P., & Clauser, B. E. (2011). The impact of statistically adjusting for rater effects on conditional standard errors of performance ratings. *Applied Psychological Measurement, 35*(3), 235–246. doi: 10.1177/0146621610390675

Rimm-Kaufman, S. E., La Paro, K. M., Downer, J. T., & Pianta, R. C. (2005). The contribution of classroom setting and quality of instruction to children. *The Elementary School Journal, 105*, 377–394. doi: 10.1086/429948

Sartain, L., Stoelinga, S. R., & Brown, E. R. (2011). *Rethinking teacher evaluation in Chicago: Lessons learned from classroom observations, principal-teacher conferences, and district implementation.* Chicago, IL: Consortium on Chicago School Research at the University of Chicago.

Schutz, A., & Moss, P. (2004). Reasonable decisions in portfolio assessment: Evaluating complex evidence of teaching. *Education Policy Analysis Archives, 12*(33). Retrieved from http://epaa.asu.edu/ojs/article/view/188/314

Stipek, D., & Byler, P. (2004). The Early Childhood Classroom Observation Measure. *Early Childhood Research Quarterly, 19*, 375–397.

Suto, I. (2012). A critical review of some qualitative research methods used to explore rater cognition. *Educational Assessment, 31*(3), 21–30. doi: 10.1111/j.1745–3992.2012.00240.x

Szpara, M. Y., & Wylie, E. C. (2005). National Board for Professional Teaching Standards assessor training: Impact of bias reduction exercises. *Teachers College Record, 107*(4), 803–841. Retrieved from www.tcrecord.org/content.asp?contentid=11821

Wenzel, S., Nagaoka, J. K., Morris, L., Billings, S., & Fendt, C. (2002). *Documentation of the 1996–2002 Chicago Annenberg Research Project Strand on Authentic Intellectual Demand Exhibited in Assignments and Student Work: A technical process manual.* Chicago, IL: Consortium on Chicago School Research.

Wolfe, E. W., Kao, C., & Ranney, M. (1998). Cognitive differences in proficient and non-proficient essay scorers. *Written Communication, 15*(4), 465–492. doi: 10.1177/0741088398015004002

APPENDIX

TABLE 3.A.1. CLASS—IRR and Descriptives, UTQ and MET Double Scored Data (UTQ sample size=1224; MET sample size = 171)

	Mean		Standard Deviation		% Exact Agreement		% Exact or Adjacent Agreement		ICC	
	UTQ	MET	UTQ	MET	UTQ	MET	UTQ	MET	UTQ	MET
Emotional Support	3.80	3.69	1.12	1.27	26.28	26.12	68.27	71.93	0.13	0.55
Positive Climate	4.47	4.15	1.08	1.28	26.39	25.73	69.61	69.59	0.09	0.57
Teacher Sensitivity	4.04	3.99	1.16	1.26	25.16	22.81	65.03	67.84	0.09	0.41
Regard for Student Perspectives	2.88	2.92	1.13	1.28	27.29	29.82	70.18	78.36	0.21	0.66
Classroom Organization	6.15	5.99	0.69	1.02	50.16	46.79	92.37	85.97	0.16	0.55
Negative Climate	6.71	6.61	0.54	0.73	62.01	63.16	97.63	95.32	0.14	0.58
Behavior Management	5.98	5.75	0.73	1.17	46.08	40.94	92.73	82.46	0.17	0.64
Productivity	5.76	5.62	0.79	1.16	42.40	36.26	86.76	80.12	0.18	0.43
Instructional Support	3.12	3.50	1.04	1.26	29.47	28.89	74.90	75.56	0.17	0.59

Instructional Learning Formats	3.60	3.94	1.05	1.21	27.45	25.73	74.35	74.86	0.16	0.59
Content Understanding	3.25	3.66	1.07	1.25	31.29	29.24	76.55	73.69	0.25	0.57
Analysis and Problem Solving	2.25	2.52	0.88	1.24	35.87	36.84	84.40	77.19	0.16	0.58
Quality of Feedback	3.39	3.28	1.15	1.31	23.28	27.49	64.30	74.86	0.10	0.58
Instructional Dialogue	–	3.05	–	1.28	–	25.15	–	77.19	–	0.65
Student Engagement	4.93	4.56	0.88	1.19	33.91	27.49	82.35	76.61	0.15	0.59

Note: All the agreement statistics are generated with segment level data in CLASS. All other descriptive statistics are generated from lesson-level data with only grade 6 to 8 teachers.

TABLE 3.A.2. CLASS—IRR and Descriptives, UTQ and MET calibration data (UTQ sample size = 933; MET sample size = 3,587)

	Mean		Standard Deviation		% Exact Agreement		% Exact or Adjacent Agreement		ICC	
	UTQ	MET	UTQ	MET	UTQ	MET	UTQ	MET	UTQ	MET
Emotional Support	4.19	3.72	1.09	1.31	33.23	32.04	80.23	76.81	0.58	0.66
Positive Climate	4.77	4.23	1.04	1.43	32.93	32.59	79.83	75.58	0.53	0.73
Teacher Sensitivity	4.53	3.98	1.07	1.16	34.54	33.73	80.98	78.42	0.54	0.55
Regard for Student Perspectives	3.28	2.95	1.16	1.33	32.23	29.80	79.90	76.44	0.66	0.71
Classroom Organization	6.14	5.82	0.60	1.10	42.76	43.93	94.40	86.88	0.41	0.71
Negative Climate	6.66	6.45	0.52	0.77	68.53	57.62	99.19	94.03	0.44	0.62
Behavior Management	6.00	5.51	0.55	1.26	30.04	39.70	96.57	87.34	0.33	0.79
Productivity	5.77	5.49	0.73	1.27	29.71	34.46	87.44	79.28	0.45	0.74

Instructional Support	3.63	3.35	1.07	1.28	34.02	32.66	80.79	76.83	0.50	0.66
Instructional Learning Formats	4.28	4.13	1.03	1.26	36.18	34.01	81.40	80.68	0.50	0.70
Content Understanding	3.79	3.51	1.08	1.24	32.50	31.92	78.44	76.86	0.52	0.65
Analysis and Problem Solving	2.72	2.69	1.05	1.25	31.32	37.11	76.27	79.62	0.46	0.65
Quality of Feedback	3.75	3.38	1.12	1.36	30.05	30.05	78.13	72.28	0.51	0.63
Instructional Dialogue	–	3.02	–	1.31	–	30.19	–	74.69	–	0.66
Student Engagement	5.15	4.66	0.82	1.15	40.04	34.54	89.72	83.41	0.55	0.68

Note: UTQ statistics are generated at segment level. For MET, only one segment is selected for calibration.

TABLE 3.A.3. FfT—IRR and Descriptives, UTQ and MET Double Scored Data (UTQ sample size = 360; MET sample size = 138)

	Mean		Standard Deviation		% Exact Agreement		ICC	
	UTQ	MET	UTQ	MET	UTQ	MET	UTQ	MET
The Classroom Environment	2.54	2.55	0.49	0.61	67.29	59.78	0.44	0.55
Creating an Environment of Respect and Rapport	2.81	2.57	0.43	0.63	77.22	63.04	0.49	0.59
Establishing a Culture for Learning	2.31	2.32	0.53	0.60	60.17	53.62	0.34	0.41
Managing Classroom Procedures	2.48	2.62	0.56	0.61	57.66	60.14	0.40	0.57
Managing Student Behavior	2.77	2.68	0.47	0.61	76.11	62.32	0.59	0.63
Organizing Physical Space	2.31	–	0.47	–	65.28	–	0.36	–
Instruction	2.20	2.29	0.48	0.58	64.52	55.07	0.26	0.38
Demonstrating Knowledge of Content and Pedagogy	2.17	–	0.50	–	61.67	–	0.23	–
Using Questioning and Discussion Techniques	1.97	2.13	0.40	0.61	75.56	55.07	0.32	0.47
Engaging Students in Learning	2.22	2.34	0.53	0.54	58.06	57.97	0.30	0.41
Using Assessment in Instruction	2.06	2.16	0.45	0.59	67.50	50.00	0.26	0.27
Communicating with Students	2.63	2.54	0.51	0.56	61.67	57.25	0.27	0.36
Demonstrating Flexibility and Responsiveness	2.13	–	0.46	–	62.67	–	0.15	–

Note: All the agreement statistics are generated with rounded data except the Pearson correlation and ICC which captures all variation in the unrounded data. All the descriptive statistics are generated from rounded lesson-level data with only grade 6 to 8 teachers.

TABLE 3.A.4. FfT—IRR and Descriptives, UTQ and MET Calibration Data (UTQ sample size = 357; MET sample size = 1,526)

	Mean		Standard Deviation		% Exact Agreement		ICC	
	UTQ	MET	UTQ	MET	UTQ	MET	UTQ	MET
The Classroom Environment	2.72	2.77	0.43	0.67	69.95	64.48	0.43	0.67
Creating an Environment of Respect and Rapport	2.93	2.85	0.26	0.63	89.81	60.75	0.46	0.63
Establishing a Culture for Learning	2.63	2.66	0.54	0.82	58.02	61.99	0.35	0.78
Managing Classroom Procedures	2.66	2.76	0.50	0.57	58.37	70.12	0.45	0.56
Managing Student Behavior	2.87	2.82	0.34	0.66	78.84	65.07	0.50	0.71
Organizing Physical Space	2.52	–	0.51	–	64.71	–	0.42	–
Instruction	2.39	2.52	0.52	0.78	57.63	54.70	0.27	0.71
Demonstrating Knowledge of Content and Pedagogy	2.42	–	0.57	–	54.37	–	0.26	–
Using Questioning and Discussion Techniques	2.11	2.32	0.52	0.92	59.16	46.66	0.42	0.73
Engaging Students in Learning	2.45	2.58	0.55	0.77	51.61	65.86	0.27	0.80
Using Assessment in Instruction	2.16	2.43	0.50	0.68	57.50	56.68	0.20	0.63
Communicating with Students	2.81	2.74	0.45	0.74	65.03	49.61	0.30	0.66
Demonstrating Flexibility and Responsiveness	2.37	–	0.53	–	58.14	–	0.18	–

Note: UTQ statistics are generated at segment level. For MET, only one segment is selected for calibration.

TABLE 3.A.5. PLATO—IRR and Descriptives, UTQ and MET Double Scored Data (UTQ sample size = 182; MET sample size = 59)

	Mean		Standard Deviation		% Exact Agreement		ICC	
	UTQ	MET	UTQ	MET	UTQ	MET	UTQ	MET
Disciplinary Demand of Classroom Talk and Activity	2.21	2.46	0.58	0.75	56.60	42.38	0.35	0.52
Purpose	2.83	–	0.42	–	64.84	–	0.03	–
Intellectual Challenge	2.11	2.53	0.53	0.71	55.49	40.68	0.24	0.41
Classroom Discourse	2.04	2.39	0.52	0.80	62.09	44.07	0.51	0.62
Text-Based Instruction	1.87	–	0.85	–	43.96	–	0.62	–
Instructional Scaffolding	1.47	1.66	0.45	0.84	67.72	47.46	0.22	−0.02
Explicit Strategy Instruction	1.07	1.72	0.30	0.86	92.31	49.15	0.49	−0.08
Models/Modeling	1.13	1.60	0.34	0.82	79.67	45.76	0.21	0.05
Guided Practice	2.38	–	0.68	–	44.51	–	0.31	–

Accommodations for Language Learning	1.29	—	0.47	—	54.40	—	−0.15	—
Representation and Use of Content	1.71	—	0.54	—	65.75	—	0.56	—
Representation of Content	2.46	—	0.55	—	69.78	—	0.71	—
Connections to Prior Knowledge	1.42	—	0.58	—	54.40	—	0.33	—
Connections to Personal and Cultural Experiences	1.24	—	0.49	—	73.08	—	0.64	—
Classroom Environment	3.91	3.72	0.28	0.60	88.46	76.27	0.51	0.77
Behavior Management	3.96	3.80	0.20	0.61	95.05	83.05	0.60	0.82
Time Management	3.86	3.64	0.36	0.59	81.87	69.49	0.42	0.71

Note: All the agreement statistics are generated with rounded data except Pearson correlation and ICC, which captures all variation in the unrounded data. All the descriptive statistics are generated from rounded lesson-level data with only grade 6 to 8 teachers.

TABLE 3.A.6. PLATO—IRR and Descriptives, UTQ and MET Calibration Data (UTQ sample size = 421; MET sample size = 552)

	Mean		Standard Deviation		% Exact Agreement		ICC	
	UTQ	MET	UTQ	MET	UTQ	MET	UTQ	MET
Disciplinary Demand of Classroom Talk and Activity	2.54	2.10	0.69	0.73	62.34	65.04	0.60	0.75
Purpose	2.96	–	0.40	–	78.09	–	0.53	–
Intellectual Challenge	2.38	2.04	0.61	0.76	61.26	65.22	0.55	0.78
Classroom Discourse	2.38	2.15	0.64	0.70	62.13	64.86	0.64	0.73
Text-Based Instruction	2.42	–	1.11	–	47.87	–	0.69	–
Instructional Scaffolding	1.69	1.25	0.63	0.56	63.33	70.92	0.50	0.32
Explicit Strategy Instruction	1.20	1.26	0.47	0.54	70.63	69.73	0.38	0.47
Models/Modeling	1.33	1.23	0.69	0.58	70.61	72.10	0.62	0.18
Guided Practice	2.59	–	0.80	–	51.17	–	0.57	–

Accommodations for Language Learning	1.64	—	0.57	—	60.91	—	0.43	—
Representation and Use of Content	2.02	—	0.79	—	57.95	—	0.56	—
Representation of Content	2.64	—	0.56	—	62.21	—	0.40	—
Connections to Prior Knowledge	1.92	—	0.97	—	45.67	—	0.61	—
Connections to Personal and Cultural Experiences	1.51	—	0.85	—	65.98	—	0.68	—
Classroom Environment	3.85	3.78	0.36	0.50	81.57	73.28	0.46	0.48
Behavior Management	3.96	3.74	0.21	0.49	94.79	74.82	0.44	0.48
Time Management	3.74	3.81	0.51	0.51	68.36	71.74	0.49	—

Note: UTQ statistics are generated at segment level. For MET, only one segment is selected for calibration. In MET, all calibration videos selected had a master-coded true score of a 4 for Time Management, and therefore, some statistics could not be computed because of the lack of variance in the true scores. One video that did not have a true score for Explicit Strategy Instruction, so we could not run rater agreement statistics for this video for this dimension.

TABLE 3.A.7. MQI—IRR and Descriptives, UTQ and MET Double Scored Data (UTQ sample size = 181; MET sample size = 60)

	Mean		Standard Deviation		% Exact Agreement		ICC	
	UTQ	MET	UTQ	MET	UTQ	MET	UTQ	MET
Richness of the Mathematics	1.14	1.23	0.35	0.42	80.11	76.67	0.46	0.53
Use of Representation or Model	0.15		0.36		75.69		0.41	
Multiple Representations or Models	0.01		0.12		97.24		0.03	
Multiple Solution Strategies	0.01		0.12		97.24		0.56	
Explicit Links Among Any Combination of Symbols, Concrete Pictures, Diagrams, Solution Strategies, etc.	0.01		0.10		97.79		−0.04	
Mathematical Explanations	0.12		0.32		83.43		0.44	
Mathematically Generalizing Statement	0.02		0.15		95.58		0.33	
High Cognitive Demand Task	0.01		0.07		98.90		0.21	
Procedural-Computational Work	2.32	1.77	0.63	0.61	57.46	70.00	0.55	0.61
Teacher Describes Mathematical Steps of a Procedure or Computation	0.56		0.50		64.64		0.57	
Students Describe Mathematical Steps of a Procedure or Computation	0.08		0.28		90.61		0.68	
Students Practice Applying an Established procedure	0.62		0.48		67.96		0.64	

Errors in the Mathematics	1.09	1.30	0.29	0.50	85.08	63.33	0.06	0.12
Major Mathematical Errors or Serious Mathematical Oversights			0.00	0.00	99.45		0.08	
Errors in Notation (mathematical symbols) or Mathematical Language			0.05	0.21	92.82		0.29	
Lack of Clarity in Presentation of Mathematical Content			0.01	0.07	98.90		0.02	
Misunderstands Student Production			0.00	0.00	100.00		−0.03	
Positive Mathematical Interactions	1.06	1.33	0.23	0.49	90.06	73.33	0.38	0.30
Identifies Mathematical Insight in Specific Student Questions, Comments, Work			0.00	0.05	99.45		0.21	
Makes Productive Mathematical Use of Student Errors			0.01	0.10	97.79		0.39	
Teacher Understands Non-Standard Student Solution Methods			0.00	0.00	100.00		−0.02	
Student Cognitive Demand	1.06	1.20	0.23	0.40	90.06	76.67	0.20	0.62
Students Provide Explanations			0.01	0.07	98.90		0.16	
Students Ask Why Questions or Make Counter-Claims			0.01	0.07	98.90		0.26	
Student Makes a Conjecture, Draws on Evidence to Form a Conclusion, and/or Engages in Reasoning About a Hypothetical and/or General Case			0.00	0.00	100.00		0.12	

Note: All the agreement statistics are generated with rounded data except for Pearson correlation and ICC, which captures all variation in the unrounded data. All the descriptive statistics are generated from rounded lesson-level data with only grade 6 to 8 teachers.

TABLE 3.A.8. MQI—IRR and Descriptives, UTQ and MET Calibration Data (UTQ sample size = 1,166)

	Mean		Standard Deviation		% Exact Agreement		ICC	
	UTQ	MET	UTQ	MET	UTQ	MET	UTQ	MET
Richness of the Mathematics	0.18	1.38	0.43	0.52	76.62	67.59	0.41	0.57
Use of Representation or Model	0.40		0.66		68.61		0.60	
Multiple Representations or Models	0.13		0.44		77.79		0.39	
Multiple Solution Strategies	0.08		0.29		87.91		0.48	
Explicit Links Among Any Combination of Symbols, Concrete Pictures, Diagrams, Solution Strategies, etc.	0.11		0.35		76.93		0.29	
Mathematical Explanations	0.33		0.55		59.14		0.35	
Mathematically Generalizing Statement	0.07		0.27		89.88		0.47	
High Cognitive Demand Task	0.15		0.45		76.07		0.27	
Procedural-Computational Work	0.57	2.03	0.67	0.74	65.12	53.37	0.62	0.68
Teacher Describes Mathematical Steps of a Procedure or Computation	0.69		0.69		55.57		0.59	
Students Describe Mathematical Steps of a Procedure or Computation	0.27		0.48		75.81		0.58	
Students Practice Applying an Established Procedure	0.74		0.83		63.98		0.69	

	(1)	(2)	(3)	(4)	(5)	(6)	(7)	(8)
Errors in the Mathematics	0.06	1.49	0.25	0.68	87.31	63.56	0.18	0.67
Major Mathematical Errors or Serious Mathematical Oversights	0.03		0.21		92.11		0.08	
Errors in Notation (Mathematical Symbols) or Mathematical Language	0.13		0.35		76.16		0.31	
Lack of Clarity in Presentation of Mathematical Content	0.09		0.31		82.68		0.13	
Misunderstands Student Production	0.01		0.11		98.28		0.22	
Positive Mathematical Interactions	0.07	1.35	0.24	0.51	88.56	68.01	0.29	0.53
Identifies Mathematical Insight in Specific Student Questions, Comments, Work	0.14		0.37		80.96		0.50	
Makes Productive Mathematical Use of Student Errors	0.07		0.26		87.22		0.31	
Teacher Understands Non-Standard Student Solution Methods	0.01		0.09		97.51		0.07	
Student Cognitive Demand	0.09	1.20	0.30	0.43	88.08	76.59	0.47	0.57
Students Provide Explanations	0.15		0.38		82.93		0.42	
Students Ask Why Questions or Make Counter-Claims	0.07		0.26		90.31		0.49	
Student Makes a Conjecture, Draws on Evidence to Form a Conclusion, and/or Engages in Reasoning About a Hypothetical and/or General Case	0.06		0.26		90.99		0.50	

Note: UTQ statistics are generated at segment level. For MET, only one segment is selected for calibration. MET sample sizes vary based on dimensions, ranging from 1,053 to 2,648.

TABLE 3.A.9. Observer Perceptions of Easier and Harder Dimensions to Score

	CLASS	FfT	PLATO	MQI
Easier	Productivity (1)	Creating an environment of respect and rapport (1)	Behavior Management (2)	
	Student Engagement (1)		Time Management (2)	
Harder	Positive Climate (1)	Establishing a culture for learning (1)	Explicit Strategy Instruction (3)	Major mathematical errors or serious mathematical oversights (1)
	Teacher Sensitivity (1)	Managing classroom procedures (1)	Modeling (2)	Errors in notation (mathematical symbols) or mathematical language (1)
	Regard for Adolescent Perspectives (1)	Organizing physical space (2)	Guided Practice (1)	Lack of clarity in presentation of content (1)
	Instructional Learning Formats (1)	Using questioning and discussion techniques (1)	Connections to Prior Knowledge (1)	Misunderstands student production (1)
	Content Understanding (1)	Engaging students in learning (1)	Connections to Personal and Cultural Experiences (1)	Use of representation or model (2)
	Analysis and Problem Solving (1)	Using assessment in instruction (2)	Purpose (1)	Multiple representations or models (1)

Student Engagement (1)	Demonstrating flexibility and responsiveness (2)	Text-Based Instruction (1)	Multiple solution strategies for a single problem (1)
	Demonstrating knowledge of content and pedagogy (3)		Explicit links among any combination of symbols, concrete pictures, diagrams, solution strategies, etc. (1)
			Mathematical explanations (2)
			Mathematically generalizing statement (2)
			High cognitive demand task (1)
			Teacher describes mathematical steps of a procedure or computation (1)
			Identifies mathematical insight in specific student questions, comments, work (2)
			Makes productive mathematical use of student errors (1)
			Teacher understands non-standard student solution methods (1)

Note: Number of observers who nominated the dimension is in parentheses.

CHAPTER

4

How Framework for Teaching and Tripod 7Cs Evidence Distinguish Key Components of Effective Teaching

RONALD F. FERGUSON WITH CHARLOTTE DANIELSON

ABSTRACT

This chapter uses data from the Measures of Effective Teaching project to study ways that adult observations using the Framework for Teaching and student perceptions using Tripod survey assessments help distinguish components of effective teaching. The approaches are found to be compatible in the components of teaching that they measure. Moreover, adults and students evaluate teaching similarly. The chapter uses value-added test score measures and student survey responses for happiness in class, effort in class, and whether the teacher inspires an interest in college as key outcomes predicted by teaching quality. The mix of teaching components that predicts value added differs systematically from the combination that predicts happiness, effort, or inspiration.

INTRODUCTION

This chapter distinguishes multiple aspects of teaching that together predict student engagement and learning. Our primary aim is to help elementary and secondary school educators understand the components of teaching effectiveness—the types of action that produce or facilitate learning and healthy development—in order to more strategically and effectively improve their own and others' teaching.

It is well known from research that some teachers routinely produce more learning than others (e.g., Kane, McCaffrey, & Staiger, 2010, 2012; Rivkin, Hanushek, & Kain, 2005). Why? According to focus-group research with regular citizens, people believe the reason is that effective teachers simply care more (Chart with Kendall-Taylor, 2008). Similarly, when we ask large audiences of professional educators to select among multiple reasons that some teachers produce more learning, they too select *caring* as the most important reason. Are they correct? Based on classrooms sampled from more than two hundred schools in six cities that participated in the Bill & Melinda Gates Foundation project on Measures of Effective Teaching (MET), findings in this chapter indicate that caring is the strongest predictor of happiness, but not learning. Instead, we find that *classroom management* is the strongest predictor of learning. The chapter presents this and other findings, distinguishing among multiple aspects of teaching and their implications for students.

Three rapidly spreading methods for assessing teacher performance are classroom observations, student surveys, and test-based measures of student learning (i.e., growth or value-added scores). The latter—test-based measures—can help us understand how much students have learned. However, they do not indicate which aspects of teaching may need to improve in order that students might learn more in any particular classroom.

Accordingly, this chapter applies two popular frameworks and associated assessment tools for measuring what teachers actually do in their classrooms. A central question is whether these two approaches—Charlotte Danielson's Framework for Teaching (FfT) and Ronald Ferguson's 7Cs framework from his Tripod Project survey assessments—are mutually reinforcing as ways of diagnosing teachers' professional strengths along with areas in need of improvement. The approaches were developed independently by the authors of this chapter and are widely used in the United States and increasingly abroad. They are research-based and have been refined over more than a decade based on analyses of prior results and feedback from elementary and secondary school practitioners and fellow researchers. Both played central roles in the Bill & Melinda Gates Foundation MET project.

The Framework for Teaching (FfT) is a definition of teaching quality and a classroom observation system designed to enrich deliberations in school systems on ways of improving instruction. Similarly, Tripod survey assessments were designed to measure perceptions of teaching quality and engagement in learning. From the Tripod surveys, MET used the 7Cs framework for effective teaching in addition to a selection of Tripod student engagement survey items that measure happiness in class, effort in class, and whether the teacher inspires students to attend college. We use these measures of happiness, effort, and inspiration to supplement value-added achievement gains as teaching outcome measures. The chapter uses data from fourth through eighth grade classrooms in the six MET districts.

The chapter is focused on three tasks. First, after introducing the frameworks, we demonstrate that specific domains and components of the FfT and Tripod 7Cs frameworks are compatible, not only conceptually, but also empirically. In particular, both frameworks have components that focus on classroom management and others that focus on instruction. Data from these distinct sources provide multiple measures for making judgments about specific categories of teaching practice and can be used together in a coherent program of professional measurement, learning, and support.

Second, we show that having multiple desired outcomes warrants a balance in teaching priorities. This is because the components of the FfT and Tripod 7Cs frameworks that most strongly predict happiness in class and being inspired by the teacher to attend college are different from those that most strongly predict value-added learning gains on standardized exams. On the one hand, the components that most strongly predict value-added achievement gains are associated with keeping students busy and on task and pressing them to think rigorously and persist in the face of difficulty. We refer to these as *press*. On the other hand, components that most strongly predict happiness in class and inspiration to attend college are associated with caring teacher-student relationships, captivating lessons, and other practices that students experience as supportive. We refer to the latter as *support*. Press and support are both important if we care not only about annual test-score gains, but also about the quality of life at school, inspiration to attend college, and a love of learning.

Third, we consider ways that combining and comparing data generated using the two frameworks can contribute to quality control by helping to uncover dishonesty or other problems with implementation. We show that either too much or too little similarity in FfT as compared to Tripod 7Cs data patterns can signal irregularities of implementation or interpretation and may warrant official scrutiny, especially under high-stakes conditions.

Finally, at the end of the chapter, we distill some key implications. Generally, we propose that paying attention to the components of the FfT and Tripod 7Cs frameworks—not just the composite scores—can enrich the quality of reflection, discourse, and support that teachers experience in collaboration with supervisors and peers concerning their teaching. This, in turn, can enhance the quality of instruction that students experience, how hard they work, how much they learn, how happy they are in class, and how earnestly they aspire to attend college.

INTRODUCTION TO THE FRAMEWORKS

Both the FfT and Tripod 7Cs frameworks are multifaceted research-based conceptions of teaching, describing what teachers do in the practice of their profession. The FfT is the outgrowth of Charlotte Danielson's experience at the Educational Testing Service (ETS), where she was a member of the design team for Praxis III (the observation-based system of teacher assessment used for the licensing of beginning teachers) and participated as well in redesigning assessments for the National Board for Professional Teaching Standards. While the FfT emerged from Danielson's work at the national level, the Tripod surveys grew out of Ron Ferguson's work in Shaker Heights, Ohio, and then with a large number of school districts across the country, where the focus was on finding levers to raise achievement levels and narrow achievement gaps. Some states and districts are using observational data from FfT and student survey data from Tripod for both teacher evaluation formulas and professional development planning.

According to MET publications, FfT and Tripod 7Cs measurement tools produce valid and reliable indicators of teaching quality—often more reliable than value added—when administered at the classroom level with fidelity (Cantrell & Kane, 2013; Ho & Kane, 2012; Kane, McCaffrey, & Staiger, 2010, 2012). For readers not familiar with the concept, value added refers to a particular approach to measuring test score gains. What distinguishes value-added measures from simpler test score growth measures is that they are adjusted for between-classroom differences in student characteristics. Many analysts prefer value added for measuring teacher effectiveness because, if implemented properly, value added approximates a condition in which there is no difference across classrooms in the characteristics of the students. Hence, value added for any particular teacher is an estimate of how much that teacher adds to students' skills and knowledge.

When we consider different classrooms taught by the same teachers in the data for this chapter, the between-classroom correlations are 0.38 for value added, 0.42 for the FfT composite, and 0.61 for the Tripod 7Cs composite. Hence, all three metrics are ways of detecting consistency at the teacher level from one classroom to another. Furthermore, as MET reports show, there is cross-validation. Specifically, the fact that each metric is clearly correlated with the others helps validate that all three are indicators of instructional quality.

FRAMEWORK FOR TEACHING

To ensure fidelity of FfT data gathering, the MET project trained hundreds of raters to score video recordings from participating classrooms. (This was done not only for FfT, but also for the other observational protocols that MET employed.) In addition, beyond the MET project, Danielson and colleagues have devised ways of training school-based raters—typically administrators—and then measuring and certifying their rating proficiency. This is important, since the findings in both this chapter and MET are only indicative of what practitioners might find if they use the FfT properly.

Danielson's work on the Praxis III and the National Board assessments at ETS proved important not only because they provided methods of assessing instruction, but more important, because they helped produce standards of practice and concrete guidance for teachers on how to achieve high standards in their classrooms. They provided foundations for teachers to engage in activities that supported teacher learning—self-assessment of teaching skills; reflection on their practice; and professional conversations with peers, coaches, and supervisors. Even in the context of high-stakes assessments of practice, educators found the exercises valuable. The many encouraging responses from educators inspired Danielson to develop the FfT (Danielson, 2013).

In the FfT, the complex activity of teaching is divided into twenty-two components, clustered in four domains of teaching responsibility:

Domain 1: Planning and Preparation

Domain 2: The Classroom Environment

Domain 3: Instruction

Domain 4: Professional Responsibilities

Domains 2 and 3 are the ones that most directly concern the actual delivery of classroom instruction. Each comprises several components. This chapter is focused on four components from Domain 2 (the first four directly below) and four from Domain 3.[1] They are the following:

- *Creating an environment of respect and rapport*, for example: respectful talk, active listening, and turn taking; acknowledgment of students' backgrounds and lives outside the classroom; body language indicative of warmth and caring; physical proximity; politeness and encouragement; and fairness.

- *Establishing a culture for learning*, for example: belief in the value of what is being learned; high expectations, supported through both verbal and nonverbal behaviors, for both learning and participation; expectation of high-quality work on the part of students; expectation and recognition of effort and persistence on the part of students; and high expectations for expression and work products.

- *Managing classroom procedures*, for example: smooth functioning of all routines; little or no loss of instructional time; students playing an important role in carrying out the routines; students knowing what to do and where to move.

- *Managing student behavior*, for example: clear standards of conduct, possibly posted and possibly referred to during a lesson; absence of acrimony between teacher and students concerning behavior; teacher awareness of student conduct, including preventative awareness; absence of misbehavior; and reinforcement of positive behavior.

- *Communicating with students*, for example: clarity of lesson purpose; clear directions and procedures specific to the lesson activities; absence of content errors and clear explanations of concepts and strategies; and correct and imaginative use of language.

- *Using questioning and discussion techniques*, for example: questions of high cognitive challenge, formulated by both students and teacher; questions with multiple correct answers or multiple approaches, even when there is a single correct response; effective use of student responses and ideas; discussion, with the teacher stepping out of the central, mediating role; focus on the reasoning exhibited by students in discussion, both in give-and-take with the teacher and with their classmates; high levels of student participation in discussion.

- *Engaging students in learning*, for example: students show enthusiasm, interest, thinking, problem solving, etc.; learning tasks that require high-level student thinking and invite students to explain their thinking; students highly motivated to work on all tasks and persist, even when the tasks are challenging; students actively "working," rather than watching while the teacher "works"; and suitable pacing of the lesson, neither dragged out nor rushed, with time for closure and student reflection.

- *Using assessment in instruction*, for example: the teacher paying close attention to evidence of student understanding; the teacher posing specifically created questions to elicit evidence of student understanding; the teacher circulating to monitor student learning and to offer feedback; and students assessing their own work against established criteria.

For the MET project, hundreds of experienced educators were trained to rate classrooms on each of the eight components listed above. They watched video recordings from the MET classrooms and assigned a score of 1, 2, 3, or 4 to each FfT component, representing "unsatisfactory," "basic," "proficient," and "distinguished," respectively. The data for this paper come from the 2009–2010 school year and include an average of two observations per classroom (hence the score for each of the eight components is most often the average from two observations of a classroom). For MET, there were no scores assigned below the component level. However, the score on each component was intended to reflect the rater's judgments concerning the overall performance of the teacher on the elements within that component.

The analysis in this chapter concerns the eight FfT components listed above and the ways that they relate both conceptually and statistically to the 7Cs of the Tripod framework described below.

THE TRIPOD 7Cs MODEL

The Tripod Project emerged in 2000 from a week-long summer workshop that Ron Ferguson designed with educators in Shaker Heights, Ohio. The week focused on Erik Erikson's first five stages of life-cycle identity development. The five clusters of issues, adapted to classrooms, concerned (1) building trusting relationships; (2) cultivating good behavior and cooperation; (3) helping students to set ambitious goals for learning; (4) encouraging and enabling persistence and resilience in the face of difficulty; and (5) helping students develop a sense of academic efficacy and take satisfaction in achievement. Teachers in small groups wrote reports on ways to achieve desired outcomes for each cluster of issues and to avoid their negative opposites. Activities were developed to continue the work during the school year. This included the idea to survey students about their experiences *in particular classrooms* (as opposed to whole-school climate surveys) in order to understand and track progress on instructional improvement.

The concept of the "Tripod Project" developed as a way to cultivate the type of teaching necessary to succeed with the five clusters of issues—later called the "Tripod Engagement Framework"—adapted from the Erikson framework. The "tripod" was "content, pedagogy, and relationships." The idea was that, in order to deliver instruction effectively, teachers needed an understanding of the subjects they were teaching (content knowledge), they needed sufficient skill to help students achieve understanding (pedagogic knowledge and skill), and they needed to connect with students on a personal level so that students would be inspired to trust and cooperate (relationships).

The first few years of Tripod surveys were designed by Ferguson in consultation with Shaker Heights teachers and administrators. They were informed by the interests that the educators expressed, as well as by the research literature on student engagement and teaching practices. Lead teachers helped by reacting to survey drafts and testing their students' interpretations of the items. Initially, there was a survey for grades K through 5 and another for grades 6 through 12. Over the ensuing years, surveys for teachers were developed, and a separate survey was designed for grades K to 2. A clear distinction developed between measures of student engagement (what individual students do, think, and feel) versus student perceptions of teaching (what teachers do and how the classroom operates as measured by the Tripod 7Cs framework).

In 2009, the Bill & Melinda Gates Foundation selected Tripod to supply the student perception surveys for the MET project. By December 2010, MET had produced evidence that the Tripod 7Cs measures are valid and reliable predictors of student learning gains. Later reports documented that student perceptions were also predictors of classroom observation scores. MET did not use the full battery of Tripod student engagement items, but it did include a few that we employ below for measuring happiness and effort in class and whether the teacher inspires students to have an interest in college.

The Tripod student perceptions of teaching that were used in MET and that are the focus of this chapter are grouped in seven scales that we call the 7Cs framework. Two (Challenge and Control) are what we call measures of "press" and the other five (Care, Confer, Captivate, Clarify, and Consolidate) are measures of "support."

- **Challenge** concerns both effort and rigor. It concerns a teacher's insistence that students should work hard and persist in the face of difficulty, for example, *"My teacher accepts nothing less than our best effort"* and *"My teacher wants us to really understand the material, not just memorize it."*

- **Control** concerns the degree to which the class is both well-behaved, for example, *"Students in this class behave the way my teacher wants them to"* and on task, *"Our class stays busy and doesn't waste time."* The connotation is not that teachers are controlling in the sense that they squash student autonomy and expression, but rather in the sense that they are able to manage the class in a way that teaching and learning occur efficiently, without being derailed by misbehavior or distractions.

- **Care** concerns whether the teacher develops supportive relationships with students and is attentive to their feelings. For example, *"My teacher in this class really tries to understand how students feel about things"* or *"My teacher seems to know if something is bothering me."* The Tripod 7Cs conception of care is focused on emotional support. An alternative conception of caring concerns a teacher's commitment to make sure that students succeed. That alternative is not captured by *Care* on its own, but rather by all of the components collectively, especially *Challenge*.

- **Confer** concerns the degree to which the teacher elicits ideas from students and welcomes their feedback. One example is *"My teacher welcomes my ideas and suggestions."* Another is *"My teacher wants us to share our thoughts."* Classrooms that students rate high on *Confer* are more "student centered" than those where only the teacher's perspective is valued.

- **Captivate** pertains to how effectively the teacher stimulates students to be interested in their lessons. A reverse coded item in this category is *"This* *class does not keep my attention—I get bored."* A positively worded item is *"My teacher makes lessons interesting."* Items are geared to measure whether the teacher is able to hold the students' attention in class and provide the basis for continuing interest.

- **Clarify** concerns how effectively the teacher is able to help students understand what she is trying to teach them, especially with regard to concepts that students may find difficult to understand. This includes having clear explanations, *"My teacher explains difficult things clearly,"* multiple explanations, *"My teacher has several good ways to explain each topic that we cover in this class,"* and a commitment to persist until understanding is achieved, *"If you don't understand something, my teacher explains it another way."*

- **Consolidate** concerns making learning coherent, for example, *"My teacher takes time to summarize what we learn each day,"* giving feedback, *"The comments that I get on my work in this class help me understand how to improve,"* and checking for understanding, *"My teacher checks to make sure we understand what s/he is teaching us."* Hence, *Consolidate* is closely related conceptually to both *Clarify* and *Challenge*.

Each of the 7Cs components is measured by multiple items in the Tripod student survey. MET used one version of the survey for grades 4 and 5 and another for grades 6 and higher. Both versions cover the same 7Cs concepts, although some items are worded more simply for the elementary school version.

Generally, both the FfT and Tripod 7Cs frameworks have components pertaining primarily to communication about rules for time use, procedures, effort, and personal conduct. In addition, both have components pertaining primarily to communication and aspects of instruction associated very directly with implementing the curriculum. For *domains* and their respective *components*, see the Framework Map in Exhibit 4.1 that follows.

PAST LITERATURE

The two-way distinction between Classroom Environment (FfT) or Press (Tripod 7Cs), on the one hand, and Instruction (FfT) or Support (Tripod 7Cs), on the other hand, is reflected in a long tradition of thought on teaching, parenting, and other types of hierarchal relations. Essentially, the first half of the distinction is concerned with the power relations between adults and the students that they teach, supervise, or parent. The other half of the distinction is focused on helping students to achieve understanding, to feel emotionally secure, and to find satisfaction in learning.

In the parenting literature, Diana Baumrind (1966, 1996) contrasts different parenting styles by the degree to which they are "demanding" (related to power) and "responsive" (focused on warmth and various forms of support). She originated the following well known typology in the 1960s: "*Authoritative* parents are both highly demanding and highly responsive, by contrast with *authoritarian* parents, who are highly demanding but not responsive; *permissive* parents, who are responsive but not demanding; and *unengaged* parents, who are neither demanding nor responsive" (1996, p. 412). She writes, "It may be said that the two intertwined generic positive childrearing goals are to foster moral character and optimal competence" (op. cit.).

EXHIBIT 4.1. Framework Map

Framework for Teaching

Domain: Classroom Environment

- Creating an environment of respect and rapport
- Managing classroom procedures
- Managing student behavior

Domain: Instruction

- Using questioning and discussion techniques
- Using assessment in instruction
- Engaging students in learning
- Communicating with students
- Establishing a culture for learning

TRIPOD 7Cs

Domain: Press

- Challenge
  - Press for Rigor
  - Press for Persistence
- Control
  - Minimize Misbehavior
  - Promote Good Behavior
  - Class Stays Busy and on Task

Domain: Support

- Confer
- Captive
- Clarify
- Consolidate
- Care

Similarly, scholars who focus on school and classroom environments have distinguished "academic press" from what some call "social support" (Lee & Smith, 1999; Lee, Smith, Perry, & Smylie, 1999), what others call "sense of community" (Shouse, 1996) and still others call personalization (Klem & Connell, 2004). Lee, Smith, Perry, and Smylie (1999) trace the distinction to writers in the early 20th century, including Flexner and Bachman (1918) writing about schools in Gary, Indiana. Baumrind (1996) reaches further back, reminding readers about debates concerning childhood self-determination that we associate with philosophers Hobbs, Rousseau, and Hegel. The issue is the need (and the right) for adults to exert control in order to foster conditions under which they can teach what the child needs to know in order to learn and mature in accordance with societal norms or survival requirements. Lee and colleagues (1999) write, "This report challenges 'either-or' proposals for school reform that view academic focus and rigor and social support for students as contradictory strategies. It argues that, to succeed in schools that press them hard to learn, students need strong social support. Conversely, even in the presence of strong social support, students will not learn much unless schools press them to achieve academically" (p. 2).

What do Lee and her colleagues mean by "social support"? Especially because the literature is sometimes unclear, we find it important to emphasize the conceptual distinction between *social or relational* supports, on the one hand, versus *pedagogic* supports and practices, on the other hand. Clearly, we in this chapter are not considering social supports outside the classroom. However, it could be argued that *Care* and *Confer* in the 7Cs framework and perhaps *Engaging Students in Learning*, *Communicating with Students*, and *Establishing a Culture for Learning* in the FfT framework entail social supports. More narrowly pedagogic in nature are *Using Questioning and Discussion Techniques* and *Using Assessment in Instruction* in the FfT framework and *Clarify*, *Captivate*, and *Consolidate* in the Tripod 7Cs framework. The literature is inconsistent on whether the least relational pedagogic practices belong in the support category rather than in the press category or whether they should be included at all in the support-press dichotomy. Whatever reasons there might be for inconsistency in the literature, our conception of support is primarily about instructional supports, some of which are more social or relational than others. Our conception includes all components in the *Instruction* and *Support* domains of the two frameworks.

Now, before moving to a discussion of findings, let us introduce key features of the data and methods that we use.

DATA AND PRIMARY METHODS

All of the data in the chapter are from the 2009–2010 school year of the MET project. Like standard value-added measures, all of the FfT and Tripod 7Cs variables are adjusted to remove variation associated with available measures of student background, including racial and ethnic backgrounds and free lunch status. The reason for the adjustments is to isolate and retain as best we can the variation in the data that is due to teaching and not predictable on the basis of student background characteristics. In addition, all of the data are classroom-level averages, where each classroom supplies one data point for each component of each measure. For example, there were 1,892 classrooms that had data for both FfT and the 7Cs measures during the 2009–2010 school year from which we drew the data for this analysis. The majority of teachers contributed two classrooms, and most classrooms have ratings from two separate FfT observations. Most of the analyses here combine the data for grades 4 through 8 for English and math classes. In addition, we combine value added from state tests and other more cognitively demanding tests that MET used to form a single value-added measure for each classroom.

The primary methods that we use are tabulations and multiple regression analyses. The presentation is organized in such a way that lack of familiarity with multiple regressions should not prevent the reader from gaining a basic understanding. We use simple indicator variables to account for differences associated with grade-level and subject differences. In addition, most regressions are structured to focus on differences between teachers who are colleagues within schools (they include an intercept for each school and they adjust for clustering by teacher). For each FfT measure, the rating that we use for any given classroom is the average for that measure across the multiple times that the classroom was observed. Similarly, each Tripod 7Cs rating is an average from all of the students who responded to the survey in that particular classroom. Finally, unless otherwise indicated, all variables are scaled to have a mean of 0 and a standard deviation of 1 defined on the classroom-level distribution.

DO ADULTS (FfT) AND STUDENTS (TRIPOD 7Cs) AGREE ABOUT TEACHING?

Now that we have introduced the frameworks and connected key concepts to past literature, this section considers how the two frameworks are conceptually and empirically related to one another. We explore how strongly adults using the FfT components agree with students using the Tripod 7Cs. The answers have bearing on how the two might be used together as instructional quality measures.

Conceptually Matching the Frameworks

Please see Exhibit 4.A.1 for the results of a matching exercise. It uses the wording from above that briefly describes each component from each framework. Using arrows, it matches each component to one or more components from the other framework. Matches are based only on the conceptual content of the measures, without reference to the data. They indicate what we regard as the strongest conceptual parallels between the two frameworks.

We use Exhibit 4.2 here in the body of the chapter to summarize the linkages from Exhibit 4.A.1. The left-hand side of Exhibit 4.2 uses the FfT components as headings, while the right-hand side uses the Tripod 7Cs components as headings. For example, on the left-hand side, major heading *Establishing a Culture for Learning* from the FfT is associated with *Challenge* and *Confer* from the 7Cs framework as subheadings, while on the right-hand side, heading *Confer* is conceptually related to four FfT components as subheadings: *Establishing a Culture for Learning, Managing Classroom Procedures, Communicating with Students, and Using Questioning and Discussion Techniques*. The exhibit shows that each component in each framework is related conceptually to one or more components from the other framework. Based on these patterns, we conclude that the frameworks are well matched conceptually, and that the two can form the basis of a coherent discourse on instructional quality.

EXHIBIT 4.2. Cross-Walking the FFT and the 7Cs: Significance Indicators from Multiple Regressions

Predicting FfT Components

Creating an environment of respect and rapport

  Care+

  Control***

Establishing a culture for learning

  Challenge***

  Confer***

Managing classroom procedures

  Control***

  Confer (n.s.)

Managing student behavior

  Control***

Communicating with students

  Confer*

  Clarify*

Using questioning and discussion techniques

  Challenge**

  Confer**

  Consolidate (n.s.)

Engaging students in learning

  Challenge*

  Captivate***

Using assessment in instruction

  Clarify***

  Consolidate (n.s.)

Predicting 7Cs Components

Care

  Creating an environment of respect and rapport***

Confer

  Establishing a culture for learning**

  Managing classroom procedures (n.s.)

  Communicating with students*

  Using questioning and discussion techniques*

Captivate

  Engaging students in learning***

Clarify

  Communicating with students***

  Using assessment in instruction***

Consolidate

  Using questioning and discussion techniques*

  Using assessment in instruction***

Challenge

  Establishing a culture for learning***

  Using questioning and discussion techniques+

  Engaging students in learning*

Control

  Creating an environment of respect and rapport**

  Managing classroom procedures (n.s.)

  Managing student behavior***

Note: Two-tailed significance indicators: + 0.10; * 0.05; ** 0.01; *** 0.001.

Empirical Matching

The fact that the frameworks are compatible conceptually does not mean necessarily that data collected using the frameworks will tell the same stories empirically. For example, there could be systematic differences in what students and adults perceive concerning any given issue. To explore the question empirically, we conducted multiple regression analyses of the patterns in Exhibit 4.2.

First, we used each of the FfT components on the left side of Exhibit 4.2 as the dependent variable in a regression equation where the 7Cs components listed under it served as the predictors. Each regression also included a school-level intercept term (a school *fixed effect*) and indicator variables for grade levels and subjects. In addition, as indicated above, each FfT and 7Cs component was adjusted for student background characteristics and scaled to have a mean of 0 and standard deviation of 1. Hence, when predicting a particular FfT component, the estimated coefficients on 7Cs components indicate how strongly each predicts that FfT component, holding constant grade level, subject, and school. Analyses for the right side of the exhibit had the same basic structure as for the left, except that the 7Cs components are the dependent variables and the FfT components are the predictors. Instead of showing regression tables here in the body of the chapter, we simply indicate the two-tailed statistical significance levels on Exhibit 4.2 using symbols that range from "n.s." (for "not significant") to "+" for 90 percent confidence, "*" for 95 percent confidence, "**" for 99 percent confidence, and "***" for 99.9 percent confidence or better. All have the expected signs. (Regression tables are in the Appendix.)

The vast majority of the relationships on Exhibit 4.2 are statistically significant. The main conclusion is that the relationships we expected based simply on our interpretations of the two frameworks are by and large affirmed by patterns in the data. Of course, the full panoply of relationships between all of the FfT components and all of the 7Cs components is much more complicated than we can fully explore. A simple correlation analysis shows that all of the 7Cs components are statistically significantly correlated with all of the FfT components at confidence levels of 95 percent and higher. FfT-to-7Cs correlations range from a low of 0.088 for the relationship between *Consolidate* and *Managing Classroom Procedures* to a high of 0.331 for the correlation between *Control* and *Managing Student Behavior*. These high and low pairings make sense; *Consolidate* and *Managing Classroom Procedures* are probably the least related conceptually of all the components in the two frameworks, and they have the lowest correlation. Conversely, *Control* from the Tripod 7Cs and *Managing Student Behavior* from the FfT both concern student behavior. They are conceptually the most related. Generally, FfT and 7C ratings that are the most conceptually similar tend to be the most highly correlated.

The Special Case of Very Unruly Classrooms

Imagine a classroom in which students are frequently off task and misbehavior appears normal. FfT observers of classrooms that students rated in the bottom quintile on *Control* probably saw such classrooms. When students rated classrooms in the bottom quintile on control, adult observers (none of whom had seen the student ratings) tended to rate it low not only on *Managing Student Behavior*; they tended to rate it low as well on *all* of the FfT components. In fact, classrooms in the bottom quintile of *Control* have such a negative pull on FfT ratings that, when classes in the bottom quintile of *Control* are included in multiple regressions using the full data set, *Control* dominates consistently as the strongest 7Cs predictor for *all* FfT components. Even when multiple regressions omit classrooms rated in the bottom *Control* quintile, where behavior is worst, *Control* is still a strong predictor of FfT ratings.

Figure 4.1 shows findings from eight multiple regressions that omitted the bottom *Control* quintile. FfT components were the dependent variables. The three 7Cs predictors were *Challenge*, *Control*, and a composite of the five components that make up *Support*. The composite for *Support* is the strongest predictor of *Engaging Students in Learning*, *Communicating with Students* and *Using Questioning and Discussion Techniques*, while *Control* is strongest for the other five. If we had included classrooms from the bottom quintile of *Control* in the analysis, *Control* would have been the strongest predictor for all eight FfT components, including those representing the *Instruction* domain in the FfT framework.

To summarize, so far in the chapter we have defined the two frameworks. We find that components of each tend to be more (less) correlated empirically with components from the other that are more (less) conceptually similar. The main exception to this generalization is that *Control* from the 7Cs framework tends to be highly predictive of FfT ratings overall, especially when classrooms from the bottom quintile on *Control* are included in the analysis. Below, we show that *Control* is the strongest predictor of value added as well—stronger than any other component of *either* framework. Similarly,

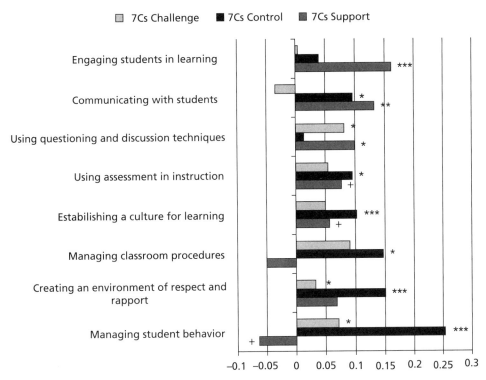

FIGURE 4.1. *Multiple Regression Coefficients Predicting FfT Components Using 7Cs Control, Challenge, and Support*

Note: This figure is computed without classrooms that were in the bottom quintile on Control. The corresponding table in the Appendix shows the results both with and without the bottom quintile on Control in the equations.

Two-tailed significance indicators: + 0.10; * 0.05; ** 0.01; *** 0.001.

Managing Student Behavior is the strongest value-added predictor from the FfT framework. The bottom line is that, when classrooms are out of control and off task, learning is difficult for students and distinguishing clearly among the multiple components of instruction may be almost impossible for adult observers as they try to rate teaching.

PREDICTING VALUE ADDED, HAPPINESS, EFFORT, AND INSPIRATION

MET data include four variables that we consider outcomes of teaching quality: value-added achievement gains, happiness in class, effort in class, and an increased inspiration to attend college. We consider each in turn.

Value Added

Value-added scores for this analysis come from the MET project. They are scaled to have a mean of 0 and standard deviation of 1 defined on the classroom-level distribution for each test by district, subject, and grade. In addition to scores from state accountability exams for math and English language arts (ELA), MET data include value-added scores for the Balanced Assessment in Math (BAM) and the SAT9. The BAM and SAT9 were included in MET to test whether results would differ for accountability and non-accountability exams. In addition, the BAM and SAT9 exams were considered more challenging than most state accountability exams. The overall finding from MET was that patterns were quite similar for accountability and non-accountability exams.

After finding few clear and statistically significant differences between subjects, exams, or grade levels in our work for this analysis, we chose to work with a value-added composite in order to simplify the presentation. First, for math, a composite score for each classroom was set equal to the average of value added from the state math test and the BAM. Then, for ELA, a composite was set equal to the average of the state test and the SAT9. For both math and ELA, we then rescaled to set the composite mean to 0 and the standard deviation equal to 1, defined on the classroom-level MET distribution. Our analysis of value added includes grades four through eight for both ELA and math. Regressions include indicator variables for grades and subjects. They also include school-level intercepts and adjust for clustering by teacher.

We begin with simple tabulations. Figure 4.2 illustrates graphically how each FfT and 7Cs component is related to value added. To construct the figure, we began by creating quintiles for each FfT and 7Cs component. For example, the lowest quintile for *Clarify* contains the bottom 20 percent of classrooms as ranked by that component; the second contains the next 20 percent; and so on up to the top quintile, which contains the 20 percent of classrooms ranked highest for that component. We computed the average value-added score for classrooms in each quintile of each component. Then, for each quintile of each component, we computed the difference between value added for classrooms in that quintile, versus value added for classrooms in its bottom quintile.

FfT and 7Cs components are rank ordered in Figure 4.2 by how much value added in the fifth quintile of a component exceeds value added in its bottom quintile. Several things are apparent. First, the largest fifth-versus-first quintile differences in value added for both FfT and 7Cs frameworks are for *Control* from the 7Cs framework and *Managing Student Behavior* from the

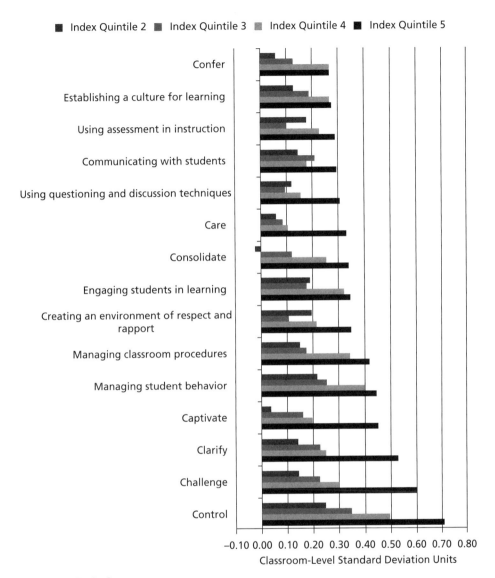

FIGURE 4.2. *Differences in Gains: The Mean Value-Added Test Score Gain for Classrooms in the Second Through Fifth Quintiles of each Respective FfT or 7Cs Component, Minus the Mean Gain in the Bottom Quintile of That Same Component*

FfT framework—the components that measure student behavior management. In addition, for both frameworks, the top few components in the ranking are those related to *Press* or *Classroom Environment*, not *Support* or *Instruction.* Second, while the top four ranked components on the figure are from the 7Cs framework, there is nuance, since the ordering would change if we made a slight change in the ordering criterion. For example, if we ranked using the fourth-versus-first quintile comparisons, *Managing Student Behavior* from the FfT framework would rank second, behind *Control*. The point is that different components distinguish among classrooms in idiosyncratic ways in different parts of their distributions.

Note also that *Control* and *Managing Student Behavior* are the components for which average value added in the second quintile most exceeds that in the first quintile. Finally, notice that value-added levels do not appear to change much when moving from the second to the third quintiles for most components. The greatest differences are in the first and the last steps—from the first to the second quintile, and from either the third to the fourth or the fourth to the fifth, depending on the component. Generally, both FfT and 7Cs components are best at distinguishing value added at their extremes. Even through the middle quintiles, the figure indicates that higher values for 7Cs components are consistently associated with higher value added. The same appears true of *Managing Student Behavior* and *Managing Classroom Procedures*, the FfT components that predict value added most strongly.

Happiness and Effort in Class and College Inspiration

Do FfT and 7Cs components predict *Happiness in Class*, *Effort in Class*, and a teacher who *Inspires Interest in College*? Figure 4.3 shows multiple regression coefficients where the dependent variables are value added (Panel A); "Happy in Class" (Panel B); "Effort in Class" (Panel C); and "Teacher Inspires Interest in College" (Panel D). FfT predictor variables are *Instruction* and *Class Environment* for regressions reported on the left side of the figure. The 7Cs predictor variables are *Support*, *Control*, and *Challenge* in the regressions reported on the right side of the figure.

Consistent with Figure 4.2, Figure 4.3 shows for value added that the FfT composite for *Class Environment* (on the left side) and the 7Cs components *Control* and *Challenge* (on the right side) are stronger predictors of value added than the composites for *FfT Instruction* or *7Cs Support*. Recall that a feature of multiple regressions is that the estimated coefficient for each predictor variable indicates the effect on the dependent variable of changing that particular predictor while the other predictors are held constant. Accordingly, an interpretation of the 7Cs result for value added in Figure 4.3 is, that when holding *Control* and *Challenge* constant, the predicted effect of increasing the

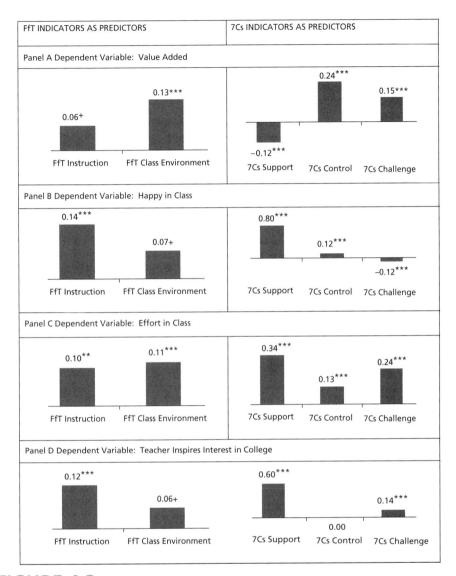

FIGURE 4.3. *Eight Multiple Regressions Predicting Student Outcomes with FfT Domains (Left Side) or 7Cs Domains (Right Side) as Predictors*

Note: Two-tailed significance indicators: + 0.10; * 0.05; ** 0.01; *** 0.001.

composite for *Support* is actually to reduce value added by a modest but statistically significant amount. We speculate below about the reasons.

Panels B, C, and D show a much different pattern. Results for *Happy in Class* in Panel B and *Teacher Inspires Interest in College* in Panel D indicate that *Instruction* and *Support* composites are much stronger predictors of these two outcomes, compared to *Class Environment*, *Control*, and *Challenge*. For *Effort in Class*, Panel C shows that the predictors are similar in their estimated impacts; coefficients for *Instruction* and *Class Environment* are almost identical. And the coefficient for *Support* is almost equivalent to the sum of the coefficients for *Control* and *Challenge*. In other words, a 1 standard deviation change in the *Support* composite is predicted to increase *Effort in Class* by about the same amount as 1 standard deviation increases in both *Control* and *Challenge*.

Another way of contrasting the relationship of value added to teacher quality, versus the relationship of happiness to teacher quality is presented

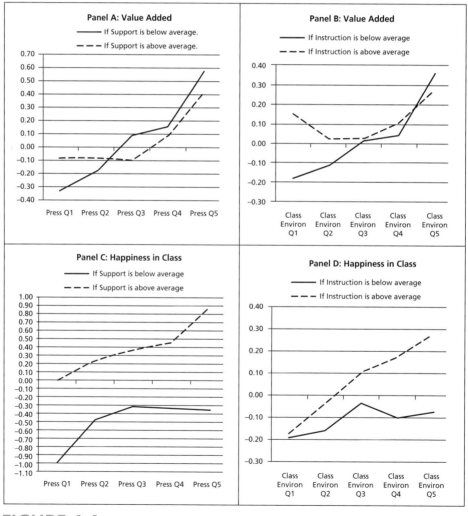

FIGURE 4.4. *Graphs of Actual Value Added and Happiness in Class*

in Figure 4.4. Panels A and C of Figure 4.4 use data from 7Cs metrics, while Panels B and D use data from FfT measures. *Press* in this exhibit is the average of *Control* and *Challenge*. The horizontal axes in Panels A and C represent quintiles for *Press*. Similarly, the horizontal axes for Panels B and D represent quintiles for *Class Environment*. The vertical axes for Panels A and B represent value added, while those for Panels C and D represent *Happiness in Class*.

The dotted lines show relationships between each outcome and *Press* (or *Class Environment*) when *Support* (or *Instruction*) is above average. Conversely, the solid lines show the relationships when *Support* (or *Instruction*) is below average. Hence, moving vertically from the dotted line to the solid line represents a reduction in *Support* or *Instruction* (i.e., from above average to below average), while moving vertically from the solid line to the dotted line represents the opposite.

Note that when *Press* is relatively low, in its first or second quintile, the dotted line is above the solid line. In other words, among teachers who rate relatively low on *Press*, those rated above average on *Support* have higher value added. Indeed, a similar pattern appears in Panel B of the figure, using the FfT framework. However, when *Press* is above average, value added tends to be slightly higher when *Support* is below average. When *Class Environment* is above average (along the horizontal axis of Panel B), the pattern for the solid versus dotted line is mixed, but generally, whether *Instruction* is rated above or below average appears not to matter very much.

The reasons for these patterns are impossible to infer from these data with any certainty. Nonetheless, it is easy to *imagine* an explanation that is relatively simple. Specifically, if a teacher that students rate low on *Press* or that observers rate low on *Class Environment* becomes much more supportive or much better at instruction, students might become more focused and learn more, even if that teacher remains a poor manager of student behavior. However, if a teacher is already quite challenging and the class is almost always well behaved and on task, then becoming more supportive might actually lower the sense of urgency in the class and some students might relax and learn less. Again, while thought provoking, any explanation at this point remains speculation, since there is no way to know from the available data.

Based on the preceding, one might be tempted to conclude that being high on *Press* and below average on *Support* is a good thing. Or, referencing Panel B of Figure 4.4, one might conclude that as long as *Class Environment* is average or above, *Instruction* is rather unimportant.

But not so fast! Before making so rash a judgment, see Panels C and D. They indicate students are happier in classrooms where *Support* as rated by the 7Cs and *Instruction* as rated by FfT metrics are above average. An analogous exhibit for *Teacher Inspires Interest in College* would appear quite similar. It seems quite reasonable to expect that students who spend lots of time in supportive classrooms will grow to love learning more and be more prone to become life-long, voluntary learners. Prioritizing *Press* and *Classroom Environment* in order to maximize value added, while neglecting to improve *Support* and *Instruction*, would surely be a short-sighted strategy. There needs to be balance.

It turns out that the relative strength of academic *Press* metrics as predictors of learning is consistent with findings in past research. For example, Lee and Smith (1999, p. 907) report: "we found that, on average, social support is positively but modestly related to learning. However, both learning and the relationship between social support and learning are contingent on the academic press of the school students attend." Similarly, Shouse (1996, p. 47) reports: "for most schools, academic press serves as a key prerequisite for the positive achievement effects of communality." Definitions and measures of support and "communality" in past studies pertain more to the relational aspects of support than to the instructional aspects. Still, across studies, there appears to be consistency in the finding that *Press* tends to be the stronger predictor of learning.

It seems highly plausible, indeed likely, that sustaining high *Press* (*Control* and *Challenge*) without intimidation and coercion requires providing a significant degree of *Support* (*Care, Confer, Captivate, Clarify,* and *Consolidate*). Similarly, achieving a high-quality *Classroom Environment* without relying on fear probably requires a relatively high quality of *Instruction*. To establish these propositions definitively would require longitudinal data, generated experimentally. Still, we can use the data that we have to deepen our intuition.

Achieving Order without Intimidation and Coercion

In order to consider whether *Support* might provide a foundation for *Press*, we ask, "Which components of the *Instruction* domain are the strongest predictors of *Classroom Environment* in the FfT framework?" and "Which components of the *Support* domain are the strongest predictors of *Press* in the Tripod 7Cs framework?" The question is whether patterns are consistent with the hypothesis that the quality of *Support* and *Instruction* might influence value added (and other outcomes) indirectly by affecting student behavior and focus in the classroom, as measured by the components of *Classroom Environment* and *Press*.

We conducted multivariate regressions to help us judge the plausibility of this hypothesis. Figure 4.5 shows the results. First, it is interesting to note that the pattern for predicting *Control* is clearly different from that for predicting *Challenge*. For *Control*, the three strongest predictors are *Clarify*, *Confer*, and *Captivate*, with *Clarify* as the strongest. A likely interpretation is that explaining concepts clearly (*Clarify*), talking with students (*Confer*) and making lessons interesting (*Captivate*) helps keep the class orderly and on task. For *Challenge*, *Captivate* is not a predictor at all. Apparently, making lessons interesting is not how teachers press students to think rigorously and persist in the face of difficulty. Instead, *Challenge* is almost equally (and quite strongly) predicted by *Clarify* and *Consolidate*. Both of the latter pertain to ways of helping students achieve understanding—explaining material clearly, summarizing, and checking for understanding. *Confer* predicts *Challenge* as well, but only half as strongly as *Clarify* and *Consolidate* and about equally as strongly as it (i.e., *Confer*) predicts *Control*. For both *Challenge* and *Control*, *Care* enters the multiple regression with a small negative and statistically significant coefficient. The concept of *Care* in the 7Cs framework is closely related to emotional support. So the finding that, other things being equal, more *Care* predicts slightly less *Control* and *Challenge* is not really surprising. Indeed, it reminds us of the finding in Figure 4.3, Panel A, concerning the negative role of *Support* in predicting value added when holding *Control* and *Challenge* constant.

For the FfT part of the analysis, our predictors are components from the *Instruction* domain whose labels constitute vivid *action* statements of what the teacher is doing instructionally—i.e., *Communicating with Students*, *Using Assessment in Instruction*, and *Using Questioning and Discussion Techniques*.

The dependent variables are the other five FfT components. Again, just as above, the question is whether predictive patterns are consistent with the hypothesis that components from the *Instruction* domain are affecting conditions measured by components from the *Classroom Environment* domain. In the same spirit, we examine how the three *Instruction* components that describe actions in their titles predict the two that have "learning" in their titles. The question is whether higher ratings on the instructional action components predict FfT rater perceptions that there is a culture of learning and that students are intellectually engaged.

Figure 4.5 indicates that all three of the FfT components with actions in their titles make distinct contributions to predicting all five of the other FfT

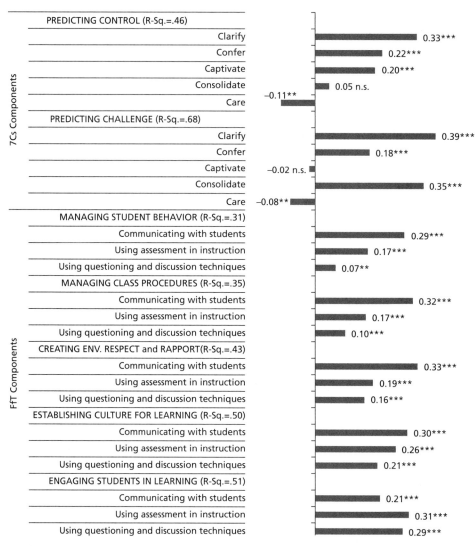

FIGURE 4.5. *Predicting Control, Challenge, and Classroom Environment Components Using Support and Instructing Components*

Note: Two-tailed significance indicators: + 0.10; * 0.05; ** 0.01; *** 0.001.

measures. For each of the standard four *Classroom Environment* components (treating *Establishing a Culture for Learning* as the fourth), *Communicating with Students* is the strongest predictor. Importantly for our hypothesis, among the FfT *Instruction* components, *Communicating with Students* is most associated conceptually with making success feasible for students who might otherwise struggle. It concerns "clarity of lesson purpose; clear directions and procedures specific to the lesson activities; absence of content errors and clear explanations of concepts and strategies; and correct and imaginative use of language." Hence, it closely parallels *Clarify* in the 7Cs framework.

Similar to findings for the 7Cs above, our interpretation is that high-quality delivery of instruction is surely among the practices that enable teachers to achieve orderly and focused classroom environments without needing to use intimidation and coercion.

To summarize, an important finding in this chapter is the strong roles of *Classroom Environment*, *Control*, and *Challenge* in predicting value added. The fact that *Support* and *Instruction* components help predict these measures in the manner shown in Figure 4.6 challenges any presumption that *Control* and *Managing Student Behavior* are best achieved through heavy-handed, coercive methods. Instead, it appears likely that both *Control* and *Managing Student Behavior* are best achieved—and indeed most effective—when students and observers alike perceive clarity in the delivery of the instruction and free-flowing communication with students who might otherwise struggle, misbehave, and go off task. It could be that improving teachers' content knowledge and associated methods for helping students with difficult material could be the most effective ways of maintaining the types of orderly, on-task classrooms that produce the most learning.

MAINTAINING DATA QUALITY

Districts around the nation are becoming more serious about using data to inform their efforts toward improvement. But data will lose their validity and value if too many of those who rate teaching fail to take care or try to manipulate outcomes. Especially in a context where stakes are high, vigilance to maintain data quality is important. Since there were no stakes for teachers or students in the MET project, there was no motive to systematically distort responses. However, the need to monitor for biases and distortions will rise as more school systems use these measures in their accountability formulas. Students in a school that uses student surveys in teacher evaluation formulas might try to influence evaluation outcomes by either inflating or deflating their responses. Administrators or coaches who rate teachers might try to low-ball ratings for teachers they want to dismiss. Or, for teachers they think deserve the benefit of the doubt, they might exaggerate ratings in order to offset low ratings from other sources, such as student ratings or value-added scores.

In either case, officials can monitor for patterns of inconsistency between 7Cs and FfT ratings in order to detect when greater scrutiny is warranted.

When 7Cs composites and FfT ratings are scaled to have standard deviations of 1 and means of 0, the difference between the standardized 7Cs and FfT composites should on average be 0, with a bell-shaped distribution around that average. Typical differences can be benchmarked using large data sets such as the MET data or a combined Tripod and FfT database for schools using both assessment systems. Irregularities can be fairly easy to detect.

Imagine measuring 7Cs-versus-FfT disagreement at the classroom level by subtracting the standardized 7Cs composite rating from the standardized FfT composite. We implemented this procedure for the MET data to examine the patterns. Column A in Table 4.1 represents the likelihood in the MET

TABLE 4.1. **Detecting Irregularities: Probabilities That the Difference Between FfT and 7Cs Composites Would Fall Repeatedly in Selected Ranges by Chance; Column A Is Based on MET Data**

	Number of Repetitions in Same Range				
	A Single Occurrence	Two	Three	Four	Five
Column	A	B	C	D	E
Difference Between FfT and 7Cs Composites	Pattern probabilities if each rating is independent				
0 or higher	0.5000	0.2500	0.1250	0.0625	0.0313
Over 0.10 standard deviation	0.4500	0.2025	0.0911	0.0410	0.0185
Over 0.25 standard deviation	0.4000	0.1600	0.0640	0.0256	0.0102
Over 0.5 standard deviation	0.3100	0.0961	0.0298	0.0092	0.0029
Over plus 1 standard deviation	0.1700	0.0289	0.0049	0.0008	0.0001
Between plus and minus 0.25 standard deviation	0.1500	0.0225	0.0034	0.0005	0.0001
Over 2.0 standard deviations	0.0300	0.0009	0.0000	0.0000	0.0000

data of observing a difference in each range listed on the left of the table. For example, the range "0 or higher" means that the FfT rating was higher than the 7Cs rating. The likelihood of this happening in the MET data is almost exactly 0.50—the same as flipping a coin. The likelihood that the FfT rating exceeds the 7Cs rating by 0.10 standard deviation is 0.45. Skipping a few lines down, we see that the likelihood of more than 1 standard deviation is 0.17 and for more than 2 standard deviations the number is 0.03. In addition, we consider the likelihood of falling in a rather narrow range around the mean: between plus and minus 0.25 of a standard deviation. The likelihood of this happening is only 0.15.

The other columns of Table 4.1 show the probabilities that multiple independent classrooms would have differences in the same range. Imagine, for example, that an administrator works in a school that surveyed students. The same administrator rates teachers. If the administrator has two classrooms to judge and is perfectly even-handed—in other words, she judges each completely on its own terms—and the students give an honest appraisal as well, then the likelihood that her FfT rating will be higher than the students' 7Cs rating for both teachers is 0.25. In other words, it will happen about a quarter of the time. However, if it keeps happening, there is likely to be some irregularity. The likelihood that her FfT rating will be higher than the students' 7Cs rating five times in a row if there are no irregularities is only 0.03—only three times in one hundred. Scrutiny would seem warranted.

The likelihood of landing repeatedly in other ranges that Table 4.1 shows is even smaller. It is interesting that excessive matching between FfT and the 7Cs ratings is also an irregularity. Falling within 0.25 standard deviations of agreement five times in a row will happen merely by chance only one in ten thousand times. The laws of probability are quite robust. Especially when there are several classrooms evaluated using both observational and student survey tools, levels of agreement and disagreement between the two methods will follow probabilistic patterns that make systematic irregularities readily detectable.

DISCUSSION AND IMPLICATIONS

This chapter set out to do three things: first, to examine whether specific domains and components of the FfT and Tripod 7Cs frameworks are well-matched not only conceptually, but also empirically; second, to explore which components of both frameworks predict value added and three measures of student engagement that are of concern to parents and educators alike; and third, to suggest how data collected using the FfT and Tripod 7Cs frameworks can be used in combination to monitor the implementation fidelity of both.

Do Adults and Students Agree about Teaching?

We find that the conceptual overlap between the frameworks is substantial and that empirical patterns in the data show similarities in adult and student assessments at the classroom level. Educators can cross-walk the two frameworks to consider the management of student conduct (e.g., *Control* from the 7Cs and *Managing Student Behavior* from the FfT); classroom-level relationships (e.g., *Care* from the 7Cs and *Creating a Climate of Respect and Rapport* from the FfT); delivery of the curriculum (e.g., *Clarify* and *Consolidate* from the 7Cs and *Using Questioning and Discussion Techniques* and *Using Assessment in Instruction* from the FfT); eliciting student perspectives and inviting help-seeking in class (e.g., *Confer* and *Clarify* from the 7Cs and *Communicating with Students* from the FfT); and making learning attractive (e.g., *Captivate* from the 7Cs and *Engaging Students in Learning* from the FfT). More examples could be listed. Generally, the 7Cs *Press* components are related to the FfT *Classroom Environment* components, and the 7Cs *Support* components are related to the FfT *Instruction* components.

Implications Based on our analysis, we judge it quite practical for educators to use both frameworks in their reflections on teaching and to draw data from both measurement systems to identify challenges, assess progress, and set goals.

Predicting Value Added and Engagement

The data that were available for this analysis included indices for value-added achievement gains, happiness in class, effort in class, and the degree to which the teacher inspires an interest in college. We found that all four were predicted in interesting ways by components of both the FfT and 7Cs frameworks.

The chapter augments MET reports by going inside the composite metrics to study how individual components and domains relate to value added. We also pay more attention to the engagement measures than was practical in the MET reports. Each of the eight FfT components and seven 7Cs components is correlated to a statistically significant degree with value added, but some more strongly than others. For both the FfT and the 7Cs frameworks, the component most conceptually associated with student conduct management was the strongest predictor of value added. In addition, student respondents to Tripod surveys and observers using the FfT protocol tend to agree when behavior is a problem. The correlation between FfT and 7Cs metrics for conduct management—*Control* and *Managing Student Behavior*—was the strongest between the frameworks. A notable finding is that being in the bottom quintile for these conduct measures, especially for *Control*, is especially problematic. Aside from the disruptive impacts on teaching and learning, problems with behavior management may restrict an FfT observer's ability to judge instruction along the multiple dimensions that the FfT aims to measure. We found that classrooms rated in the bottom quintile on *Control* were rated low on all FfT components, and to a greater degree students rated the same classrooms low on the 7Cs components.

An unexpected but robust finding is that holding constant *Control* and *Challenge* while increasing *Support* tends to depress value added. Similarly, *Instruction* has a smaller predicted impact on value added than *Classroom Environment*. We speculate that when students rate a teacher low on both *Support* and *Press* or when an observer sees reasons to rate a classroom low on both *Instruction* and *Class Environment*, increasing the level of *Support* or the quality of *Instruction* may encourage or enable students to pay more attention to their studies. However, when instructional quality is already high for most components, increasing *Support* might relieve some of the stress that drives students to focus and persevere. For the time being, this explanation remains speculation but seems consistent with patterns in the data.

While *Control* and *Challenge* from the 7Cs framework and *Classroom Environment* from the FfT were the strongest predictors of value added, components from the *Support* domain of the 7Cs framework and the *Instruction* domain of the FfT framework most strongly predicted *Happiness in Class* and *Teacher Inspires Interest in College*. *Effort in Class* was predicted by a relatively balanced combination of *Support* and *Press* factors.

Finally, our findings are consistent with the possibility that *Support* and *Instruction*—especially *Clarify* and *Communicating with Students*—might be important enablers for *Press* and *Classroom Environment*.

Implications The finding that *Control*, *Challenge*, and the components of *Classroom Environment* are stronger and more consistently positive predictors of value added than the components of *Support* and *Instruction* may tempt some educators to increase their focus on heavy-handed, coercive ways of managing classrooms. There are two reasons that this may be a mistake. First, most of us, including parents, educators, and others, want classroom climates that foster a love of learning. Findings here concerning predictors of happiness, effort, and interest in college caution us to value classroom experiences associated with higher values in the *Instruction* and *Support* domains. Second, it seems highly likely that better performance in the *Instruction* and *Support* domains might actually buttress performance in the *Press* and *Classroom Environment* domains. Hence, maintaining a balance seems important. If any one or two components should be the focus, *Clarify* from the 7Cs framework and *Communicating with Students* from the FfT framework are prime candidates to consider. This is because they not only help to predict the non-value-added outcomes—happiness, effort, and college inspiration—but they are also strong predictors of *Control*, *Challenge*, and *Classroom Environment*, which in turn, are strong predictors of value added.

Maintaining Data Quality

One hears a good deal of informal conversation these days concerning the ways that measurement tools can be misused, especially under high-stakes conditions. Therefore, it is important to make sure that stakeholders are well prepared to use tools correctly and that carelessness or intentional misuse are discouraged or curtailed. It is difficult to know how severely the incentives entailed with high-stakes use of FfT and Tripod instruments could distort the ways that people use them. Clearly, reports of cheating over the past year on standardized testing in the Atlanta school system should make us cautious.

There are multiple ways to detect irregularities. Using large benchmarking data sets, it is possible to check how frequently disagreement between FfT and 7Cs composites will tend to be in particular ranges. There are some ranges that occur very rarely, even for a single class. For example, in the MET data, the difference between FfT and 7Cs ratings exceeds 2 standard deviations in only 3 percent of classrooms. Such a large difference should trigger at least a modest bit of examination. However, even more important, having multiple classrooms fall consistently within the same range of FfT-7Cs disagreement should be a very rare event. Table 4.1 shows, for example, that finding five classrooms where the FfT rating in standard deviation units exceeds the 7Cs rating all five times should be a rare event. An administrator who consistently rates teachers higher than the students do is very likely out of calibration, and an intervention is almost certainly warranted.

Limitations

Despite the unusual richness of the data, the work that we discuss in this chapter is very much work in progress. Because all of the data are cross-sectional and generated from natural variation, not through planned or experimental variation, estimates must necessarily be interpreted as correlational, not causal. Causal statements in this context are judgments, not findings. In addition, this has been an aggregate analysis. We have lumped together different subjects, different tests, different grades, and different schools and districts. Whether our conclusions will apply to more homogeneous categories of analysis is beyond the scope of this chapter, but nonetheless important to address in future work. Finally, it is important to note that the MET data were collected under special conditions. Raters were trained and monitored to ensure that they scored classrooms correctly. Student surveys were administered according to protocol, and data records were carefully managed. The reliability and validity of the data deepened upon quality control. The findings reported here are unlikely to apply in instances when observation and data collection procedures are not of high quality.

CONCLUSION

This chapter concerns ideas and tools for helping educators to reflect on their work, refine their craft, and increase their effectiveness. We show that concepts and tools from the Framework for Teaching and Tripod survey assessments—tools that the authors of the chapter have designed independently over many years—are quite compatible. Furthermore, MET data collected and organized using the two frameworks show similar empirical relationships to student engagement and learning. Most prominent, analysis of data from both frameworks shows that *classroom management* is the strongest predictor of achievement gains. In addition, for each framework, the teaching component associated with *clarity* is the strongest predictor of effective classroom management.

A central finding is that the challenging and structured teaching practices that most effectively raise test scores are different from the mix of caring and emotionally supportive practices that most effectively foster happiness, voluntary effort, and inspiration to attend college. This does not mean we should downplay the importance of raising test scores. Remember that reading and math scores measure skills for which employers will someday pay and upon which families will someday depend. But schools should strive to achieve a balance between the types of *Press* most strongly associated with short-term growth in measurable skills versus the types of *Support* that foster a healthy and optimistic outlook on life and learning. The ideas and evidence that we examine in this chapter can help us identify and support balanced teaching that fosters the multiple skills and orientations students need to succeed.

Finally, our first priority (and the main reason we do this work) is to help educators to improve instructional quality. However, as the tools become used increasingly for accountability purposes, not simply instructional improvement, the integrity of the data needs to be protected. Monitoring becomes important. We show near the end of the chapter that comparing FfT and Tripod 7Cs ratings from clusters of individual classrooms is a way to discover patterns of irregularity that may warrant careful scrutiny. Data can be standardized in ways that enable analysts to estimate the likelihood that the pattern of FfT and Tripod 7Cs ratings from a particular batch of classrooms could have occurred normally, without systematically inappropriate forces intervening.

Recall that we opened the chapter by asking why some teachers routinely produce more learning than others do. Having reviewed this chapter, what is your answer? What are some implications for your work?

NOTE

1. Domains 2 and 3 each have five components in the FfT framework. MET omitted one from each domain. The omitted components from these domains are "organizing physical space" and "demonstrating flexibility and responsiveness." More about the framework and components, elements and performance levels can be found in *Enhancing Professional Practice* (Danielson, 2007) or at www.danielsongroup.org.

REFERENCES AND ADDITIONAL RESOURCES

Baumrind, D. (1966). Effects of authoritative parental control on child behavior. *Child Development, 37,* 887–907.

Baumrind, D. (1996, October). The discipline controversy revisited. *Family Relations, 45*(4), 405–414.

Cantrell, S., & Kane, T. J. (2013). *Ensuring fair and reliable measures of effective teaching: Culminating findings from the MET Project's three-year study.* Seattle, WA: Bill & Melinda Gates Foundation.

Chart, H. with Kendall-Taylor, N. (2008). *Reform what? Individualist thinking in education: American cultural models on schooling.* Washington, DC: Frameworks Institute.

Danielson, C. (2007). *Enhancing Professional Practice: A framework for teaching.* ASCD.

Danielson, C. (2013). *The Framework for Teaching Evaluation Instrument.* Princeton, NJ: The Danielson Group.

Ferguson, R. F. (2012). Can student surveys measure teaching quality? *Phi Delta Kappan, 94*(3), 24–28.

Flexner, A., & Bachman, F. (1918). *The Gary schools: A general account.* New York, NY: General Education Board.

Ho, A. D., & Kane, T. J. (2012). *The reliability of classroom observations by school personnel.* Seattle, WA: Bill & Melinda Gates Foundation.

Kane, T. J., McCaffrey, D. F., & Staiger, D. O. (2010). *Learning about teaching: Initial findings from the Measures of Effective Teaching Project.* Seattle, WA: Bill & Melinda Gates Foundation.

Kane, T. J., McCaffrey, D. F., & Staiger, D. O. (2012). *Gathering feedback for teaching: Combining high-quality observations with student surveys and achievement gains.* Seattle, WA: Bill & Melinda Gates Foundation.

Klem, A. M., & Connell, J. P. (2004). Relationships matter: Linking teacher support to student engagement and achievement. *Journal of School Health, 74*(7), 262–273.

Lee, V. E., & Smith, J. B. (1999). Social support and achievement for young adolescents in Chicago: The role of school academic press. *American Educational Research Journal, 36*(1), 907–945.

Lee, V. E., Smith, J. B., Perry, T. E., & Smylie, M. A. (1999). *Social support, academic press, and student achievement: A view from the middle grades in Chicago.* Chicago, IL: Consortium on Chicago School Research.

Rivkin, S. G., Hanushek, E. A., & Kain, J. F. (2005, March). Teachers, schools and academic achievement. *Econometrica, 72*(2), 417–458.

Shouse, R. C. (1996). Academic press and sense of community: Conflict, congruence, and implications for student achievement. *Social Psychology of Education, 1*(1), 47–68.

APPENDIX

EXHIBIT 4.A.1. Comparing the Framework for Teaching and Tripod 7Cs

Framework for Teaching	Tripod 7Cs
Creating an environment of respect and rapport. For example: respectful talk, active listening, and turn taking; acknowledgment of students' backgrounds and lives outside the classroom; body language indicative of warmth and caring; physical proximity; politeness and encouragement; and fairness.	**Care** concerns whether the teacher develops supportive relationships with students and is attentive to their feelings. For example, "My teacher in this class really tries to understand how students feel about things" or "My teacher seems to know if something is bothering me." The 7Cs conception of care is focused on emotional support. An alternative conception of caring concerns a teacher's commitment to make sure that students succeed. That alternative is captured by all of the Cs, collectively.
Managing student behavior. For example: clear standards of conduct, possibly posted, and possibly referred to during a lesson; absence of acrimony between teacher and students concerning behavior; teacher awareness of student conduct, including preventive awareness; absence of misbehavior; and reinforcement of positive behavior.	**Control** concerns the degree to which the class is both well-behaved, for example, "Students in this class behave the way my teacher wants them to" and on task, for example, "Our class stays busy and doesn't waste time." The connotation is not that teachers are controlling in the sense of squashing student autonomy and expression, but rather that they are able to manage the class in a way that teaching and learning occur efficiently, without being derailed by misbehavior or distractions.
Managing classroom procedures. For example: smooth functioning of all routines; little or no loss of instructional time; students playing an important role in carrying out the routines; students knowing what to do, where to move.	**Confer** concerns the degree to which the teacher elicits ideas from students and welcomes their feedback. One example is "My teacher welcomes my ideas and suggestions." Another is "My teacher wants us to share our thoughts." Classrooms that students rate high on Confer are more "student centered" than those where only the teacher's perspective is valued.
Establishing a culture for learning. For example: belief in the value of what is being learned; high expectations supported through both verbal and nonverbal behaviors, for both learning and participation; expectation of high-quality work on the part of students; expectation and recognition of effort and persistence on the part of students; and high expectations for expression and work products.	**Challenge** concerns both effort and rigor. It concerns a teacher's insistence that students should work hard and persist in the face of difficulty, for example, "My teacher accepts nothing less than our best effort," and think hard, for example, "My teacher wants us to really understand the material, not just memorize it."
Using questioning and discussion techniques. For example: questions of high cognitive challenge, formulated by both students and teacher; questions with multiple correct answers, or multiple approaches, even when there is a single correct response; effective use of student responses and ideas; discussion, with the teacher stepping out of the central, mediating role; focus on the reasoning exhibited by students in discussion, both in give-and-take with the teacher and with their classmates; high levels of student participation in discussion.	**Consolidate** concerns making learning coherent, for example, "My teacher takes time to summarize what we learn each day," giving feedback, "The comments that I get on my work in this class help me understand how to improve," and checking for understanding, "My teacher checks to make sure we understand what she is teaching us." Hence, Consolidate is closely related conceptually to both Clarify and Challenge.
Communicating with students. For example: clarity of lesson purpose; clear directions and procedures specific to the lesson activities; absence of content errors and clear explanations of concepts and strategies; and correct and imaginative use of language.	**Captivate** pertains to how effectively the teacher stimulates students to be interested in the lessons. A reverse coded item in this category is, "This class does not keep my attention—I get bored." A positively worded item is, "My teacher makes lessons interesting." Items are geared to measure whether the teacher is able to hold the students' attention in class and provide the basis for continuing interest.
Engaging students in learning. For example: students show enthusiasm, interest, thinking, problem solving, etc.; learning tasks that require high-level student thinking and invite students to explain their thinking; students highly motivated to work on all tasks and persist, even when the tasks are challenging; students actively "working," rather than watching while the teacher "works"; and suitable pacing of the lesson, neither dragged out nor rushed, with time for closure and student reflection.	**Clarify** concerns how effectively the teacher is able to help students understand what she is trying to teach them, especially with regard to concepts that students may find difficult to understand. This includes having clear explanations, "My teacher explains difficult concepts clearly," multiple explanations, "My teacher has several good ways to explain each topic that we cover in this class," and a commitment to persist until understanding is achieved, "If you don't understand something, my teacher explains it another way."
Using assessment in instruction. For example: the teacher paying close attention to evidence of student understanding; the teacher posing specifically created questions to elicit evidence of student understanding; the teacher circulating to monitor student learning and to offer feedback; and students assessing their own work against established criteria.	

TABLE 4.A.1. Backup for Exhibit 4.2, Column 1

Column	Creating an environment of respect and rapport 1.	Establishing a culture for learning 2.	Managing classroom procedures 3.	Managing student behavior 4.	Communicating with students 5.	Using questioning and discussion techniques 6.	Engaging students in learning 7.	Using assessment in instruction 8.
Care	0.051+							
Control	0.255***		0.272***	0.334***				
Challenge		0.115***				0.103**	0.089*	
Confer		0.111***	-0.033		0.096*	0.137**		
Clarify					0.102*			0.174***
Consolidate						-0.047		0.005
Captivate							0.143***	
Subject and Level Indicators	Yes	Yes	Yes	Yes	Yes	Yes	Yes	Yes

(continued)

(Table 4.A.1 continued)

Column	Creating an environment of respect and rapport 1.	Establishing a culture for learning 2.	Managing classroom procedures 3.	Managing student behavior 4.	Communicating with students 5.	Using questioning and discussion techniques 6.	Engaging students in learning 7.	Using assessment in instruction 8.
School intercepts	Yes	Yes	Yes	Yes	Yes	Yes	Yes	Yes
Constant	0.22**	0.133	0.191**	0.101	0.156+	0.122	0.113	0.128
R-Square	0.285	0.260	0.274	0.309	0.216	0.199	0.231	0.225
Adj. R-Square	0.194	0.165	0.181	0.221	0.116	0.096	0.132	0.126

Note: Regressions behind Column 1 of Exhibit 4.2 in the body of the chapter. Each school has a separate intercept term and all regressions have level (i.e., elementary versus middle school) and subject (i.e., ELA versus math) indicator variables.

$N = 1,175$ teachers; 1,892 classrooms; standard errors adjusted for clustering by teacher.

Two-tailed significance indicators: + 0.10; * 0.05; ** 0.01; *** 0.001.

TABLE 4.A.2.   Backup for Exhibit 4.2, Column 2

	Care	Confer	Captivate	Clarify	Consolidate	Challenge	Control
Column	1.	2.	3.	4.	5.	6.	7.
Managing classroom procedures	0.18***						0.099**
Communicating with students		0.101**				0.109***	
Establishing a culture for learning		0.017					0.04
Creating an environment of respect and rapport		0.07*		0.109***			
Using questioning and discussion techniques		0.059*			0.068*	0.051++	
Using assessment in instruction			0.195***			0.065*	
Engaging students in learning				0.107***	0.098***		
Managing student behavior							0.238***
Subject and level indicators	Yes	Yes	Yes	Yes	Yes	Yes	Yes
School-specific intercepts	Yes	Yes	Yes	Yes	Yes	Yes	Yes
Constant	0.249*	0.088	0.167++	0.134	0.248**	0.172++	−0.032
R-Square	0.217	0.258	0.228	0.232	0.247	0.266	0.274
Adj. R-Square	0.118	0.163	0.131	0.135	0.151	0.171	0.274

Note: Regressions behind Column 2 of Exhibit 4.2 in the body of the chapter. Each school has a separate intercept term and all regressions have level (i.e., elementary versus middle school) and subject (i.e., ELA versus math) indicator variables.

$N = 1{,}175$ teachers; 1,892 classrooms; standard errors adjusted for clustering by teacher.

Two-tailed significance indicators: + 0.10; * 0.05; ** 0.01; *** 0.001.

TABLE 4.A.3. Regressions Behind Figure 4.1

Column	Creating an environment of respect and rapport	Managing classroom procedures	Managing student behavior	Establishing a culture for learning	Using questioning and discussion techniques	Communicating with students	Engaging students in learning	Using assessment in instruction
	1.	2.	3.	4.	5.	6.	7.	8.

Panel A: Regressions exclude classrooms for which Control was in the bottom quintile. This version is shown on Exhibit 4.2.

Support	0.069+	−0.050	−0.062+	0.057	0.100*	0.132**	0.162***	0.077+
Control	0.151***	0.148***	0.255***	0.103*	0.014	0.098*	0.040	0.096*
Challenge	0.032	0.092*	0.072*	0.050	0.082*	−0.034	0.004	0.054
Constant	0.279***	0.203**	0.155*	0.210*	0.133	0.188+	0.182*	0.138
R-Square	0.257	0.248	0.272	0.258	0.210	0.225	0.232	0.233
Adj. R-Square	0.139	0.129	0.156	0.140	0.084	0.102	0.110	0.111
Classrooms	1554	1554	1554	1554	1554	1554	1554	1554
Teachers	1114	1114	1114	1114	1114	1114	1114	1114
Schools	206	206	206	206	206	206	206	206

Panel B: Regressions below include even the bottom quintile on Control. Not shown in the body of the chapter.

Support	0.014	−0.096*	−0.095**	0.024	0.068+	0.091*	0.118**	0.050
Control	0.244***	0.261***	0.338***	0.202***	0.094**	0.171***	0.135***	0.145***
Challenge	0.052	0.097**	0.103**	0.061+	0.058	−0.011	0.015	0.056
Constant	0.221**	0.189**	0.102	0.148	0.118	0.162+	0.125	0.132
R-Square	0.285	0.277	0.312	0.279	0.202	0.230	0.240	0.238
Adj. R-Square	0.194	0.184	0.224	0.186	0.100	0.132	0.142	0.140
Classrooms	1892	1892	1892	1892	1892	1892	1892	1892
Teachers	1275	1275	1275	1275	1275	1275	1275	1275
Schools	208	208	208	208	208	208	208	208

Note: Each school has a separate intercept term and all regressions include level (i.e., elementary versus middle school) and subject (i.e., ELA versus math) indicator variables.

Standard errors adjusted for clustering by teacher.

Two-tailed significance indicators: + 0.10; * 0.05; ** 0.01; *** 0.001.

TABLE 4.A.4. Regressions Behind Figure 4.3

Column	Value Added	Happy in Class	Effort in Class	Inspired Re: College	Value Added	Happy in Class	Effort in Class	Inspired Re: College
	1.	2.	3.	4.	5.	6.	7.	8.
FfT Instruction	0.063+	0.137***	0.095**	0.118***				
FfT Class Environment	0.127***	0.069+	0.110***	0.057+				
7Cs Support					−0.120***	0.802***	0.335***	0.600***
7Cs Control					0.244***	0.121***	0.125***	−0.004
7Cs Challenge					0.148***	−0.115***	0.238***	0.135***
Subject and Level Indicators	Yes	Yes	Yes	Yes	Yes	Yes	Yes	Yes
School Intercepts	Yes	Yes	Yes	Yes	Yes	Yes	Yes	Yes
Constant	−0.005	0.137	0.061	0.041	0.057	−0.01	−0.01	−0.034
R-Square	0.214	0.163	0.169	0.189	0.203	0.639	0.435	0.532

Adj. R-Square	0.114	0.055	0.062	0.084	0.136	0.608	0.378	0.492
Classes	1938	1868	1868	1868	3002	2961	2961	2961
Teachers	1307	1261	1261	1261	1920	1902	1902	1902
Schools	212	207	207	207	226	225	225	225

Note: Each school has a separate intercept term and all regressions include level (i.e., elementary versus middle school) and subject (i.e., ELA versus math) indicator variables.

Standard errors adjusted for clustering by teacher.

Two-tailed significance indicators: + 0.10; * 0.05; ** 0.01; *** 0.001.

TABLE 4.A.5. Regressions Behind Figure 4.5

	Control	Challenge	Managing student behavior	Establishing culture for learning	Managing classroom procedures	Creating an environment of respect and rapport	Engaging students in learning
Care	−0.110**	−0.079*					
Clarify	0.340***	0.403***					
Captivate	0.203***	−0.018					
Confer	0.227***	0.184***					
Consolidate	0.051	0.374***					
Communicating with Students			0.291***	0.300***	0.319***	0.335***	0.212***
Using Assessment in Class			0.173***	0.264***	0.167***	0.189***	0.307***
Using Questioning and Discussion Techniques			0.068*	0.205***	0.099**	0.161***	0.286***

Subject and Level Indicators	Yes	Yes	Yes	Yes	Yes	Yes	Yes
School Intercepts	Yes	Yes	Yes	Yes	Yes	Yes	Yes
Constant	−0.144*	0.114*	0.032	0.053	0.102	0.135*	0.037
R-Square	0.503	0.708	0.389	0.558	0.424	0.490	0.564
Adj. R-Square	0.461	0.683	0.311	0.502	0.351	0.425	0.508
Classes	3004	3004	1939	1939	1939	1939	1939
Teachers	1921	1921	1308	1308	1308	1308	1308
Schools	226	226	212	212	212	212	212

Making Decisions with Imprecise Performance Measures

The Relationship Between Annual Student Achievement Gains and a Teacher's Career Value Added

DOUGLAS O. STAIGER AND THOMAS J. KANE

ABSTRACT

Critics often point to low year-to-year correlations in teacher value-added measures as *prima facie* evidence against their use. We argue that decision-makers should focus instead on the correlation between a single year's performance and a teacher's career performance. Using data from several urban school districts, we construct annual and career performance measures for teachers with at least six years of value-added data. Year-to-career performance correlations range from 0.5 to 0.8—substantially stronger than year-to-year performance correlations. Three-quarters of the teachers ranked at the 25th percentile on annual value added had career performance below average. Finally, cumulative estimates of teacher value added (based on performance to date) are better predictors of career performance and very stable over time.

INTRODUCTION

There is continuing confusion and debate over whether value-added measures are sufficiently reliable to be used in high-stakes personnel decisions. On the one hand, critics often point to the year-to-year volatility in value-added measures as *prima facie* evidence against their use. They ask, how can we sanction teachers who are in the bottom quartile of value added this year when we know that value added for nearly two-thirds of these teachers will no longer be in the bottom quartile when measured again next year? On the other hand, the results of the MET project and others have highlighted that even unreliable performance measures such as value added can identify substantial and lasting differences across teachers.

Our goal in this chapter is to reconcile these two views. Despite the fact that value-added measures are unreliable by conventional standards and unstable over time, they are strong predictors of an individual teacher's career performance that can be used to improve decision making. Much of the confusion is due to an over-interpretation of seemingly low year-to-year correlations in value-added measures. For most decisions, year-to-year volatility in annual performance is the wrong statistic for judging the informational value of value-added data. A retention decision, for instance, rests on a different relationship, the correlation between a single year's performance (or performance to date) and a teacher's career performance. We propose a way to infer the year-to-career correlation using the year-to-year correlation. We also test that method using data from several urban school districts that have six or more years of data on teacher value added. We show that the year-to-career performance correlation can be estimated with a simple calculation, that the estimate corresponds with the actual correlation observed between a single year of value added and a teacher's multi-year average, and that it is substantially stronger than the year-to-year correlation in performance.

In addition, we study the usefulness of value-added data in a retention decision. To do so, we model the decision problem faced by a supervisor. When analyzed in that way, it becomes clear that every retention decision involves two teachers—the incumbent teacher and a prospective new hire. Although the latter is usually anonymous, a principal's or supervisor's decision requires comparing the likelihood that either of the teachers will turn out to be high performing. A common conceptual error is to focus on the degree of uncertainty surrounding an individual teacher's likely career performance.

Yet it is the teacher's performance relative to the potential replacement that matters. In the worst-case scenario, the supervisor would have to hire a rookie every year to fill the slot. In that context, the right decision rule would be to ask whether the teacher was likely to be more or less effective than an infinite series of novice teachers. We find that even one year of value-added data can substantially reduce the chance of making a mistake.

Unlike many debates in education, there is surprisingly little dispute about the underlying facts. In most studies, the correlation in test-based measures of teaching effectiveness between one school year and the next ranges between 0.35 and 0.50 in elementary grades, and it is somewhat higher in middle school grades (where value added is based on multiple classrooms per teacher). Such fluctuations are due to a number of factors, such as the finite number of students in their classrooms in a given year. For instance, an elementary teacher will have between fifteen and twenty-five students. With samples that small, a few unusually rowdy or studious students can make a difference from year to year.

A correlation as low as 0.35 can produce seemingly troubling statistics in terms of year-to-year changes. For instance, only about one-third of teachers ranked in the top quartile (highest 25 percent) of value added based on one academic year's performance would appear in the top quartile again the next year. Moreover, 10 percent of bottom-quartile teachers (bottom 25 percent) one year would appear in the top quartile the next.

Such instability in measures of performance is not unique to teaching. In a wide range of settings, ranging from using SAT scores to predict college GPA (Camara & Echternacht, 2000), surgical mortality rate at hospitals (Dimick, Staiger, Basur, & Birkmeyer, 2009), to the batting averages and earned-run averages for major league baseball players (Schall & Smith, 2000), annual performance measures show similarly low correlations, yet are regularly used for high-stakes evaluation.[1]

We should be asking three key questions when trying to interpret value added:

1. Does a Teacher's Value Added One Year Predict Value Added Over His or Her Career?

It would be troubling if the measures were so volatile that one year's performance does not predict future performance. But this is not true. Despite the fact that annual performance of all teachers varies widely from year to year, this variation is not enough to hide large differences across teachers in their underlying career performance. As the evidence presented below demonstrates, value added from one year of teaching predicts large differences in performance over the teacher's career. For example, teachers ranked in the bottom 25 percent based on a single year of value added will typically perform worse than an average rookie teacher over the remainder of their careers. Averaging value added over two years of teaching predicts even larger differences in career performance.

2. Would Our Impression of a Given Teacher's Performance Change Wildly from One Year to the Next? Would We Simply Be Whipsawing and Confusing School Administrators and Teachers by Providing Them with Annual Performance Data?

This too would be troubling—if it were true. But beliefs about teacher performance are *cumulative*. When provided with two years of value-added data, an administrator should use the *average* over the two years, rather than focusing solely on the most recent year. Why? Because the two-year average is a better predictor of career performance. Yet, despite the volatility in single-year measures, teacher rankings based on cumulative estimates of teacher value added change very little from year to year. For instance, in the districts we look at, less than 1 percent of those who were in the top quartile of performance after only one year of data would be in the bottom quartile over two years. Less than 4 percent would be in the bottom quartile over four years. Despite the volatility, there is a low probability that someone averaging performance over multiple years would change his or her mind about who is more and less effective.

3. Can Value Added Be Used to Improve Decision Making?

Would a single-year measure of performance lead to too many mistakes? It is impossible to say without knowing the decision to be made and the costs of different types of mistakes. Using the example of a principal deciding whether to renew a new teacher's contract for a second year, we show that not renewing the bottom 25 percent of teachers based on one year of value added would increase the chance of having a more effective teacher in the classroom (and thereby reduce mistakes), even if the principal had to replace the incumbent teacher with a string of newly hired rookie teachers.

Our conclusion is that value-added measures are useful despite their volatility. Test-based measures of a teacher's effectiveness from one year do predict their effectiveness over their careers. Moreover, cumulative estimates of teacher value added change very little over time and predict large career performance differences. Finally, decision making improves when value added is used in an appropriate manner.

The first section of this chapter develops a statistical model of teacher impacts on student test scores in order to look at the issue theoretically. In this section, we (1) define what we mean by a teacher's underlying long-term (career) performance, (2) show that the correlation with underlying long-term performance is different from year-to-year correlation in annual performance, (3) show how to easily calculate the correlation between any observed measure and a teacher's underlying long-term performance, and (4) argue that the correlation with underlying long-term performance summarizes both the predictive power and risk of misclassification for any annual performance measure.

The second section provides evidence from three large districts in order to look at the issue empirically. Rather than using data from the MET study, which was only available for a small number of years, we use historical data from three large anonymous districts with up to nine years of value-added data for each teacher (required for estimating career value added). We report on three types of analyses: (1) comparing differences in career value added from ranking teachers on one year versus ranking them on career, and showing what fraction of the total career differences you can capture with one year; (2) showing how rankings on one year of value added misclassify teachers in terms of their career value added (versus next year value added); and (3) comparing the stability and predictive power of cumulative measures of value added versus one-year measures of value added.

The third section looks at the issue of using value added in the context of a simple decision-making problem under uncertainty. We consider the problem facing a principal in deciding whether to renew a new teacher's contract for a second year. This problem can be thought of as having to choose between two teachers (the incumbent teacher and the prospective new hire), with the goal of choosing the teacher who will have a higher effectiveness in the classroom over his or her career. Using this framework, we show that most teachers who are in the bottom quartile in their first year of value added will have lower value added over their careers than a typical new hire will. The bottom 25 percent of teachers based on one year of value added will have career performance worse than if their position were filled every year by a new rookie teacher. In contrast, using a "legal" standard of only removing incumbent teachers if one is 95 percent certain that they are below average results in mistakenly retaining teachers who have up to a 90 percent chance of having worse value added over their careers than if one had filled the positions with new rookies each year. Relative to the current practice of identifying only a small fraction of teachers as ineffective, our evidence suggests a more aggressive policy of identifying at least the bottom quarter of teachers as ineffective.

A STATISTICAL MODEL OF TEACHER IMPACTS

Suppose teachers did not differ in the degree to which their impacts on students improved or declined over their careers. Rather, suppose their measured impact on students were simply fluctuating randomly around their long-term average.[2] If that were the case, we ask, what would the current (albeit imperfect) measure of a teacher's effectiveness tell us about his or her long-term effectiveness?

The above scenario would have two important implications: first, it would mean that the estimated impact of a teacher in any given year or with any given group of students is a noisy estimate of a teacher's long-term impact on student achievement; and, second, it would mean that one could estimate just how much noise there is in any given year by observing the correlation in estimated impacts from any two years. In particular, the correlation between any current measure of value added and the expected long-term effectiveness is simply the square root of its correlation with another single year of value added. The only requirement is that the two annual value-added measures are estimated for different classrooms of students, so that the errors are independent.

To see why the square root of the year-to-year correlation is an estimate of the year-to-career correlation in value added, consider the following simple model. Suppose the short-term measure of a teacher's value added can be expressed as $T_{ij} = \alpha_i + \varepsilon_{ij}$, where i is a subscript for teacher and j is a subscript for school year or classroom of students, α_i is the effect of that teacher over the long term, ε_{ij} is a transitory error in measurement that is uncorrelated for different values of j and unrelated to α_i. (This simple model supposes that there's a "fixed" teacher effect, which does not drift or evolve over time.) Then, the correlation between T_{ij} and α_i can be written as:

$$\rho_{T_{ij},\alpha_i} = \frac{\sigma_{T_{ij},\alpha_i}}{\sigma_{T_{ij}}\sigma_{\alpha_i}} = \frac{\sigma_\alpha^2}{\sigma_{T_{ij}}\sigma_{\alpha_i}} = \sqrt{\frac{\sigma_\alpha^2}{\sigma_{T_{ij}}^2}} = \sqrt{\rho_{T_{ij},T_{ik}}}$$

The latter term is the square root of the correlation between the short-term measure for two different school years or distinct groups of students, j and k.

The intuition for this result is fairly simple. The year-to-year correlation in value added is based on two noisy estimates of a teacher's underlying career performance, that is, it is the correlation between one noisy measure from this year and another noisy measure from the next year. Because both this year's and next year's value-added measures are noisy, the correlation between the two tends to be low. However, the year-to-career correlation should be greater than the year-to-year correlation because it is based on only one noisy estimate, that is, it is the correlation between one noisy measure from this year and the teacher's actual career performance (not a noisy estimate from next year). Thus, for example, if the year-to-year correlation is 0.36, taking the square root implies a larger year-to-career correlation of 0.6. The year-to-year correlation is misleading in that it suggests that this year's value added is only weakly related to a teacher's future performance, while in fact it is only weakly related to the teacher's noisily measured performance from next year and is more strongly related to the teacher's career performance.

The estimated correlation of annual value added with long-term effectiveness captures the two things we most care about in any measure: predictive power *and* the risk of putting teachers in the wrong categories using the measure.

Predictive Power Suppose we were to use an annual measure of value added to identify teachers with more effective and less effective practice. The difference in expected long-term student achievement gains for those in the two groups will be proportional to the correlation with long-term value added. This is what we mean when we say it is a measure of predictive power. For example, if we rank teachers into quartiles based on one year of value-added data, a year-to-career correlation of 0.6 implies that the difference in career value added between top- and bottom-quartile teachers will be 60 percent as large as it would be if we ranked teachers into quartiles based on actual career value added. Thus, a year-to-career correlation of 0.6 implies that we can capture 60 percent of the potential differences in career value added with just one year of value-added data.

Miscategorization The estimated correlation with long-term effectiveness is also an indirect measure of the risk of misclassifying those with different long-term effectiveness based on short-term measures. Under the assumption that the distribution of effectiveness is bell-shaped, the difference in the *probability* that a teacher in either group is above or below some threshold in long-term effectiveness is proportional to the correlation with long-term effectiveness.[3] In fact, the difference in the probability that a top- or bottom-quartile teacher on any given measure has above (or below) average value added in the long term is approximately equal to the measure's correlation with long-term effectiveness. For example, if we rank teachers into quartiles based on one year of value-added data, a year-to-career correlation of 0.6 implies that a top-quartile teacher will have a 60 percent greater chance than a bottom-quartile teacher of having above average value added over his or her career.

The hypothetical scenario in which teachers' underlying effectiveness does not change over their careers is unlikely to be exactly true. However, the evidence in Chetty, Friedman, and Rockoff (2013) and Goldhaber and Hansen (in press) suggest it is not far off as an approximation. Therefore, it will be an empirical question as to whether this approximation is a good guide in practice, that is, whether the square root of the year-to-year correlation in value added is approximately equal to the year-to-career correlation—an empirical question to which we now turn.

EVIDENCE FROM THREE LARGE DISTRICTS

To explore the implications of volatility, we used actual data on teacher-level "value added" from three large districts. Estimating a teacher's career value added requires many years of value-added data. Therefore, rather than using data from the MET study, which was only available for a small number of years, we use historical data from three large anonymous districts with up to nine years of value-added data for each teacher. Each of the districts had a large sample of teachers in grades 4 through 8 teaching ELA and math, for whom we could estimate between six and nine years of value-added data. We used standard methodology for calculating teacher value added using student achievement, including statistical controls for each student's performance on state tests from the prior school year as well as controls for gender, race, ethnicity, free or reduced-price lunch status, and the means of all the above characteristics for the other students in the class. In each year, we average value-added estimates over all the classrooms taught by a teacher (typically, one classroom in elementary grades and two to five classrooms in middle grades).

Comparing Year-to-Year and Year-to-Career Correlations

In the first row of Table 5.1, we report the year-to-year correlations for the three districts in ELA and math. These correlations are typical of what is seen in the literature, ranging from 0.25 to 0.62, with higher year-to-year correlations in math than in ELA. The second row of Table 5.1 reports the implied year-to-career correlations, that is, the square root of the first row. These are predictably larger than the year-to-year correlations, and range from 0.50 to 0.78. More important, they are almost identical to what we obtain when we calculate actual year-to-career correlations, reported in the third row of Table 5.1. These are based on correlating single-year value added with a teacher's average value added over his or her entire career. All of the teachers in the sample have six to nine years of value-added data, with the average career value added being based on 6.7 to 7.6 years of data (in the bottom row of the table). Thus, the square root of the year-to-year correlation is an excellent guide to the correlation one will actually observe between one year of value added and value added over the teacher's career.

The results in Table 5.1 highlight the importance of the distinction between year-to-year and year-to-career correlations in value added. All of

TABLE 5.1. **Year-to-Year Versus Year-to-Career Correlations**

	Math			ELA		
	District 1	District 2	District 3	District 1	District 2	District 3
Correlation of value added:						
Year-to-year	0.42	0.62	0.47	0.27	0.48	0.25
Implied year-to-career (square root)	0.65	0.78	0.69	0.52	0.69	0.50
Actual year-to-career	0.65	0.78	0.70	0.55	0.71	0.57
Number of teachers	2832	3984	377	2640	4197	370
Average number of years per teacher	7.2	6.7	7.5	7.1	6.7	7.6

the debate has focused on the low year-to-year correlations. However, Table 5.1 demonstrates that the actual year-to-career correlations are much higher. Thus, annual value-added measures are a fairly powerful predictor of a teacher's career performance, despite low year-to-year correlations in value added. Moreover, as theory would suggest, in the absence of data on career value added, the square root of the year-to-year correlations is a useful way of estimating the year-to-career correlation.

In Figure 5.1, we show the average difference in career value added for math teachers sorted into quartiles based on one year of value added in District 1 (blue bars). For comparison, we show the difference in career value added when we sort the same math teachers into quartiles based on their career value added (red bars)—the best we could do. One year's ranking identifies 65 percent of the eventual difference in career value added that we could eventually identify, that is, the difference in career value added between the highest and lowest quartile rank based on one year of value added is 65 percent of the best

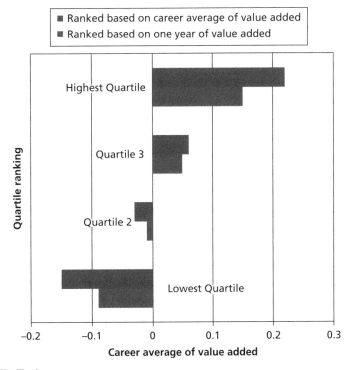

FIGURE 5.1. *One Year's Ranking Identifies 65 Percent of Eventual Difference in Career Value Added for Math in District 1, Consistent with* $\rho_{VA_{t,\mu}} = 0.65$

case (ranking based on career value added). This is perfectly consistent with a year-to-career correlation in value added of 0.65 for math in District 1. Results are very similar for other subjects and districts. Thus, the year-to-career correlation is an excellent guide to the predictive power of one year of value added.

Do Rankings on One Year of Value Added Misclassify Teachers in Terms of Their Career Value Added? In Tables 5.2, 5.3, and 5.4, we provide evidence of how badly a single year of value added misclassifies teachers in terms of their career performance. In Table 5.2, we show how teachers ranked in the bottom 25 percent based on one year of value added rank on career value added. For each district and subject, we report the percent of these teachers, all of whom were ranked in the bottom 25 percent based on one year of value added, who ranked in each quartile based on their career value added. For example, for math in District 1, 55 percent of the teachers ranked in the bottom quartile on one year of value added turned out to be in the bottom quartile over their entire careers, and 82 percent (55 percent + 27 percent) were below average over their

TABLE 5.2. **Misclassification Rates for Teachers in Bottom 25 Percent on One Year of Value-Added Data**

	Teacher Ranked in Bottom 25% Based on One Year of Value Added Data					
	Math			ELA		
	District 1	District 2	District 3	District 1	District 2	District 3
% of teachers falling in each quartile of *career average* value added (6+ years)						
bottom quartile	55%	65%	59%	48%	60%	50%
2nd quartile	27%	25%	27%	27%	26%	27%
3rd quartile	13%	8%	11%	17%	10%	16%
top quartile	5%	1%	3%	8%	4%	7%

TABLE 5.3. **Misclassification Rates for Teachers in Bottom 10 Percent on One Year of Value-Added Data**

| | Teacher Ranked in Bottom 10% Based on One Year of Value Added Data | | | | | |
| | Math | | | ELA | | |
	District 1	District 2	District 3	District 1	District 2	District 3
% of teachers falling in each quartile of *career average* value added (6+ years)						
bottom quartile	67%	81%	70%	61%	76%	61%
2nd quartile	22%	15%	20%	22%	16%	23%
3rd quartile	8%	4%	8%	12%	6%	11%
top quartile	3%	1%	1%	5%	2%	5%

careers. In contrast, only 5 percent of these teachers ended in the top quartile over their careers. Results for other districts and subjects are similar. Note that for math in District 1, the difference between the percentage below average (82 percent) and the percentage above average (18 percent) is 64 percent, which is very close to the year-to-career correlation reported in Table 5.1, as predicted by our statistical model. Thus, while there is some misclassification, rankings based on one year of value added have only modest amounts of misclassification that are in line with the simple estimate of year-to-career correlation.

Tables 5.3 and 5.4 repeat this analysis, but limiting the sample to teachers who performed in the bottom 10 percent and 3 percent based on a single year of value added. These tables might be more representative of real-world practice, where only a small percentage of the worst-performing teachers are being identified for dismissal or as needing improvement. Teachers ranked in the bottom 10 percent or 3 percent of one-year value added are even more likely to be in the bottom quartiles over their careers. Of the teachers ranked in the bottom 3 percent based on one year of value added, only 2 to

TABLE 5.4. **Misclassification Rates for Teachers in Bottom 3 Percent on One Year of Value-Added Data**

	Teacher Ranked in Bottom 3% Based on One Year of Value Added Data					
	Math			ELA		
	District 1	District 2	District 3	District 1	District 2	District 3
% of teachers falling in each quartile of *career average* value added (6+ years)						
bottom quartile	75%	91%	81%	71%	86%	70%
2nd quartile	18%	7%	12%	17%	9%	18%
3rd quartile	4%	2%	5%	8%	4%	11%
top quartile	3%	0%	2%	3%	1%	1%

12 percent (depending on district and subject) rank above average on career value added, and 3 percent or less rank in the top quartile over their careers. Thus, teachers in the tails of the distribution on one-year value added are relatively unlikely to be miscategorized in terms of their career performance.

Comparing the Stability and Predictive Power of Cumulative Measures of Value Added

Does Early-Career Performance Predict Later Performance? In Tables 5.5 (District 2) and 5.6 (District 1), we limit the sample to those teachers with value-added data during their first through fourth years of teaching (in District 3, samples were too small for this analysis). We first sort teachers into quartiles using their value added during their first year of teaching. We also do so using their value added averaged over their first two years of teaching. The first column reports the mean value added of each group during their third and fourth years of teaching. In District 2, those with math value added in the top quartile during their first year of teaching led students to a performance 0.14 standard deviations *above* similar students during their third and fourth years of teaching. Those with value added in the bottom quartile during their first year had students with value-added gains 0.14 standard deviations *below* similar students during their third and fourth years. In other words, value-added data— even from the first year of teaching—*does* help predict student achievement gains in future years. In fact, the stakes involved in being assigned a third- or fourth-year teacher who had performed in the top versus bottom quartile during his or her first year of teaching are quite large—roughly a quarter of a standard deviation (approximately a quarter of the black-white achievement gap).

The predictive value increases somewhat by averaging over the first two years of teaching. For instance, those who were in the top quartile after two years had students with gains 0.17 standard deviations above similar students during their third and fourth years, while those who were in the bottom quartile after two years watched their students lag behind −0.18 standard deviations during their third and fourth year. Instead of a .28 standard deviation difference, there's a 0.35 standard deviation difference between those assigned a top or bottom quartile teacher as ranked at the end of their first two years of teaching.

All these differences were somewhat smaller in reading. (Researchers commonly find larger teacher effects on math achievement.) They are also somewhat smaller in District 1 (Table 5.6) than in District 2 (Table 5.5). However, the same two findings hold true: First-year teacher performance does predict future performance. And combining data over the first two years increases the predictive value somewhat.

Does Cumulative Performance Change Over Time? In the subsequent columns in Tables 5.5 and 5.6, we report the percent of teachers appearing in each quartile of value added when another year's worth of value-added data are added. As noted above, one gains predictive power by averaging the measures over more than one year. How much would those measures change when averaging in another year? Among those who were in the first quartile at the end of their first year of teaching, 71 percent were in the top quartile over the first two years of teaching. Less than 1 percent appeared in the bottom quartile over the first two years of teaching. In fact, only 5 percent of those who started out in the bottom quartile at the end of their first year would appear in the top half over two years.

TABLE 5.5. Stability of Teacher Value Added Rankings in District 2

Value added in 3rd and 4th year	Percent in each quartile on a cumulative career value-added measure the following year			
	Top quarter	2nd quarter	3rd quarter	Bottom quarter
Math				
Ranking after 1st year				
top quarter	0.14	71%	24%	5%	0%
second quarter	0.03	23%	44%	28%	5%
third quarter	−0.05	5%	27%	44%	24%
bottom quarter	−0.14	0%	5%	23%	71%
Ranking after 2nd year				
top quarter	0.17	80%	18%	1%	0%
second quarter	0.03	15%	60%	25%	0%
third quarter	−0.06	2%	22%	56%	20%
bottom quarter	−0.18	0%	0%	18%	82%
Reading				
Ranking after 1st year				
top quarter	0.08	67%	25%	7%	1%
second quarter	−0.01	23%	44%	28%	5%
third quarter	−0.04	9%	24%	41%	26%
bottom quarter	−0.06	2%	7%	24%	68%
Ranking after 2nd year				
top quarter	0.09	77%	21%	2%	0%
second quarter	0.01	24%	54%	22%	0%
third quarter	−0.03	5%	25%	54%	16%
bottom quarter	−0.11	1%	1%	18%	79%

TABLE 5.6. **Stability of Teacher Value Added Rankings in District 1**

| Value added in 3rd and 4th year | Percent in each quartile on a cumulative career value-added measure the following year | | | |
	Top quarter	2nd quarter	3rd quarter	Bottom quarter
Math					
Ranking after 1st year					
top quarter	0.10	68%	21%	9%	2%
second quarter	0.04	23%	42%	29%	5%
third quarter	0.01	7%	28%	37%	28%
bottom quarter	−0.03	2%	9%	25%	65%
Ranking after 2nd year					
top quarter	0.14	76%	20%	4%	0%
second quarter	0.05	18%	52%	27%	3%
third quarter	0	3%	22%	53%	22%
bottom quarter	−0.08	0%	3%	15%	83%
Reading					
Ranking after 1st year					
top quarter	0.05	63%	29%	7%	1%
second quarter	0.04	27%	38%	28%	8%
third quarter	0	7%	28%	43%	22%
bottom quarter	−0.04	3%	6%	22%	69%
Ranking after 2nd year					
top quarter	0.07	77%	19%	4%	0%
second quarter	0.03	22%	44%	32%	3%
third quarter	0.01	4%	5%	7%	4%
bottom quarter	−0.05	1%	1%	2%	1%

The impact of adding another year's worth of data is even smaller after two years. Eighty-two percent of those in the bottom quartile after two years would appear in the bottom quartile after three years. Less than 1 percent of those in the bottom quartile after two years appeared in the top half over three years.

Overall, Tables 5.5 and 5.6 suggest that accumulated value-added estimates, averaged over a teacher's career to date, are better predictors of future value added and are considerably more stable than single-year value-added estimates.

USING VALUE ADDED: DECISION MAKING UNDER UNCERTAINTY

Would a single-year measure of performance lead to too many mistakes? It is impossible to say without knowing the decision to be made and the costs of different types of mistakes.

More than two centuries ago, Daniel Bernoulli wrote a famous paper on the dilemma facing an 18th century merchant when deciding whether or not to insure a ship's cargo in winter, given the probability of an accident (Bernoulli, 1738). Since that time, a rich theory of decision making under uncertainty has been elaborated. In this section, we apply a simple decision-theoretic model to employment decisions at schools.

Consider the following hypothetical example: Suppose that an elementary school principal learns that an experienced teacher she recently hired completes her first year with *measured* effectiveness in the bottom quartile. It is only a single year of teaching and, as we've seen, one year is an imperfect signal of a teacher's likely career performance. The principal faces a dilemma: Should she renew the teacher's contract for a second year?

First, note that there is no such thing as a low-stakes decision. Whether she retains the teacher or replaces the teacher, there are consequences for two adult teachers (the incumbent who may be looking for work and a prospective replacement teacher who will be relieved to have finally found a job) and twenty-five youngsters who will be in the classroom.

Second, note that the principal is not assessing the performance of one teacher, but two: the incumbent teacher and, implicitly, the prospective replacement teacher. If the principal knows the potential replacement, she could compare the two teachers' recent performance. However, even if the principal does not know the potential replacement, she is not completely in the dark. Even if the principal will be required to take whomever the district's human resource department sends her, the distribution of possible outcomes is the distribution of career value added for all teachers. The expected value of the teachers' career effectiveness is simply the mean career effectiveness across teachers. And the probability of different outcomes is reflected in the distribution of career effectiveness across all teachers.

In Figure 5.2, we report the distribution of career average achievement gains for those who appeared in the bottom quartile in a given year. We compare it to the distribution of career average achievement gains for all teachers. The vertical lines represent the 25th, 50th, and 75th percentiles in career value added for all teachers.

What is the probability that a principal and her students will end up having a highly effective teacher in the future? That depends on the *difference* in the probability that the incumbent and the replacement teacher are highly effective. According to Table 5.2, if the incumbent teacher was in the bottom quartile one year, there is only a 4 to 8 percent chance that the teacher will turn out to be in the *top quartile* at the end of six or more years. But the likelihood that a randomly drawn replacement teacher will be in the top quartile is considerably higher—25 percent.

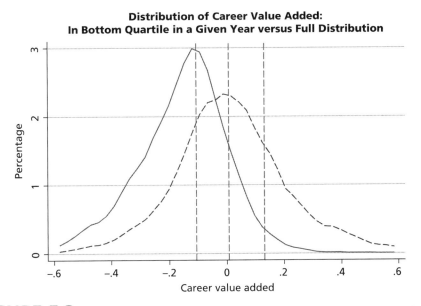

**Distribution of Career Value Added:
In Bottom Quartile in a Given Year versus Full Distribution**

FIGURE 5.2. *Distribution of Career Value Added for Teachers Ranked in the Bottom Quartile Based on One Year of Value Added (Solid Line) Compared to All Teachers (Dashed Line)*

Which decision maximizes the chance that students have access to a top-quartile teacher? On the one hand, if the principal keeps the incumbent and foregoes the opportunity to hire a replacement, she has a 4 to 8 percent chance that the teacher is highly effective. On the other hand, if the principal chooses the replacement teacher, she has a 25 percent chance of having a top-quartile teacher. Therefore, the more concerned a principal is about the prospect of losing a great teacher, the more likely he or she will be to hire the replacement teacher and replace the incumbent.

Whenever a school leader has to make a decision based on a single year of data, he or she runs the risk of falsely identifying a great teacher as ineffective. On the one hand, once a teacher has a poor track record—even on an imperfect measure—that teacher has *lower* odds of being a great teacher than does a replacement teacher drawn at random. On the other hand, if a teacher has a strong track record, then he or she has higher odds of being a great teacher than an unknown replacement teacher does.

The Expected Impact If the Principal Must Hire a Novice Teacher as the Replacement

How might the principal's decision differ if she knew that there were no experienced teachers available, that the only available replacements will be novice teachers right out of graduate school? In that case, the appropriate comparison would be to the expected effectiveness of the average *novice* teacher. Many researchers have studied the difference in effectiveness between the average novice teacher and other experienced teachers. Most of that research suggests that the students assigned to the average novice teacher lose 0.06 to 0.08 standard deviations in achievement during the teacher's first year of teaching relative to similar students assigned to the average teacher.

Note that the principal's best prediction of the bottom-quartile incumbent teacher's achievement gain (about −0.10 standard deviations, based on Figure 5.2) is still lower than the expected achievement gain of the average novice (−0.06 to −0.08) standard deviations. The principal could expect to raise fourth grade performance by 0.02 to 0.04 standard deviations *next year* by replacing the teacher and taking a chance with a novice. Admittedly, that's not a large difference. However, the principal could expect within two or three years that the average novice's achievement gains will converge toward that of the average teacher and the gap would be back to 0.10 standard deviations.

In sum, at least in terms of *expected* impact on students, the incumbent teacher in our example has a serious disadvantage with respect to any potential replacement teacher. On average, when ranked on just one year of value-added data, teachers in the bottom quartile will typically perform worse than a novice teacher over their entire careers. Even a single year of performance in the bottom quartile means that a teacher is a worse bet than an unknown teacher with a clean slate, even if that replacement is a novice teacher. While this conclusion may be surprising to some, it derives directly from the strong year-to-career correlation in value added (along with large differences in career performance across teachers). An alternative strategy for the principal would be to target bottom-quartile teachers for professional development and in-service training. However, such training would have to be much more effective than traditional professional development, given that bottom-quartile teachers otherwise would perform worse than rookies and have little chance of being highly effective over their careers.

Presumed Average Until Proven Below Average?

Many analysts have sought to apply the framework of classical hypothesis testing to making employment decisions with imperfect information (Baker, Barton, Darling-Hammond, Haertel, Ladd, Linn, Ravitch, Rothstein, Shavelson, & Shepard, 2010; Hill, 2009; Schochet & Chiang, 2010). They argue that a high-stakes decision can be justified only when a teacher's performance is *statistically significantly* different from average. In effect, they would establish a "no deny zone" (and, presumably, a "no bonus zone") by adding and subtracting two times the standard error of measurement to the average teacher's performance. Within that range, no teacher would be statistically different from the average teacher. As a practical matter, given the size of standard errors of measurement, such a span would include most of the distribution of teachers and leave only the extreme tails uncovered.

However, many employment decisions—such as the retention decision—do not fit the classical hypothesis-testing framework. The classical hypothesis test was designed for a specific type of decision: when the costs of rejecting a true hypothesis are paramount and the cost of failing to reject a false hypothesis are secondary. In many areas of science, it makes sense to assume that a medical procedure does not work, or that a vaccine is ineffective, or that the existing theory is correct, until the evidence is very strong that the starting presumption is wrong. That is *why* the classical hypothesis test places the burden of proof so heavily on the alternative hypothesis and preserves the null hypothesis—in our case, that the incumbent teacher is presumed effective—until the evidence is overwhelmingly to the contrary.

In the case of a retention decision, that would be inappropriate. To be sure, there are costs to failing to retain an effective teacher (that is, mistakenly rejecting the presumption that a teacher is effective). A poor decision with an incumbent teacher can have a negative effect on morale. Parents may complain. An incumbent teacher may be more likely to pursue legal action than a prospective teacher who was passed over. However, these costs are not overwhelmingly larger than the cost of retaining an ineffective teacher—a decision whose costs are borne primarily by the students. This is especially true in the case of a tenure decision, when an ineffective teacher is granted decades of job security in teaching children. Indeed, the classical hypothesis-testing framework would be especially inappropriate in a tenure decision, given that the cost of failing to reject a false hypothesis (that the teacher is effective) is likely to be larger than the cost of rejecting a true hypothesis.

In Figure 5.3, the horizontal axis reports the percentile of each teacher's value added from one year. The vertical axis reports two types of

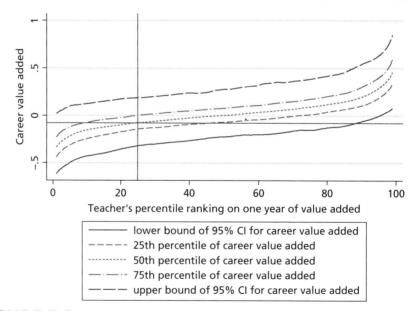

FIGURE 5.3. *Distribution of Career Value Added for Teachers Ranked at Each Percentile Based on One Year of Value Added*

statistics. The blue lines report the top and bottom points for the 95 percent confidence interval (CI) for a representative teacher in each percentile. The red lines report the 25th, 50th, and 75th percentile of the career value added of the teachers in each percentile. (These data represent actual career average value added for teachers in the three districts for whom we could calculate value added for more than six years. These are not simulations.) We have also noted in the graph the average value added of a novice teacher in the district, which was −0.08 student level standard deviations. Value added is reported relative to the gain achieved by the average teacher in the district. (By definition, the average teacher's value added is 0.)

First, focusing on the upper and lower bounds of the 95 percent confidence interval (the blue lines), note that the 95 percent confidence interval for teachers in the bottom percentile includes 0. (The upper bound of the 95 percent confident interval is above 0 for every percentile.) In other words, although there may be teachers within the bottom 1 percent of teachers who are "statistically significantly" worse than average, the average teacher in the bottom 1 percent is not. Similarly, only a few percentiles of teachers at the top of the distribution in single-year value added are "statistically significantly" better than average (that is, the curve for the lower bound of the 95 percent confidence interval rises above 0.)

Second, focusing on the distribution of actual career value added in each percentile (the red lines), note than almost 75 percent of the teachers in the bottom 1 percent on single-year value added had career value added below −0.25. Neal and Johnson (1996) found that an entire year of schooling produces a 0.25 standard deviation in test gains for the typical student. In other words, 75 percent of the teachers in the bottom 1 percent caused students to fall behind by the equivalent of a whole year while the students were in their classrooms. At the other extreme, for teachers with single-year value added in the top 1 percent, 75 percent of such teachers had career value added above 0.25. In other words, the average students in their classes were achieving two years' worth of achievement gains in a single year.

In the preceding, we proposed using "better than the average novice teacher" as the threshold for a retention decision. Figure 5.3 further illustrates the implications of such a rule. Note that median career value added is equal to the average value added of a novice teacher for teachers in the 25th percentile.

In other words, 25 percent of teachers would fail the "better than the average novice" test based on a single year of value added, depending on the district. For teachers with single-year value added at that threshold, we could not reject the hypothesis that the teacher was equivalent to the average teacher. (Zero is contained within the 95 percent confidence interval for such teachers.) However, even though we could not pass the classical hypothesis-testing threshold, 75 percent of such teachers had career value added worse than the average teacher! (The 75th percentile of the career value added for teachers at that point in the horizontal axis is less than 0.)

What is a "mistake" in the context of a tenure decision, and how do the two rules compare in terms of mistakes made? A supervisor would be making a mistake whenever a tenure offer is made to a teacher whose career value added is below that of a novice teacher. In such cases, students would have been better off if the principal committed to hire a rookie teacher to fill the slot every year. (This is a conservative estimate. In principle, a supervisor could do even better by promoting and retaining the successful future rookies.) When a teacher's single-year value added is at the 25th percentile, the likelihood of making a mistake is 50-50. When a supervisor offers tenure to a teacher below the 25th percentile, the chances of a mistake rise. For instance, at approximately the 10th percentile, more than 75 percent of teachers will have career value added worse than the average novice. Yet, the 10th percentile teacher is not "statistically significantly" different from the average teacher.

An example from another field may be useful. Suppose you have had a heart attack and an ambulance arrives to transport you to a hospital emergency room. You can go to one of two hospitals, Hospital A or Hospital B. At Hospital A, the mortality rate for heart attack patients is 75 percent. At Hospital B, the mortality rate is 20 percent. Of course, these mortality rate estimates are subject to fluctuation. But suppose you knew that among hospitals of this size that had 75 percent mortality, you had a 90 percent chance that they were better than average over the long run, while the hospital with 20 percent mortality only had a 10 percent chance of being better than average. Suppose neither rate is "statistically significantly" different from average. In other words, there was not a sufficient number of admissions at either hospital to make the evidence overwhelming that Hospital A is better than average or that Hospital B is worse than average. Would you truly be indifferent which hospital the ambulance driver chose?

CONCLUSION

Our results challenge the claim that year-to-year volatility in value-added measures is *prima facie* evidence against their use. While value-added measures are unreliable by conventional standards and unstable over time, they are strong predictors of an individual teacher's career performance and thus can be used to improve decision making.

Our analysis has three key *implications for practice*:

- Year-to-year instability in value added and other teacher performance measures is misleading. One should instead focus on the correlation between annual performance measures and career performance, which is equal to the square root of the year-to-year correlation.

- Annual value-added measures are a fairly powerful predictor of a teacher's career performance, despite low year-to-year correlations in value added. The year-to-career correlations for value-added measures are in the range of 0.5 to 0.8.

- The classical hypothesis-testing framework, which presumes that a teacher is "average until proven below average," identifies too few teachers as ineffective. Instead, we suggest using whether a teacher's expected career value added lies below a given threshold, such as the performance of a typical novice. Based on this standard, teachers ranked in the bottom 25 percent of annual value added would be expected to perform below the novice level over the course of their careers.

Schools are unaccustomed to differentiating between teachers. It would be difficult to implement a new teacher evaluation system, even if performance could be measured perfectly. The manifest imperfection of the measures makes a difficult implementation even more difficult.

Not surprisingly, many districts have chosen to use teacher performance measures cautiously. The "average until proven below average" criterion is designed to protect the interests of incumbent teachers, just as "innocent until proven guilty" is designed to protect the liberty of the accused in our legal system. However, if the paramount goal were to raise student achievement, to maximize the chance that all students have an effective teacher, and to be fair to both prospective novice teachers as well as incumbent teachers, school systems would be using a different standard. For example, promoting only those teachers who have expected effectiveness higher than the average novice teacher would lead to very different decisions and a different set of outcomes for students. Most teachers with single-year value added in the bottom quartile will not be "statistically significantly" different from average achievement yet will perform at levels below a novice teacher throughout their careers. The classical hypothesis-testing framework, which presumes that a teacher is "average until proven below average" is simply inappropriate for such decisions.

NOTES

1. See Goldhaber and Hansen (in press) and Sturman, Cheramie, and Cashen (2005) for a summary of other examples.

2. The key assumption here is that the errors in measurement are independent across different time periods and with different groups of students, and that the errors are unrelated to a teacher's long-term effectiveness. This also implies that there is no gradual "drift" in effectiveness. It is straightforward to allow for drift, for example, to let underlying teacher effectiveness follow a statistical model such as an auto-regressive process. This would have little impact on the analyses we present here.

3. We have demonstrated this by simulation.

REFERENCES AND ADDITIONAL RESOURCES

Baker, E. L., Barton, P. E., Darling-Hammond, L, Haertel, E., Ladd, H. F., Linn, R. L., Ravitch, D., Rothstein, R., Shavelson, R. J., & Shepard, L. A. (2010, August). *Problems with the use of student test scores to evaluate teachers.* Economic Policy Institute Briefing Paper No. 278. Washington, DC: Economic Policy Institute.

Bernoulli, D. (1738). Specimen theoriae novae de mensura sortis. *Comentarii Academiae Scientiarum Imperialis Petropolitanae, 5*, 175–192.

Bernoulli, D. (1954, January). Exposition of a new theory on the measurement of risk. *Econometrica, 22*(1), 23–36).

Camara, W. J., & Echternacht, G. (2000, July). *The SAT I and high school grades: Utility in predicting success in college.* New York, NY: The College Board.

Chetty, R., Friedman, J. N., & Rockoff, J. E. (2013, July). *Measuring the impacts of teachers I: Evaluating bias in teacher value-added estimates.* Working paper.

Dimick, J. B., Staiger, D. O., Basur, O., & Birkmeyer, J. D. (2009). Composite measures for predicting surgical mortality in the hospital. *Health Affairs, 28*(4), 1189–1198.

Goldhaber, D., & Hansen, M. (in press). Is it just a bad class? Assessing the long-term stability of estimated teacher performance. *Economica.*

Hill, H. C. (2009, Autumn). Evaluating value-added models: A validity argument approach. *Journal of Policy Analysis and Management, 28*(4), 700–709.

Neal, D. A., & Johnson, W. R. (1996). The role of premarket factors in black-white wage differences. *Journal of Political Economy, 104*(5), 869–895.

Schall, T., & Smith, G. (2000). Do baseball players regress to the mean? *The American Statistician, 54,* 231–235.

Schochet, P. Z., & Chiang, H. S. (2010). *Error rates in measuring teacher and school performance based on student test score gains* (NCEE 2010-4004). Washington, DC: National Center for Education Evaluation and Regional Assistance, Institute of Education Sciences, U.S. Department of Education.

Sturman, M. C., Cheramie, R. A., & Cashen, L. H. (2005). The impact of job complexity and performance measurement on the temporal consistency, stability, and test-retest reliability of employee job performance ratings. *Journal of Applied Psychology, 90,* 269–283.

CHAPTER

6

To What Extent Do Student Perceptions of Classroom Quality Predict Teacher Value Added?

STEPHEN W. RAUDENBUSH AND MARSHALL JEAN

ABSTRACT

Surveys of student perceptions produce multiple measures of classroom quality. Our aim in this chapter is to decide which of these measures are most useful in predicting student learning. Conventional statistical methods can produce misleading results, because the measures of classroom quality are quite highly correlated. We therefore introduce a new method, the Multilevel Variable Selection Model, and we apply this method to the Tripod survey of student perceptions, which provides seven indicators of classroom effectiveness based on twenty-eight items. We find that classrooms that are well-controlled and intellectually challenging produce comparatively large learning gains. Our new methods can readily be extended to study the combined contribution of student perception data, classroom observation data, and other measures to student learning gains.

INTRODUCTION

A key challenge in measuring teacher effectiveness is to clarify the predictive validity of student perceptions, classroom observations, and other indicators. We'd like to know which aspects of classroom life, as measured by these methods, are most useful in predicting student learning, and we'd like to know just how predictive the entire ensemble of information might be. The problem is that the many indicators of classroom quality are highly correlated, and this makes it difficult to decide which kinds of data are most useful and how predictive the data are taken together. Unfortunately, standard methods of statistical prediction do not help much and can produce highly misleading results when the predictors of interest are highly correlated. In this chapter, we introduce a new method, the Multilevel Variable Selection Model (MVSM) to address this problem. We apply this method to the Tripod survey of student perceptions, which provides seven indicators of classroom effectiveness based on twenty-eight items. We find that classrooms that are well-controlled and intellectually challenging produce comparatively large learning gains. Controlling for *control* and *challenge*, teachers who "captivate" their students (as indicated by Tripod) actually do a little worse than those who do not. We consider possible explanations for the negative effect of *captivate*. These three indicators seem to capture nearly all of the information that Tripod provides about student learning.

While past research suggests that student perceptions give important information about teacher effectiveness, our analytic approach suggests that Tripod as a whole explains more of the variance in teacher value added than is suggested using conventional analytic approaches. We check our results against an alternative method, "multilevel principal components analysis," with strikingly convergent results. We discuss uses of these methods in revising applications of Tripod. Our new methods can readily be extended to study the combined contribution of student perception data, classroom observation data, and other measures to student learning gains.

Why Measure Student Perceptions of Classroom Quality?

We often hear fond stories about a particular teacher who made a difference in the life of a child, and it seems intuitively obvious that some teachers are more effective than others. Recent research supports this idea. Chetty, Friedman, Hilger, Saez, Schanzenbach, and Yagan (2011) computed for each of many kindergarten classrooms a "value-added score"—an estimate of how much children learned in their kindergarten year, on average, as measured by an achievement test. A key feature of this study is that the children had been assigned at random to their teachers. Remarkably, the researchers were able to obtain information on how these children fared as adults many years later. Children attending effective classrooms as indicated by value added attained more education and earned significantly more as adults, on average, than did children whose classrooms had lower value-added scores. This result supports other studies that also used random assignment of children to classrooms (Kane & Staiger, 2008; Nye, Hedges, & Konstantopoulos, 2004), showing that teachers vary significantly in how effective they are at fostering learning, as measured by achievement tests.

Of course, teachers are not typically assigned at random to classrooms. A crucial methodological contribution of the work cited above and related work (c.f., Chetty et al., 2011) is that teacher value-added scores provide useful information even when it is not possible to assign teachers at random. The Measurement of Effective Teaching (MET) Project is the largest study to date to support this conclusion (Bill & Melinda Gates Foundation, 2010).

With these exciting results in mind, value-added scores are not a silver bullet. Their reliability in discriminating among teachers in any given year is modest (Glazerman, Goldhaber, Loeb, Staiger, Raudenbush, & Whitehurst, 2011; Kane & Staiger, 2008; McCaffrey et al., 2003). Moreover, it is difficult to collect such data frequently, and some teachers do not teach subjects that are covered by state achievement tests; for those teachers, we cannot compute value-added scores. Moreover, test scores provide little information that teachers might use to change their practices. The information tells us about global achievement, rather than pinpointing specific aspects of teaching that might need improvement. And value-added scores become available to teachers too late—after the tested children have moved on to another grade—to be used for improvement. Finally, achievement test scores capture only part of what makes a classroom effective for child and youth development.

Not surprisingly, then, policymakers and researchers are intensely interested in collecting a wide array of information that can supplement achievement test scores as indicators of teaching effectiveness (Berk, 2005; Bill & Melinda Gates Foundation, 2013; Glazerman et al., 2011). Ideally, such measures of effectiveness would be reasonably reliable and would predict value-added scores while adding additional valuable information about the quality of a classroom experience.

Among the most promising approaches to assessing teaching quality is to obtain student perceptions via self-administered questionnaires. The Tripod survey, developed by Ronald Ferguson of Harvard University, is one of the information sources for the MET study. Ferguson developed Tripod to reveal how teachers compare on what he called the "7Cs." Thus, Tripod prompts each student to share perceptions of how much his teacher *cares* for him, how well the teacher *controls* the class; how effectively the teacher *clarifies* key concepts and assignments; how effectively the teacher *challenges* students; how well the teacher *captivates* students by making schoolwork interesting; whether the teacher effectively *confers* with students to check their understanding of the schoolwork; and whether the teacher helps students *consolidate* understanding by summarizing key concepts and providing feedback on student work. The version of the survey we study in this chapter has twenty-eight questionnaire items that reveal information on these 7Cs (see Table 6.1). The Tripod survey can be administered frequently, analyzed rather quickly, with results fed back to teachers and administrators in time to support teacher

TABLE 6.1. **Design of the Tripod Survey**

C Construct	Item Text
Care	I like the way my teacher treats me when I need help.
Care	My teacher in this class makes me feel that he/she really cares about me.
Care	The teacher in this class encourages me to do my best.
Care	My teacher gives us time to explain our ideas.
Control	My classmates behave the way my teacher wants them to.
Control	Our class stays busy and does not waste time.
Control	Everybody knows what they should be doing and learning in this class.
Clarify	My teacher explains things in very orderly ways.
Clarify	In this class, we learn to correct our mistakes.
Clarify	My teacher explains difficult things clearly.
Clarify	My teacher has several good ways to explain each topic that we cover in this class.

(continued)

(*Table 6.1 continued*)

C Construct	Item Text
Clarify	I understand what I am supposed to be learning in this class.
Clarify	My teacher knows when the class understands, and when we do not.
Clarify	This class is neat—everything has a place and things are easy to find.
Clarify	If you don't understand something, my teacher explains it another way.
Challenge	My teacher pushes everybody to work hard.
Challenge	In this class, we have to think hard about the writing we do.
Challenge	In this class, my teacher accepts nothing less than our full effort.
Captivate	Schoolwork is interesting.
Captivate	We have interesting homework.
Confer	When he/she is teaching us, my teacher asks us whether we understand.
Confer	My teacher asks questions to be sure we are following along when he/she is teaching us.
Confer	My teacher checks to make sure we understand what he/she is teaching us.
Confer	My teacher tells us what we are learning and why.
Confer	My teacher wants us to share our thoughts.
Confer	My teacher wants me to explain my answers—why I think what I think.
Consolidate	My teacher takes the time to summarize what we learn each day.
Consolidate	When my teacher marks my work, he/she writes on my papers to help me understand.

improvement efforts. Tripod also potentially provides detailed information on multiple aspects of classroom life. Hence, the survey has potentially important utility in assessing and improving the quality of teaching practice.

Assessing the Validity of Tripod

A critical question involves predictive validity: To what extent do student perceptions predict student learning? Evidence from the first MET report (Measurement of Effective Teaching Project, 2010) suggests an affirmative answer. MET researchers administered the Tripod survey in over 2,500 classrooms. To assess the validity of student perception data, they correlated measures of the 7Cs with measures of student achievement. Interestingly, the student achievement measures were gathered not from the same students who responded to the survey, but rather from a different set of students taught by the same teacher. This guaranteed that student achievement could not be the cause of the student perceptions. A key finding was that various measures of student perceptions significantly predicted student learning.

However, standard statistical procedures can't tell us just *how* powerful Tripod measures are as predictors of achievement, nor can they tell us *which* aspects of student perception—that is, which of the 7Cs—are most important. We explain why in this chapter by presenting a new statistical method that enables us to answer these questions with some confidence. We shall use this method to summarize the overall power of Tripod to predict value added and to isolate those components of Tripod that are most predictive. The method is called the "Multilevel Variable Selection Model" or MVSM.

Conventional Analysis of Tripod

Using standard statistical methods, we find that each of the 7Cs measured in one year is positively associated with the achievement growth within a teacher's classroom in a different year, as measured by the value-added score. However, when we use all seven to simultaneously predict value added, the key finding seems to be that some of these are extremely strongly positively associated with value added, while others are significantly negatively associated with value added (controlling the others). These findings are implausible; it seems unlikely that any of the 7Cs is as powerful as the conventional results would indicate, nor does it seem reasonable that increasing some of the 7Cs has a really bad effect on children. The source of these implausible results is that the seven dimensions are highly correlated, particularly after we adjust for measurement error, and it is well known that a prediction model based on highly inter-correlated predictors becomes unstable: the coefficients associated with the seven predictors have very large standard errors and, as a result, can become very large in magnitude—positive or negative— even if the underlying true relationships are small. This is the problem of "collinearity" discussed in every textbook on multiple regression, the statistical method nearly universally used for predicting an outcome using multiple explanatory variables. When predictors are highly correlated, some predictors that truly have small positive effects can be estimated to have very harmful effects. Using standard methods, it is difficult to discern which of the 7Cs are important.

One consequence of obtaining unstable and therefore highly variable estimates of the importance of each prediction is that we will tend to over-estimate the capability of the 7Cs together to predict the outcome. Thus, we are likely to overstate the predictive validity of the 7Cs.

Often, researchers will react to collinearity in ways that have the opposite fault: to understate the importance of the 7Cs. One way to do this is simply to look at one predictor at a time. Another is to create a single index, such as the mean of all of the predictors. These approaches eliminate the problem of dealing with highly inter-correlated predictors, but these approaches do not, in general, fully use all of the information in the predictors, and that is why they understate the utility of the predictors in accounting for the outcome. Moreover, these approaches don't help us decide which information is most crucial to collect.

Rationale for Using New Methods

After applying our new MVSM, we will see that the implausibly large regression coefficients, both negative and positive, are "shrunk" to more plausible values, strengthening the idea that the 7Cs share a common source of variation with value added. Yet the model will enable us to read signals suggesting that some predictors are more important than others, and that some may undermine effective prediction. This more nuanced understanding, in principle, enables us to isolate a subset of predictors that maximizes our ability to validly predict the outcome while eliminating redundant information in the predictors.

Our aim, then, is to arrive at the best possible summary of the information in Tripod. Our hope is that this will make Tripod more useful to teachers, while giving teachers and researchers an accurate account of just how helpful Tripod is in predicting student achievement gains. Finally, if we knew that a subset of Tripod items was particularly important as a predictor of student learning, we might be able to devise more efficient surveys of students.

This last point bears elaboration. Measures of student perceptions constitute only one source of information about classroom effectiveness. Educators are also interested in observing classrooms to rate the quality of instruction overall as well as in particular subjects such as reading and math. Supervisors may wish to look at artifacts of students' work, such as essays or problem sets, and they may collect lesson plans and other information. The MET study itself has collected a wealth of information on each of many classrooms. It would be good to know which of these sources of information are most predictive of student learning.

So learning about which aspects of Tripod are most predictive of student learning is part of the larger problem of learning about how to tailor a whole system of data collection that provides useful information at reasonable cost and that avoids taking up teachers' time with many pieces of information that might be redundant or uninformative. We believe the statistical procedures proposed here can help solve this larger problem, enabling us to combine many sources of information to devise a single model that best predicts student achievement gains.

In sum, we propose in this chapter a novel methodology for learning about which aspects of a data source like Tripod are most predictive of a valued outcome such as student learning: MVSM. It is "multilevel" because student perceptions vary at several levels: among students within a classroom, among classrooms within a school, and among schools. It is a "variable selection model" because it helps us select a subset of a large number of variables that is most useful in predicting a valued outcome. We test this model against an alternative approach that is a little more complicated but has a similar goal: a "multilevel principal components model." The results are strikingly convergent: each provides similar results about how effective Tripod is overall in predicting student learning gains, as measured by value added, and which aspects of Tripod are more effective in doing so.

The MVSM appears to work well and is almost as easy to use as multiple regression, with which most analysts are already familiar. The method is applicable when we are faced with many correlated predictor variables. In this chapter, we apply this new methodology to a large-scale data set from an urban U.S. school district. The data set combines survey data from Tripod with value-added statistics collected in a different year. As in MET, this design enables us to see whether student perceptions of teaching effectiveness collected one year predict how much a teacher's students learn in a different year. The results may help inform the design and use of the Tripod survey and other surveys of students' perceptions. We also anticipate that this methodology will be useful to researchers who are combining dense information from other sources, such as classroom observations, to obtain measures of teacher effectiveness validated as predicting student learning gains.

In the next section, we provide a conventional analysis of the Tripod data. We use standard methods to assess the reliability of Tripod measures, the correlations between them, and their predictive validity. The following section introduces our new method: We show how to use the MVSM, share the results of its application to Tripod, and contrast the findings with those based on conventional methods. To provide a check on these results, the last section of the paper prior to the Discussion section applies an alternative novel method known as "principal components regression." This approach reproduces the results based on the MVSM but uses a less direct way to get there. Our Discussion section summarizes our findings and makes recommendations for studies of classroom effectiveness.

A CONVENTIONAL ANALYSIS OF THE TRIPOD DATA

We studied 405 fourth and fifth grade teachers working within ninety-five elementary schools in a large urban district. This district was one of those studied in MET, although the data were collected independently. Researchers administered the Tripod survey in each of these classrooms, yielding, on average, eighteen complete student surveys, consisting of twenty-eight responses to the items described in Table 6.1. To assess validity, we use value-added data collected on the same teachers during the year before collection of the Tripod data. Thus, the students who shared their perceptions of teacher effectiveness were independent of those whose achievement test scores supply the evidence of teacher impact on student learning.

A standard analysis will first assess the reliability of the Tripod measures. We'll see that reliability is quite respectable. Next, we'd like to know how strongly inter-correlated the 7Cs are. We find them to be very highly correlated, especially if we take into account measurement error. These high inter-correlations pose a challenge for the next step: assessment of validity. We'll see that each of the 7Cs predicts value added, but that doesn't tell us which of the 7Cs are most important or how strongly predictive the 7Cs are taken as a whole. A conventional multiple prediction exercise is the next logical step, but it produces highly misleading results, defining the challenge for our novel MVSM approach.

Reliability Analysis

Our first step was to compute the reliability of measures of each of the 7Cs and their inter-correlations. For this purpose, we used the three-level multivariate measurement model described by Raudenbush, Rowan, and Kang (1991). At the first level, item responses for each child vary randomly around child-specific "true scores," one for each of the 7Cs. At the second level, these child-specific "true scores" vary randomly around a teacher's mean. At the third level, teacher-specific true scores vary randomly around a global, district-wide mean. This analysis tells us how much of the variance in each of the 7Cs lies between items, between children, and between teachers. The variance between teachers provides the "signal" we are interested in, that is, the information about how much teachers vary in their effectiveness, as indicated by each of the 7Cs. The variation between items may be regarded as item inconsistency, while the variability among students within a classroom may be regarded as "rater variance." In effect, Tripod casts each student within a class as an informant, or rater, of the quality of the classroom; inconsistencies among student responses within a class are therefore regarded as "rater error" and are thus part of the measurement error.

Table 6.2 summarizes the results of this analysis. The intra-teacher correlation measures how similar student responses are and is equivalent to the fraction of variation in the "true" student perceptions between teachers. Table 6.2 thus shows that 24 percent of the variation in *Clarify* responses lies between teachers, while 35 percent of the variation in *Control* lies between teachers. All other intra-teacher correlations lie between these two numbers. Variables that have more items and larger fractions of variation between teachers will be more reliable. The reliabilities in Table 6.2 are very similar, ranging between 0.74 and 0.81.

Correlations Among the "True" 7Cs

The analysis also gives us estimates of the correlations among the 7Cs. These are adjusted for measurement error and displayed in Table 6.3. We see that the 7Cs are quite highly inter-correlated. The weakest correlation of 0.56 is

TABLE 6.2. Reliability Analysis

Variable	Number of Items	Student-Level Variance	Teacher-Level Variance	Intra-Teacher Correlation	Teacher-Level Reliability
Care	4	.32	.13	.28	.79
Control	3	.27	.14	.35	.81
Clarify	8	.22	.07	.24	.78
Challenge	3	.27	.10	.26	.75
Captivate	2	.49	.16	.24	.74
Confer	6	.26	.09	.26	.79
Consolidate	2	.43	.17	.29	.77

TABLE 6.3. Correlations Among 7Cs after Correction for Measurement Error

	Control	Clarify	Challenge	Captivate	Confer	Consolidate
Care	.73	.93	.63	.68	.89	.84
Control		.81	.56	.62	.75	.69
Clarify			.76	.74	.95	.85
Challenge				.57	.79	.69
Captivate					.73	.76
Confer						.87

between *Challenge* and *Control*, while the largest is 0.95 between *Clarify* and *Confer*. These results illustrate how difficult it will be to assess the independent contributions of each of the 7Cs to the prediction of value added. It will be nearly impossible to separate the contributions of *Clarify* and *Confer*, because they appear to provide nearly the same information about teachers. However, it may well be possible to separate the contributions of *Challenge* and *Control*. The latter are correlated, but not so highly, implying that some teachers challenge their students intellectually, but are not so skilled at creating well-controlled classrooms; other classrooms are well controlled, but apparently not too challenging.

Assessing Validity

The next step in a standard analysis is to study validity. High reliability (see Table 6.2) is a necessary, but not sufficient, condition for validity. To be valid, a measure must minimally predict a *criterion*, that is, a known measure of teacher effectiveness. We choose as our criterion a teacher value added to student math learning, derived from a sample of each teacher's children in a different year from the year in which the Tripod data were collected.

There are three conventional ways of assessing validity. One is to assess the explanatory power of each of the 7Cs separately. We call these univariate model estimates. A second approach is to bite the bullet and include all of them in the regression, encountering the collinearity problem. A third is to combine all seven into a single scale or index—or possibly into two or three scales—using principal components or factor analysis. We'll show how each of these approaches works, starting with univariate models.

Univariate Prediction We estimate the simple linear prediction model

$$Y_{ij} = \beta_p x_{pij} + u_j + r_{ij}, \tag{1}$$

where Y_{ij} is the value-added score for teacher i in school j; the predictor x_{pij} is one of the 7Cs ($x_{1ij} = (care)_{ij}$, $x_{2ij} = (control)_{ij}$, ... $x_{7ij} = (consolidate)_{ij}$); β_p is a regression coefficient—which indicates the strength of association between the predictor and the outcome; u_j is a school-level random effect having 0 mean and variance τ^2; and r_{ij} is a teacher random effect having 0 mean and variance σ^2.[1] The outcome and each predictor are standardized to have means of 0 and standard deviations of 1.0.

Table 6.4 provides the results. The first column omits all predictors and tells us how much of the variance in value added lies within and between schools. We see that 19 percent of the variance lies between schools and 81 percent lies within schools. The next column tells us that the first of the 7Cs (*Care*) significantly positively predicts value added, with a coefficient (equivalent here to a correlation coefficient) of 0.169 and a standard error of 0.049.

TABLE 6.4. Univariate Regressions Predicting Value Added

	Null Model	Care	Control	Clarify	Challenge	Captivate	Confer	Consolidate
Care		.169 (.049)						
Control			.236 (.048)					
Clarify				.225 (.049)				
Challenge					.250 (.049)			
Captivate						.102 (.051)		
Confer							.214 (.049)	
Consolidate								.143 (.050)
$\hat{\tau}^2$	.19	.17	.18	.17	.18	.20	.18	.19
$\hat{\sigma}^2$	.81	.81	.78	.79	.78	.81	.79	.81

After controlling for *Care*, the variance between and within schools is slightly reduced (to 0.17 and 0.81, respectively). The overall explanatory power of *Care* is $R^2 = 1 - \tau^2 - \sigma^2$ and is estimated thus to be $1 - 0.17 - 0.81 = 0.02$ or 2.0 percent. The other columns are similarly interpreted. Note that the "C" with the largest coefficient is *Challenge* (coefficient of 0.250), while the second-largest is associated with *Control* (0.236). *Captivate* has the smallest coefficient (0.102). All achieve conventional levels of statistical significance (each is at least twice its standard error). The maximum explained variance (for *Control*) is about 0.059 or 5.9 percent.

These results are certainly interesting and corroborate the findings of the MET study (Bill & Melinda Gates Foundation, 2010), which also found that student perceptions predict value added. Indeed, each of the 7Cs taken separately significantly predicts value added. The explained variation is modest, but the coefficients are non-negligible in every case.

The problem is that the univariate analysis tells us nothing about how well the 7Cs taken together predict value added, nor does it supply any information about the relative importance of the 7Cs. To answer these questions, it is standard to formulate a multiple prediction model, the topic to which we now turn.

Multivariate Prediction We now expand Equation 1 to include all 7Cs as predictors of the outcome. The model is thus:

$$Y_{ij} = \beta_1(care)_{ij} + \beta_2(control)_{ij} + \beta_3(clarify)_{ij} + \beta_4(challenge)_{ij}$$
$$+ \beta_5(captivate)_{ij} + \beta_6(confer)_{ij} + \beta_7(consolidate)_{ij} + u_j + r_{ij}$$
$$= \sum_{p=1}^{7} \beta_p x_{pij} + u_j + r_{ij}, \tag{2}$$

where the symbols take on the same meaning as in Equation 1.[2]

Results are in Table 6.5 (Column 1). One notable feature of these results is the extraordinarily large standard errors, as compared to those in Table 6.4. In the worst case, for *Clarify*, the standard error of 0.372 is 76 times larger than the standard error in the univariate model (Table 6.4)! Closely related, the coefficients estimates in Table 6.5 are highly variable, ranging from a minimum of about −0.23 (for *Care* and *Captivate*) to a maximum of 0.55 for *Clarify*. Yet only the coefficients for *Challenge* and *Captivate* achieve a nominal level of statistical significance. Finally, if we were to believe these results, we would conclude that the model explains about 10.8 percent of the variance

TABLE 6.5. **Multiple Predictor Models Predicting Value Added**

	Conventional Least Squares	Ridge Regression (Empirical Bayes)	Trimmed model: Conventional Weighted Least Squares	Trimmed model: Ridge Regression (Empirical Bayes)
Care	−.230 (.203)	−.049 (.078)		
Control	.146 (.105)	.179 (.072)	.244 (.069)	.219 (.069)
Clarify	.550 (.372)	.131 (.062)		
Challenge	.202 (.100)	.197 (.071)	.251 (.067)	.228 (.068)
Captivate	−.227 (.092)	−.160 (.076)	−.247 (.074)	−.198 (.073)
Confer	−.131 (.257)	.039 (.078)		
Consolidate	−.100 (.134)	−.106 (.084)		
$\hat{\tau}^2$	.14	.15	.15	.15
$\hat{\sigma}^2$	.77	.76	.77	.76
$\hat{\Delta}^2$		.03		.04

in value added, almost double the explained variance of 5.9 percent in the most predictive model in Table 6.4. All of these anomalies are attributable to the collinearity problem: standard regression methods provide extremely imprecise estimates of coefficients when predictors are highly correlated (please recall the high inter-correlations noted in Table 6.3). These nasty features of conventional prediction often lead analysts to abandon multiple prediction and apply the third conventional approach: combining all measures into a single composite score.

Composite Score The third approach would combine the 7Cs into one single index. The problem with this approach is a potential loss of information. Despite the high correlations among the 7Cs, it might be the case that certain

Cs carry uniquely important information, and that teachers would especially benefit from improving the corresponding aspects of their teaching. However, we defer discussion of the composite approach until we come to the section of our chapter on principal components analysis.

THE MULTILEVEL VARIABLE SELECTION MODEL (MVSM)

Recall that the univariate regressions (Table 6.4) give sensible estimates of the predictive validity of each of the 7Cs, taken one at a time. However, because each of these regressions uses only one piece of information generated by Tripod, we suspect that these models underestimate the predictive power of Tripod as a whole. Therefore, the maximum explanatory power of these models ($R^2 = 5.9$ percent) is a lower bound on the predictive power of Tripod as a whole. Moreover, the seven regressions in Table 6.4 give us no information on how best to combine information from Tripod to explain student growth in achievement.

In contrast, the regression with seven predictors (Column 1, Table 6.5) yields coefficient estimates that appear greatly exaggerated in absolute value. It seems that the very large standard errors caused by collinearity create large chance differences in the coefficient estimates. One result is that our interpretation of the relative importance of each of the 7Cs is distorted. A second result is that the overall explanatory power of the model, which increases with the absolute value of the regression coefficients, is exaggerated. Therefore, we must regard the explanatory power of this model ($R^2 = 10.8$ percent) to be an *upper bound* of the explanatory power of Tripod for these value-added outcomes.

How, then, can we obtain estimates of the predictive power of the 7Cs that are plausible and that produce a realistic assessment of the explanatory power of Tripod, which must lie somewhere between $R^2 = 5.9$ percent and $R^2 = 10.8$ percent?

For this purpose, we adopt a special case of "ridge regression" (Hoerl & Kennard, 1970). Technically, ridge regression adds a small positive constant, k, to the sum of squares of each explanatory variable in the computation of the regression coefficients (see the Appendix B for details). This stabilizes estimation and "shrinks" unreliable coefficient estimates toward 0. An interesting feature of ridge regression is that it induces a small bias in regression coefficients, while significantly reducing the sampling variance of the estimates. As a result, we can readily prove that the ridge-based coefficient estimates will be more accurate (have smaller expected mean squared error) than will the coefficients estimated by least squares (Lindley & Smith, 1972). The question naturally arises: How do we select the size of k? Lindley and Smith proposed a solution using a method known as "empirical Bayes" that is now increasingly used in the social sciences. This approach is quite elegant statistically and is based on a rationale that makes considerable intuitive sense in the context of our example.

As mentioned, we have strong reason to suspect that the magnitudes (absolute values) of the seven regression coefficients generated by the conventional multiple regression (Column 1, Table 6.5) are exaggerated, and we know why: collinearity among the predictors has induced great uncertainty about these coefficients, as reflected in the huge standard errors we see in the table. Lindley and Smith reasoned that, although some large part of the variation in these estimated coefficients represents random error ("noise"), some part of the variation in these estimates reflects variation in the true regression coefficients. If we can estimate the amount of noise in these estimates, we might then "back out" the variance of the true coefficients, call it Δ^2. This provided Lindley and Smith with an answer to the question, "How large should the value of k be in ridge regression?" Lindley and Smith's reasoning led them to derive the optimal value of k as

$$k = \sigma^2/\Delta^2. \tag{3}$$

Equation 3 says that the k should be inversely proportional to Δ^2, the variance of the true values of the coefficients, β_p, p $= 1, \ldots, 7$. (The teacher-level variance σ^2 is just a scaling factor; think of it as the constant of proportionality that simply depends on the units of the outcome.) If the coefficients in the seven-predictor model vary mostly because of noise—that is, the true coefficients are nearly equal—Δ^2 will be very small, k will be large, and all of the coefficients in Equation 2 will be "shrunk" toward a common value. That value should presumably be the value we would obtain if we created a single index of the 7Cs—an average—and used that average as a predictor. (This is essentially what we obtain if we use the first principal component of the 7Cs as a predictor; see below). In contrast, if the coefficients in the seven-predictor model vary in part because the true coefficients are, in fact, highly variable, Δ^2 will be large, k will be small, and the solution will look very much like that given by the conventional regression model. We develop this idea mathematically in the Appendices; our contribution is original in one way: We have integrated Lindley and Smith's approach into a hierarchical linear model that represents the fact that teachers are nested within schools. This enables us to simultaneously estimate how much variation lies within and between schools; and we have the option, not employed here for simplicity, of allowing the regression coefficients to randomly vary over schools, based on a theory that schools may be heterogeneous in the extent to which value added predicts learning.

The results of our MVSM analysis are given in Column 2 of Table 6.5. The evidence suggests that the true regression coefficients vary modestly, $\hat{\Delta}^2 = 0.03$, meaning that most of the variation in the estimates shown in Column 1 is noise. As a result, the coefficient estimates based on MVSM are much closer to 0 than those based on the conventional analysis of Column 1. In particular, the coefficient for *Clarify* is shrunk from 0.550 to 0.131. Moreover, the standard errors based on MVSM have "calmed down" considerably. None exceeds 0.084—still larger than in the univariate regressions, but much smaller than in the conventional seven-variable regression.

Finally, the explanatory power of the model is now estimated to be $R^2 = 7.8$ percent—about midway between the lower bound of 5.9 percent, based on the univariate models and the upper bound of 10.8 percent, based on the conventional seven-variable regression. Interestingly according to the MVSM, one source of unexplained variation is the variability $\hat{\Delta}^2 = 0.03$ in the unknown true regression coefficients. We can think of this component as reflecting uncertainty that arises from collinearity in the 7Cs.

These results would suggest that an academically challenging environment within a well-controlled classroom significantly positively predicts value added (see coefficients for *Challenge* and *Control*). Holding these constant, attempts to "captivate" students by making schoolwork and homework "interesting" negatively predict value added.

MULTILEVEL PRINCIPAL COMPONENTS REGRESSION

We had mentioned that a strategy for eliminating collinearity among multiple predictors is to combine them into a single index. We can use a simple average. A more sophisticated version of this approach is to transform the original 7Cs into seven uncorrelated "principal components," which we shall call the "7 Ss," where each S is a weighted average of the 7Cs. The standard approach is to rank order the principal components in order of their variances, known as Eigenvalues in the language of this methodology. We display the results in Table 6.6. The table shows the 7 Ss, each a linear combination of the 7Cs.

TABLE 6.6. Principal Components Transformation of the 7Cs

	Transformation of original 7Cs (Eigenvector * 7C vector)	Variance (Eigenvalue)	Coefficient, $\hat{\theta}_{p'}$ (se)
1	$S_1 = .39 * care + .35 * control + .40 * clarify + .35 * challenge + .36 * captivate + .40 * captivate + .39 * consolidate$	5.88	.082 (.021)
2	$S_2 = -.17 * care - .61 * control - .07 * clarify + .76 * challenge - .07 * captivate + .11 * captivate - .06 * consolidate$	.38	.057 (.079)
3	$S_3 = -.04 * care + .50 * control + .15 * clarify + .35 * challenge - .70 * captivate + .08 * captivate - .32 * consolidate$	.34	.415 (.085)
4	$S_4 = -.56 * care + .43 * control - .16 * clarify + .30 * challenge + .54 * captivate - .19 * captivate - .23 * consolidate$	.23	.091 (.095)
5	$S_5 = -.35 * care + .20 * control - .28 * clarify - .02 * challenge + .29 * captivate - .06 * captivate + .82 * consolidate$	.11	-.057 (.145)
6	$S_6 = .51 * care + .10 * control - .16 * clarify + .29 * challenge + .02 * captivate - .78 * captivate + .09 * consolidate$	.04	-.043 (.229)
7	$S_7 = .33 * care + .14 * control - .82 * clarify + .06 * challenge + .05 * captivate + .41 * captivate - .13 * consolidate$	.01	-.548 (.397)

The set of coefficients that transform each of the 7Cs into each S is called an "Eigenvector." Notice that the Eigenvector for the first S contains the values (0.39, 0.35, 0.40, 0.35, 0.36, 0.40, 0.39). These numbers are very similar, so we see that the first S is, in essence, proportional to the mean of the 7Cs.

The second S assigns a large positive weight to *Challenge* and a large negative weight to *Control*. In our earlier discussion of the correlation matrix in Table 6.3, we noted that some teachers were high on *Control* but low on *Challenge*. The second S will assign a large value to such teachers. The third S appears to distinguish teachers who are high on *Control* and *Challenge*, but low on *Captivate*. Note that the first S has a much larger Eigenvalue (variance) than does any other S. Moreover, the Eigenvalues diminish as we look down the table from S_1 to S_7.

Having clarified the definition of each principal component, let's now use the 7 Ss to predict value added using the model

$$Y_{ij} = \sum_{p=1}^{7} \theta_p s_{pij}^* + u_j + r_{ij}, \qquad (4)$$

where s_{pij}^*, $p = 1, \ldots, 7$ is principal component p associated with the empirical Bayes estimates x_{pij}^*, $p = 1, \ldots, 7$. The results are in the last column of Table 6.7. Note that the first S (recall this is essentially the mean of the 7 Ss) is highly statistically significantly predictive of value added, with a t-ratio of $0.082/0.021 = 3.90$. The very small standard error associated with this first S results from its large Eigenvalue. Predictors that have large variance provide more precise estimates of regression coefficients than do those with small variance. The second S, which distinguishes teachers whose classrooms have high *Control* and low *Challenge*, is not different from 0. This is consistent with our earlier results suggesting that *Control* and *Challenge* are both important in predicting value added. The third S, representing teachers who are high on *Challenge* and *Control* but low on *Captivate*, is positive and statistically significant, again consistent with our earlier results, which assigned positive coefficients to *Challenge* and *Control* and a negative coefficient to *Captivate* to net the contribution of the other two (see Table 6.5, Columns 2 and 3). None of the other Ss contribute significantly to the prediction of value added.

Note the dramatic inflation of standard errors in Table 6.6 for Ss that have small Eigenvalues. In particular, the standard error for the coefficient for S_7

is 0.397, similar to the largest standard error we obtained using conventional regression (Table 6.5, Column 1)! This result helps us to see how principal components regression works. Using principal components, we have solved the problem of collinearity—correlations among all of the 7 Ss are zero. However, we have "traded off" the problem of collinearity for the problem of small variance in some of the predictors. The data provide no leverage for estimating the contribution of Ss that have small Eigenvalues, as indicated by their large standard errors.

This is a perfect tradeoff, as shown in the first two columns of Table 6.7. It is straightforward to translate the $\hat{\theta}_p$ coefficients from Equation 5 (and Table 6.6) back into the corresponding $\hat{\beta}_p$ values. As shown in the first two columns of Table 6.7, the translation perfectly reproduces the results of the conventional regression using the 7Cs.

While the principal component method trades off the collinearity problem for a small variance problem, the small variance problem is easy to solve: simply eliminate from the model those components that have small variance

TABLE 6.7. **Principal Components Regression and "Back-Translation" to 7Cs**

	Conventional Least Squares	Principal Components: Back Translation to 7Cs	Trimmed model: Ridge Regression (Empirical Bayes)	Trimmed Model: Principal Components: Back Translation to Cs
Care	−.230	−.230		.005
Control	.146	.146	**.219**	**.202**
Clarify	.550	.550		.090
Challenge	.202	.202	**.228**	**.219**
Captivate	−.227	−.227	**−.198**	**−.266**
Confer	−.131	−.131		.074
Consolidate	−.100	−.100		−.098

and, correspondingly, large standard errors! We therefore recomputed the model (Equation 4) using only the first three Ss. We then translated the results back and compared them to what we obtained using our new MVSM. These are shown in the last two columns of Table 6.7. We see that the results are extremely similar: large positive contributions for *Control* and *Challenge*; controlling for these, we see a negative contribution of *Captivate*.

DISCUSSION

A key challenge in assessing classrooms is to clarify the predictive validity of a large number of explanatory variables. This arises because researchers increasingly have the option of collecting data on student perceptions, classroom observations, and other sources. There is potential to collect a great deal of information, some of which is redundant or otherwise uninformative. We'd like to know which aspects of classroom life as measured by these methods is most useful in predicting student learning, and we'd like to know just how predictive the entire ensemble of information might be. We have provided two methods for achieving these aims: a multilevel variable selection model and a multilevel principal components regression model.

When we applied these two methods to the Tripod data, we found that the two methods gave us very similar results. Tripod, taken as a whole, explains about 7.8 percent of the variation in learning gains achieved by students in a different year from the year in which the student perceptions were collected. This is equivalent to a correlation between predicted and observed value added of $r = 0.29$. (This underestimates the correlation between Tripod and the "true" value added because the latter is measured with error.)

We found that teachers whose classrooms are well controlled and intellectually challenging produce comparatively large learning gains. Controlling for control and challenge, teachers who "captivate" their students, as indicated by Tripod, actually do a little worse than those who do not. This latter result seems a little puzzling. *Captivate* is measured by two items: "Schoolwork is interesting" and "We have interesting homework." Why would affirmative answers to these questions produce negative associations with value added—after adjusting for *Control* and *Challenge*? One possibility is that student perceptions that school and homework are interesting is a consequence of *Control* and *Challenge*. Teachers who challenge their students intellectually in well-controlled classrooms may make school interesting. We generally do not wish to control for consequences of causes in regression. Regression tells us what happens to an outcome when we increase the value of a predictor, holding constant other predictors.

The idea of increasing *Control* and *Challenge* while holding constant *Captivate* may not make sense. Alternatively, it may be that teachers who are good at making things interesting without increasing *Control* and *Challenge* are comparatively ineffective. We do not intend to adjudicate such explanations here, but rather to suggest that careful probing of predictive validity using these methods may trigger a useful reexamination of certain details of the classroom assessment procedure. More generally, we expect that this methodology will be useful in assessing the predictive validity of a wide range of indicators of classroom quality, and the results may lead to improvements in how these indicators are conceived and used.

NOTES

1. Our method accounts for measurement error of each of the 7Cs (see note 2).

2. Of course, we do not observe the true values x_{pij}, $p = 1, \ldots, 7$ of the 7Cs, so we cannot estimate the theoretical model (1) from the data. A commonly used option is to simply substitute the observed values, which we denote X_{pij}, $p = 1, \ldots, 7$ into Equation 1, then to estimate the model. These observed values are the simple mean responses of the students in each classroom. We know, however, that when observed values X measure true values x with error, such a procedure will give us biased estimates of $\beta_1, \beta_2, \ldots, \beta_7$. Hence, our estimate of R^2, the explanatory power of the model, will also be biased toward 0.

   To solve this problem, we substitute a multivariate version of Truman Kelley's (1925) "estimated true score" for the unobserved true values, x_{pij}, $p = 1, \ldots, 7$. Conditional on the values X_{pij}, $p = 1, \ldots, 7$ that we actually do observe, the expected value of our outcome based on (1) becomes

$$E(Y_{ij} \mid X_{1ij}, \ldots, X_{pij}) = \sum_{p=1}^{7} \beta_p E\,(x_{pij} \mid X_{1ij}, \ldots, X_{pij})$$

$$\equiv \sum_{p=1}^{7} \beta_p x^*_{pij}, \qquad\qquad (*)$$

where $x^*_{pij} = E(x_{pij} \mid X_{1ij}, \ldots, X_{pij})$ is the conditional mean of the true score x_{pij} given the observed scores $X_{1ij}, \ldots, X_{pij}$. These can be estimated via the empirical Bayes method (Morris, 1983), but now using the multivariate approach (Raudenbush, Rowan, & Kang, 1991), sometimes known as "multivariate shrinkage." Substituting the empirical Bayes estimates x^*_{pij} for x_{pij} in Equation (*) "identifies" our model—that is, equates the parameters of (1), which we can, in principal, estimate, with the parameters of (2), which is a theoretical model because we do not observe x_{pij}. Actually, our solution to the problem of measurement error—namely, the substitution of x_{pij}^* for x_{pij}, actually makes the collinear problem worse. The reason is that the correlations among the empirical Bayes estimates are even a little higher than are the correlations among the true values of the 7Cs. This is a well-known result (Raudenbush, 1999): each of the observed values of the 7Cs carries information about the other values of the 7Cs; multivariate shrinkage fully exploits this information, inducing, however, more dependence among the empirical Bayes estimates.

REFERENCES AND ADDITIONAL RESOURCES

Berk, R. (2005). Survey of 12 strategies to measure teaching effectiveness. *International Journal of Teaching and Learning in Higher Education, 17,* 48–62.

Bill & Melinda Gates Foundation. (2010). *Learning about teaching: Initial findings from the measures of effective teaching project.* Seattle, WA: Author.

Bill & Melinda Gates Foundation. (2013). *Measures of Effective Teaching (MET) project: Final report.* Seattle, WA: Author.

Chetty, R., Friedman, J. N., Hilger, N., Saez, E., Schanzenbach, D. W., & Yagan, D. (2011). How does your kindergarten classroom affect your earnings? Evidence from Project STAR. *Quarterly Journal of Economics*, *126*(4), 1593–1661.

Dempster, A. P., Laird, N. M., & Rubin, D. B. (1977). Maximum likelihood from incomplete data via the EM algorithm. *Journal of the Royal Statistical Society, Series B, 39,* 1–38.

Glazerman, S., Goldhaber, D., Loeb, S., Staiger, D., Raudenbush, S., & Whitehurst, G. J. (2011). *Passing muster: Evaluating teacher evaluation systems.* Washington, DC: The Brookings Institution.

Hoerl, A. E., & Kennard, R.W. (1970). Ridge regression: Biased estimation for nonorthogonal problems. *Technometrics, 12*(1), 55–67.

Kane, T. J., & Staiger, D. O. (2008). Estimating teacher impacts on student achievement: An experimental evaluation. Working Paper 14607. Washington, DC: National Bureau of Economic Research.

Kelley, T. L. (1925). The applicability of the Spearman-Brown formula for the measurement of reliability. *Journal of Educational Psychology*, *16*(5), 5, 300–303.

Lindley, D. V., & Smith, A. F. (1972). Bayes estimates for the linear model. *Journal of the Royal Statistical Society, Series B, 34,* 1–41.

McCaffrey, D. F., Koretz, D. M., Lockwood, J. R., & Hamilton, L. S. (2003). *Evaluating value-added models for teacher accountability.* Santa Monica, CA: Rand Corporation.

Measurement of Effective Teaching Project. (2012). *Gathering feedback for teaching: Combining high-quality observations with student surveys and achievement gains.* Seattle, WA: Bill & Melinda Gates Foundation.

Morris, C. N. (1983). Parametric empirical Bayes inference: Theory and applications. *Journal of the American Statistical Association*, *78*(381), 47–55.

Newman, F., Lopez, G., & Anthony Bryk. (1998). *The quality of intellectual work in Chicago schools: A baseline report.* Chicago, IL: Consortium for Chicago School Research.

Nye, B., Hedges, L. V., & Konstantopoulos, S. (2004). How large are teacher effects. *Educational Evaluation and Policy Analysis, 26,* 237–257.

Pianta, R. C., La Paro, K., & Hamre, B. K. (2008). *Classroom assessment scoring system.* Baltimore, MD: Paul H. Brookes.

Raudenbush, S. W. (1999). Hierarchical models. In S. Kotz (Ed.), *Encyclopedia of statistical sciences* (Vol. 3, pp. 318–323). Hoboken, NJ: John Wiley & Sons.

Raudenbush, S. W. (2009). Adaptive centering with random effects: An alternative to the fixed effects model for studying time-varying treatments in school settings. *Journal of Education, Finance and Policy, 4,* 468–491.

Raudenbush, S. W., Bryk, A., & Congdon, R. (2011). *HLM 7* [Software]. Lincolnwood, IL: Scientific Software, Inc.

Raudenbush, S.W., Rowan, B., & Kang, S. J. (1991). A multilevel, multivariate model for studying school climate in secondary schools with estimation via the EM algorithm. *Journal of Educational Statistics, 16*(4), 295–330.

Raudenbush, S. W., & Sadoff, S. (2008). Statistical inference when classroom quality is measured with error. *Journal of Research on Educational Effectiveness, 1,* 138–154.

APPENDIX A: MULTIVARIATE SHRINKAGE TO REMOVE MEASUREMENT ERROR IN PREDICTORS

Equation 1 can be written as

$$Y = \beta_0 + \beta^T \pi + \varepsilon, \tag{1}$$

where β is a 7 by 1 vector of regression coefficients, π is a 7 by vector of "true scores" (that is, the latent, true values of each of the 7Cs), β_0 is a fixed intercept, and ε is a random disturbance composed of a school-level and a classroom-level component. We do not observe the true values π, but instead observe estimates $\hat{\pi}$ based on a survey using twenty-eight items. Following Raudenbush and Sadoff (2008), we can estimate β without bias by conditioning (2) on the estimates $\hat{\pi}$:

$$\begin{aligned} E(Y \mid \hat{\pi}) &= \beta_0 + \beta^T E(\pi \mid \hat{\pi}) + E(\varepsilon \mid \hat{\pi}) \\ &= \beta_0 + \beta^T \pi^*, \end{aligned} \tag{2}$$

where $\pi^* = E(\pi \mid \hat{\pi})$ can be computed by estimating the joint distribution of π, $\hat{\pi}$ under multivariate normality and $E(\varepsilon \mid \hat{\pi}) = E(\varepsilon) = 0$, under the assumption that the model error ε is independent of the 7Cs. We can relax the latter assumption by including fixed effects of schools and adding student covariates.

APPENDIX B. RIDGE REGRESSION WITH EMPIRICAL BAYES FOR TWO-LEVEL DATA

B.1. Exchangeability within Regressions

The Model Let us begin with the standard OLS regression model

$$Y_i = \beta_0 + \sum_{p=1}^{p} \beta_p x_{pi} + e_i \equiv \beta_0 + \mathbf{x}_i^T \beta + e_i, \qquad e_i \sim iid\ N(0, \sigma^2), \quad \textbf{(1)}$$

for $i = 1, \ldots, n$ where Y_i is a continuous outcome, in our case the value-added score for teacher classroom i, hypothesized to be a linear function of P known covariates $x_{1i}, \ldots, x_{Pi}$, elements of the P by 1 vector $\mathbf{x}_i$, plus an additive random disturbance term e_i assumed independently and identically distributed with mean 0 and variance σ^2. We can also stack these equations to represent the model in matrix notation, yielding

$$Y = \mathbf{1}_n \beta_0 + X\beta + e, \qquad e \sim N_n(0, \sigma^2 I_n), \quad \textbf{(2)}$$

where Y is an n by 1 vector of outcomes, X is the n by P matrix of predictors, $\mathbf{1}_n$ is an n by 1 vector having elements equal to unity, and e is a random disturbance term. Hence β_0 is a scalar intercept and β is a vector of coefficients to be estimated.

We know that the OLS estimator (given the intercept β_0)

$$\hat{\beta} = (X^T X)^{-1} X^T (Y - \mathbf{1}_n \beta_0) \quad \textbf{(3)}$$

is "best linear unbiased," and, in the case where e is multivariate normal, OLS provides the unique, minimum variance unbiased estimator. However, the problem we face is that P may be large, so large that $X^T X$ may be ill-conditioned; even if $X^T X$ is non-singular, the OLS estimates may be so noisy that they become uninterpretable and non-replicable in new samples. For example, considering the Tripod data alone, there are at least twenty-eight items in some versions of the survey, each of which could become a regressor, and they are positively inter-correlated. Even with a large n, OLS estimates, while computable, will likely be unstable across samples, so that any attempt to rank these OLS estimates in importance may be futile. In the illustrative example here, we used seven scales, rather than twenty-eight item responses, as predictors, but the method allows a very large number of predictors, and we develop that idea here.

Rather than specify, say, $P = 28$ regressors, one for each item in the Tripod survey, for example, we might impose a radical simplification: combine these twenty-eight items into a single mean of all P items and regress the outcome on this mean, yielding a single regression coefficient, call it δ_0. This strategy would ensure stable estimation, but would prohibit us from learning anything about the relative importance of the twenty-eight items in predicting the value-added outcome.

A Compromise So far we are faced with a choice between conceiving the predictor of value added to have twenty-eight dimensions versus one. A principled compromise is to impose an exchangeable prior distribution on β of the form

$$\beta = \mathbf{1}_p\delta_0 + v \sim N(\mathbf{1}_p\delta_0, \Delta^2 I_p). \tag{4}$$

We can think, as Bayesians, that δ_0 is our best *a priori* guess about the value of any specific coefficient β_p in the P by 1 vector β, while Δ^2 represents the degree of uncertainty we have about the proposition that β_p is near δ_0. A frequentist interpretation is that, in the case of Tripod, the twenty-eight items represent a sample from a large universe of items that measure the quality of the classroom climate; δ_0 is the population mean of the coefficients associated with these items; and Δ^2 is the population variance of those coefficients.

So our linear model now follows from substituting (4) into (3)

$$Y = \mathbf{1}_n\beta_0 + X\mathbf{1}_p\delta_0 + Xv + e \sim N_p(\mathbf{1}_n\beta_0 + X\mathbf{1}_p\delta_0, V),$$
$$V = \Delta^2 XX^T + \sigma^2 I_p. \tag{5}$$

The New Estimator The maximum likelihood estimator of the parameters of (5), given the variance-covariance parameters and β_0, is

$$\hat{\delta}_0 = (\mathbf{1}_P^T X^T V^{-1} X\mathbf{1}_P)^{-1}\mathbf{1}_P^T X^T V^{-1}(Y - \mathbf{1}_n\beta_0), \tag{6}$$

while the empirical Bayes posterior mean of the exchangeable coefficients, given the MLE is

$$\beta^* = \mathbf{1}_P\hat{\delta}_0 + (X^T X + \sigma^2 \Delta^{-2} I_p)^{-1} X^T(Y - \mathbf{1}_n\beta_0). \tag{7}$$

This new estimator (7) lies on a continuum between the two extremes we discussed above. Suppose, for example, that the twenty-eight Tripod items each contribute uniquely to the prediction of value added. Then the heterogeneity among them would be large, so that Δ^{-2} will be very small and (6) will converge to the OLS estimator (3) using the full complement of twenty-eight predictors. In contrast, suppose that, after controlling for the mean of the twenty-eight items, the individual items make no additional contribution. In this case $\Delta^{-2} \to \infty$, $V = \sigma^2 I_P$ and (7) converges to

$$\beta^* = \mathbf{1}_P \hat{\delta}_0 = \mathbf{1}_P (\mathbf{1}_P^T X^T X \mathbf{1}_P)^{-1} \mathbf{1}_P^T X^T (Y - \mathbf{1}_n \beta_0)$$
$$= \mathbf{1}_P (\bar{X}^T \bar{X})^{-1} \bar{X}^T (Y - \mathbf{1}_n \beta_0) / P, \qquad (8)$$

where $\bar{X}$ is the mean of the $P = 28$ items. So every element of β^* is now a constant and is proportional to what we would obtain by simply combining the twenty-eight items into a single mean. We therefore see how β^* locates our inference on a continuum between the most elaborate and the most parsimonious model.

An important feature of β^* is that it will exist, even when P is so large that $X^T X$ becomes singular. This results from the augmentation of $X^T X$ by the prior variance ratio $\sigma^2 \Delta^{-2} I_P$ in (7). However, if $X^T X$ is non-singular, the OLS estimate will exist, and we can gain insight by rewriting (7) as

$$\beta^* = \mathbf{1}_P \hat{\delta}_0 + (X^T X + \sigma^2 \Delta^{-2} I_P)^{-1} X^T X \hat{\beta}$$
$$= \Lambda \hat{\beta} + (I_P - \Lambda) \mathbf{1}_P \hat{\delta}_0, \qquad (9)$$

where Λ is a multivariate "reliability matrix" converging to I_P when the OLS estimate is estimated precisely (e.g., the $P = 28$ coefficients are heterogeneous and/or the sample size is large).

It is straightforward to elaborate the structure imposed on the regression coefficients using the model

$$\beta = z\delta + v \sim N(\delta_0, \Delta^2 I_P), \qquad (10)$$

where z is a matrix of predictors. Equation 5 is a special case in which $z = \mathbf{1}_P$. For example, we might assume *a priori* that the twenty-eight items in

Tripod measure two constructs, so that δ would be a 2 by 1 vector. The general model thus extends (5) to become

$$Y = \mathbf{1}_n \beta_0 + Xz\delta + Xv + e \sim N_P(\mathbf{1}_n \beta_0 + Xz\delta, V), \quad V = \Delta^2 XX^T + \sigma^2 I_P. \quad (11)$$

B.2. Clustering by School: Exchangeability Between Regressions

We now confront the fact that the MET involves clustering by school. We may want to represent school differences by means of fixed effects or random effects, with or without randomly varying regression coefficients (Raudenbush, 2009). The random coefficient model allows the association between school quality indicators in X and the outcome Y to vary by school. Such variation may be partly (or entirely) predictable on the basis of school characteristics or partly (or entirely) random. For example, the associations between student perceptions and outcomes may vary by the level of the school (elementary versus secondary) or by the overall level climate of the school. Given randomization of teachers within schools, as in the MET study, an interesting model has fixed intercepts and random coefficients. To allow a flexible and comprehensive range of options, we shall allow the regressions to be partly predictable and partly exchangeable between schools. This involves an elaboration of our basic model (Equation 11).

Denote the value added outcome for classroom i in school j as Y_{ij} for teachers $i = 1, \ldots, n_j$ within schools $j = 1, \ldots, J$. Stack these outcomes within school j to define the outcome vector Y_j. The predictor variables are elements measured by classroom observations, student perceptions, and other sources, represented in the n_j by P matrix X_j. Within school j, we represent the outcome as a standard linear regression

$$Y_j = \mathbf{1}_{n_j} \beta_{0j} + X_j \beta_j + e_j, \qquad e_j \sim N_{n_j}\left(0, \sigma^2 I_{n_j}\right), \qquad (12)$$

where β_j is a P by 1 vector of school-specific coefficients.

The problems we face are that P may be very large and n_j may be very small. Thus, Equation 1, which specifies JP coefficients, will not be estimable without some restrictions on the parameters. To reduce the dimensionality of β_j within each school, we adopt exchangeability *within* regressions, as above:

$$\beta_j = z\delta_j + v, \qquad v \sim N(0, \Delta^2 I_p), \tag{13}$$

where δ_j is a Q-dimensional coefficient vector, $Q < P$. Substituting (13) into (12), our school-specific model becomes

$$Y_j = \mathbf{1}_{n_j} \beta_{0j} + X_j z \delta_j + X_j v + e_j, \tag{14}$$

an obvious extension of (11).

Now the coefficient vector $\delta = \delta_1, \ldots, \delta_J$ has dimension JQ, smaller than JP, but still a large number, with new parameters added for every additional school added to the sample. This problem of "proliferating parameters" will lead to inconsistent estimates. To address this problem, we adopt exchangeability *between* schools, thereby allowing key parameters to be fixed over schools, while others are exchangeable. We therefore have

$$\beta_{0j} = W_{0j}^T \gamma_0 + u_{0j} \tag{15}$$
$$\delta_j = W_j \gamma + u_j, \qquad (u_{0j} \quad u_j) \sim N(0, \tau).$$

Here W_{0j} is a vector of school characteristics that predict variation in school-specific intercepts β_{0j}, and the associated regression coefficients are the elements of the vector γ_0. Similarly, W_j is a school-specific matrix of explanatory variables that account for between-school heterogeneity in the school-specific regression coefficients, δ_j, and the associated coefficients are γ. Now combining (15) into (14), we have the mixed linear regression model

$$Y_j = W_{0j}^T \gamma_0 + X_j z W_j \gamma + \mathbf{1}_{n_j} u_{0j} + X_j z u_j + X_j v + e_j$$
$$= \left(\mathbf{1}_{n_j} W_{0j}^T \quad X_j z W_j \right) \begin{pmatrix} \gamma_0 \\ \gamma \end{pmatrix} + \left(\mathbf{1}_{n_j} \quad X_j \right) \begin{pmatrix} u_{0j} \\ u_j \end{pmatrix} + X_j v + e_j. \tag{16}$$

We can represent (16) succinctly as a mixed linear model:

$$Y_j = A_{fj} \theta_f + A_{rj} \theta_{rj} + X_j v + e_j,$$
$$\theta_{rj} \sim N_R(0, \tau), \qquad v \sim N_P(0, \Delta^2 I_P), \qquad e_j \sim N_{n_j}\left(0, \sigma^2 I_{n_j}\right), \tag{17}$$

where $A_{fj} = (\mathbf{1}_{n_j} \ W_{0j}^T \ X_j z W_j)$ is the n_j by F design matrix for the fixed coefficient vector $\theta_{fj} = (\gamma_0 \ \gamma)^T$ and $A_{rj} = (\mathbf{1}_{n_j} \ X_j)$ is the n_j by R design matrix for the between-school random effects vector θ_{rj}.

B.3. Estimation of Fixed Coefficients

Given the variance-covariance components, the maximum likelihood estimator of the fixed coefficient vector in (18) is

$$\hat{\theta}_f = \left(\sum_{j=1}^{J} A_{fj}^T H_j A_{fj}\right)^{-1} \sum_{j=1}^{J} A_{fj}^T H_j Y_j,$$

$$H_j = M_j - M_j X_j C_1^{-1} M_j$$

$$M_j = I_{n_j} - A_{rj} C_j^{-1} A_{rj}^T \tag{18}$$

$$C_j = A_{rj}^T A_{rj} + \sigma^2 \tau^{-1}$$

$$C_{1j} = \sum_{j=1}^{J} X_j^T M_j X_j + \Delta^{-2} I_P.$$

B.4. Estimation of Variance-Covariance Components

To estimate the variance-covariance components, we adopt the EM algorithm (Dempster, Laird, & Rubin, 1977). This requires expressions for the conditional distributions of the variance components, given the data and given current estimates of the unknown parameters $\psi = (\theta_F, \tau, \Delta^2, \sigma^2)$. We have
(i) $v \mid Y, \psi \sim N(v^*, V_{vv})$, where

$$v^* = V_{vv} \sum_{j=1}^{J} X_j^T M_j (Y_j - A_{fj} \theta_f)$$

$$V_{vv} = \left(\sum_{j=1}^{J} X_j^T M_j X_j + \sigma^2 \Delta^{-2} I_P\right)^{-1} \tag{19}$$

(ii) $u_j \mid Y, \psi \sim N(u_j^*, V_{rrj})$, where

$$\theta_{rj}^* = C_j^{-1} A_{rj}^T \left(Y_j - A_{fj} \theta_f - X_j v^*\right)$$

$$V_{uuj} = C_j^{-1} + C_j^{-1} A_{rj}^T X_j C_1^{-1} X_j^T C_j^{-1} \tag{20}$$

M-Step

If the school random effects θ_{rj}, $j = 2, \ldots, J$, the within-regression random effects v, and the fixed coefficients θ_{rj} were known, the maximum likelihood (subscripted "CD" for "complete-data") estimators of the variance-covariance components could be computed in a single step:

$$\hat{\tau}_{CD} = J^{-1}\sum_{j=1}^{J}\theta_{rj}\theta_{rj}^{T} \qquad \hat{\Delta}_{CD}^{2} = P^{-1}v^{T}v \qquad \hat{\sigma}_{CD}^{2} = N^{-1}\sum_{j=1}^{J}e_{j}^{T}e_{j}. \quad (21)$$

E-Step

These "complete-data" MLEs cannot be computed, because the sufficient statistics required for them are unknown. The idea behind EM is to substitute for these sufficient statistics their conditional expectations, given the observed data and current estimates of the parameters:

$$E\left(\sum_{j=1}^{J}\theta_{rj}\theta_{rj}^{T} \mid Y, \psi\right) = \sum_{j=1}^{J}(\theta_{rj}^{*}\theta_{rj}^{*T} + V_{rrj})$$

$$E\left(v^{T}v \mid Y, \psi\right) = v^{*T}v^{*} + tr(V_{vv})$$

$$E\left(\sum_{j=1}^{J}e_{j}^{T}e_{j} \mid Y, \psi\right) = \sum_{j=1}^{J}e_{j}^{*T}e_{j}^{*} + JR\sigma^{2} + P\Delta^{2} + \sigma^{2}\tau^{-1}tr\left\{\sum_{j=1}^{J}A_{rj}^{T}A_{rj}\right\} \qquad (22)$$

$$+ \sigma^{2}\Delta^{-2}tr\left\{\sum_{j=1}^{J}X_{j}^{T}X_{j}\right\}.$$

Each iteration of the algorithm increases the log-likelihood until the achievement of a desired rate of convergence.

2

CONNECTING EVALUATION MEASURES WITH STUDENT LEARNING

CHAPTER

7

Combining Classroom Observations and Value Added for the Evaluation and Professional Development of Teachers

ERIK A. RUZEK, CHRISTOPHER A. HAFEN,
BRIDGET K. HAMRE, AND ROBERT C. PIANTA

ABSTRACT

School district administrators and state officials are faced with the challenging task of creating teacher evaluation systems that distribute teachers across a continuum of effectiveness and provide comprehensive and actionable information. We contend that these systems must incorporate both observational measures of instruction and measures of student achievement gains that are attributable to teachers (value added). Using value-added data and scores on the Classroom Assessment Scoring System (CLASS) from the first year of the MET project, we present four strategies that districts might employ to create categories of teacher effectiveness. We consider the implications of each strategy on teacher evaluation and the allocation of professional development resources for the continued improvement of classroom instruction and student learning.

INTRODUCTION

Legislation at the federal, state, and local levels increasingly promotes the formation of teacher evaluation systems that can provide a well-rounded appraisal of a teacher's instruction, including both observational measures of the quality of instruction and quantifiable impacts on students' learning. An effective evaluation and feedback system should provide the basis for making decisions about facets of human capital development, such as professional development and merit pay. In creating comprehensive evaluation systems, school districts are tasked with building a fair *and* rigorous system, often from the ground up, that incorporates both teacher observational protocol(s) and teacher value-added scores describing the student achievement gains associated with a given teacher.

District leaders face numerous decisions in this work, including determining which classroom observational protocol to use, measuring the degree to which their observational measure of choice corresponds to value-added assessments, determining the optimal cutoffs that serve as trigger points for certain contingencies (e.g., supplementary professional development or merit pay), and choosing one or two from the myriad professional development programs available, among others. Each of these decisions independently requires careful consideration, and to make matters more difficult, the answer for one often depends on the answer for another. It is with these considerations in mind that in this chapter we seek to add clarity on the issues by, and take the steps necessary for, using data from value-added and observational assessments to make decisions regarding teacher performance. We do so through a systematic analysis of data from the Measures of Effective Teaching (MET) study, which included a number of high-quality observational measures of teachers' instruction, in addition to data on changes in students' academic achievement attributable to teachers (value-added scores).

In order to make the decisions and associated issues more salient, we thread our discussion and analysis through the lens of a hypothetical school district called Greenwood, as its administrators and teachers wrestle with a state mandate to incorporate observational measures of teachers' instruction into their existing teacher performance evaluation system, which at present relies exclusively on measuring effectiveness in terms of teacher-associated changes in student test scores—that is, value-added metrics (VAM). Greenwood leaders want to determine how these two indicators, observations of classroom instruction and VAM, can be used in concert to (1) inform their assignment of appropriate professional development (PD) for teachers who are struggling with aspects of their instruction, (2) develop and cultivate talent for roles such as instructional coaches, and, potentially, (3) serve as a source of information for rewarding those teachers who are both exceptionally responsive to their students and who promote academic achievement.

Greenwood approaches these decisions and aims realizing that teachers' practices in the classroom can function both as a focus of performance evaluation and as a target for professional development. It is clear to Greenwood leaders that increasing student achievement (as measured by value-added scores) must be a primary goal of teachers' practice; VAM is used as a standard for teachers' effectiveness and, thus, a component of their evaluation. However, Greenwood also wants their evaluation system to drive improvements in classroom practices likely to contribute not only to academic achievement assessed by VAM, but also to a broad range of student learning and developmental outcomes (e.g., students' academic engagement, team problem solving, motivation, and interpersonal skills). Greenwood also knows that teachers' instructional practices are amenable to change—and perhaps the most actionable component of their performance evaluation (Sabol, Hong, Pianta, & Burchinal, 2013). So it seems critical to include observation as a core component of a comprehensive and relevant human capital development and management system. District leaders also want to make sure that teachers are given feedback on their observed practices and are offered PD to improve those practices. They plan to use the observational component of the teacher evaluation system for driving feedback and PD efforts.

The choice of the appropriate observational measure of instruction needs to be made on a district-by-district basis, and the analyses we describe below and carry out, using observational and student-achievement data collected on MET teachers, could be performed on any of the high-quality observational measures in the MET study. Because of our familiarity with it and the strong empirical base for its reliability and validity, we focus here on the Classroom Assessment Scoring System (CLASS; Pianta, LaParo, & Hamre, 2008). CLASS measures the nature and quality of teacher-student interactions across instructional, social/emotional, and organizational domains (Hamre, Pianta, Mashburn, & Downer, 2007). CLASS also has an aligned professional development approach, MyTeachingPartner (which we describe later in the chapter when we discuss Greenwood's options for PD), and is technically sound (important for all the decisions and uses Greenwood intends, particularly merit pay). Greenwood's plan for providing feedback and PD aligned to the observation (CLASS) starts with routine observations early in the school year, followed by opportunities for teachers to improve their practices (and student achievement and related outcomes) over the course of the academic year (Allen, Pianta, Gregory, Mikami, & Lun, 2011; Downer, Pianta, Fan, Hamre, Mashburn, & Justice, 2012; Pianta, Mashburn, Downer, Hamre, & Justice, 2008).

For the purposes of decision making and assignment of teachers to PD or other contingencies, Greenwood plans to sort teachers into different levels of teaching effectiveness. District leaders seek to create a system that is (1) easily understandable to administrators, teachers, and parents; (2) distributes teachers across a continuum of effectiveness, as opposed to describing all teachers as highly effective (Weisberg, Sexton, Mulhern, & Keeling, 2009); and (3) ensures that there are meaningful student learning distinctions between teachers in the different effectiveness levels. Many strategies for creating groupings that meet these aims are possible, and in this chapter we use data from the MET study to consider four possible grouping strategies. One of the fundamental aims of this chapter is to identify the ways in which each classification scheme, and its utility in addressing district decision-making needs, varies as a function of the distribution of scores and the association between observation scores (in this case using CLASS) and VAM. Depending on the nature of the distributions, the CLASS-VAM association, and the ways it is parameterized, one obtains different results for characterizing teachers' effectiveness. These differences in classification have consequences for the decisions Greenwood leaders seek to make.

FOUR STRATEGIES FOR GROUPING TEACHERS' EFFECTIVENESS USING CLASS AND VAM

This section outlines the four ways in which we examine CLASS-VAM associations, starting with the simplest strategy and slowly building up to more complex, and data-intensive, strategies.

Strategy 1: Assume a Linear Relation Between CLASS Scores and VAM

The simplest and most common form of understanding and estimating the association between observation and VAM scores is to treat the relation between the two measures as linear throughout the entire distribution, as signified by the overall correlation between the two indicators of effectiveness. A linear association indicates that a 1 point increase in CLASS is associated with a fixed amount of gain in VAM, regardless of where a particular CLASS score is located on the scale. This would mean that an increase near the bottom of the CLASS scale (e.g., from a score of 2 to a score of 3) or near the top (e.g., from a score of 5 to a 6) would produce the same amount of VAM gain. Greenwood leaders want to consider the use of this approach because it is simple to understand and it could streamline their PD efforts. Whether they target teachers at the low, middle, or upper end of the CLASS score range for PD, under this model they would expect to get a similar boost to VAM from increasing CLASS scores. This model might support a "one size fits all" style of professional development in which all teachers would receive the same PD approach, which may be more parsimonious from a political standpoint.

A downside of this approach is that it provides little information to target less or more intense (and costly) professional development and the relative costs/benefits that might follow from having more information. It likewise ignores the possibility that, at some points on the distribution of CLASS scores, the correlation between CLASS and VAM may be stronger or weaker. Furthermore, this approach is potentially problematic in that it doesn't clearly identify groups of teachers based on CLASS-VAM combinations, as required by the state mandate.

Strategy 2: Define Effectiveness Categories Based on CLASS Manual

The second strategy defines effectiveness categories based on the actual descriptions in the CLASS Manual for low (ineffective), middle (effective), and high-quality (highly effective) instructional interactions and examines value-added scores for teachers in each of those groups under the assumption that they should be meaningfully different. One might consider this an approach based on theoretical or *a priori* distinctions among teachers in their interactions with students. More specifically, when scoring the CLASS, observers assign a rating of 1 (low) to 7 (high) on dimensions of teacher-student interaction, such as Quality of Feedback or Regard for Students' Perspectives (Pianta, Mashburn, Downer, Hamre, & Justice, 2008). These scale points are defined in the manual by specific behavioral markers that reflect low, middle, and high levels of the dimension indicators. In a sense, this distribution of behaviors reflects a theory, or map, of the effectiveness of teachers' behavior. This scaling from low to high, based on the CLASS Manual, could be used to create categories of teachers' effectiveness by relying on the manual to derive cutpoints to distinguish groups.

In deferring to the CLASS Manual for creating effectiveness categories, this strategy potentially takes control of the process out of Greenwood's collective hands, unless district leaders and teachers concur with the CLASS Manual's categorization. This strategy could be problematic if the association between CLASS scores and VAM does not align with the CLASS-defined low, medium, and high categories. Put differently, the CLASS scoring system attempts to discriminate between levels of instruction believed to be meaningful, but it may be that the differences between those levels are negligible with respect to whether they contribute to higher or lower levels of VAM.

Strategy 3: Create "Teacher Effectiveness" Categories Based on CLASS Distribution

The third strategy creates categories of teacher effectiveness based on different groupings of CLASS scores in the district and again examines value-added differences between groups. For example, categories could be created based on dividing the distribution of CLASS scores into quartiles (labeling CLASS scores below the 25th percentile ineffective, CLASS scores between the 26th and 50th percentiles as developing effectiveness, scores between the 51th and 75th percentiles as effective, and CLASS scores above the 76th percentile highly effective). A district might do this because they have sufficient funds to provide intensive PD to the lowest 25 percent and to provide merit pay to the top 25 percent. Other districts might use other percentile-based cuts for similar decisions. Districts may want to use their teacher evaluation systems to identify excellence for merit pay (noted above) or to select teachers for roles as coaches; in each case financial or other considerations may come into play. Alternatively, a district may want to examine the distribution of teacher effectiveness scores (VAM and/or CLASS), in which case certain "natural" breakpoints may be evident. In other words, districts may find it useful to look at their own data, consider it in light of available resources and goals, and then categorize teachers accordingly.

Like the first strategy, this approach also assumes a linear association between CLASS scores and VAM, but it differs in that it does not necessarily rely on the linear slope being the same throughout the distribution (this is also true for the second strategy). However, despite the percentiles that might be established based on any of a variety of considerations, and just as with the second strategy, it seems warranted for Greenwood to examine the extent to which any cutoffs create meaningful distinctions in performance between groups. And, in part, this depends on the association between the observation and student VAM scores, which district personnel must acutely attend to as decision makers weigh the various options.

Strategy 4: Look for CLASS Score Thresholds or Breakpoints

Importantly, the first three strategies assume a linear association between CLASS scores and VAM, such that increases in one measure correspond to increases in the other. It is critical that this assumption be examined; that is, Greenwood staff must determine whether the categories of teacher effectiveness based on CLASS and VAM have any correspondence with actual improvements in student learning. An alternative to the assumption of linearity is the possibility that the correspondence between the two indicators is nonlinear; that is, there may be points along the joint distribution at which the magnitude of the association varies. Thus, the final strategy considered by Greenwood employs an approach that can capture nonlinear associations between CLASS and value-added scores. It examines the association between CLASS scores and value-added scores at different points along the CLASS score distribution to find CLASS score values (or thresholds) at which the association between the two measures grows substantially or flattens out. For example, if the association between CLASS scores and VAM is noticeably weaker above a given level of practice, it would suggest that PD should focus on improving quality up to that threshold level, but improving quality above that point may not be as influential for improving student outcomes. Greenwood wants to use its own data to drive policy, decision making, and investments. Therefore, they must undertake a critical and empirical analysis of their own data on teacher instructional quality and student achievement.

As we have noted, each of these strategies takes a different approach to characterizing the ways in which CLASS scores might relate to VAM. Although categorization of teachers according to their effectiveness, using some combination of VAM and observation, has been at the core of many states' or districts' current educational reform efforts, we are not aware of any prior analysis of these associations to drive decision making or to clarify any of the associated issues. Thousands of observations are now being conducted in schools without any significant attention to the issues we examine here. It is not hard to imagine how a lack of attention to these matters could lead to unanticipated errors and costs for administrators, teachers, and students.

Our primary aim is to help school districts use classroom observational and value-added measures to devise teacher evaluation, accountability, and professional development systems that provide comprehensive and action-able information for teachers, administrators, and PD staff. We start with the premise that district professionals (superintendents, principals, teachers, staff) face a set of complex, interlocking challenges: limited (and dwindling) finan-cial resources; demands for accountability and improvement that require new approaches (and possible investments); a policy context that constrains some alternatives and forces others; a limited supply of talented classroom teachers, but a potentially large number of teachers who can improve their impact on students; and a commitment to teachers currently working in the classroom. Navigating these challenges ultimately leads to tradeoffs around key deci-sions; we hope to provide some illustrations of these tradeoffs and how an informed analysis can help address them.

HOW MET DATA IS USED TO HELP GREENWOOD ASSESS THE FOUR STRATEGIES

In order to help inform districts such as Greenwood, we draw on data from the MET study. Readers are referred to reports on the MET published by the Bill & Melinda Gates Foundation (2013) for details on the sample of teachers and students, assessment protocols, procedures, and psychometric proper-ties of the instruments used in the present study. In order to examine the four categorization schemes Greenwood is considering, we included data from all MET English and mathematics teachers in grades 4 through 9.[1] We use each teacher's overall score from the CLASS as a measure of instructional quality and his or her value-added metrics (VAM) as a measure of his or her impact on student learning, both of which we briefly describe below.

Measuring Instructional Quality Using the Classroom Assessment Scoring System

MET teachers recorded at least two lessons on a topic from a list of subject-specific "focal topics."[2] These recorded sessions were then scored by CLASS-trained and -certified raters. In this chapter we use overall scores from the

CLASS (Pianta, LaParo, & Hamre, 2008), which measures the quality of teachers' cognitive and social-emotional interactions with students, assigning ratings ranging from 1 to 7 on dimensions of interaction. CLASS provides an overall assessment of a teacher's instructional interactions, which is the product of a teacher's scores on the three broad CLASS domains: Emotional Support, Instructional Support, and Classroom Organization. Each of these domains, in turn, encompasses a set of finer-grained assessments of particular dimensions of interactions in that domain. The Emotional Support domain includes Positive Climate, Teacher Sensitivity, and Regard for Student Perspectives. The Classroom Organization domain includes Behavior Management, Productivity, and Negative Climate. The Instructional Support domain includes Instructional Learning Formats, Content Understanding, Analysis and Inquiry, Quality of Feedback, and Instructional Dialogue.

In practice, school districts that employ CLASS often utilize the overall score from the measure but can use the domain scores to target more specific feedback and PD for teachers. For the purposes of the current investigation, we utilize the overall score, much as most school districts would, by taking the average across all CLASS dimensions. Of note is that the overall score, an average of domain scores (which are, in turn, averages of dimensions in domain), more heavily weights the Instructional Support domain in that Instructional Support includes five dimensions, while the other two domains each have three dimensions.

MET Value-Added Metrics

To measure a teacher's impact on student learning on the appropriate state test of mathematics or ELA, we used the official MET-estimated VAM score for each teacher, which is an entirely separate measure from the CLASS scores. Because MET teachers taught in different states, MET researchers standardized test scores (mean of 0 and a standard deviation of 1) for each district, subject, year, and grade level. They estimated a statistical model to predict a student's end-of-year score on the state assessment, accounting for that student's test score in that subject from the prior year, a set of student characteristics,[3] and the mean prior test score and mean student characteristics in the specific course section or class that the student attended. These value-added models were estimated separately by district, grade level, and subject (mathematics or ELA). The teacher value-added scores are the residuals by teacher, subject, and year (or teacher, section, subject, and year if a teacher taught more than one course section) from the statistical model (see Bill & Melinda Gates Foundation, 2010 for technical details).

Analyses Employed in Evaluating Each of the Strategies

Strategy 1: Simple Linear Association We first examine the distribution of CLASS scores among MET teachers, looking for whether CLASS scores are normally distributed (i.e., bell-shaped), and report on the range and variability of CLASS scores across MET teachers. A linear regression is estimated to determine the overall association between CLASS scores and VAM in the MET sample.

Strategy 2: Using CLASS Manual Guidelines Here we use guidelines from the CLASS Manual to set effectiveness thresholds (as opposed to determining them from the distribution of CLASS scores) and consider the consequences of taking such an approach for the MET sample.

Strategy 3: Using Actual Distribution of CLASS Scores In this strategy, we first categorize CLASS scores into a variety of predetermined groups based on the overall CLASS score distribution in the MET sample, focusing on a categorization that identifies teachers in the top 10 percent, 40 percent, 40 percent, and bottom 10 percent of the MET CLASS score distribution. For each of the different categorization schemes, we use ANOVAs with follow-up Tukey's HSD contrasts to test whether average VAM in each category is significantly different from average VAM in other categories.

Strategy 4: Thresholds Finally, we investigate the possibility of thresholds or breakpoints in CLASS scores when the association between CLASS scores and VAM accelerates, levels off, or even declines. The presence of such thresholds is determined using a spline regression model that locates inflection points along the CLASS scale where associations between CLASS and VAM change.

These analyses help to establish the nature of the association between CLASS scores and VAM in the MET sample. Each of the strategies has implications for developing a comprehensive teacher evaluation system, including how to categorize levels of effectiveness, how and when to assign PD, and how to award merit pay to teachers.

In order to ensure that the association between CLASS and VAM is not confounded with the particular geographical locations where teachers taught, the subject matter they instruct students on, or the grade level of the students they taught, we adjust our regression models for each of these factors. It is important to note that the MET data, as we have analyzed them, do not allow us to make causal claims about the effects of raising CLASS scores on VAM because data on teacher instruction and student achievement were merely observed. In other words, no experimental intervention was employed to raise the quality of teachers' instructional interactions with their students. As we will discuss later in the chapter, recent experimental research using a coaching model to increase the quality of teachers' instruction along CLASS dimensions (MyTeachingPartner) provides evidence that increasing CLASS scores does lead to greater student achievement. Although experimental interventions to raise CLASS scores give us greater confidence in the causal link between CLASS scores and student achievement, we urge readers to be aware that the present analysis cannot make causal claims. Indeed, the vast majority of data that school district leaders will have at their disposal to carry out analyses such as those employed here will be observational, and therefore cannot be equated with causal interpretations.

A COMPARISON OF THE FOUR STRATEGIES AND THE PD IMPLICATIONS

In seeking to use CLASS scores as a part of their teacher evaluation system, the Greenwood school district has to evaluate how CLASS scores are related to student achievement gains (VAM). Each of their proposed strategies makes different assumptions about the relation between CLASS scores and VAM, and each therefore requires a distinct analysis. The first three strategies assume that the increases in CLASS scores are associated with increases in VAM. They differ slightly in that the first strategy assumes that the association is constant throughout the distribution of CLASS scores, whereas the second and third strategies allow for the possibility that the linear association is different at distinct points in the CLASS distribution. The final strategy uses a statistical analysis approach to identify points in the CLASS score distribution that note CLASS score thresholds where associations with VAM show marked changes. Below, we use MET data to assess these four strategies.

Strategy 1: Assume a Constant Linear Relation Between CLASS Scores and VA

An important first step is to examine the distribution of CLASS scores for Greenwood teachers, as this provides information about the shape of the distribution (whether it is "normal" or bell-shaped), the range of scores, and the variability in scores. The second step is to establish whether the relation between CLASS scores and VAM is linear, that is, a 1 point increase in CLASS scores anywhere along the score range produces the same amount of VAM change. We illustrate this two-step process using the sample of teachers in the MET data.

Figure 7.1 shows the distribution of overall CLASS scores for grades 4 to 9 English and mathematics teachers in the first year of MET data collection (a total of 1,580 teachers). The mean CLASS score for MET teachers was 4.25, with a standard deviation of 0.53. The mean CLASS score for mathematics teachers was 4.20, with a standard deviation of 0.53, and the mean CLASS score for English teachers was 4.29, with a standard deviation of 0.53. Although the magnitude of this difference is not large, this indicated that English teachers had significantly higher CLASS scores on average. It is important to keep in mind that a CLASS score of 4.30 sits at the exact middle of the CLASS score range, while the minimum CLASS score in the MET data was 2.18 and the maximum was 5.70 (see Figure 7.1).

The simplest strategy that could possibly help Greenwood to deal with the state mandate for integrating observational and value-added metrics into teacher evaluation is to estimate the linear association between CLASS scores and VAM. We estimated this association across all teachers in the MET sample instead of breaking out the analysis by upper elementary and middle and high school teachers, statistically adjusting for the grade level, academic subject, and district a teacher taught in. Doing so indicated that a 1 point increase in CLASS scores was associated with a 0.18 gain in VAM in the MET sample. This is a significant association; however, it is important to note that, by estimating the association in this manner, one assumes that the linear association between CLASS and VAM is the same throughout the CLASS distribution. This assumption is explicitly tested as we explore Greenwood's alternative strategies.

PD Implication If a district is facing state pressure to raise VAM scores across the board, then results from the analysis of Strategy 1 suggest that PD to improve CLASS scores may be equally effective in raising VAM, no matter the current quality of a teacher's instructional interactions with students. The first analysis does not provide enough information to conclude that there is a greater VAM payoff to focusing PD on teachers with lower CLASS scores than on those with

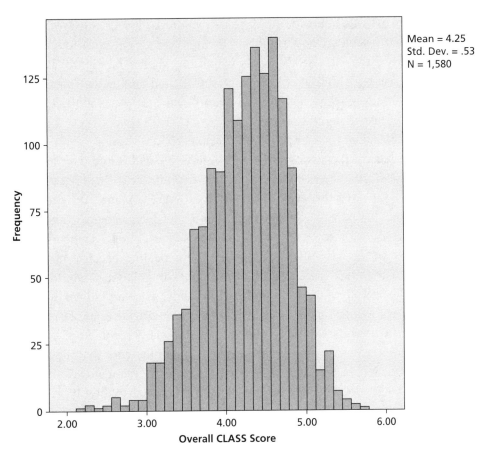

FIGURE 7.1. *CLASS Score Distribution for MET English and Mathematics Teachers (Histogram)*

middling CLASS scores. Put differently, the first strategy might be too simplistic to be useful for targeting PD to those teachers whose VAM scores are most likely to be affected by additional PD. Similarly, the first strategy does not help to address state mandates to create meaningful teacher effectiveness categories.

Strategy 2: Define Effectiveness Categories Using Guidelines from the CLASS Manual

The first strategy, although simple to understand, ignores the state mandate to create a set of effectiveness categories that can be used for rewarding teachers and targeting PD more strategically for greater returns on VAM.

One alternative that Greenwood wants to explore is the creation of effectiveness categories based on definitions of high-, medium-, and low-quality instruction from the CLASS Manual, which are shown in Figure 7.2, and could correspond to highly effective, effective, and ineffective categories, respectively. Many Greenwood administrators and teachers believe that the high quality of instruction that is indicated by a CLASS score of 6 is the minimum acceptable score for which district teachers should strive.

As indicated by the histogram from Figure 7.1 and Table 7.1, the vast majority of MET teachers (98.7 percent) had overall CLASS scores that fell into the Mid (3.00 to 5.99) category from the CLASS Manual; only a handful of teachers (1.3 percent) were in the Low (1 to 2.99) category, and none were in the High (6.00 to 7.00) category. This suggests that a categorization scheme based on the CLASS Manual, although appealing because it reflects meaningful distinctions in teachers' instructional interactions, would be of little use in the sample of teachers in the MET study, as nearly all MET teachers would be categorized as effective. In order for an effectiveness strategy to be useful for PD purposes, there must be at least some percentage of teachers in the top and bottom categories. However, it is also the case that alternative classification schemes could be devised based on the manual descriptions; Greenwood could decide that scoring a "5" or above was highly effective (6 percent), scoring a "3" or below was ineffective (30 percent) and the remainder (64 percent) of teachers could be classified as effective. In this *a priori* classification approach, the primary focus is mapping the distribution to the descriptions in the manual.

Low		Mid			High	
1	2	3	4	5	6	7
The low-range description fits the classroom/teacher very well. All, or almost all, relevant indicators in the low range are present.	The low-range description mostly fits the classroom/teacher, but there are one or two indicators that are in the mid-range.	The mid-range description mostly fits the classroom/teacher, but there are one or two indicators in the low range.	The mid-range description fits the classroom/teacher very well. All, or almost all, relevant indicators in the mid-range are present.	The mid-range description mostly fits the classroom/teacher, but there are one or two indicators in the high range.	The high-range description mostly fits the classroom/teacher, but there are one or two indicators in the mid-range.	The high-range description fits the classroom/teacher very well. All, or almost all, relevant indicators in the high range are present.

FIGURE 7.2. *Effectiveness Categories as Defined by the CLASS Manual*

TABLE 7.1. **Percentage of Teachers Who Fell in Each of the CLASS Scoring Defined Ranges**

Low		Mid			High	
1	2	3	4	5	6	7
0%	1.3%	28.7%	64.0%	6%	0%	0%

As we will show in evaluating Greenwood's third strategy, districts might use the CLASS score distribution in their district as a guide in deciding what percentages of teachers should be in the top and bottom categories.

PD Implication Unfortunately, the instruction of teachers in the MET sample was almost exclusively confined to the CLASS Manual–defined Mid category, with a few instances of teachers having Low-quality instruction, and no teachers exhibiting High-quality instruction. The MET sample distribution cannot therefore help us in determining the usefulness of Greenwood's second strategy, at least when using the whole number ratings provided by the manual and rounding teachers' overall average CLASS scores to fit those whole number classification schemes.

However, the actual scores yielded by the computations of averages to obtain overall CLASS scores creates a much more informative distribution that includes many scores in the range between whole numbers. As we will show in more detail when we present Strategy 4, two points along the CLASS scale (total score of 2.91 and total score of 4.5) are particularly relevant for administrators seeking the best place to focus their training and PD efforts, and both would be considered midrange CLASS scores. An average CLASS score of 2.91 (or 3) indicates that some of the features of instruction were in the mid-quality range, but many were in the low-quality range, whereas an average score of 4.5 indicates that the majority of features were in the mid-quality range, with some in the high-quality range. Teachers and administrators may view middling scores as insufficient for their students and believe that CLASS-defined high-quality instruction (CLASS score of 6 or 7) should be the criteria by which all teachers are judged. Although we would encourage such a bold vision for Greenwood or other school districts, it is important to note that districts must use data to help them locate active CLASS score ranges in which even incremental instructional improvements can lead to student learning gains (VAM), which we illustrate in Strategy 4.

Strategy 3: Create Teacher Effectiveness Categories Based on the CLASS Score Distribution

A third approach that Greenwood can employ, one that is commonly used in state accountability systems, is to sort teachers into effectiveness categories based on their actual CLASS score, which in most cases is an average computed across multiple cycles and composited across multiple dimensions into a domain or overall score. Such a system is easy to comprehend by a wide variety of audiences. Although Greenwood might like to follow the CLASS Manual guidelines to help create *a priori* categories, we saw earlier that such an approach would be inappropriate if the distribution of Greenwood teachers' CLASS scores looked like the distribution of CLASS scores in the MET sample. Therefore, Greenwood needs to create effectiveness categories based on real-world data about CLASS scores in their district and, then, test whether these categories are associated with significant differences in student achievement.

To illustrate, we sort MET teachers into a set of four effectiveness categories based on where their CLASS score fell within the actual distribution of MET teachers. We start by choosing a distribution that identifies smaller portions of teachers in the top and bottom categories (top 10 percent, 40 percent, 40 percent, and bottom 10 percent), as these are the categories that often have the highest stakes associated with them. Greenwood has limited money for rewarding those teachers at the top and for helping those at the bottom, so a 10-40-40-10 split allows them to deploy most of their resources to those teachers in the tails. For ease of presentation, we label these categories as Highly Effective, Effective, Developing Effectiveness, and Ineffective. Figure 7.3 shows the average standardized VAM score (mean score = 0 with a standard deviation = 1) for teachers in each of the effectiveness categories. Highly Effective teachers had overall CLASS scores that ranged from 4.88 to 5.70, Effective teachers range from 4.30 to 4.87, Developing Effectiveness teachers range from 3.57 to 4.29, and Ineffective teachers range from 1.00 to 3.56.

An ANOVA test for mean VAM score differences across the four groups indicates that this categorization scheme identifies significant differences in VAM between teachers in each of the categories, when compared to the adjacent categories. For example, Highly Effective teachers have better

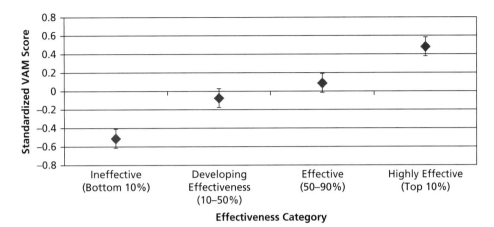

FIGURE 7.3. *Average Standardized Value-Added Score for Teachers in the Four Effectiveness Categories*

achieving students than Effective teachers (and all other groups) do. Indeed, Figure 7.3 suggests that moving from one category of effectiveness to the next appears to have a roughly similar impact on VAM. Based on this information, Greenwood might conclude that they have hit upon a good categorization scheme. However, in order to truly know whether this is the case, further investigation is necessary.

To check whether the pattern of means was an artifact of the particular categorization scheme chosen, we examined the mean standardized VAM score differences we would observe under alternative categorizations. Table 7.2 shows the results for these different categorizations. In the 10-40-40-10 split described above, the largest mean VAM score difference for adjacent categories was between teachers in the Ineffective group (CLASS score below the 10th percentile) and Developing Effectiveness (CLASS score between the 10th and 40th percentiles) groups, which were separated by about one-half of a standard deviation difference in VAM scores. In a different categorization, in which the top and bottom capture 15 percent each, as opposed to 10 percent each, the largest mean differences were between the Highly Effective group and the Effective group, which had more than half of a standard deviation mean difference. When we boost the top and bottom categories to 20 percent each, the largest mean difference is similarly between the Highly Effective group and the Effective group, which was about half of a standard deviation.

TABLE 7.2. **Standardized Value-Added Score for Each Category Across the Categorization Schemes**

Categories (percentiles)	Ineffective	Developing Effectiveness	Effective	Highly Effective
10-40-40-10	−0.52	−0.07	0.09	0.48
15-35-35-15	−0.31	−0.03	0.01	0.56
20-30-30-20	−0.16	−0.04	0.02	0.55
25-25-25-25	−0.10	−0.02	0.05	0.43

Finally, we examined a categorization whereby the percentage of teachers in each category was equivalent, finding that the largest mean difference was 0.38 SD between the Highly Effective group and the Effective group. In all cases, it appeared that the gains in VAM from increases in CLASS scores were largely attributable to teachers in the upper and lower groups, although, as the extreme groups were expanded to include more teachers, the strength of the association between CLASS scores and VAM decreased. It is the responsibility of the individual district to determine whether or not this pattern is true in their case.

PD Implication Using the distribution of CLASS scores in the MET sample as a guide for the creation of effectiveness categories, we found that a categorization strategy to identify teachers based on whether their CLASS scores were in the bottom 10 percent, next 40 percent, the following 40 percent, or the top 10 percent did the best job of maximizing VAM differences. The greatest VAM differences were found between teachers in the bottom 10 percent and next 40 percent categories. The next-largest VAM differences were found between teachers in the upper 40 percent and the top 10 percent categories. Thus, in order to get the largest impact for their PD investment, Greenwood might heavily target those teachers at the very bottom of the CLASS score distribution, as well as those teachers near the middle and top of the Effectiveness category (i.e., teachers with CLASS scores between the 70th and 90th percentiles). This analysis indicates that the labeling of teachers' effectiveness changes under different percentile-based schemes for classification, with each set of percentile cutoffs having different implications for varying courses of action. We encourage districts to carefully investigate the conclusions they might draw from using different categorization schemes, ideally with observation and VAM data collected on the teachers for whom these categorization schemes will impact.

Strategy 4: Look for CLASS Score Thresholds or Breakpoints

The final strategy looks for natural thresholds at which associations between CLASS scores and VAM show marked changes. Of particular interest are thresholds at which there are dramatic increases in VAM once a particular CLASS score is attained. These "active ranges" are important because potentially large achievement gains can be had by improving the instruction of teachers with CLASS scores adjacent to the threshold point. Given the pressure Greenwood is under to improve student achievement, the district is interested in providing PD to teachers for whom they are most likely to see achievement benefits. The threshold approach is therefore appealing because it may optimize those decisions based on actual associations between CLASS and VAM.

The statistical technique we use to identify a threshold is spline regression, which estimates the association between CLASS scores and VAM within different ranges of CLASS scores to find points along the CLASS score distribution at which the VAM differences between teachers above the threshold and teachers below the threshold is greatest. For example, if a district were interested in locating thresholds at the lower and upper end of the CLASS score distribution, an analyst might initially focus on CLASS scores around the 10th percentile mark (CLASS score of 3.56 in the MET) and separately around the 90th percentile mark (CLASS score of 4.88 in the MET). Whatever the starting point, it is important to maintain a decent-sized sample of teachers in the "higher quality" (or post-threshold) group. As shown in Figure 7.4, an active range was observed when MET teachers' average CLASS scores rose above 4.5.

Quality (as defined by the overall CLASS score) predicted achievement more strongly in classrooms in which the measured instructional quality was above 4.5, relative to those classrooms in which the CLASS score was below 4.5 (Higher: slope = 6.97, d [effect size] = 0.29; Lower: slope = 1.78, d = 0.04). This indicates that quality of instruction predicted achievement

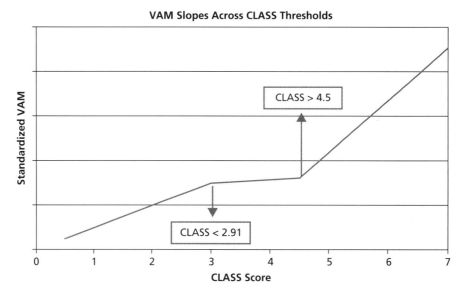

FIGURE 7.4. *Regression Slope for the Association Between CLASS Scores and VAM at the Upper and Lower CLASS Thresholds*

only in classrooms described as showing moderate-to-good classroom interactions (CLASS score > 4.5). We also investigated whether a point at the lower end of the CLASS scale provided a similar threshold at which VAM differences between those above and below the point were maximized. An active range was also observed at the lower end of the CLASS score range, between a CLASS score of 1 and 2.91 (see Figure 7.4). In this lower active range, the linear association between CLASS scores and VAM (d = 0.26) was nearly as strong as the CLASS-VAM association in the upper active range (CLASS score > 4.50). CLASS scores between 2.91 and 4.5 did not significantly predict increases in VAM (d = 0.03). These findings suggest that the association between quality and student achievement is at least in part nonlinear in the MET data. That is, CLASS scores and VAM do not rise in tandem at a constant rate across the CLASS score distribution. Thus, a simple linear approach (Strategy 1) can be misleading.

PD Implication Supposing that district leaders want to focus on those teachers for whom PD might produce the most VAM gains, the threshold analysis would point them toward honing in on those teachers below a 3 (2.91) and those teachers in the 5 and above range. Any movement at the bottom is beneficial for obvious reasons. At the same time, an explicit PD focus on those teachers who are just outside the upper active range (i.e., teachers with a CLASS score of 4) may lead to appreciable gains in VAM. A teacher with a CLASS score of 3 is the furthest away from the active range and would likely need to be given more time and PD resources than a teacher with a CLASS score of 4. Combining PD with incentives might lead a district to slightly revise these recommendations. Districts like Greenwood could choose to reward top teachers for increasing VAM *and* for showing other evidence of high-quality instruction. At the same time, they might focus PD on those teachers below the lower CLASS score threshold (2.91), where incremental improvements in practice can produce substantive VAM gains.

INCREASING INSTRUCTIONAL QUALITY: A CASE STUDY OF MYTEACHINGPARTNER

The previous sections describing the process of using observational data and value-added to inform PD are helpful but do not address the problem of *how* to increase instructional quality. For that, Greenwood and districts like it must identify PD programs that reliably improve teachers' instructional interactions with students. Although there are many PD programs available, in this section we highlight the MyTeachingPartner program (MTP) due to its close association with the CLASS observational measure and its proven effectiveness at improving classroom interactions, along with a host of other educational and behavioral outcomes. In this section, we briefly present the process of MTP and summarize key results from published studies. Most important, we discuss how MTP's positive impacts on increasing teachers' CLASS scores might be relevant for a district such as Greenwood. The MTP model demonstrates how PD can be adjusted to accommodate each district's unique situation, including the decisions they must make about how best to identify the effectiveness of teachers, target PD to the appropriate groups of teachers, and balance the tradeoffs inherent in current accountability frameworks. It is worth noting that MTP recognizes the world of limited resources that districts inhabit. In addition to the resource-heavy full coaching model we describe in the following section, MTP also offers districts access to a library of real-world, high-quality instruction exemplars and web-based templates that prompt teachers to reflect on their own practice in relation to those video exemplars.

MyTeachingPartner (MTP)

MTP targets the quality of teacher-student interactions. The program is designed to guide teachers in creating emotionally positive, motivating, and cognitively challenging classrooms characterized by sensitivity to individual students' socio-emotional and academic needs (Pianta, Mashburn, Downer, Hamre, & Justice, 2008). MTP offers teachers *ongoing, personalized* coaching and feedback aligned with a validated set of observable teacher behaviors that are associated with increases in student achievement. Although MTP was designed using the CLASS as the measure of effective teacher-student interactions, recent iterations have utilized district-specific observation protocols that are cross-walked to the CLASS to yield identifiable and validated targets for MTP coaching. The MTP process includes working through multiple "coaching cycles" throughout the school year, with each cycle consisting of five steps: (1) record, (2) write, (3) respond, (4) conference, and (5) action plan.

In the first step, the teacher submits a video recording of his or her instruction to consultants. In the second step, the consultant examines the video recording and isolates illustrative examples of one or more dimensions of the instructional framework of focus. To accompany these clips, the consultant writes prompts that are intended to reinforce positive aspects of the teacher's instruction that align with the instructional framework. At the same time, the prompts push the teacher to reflect on areas of instruction that he or she might alter to better align with specific dimensions of the framework. In the third step, the teacher views the submitted video clips and answers written prompts to help him or her reflect on how his or her interactions with students do or do not align with the instructional framework. In the fourth step, the consultant meets with the teacher one-on-one (via the phone, computer, or face-to-face) to discuss the feedback and reflections. In the final step of the cycle, the teacher and consultant develop an action plan to build on strengths and address challenges. Specifically, they identify strategies to implement new behaviors that embody a targeted area of the instructional framework in the teacher's upcoming instruction. This process continues throughout the school year, and depending on the particular context, could repeat for five to eight cycles.

Research Findings on MTP

Research evidence suggests that MTP is successful at producing desired changes in student outcomes across grade levels. Early work demonstrated effectiveness in improving preschool program effects on children's school readiness skills (Mashburn, Downer, Hamre, Justice, & Pianta, 2010; Pianta, Mashburn, Downer, Hamre, & Justice, 2008). More recent work has demonstrated efficacy in middle and high school for improving student performance on high-stakes tests (Allen, Pianta, Gregory, Miami, & Lun, 2011) and promoting positive peer interactions (Mikami, Gregory, Allen, Pianta, & Lun, 2011). Recent evaluation work indicates that MTP can be delivered consistently at scale (LoCasale-Crouch, Kraft-Sayre, Pianta, Hamre, Downer, Leach et al., 2011).

More specifically, in a randomized control trial of MTP conducted with seventy-eight middle and high school teachers and over fourteen hundred of their students, teachers who participated in the MTP condition had significantly higher CLASS scores than teachers in the control condition, controlling for the quality of their instruction at the beginning of the year. Critically, end-of-course, standardized state exam scores for students whose teachers were in the MTP condition were higher than were those for students in control classrooms one year after the intervention (Allen, Pianta, Gregory, Mikami, & Lun, 2011). This significant difference equated to an average increase in student achievement from the 50th to the 59th percentile for a student moved from the control condition to the MTP condition. MTP participation was also associated with increases in observed student engagement (Gregory, Allen, Mikami, Hafen, & Pianta, 2014) and more positive peer interactions (Mikami, Gregory, Allen, Pianta, & Lun, 2011). Findings in the three random-assignment outcome studies held for all teachers in the intervention, no matter the racial composition of the classroom, the percentage of classroom students who qualified for free or reduced-priced lunch (an indication of low-income status), and the number of low-achieving students in the classrooms at the start of the year. Given that the findings held across these different classrooms with ethnically and socio-economically diverse groups of students, MTP appears to *promote* all students' achievement, engagement, and prosocial peer relations—regardless of their risk status.

MTP in Greenwood

Returning to Greenwood School District, we walked them through a set of analyses with CLASS scores and VAM from the MET study to illustrate different options for allocating resources to professional development. Greenwood's superintendent recently heard some positive press about the

MTP coaching program and its impacts on teaching and student learning and engagement, which led to the school board's decision to implement the program. Unfortunately, as is the case with most school districts, the superintendent realized that the district did not have the resources to immediately implement MTP with all of their teachers. The issue becomes how to identify the right teachers to target for full MTP coaching. Given their limited resources, Greenwood's board wants to use MTP to obtain the biggest gain in student achievement. Fortunately, the information presented previously in this chapter points to a solution.

The threshold analysis identified two break points at which the association between CLASS scores and student achievement was positive: 2.91 and 4.5. The most "active" ranges (CLASS score values above which the association between observed instruction and achievement were strongest) were below 2.91 and above 4.5, while the range from 2.91 to 4.5 was relatively "inactive." Prior evaluation research on MTP suggests that the impact of receiving MTP coaching is approximately 0.20 CLASS points (Allen, Pianta, Gregory, Miami, & Lun, 2011). This provides the Greenwood's data team with potentially vital information for understanding whom to involve in MTP coaching. Teachers who are very close (e.g., 2.65 to 2.90) to the threshold of 2.91 may not benefit as much as those who are not as close (e.g., below 2.65). Conversely, there is potentially great benefit in moving teachers who are close to the upper threshold (e.g., 4.3 to 4.49) into the active range, as well as working with teachers who are already above the threshold to move them even higher. Does this mean that the teachers in the middle of the distribution (2.65 to 4.3) should be ignored? Of course not, but it does suggest that these teachers may require a mix of high- and low-intensity professional development over a sustained period of time to actually yield the positive impacts the school district is seeking.

MTP is clearly a high-intensity PD program, but a number of lower-intensity and fairly low-cost PD options are available to districts that, if utilized well, could have an impact on classroom instruction. Greenwood wants to employ such PD with teachers in the middle of the "inactive" range of the CLASS score distribution, that is, those teachers who are least likely to see large VAM gains from a single year of MTP coaching (e.g., teachers with CLASS scores between 2.91 to 3.75). The key is to provide other types of lower-cost *ongoing* supports for these teachers in an effort to prime them for coaching. For example, in the MTP studies, teachers receiving coaching also had access to a video library of real-world examples of high-quality instruction. Teachers in the non-active CLASS score range could be given access to such an exemplar library that could be incorporated into other ongoing PD efforts, such as instructional or professional learning communities (or teams). Likewise, the development of massively open online courses (MOOCs) taught by faculty at the nation's top institutions has opened up a new world of possibilities for teachers to gain additional background knowledge on the academic subjects they teach, learn about child and adolescent development, and even take instructional methodology courses that they would otherwise have access to only if they enrolled in a degree- or certificate-granting course from a local university. In contrast to the traditional one-off PD sessions that districts pay big money for, MTP and the lower-intensity PD strategies discussed earlier represent sustained approaches to increasing teachers' knowledge about the subjects they teach, as well as their students' psychological and cognitive development, and expose teachers to diverse and effective instructional methods for improving their own instructional practice.

IMPLICATIONS FOR PRACTICE AND POLICY

School districts face considerable challenges as they seek to incorporate observational measures of instruction into existing teacher evaluation and reward systems. These systems have increasingly relied on student achievement metrics; however, researchers, administrators, and teachers have called for an equal focus on measuring actual instructional quality (see Hill, Kapitula, & Umland, 2011, for an illustrative example of the potential pitfalls of relying solely on VAM metrics). This chapter was written to help those individuals who are struggling to craft comprehensive measures of instructional quality that can inform efforts to deliver appropriate PD and potentially reward highly effective teachers. Given that districts are often asked to create categories describing a teacher's effectiveness, we explored different strategies for the creation of categories using a combination of scores from the CLASS observational measure and VAM. Using data from the MET study, we considered how these different strategies would impact Greenwood school district, a hypothetical school district facing a state mandate to define teacher effectiveness using categories and more tightly integrate PD around these categories.

Strategy 1 estimated the linear association between CLASS and VAM, mostly for illustrative purposes, but did not lead to a viable categorization strategy. Districts might like the idea of creating categories based on, and organizing PD around, the scoring rubric from instructional quality measures like the CLASS (Strategy 2). Evidence from the MET sample indicated that such an approach would only be useful if teachers' CLASS scores were actually distributed across these brackets. The vast majority of MET teachers (98 percent) had CLASS scores that fell into the middle-quality group, and it was thus difficult to devise a PD strategy in such a circumstance.

Creating effectiveness categories based on the distribution of CLASS scores in a district is another viable strategy (Strategy 3), but it requires a more intensive data effort from the district, as they must figure out which breakdown provides the most leverage for detecting differences in VAM. In the MET sample, a 10-40-40-10 categorization scheme provided the most leverage to detect VAM differences. Based on examining the mean VAM differences between groups, it was determined that PD aimed at moving teachers from the bottom 10 percent to the next 40 percent was likely to provide the most gains in VAM. We also presented a more iterative approach to identify break points in the distribution of CLASS scores where associations with VAM change appreciably (Strategy 4). These threshold points help determine an active range, whereby changes in CLASS scores may be more likely to promote changes in VAM. Two such ranges were observed in the MET data. The first was at the bottom of the CLASS score range, between a score of 1 and 3, and the second occurred within the CLASS score range of 5 to 7. We considered a number of PD and incentive strategies that districts could employ once they identify these active ranges.

Doing the heavy data work to identify a categorization scheme that will be useful to a district is a necessary step, but to make a difference, districts must identify PD programs that really work for them and their teachers. We highlighted MyTeachingPartner (MTP), a program focused on offering teachers' *ongoing, personalized* coaching and feedback that is grounded in a common instructional framework. MTP was originally designed to accompany the CLASS framework, although recent iterations have utilized frameworks that are more district-specific. In randomized trials, MTP has proven effective at improving teachers' instructional quality, which has, in turn, produced student achievement gains and more positive student behavior and engagement (Allen, Pianta, Gregory, Mikami, & Lun, 2011; Gregory, Allen, Mikami, Hafen, & Pianta, 2014; Mashburn, Downer, Hamre, Justice, & Pianta, 2010;

Mikami, Gregory, Allen, Pianta, & Lun, 2011; Pianta, Mashburn, Downer, Hamre, & Justice, 2008). An important feature of any high-quality PD program is its ability to accommodate the particular needs and limitations within a district. In this vein, we described ways in which MTP could be tailored to be more or less resource intensive (e.g., face-to-face coaching or video-assisted models) and more or less aligned with a district's instructional framework. We also highlighted the possibility of using other sources of PD, including exemplar video libraries and MOOCs, to provide teachers with opportunities to engage with high-quality, but lower-cost ongoing PD.

CONCLUSION

We acknowledge that school districts are faced with a challenging set of demands in creating comprehensive teacher evaluation systems. Many of the tools needed to meet these demands already exist, including high-quality measures of teachers' instruction, value-added measures of student learning, and professional development programs that teachers engage with on an ongoing basis. While the tools may not exist in a pre-packaged form, a district that is willing to dedicate personnel and time to this critical endeavor can find them. In the end, we hope this chapter can provide guidance to those individuals tasked with creating evaluation systems that are useful to teachers and administrators in the schools and also to the wider community of parents and citizens who want all children to have access to high-quality instruction. Our focus on a specific observational measure and PD program in this chapter is not meant to discount others; we encourage decision-makers to take a full accounting of the various measures and PD options available to them so that they can choose the tools that best work for their districts.

NOTES

1. For year one MET teachers with data on two different class sections, we used only data from the class with the lower section ID number.

2. For example, a focal topic for fifth grade math teachers was adding and subtracting fractions, while a focal topic for seventh to ninth grade ELA teachers was writing about literature.

3. Available student characteristics varied by district but included student demographic information, free or reduced-price lunch status, English language learner (ELL) status, special education status, and gifted student status.

REFERENCES AND ADDITIONAL RESOURCES

Allen, J. P., Gregory, A., Mikami, A. Y., Lun, J., Hamre, B. K., & Pianta, R. C. (2013). Observations of effective teaching in secondary school classrooms: Predicting student achievement with the CLASS-S. *School Psychology Review, 42*, 76–98.

Allen, J. P., Pianta, R. C., Gregory, A., Mikami, A. Y., & Lun, J. (2011). An interaction-based approach to enhancing secondary school instruction and student achievement. *Science, 333* (6045), 1034–1037. doi: 10.1126/science.1207998

Bill & Melinda Gates Foundation. (2010). Learning about teaching: *Initial findings from the Measures of Effective Teaching project.* Retrieved from www.metproject.org/downloads/ Preliminary_Findings-Research_Paper.pdf

Bill & Melinda Gates Foundation. (2013). *Ensuring fair and reliable measures of effective teaching: Culminating findings from the MET project's three-year study.* Retrieved from www.metproject .org/downloads/MET_Ensuring_Fair_and_Reliable_Measures_Practitioner_Brief.pdf

Downer, J. T., Locasale-Crouch, J., Hamre, B., & Pianta, R. (2009). Teacher characteristics associated with responsiveness and exposure to consultation and online professional development resources. *Early Education and Development, 20* (3), 431–455. doi: 10.1080/10409280802688626

Downer, J. T., Pianta, R. C., Fan, X., Hamre, B. K., Mashburn, A., & Justice, L. (2012). Effects of web-mediated teacher professional development on the language and literacy skills of children enrolled in prekindergarten programs. *NHSA Dialog, 14*(4), 189–212.

Gregory, A. Allen, J. P., Mikami, A. Y., Hafen, C. A., & Pianta, R. C. (2014). Effects of a professional development program on behavioral engagement of students in middle and high school, *Psychology in the Schools, 51(2),143–163.*

Hadden, D. S., & Pianta, R. C. (2006). MyTeachingPartner: An innovative model of professional development. *Young Children, 61*(2), 42–43.

Hamre, B. K., Pianta, R. C., Burchinal, M., Field, S., Locasale-Crouch, J. L., Downer, J. T., . . . Scott-Little, C. (2012). A course on effective teacher-child interactions: Effects on teacher beliefs, knowledge, and observed practice. *American Educational Research Journal, 49*(1), 88–123. doi: 10.3102/0002831211434596

Hamre, B. K., Pianta, R. C., Mashburn, A. J., & Downer, J. T. (2007). *Building a science of classrooms: Application of the CLASS framework in over 4,000 US early childhood and elementary classrooms.* New York, NY: Foundation for Child Development. Retrieved from http://fcd-us .org/sites/default/files/BuildingAScienceOfClassroomsPiantaHamre.pdf

Hill, H. C., Kapitula, L., & Umland, K. (2011). A validity argument approach to evaluating teacher value-added scores. *American Educational Research Journal, 48*(3), 794–831. doi: 10.3102/0002831210387916

LoCasale-Crouch, J., Kraft-Sayre, M., Pianta, R. C., Hamre, B. K., Downer, J. T., Leach, A., . . . Scott-Little, C. (2011). Implementing an early childhood professional development course across 10 sites and 15 sections: Lessons learned. *NHSA Dialog: Research-to-Practice Journal for the Early Childhood Field, 14*(4), 275–292. doi: 10.1080/15240754.2011.617527

Mashburn, A. J., Downer, J. T., Hamre, B. K., Justice, L. M., & Pianta, R. C. (2010). Consultation for teachers and children's language and literacy development during pre-kindergarten. *Applied Developmental Science, 14*(4), 179–196. doi: 10.1080/10888691.2010.516187

Mikami, A. Y., Gregory, A., Allen, J. P., Pianta, R. C., & Lun, J. (2011). Effects of a teacher professional development intervention on peer relationships in secondary classrooms. *School Psychology Review, 40*(3), 367–385.

Pianta, R. C., LaParo, K.M., & Hamre, B. K. (2008). *Classroom assessment scoring system.* Baltimore, MD: Brookes Publishing Company.

Pianta, R. C., Mashburn, A. J., Downer, J. T., Hamre, B. K., & Justice, L. (2008). Effects of web-mediated professional development resources on teacher-child interactions in pre-kindergarten classrooms. *Early Childhood Research Quarterly, 23*(4), 431–451. doi: 10.1016/j.ecresq.2008.02.001

Sabol, T. J., Hong, S.L.S., Pianta, R. C., & Burchinal, M. R. (2013). Can rating pre-K programs predict children's learning? *Science, 341*(6148), 845–846. doi: 10.1126/science.1233517

Weisberg, D., Sexton, S., Mulhern, J., & Keeling, D. (2009). The widget effect: Our national failure to acknowledge and act on differences in teacher effectiveness. Brooklyn, NY: New Teacher Project.

CHAPTER

8

Classroom Observation and Value-Added Models Give Complementary Information About Quality of Mathematics Teaching

CANDACE WALKINGTON AND MICHAEL MARDER

ABSTRACT

We developed the UTeach Observation Protocol (UTOP), which provides a systematic way to organize observations about teachers and students in a classroom and provides numerical ratings of classroom quality in multiple dimensions. Through the Measures of Effective Teaching project, we obtained UTOP ratings and comments on 982 videos of grades 4 to 8 mathematics classrooms. We also obtained results for each teacher in the videos from value-added models, which use changes in student test scores to evaluate teachers. We studied the connections between the UTOP ratings and the value-added model ratings. We were surprised by many findings. For example, the particular classroom attributes that lead to the largest student test score gains at sixth

(continued)

Note: We are grateful to the Bill & Melinda Gates Foundation for funding that enabled us to carry out this work. Partial funding for the development and pilot studies of the UTOP were provided by the National Science Foundation through a Noyce Scholarships grant, DUE-0630376. Inclusion of the UTOP in the MET project was organized by the National Math and Science Initiative, in cooperation with Laying the Foundations, partially funded by the Carnegie Corporation. We particularly thank John Winn, Matthew Valerius, and Christy Hovanetz for their assistance. We also thank members of the original UTOP pilot team, including Mary Walker, Larry Abraham, Prerna Arora, Shasta Ihorn, and Jessica Gordon. The opinions expressed in this chapter are the responsibility of the authors and are not necessarily shared by the National Science Foundation, Bill & Melinda Gates Foundation, National Math and Science Initiative, or Carnegie Corporation.

(continued)

grade lead to the lowest test score gains at fifth grade. Our main conclusion is that classroom observation and value-added models supply complementary and separately valuable information on what happens in classrooms. Neither can be used in isolation, nor does averaging the results together retain enough information. In the best classrooms, both observation results and student test-score gains are favorable.

INTRODUCTION

Urgent debates about teaching effectiveness pervade media channels (Gladwell 2008; Meyers, Gamst, & Guarino, 2006), policy documents (Gordon, Kane, & Staiger, 2006), and educational research (Pianta & Hamre, 2009), as we move into an era of high-stakes testing with teacher, student, and school-level accountability measures. Teachers have a considerable impact on student achievement (Heck, 2008; Rivkin, Hanushek, & Kain, 2005; Rowan, Correnti, & Miller, 2002; Sanders & Rivers, 1996; Wright, Horn, & Sanders, 1997); however, the classroom behaviors that contribute to effective teaching have proven surprisingly difficult to measure. Initiatives such as Race to the Top propose to measure teacher quality by making use of value-added models, where teachers are evaluated based on changes in their students' standardized test scores (Rivkin, Hanushek, & Kain, 2005; Sanders & Rivers, 1996). Even the most vigorous advocates of value-added models acknowledge the need for multiple measures of teaching performance, particularly when decisions might lead to financial rewards or dismissal. But there is not yet agreement on what the alternative measures might be.

Many researchers have argued for the use of classroom observations: "Placing validated, standardized observational assessment of teachers' classroom instruction and interactions more squarely in the realm of large-scale education science and in protocols evaluating the impacts of teacher education could have tremendous downstream consequences in terms of traction on questions that vex the field" (Pianta & Hamre, 2009, p. 109). Thus a significant effort is under way to determine the relationship between teacher value-added scores and classroom teaching behaviors measured by observation protocols (Bill & Melinda Gates Foundation, 2012).

We have been associated with UTeach, a program to prepare secondary mathematics and science teachers at UT Austin. Working with other scientists, educational researchers, and master teachers, we developed the UTeach Observation Protocol (UTOP). Following a pilot study in which the UTOP was used to evaluate UTeach graduates (reviewed briefly here), the National Math and Science Initiative enabled us to collaborate with the Measures of Effective Teaching (MET) project (Bill & Melinda Gates Foundation, 2012) and rate a large set of video lessons from the MET database using the UTOP. This collaboration allowed UTOP ratings to be tied to teacher value-added scores on both standardized state assessments and on assessments designed to measure conceptual understanding. The goal of this chapter is to explore the connections we found between observation scores and value-added measures and to explain the conclusions we reached.

PRECONCEPTIONS ABOUT TEACHER QUALITY

From our vantage point within UTeach, preparing mathematics and science majors to become teachers, we came to this study with some preconceptions:

- Teaching quality is not a single number. Excellent pre-service teachers possess many different qualities, some of which are best found from observation, some of which are best found from their writings, and some of which are best found from their performance on examinations.

- When we must make binary decisions (to certify or not certify), we do not use a cutoff on a single continuous metric. In UTeach there are numerous critical checkpoints where sufficiently poor performance bars recommendation for certification.

- The components of pre-service teaching quality can be measured separately and are separately actionable. A pre-service teacher who fails chemistry can retake chemistry. A pre-service teacher who focuses all of her attention during a teaching experience on two loud students at the front of the class can learn from the mistake and involve the whole class the next time.

- Changes in secondary student test scores are neither viable nor necessary for the evaluation of pre-service teachers, since the contact of pre-service teachers with public school students is too infrequent for them plausibly to be held responsible for results on these exams, and the legal context holds the classroom teacher of record accountable.

In the school reform context, by contrast, the preconceptions are different. Teaching quality is defined in terms of changes in student test scores. From the start we perceived a difficulty. In the Measures of Effective Teaching project, "measures" is plural but "effective teaching" is singular. The project name implies that there are many ways to measure, but they are aiming in the end at one thing. Yet, if teacher quality is defined in terms of student achievement, and student achievement is defined as the score coming from value-added models, then, by definition, measurements from value-added models are perfectly correlated with true teacher quality and student achievement. The other measures end up without a compelling technical role, except perhaps to provide diagnostic guidance on how to raise test scores.

We agree that, ultimately, schooling must be judged by its value to students. Even so, we do not grant exclusive status to annual rises on test scores. Some student learning objectives, such as the ability to work with a group or give an oral presentation on a project, are better evaluated during observation than on paper tests. Furthermore, the value of schooling should be judged by the final results at the end of twelfth grade. If critics of "teaching to the test" are right, then there may be teaching practices at one grade that raise the scores that year, but put students at a disadvantage later down the educational line. In this chapter we will discuss specific cases in which this may be happening. For the moment, we simply present the possibility that separate measures have separate value and explain why investigation cannot begin by uncritically privileging one over another.

THE DEVELOPMENT OF THE UTOP

We began to develop the UTOP in 2006 in response to a requirement to evaluate National Science Foundation–funded Noyce Scholars within UTeach. We began by looking for classroom observation protocols that assessed teaching behaviors consistent with the goals and foci of UTeach; not finding any, we decided to modify the Classroom Observation Protocol (COP) (Horizons Research, 2000a, 2000b). We added, subtracted, and modified indicators. The instrument has experienced several revisions, but we refer to them all as the UTeach Observation Protocol (UTOP). The original version of the UTOP contained thirty-two indicators, each rated on a 1 to 5 scale with "Don't Know" and "Not Applicable" options. The indicators were organized into four sections: Classroom Environment, Lesson Structure, Implementation, and Mathematics/

Science Content. Each of the four sections concluded with a 1 to 5 Synthesis Rating, which was intended to capture the observers' overall rating of the teaching behaviors in that section, without necessarily being a numerical average. For example, if the teacher spent the class period communicating incorrect content, the synthesis rating could be rated to reflect this more strongly than a numerical average of the ratings in the Content section would permit. The protocol also included an extended post-observation teacher interview, which posed a variety of questions about the context and events of the lesson. For the current, full version of the UTOP, visit http://uteach.utexas.edu/UTOP.

We initially tested the UTOP in a pilot study in which we conducted observations in the classrooms of UTeach alumni. In order to provide a comparison group for our graduates, efforts were made to find teachers from other preparation backgrounds working in the same schools, teaching similar classes in their content areas. Thirty-six teachers were observed (twenty-one UTeach alumni and fifteen from other preparation backgrounds) over five semesters, with a total of eighty-three observations. Seven of the UTeach alumni had received Noyce Scholarships and thus might be considered to represent the top tier of UTeach students in terms of academic qualifications and commitment to teach. All teachers had fewer than five years of teaching experience, and most were in their first or second year of teaching. Two raters, one with a background in mathematics and one with a background in science, were present at most observations.[1]

The results of this comparative study showed promise for the UTOP's ability to differentiate between teachers from different preparation backgrounds. Figure 8.1a shows the average scores in each of the four UTOP sections for UTeach graduates who were Noyce Scholars (green), UTeach graduates who were not Noyce Scholars (blue), and graduates of other teacher preparation pathways (red). Noyce Scholars scored highest on the UTOP, with UTeach non-Noyce in the middle, and non-UTeach at the bottom. Figure 8.1b shows how the scores of the three groups of teachers varied as a function of years of teaching experience. A conclusion suggested by the data is that the difference between Noyce Scholars and other new teachers is most evident in the first year and that UTeach alumni overall stand out more because of their growth over the first three years of teaching than because of their teaching practices at the outset. We note that, despite attempts to keep observers from knowing the background of the teachers they watched, attempts at blinding were not uniformly successful, and this may have biased the scores.

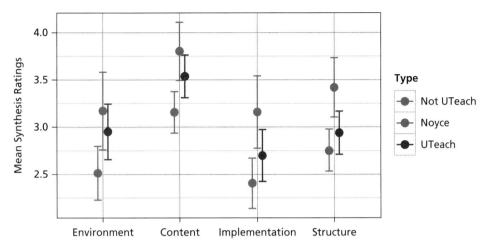

FIGURE 8.1a. *Mean Synthesis Ratings for UTeach Graduates Who Receive Noyce Scholarships (N = 7), UTeach Graduates Who Do Not (N = 14), and Non-UTeach Graduates (N = 15)*

Note: Error bars are determined from the standard uncertainties produced by lmer function (Bates & Maechler, 2010) in the R software package, specifying teacher identity as a random effect.

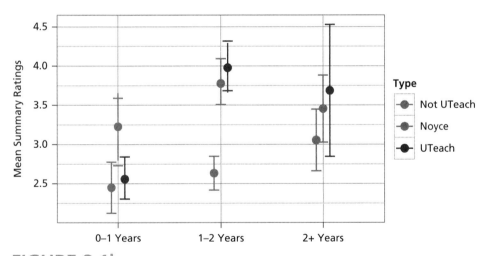

FIGURE 8.1b. *Mean Synthesis Ratings for Non-UTeach, UTeach (Not Noyce), and UTeach Noyce Scholars as a Function of Number of Years of Classroom Teaching Experience*

Note: Standard errors are again produced by the R function lmer using teacher identity as a random effect. The small sample size of this pilot study means that no significant differences between teachers with more than two years of experience can be determined. Significant effects include the growth of non-Noyce UTeach graduates between their first and second years, and the difference between UTeach and non-UTeach graduates with one or two years of teaching experience.

While our pilot study showed promise in establishing the reliability and validity of the UTOP, there were several shortcomings. First, the sample size was too small to establish many statistically significant results. Second, the observers in this study were from a small, university-based research team rather than from the general population of observers who might be interested in using the UTOP, so their reliability might have been higher than could realistically be obtained in other contexts. Third, the sample was composed of a relatively small collection of volunteers who offered informed consent, making it unclear how well the results could be generalized. Fourth, there was no information available on the value-added gains of the teachers involved in the study, making it impossible to draw any links with test-based measures of student achievement. We were fortunate to be able to overcome several of these limitations when the UTOP was adopted for use with the MET project.

We made several modifications to the UTOP when we partnered with MET after this pilot study was conducted. First, we reduced the number of indicators from thirty-two to twenty-two, because there were indicators that could not be well-captured in a video context without access to a teacher interview. Second, we created detailed scoring rubrics that supplied guidelines for 1 to 5 ratings on each indicator and removed many of the "Don't Know" and "Not Applicable" options. Third, using the data from our pilot study, we wrote sample vignettes of supporting evidence that could be used to justify 1 to 5 ratings on each indicator. A group of ninety-nine teachers assembled by the National Math and Science Initiative and Laying the Foundation used this modified instrument to rate 982 videotaped mathematics lessons from the MET project database.

THE UTOP IN THE MET PROJECT

Research Questions

In 2009, with assistance from the National Math and Science Initiative, we were given the opportunity to rate a subset of the MET project's classroom videos—1,001 videos of classrooms in grades 4 through 8 mathematics—using the UTOP. In this section, we briefly discuss some of the key findings relating to the UTOP that were found in MET's report on the classroom observation instruments (Bill & Melinda Gates Foundation, 2012). After the MET study released reports on the relationship between observation and value-added scores for teachers from the study, we were provided access to the MET data set and performed additional analyses of the same data.

We found ourselves with a number of questions:

1. The Gates Foundation study showed (Figure 3) that teachers with the best UTOP scores obtained higher value-added scores than did teachers who scored highly on other observation instruments in the MET study. Thus, the UTOP seemed particularly equipped to identify the strongest teachers. Furthermore, value-added scores plotted versus UTOP scores were fairly flat (did not have a positive slope) for low to medium UTOP scores; the rise was at the top end of UTOP scores. Put another way, high UTOP scores seemed to be associated with high value-added scores, but the UTOP did not discriminate well among teachers with low to medium value-added scores. Finally, the MET report provided no estimate of measurement uncertainty (error) of the value-added scores, making it difficult to determine whether apparent differences for different UTOP levels were statistically significant. We decided to investigate these points.

2. The UTOP measures twenty-two different aspects of classroom behavior, but in the MET report none of these individual behaviors was compared to teacher value-added gains. The report only compared a summary UTOP rating to teacher value-added scores. We wondered whether any of these twenty-two behaviors stood out in connection with raising student test scores. If so, we might be able to use this information to help teachers improve.

3. Overall, the connections between value-added model scores and observation scores were fairly weak for the UTOP, as well as for the other observation instruments. There were many cases where value-added scores and observation scores were not in agreement. We sought a way to consider results from the UTOP and value-added models on an equal footing and to examine carefully lessons where these two measures agreed or disagreed.

While our investigation proceeded essentially as planned, we modified our questions as analysis proceeded. Most important, we found that results from different grade levels were substantially different from one another, and it often seemed best to disaggregate by grade before performing other analyses. We settled on the following sharpened research questions:

R1. What is the relationship between value-added gains of teachers involved in the MET study and UTOP observation scores for these same teachers, for teachers with different levels of UTOP scores? In particular, how do the relationships between value-added models and UTOP scores change as one focuses on subgroups of teachers who have different levels of observation or value-added scores?

R2. What is the relationship between value-added gains of teachers involved in the MET study and UTOP scores for these same teachers on the twenty-two individual UTOP indicators? In particular, how do the results depend on grade level taught (4 through 8)?

R3. Using a subset of teaching behaviors from the UTOP that we present as a minimal or "consensus view" of effective teaching, what is the level of consistency between value-added measures of teaching effectiveness from teachers in the MET sample and UTOP classroom observation measures from these same teachers? What are the characteristics of classrooms in which these measures strongly agree or strongly conflict?

Rating Method

Over the course of seven weeks, ninety-nine raters scored 1,001 videos of grades 4 through 8 mathematics lessons from the MET video library using the UTOP. Of the ninety-nine raters, forty-one had backgrounds in science and fifty-eight were from mathematics backgrounds. These raters were highly qualified master teachers; the average rater had nineteen years of teaching experience, and over half held master's degrees or higher. For more information on rater background characteristics, see the Gates Foundation study. All ratings were entered into an online version of the UTOP on SurveyMonkey.

The raters were trained through a process whereby they first watched and rated videos from the MET database in large and small groups and discussed their ratings with other raters and UTOP developers. The raters were introduced to the scoring rubrics for each UTOP indicator, as well as the example vignettes of supporting evidence for each indicator. Trainees would later be given the standard "normed" UTOP ratings for each video, with supporting evidence cited for each rating. This training process lasted for a little under two days, at which point the raters were considered ready to rate on their own. However, one-third of the videos they rated would be double-scored, and they would have to discuss their ratings with the other rater who rated the same video after their original scores were entered. The two raters were asked to come to agreement on all indicator and synthesis ratings and record them. Of the 1,001 videos, 331 were double-scored, and ten were triple-scored. For the analyses presented here, if a lesson had two or three raters, we use the UTOP scores they agreed on after discussion. If a lesson only had one rater, we use this rater's UTOP scores. There were eight cases where two raters scored a lesson but did not subsequently discuss their ratings. In these cases, we use the average of the two raters' scores.

Video Version of UTOP

The version of the UTOP used in the MET study contained twenty-two indicators, shown in Table 8.1 below. See the Gates Foundation (2012) study for descriptive statistics on how teachers in the sample scored across these twenty-two indicators. The short descriptions of the indicators are used in all figures in this chapter.

As can be seen from Table 8.1, for some of our analyses we found it useful to conceptually group different indicators. We selected a subset of nine indicators from the UTOP that plausibly represent a consensus view of acceptable teaching (right-most column in Table 8.1). That is, even if it is not taken as settled whether inquiry or direct instruction is to be preferred, it would be difficult to find anyone to defend poor performance on these particular indicators. For example, it would be hard to defend a lesson where much of the class is not paying attention or one where the teacher makes mathematical errors during an explanation. What we call the "consensus score" for a lesson is the average of these nine UTOP indicators. We also selected six indicators that represent UTeach faculty values but are not universally accepted as necessary components of effective teaching and labeled them "innovative." These are teaching behaviors that are commonly encouraged by mathematics educators, but not universally accepted.

Sample of Video Lessons

The original sample was 1,001 video lessons; however, six were excluded because of severe audio or video problems or because the video did not show a mathematics lesson. An additional thirteen videos were omitted because they did not have corresponding value-added data, for a final video count of 982. The grade levels of the 982 video mathematics lessons are shown in Table 8.2. The 982 lessons were from the classrooms of 249 teachers. Two hundred and thirty-seven teachers had four videos of their classroom scored with the UTOP, while ten teachers had three lessons scored and two teachers had two lessons scored. Video lessons typically lasted between fifty minutes

TABLE 8.1. List of UTOP Indicators Used in MET Video Ratings

Indicator	Short Description	Indicator Group
Section 1: Classroom Environment Synthesis	**Environment Synthesis**	**Synthesis**
1.1. The classroom environment encouraged students to generate ideas, questions, conjectures, and/or propositions that reflected engagement or exploration with important mathematics concepts.	Ideas	Innovative
1.2. Interactions reflected collegial working relationships among students.	Interactions	–
1.3. Based on conversations, interactions with the teacher, and/or work samples, students were intellectually engaged with important ideas relevant to the focus of the lesson.	Engagement	–
1.4. The majority of students were on task throughout the class.	On Task	Consensus
1.5. The teacher's classroom management strategies enhanced the classroom environment.	Management	Consensus
1.6. The classroom environment established by the teacher reflected attention to issues of access, equity, and diversity for students (e.g., cooperative learning, language-appropriate strategies and materials).	Equity	Consensus
Section 2: Lesson Structure Synthesis	**Lesson Synthesis**	**Synthesis**
2.1. The lesson was well organized and structured.	Organized	Consensus
2.2. The lesson allowed students to engage with or explore important concepts in mathematics (instead of focusing on techniques that may only be useful in exams).	Important	Consensus

2.3. The lesson included an investigative or problem-based approach to important concepts in mathematics.	Inquiry	Innovative
2.4. The teacher obtained and employed resources appropriate for the lesson.	Resources	Consensus
2.5. The teacher was critical and reflective about his/her practice after the lesson, recognizing the strengths and weaknesses of the instruction.	Reflection	—
Section 3: Implementation Synthesis	**Implementation Synthesis**	**Synthesis**
3.1. The teacher's questioning strategies developed student conceptual understanding of important mathematics content.	Questioning	Innovative
3.2. The teacher used formative assessment effectively to be aware of the progress of all students.	Assessment	—
3.3. The teacher involved all students in the lesson.	Involvement	Consensus
3.4. An appropriate amount of time was devoted to each part of the lesson.	Timing	—
Section 4: Mathematics Content Synthesis	**Content Synthesis**	**Synthesis**
4.1. The mathematics content chosen was significant and worthwhile for this course.	Worthwhile	Consensus
4.2. During the observation, it was made explicit to students why the content is important to learn.	Explicit	Innovative

(continued)

(*Table 8.1 continued*)

Indicator	Short Description	Indicator Group
4.3. Content communicated through direct and non-direct instruction by the teacher is consistent with deep knowledge and fluency with the mathematics concepts of the lesson.	Fluent	Consensus
4.5. Teacher written content information was accurate.	Correct	–
4.6. Elements of mathematical abstraction were used appropriately in the lesson.	Abstraction	–
4.7. Appropriate connections were made to other areas of mathematics or to other disciplines.	Connections	Innovative
4.8. During the lesson, there was discussion about the content topic's role in history or current events.	Society	Innovative
Summary: Mean of four synthesis indicators	Summary	
Consensus: Mean of nine consensus indicators	Consensus	
Innovation: Mean of six innovative indicators	Innovative	

Note: Consensus indicators are intended to be a subset that almost all reasonable observers would consider an essential component of effective teaching; 4.4 was omitted only because it was so frequently indicated as "NA" when written materials were not visible. Innovative indicators are those that reflect qualities of classrooms valued within UTeach but not necessarily shared by all observers.

TABLE 8.2. **Grade Level of 982 Video Lessons Scored on UTOP**

Grade Level	Number of Videos	Number of Class Sections	Number of Teachers
Grade 4	189	55	48
Grade 5	211	58	52
Grade 6	200	103	52
Grade 7	209	104	52
Grade 8	173	89	45

and one hour, and all covered elementary or middle grades mathematics content. Teachers were volunteer participants from six school districts in six different states; for more demographic characteristics of the teachers see Bill & Melinda Gates Foundation (2012).

The 249 teachers in the sample taught a total of 409 class sections (i.e., consistent groups of students in a contained mathematics class); eighty-nine teachers were filmed teaching only one class section, while 160 teachers were filmed teaching two class sections. For a given class section, teachers were filmed from one to four times: specifically, twelve class sections were filmed once, 305 were filmed twice, eight were filmed three times, and eighty-four were filmed four times. Each of these class sections corresponded to one set of value-added scores. We aggregated the scores from different UTOP observations of the same class section in three different ways, recording for each UTOP indicator the maximum, the minimum, and the average. In what follows, we have settled on use of the average, although it is not hard to construct arguments that for some indicators teachers should be accountable for the worst behavior that is seen, while for others they should receive credit for the best. We also aggregated all comments of all raters of all videos for each class section for use in our qualitative analysis.

Descriptive Statistics of UTOP and Value-Added Models

We computed averages (Table 8.3) and examined a variety of statistical models for UTOP indicators and value-added scores (Table 8.4). The value-added variables used in the analyses were either teacher value-added gains on state

TABLE 8.3.   **UTOP Summary Rating and Average Value-Added Gains for Lessons in Grades 4 Through 8**

Grade Level	Avg. UTOP Summary (St. Dev)	Avg. BAM 2010 (St. Dev)	Avg. State VAM 2009 (St. Dev)	Avg. State VAM 2010 (St. Dev)
Grade 4	2.75 (0.671)	−0.036 (0.207)	0.029 (0.205)	0.002 (0.178)
Grade 5	2.76 (0.658)	0.065 (0.195)	0.009 (0.222)	0.023 (0.205)
Grade 6	2.51 (0.721)	−0.008 (0.274)	−0.008 (0.200)	−0.002 (0.253)
Grade 7	2.39 (0.649)	0.010 (0.292)	0.022 (0.113)	0.0003 (0.156)
Grade 8	2.33 (0.662)	−0.007 (0.231)	0.037 (0.165)	0.015 (0.170)

TABLE 8.4.   **Simple Regression Models of UTOP**

Group	Coefficient	Standard Error
White	0.59	0.09
Gifted	0.41	0.15
Black	−0.29	0.09
Hispanic	−0.38	0.09
Low Income	−0.43	0.10

Note: Summary scores as a function of student demographic variables, all of which are fractions in the range [0,1]. The coefficients are slopes describing variation of the UTOP Summary across all grades as a function of the fraction of White, Gifted, Black, Hispanic, and Low-Income (eligible for free or reduced lunch) students in class.

standardized tests in 2009 (the year before the video observations; State VAM 2009), in 2010 (the year of the video observations; State VAM 2010), or the teacher's value-added gains on the Balanced Assessment of Mathematics in 2010 (BAM 2010).

TABLE 8.5. **Numbers of Classes Observed, by District and Grade Level**

District/Grade	4	5	6	7	8
1	0	0	26	32	30
2	10	10	8	0	0
3	8	12	0	0	0
4	17	16	32	28	10
5	10	10	17	20	19
6	10	10	20	24	30

Note: There is no grade for which all districts participated. There are three districts for which all grades were observed.

The most important observations are[2]

1. The average UTOP scores in the MET sample are substantially lower than the scores observed in the UTOP pilot study (Figure 8.1b). UTeach graduates with one to two years of experience in the pilot study had overall UTOP scores near 4, while typical UTOP scores in the MET sample are near 2.5, and drop going from elementary to middle school.

2. We found dependence of the UTOP scores on a fraction of minority students and a fraction of low-income students in the classroom; quality in the classroom went down as the fraction of minority students and low-income students went up. This is not true for any of the VAM scores, since the value-added models control for these demographic variables.

Both these results are disquieting. What sorts of lessons does one learn from the sample of MET teachers if, on average, they have so much room to improve? If observation scores systematically depend on the concentration of student poverty, are observation scores fair? Should one systematically compensate?

Table 8.5 displays the distribution of observations organized by district and grade level. There are three districts for which several grade levels were not sampled at all. Upon seeing these results we were initially concerned, since as we will show, there are strong dependencies upon grade level. The very inhomogeneous relation between district and grade level raised the possibility that the apparent dependence upon grade level was in fact a dependence upon district. To examine this scenario, we repeated analyses by restricting ourselves to Districts 4, 5, and 6, for which all available grades are sampled fairly evenly. The results were unchanged, except that the margins of error increased due to decreased sample size. A particular example is discussed in the caption to Figure 8.7. We do not otherwise mention this point further.

RESULTS

We now investigate each of the three research questions in turn. First, we examine the overall relationship between UTOP observation scores and teacher value-added gains for teachers in the MET sample, examining the possibility of nonlinear relationships between the two measures. Second, we look at the relationship between UTOP scores on individual indicators and teacher value-added gains. And finally, we investigate both quantitatively and qualitatively the cases in which observation scores and value-added models agree and disagree.

Overall Relationships between UTOP Scores and Value-Added Method Scores

Our first research question addressed the relationship between value-added scores from teachers in the MET sample and UTOP scores from rating video lessons of these same teachers. We began this analysis by examining a relationship featured in the research paper from the second-year MET report, which displayed average value-added score as a function of teacher observation score ranked by percentile (the upper-right panel of Figure 3 in the Gates Foundation study [2012]). We were struck by the fact that, for the best teachers, the UTOP was associated with higher gains on BAM 2010 than other observation instruments, a gain in valued-added score of around 0.11. Note that for all its value-added models, the MET project proposes that a gain of 0.25 corresponds approximately to a gain of nine months of schooling.

To check this result, we first divided the 409 class sections into ten groups (deciles), based on the Summary rating for that class section, and plotted UTOP Summary decile versus BAM 2010. We also made similar plots for each of the four UTOP Synthesis ratings separately, and for the Consensus and the Innovative indicator groups. We followed the plots with statistical analyses that examined whether different linear slopes and intercepts would be appropriate for different regions of these plots—whether the relationship between UTOP and value added would be significantly different depending on whether UTOP scores were relatively high or relatively low. We tested for this difference by fitting linear models with grade level, UTOP score, UTOP scoring region, and the interaction of UTOP score and UTOP scoring region as predictors of value-added gains. UTOP scoring regions were obtained by dividing normalized UTOP scores into regions using a variety of intervals—including deciles, quantiles, thirds, and halves.

Figure 8.2a shows the results of dividing teachers into deciles according to the UTOP Summary score and plotting the average BAM 2010 value-added score for each decile. We find the same difference shown in the MET report between top and bottom teachers, and a relatively clear positive relationship between BAM value-added score and UTOP Summary score for teachers in the 7th to 10th decile of UTOP scores. However, the relationship between UTOP Summary score and BAM value-added score is not particularly smooth, and standard errors on the order of 0.05 limit the number of cases in which difference between teachers in different deciles could be called significant. Figure 8.2b shows the same relationship, but restricted to sixth grade, where we find that the correlation between UTOP and BAM value-added is the strongest. Indeed, now the difference between lowest- and highest-ranked teachers is 0.3, or "eleven months of schooling." For fifth grade, as shown in Figure 8.2c, value-added scores, if anything, decrease as UTOP scores increase, but none of the differences are significant. We tested whether we could use statistical models to fit different slopes to different regions of the graph in Figure 8.2a—perhaps allowing for a flatter slope for the first two-thirds of the UTOP deciles and a steeper slope for the final one-third. However, the uncertainties were too high to permit us to detect any significant differences of this kind.

We next proceeded to examine the various UTOP composite and Synthesis ratings in the same manner. Figure 8.3 shows BAM 2010 value-added scores versus the Consensus, Summary, and Innovation groupings of UTOP indicators. The strongest correlation with BAM value-added scores arises for the Consensus indicator that focuses on competence in routine classroom practices, and the weakest correlation arises for the indicators we

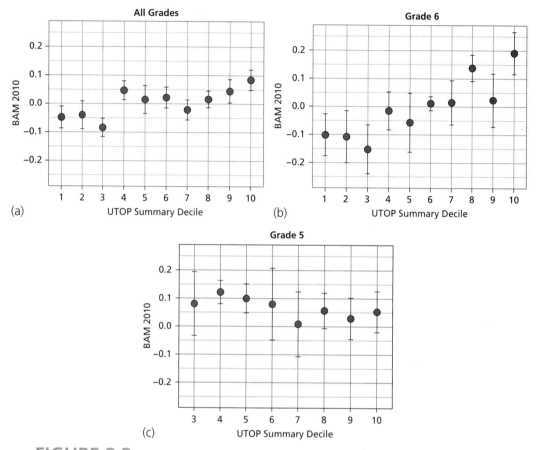

FIGURE 8.2. *Average BAM Value-Added Score versus Decile Ranking on UTOP Average Summary Indicator (a) All Grades, (b) Sixth Grade Only, (c) Fifth Grade Only*

associated with innovative teaching practices. One reason that the Innovation indicator leads to such inconclusive results becomes more apparent from Figure 8.4, which inverts the axes and plots mean UTOP composite scores versus BAM decile. What now is obvious is that the overall scores on the Innovation indicator are extremely low. One cannot expect to learn how these supposedly innovative practices affect value-added scores unless one has a reasonable sample of teachers performing them well.

Figure 8.5 shows BAM 2010 value-added as a function of UTOP scoring quantile on the four Synthesis ratings. The Classroom Environment and Lesson Structure Synthesis ratings show a somewhat steady growth of

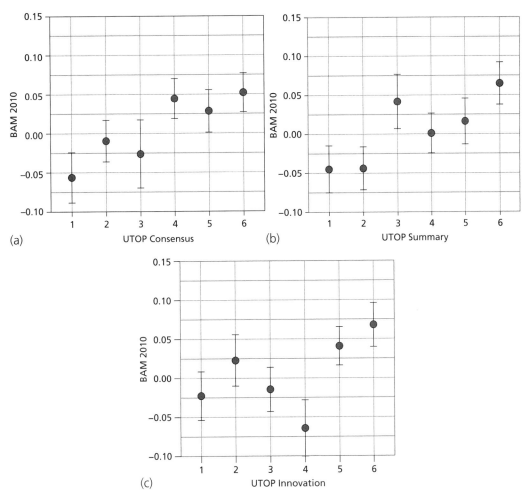

FIGURE 8.3. *Average BAM 2010 Value-Added Score versus Quartile Ranking on UTOP (a) Consensus, (b) Summary, and (c) Innovation Indicators*

value-added score with UTOP score. Attempts using statistical models to fit different slopes to different regions of the graphs for Synthesis, Consensus, and Innovative ratings were not successful.

We conclude that the teachers with the highest UTOP scores do indeed have higher value-added scores than those with the lowest. However, the measurement uncertainties are large, and attempts to identify a pattern in how value-added scores depend on UTOP scores were not successful.

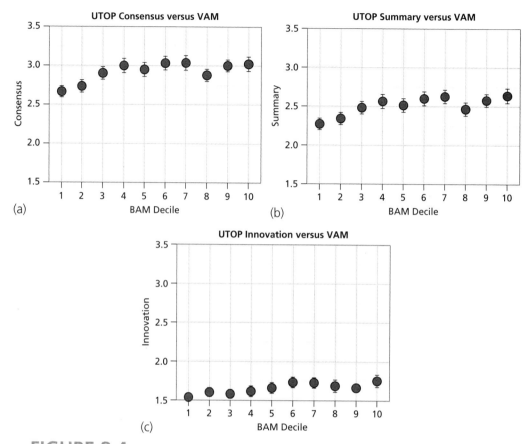

FIGURE 8.4. *Average UTOP (a) Consensus, (b) Summary, and (c) Innovation Scores versus BAM Value-Added Score Decile Rankings*

Correlation between UTOP Indicators and Value-Added Scores

Our second research question concerned the relationship between value-added gains and scores on different individual UTOP indicators. We wanted to know whether particular teaching behaviors or classroom characteristics were associated with improved student test scores.[3] Table 8.6 displays coefficients showing all the cases in which improvement of a particular UTOP indicator was associated with a statistically significant increase in value-added model score. Figure 8.6 shows the same data for BAM value-added only, in graphical form.[4]

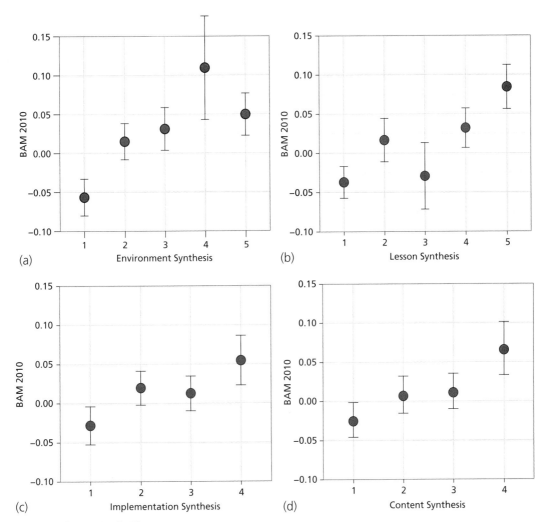

FIGURE 8.5. *BAM Value-Added Score versus Ranking on UTOP Synthesis Ratings, (a) Environment, (b) Lesson Structure, (c) Implementation, and (d) Content*

Note: The use of four or five groups results from attempting to group into quintiles with the R function cut2.

Table 8.6 highlights those indicators that achieved the highest level of statistical significance for all three value-added measures. Three of these indicators (On Task, Management, Classroom Environment Synthesis) describe orderly, supportive, well-managed classrooms. The fourth (Important) specifically examines whether a classroom session focuses on test preparation or on

TABLE 8.6. **Tabulation of All Significant Correlations between Individual UTOP Indicators/Synthesis Ratings and Value-Added Scores from the Balanced Assessment of Mathematics (BAM) and 2010 and 2009 State Mathematics Exams**

UTOP Indicator	BAM 2010	State VAM 2010	State VAM 2009
1.1. Ideas	NS	.0467 (.0138)***	.0432 (.0126)*
1.2. Interactions	.0427 (.0140)**	.0361 (.0113)**	.0410 (.0100)***
1.3. Engagement	NS	.0398 (.0138)**	.0335 (.0126)**
1.4. On Task	.0473 (.0141)***	.0563 (.0106)***	.0477 (.0096)***
1.5. Management	.0476 (.0136)***	.0562 (.0103)***	.0468 (.0093)***
1.7. Equity	.0442 (.0189)*	.0414 (.0144)**	.0527 (.0129)***
2.1. Organized	.0393 (.0183)*	.0492 (.0139)***	.0427 (.0126)***
2.2. Important	.0638 (.0166)***	.0438 (.0128)***	.0452 (.0115)***
2.3. Inquiry	.0545 (.0218)*	.0334 (.0168)*	.0398 (.0151)**
2.4. Resources	NS	NS	.00588 (.00150)***
2.5. Reflection	NS	NS	NS
3.1. Questioning	NS	.0403 (.0141)**	NS
3.2. Assessment	NS	.0352 (.0157)*	.0365 (.0142)*
3.3. Involvement	NS	.0402 (.0123)**	.0412 (.0113)***
3.4. Timing	NS	.0509 (.0138)***	.0368 (.0126)**
4.1. Worthwhile	.0464 (.0219)*	.0434 (.0168)*	.0440 (.0153)**
4.2. Explicit	NS	.0437 (.0161)**	.0431 (.0145)**

UTOP Indicator	BAM 2010	State VAM 2010	State VAM 2009
4.3. Fluent	NS	.0439 (.0149)**	.0505 (.0134)***
4.4. Correct	NS	NS	NS
4.5. Abstraction	NS	NS	.0316 (.0123)*
4.6. Connections	.0468 (.0196)*	.0554 (.0149)***	.0440 (.0136)*
4.7. Society	NS	NS	.0663 (.0232)**
Section 1: Classroom Environment Synthesis	**.0622 (.0183)***	**.0618 (.0139)***	**.0521 (.0127)***
Section 2: Lesson Structure Synthesis	**.0595 (.0198)**	**.0612 (.0151)***	**.0559 (.0137)***
Section 3: Implementation Synthesis	**NS**	**.0671 (.0156)***	**.0543 (.0142)***
Section 4: Mathematics Content Synthesis	**.0552 (.0232)***	**.0565 (.0177)**	**NS**

Note: Each column shows the significant regression slope coefficients, while parentheses show the uncertainty in the slope estimate. The asterisks indicate the level of significance (* = $p < .05$, ** = $p < .01$, *** = $p < .001$). NS means "Not Significant." Entries shaded showed the highest level of statistical significance for all three value-added models.

important mathematical ideas. Thus, if we have to say, in general, independent of grade level, what features of classroom performance to focus on in the hopes of raising test scores, these are the ones.

Most of the UTOP indicators have a significant and positive relationship with value-added scores on the 2009 and 2010 state assessment. The value-added scores derived from state tests seem to emphasize procedural skill somewhat more than the scores from BAM do. For example, value-added scores have a significant relationship with Inquiry in the BAM results, but not for the state tests, while Timing shows significant correlation for the state

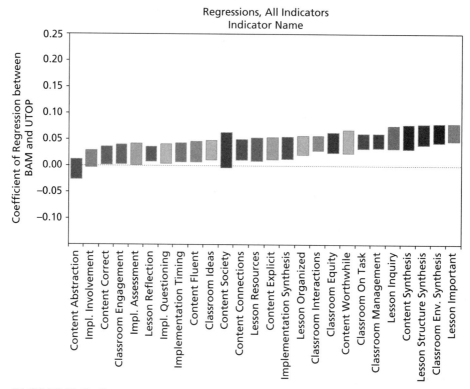

FIGURE 8.6. *Regression Slopes for All UTOP Indicators Showing Their Relationship to Value Added on BAM 2010*

Note: Each bar has a height of two standard uncertainties.

tests and not for BAM. In the following analysis we focus on BAM, partly because we value its emphasis on conceptual understanding, and partly because it was a single exam administered across the whole study, rather than a collection of disparate examinations from different states.

The table of regression coefficients is overall not very illuminating, because patterns do not always leap out and because the different value-added models do not always agree. In Figure 8.7 we focus on a single indicator, 2.3, which concerns investigative or problem-based approaches to mathematics and examine it in more detail. Here are some lessons from the figure:

1. The graphs associated with the three different exams are strikingly similar to one another. The three exams seem fundamentally to be measuring the same thing.

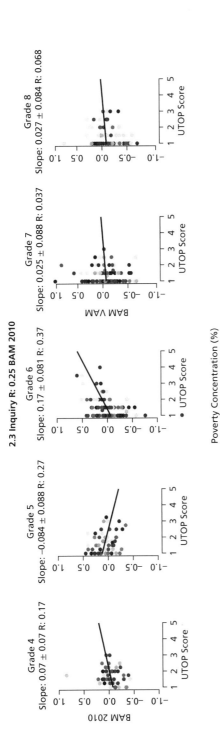

FIGURE 8.7. *Scatterplots Showing the Relationship between the UTOP Lesson Inquiry Indicator and BAM 2010 (a), State 2009 (b), and State 2010 (c) Scores*

Note: "The lesson included an investigative or problem-based approach to important concepts in mathematics." Regression lines are shown, together with estimates for uncertainty of the slope. Separate teacher classrooms are treated completely independently; including teacher identity as a random effect makes no appreciable difference. When restricted only to Districts 4, 5, and 6 (see Table 8.5 and accompanying discussion) the regression slopes change only in the second decimal place. For example, the slope for sixth grade becomes 0.16 ± 0.098 with $R = 0.4$, the slope at grade 7 becomes 0.06 ± 0.1 with $R = 0.095$. This and subsequent plots color-code classes according to student poverty concentration. The overall lesson of the color coding is that in all cases the relationship between UTOP score and poverty is weak, as patterns do not stand out.

(continued)

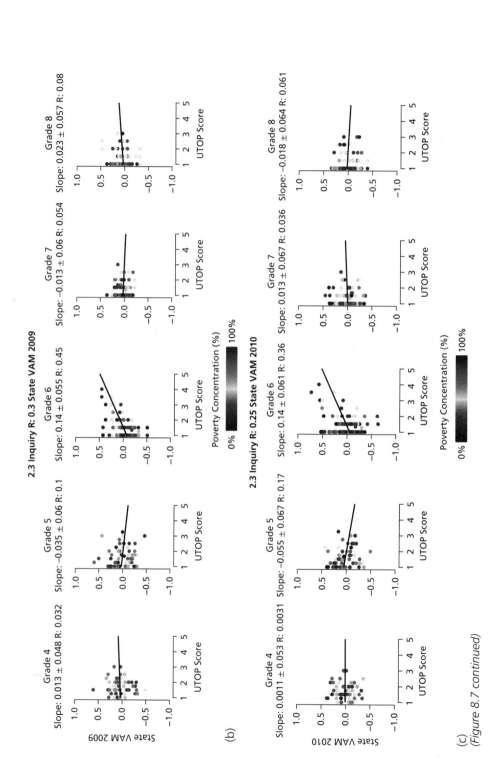

(b)

(c)

(Figure 8.7 continued)

2. Test scores vary quite differently with inquiry practices in different grade levels: negatively at fifth grade, positively in sixth grade. This is one reason why, when all grades are lumped together, this indicator does not emerge as strongly associated with value-added scores.

3. There is not an extremely obvious visual pattern related to the color of the dots. Therefore, the relationship between poverty concentration and classroom performance, although it exists, is weak.

4. The individual class sections form a cloud surrounding the regression line, rather than clustering tightly upon it. This is the meaning of a correlation coefficient $R \approx 0.3$.

Having found that the relationship between UTOP scores and value-added scores depends on grade level, we turn to a more systematic investigation of this point. We focus on fifth and sixth grades, which are more different from each other than any two other grade pairs. Figure 8.8 displays regression slopes for each UTOP indicator. The main messages from this figure are

1. By and large, the better fifth grade teachers look according to the UTOP, the lower their student test score gains.[5]

2. By and large, the better sixth grade teachers look according to the UTOP, the higher their student test score gains.

3. In many cases, the teaching practices associated with the best score gains at sixth grade (for example, Inquiry) are associated with the lowest score gains at fifth grade, and vice versa.

A similar pattern persists for many other indicators and for the three separate value-added models; correlations with UTOP are most positive at sixth grade, have an intermediate value in fourth and seventh grade, are weaker in eighth grade, and weakest of all in fifth grade.[6]

What are some possible explanations? In our sample, all the fifth grade scores are from self-contained elementary schools, while all sixth grade scores are from middle schools. In middle school, sixth grade students are making a difficult transition, leaving the support of self-contained classrooms. The teaching behaviors valued by the UTOP may be especially important during this transition. The nature of the mathematical content itself also varies according to grade level—fifth grade may be a year when students are still focusing on concrete, more calculational aspects of mathematics. Sixth grade,

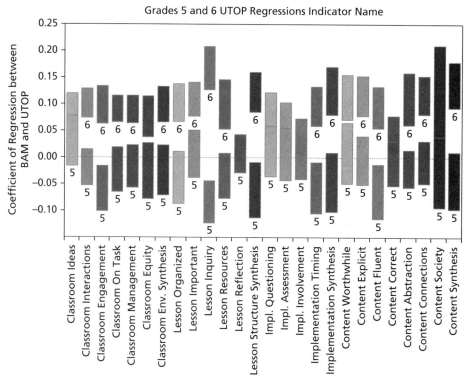

FIGURE 8.8. *Regression Slopes for All UTOP Indicators with Respect to BAM Value-Added Scores in Fifth and Sixth Grade*

Note: The height of each bar is two standard uncertainties.

by contrast, can potentially mark the beginning of a transition to higher-level, more abstract mathematical content. This may be a key point in students' mathematical development, when the behaviors on the UTOP are most important. While UTOP scores had the strongest relationships to value added in sixth grade, they seemed to have especially weak or even negative relationships in fifth and eighth grades. We note that in some states fifth and eighth grade state tests have particularly high stakes in that they constitute key exit exams that the students cannot progress to the next grade level without passing. Regardless of the official state testing procedures, in the fifth and eighth grade years at all schools in the sample, students are being evaluated on whether they are ready to exit one school setting (elementary or middle school), and enter another (middle or high school). We investigate the fifth versus sixth grade difference qualitatively at the end of the next section.

Qualitative Analysis of UTOP and VAM Scores Treated on Equal Footing

Our final research question led us to grapple directly with the relatively low level of consistency between observation scores and value-added scores. One possible conclusion would be that observation scores are weak and unreliable measures of student achievement and, in view of their expense, should be discarded. This conclusion is partly created by a rhetorical device, the use of the words *student achievement* for scores from value-added models. Some additional terminology can help emphasize that computer-scored tests are not the only valuable student outcome. Our terminology was suggested by the observation that sometimes teachers can raise student test scores by teaching them content errors that are helpful on exams,[7] but *this is not acceptable*.

In Table 8.1, we defined UTOP indicators that represent a "consensus" view of effective teaching. Figure 8.9 plots the BAM 2010 value-added scores versus the Consensus indicator. Patterns similar to those seen for other indicators, such as in Figure 8.7 are evident here, too. Because the Consensus indicator was chosen to represent classroom attributes that almost any reasonable person would view as essential, we used it to define "acceptable" and "unacceptable" teaching.

Specifically, we define acceptable teaching to correspond to an average score of 3 or more on the Consensus indicators and unacceptable teaching to be a score less than 3. By contrast, we define "effective teaching" to correspond to a positive score from value-added models on BAM 2010 and "ineffective teaching" to correspond to negative scores. Thus, we end up with four possibilities for each class section rated with the UTOP and BAM value-added scores: Unacceptable Ineffective Teaching, Unacceptable Effective Teaching, Acceptable Ineffective Teaching, and Acceptable Effective Teaching.

The distribution of teachers according to these quadrants is shown by grade level in Figure 8.10. Many things stand out in this figure:

1. Acceptable but Ineffective teachers are most likely in fourth and fifth grades, compared with sixth, seventh, and eighth grades.

2. Unacceptable but Effective teachers are most likely in fifth, seventh, and eighth grades.

3. Unacceptable Ineffective teachers are most likely in sixth, seventh, and eighth grades, while Acceptable Effective teachers are most likely in fourth and fifth grades. Grade school looks much better than middle school, viewed this way.

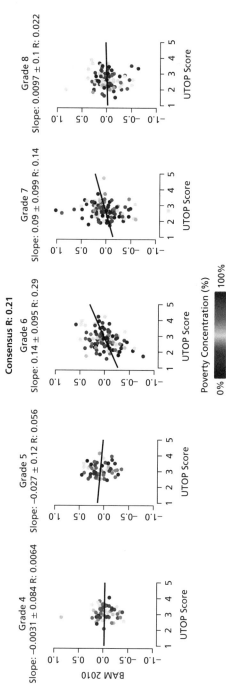

FIGURE 8.9. *Scatterplots Showing the Relationship between the UTOP Consensus Indicator for Acceptable Teaching and BAM 2010 Value Added*

Note: Regression lines are shown, together with estimates for uncertainty of the slope. Separate teacher classrooms are treated completely independently; including teacher identity as a random effect makes no appreciable difference.

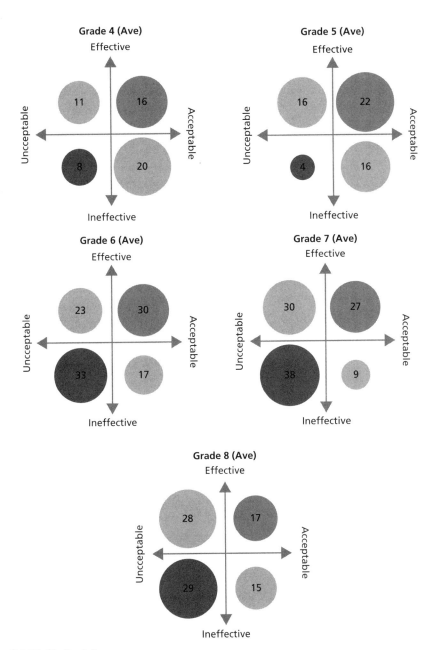

FIGURE 8.10. *Quadrant Plots Showing Distributions of Class Sections According to the Four Possible Combinations of Acceptable/Unacceptable and Effective/Ineffective Teaching*

Note: The area of each circle is proportional to the percentage of class sections at that grade level in each quadrant, while the number of class sections is indicated inside.

Having divided all class sections into these four quadrants, we proceeded to carry out a qualitative investigation, making use of the sometimes extensive comments provided by UTOP raters for each indicator. For example, for the UTOP indicator about classroom management, raters typically wrote supporting evidence that cited specific instances of misbehavior by students and particular techniques the teacher used in order to control behavior. To select class sections for the analysis, we calculated the average BAM 2010 and average UTOP Consensus rating for each class section and normalized both measures. We defined deviance as the difference between normalized BAM 2010 and normalized UTOP Consensus score. We selected the six class sections that had the highest and lowest deviance—those with high normalized BAM and low normalized UTOP (Unacceptable Effective) and those with a low normalized BAM and high normalized UTOP (Acceptable Ineffective). For comparison purposes, we also looked at class sections with especially high BAM and UTOP (Acceptable Effective), and especially low BAM and UTOP (Unacceptable Ineffective).[8]

We now provide a narrative that describes the characteristics of the classrooms with the highest and lowest deviance between observation scores and value-added scores in the four quadrants.[9]

Quadrant 1: High BAM, Low UTOP (Unacceptable Effective Teachers)

These classrooms were sometimes characterized by an explicit focus on standardized test preparation during the lesson. In some cases test preparation was isolated to the warm-up, in other cases it was the focus of the lesson. One observer writes "[The] teacher moved from warm-up to independent practice. Students understood lesson was to practice concepts that could appear on tests." Some observers noted that these lessons focused on training students to perform procedures without understanding, rather than conceptual development of significant mathematical ideas. There was also little attempt at formative assessment or higher-level questioning in these classrooms. "There was no exploration in this lesson. The student[s] went through the procedure of solving Pythagorean theorem problems. The teacher asked fill-in-the-blank questions."

The teacher made major content-related errors in one or more observations of half of these class sections—for example, one observer wrote that "The teacher [made] many errors as she communicated the content of the course. She emphasized that the base is the straight line (not line segment) that is on the bottom of the triangle and that height of the triangle had to be measured from the top of the triangle to the bottom. She also indicated that it is a straight line rather than a slanted line." The other observer from the same lesson noted that the teacher told students the height was the tallest part of the triangle, resulting in much student confusion. Teachers in other class sections simply seemed to be unable to deal with student confusion surrounding the mathematics content; as a result, students seemed to leave the lesson without a firm grasp on the concepts. One observer writes that "Teacher didn't deal with all the students who were having problems. He didn't address or try to correct their understanding. He just showed more problems to work."

In four of these six class sections, at least one observer noted the teacher treating their students disrespectfully. One observer writes, "There were several occasions where students were confused and asked for help and the teacher either dismissed the student or became confrontational with the student," while another describes a different classroom where "[The teacher's] demeanor toward some students was adversarial, demeaning, and inappropriate. 'You're just making a mess. You're like a big disaster. What are you doing!'" Overall, these lessons often had a major weakness—namely disrespectful behavior, content mistakes, or very low student engagement with the concepts—that compromised their UTOP scores.

Quadrant 2: Low BAM, High UTOP (Acceptable Ineffective Teachers)

These classrooms were also sometimes characterized by an explicit focus on standardized test preparation. "This lesson was review for an EOG. The students were not uncovering any new concepts. The students were just performing calculations given the formulas." In nearly all of the class sections (five out of six), observers commented that instruction was procedural and focused on direct instruction and guided practice. One observer writes, "The quality of the interactions and engagements was consistent, but the intellectual level stayed at a low level for most of the students. While students stayed active most of the time, neither students nor the teacher stretched or challenged the concepts in this lesson."

The content being covered in these classrooms was somewhat dull and delivered in a traditional format. One observer noted that "The lesson structure was very monotonous." In half of these class sections, instruction was largely symbolic and mechanical, with few connections to the context in which mathematics arises. One observer wrote that "Her engagements with the students are not mathematical in nature; they are designed to keep the classroom under control and on-task. She calls on students to volunteer answers, but it is as if they are filling in the blanks. . . . There is no spark of interest, no freedom to explore and ask questions, etc."

These lessons were usually orderly with few management problems. One observer writes, "This was a direct instruction lesson, but one that was run to a point that the students were on task. This teacher keeps the class with him and has management techniques that maintain student involvement." Most of these teachers were fluid and accurate when communicating mathematical content. One observer writes, "The examples, discussions, explanations, and verbal content were excellent and showed the deep knowledge and fluency of the lesson, which was solving equations and inequalities. She was able to explain, answer questions without any hesitation or incorrect statements," while another describes, "The teacher moved through the calculations smoothly and without mistake . . . the lecture was very concise and correct." Overall, these lessons could be described as "orderly but unambitious" or "coherent but unimaginative."

Quadrant 3: Low BAM, Low UTOP (Unacceptable Ineffective Teachers)

These classrooms were often focused on standardized test preparation. One observer writes, "There was no opportunity to engage or explore any math concepts. . . . this was entirely test prep review . . . the teacher talked a great deal about learning the material so that they could pass the state test." Nearly all of these lessons consisted of tasks where students were given simple, procedural, drill problems. "There was no way for students to engage or explore the content. The problems were very basic, with only one or two steps." No significant connections were made to the real world, history, or to other disciplines, and the significance of the content was not made explicit to students. "There was no engagement. The problems were written on a transparency; they were simply numbers, not related to anything else. Students were asked to read an explanation from the board and then work the problem."

Nearly all of these classrooms had major issues with student behavior—students were yelling, fighting, and being disruptive or were simply bored and refused to engage in the lesson. One observer describes how "This room was a zoo. . . . yelling answers at the top of their lungs . . . does not make intellectually engaged." Another observer writes that "The teacher attempts to manage the students and has some strategies, but fails to follow through on any of them. . . . the teacher continues lecturing while the students are talking." These lessons had significant amounts of wasted time, with one observer describing how "This lesson was way too time-consuming; he did not efficiently move from one problem to the next."

Students' roles were often passive and involved copying the teacher's procedures and answering low-level questions. One observer writes, "This was a review lesson in preparation for a state test, and students followed along answering the teacher's recall-type questions," while another notes that "The students seem to know that the teacher is expecting choral responses. . . . students answered in unison." There were few issues with teacher content knowledge—this may be due to the fact that most of these classrooms were so poorly managed, or so procedural and without student input, that there was little opportunity for the teacher to demonstrate content knowledge. One observer noted that "The teacher never worked a problem or explained to a student how to solve a problem. She only focused on discipline and trying to get kids to do their corrections without helping them know how to do the corrections." By nearly any measure or definition, these classrooms displayed very ineffective teaching.

Quadrant 4: High BAM, High UTOP (Acceptable Effective Teachers)

These classrooms had little focus on standardized exam preparation—standardized testing was rarely mentioned. These teachers all had orderly, well-managed classrooms in which students were always on task and engaged. One observer describes how "The teacher had a good rapport with her class and almost no visible instances of students being off task or needing correction of misbehavior. Most all the students were involved in the lesson and interested in participating in discussion and working the problems to get the correct answer." Students in all of these classrooms were often encouraged to generate contributions and solutions: "The students in this classroom were constantly generating ideas, conjectures, and propositions. . . . the teacher asked for multiple strategies and she explored each one before she went on . . . the environment was friendly and she encouraged all answers to be looked at and explored."

The majority of these class sections was engaged in one or more lessons that involved investigation or problem-based learning: "The structure of this lesson was excellent. . . . it led the students through an exploration where they had to try and solve problems on their own with different strategies before being taught about [t]he rules and the procedures." The majority of these class sections also included lessons that focused on making authentic, real-world connections. One observer describes how the teacher "guided them through real-world examples from their own lives to make the concepts of area and perimeter come alive for the student[s]," while another wrote that "These concepts went further than focusing on simply getting an answer correct and focused on life skills."

At least half of these class sections displayed other important characteristics. Observers noted instances of students being engaged in mathematical justification, explanation, or proof. One observer wrote that "Students would cite concepts they had learned using evidence to support their positions, and they would respond to the other students' points," while another described how "Students are asked to explain their answers." These teachers also made specific moves to make the importance of the content explicit to students. "The teacher led them through a series of questions to show them why Pythagorean Theorem is so important. She did not start with showing them the formula first, but instead showed them why it would be so difficult to solve certain problems without it." Finally, observers noted that these teachers engaged in high-quality formative assessment of student progress: "Teacher frequently stops video for formative assessment, asking questions that review the material instead of just asking if they understand." These classrooms were characterized by students engaged in learning and grappling with important mathematics concepts.

Summary of Quadrants

Figure 8.11. summarizes some key characteristics of the six outlying class sections in each of the four quadrants.

High Value Added in Fifth Versus Sixth Grade

During the course of our prior analyses, we had found large differences in the relationship between scores on individual UTOP indicators and teacher value-added measures by grade level. One particularly striking comparison was fifth versus sixth grade. We conclude these analyses with a qualitative analysis of

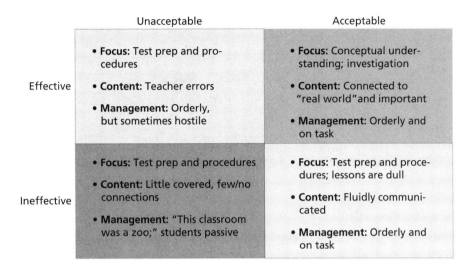

FIGURE 8.11. *Key Characteristics of the Six Outlying Class Sections in Each of the Four Quadrants of Effective and Acceptable Teaching*

fifth and sixth grade classrooms where the teacher has especially high BAM 2010 value-added scores. These classrooms were selected by looking for the six class sections with the highest BAM 2010 value added in fifth grade and the top six class sections in sixth grade.

In the top six BAM value-added class sections in fifth grade, instruction was weak to mediocre, as measured by the scores and supporting evidence on the UTOP. In four of the six class sections, the students were described as generally being on task. This is not surprising given the preceding descriptions of "acceptable effective" and "unacceptable effective" as orderly classes. We did not find an explicit focus on standardized testing in these classrooms, although the type of instruction described is quite consistent with traditional testing drill strategies. The observers noted little intellectual engagement (three of six class sections), few or no real-world connections (five of six class sections), or mentions of the importance of the content (three of six class sections). Observers found incorrect or poorly communicated mathematical content (three of six class sections) and significant amounts of wasted time (three of six class sections). Some of these classrooms were quite poor, some were mediocre, and none exhibited teaching practices accepted in the mathematics education community or recommended by educational research.

The story with the top six BAM value-added class sections in sixth grade was somewhat different. Three of the six top class sections in sixth grade had actually fallen into the outlier analysis of our "acceptable effective" category and were analyzed in the previous section. These were very strong classrooms in terms of both BAM value-added and UTOP scores, where students were engaged with important mathematical ideas and participating in authentic problem solving. They were consistent with current views of research on effective instruction in elementary mathematics. However, the other three class sections were the opposite—these classes had very poor instruction and unacceptable teachers, as measured by the UTOP. Students in these classrooms were off task or bored (three of three class sections), and the teacher sometimes focused on test preparation and used rote and keyword type approaches to mathematics learning (two of three class sections). One observer writes, "There was a lot of body language and lack of participation that indicated either boredom or lack of understanding/care about the content. . . . I noticed at least two on each side of the camera who were slumped in their desks with heads in hands." In these class sections, there were also poor questioning techniques (three of three) and poor formative assessment (two of three): "A few students asked questions, but they were procedural. No higher-order questions were asked or proposed. Students were engaged, but only rotely solving by a process without understanding what or why the process resulted in a solution." There was little student generation of ideas or questions (three of three), and few real-world connections (two of three). An observer wrote that "The examples were non-existent in a real-life setting, and it was a rote exercise in the mechanical simplifying of a simple linear equation."

These observations at fifth and sixth grade levels demonstrate the danger of using value-added assessments as the "gold-standard" of teaching effectiveness. Although in the sixth grade data with high BAM, we see some classrooms in which productive learning of mathematics seems to be occurring, the supposedly exemplary instruction singled out by valued-added scores on their own is highly variable, and in some cases indefensible.

DISCUSSION AND CONCLUSION

We conclude by repeating some of the points with the greatest potential implications for policy and practice:

1. The typical classroom practices observed in the MET study were rather weak, as judged by the UTOP, and therefore one should be hesitant to draw strong conclusions about what exemplary schools look like from

this project. Practices that many mathematics educators might label "innovative" were almost never observed.

2. The classroom attributes most reliably and consistently associated with increased value-added scores were supportive, orderly, well-managed classrooms that focus on important content rather than explicit preparation for tests.

3. The classroom practices favored by the UTOP were more often seen in elementary school than in middle school. The drop in quality in middle school is striking. The professional development needs of teachers in various grade levels may be substantially different.

4. There is some potentially encouraging news about middle school. The highest value-added scores in sixth grade correlate well with high scores on many specific UTOP indicators. This does not prove that helping teachers improve their practice in accord with the UTOP will raise scores, but it certainly leaves open the possibility. At sixth grade, the UTOP indicates that raising student scores requires both overall excellence across all domains and a willingness to use innovative methods to engage and motivate students.

5. Teachers from the UTeach program, whose study included coursework specifically aimed at instilling practices measured by the UTOP, score considerably higher on the UTOP than other teachers we examined. Therefore, it is plausible that professional development that uses the UTOP to identify areas with potential for teacher growth, and then provides relevant coursework similar to that used in the UTeach program, could raise UTOP scores.[10]

6. An evaluation system based on averages of value-added and observation scores can gloss over undesirable outcomes. Teachers making content errors or creating a hostile environment can obtain good value-added scores. Teachers subjecting students to correct but boring lessons can obtain acceptable UTOP scores. Good teaching needs to be *both* acceptable and effective. The best teachers focus on conceptual understanding rather than explicit preparation for tests, while maintaining orderly engaged classrooms.

A common criticism of teacher evaluation processes is that they rate almost all teachers as excellent and provide little useful feedback (New

Teacher Project, 2009). Yet, UTOP observations in this study were more demanding than the value-added measures. In grades 5 through 8, more teachers were rated unacceptable than were rated ineffective. Furthermore, observation is in a better position to raise certain sorts of uncomfortable questions than value-added models are. Our UTOP measurements found that teaching became systematically worse in moving from elementary to middle school. Value-added models compare teachers in similar environments to each other and may not raise such possibilities. Similarly, if worse teachers are systematically placed in classrooms of students from low-income families, value-added models can react by controlling for environmental effects so that the effect disappears. Observation scores typically do not.

Classroom observation has the potential to be more ambitious than value-added modeling. Let us take the example of the Society indicator, which asks for a discussion of a topic's role in history or society. This was the lowest-ranked indicator for the MET sample, with an average score of 1.1. Our own view is that it is valuable for students to understand something of the social and historical significance of mathematics, whether or not this understanding is rewarded in today's mathematics examinations. We do not want students to become good citizens because it will raise their mathematics scores; we want students strong in mathematics because it will help make them good citizens. UTeach graduates in our pilot study had an average on this indicator of 3.5, perhaps because UTeach has a semester-long class focused on this topic. A similar course should help other teachers improve on this indicator. We offer this example to illustrate the way that observation scores and professional development could interact and the way that an observation instrument can more flexibly broaden the goals of school than exams can.

But we do not conclude that analysis of student test scores is superfluous. Neither measure, UTOP scores nor BAM value-added, appears on its own adequate to capture good teaching. Analyses of classrooms in which the two measures differed revealed that acceptable UTOP scores can be assigned to teachers with strong content knowledge and good management skills, but who lack the pedagogical skills to effectively engage students in mathematics learning. High BAM value-added scores can be obtained by teachers with weak content knowledge, who treat their students disrespectfully, or who also lack the pedagogical skills to engage students in mathematics learning. When both of these measures were in accord, the results were much more compelling. Few could argue that the classrooms with both low BAM and low UTOP scores belonged to teachers not in need of substantial assistance. The classrooms with high BAM and high UTOP scores displayed many of the characteristics favored by reform movements in education, based on research on how children learn. Classroom observation and value-added scores should be considered together, on equal footing, to help teachers develop as they progress in their careers, as measures of effective teaching.

NOTES

1. Raters obtained a weighted kappa agreement of 0.41 on individual UTOP indicators, which is moderate agreement, and 0.63 on the synthesis ratings, which is substantial agreement (Landis & Koch, 1977).

2. In some models, we used UTOP scores to predict BAM value-added scores or value-added scores from the state tests. Grade level was also often a predictor in the models, and the data set we used to construct the models was always aggregated to the class section level. Note that BAM was administered only in 2010, so the pre-score for the BAM value-added models was the state test in 2009. Descriptive information about UTOP ratings and value-added gains as they vary by grade level are shown in Table 8.3.

3. We fit linear regression models with grade level and UTOP indicator or Synthesis ratings as predictors. We also included a term for the interaction of the UTOP score with grade level (4 to 8). This made for a base set of twenty-six different models, as there are twenty-two indicators on the UTOP and four Synthesis ratings. We fit this set of models for three different dependent variables: State VAM 2009, State VAM 2010, and BAM 2010. We tested for the significance of the interaction term, display the results visually by using the regression coefficients to show patterns that emerged, and use the standard error of the regression coefficients to show the uncertainty.

4. The BAM value added of the class sections had a mean of .005 and standard deviation of .255; values ranged from -1.254 to 1.021.

5. Few of the regression coefficients are significantly different from one another, and few of them are significantly different from 0. Pooling indicators together to reduce the level of uncertainty, one can conclude that the relation between improved performance on the UTOP and increased BAM value-added scores is negative. Overall, the distribution of value-added scores was higher in fifth grade than in any other grade. t tests give significant differences ($p < .05$) for the averages of BAM scores between fourth and fifth, fifth and sixth, and fifth and eighth grades.

6. We examined many interaction models and grouping of grades. The grouping that seemed best to fit the data was to assemble the fourth, fifth, seventh, and eighth grade lessons into one group, and the sixth grade lessons into another group. We looked at models that had indicator score, grade level group, and the interaction of these two terms as predictors. We found that, for sixteen of the twenty-two UTOP indicators, the interaction term was significant ($p < .05$; Indicators 1.1, 1.2, 1.3, 1.4, 1.5, 2.1, 2.3, 3.1, 3.4, 4.2, 4.3, 4.5, 4.6) or marginally significant ($p = .0740, .0644, .0533$; Indicators 2.2, 2.4, and 4.1, respectively). The interaction term was also significant for three of the Synthesis ratings: Lesson Structure, Implementation, and

Mathematics Content (p = .0302, .0147, and .0150, respectively). In all cases, the trend was the same—the indicator or Synthesis rating had a stronger, positive relationship with value-added for sixth grade class sections, compared to other grade levels. We ran these same models with 2009 and 2010 State VAM as the dependent measure, and the results were similar.

7. For example, "In a fraction, the denominator is the largest integer."

8. We selected these sections by summing the normalized UTOP Consensus rating and the normalized BAM 2010, and choosing the highest and lowest sums. Note that results were similar if we instead used the normalized UTOP Summary and the normalized BAM 2010, rather than UTOP Consensus rating. A problem we encountered is that a number of the Unacceptable Effective and Acceptable Ineffective class section outliers actually had the greatest sum as well as the greatest difference. This is because one measure (BAM or UTOP) was anomalously high or low. We omitted these class sections when choosing Acceptable Effective and Unacceptable Ineffective class sections for extra examination.

9. Once six extreme class sections were selected for each of the four quadrants, we compiled the UTOP supporting evidence for all lessons from that class section. There were most commonly two separate lessons for each class section (the total ranged from one to four), and UTOP observations were typically carried out by two different observers (although the number ranged from one to seven). We used thematic analysis techniques (Braun & Clarke, 2006). Themes were given more prominence if they were observed in multiple lessons and cited by multiple raters; however, for class sections that had only one lesson and one rater, this was not possible. The major themes coded for each class section were then compared within each quadrant to determine which themes consistently arose across all or many class sections.

10. Some studies provide direct evidence that innovative practices favored by the UTOP can raise value-added scores as well (Silverstein, Dubner, Miller, Glied, & Loike, 2009; Granger, Bevis, Saka, Southerland, Sampson, & Tate, 2012).

REFERENCES AND ADDITIONAL RESOURCES

Bates, D., & Maechler, M. (2010). lme4: Linear mixed-effects models using s4 classes. R package version 0.999375–35. http://CRAN.R-project.org/package=lme4

Braun, V., & Clarke, V. (2006). Using thematic analysis in psychology. *Qualitative Research in Psychology*, *3*(2), 77–101.

Bill & Melinda Gates Foundation. (2012). *Gathering feedback for teaching: Combining high-quality observations with student surveys and achievement gains*. Research paper. www.metproject. org/downloads/MET_Gathering_Feedback_Research_Paper.pdf

Gladwell, M. (2008, December 15). Most likely to succeed: How can we hire teachers when we can't tell who's right for the job? *New Yorker*. www.newyorker.com /reporting/2008/12/15/081215_fact_gladwell

Gordon, R., Kane, T. J., & Staiger, D. O. (2006). *Identifying effective teachers using performance on the job*. www.brookings.edu/views/papers/200604hamilton_1.pdf

Granger, E. M., Bevis, T. H., Saka, Y., Southerland, S. A., Sampson, V., & Tate, R. L. (2012). The efficacy of student-centered instruction in supporting science learning. *Science*, *338*, 105–108.

Heck, R. H. (2008). Teacher effectiveness and student achievement: Investigating a multilevel cross-classified model. *Journal of Educational Administration, 47*, 227–249.

Horizons Research. (2000a). *Inside the classroom interview protocol.* www.horizon-research.com /instruments/clas/interview.php

Horizons Research. (2000b). *Validity and reliability information for the LSC classroom observation protocol.* www.horizon-research.com/instruments/clas/cop.php

Landis, J. R., & Koch, G. G. (1977). The measurement of observer agreement for categorical data. *Biometrics, 33*, 159–174.

Meyers, L., Gamst, G., & Guarino, A. (2006). *Applied multivariate research.* Thousand Oaks, CA: Sage.

New Teacher Project. (2009). *The widget effect.* http://widgeteffect.org

Pianta, R., & Hamre, B. (2009). Conceptualization, measurement, and improvement of classroom processes: Standard observation can leverage capacity. *Educational Researcher, 38*(2), 109–119.

Rivkin, S., Hanushek, E., & Kain, J. (2005). Teachers, schools, and academic achievement. *Econometrica, 73*, 417–458.

Rowan, B., Correnti, R., & Miller, R. (2002), What large-scale, survey research tells us about teacher effects on student achievement: Insights from the prospects study of elementary schools. *Teachers College Record, 104*(8), 1525–1567.

Sanders, W., & Rivers, J. (1996). *Cumulative and residual effects of teachers on future student academic achievement.* Knoxville, TN: University of Tennessee Value-Added Research and Assessment Center.

Silverstein, S. C., Dubner, J., Miller, J., Glied, S., & Loike, J. D. (2009). Teachers' participation in research programs improves their students' achievement in science. *Science, 326*, 440–442.

Wright, S., Horn, S., & Sanders, W. (1997). Teacher and classroom context effects on student achievement: Implications for teacher evaluation. *Journal of Personnel Evaluation in Education, 11*, 57–67.

CHAPTER

9

Does the Test Matter?

Evaluating Teachers When Tests Differ in Their Sensitivity to Instruction

MORGAN S. POLIKOFF

ABSTRACT

Implicit in the main MET project reports is the assumption that the policy recommendations offered apply equally across states. However, there is evidence from previous work that state tests differ in the extent to which they reflect the content or quality of teachers' instruction (their *instructional sensitivity*). This chapter applies the methods of the main MET reports to data disaggregated by state to explore whether state tests vary in their sensitivity and whether variation in sensitivity affects the recommendations for weighting components in multiple-measures teacher evaluation systems. The chapter shows that state tests indeed vary considerably in their correlations with observational and student survey measures of effective teaching. Furthermore, some state tests correlate weakly or not at all with these measures, suggesting weak sensitivity to instructional quality. These state-to-state differences in correlations produce weighting recommendations that also differ across states. However, an equally weighted composite of measures may work well in most cases. The chapter concludes by recommending that states explore their own data to ensure their tests are adequately sensitive to high-quality instruction.

INTRODUCTION

As states and districts design new teacher evaluation systems, they must decide how to weight the various measures of teacher performance (e.g., value-added scores, observations, student surveys) in constructing an overall measure of effectiveness. How to weight the multiple measures has been a focal point of the larger MET project, and various chapters in this volume discuss relevant factors in the decision. To this point, however, the MET project has assumed that the techniques for making decisions about weights for multiple measure evaluation systems should be the same across settings. For instance, rather than calculating optimal weights for evaluation systems separately by state, the reports are aggregated across states and grades. This assumption may be problematic, however; as I will show in this chapter, the state tests used to construct value-added measures differ considerably in the extent to which they reflect the quality of teachers' instruction. This property of assessments—their *instructional sensitivity*—is the focus of the present discussion.

In this chapter, I briefly discuss instructional sensitivity as a property of assessments and its relevance to the MET project's central aims. Next, I reanalyze the MET data separately by state and show that the state tests indeed differ in their sensitivity. Third, I use the methods of the main MET reports to show how the variation in sensitivity across states results in different optimal weighting schemes that produce different levels of stability in teacher effectiveness ratings. Finally, I discuss practical implications of the findings and make policy suggestions for teacher and school accountability policies. The four questions guiding this chapter are

1. To what extent are state tests of student achievement in mathematics and English language arts (ELA) sensitive to observational ratings and student surveys of teachers' pedagogical quality?

2. To what extent do state tests significantly differ in their sensitivity to observational measures of pedagogical quality and student survey evaluations?

3. How do the optimal weights in composite measures of teacher performance differ across states?

4. How does the year-to-year stability of composite teacher performance ratings differ across states and across approaches to creating those composites?

The answers to these questions have important implications for policymakers designing multiple measures systems to evaluate teachers and improve instruction. One implication is technical: if state tests differ in their sensitivity to instruction, should different states use different weights in constructing composite measures of effectiveness? A second implication is practical: for states where the sensitivity of tests to instruction is weak, how can results from these tests be effectively used to guide teacher professional development or improvement plans?

BACKGROUND

What Is Instructional Sensitivity?

The origins of instructional sensitivity are with the initial development of criterion-referenced assessments in the 1960s (Cox & Vargas, 1966). The dominant mode of assessment prior to that point was the norm-referenced assessment; these tests were intended to rank individuals. In contrast, criterion-referenced assessments, such as those required under the No Child Left Behind Act, were intended to measure student mastery of a content domain (Glaser, 1963). Given these differing intended uses, the architects of criterion-referenced assessment argued that the traditional test construction techniques for building norm-referenced assessments were not appropriate for criterion-referenced assessments.

In particular, these test developers argued that the item statistics used to select and evaluate the quality of norm-referenced test items (e.g., discrimination, difficulty) were not appropriate for criterion-referenced assessments (Cox & Vargas, 1966; Popham, 1971). For example, in norm-referenced assessments, items with very low difficulty are generally thrown out—in the extreme case in which every respondent correctly answered the question, the item would not provide any information about relative performance of test-takers. In criterion-referenced assessments, however, such an item might merely indicate that all test-takers have learned the material being tested, and the item might not be thrown out. In other words, the creators of criterion-referenced assessment argued that criterion-referenced tests and items should, first and foremost, accurately differentiate students who had and had not been instructed effectively in the content targeted by the assessment. They called this item property "instructional sensitivity." For a full review of the history of instructional sensitivity and the multitude of approaches to investigating it, see Polikoff (2010).

There are three primary methods of instructional sensitivity analysis (Polikoff, 2010): item statistic, judgmental, and instruction-focused. The earliest techniques involved item statistics (e.g., Cox & Vargas, 1966; Haladyna & Roid, 1981). For instance, one promising approach (Cox & Vargas, 1966) was a simple difference in item difficulty between students who had and had not been instructed in the target content (or between the same students, taken before and after receipt of instruction). These item statistics did not catch on widely. They were primarily criticized for not including measures of teachers' instruction (Airasian & Madaus, 1983). As an example, consider an item where the same set of students in a class answered the item correctly before and after instruction; in other words, no students learned the content of the item during the instructional period. In this case, is the item insensitive to the instruction provided by the teacher? Or was instruction just of poor quality (or not focused on the content measured by the item)? Without evidence of what and how the teacher taught, there is no way to distinguish which of these two explanations is correct.

A second class of sensitivity analysis is judgmental in nature. A recently proposed judgmental technique would create "sensitivity panels," much like the panels currently used to set performance standards for state and national assessments (Popham, 2007). These panels would have teams of experts examine the items to rate them on several dimensions seemingly related to their sensitivity, arriving at an overall evaluation of the sensitivity of individual items or whole assessments. While judgmental methods have been proposed since the late 1970s, recent work suggests these methods do not generally agree with item statistic approaches in identifying items that appear to be sensitive to instruction (Chen, 2012). More research is needed on these methods before they can be widely used in the field.

The third method, which is used in this chapter, is instruction focused and employs measures of instruction in concert with student achievement data to investigate sensitivity (e.g., D'Agostino, Welsh, & Corson, 2007; Gamoran, Porter, Smithson, & White, 1997; Greer, 1995; Muthen, Huang, Jo, Khoo, Goff, Novak et al., 1995; Ruiz-Primo, Shavelson, Hamilton, & Klein, 2002; Wiley & Yoon, 1995). The most promising of these are methods based on detailed observations and ratings of instructional practices (Polikoff, 2010). The premise of the analysis is quite straightforward. The first step is to identify the features of quality instruction that are to be measured—these should be features of instruction that research suggests are important indicators of effective teaching in the content area. The second step is to observe a number of teachers to evaluate them against these features. The third step is to create value added or other measures of student achievement growth on tests specifically designed to measure what the teachers are supposed to have taught (i.e., the content in state subject-area standards). The fourth and final step is to predict student achievement gains with the measures of instructional quality.

The basic approach of this kind of sensitivity analysis is identical to the approach taken in measuring the *predictive validity* of the instructional measure for predicting the outcome (student achievement gains). In essence, the concept of instructional sensitivity flips the interpretive focus from the predictor to the outcome, arguing that assessments themselves vary considerably in their ability to detect differences in the predictor (instruction) and that this variation is worthy of investigation and reporting.

If all state tests were sensitive to high-quality instruction (and equally so), we would expect that (1) well-conceptualized and measured indicators of instructional quality would be positively associated with student achievement gains and (2) the associations would be roughly constant across different tests. In contrast, if state tests were weakly and/or variably sensitive to instruction, we would expect that (1) there would be no or little association of instructional practice with student achievement gains and (2) these associations would differ from test to test. Given this intended focus, it is important to emphasize that the work presented in this chapter is *not* intended to be used to compare the predictive validity of various measures of pedagogical quality (i.e., to say one measure of teachers' pedagogical quality is "better" than another one). Rather, it is assumed that each of the measures of pedagogical quality captures some important indicators of teacher performance. The question, then, is to what extent the assessments can detect that which is measured by the instruments.

The main MET research analyses appear to have anticipated strong and uniform sensitivity, given that the study reports have (1) taken the measures of pedagogical quality to be worthy measures that should be associated with achievement gains and (2) not reported on differences in associations across the study's six districts and states. The present chapter retains the assumption that the pedagogical quality measures indeed capture important dimensions of instructional quality but probes the possibility that the relationship of achievement gains with instructional quality (as measured through observations and student surveys) varies across states.

Why Is Sensitivity Important?

The results from state and district assessments are used for an array of purposes. Among these are (1) making promotion or retention decisions for individual students, (2) informing instructional improvement efforts for teachers, and (3) evaluating the performance of districts, schools, or teachers for feedback or accountability. For the latter two purposes, the inferences made from the assessment results rely on the assumption that those results accurately reflect the instruction received by the students taking the test. This assumption is at the heart of the investigation of instructional sensitivity.

To illustrate the importance of assessments that are sensitive to instruction, consider the following example. Teachers in Westlake Elementary adopt the Connected Math Program as their new elementary mathematics model. The teachers, supported by extensive, high-quality professional development, implement dramatic instructional changes to align with the new model, and students seem to be responding. These instructional changes improve the quality of their instruction as judged by high-quality observational tools, such as the Framework for Teaching. Benchmark assessments taken throughout the year show considerable improvement in student performance, suggesting the reforms are working as planned. At the end of the year, students complete the annual state assessment. Two months later, teachers receive results of the state assessments, which show that achievement gains for the past year were no higher (in fact, they were lower) than in previous years. Teachers are confused about the results and unsure of how to make instructional changes to respond.

This example highlights several facts about instructionally sensitive assessments. First, sensitive assessments are essential for helping teachers use assessment data to improve their instruction. In this case, teachers were unable to understand how to improve their instruction because they received conflicting messages from different assessments. Second, sensitive assessments should positively reflect instruction that is "high quality," as judged by research-based instructional observation protocols, and that is well aligned with the content covered on the assessment. Third, inferences made about teacher performance based on the insensitive state assessments will, by definition, not accurately reflect the actual quality of instruction that teachers provided to students. Thus, without sensitive assessments, the validity of virtually all the inferences made about teachers and schools on the basis of assessment data alone are questionable. Clearly, given the MET project's stated goal of improving the measurement of effective teaching, it is essential that the sensitivity of the assessments be taken into account.

STUDYING INSTRUCTIONAL SENSITIVITY OF MULTIPLE STATE TESTS

The present analysis uses section-level value-added scores, observational scores, and student survey results from the MET study's first year. First, I illustrate variation in sensitivity across states by comparing correlations of the value-added model (VAM) scores with composite scores and subscores from the Tripod surveys, Framework for Teaching (FfT), Classroom Assessment Scoring System (CLASS), Protocol for Language Arts Teaching Observations (PLATO), and Mathematical Quality of Instruction (MQI). I calculate the correlations by state and subject and conduct two sets of tests for statistical significance. First, I test whether each correlation is significantly different from 0. To simplify reporting, I indicate the correlation of VAM with each of the five survey or observational measures of instructional quality, and whether each of the correlations is significantly different from 0. Next, I test whether there are significant differences in correlations among states and summarize the results in the text. I exclude State 3 from all state-level analyses because of the small sample of MET teachers from that state, but the data from State 3 are used in calculating overall averages and correlations.

Once I have established the presence of differential sensitivity across states, the question is how states should use this information in combining multiple measures. To investigate this issue, I present a series of examples that illustrate how multiple alternatives for weighting the components would play out in terms of prediction and stability. Following the project reports, I calculate optimal weightings for predicting different criteria and show how these weightings differ across the states in the MET sample. The two outcome criteria I attempt to predict are (1) value-added only and (2) an equally weighted composite of value added, observation results from the Framework for Teaching, and Tripod surveys. Here, I use results from one section or year of a teacher's class to predict results from another section or year. I follow the procedures outlined in the main MET reports to calculate these optimal weights (Mihaly, McCaffrey, Staiger, & Lockwood, 2013). The weights can be interpreted as the weights that should be assigned to each component of the index in order to maximize its correlation with the outcome.

TO WHAT EXTENT ARE STATE TESTS SENSITIVE TO PEDAGOGICAL QUALITY?

This section explores the sensitivity of state mathematics and ELA tests by presenting correlations of state test VAM scores with each of the observational rubric total scores and the Tripod survey composite score. Before discussing these correlations, one important issue is deciding what level of correlation is evidence of sensitivity. This is a difficult issue, because there is not an established threshold in the literature. One approach might be to say that each assessment's VAM scores should be positively correlated with each of the measures taken as indicators of high-quality instruction. This approach is liberal, as correlations of even minute magnitudes will be statistically significant in large enough samples. A more conservative approach would be to determine an *a priori* threshold for indicating sensitivity, such as a correlation of 0.2 or higher. Because the literature does not offer such a threshold, I take the more liberal approach here. In the future it may be a useful exercise to establish levels of sensitivity signified by correlations of increasing magnitude (e.g., a correlation of 0.2 signifies "moderate sensitivity" and a correlation of 0.4 signifies "strong sensitivity").

Mathematics

A first way to analyze the correlations for mathematics, shown in Table 9.1, is to consider the correlations at the aggregate level (i.e., the correlations using data from all partner states together). The total score correlations are the first values in each cell in the table, and the aggregate correlations are in the leftmost column. These correlations show a consistent pattern of positive relationships between state test VAM and total scores on the Tripod, FfT, and CLASS, with correlations ranging from 0.15 to 0.19. That is, for each of these three instruments, teachers who score higher on the instrument tend to score higher on value added (although only modestly so). In contrast, there is no correlation between VAM and scores on the MQI; the correlation is a statistically insignificant 0.03. Based on these results, we might conclude that state tests are sensitive to instructional quality as measured on the Tripod, FfT, and CLASS, but not as measured by the MQI.

Another way to look for sensitivity is to consider correlations at the subscale level. These are the second entries in each cell in the table, where I simply report the number of subscales that have positive, significant associations

TABLE 9.1. Raw Correlations of State Test VAM Scores with Instructional Quality Measures by State, Mathematics

	Overall State VAM	Districts				
		1	2	4	5	6
Tripod composite	0.19*	0.33*	0.21*	0.09	0.20*	0.16*
Tripod subscales (7)	7	7	5	1	5	5
n	1135	144	236	262	238	255
FfT composite	0.18*	0.31*	0.03	0.13	0.26*	0.23*
FfT subscales (8)	8	4	0	1	7	6
n	805	85	173	184	180	183
CLASS composite	0.15*	0.18	0.04	0.08	0.19*	0.28*
CLASS subscales (12)	9	2	1	1	5	11
n	804	85	173	183	180	183
MQI composite	0.03	−0.04	0.01	0.07	−0.03	0.18*
MQI subscales (5)	3	0	0	0	0	3
n	794	84	166	183	178	166

Note: *significantly different from 0, $p < .05$.

with the state test VAM. For the aggregate sample, there are significant correlations on the large majority of subscales. On the Tripod and FfT, there are significant correlations on each subscale; the strongest correlation across all subscales is the correlation of state test VAM with the FfT subscale for managing student behavior ($r = 0.20$). In contrast, there are five subscales spread across the CLASS and MQI that do not show significant correlations. These subscales are (1) CLASS–Regard for Student Perspectives ($r = 0.03$), (2) CLASS–Analysis and Problem Solving ($r = 0.03$), (3) CLASS–Instructional Dialogue ($r = 0.06$), (4) MQI–Errors and Imprecision ($r = 0.03$), and (5) MQI–Working with Students and Mathematics ($r = 0.04$). In short, with the exception of the behaviors represented by these five subscales, the state assessments in our partner districts are (on average) sensitive to all of the behaviors represented by the rubrics and surveys. The correlations are generally small, however.

The next five columns in the table show the same correlations, but at the state level. States are not identified due to privacy. These five columns illustrate several interesting findings about the sensitivity of each state's assessments to total score measures of pedagogical quality. First, state tests differ in their patterns of sensitivity. The most sensitive state assessments seem to be in State 6, where there are significant correlations of state test VAM with total scores on all four rubrics. In contrast, in State 4, there are no significant correlations of VAM with rubric or survey total scores. The other three states have some significant and some nonsignificant correlations between VAM and the various rubrics. Second, some of the correlations are much larger at the individual state level than for the aggregate sample—for instance, the correlation of VAM with the Tripod composite in State 1 is ($r = 0.33$, considerably larger than the correlation in the other districts ($r = 0.18$). At the total score level, there is a good deal of variation in the magnitude and statistical significance of the correlations, indicating varying degrees of sensitivity.

To illustrate these correlations in another way, Figures 9.1 and 9.2 illustrate "high" and "low" correlations of Tripod scores with VAM scores in mathematics. The two scatterplots are for States 2 and 4, respectively, and each includes a smoothed curve of best fit (a lowest line) plotted on identical axes. In State 2 ($r = 0.29$) the relationship appears positive and almost linear, with each unit of increase in Tripod associated with increasing VAM scores. In State 4 ($r = -0.05$), the relationship appears nonexistent; the curve of best fit is almost completely flat, except for small shifts near the extremes. In short, in State 2, the test is sensitive to differences in teachers' Tripod ratings; in State 4, differences in teachers' VAM scores are in no way reflective of differences in the quality of their instruction, as rated by the Tripod.

There are also notable patterns at the subscale level across states. In general, the patterns at the subscale level support those at the total score level. For instance, there is little evidence of sensitivity for State 4 at the subscale level, with just three significant correlations across the thirty-three subscales. Also, the five subscales mentioned earlier that did not have significant aggregate correlations with VAM scores show relatively little evidence of correlation at the state level either. Three of the five subscales have one significant correlation each, all with VAM for State 6. The other two subscales

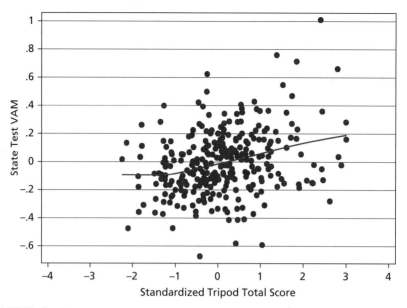

FIGURE 9.1. *Scatterplot of State Test VAM with Tripod Total Score for State 2*

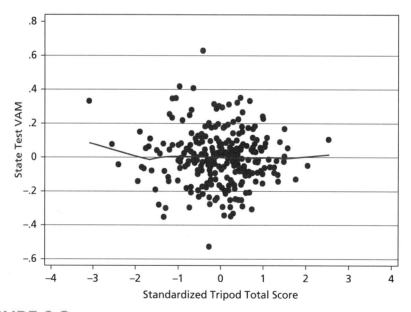

FIGURE 9.2. *Scatterplot of State Test VAM with Tripod Total Score for State 4*

(CLASS–Regard for Student Perspectives, MQI–Errors and Imprecision) have no significant correlations with VAM from any state test. Taken together, these results suggest that there is some sensitivity of state tests to pedagogical quality measures in all cases except State 4. However, not all states' tests are sensitive to all of the pedagogical quality measures—in particular, only one state's tests are sensitive to MQI scores.

English Language Arts

The results for parallel analyses in ELA are shown in Table 9.2. Unlike in mathematics, there is significant sensitivity of state tests to pedagogical quality as measured by total scores on all four of the instruments. The largest correlation is for the Tripod ($r = 0.15$), while the other three tools have roughly equal correlations of 0.07 to 0.09. While all of these correlations are significant, they are as small as or smaller than the correlations for Tripod, FfT, and CLASS in mathematics, perhaps indicating somewhat less overall sensitivity than was found in mathematics.

This interpretation also appears to hold when looking at correlations with the instrument subscales. While all seven Tripod subscales are significantly correlated at the aggregate level with state test VAM, there is less sensitivity on the other three instruments. Indeed, just nine of twenty-seven subscales on the other three instruments show sensitivity at the aggregate level to state test VAM. In short, the average state ELA test across the partner states showed sensitivity to Tripod and its subscales, but only modest sensitivity to the other measures of pedagogical quality.

The state-level correlations are shown in the right-most five columns of Table 9.2. Again, correlations appear weaker in some states than in others. For instance, the assessments in State 4 show no sensitivity to any of the pedagogical quality scales at either the total score or subscale levels. Indeed, some of the correlations for that district are negative, and one of these negative correlations is statistically significant (Tripod care subscale, $r = -0.12$). There is also weak evidence of sensitivity of the assessments in State 1, with just four significant subscale correlations, but this is partially attributable to the smaller sample size for the district in that state. In contrast, there is mixed evidence of sensitivity of the assessments in States 2, 5, and 6. Across all states and instruments, there is only one case in which the state assessments are sensitive to more than half of the subscales for a particular instrument—State 2 for the Tripod. Overall, the conclusion must be that there is weaker sensitivity of

TABLE 9.2. Raw Correlations of State Test VAM Scores with Instructional Quality Measures by State, English Language Arts

	Overall State VAM	Districts				
		1	2	4	5	6
Tripod composite	0.15*	0.14	0.29*	−0.05	0.16*	0.13*
Tripod subscales (7)	7	0	7	0	3	2
n	1248	156	265	306	265	256
FfT composite	0.07*	0.11	−0.01	0.04	0.13	0.17*
FfT subscales (8)	2	1	0	0	1	3
n	864	102	191	204	190	177
CLASS composite	0.09*	0.18	0.11	−0.03	0.13	0.12
CLASS subscales (12)	5	2	2	0	3	0
n	864	102	191	204	190	177
PLATO composite	0.08*	0.09	0.06	0.05	0.15*	0.12
PLATO subscales (7)	2	1	0	0	3	1
n	857	102	186	203	190	176

Note: *significantly different from 0, $p < .05$.

state ELA assessments than of state mathematics assessments to differences in the quality of teachers' instruction.

TO WHAT EXTENT DO STATE TESTS *SIGNIFICANTLY DIFFER* IN THEIR SENSITIVITY?

The results discussed above are suggestive that there are between-state differences in the sensitivity of assessments to pedagogical quality. However, to this point all of the comparisons have been descriptive. This section discusses the results of statistical tests for the difference in correlations to identify those states in which the correlations are significantly different from one another.

The results are summarized here; tables displaying the results in detail are available from the author.

The results of these comparisons illustrate several important findings about the variation in sensitivity across states. First, many of the differences discussed in the previous section are indeed statistically significant, indicating that state assessments vary in their sensitivity in ways highly unlikely to be due to chance. Second, there are significant differences in sensitivity at the total score level on all four measures of mathematics instruction, as compared to just one measure of ELA instruction. Third, there are significant differences in sensitivity at the subscale level on all measures of instruction, save for the PLATO in ELA.

At the total score level in mathematics, States 1 and 6 have the most sensitive assessments, while States 2 and 4 have the least. In contrast, the assessments in State 5 are more sensitive than those in State 2 to FfT ratings and less sensitive than those in State 6 to the MQI. At the total score level in ELA, State 4's assessments are significantly less sensitive than those in States 1, 2, 5, and 6 to the Tripod. These differences in sensitivity at the total score level are the ones most likely to influence the multiple measures composites, which is a focus of the next section.

At the subscale level, there are many significant differences in sensitivity. For example, there are fourteen subscales on the Tripod, FfT, and CLASS in mathematics for which State 2's assessments are less sensitive than one or more other states' assessments. The other state with all negative results is State 4 in both mathematics and ELA. In each of these states, the state assessments are not more sensitive than any other state's assessments to either subscales or total scores on any measure of instructional quality. Overall, these results show that the correlations found and described in the main MET reports glossed over the sometimes substantial differences in correlations found across study states.

COMBINING MULTIPLE MEASURES WHEN TESTS DIFFER IN THEIR SENSITIVITY

This section is devoted to exploring how states or districts might think about combining multiple measures of instruction when assessments differ in their sensitivity to instruction. To be sure, there are many critiques of the approach of combining multiple measures into a single composite index (e.g., Baker,

Oluvole, & Green, 2013). Indeed, it may make more sense to consider each measure of teacher performance as a separate indicator of teacher performance that provides imperfect but useful information. Nevertheless, many states and districts, in part responding to incentives from the federal government, have begun designing and implementing such systems, so providing practical advice is paramount.

I begin by using the techniques of the main MET project analyses to determine optimal weights for predicting various outcomes and exploring how these optimal weights differ across states. I use two outcomes for my examples. The first is simply value added on the state assessment in a different section or year. The second outcome is an equally weighted composite of state test VAM scores, Framework for Teaching scores, and Tripod survey scores, again calculated in a different section or year. To create the composite, each measure was standardized and the scores were averaged. I use only FfT scores here, both as an example and because the FfT is the most widely used of the MET study protocols in new teacher evaluation systems. In general, the main conclusions and recommendations discussed in the conclusion section hold, no matter what tool is used, with the possible exception of the MQI.

Optimal Weights for Predicting State Test VAM

The first and third panels in Table 9.3 show the optimal weights for predicting value added on the state assessments in mathematics and ELA. I show the weights both overall and for the five states with large samples (excluding State 3). Overall, in mathematics, state test VAM is the largest component of the optimally weighted composite for predicting state test VAM in another section. The optimal weight for VAM is calculated as approximately 0.75. Less weight is given to observational scores from the FfT (0.11) and the Tripod surveys (0.14). These results are consistent with the project's main reports.

Looking across states, there is some variation in the magnitude of the weights in the optimal composites. State test VAM is always the largest component of the composite, but the weight varies from 0.60 in State 1 to 0.81 in State 2. Another difference across states is in the magnitude and rank ordering of the weights on the FfT and Tripod. In States 1, 5, and 6 (as is true in the aggregate), the Tripod receives a larger optimal weight than the FfT. In contrast, in States 2 and 4, the FfT receives the larger weight.

Overall, in ELA, the optimal weights for predicting state test VAM again favor the state test VAM. This component receives exactly half of the weight

TABLE 9.3. **Optimal Weights by State for Predicting State Value Added**

	Overall	State 1	State 2	State 4	State 5	State 6
			State value added in mathematics (A)			
VAM	0.75	0.75	0.77	0.64	0.60	0.81
FfT	0.11	0.05	0.22	0.32	0.05	0.02
Tripod	0.14	0.20	0.01	0.05	0.35	0.17
			Equally weighted composite in mathematics (B)			
VAM	0.31	0.27	0.41	0.19	0.29	0.43
FfT	0.32	0.32	0.28	0.36	0.28	0.32
Tripod	0.37	0.41	0.31	0.44	0.43	0.25
			State value added in ELA (A)			
VAM	0.50	0.75	0.42	0.55	0.17	0.46
FfT	0.13	0.07	0.38	0.01	0.04	0.24
Tripod	0.37	0.18	0.20	0.44	0.79	0.29
			Equally weighted composite in ELA (B)			
VAM	0.11	0.25	0.09	0.01	0.16	0.04
FfT	0.43	0.34	0.30	0.42	0.42	0.64
Tripod	0.46	0.41	0.61	0.58	0.42	0.32

Note: Values may not add to 1 due to rounding.

in the composite at the aggregate level. The Tripod survey receives the next highest weight at 0.37, while the FfT receives the smallest weight at 0.13. Again, this rank ordering is consistent with that presented in the project's main reports. Looking across states in ELA, there is a wider range in the weights than is true in mathematics. In State 5, for example, the assessment does not receive the largest weight in the composite. In two other states—States 2 and 6—the state test receives a plurality of the weight, but not a majority. These three states showed significant sensitivity to either Tripod or FfT. In States 1 and 4, the state test VAM does receive the largest weight in the composite. Again, the rank ordering of the other two components' weights varies across states, with FfT receiving a larger weight than Tripod in State 2.

Taken together with the sensitivity results presented earlier, these results suggest several conclusions about the variation in optimal weights across states when state tests differ in their sensitivity to instruction. First, the optimal weights for predicting state test VAM differ considerably from state to state, including differences in both the magnitude and rank order of the weights. States adopting the overall optimal weights calculated in the MET reports by pooling data across states might, in fact, be implementing weights that are not optimal for their particular data.

Second, the variation across states in optimal weights appears larger in English than in mathematics, corresponding to the greater variation in sensitivity in ELA described above. Thus, states might consider different weighting schemes for different subjects. Third, for the two state assessments in ELA that show no significant sensitivity to either FfT or Tripod, the optimal weights in the composite predicting state test VAM favor state test VAM over other measures. Conceptually, this makes sense. If the state test VAM is not highly correlated with the other measures in the composite, then the state test will comprise the largest portion of the composite for predicting future VAM. What limits the magnitude of these weights from being higher is the generally low reliability of state test VAM estimates in ELA (roughly half as large as in mathematics). In short, the weights on state VAM in the optimal composites are larger when (1) the state test VAM is more reliable and (2) the state test is less sensitive to instruction.

Optimal Weights for Predicting an Equally Weighted Composite

Rather than viewing test scores as the essential measure of teacher quality, we might view each of the three measures (VAM, observations, and student surveys) as being important. Thus, instead of creating an optimal composite to predict VAM, we might create an optimal composite to predict some aggregate measure that combines VAM, observations, and surveys. The most straightforward aggregate is simply the average of the three standardized measures. Predicting an equally weighted composite has several advantages over predicting VAM alone. For instance, equal composites reflect the complex nature of teaching, and they are less likely to create negative incentives (e.g., teaching to the test) than outcomes based only on test scores.

In the second and fourth panels of Table 9.3, I show the optimal weights for predicting an equally weighted composite of state test VAM, FfT, and Tripod. In mathematics, the weights for the overall composite (i.e., including all states) are quite close to equal—0.31 for state test VAM, 0.32 for FfT, and 0.37 for Tripod. However, there is a good deal of variation across states in the optimal weights for predicting the equally weighted composite. State test VAM receives the largest weights in the composites for States 2 and 6, while Tripod receives the largest weights in States 1, 4, and 5. However, in all five states the three components are roughly equally weighted, with no weights below 0.19 or above 0.44. Thus, if the goal is predicting an equally weighted composite, the optimal weights are likely to be roughly equal.

In English language arts, the optimal weights for predicting the equally weighted composite are greater for observation scores and Tripod scores than for state test VAM. Across the states, the overall weight for the state test VAM is just 0.11, as compared to 0.43 for FfT and 0.46 for Tripod. Again, there is a good deal of variation across states in weights, but the optimal weight on state test VAM is always 0.25 or lower. The largest weight generally goes to Tripod, but this too varies from 0.32 to 0.61. In neither mathematics nor ELA is there a clear pattern between the sensitivity results presented earlier and the composite weights derived here.

HOW DOES THE STABILITY OF TEACHER PERFORMANCE RATINGS DIFFER ACROSS STATES?

A key purpose of new multiple-measure evaluation systems is to make judgments about the performance of individual teachers. Sometimes, these judgments are to be used for high-stakes decisions (e.g., employment), and sometimes they are to be used for lower-stakes decisions (e.g., professional development). Regardless of the intended uses of these results, it is important that results from evaluation systems reflect real, persistent differences in teacher performance, rather than idiosyncratic variations from one year to the next. Thus, the year-to-year stability of these ratings is important, and this section investigates whether the stability of ratings based on the various composites estimated above differ within and across states.

Table 9.4 shows the year-to-year correlation of five different composites in each subject. The top four rows are drawn from the composites presented above—optimal weights for predicting state test VAM and an equally weighted composite. I present both the aggregate weights (i.e., assigning the same weights to each state based on the optimal weight calculated using data from all districts [left-most column of Table 9.3]) and the state-specific weights. The last row of each section is merely an equally weighted composite of the three measures.

Based on these stability indices, several conclusions are possible. First, the stability of teacher ratings is generally higher in mathematics than in ELA. On average, the difference is relatively small (0.03 to 0.08 difference in correlations). This is likely due to the higher reliability of the individual composites of the index in mathematics. Second, the stability of the ratings tends to be only slightly higher when using the state-specific weights as compared to the aggregate sample weights. Thus, there is not much gained in terms of stability by using state-specific weights. Third, the stability tends to be lowest for weights based on predicting VAM. Fourth, the stability of ratings varies considerably across states. Even using the same equally weighted composite, the stability varies from 0.61 to 0.44 in mathematics and from 0.56 to 0.38 in ELA. In both cases, the highest stability is in State 1 and the lowest is in State 6.

Another way to consider stability is to think of it in other metrics that may be more intrinsically meaningful. One such metric is the misclassification rate. Consider the stability of 0.39 for the aggregate composite for predicting only the state VAM in ELA. This was the lowest overall stability in ELA. Given a stability of 0.39, of the teachers rated as below the median in one year/section, approximately 64 percent were rated below the median in another year/section. Of the teachers rated in the bottom 25 percent, approximately 48 percent were rated in the bottom 25 percent in another year/section. And of the teachers rated in the bottom 10 percent, approximately 26 percent were rated in the bottom 10 percent in another year/section.

Now consider the stability of 0.54, which we would have obtained had we used each state's optimal weights for predicting the evenly weighted composite of VAM, Tripod, and FfT (fourth entry in the first column). With this level of stability, 70 percent of the bottom-half teachers are in the bottom

TABLE 9.4. **Year-to-Year Stability of Teacher Rankings Based on Various Weighted Composite Measures of Teacher Effectiveness**

	Overall	State 1	State 2	State 4	State 5	State 6
Mathematics						
Aggregate composite predicting VAM	0.47	0.45	0.53	0.42	0.46	0.52
State composites predicting VAM	0.48	0.46	0.51	0.48	0.49	0.50
Aggregate predicting equal composite	0.54	0.63	0.58	0.57	0.58	0.42
States predicting equal composite	0.57	0.65	0.58	0.58	0.58	0.49
Equal composite	0.55	0.61	0.59	0.57	0.58	0.44
ELA						
Aggregate composite predicting VAM	0.39	0.49	0.46	0.33	0.43	0.25
State composites predicting VAM	0.40	0.38	0.43	0.34	0.47	0.31
Aggregate predicting equal composite	0.52	0.62	0.57	0.47	0.61	0.40
States predicting equal composite	0.54	0.60	0.56	0.47	0.61	0.50
Equal composite	0.48	0.56	0.51	0.40	0.55	0.38

half in another year/section; 55 percent of the bottom 25 percent of teachers are in the bottom 25 percent in another year/section; and 46 percent of the bottom 10 percent of teachers are in the bottom 10 percent in another year/section. In short, the stability increase from 0.39 to 0.54 results in meaningful increases in the stability of relative rankings of teachers, especially at the extremes of the distribution (where policy is most often focused). The overall conclusion is, therefore, that a weighting system that is optimal for predicting next year's VAM will result in more teachers being incorrectly classified as high- or low-performing than one that is optimal for predicting a composite of multiple measures of teacher performance will.

SUMMARY OF FINDINGS

The purpose of this chapter was to investigate the extent to which some of the main results of the MET reports masked meaningful variation across states. In particular, the work focused on exploring the extent to which the state assessments used in the study were sensitive to observational and student survey measures of teacher quality. A second focus was on exploring the extent to which differences across states in correlations among instruments were reflected in differences in the optimal weights for multiple-measure teacher evaluation systems.

Returning to the research questions, several clear conclusions result from this work. First, the raw correlations of VAM scores with pedagogical quality ratings are generally low, with typical correlations falling in the range of 0.10 to 0.20; thus, we might conclude that the tests used in the partner states are only weakly sensitive to pedagogical quality, as judged by the MET study instruments. Given that there is no rule against which to evaluate these correlations, we cannot say whether the tests are "sensitive enough" to pedagogical quality. Rather, what we can say is that there are several high-quality, research-based measures of teachers' instruction that show small-to-no relationship with student learning gains. The sensitivity appears to be somewhat weaker in English language arts than in mathematics. Again, one important explanation for these findings is that the reliability of all study instruments, with the possible exception of Tripod, was merely moderate.

A second conclusion is that state tests indeed differ, sometimes substantially, in their sensitivity to the measures of pedagogical quality at both the total score and subscale levels. Some states' assessments appear to be sensitive to all of the measured indicators of pedagogical quality, whereas other states' assessments are insensitive to all indicators. Perhaps the most troubling case is State 4, where the assessments show limited to no sensitivity to student surveys or observational ratings in either subject. Of course, the tests in this state may be sensitive to some other measure of teacher quality that was not used in the MET study, just as the results described here with regard to particular instruments may not hold across all states in the United States.

A third conclusion is that the estimated optimal weights differ from state to state, again sometimes substantially. When the goal is predicting future value added, the weights in all states and both subjects favor prior value added, although to varying degrees (more so in mathematics and in states in which sensitivity is low). When the goal is predicting an evenly weighted composite of value added, Tripod surveys, and FfT scores, the optimal weights sometimes favor value added and sometimes favor the other measures. The weights also appear to vary somewhat more in ELA than in mathematics.

A fourth and final conclusion is that the year-to-year stability in estimates of teacher performance using the weighted composites varies across states; however, it is generally higher in several cases. First, the stability of teacher performance ratings is higher when the composite includes a greater weight on FfT and Tripod scores, since those individual components have higher reliability than VAM scores do. Second, the stability is only marginally higher when using state-specific optimal weights, as compared to the average optimal weights from across the partner states. Third, the stability of an evenly weighted composite is greater than that of a composite based primarily on VAM and not much lower than that of an optimally weighted composite. Even when the same weights are applied to all states, however, the stability of the resulting composites differs across states in sometimes meaningful ways.

IMPLICATIONS FOR POLICY

Several important policy recommendations flow from this chapter. First, states should consider weighting schemes that place substantial weight on each of the components of effective teaching. Should policymakers decide that effective teaching is defined by teachers who produce large achievement gains, are rated highly by students, and score well on observational protocols, then each of these measures should receive meaningful weights in the evaluation system. Perhaps the most sensible and straightforward approach is to simply weight each of the measures of effective teaching equally. This matches the recommendations in the main MET project reports. As this chapter shows, an equal weighting approach performs well from a stability standpoint. At the same time, this approach does not appear to be meaningfully affected by variation in the sensitivity of assessments. This approach also reduces some of the potential gaming issues that might come with a system that is more heavily weighted to one component or another (e.g., teachers focusing on teaching to the test in a system where substantial weight is placed on the test). Finally, this approach recognizes that teaching is a complex, multifaceted set of skills that probably should not be reduced to just one type of measure. This approach will, however, diminish the ability of the composite to predict future student test performance, particularly so in states in which the assessments are weakly sensitive to instruction.

A second recommendation is that states and districts should carefully study the sensitivity of their assessments to measures of pedagogical quality. This is perhaps even more important in ELA, where sensitivity appears to be relatively lower than in mathematics. The first step in such a process is establishing a clear understanding of the type of instruction that is desired. Policymakers, researchers, and educators should work together to develop a clear definition of "high-quality" instruction. This means establishing a conception of effective teaching and ensuring that appropriate measures are constructed to capture each component reliably. Many states have already done this through their adoption of evaluation tools such as the Framework for Teaching in the No Child Left Behind waivers or Race to the Top applications.

This vision of effective instruction should also be made clear to teachers, so that they can work to align their instruction with the vision. Next, the goal should be to ensure that all state assessments, especially those used for decisions about teachers and schools, are sensitive to that kind of instruction. While there is some evidence as to how to evaluate the sensitivity of assessments (Polikoff, 2010), there is not a strong literature on building sensitive assessments. Building such assessments will require iterative test development and an explicit focus on sensitivity. Without sensitive assessments, many of the inferences made about teacher and school effectiveness on the basis of test scores only may be of questionable validity. Furthermore, it will be difficult for teachers to sustain instructional improvement if the tests used to gauge performance are not sensitive to improvements in instruction through professional development.

A third and final policy suggestion is that policymakers must work to provide teachers with clear interpretations of results from multiple measures evaluation systems. This means helping teachers understand how the scores on the multiple measures are each calculated, how they are related to one another, and what can be learned from combining information from multiple measures. These are challenging and complex issues that teachers cannot solve on their own, so policymakers must work to ensure that results are presented to teachers in ways that are well understood and that decisions made on the basis of those results—both by teachers and by district personnel—are justifiable. The MET project reports offer a set of clear suggestions for states and districts undertaking these endeavors. If these conditions are not met, there is little hope that the results from multiple measures evaluation systems will be used in ways that are desired by policymakers.

The results presented here clearly demonstrate that some states' tests are better than others when it comes to correlating with other desired outcomes. The reasons for these differences are not well known, but they should be an intense focus of study in the coming years. Several hypotheses seem particularly probable. One hypothesis is that the tests that are less sensitive are more poorly aligned to the state content standards (Polikoff, Porter, & Smithson, 2011). Another hypothesis is that the less-sensitive assessments are more poorly aligned to the content teachers are teaching (since teachers' instruction is poorly aligned with standards and assessments on average [Polikoff, 2012]). A third hypothesis is that the variation in sensitivity is attributable to features of the test items or content (e.g., multiple choice versus constructed response, procedural versus more advanced cognitive demand). There are surely other hypotheses, as well, and each merits investigation. Regardless of the reasons for the insensitivity, as we move toward increased use of assessments for both formative and summative purposes, it is essential that these tests accurately reflect the quality and content of instruction being provided in the classroom. If not, the test results will send conflicting information that will prevent teachers from learning to improve.

REFERENCES AND ADDITIONAL RESOURCES

Airasian, P. W., & Madaus, G. F. (1983). Linking testing and instruction: Policy issues. *Journal of Educational Measurement, 20*(2), 103–118.

Baker, B., Oluwole, J., & Green, P., III. (2013). The legal consequences of mandating high stakes decisions based on low quality information: Teacher evaluation in the Race-to-the-Top era. *Education Policy Analysis Archives, 21*, 5.

Chen, J. (2012). *Impact of instructional sensitivity on high-stakes achievement test items: A comparison of methods.* (Unpublished doctoral dissertation). Lawrence, KS: University of Kansas.

Cox, R. C., & Vargas, J. S. (1966). *A comparison of item-selection techniques for norm referenced and criterion referenced tests.* Paper presented at the Annual Conference of the National Council on Measurement in Education, Chicago, IL.

D'Agostino, J. V., Welsh, M. E., & Corson, N. M. (2007). Instructional sensitivity of a state standards-based assessment. *Educational Measurement, 12*(1), 1–22.

Gamoran, A., Porter, A. C., Smithson, J., & White, P. A. (1997). Upgrading high school mathematics instruction: Improving learning opportunities for low-achieving, low-income youth. *Educational Evaluation and Policy Analysis, 19*(4), 325–338.

Glaser, R. (1963). Instructional technology and the measurement of learning outcomes: Some questions. *American Psychologist, 18,* 519–521.

Greer, E. A. (1995). *Examining the validity of a new large-scale reading assessment instrument from two perspectives.* Urbana, IL: Center for the Study of Reading.

Haladyna, T. M., & Roid, G. H. (1981). The role of instructional sensitivity in the empirical review of criterion-referenced test items. *Journal of Educational Measurement, 18*(1), 39–53.

Mihaly, K., McCaffrey, D. F., Staiger, D. O., & Lockwood, J. R. (2013). *A composite estimator of effective teaching.* Seattle, WA: Bill & Melinda Gates Foundation.

Muthen, B. O., Huang, L., Jo, B., Khoo, S., Goff, G. N., Novak, J. R., et al. (1995). Opportunity-to-learn effects on achievement: Analytical aspects. *Educational Evaluation and Policy Analysis, 17*(3), 371–403.

Polikoff, M. S. (2010). Instructional sensitivity as a psychometric property of assessments. *Educational Measurement: Issues and Practice, 29*(4), 3–14.

Polikoff, M. S. (2012). Instructional alignment under No Child Left Behind. *American Journal of Education, 118*(3), 341–368.

Polikoff, M. S., Porter, A. C., & Smithson, J. (2011). How well aligned are state assessments of student achievement with state content standards? *American Educational Research Journal, 48*(4), 965–995.

Popham, J. W. (1971). Indices of adequacy for criterion-reference test items. In J. W. Popham (Ed.), *Criterion-referenced measurement (an introduction)* (pp. 79–98). Englewood Cliffs, NJ: Educational Technology Publications.

Popham, J. W. (2007). Instructional insensitivity of tests: Accountability's dire drawback. *Phi Delta Kappan, 89*(2), 146–155.

Rovinelli, R. J., & Hambleton, R. K. (1977). On the use of content specialists in the assessment of criterion-referenced test item validity. *Dutch Journal of Educational Research, 2*(1), 49–60.

Ruiz-Primo, M. A., Shavelson, R. J., Hamilton, L., & Klein, S. P. (2002). On the evaluation of systematic science education reform: Search for instructional sensitivity. *Journal of Research in Science Teaching, 39*(5), 369–393.

Wiley, D. E., & Yoon, B. (1995). Teacher reports on opportunity to learn: Analyses of the 1993 California Learning Assessment System (CLAS). *Educational Evaluation and Policy Analysis, 17*(3), 355–370.

CHAPTER

10

Understanding Instructional Quality in English Language Arts

Variations in PLATO Scores by Content and Context

PAM GROSSMAN, JULIE COHEN, AND LINDSAY BROWN

ABSTRACT

In this chapter, we explore both what is revealed about the quality of instruction in English language arts (ELA) through the MET data, as well as how the content, grade level, and composition of students moderate the relationship between measures of teaching and student achievement. We focus specifically on one observation protocol, the Protocol for Language Arts Teaching Observation (PLATO). Our analysis suggests that it would make sense for districts to target resources toward the improvement of middle school instruction in ELA, given the steady downward trend in instructional quality by grade level. Classroom observation protocols represent one component that can provide diagnostic feedback to teachers, school leaders, and district administrators. Using these data to understand how instructional quality might vary by content domain, by grade level, or by student demographics provides districts with a deeper understanding of how best to use scarce resources to improve the quality of instruction for all students.

INTRODUCTION

Although much of the focus in recent educational policy has been on ways to evaluate individual teachers, less effort has gone into understanding the quality of *teaching* and how it might vary in response to the needs of particular students or the demands of particular contexts. Most policies regarding teacher evaluation, in fact, assume that teaching is a generic activity and that quality instruction should look similar across contexts and, therefore, prescribe generic models of teacher evaluation. Yet as Joseph Schwab (1978) observed long ago, understanding teaching requires attention to four central commonplaces of the classroom: the teacher, the students, the subject matter, and the milieu or context in which teaching occurs. As we seek to understand the relationships among different measures of teaching quality and student achievement, we must think critically about how these commonplaces may influence the variability of instructional practice and their implications for teacher evaluation systems.

In this chapter, we explore both what is revealed about the quality of instruction in English language arts (ELA) through the MET data, as well as how the content, grade level, and composition of students affect PLATO scores. We focus on three potential factors that may affect the quality of instruction received by students: grade level, specific content domain within the subject of English language arts (reading, writing, etc.), and student demographics.

Although the initial analyses from the MET project suggest broad associations between different measures of teaching quality (Kane & Staiger, 2012), many questions remain unanswered. For example, is the quality of teaching similar across different grades, or are there systematic differences by grade level? How does the quality of instruction vary across the different content domains included in the broad category of English language arts? Are classrooms with students from different racial or ethnic backgrounds exposed to similar instructional quality, or are there systematic differences depending on the composition of students in a classroom? Although questions such as these may represent inconvenient complications in the effort to create a one-size-fits-all system of teacher evaluation, the answers to these questions are consequential as districts develop and refine their systems for evaluating and supporting teachers. Investigating these questions will also help us develop a deeper understanding of teaching, in all its complexity, and how to best target resources for improvement.

Snapshot of Instruction Through the Lens of PLATO

The MET data provide a unique opportunity to look at the quality of ELA instruction across multiple districts and thousands of classrooms. The data from systematic observation protocols used in MET are able to provide a snapshot of instructional quality across classrooms, allowing teachers, principals, and district leaders to develop a more global sense of instruction in their schools or districts. Such data can provide districts and schools with information about both strengths and weaknesses in the quality of classroom teaching.

We focus specifically on one observation protocol, the Protocol for Language Arts Teaching Observation (PLATO). PLATO is a subject-specific observational tool initially developed as part of a research study to identify classroom practices related to teachers' impact on student achievement. The protocol is based on prior research on effective teaching in English language arts, across the content domains of reading, writing, and literature (Grossman, Greenberg, Hammerness, Cohen, Alston, & Brown, 2009; Grossman, Loeb, Cohen, & Wyckoff, 2013). The protocol highlights thirteen elements of high-quality teaching in English language arts, organized into four underlying factors: (1) the disciplinary and cognitive demand of classroom talk and activity; (2) representations and use of content; (3) the quality of instructional scaffolding; and (4) classroom environment. These four factors were first identified around conceptual clusters and then tested empirically using our classroom observation data.

For PLATOPrime, the version of the instrument used in the MET study, we included six of these thirteen elements, which clustered into three of our factors, excluding the representation and use of content.[1] The disciplinary and cognitive demand factor captures the extent to which teachers ask students to engage in intellectually challenging activities and talk (cf. Nystrand, 1997; Taylor, Pearson, Peterson, & Rodriguez, 2005). The instructional scaffolding factor evaluates the extent to which teachers provide specific instructional supports, including instruction around and modeling of specific meta-cognitive strategies or skills, to facilitate student learning of ELA content (cf. Beck & McKeown, 2002; Hillocks, 2000). Our classroom environment factor looks at both time and behavior management to assess the teacher's efficient organization of classroom routines and materials to ensure that instructional time is maximized and the degree to which student behavior facilitates academic work (cf. Denham & Lieberman, 1980). We selected the six specific elements that comprise PLATOPrime based on the high levels of reliability of the scales and prior research suggesting these instructional elements were associated with student outcomes. In Table 10.1, we provide an overview of these elements.

In Table 10.2, we provide the average scores of MET teachers on the PLATOPrime instrument. Across all grades and content domains, teachers scored highest on behavior and time management (factor 3: classroom environment) and lowest on strategy instruction and modeling (factor 1:

TABLE 10.1. **Overview of PLATOPrime Elements**

Name of Element	Factor	Description
Modeling	Instructional Scaffolding	Teacher visibly enacts the work in which students will engage.
Strategy Use and Instruction	Instructional Scaffolding	Teacher explains *how* students can implement learning strategies (i.e., making predictions, using quotes to support an argument).
Intellectual Challenge	Cognitive/ Disciplinary Demand	Teacher provides tasks that require analysis, inference, and/or idea generation.
Classroom Discourse	Cognitive/ Disciplinary Demand	Teacher provides opportunities for students to engage in extended, elaborated conversations. Teacher picks up on, elaborates, or clarifies student contributions to discussions.
Time Management	Classroom Environment	Teacher organizes classroom routines and materials to ensure that little class time is lost to transitions, and that instructional time is maximized.
Behavior Management	Classroom Environment	Teacher addresses student misbehavior and facilitates environment that allows for academic work.

TABLE 10.2.   **Mean PLATO Scores Across MET Sample**

PLATO Element	PLATO Average	SD
Intellectual Challenge	2.29	0.45
Classroom Discourse	2.25	0.49
Behavior Management	3.71	0.49
Modeling	1.52	0.52
Strategy Use and Instruction	1.76	0.54
Time Management	3.51	0.57
Factor 1: Instructional Scaffolding	1.64	0.47
Factor 2: Disciplinary Demand	2.25	0.49
Factor 3: Classroom Environment	3.61	0.48
PLATO Composite (Average Across Elements)	2.51	0.35

Instructional Scaffolding). The average composite PLATO score was 2.5 on a 4-point scale. According to the PLATO measure, the classrooms included in the MET data are generally well-managed environments. However, the low scores on strategy use and instruction and modeling are striking, given that research in literacy suggests the importance of both of these practices in developing students' reading and writing ability (e.g., Graham, 2006; Snow & Biancarosa, 2003). The scores in classroom discourse also suggest that students are rarely engaged in substantive discussions and that most classroom talk most closely resembles the IRE (initiative, response, evaluation) pattern of a teacher question, followed by a short student response.

Predictive Power of Each Moderator

To determine how grade level, student characteristics, and content domains predict the average PLATO score, we first conducted what is commonly referred to as an "omnibus" test. The test asks how much of the change in the PLATO average is explained by grade level, student characteristics, and content domains, independently of the others. For example, the test analyzes the degree to which knowing whether the lesson focuses on reading versus writing skills explains a significant portion of variation in the PLATO scores, while holding district, grade level, and student demographics constant.

The model we used for this analysis is

$$\text{PLATO Average} = \beta_1 \cdot \text{District} + \beta_2 \cdot \text{Grade} + \beta_3 \cdot \text{ContDom} + \beta_4 \cdot \text{StuDem} + \varepsilon$$

To accommodate the content domains, which are scored for every fifteen minutes of instruction, the analysis is at the lesson level. Content domains are scored a 1 if the lesson received a 1 for the same content domain (e.g., "reading") for both segments of instruction in the lesson. It is scored a 0 otherwise. The standard errors are clustered at the teacher level to account for potential correlation in scores.

Table 10.3 demonstrates that all commonplaces except the district contribute statistically meaningful information about the variation in PLATO scores, even after controlling for the other commonplaces. We can also see that the grade level of students contributes disproportionately more information than the other moderators, with an F-statistic of 114. In other words, grade level explains more of the differences in a PLATO average than do student demographics or content domain, although all three contribute statistically meaningful information. We explore these significant moderators—grade level, content of instruction, and student demographics—in more detail in the sections below.

TABLE 10.3. **Significance of Moderators**

Moderator	F-statistic	p-value
District	0.08	0.778
Grade	114.60	0.00
Content Domain	13.83	0.00
Student Demographics	7.14	0.00

Grade Level as Context for Instructional Quality

After analyzing teachers' instructional patterns across the MET sample, we focused on the extent to which PLATO scores vary by grade level. There are several plausible reasons for why teaching practices in English language arts might look different at different grade levels. First, teacher preparation in elementary language arts might emphasize different instructional techniques than would secondary, subject-specific preparation. Moreover, the curricular demands likely vary at different grade levels, contributing to differential instructional formats. In particular, one might hypothesize that scores on the elements in our disciplinary demand factor, intellectual challenge and classroom discourse, would differ from the elementary to the secondary grades.

Teachers might assume that older students would be better able to navigate activities that target inferential skills, contributing to higher scores on our intellectual challenge scale. In the same way, teachers might perceive middle school students as better equipped to engage in extended academic discussions, leading to higher scores on classroom discourse. Conversely, we might hypothesize that scores on our classroom environment scales, time and behavior management, would be lower in the middle grades, as research suggests that working with early adolescents may be associated with a particular set of challenges for creating organized, orderly classrooms (Lassen, Steele, & Sailor, 2006; Warren, Edmonson, Griggs, Lassen, McCart, Turnbull et al., 2003). Finally, the impact of standardized assessments also varies by grade level, which might result in differences in instruction. Teachers in the "tested" grade levels may experience differential pressure to cover more content, leading to more breadth of material presented—and potentially less depth.

Although hypotheses abound, little research has actually explored variations in teaching practice by grade level. The MET database provides a unique opportunity to explore instructional quality across multiple grades. To examine the role of grade level on instruction, we ran basic descriptive statistics, looking at mean PLATO scores in each grade level. We then examined grade level as a predictor of each of the six PLATO elements.

How do PLATO scores vary by grade level? We find that across both the average PLATO score and across all individual elements, PLATO scores are significantly lower for lessons in grades 6 through 8, compared to grades 4 and 5 ($p < .05$). In fourth and fifth grades, average PLATO scores are systematically higher, closer to the 3 score point, which represents evidence of quality instruction, with some weakness. In the middle grades, in particular in seventh and eighth grades, average PLATO scores are closer to the 2 score point, which represents "limited evidence" of quality instruction in the elements (see Table 10.4).

Table 10.4 looks at PLATO scores for each element as a function of grade level. For the purposes of comparison, fourth grade serves as the reference group. Across the PLATO elements, the fourth and fifth grade PLATO scores are not statistically significantly different from each other, suggesting that instructional quality is similar at these two elementary grades. However, teachers in all the middle grades had significantly lower scores than the fourth grade teachers on all the PLATO elements. Thus, our hypothesis that disciplinary demand might be higher, for example, in classrooms with older students does not prove to be true in the MET sample. However, behavior and time management are indeed stronger in elementary classrooms than in the middle school classes.

These findings clearly suggest that instructional quality in English language arts is generally weaker in the middle grades than at the elementary level. For districts needing to think strategically about where to allocate scarce resources, our analyses suggest that middle school teachers might be most in need of targeted assistance in their language arts teaching practice, as measured by PLATO.

Language Arts Content Domains as Context for Instructional Quality

English language arts is a broad subject, covering a vast terrain of content domains from lessons on vocabulary, mechanics, and grammar to activities that engage students with literary texts or teach them to write persuasive editorials. Although these all fall under the capacious umbrella of ELA instruction, we can imagine teachers using a different repertoire of practices when teaching different content domains, although little research has actually explored this empirically. Moreover, some research suggests that content domain coverage can be an important predictor of student achievement (Rowan, Correnti, & Miller, 2002). For these reasons, PLATO also requires raters to code each fifteen-minute instructional segment for all content domains of English language arts covered in that segment. Content domain codes include reading, writing, literature, speaking and listening, and grammar and mechanics. Content domains are coded as binary variables. They are scored 1 when that content domain is present in the fifteen-minute segment

TABLE 10.4. PLATO Averages as a Function of Grade Level (Fourth Grade Is Reference Group)

	PLATO Average	Intellectual Challenge	Classroom Discourse	Modeling	Strategy Use and Instruction	Behavior Management	Time Management
			Classroom Environment				
Grade 4	2.67	2.40	2.35	1.74	1.99	3.82	3.69
Grade 5	2.67	2.41	2.40	1.70	1.97	3.83	3.73
Grade 6	2.46***	2.25***	2.23***	1.42***	1.69***	3.71**	3.45
Grade 7	2.32***	2.13***	2.07***	1.31***	1.57***	3.57***	3.27
Grade 8	2.33***	2.21***	2.11***	1.32***	1.49***	3.55***	3.29

Note: * denote significant differences from fourth grade teachers: *p* < .05, **p* < .01, ***p* < .001.

of instruction being scored, or 0 if absent. Raters can check more than one content domain, if applicable.[2] These data allow us to look at the extent to which instruction in any fifteen-minute segment focused on a single content domain or included topics across multiple domains. For example, a teacher might ask students to write a haiku. This lesson would be coded as "writing only." However, another teacher might ask students to read and analyze several haikus before being asked to write their own. This lesson would be coded as "reading and writing." Of the double-scored segments in the MET, rater agreement ranged from a low of 82 percent (writing) to a high of 95 percent (grammar and word study), suggesting that raters generally agreed on content domains covered in a lesson segment. These data enable us to look at the quality of teaching within specific content domains, as well as to assess to what extent teachers are touching upon the different components of ELA across multiple lessons.

Prior research suggests that writing, in particular, seems to present an instructional challenge for teachers. In prior work using PLATO (Grossman et al., 2009), we found that instructional quality appears lower in writing than in any of the other content domains. Writing lessons, across the board, received lower scores on almost all of the PLATO elements; modeling was the only instructional element that was stronger in writing than in other content areas. The MET data provides the opportunity to explore the extent to which these findings hold up across a larger sample that spans multiple grade levels and districts nationwide.

To understand how much instruction targeted reading, writing, a combination of the two, or other language arts skills (grammar, word study, etc.), we ran basic descriptive statistics looking at the content domain coverage both within and across grade levels. We were broadly interested in the differences between lessons that focused on writing versus those that focused on the comprehension and interpretation of text. Thus, for the purposes of this analysis, lessons that focused on literary analysis, as well as those that targeted fluency and decoding, were both considered reading lessons. We then looked at average PLATO scores as a function of content domain coverage to determine whether instructional quality varied by the type of ELA content being taught.

Across the 3,500 language arts lessons collected from the fourth through eighth grade teachers in the MET study, we see much more teaching of reading than of writing (Table 10.5). There are approximately four times as many lessons coded as purely reading than as purely writing. The MET protocol

TABLE 10.5. **Percentage of Language Arts Lessons by Content Area and Grade Level**

Percentage of Writing Lessons by Grade		Percentage of Reading Lessons by Grade		Percentage of Mixed (Reading and Writing) Lessons by Grade		Percentage of Grammar/Word Study/ Vocabulary Lessons by Grade	
Grade	Mean	Grade	Mean	Grade	Mean	Grade	Mean
4	0.18	4	0.67	4	0.087	4	0.064
5	0.161	5	0.667	5	0.089	5	0.083
6	0.162	6	0.477	6	0.188	6	0.174
7	0.092	7	0.434	7	0.228	7	0.246
8	0.113	8	0.447	8	0.267	8	0.173
9	0.106	9	0.698	9	0.196	9	0
Average Across Grades	0.136		0.566		0.176		0.123

asked teachers to capture at least one reading and one writing lesson on focal topics, which may have actually inflated the number of writing lessons included in the sample.

Although we might expect there to be more writing instruction as students grow older, we find the opposite to be true. Surprisingly, the percentage of writing lessons is highest in grade 4 (18 percent) and lowest in grade 7 (9 percent). We see a similar pattern with reading instruction; the percentage of reading lessons is lower in the middle grades (6 to 8) than in the elementary grades (4 and 5). While writing instruction is not that common across the lessons captured in MET classrooms, neither are lessons focusing on grammar, mechanics, or word study. This is particularly true in the elementary grades, where only 7 percent of lessons are coded as grammar, mechanics, or word study.

Instruction that included a focus on both reading and writing was much more common in the middle school ELA classes than in elementary classrooms. In grades 4 and 5, only 8 percent of lessons were coded as targeting reading and writing skills together. These numbers go up dramatically at the higher grade levels.

Our analyses also indicate that there are systematic differences in the quality of instruction by the content domain being taught. To get a sense of variation in instructional quality by content domain, we compared PLATO scores for reading/literature lessons to scores for lessons that focused on writing, grammar, or vocabulary lessons. In this analysis, lessons that target reading/literature are the reference group. Table 10.6 illustrates that the composite PLATO score (scores averaged across elements) are not meaningfully different between reading or writing lessons. However, we see distinct, and statistically significant, differences in scores on individual elements.

Classroom discourse scores are significantly lower ($p < .001$) in writing lessons than in reading lessons. Behavior management scores were also lower during writing lessons ($p < .05$) than during reading lessons. However, the opposite pattern holds for the instructional scaffolding elements. Scores on modeling and strategy use and instruction are significantly higher ($p < .001$) during writing lessons than during reading lessons.

Interestingly, instructional quality is significantly lower across the six PLATO elements during lessons that target both reading and writing skills, and both the disciplinary demand of instruction and classroom environment are significantly lower during grammar, vocabulary, or word study lessons. In other words, instructional quality is significantly higher in lessons that exclusively target reading and/or literature skills than in lessons that target skills across the ELA content domains.

These findings suggest there may be consequential differences in terms of the instructional practices that teachers use when teaching different content domains in English language arts. Although teachers may be modeling more during writing lessons, they also seem to have less effective behavior management and provide fewer opportunities for students to engage in classroom discussion during these lessons. Although there were fewer lessons that targeted grammar, mechanics, or word study, these lessons also scored lower in instructional quality across the board.

Why might instructional quality look different when teaching different content? Perhaps some of the instructional challenges during writing

TABLE 10.6. PLATO Scores as a Function of Lesson Content (Reading Is Reference Group)

	Plato Average	Disciplinary Demand Factor		Instructional Scaffolding Factor		Classroom Environment Factor	
		Intellectual Challenge Average	Classroom Discourse Average	Modeling Average	Strategy Use and Instruction Average	Time Management Average	Behavior Management Average
	Beta/(se)	Beta/(se)	Beta/(se)	Beta/(se)	Beta/(se)	Beta/(se)	Beta/(se)
Writing	0.032	−0.026	−0.172	0.317	0.125	0.015	−0.066
	−0.021	−0.031	−0.032	−0.035	−0.038	−0.033	−0.028
Reading and Writing Instruction	−0.197	−0.224	−0.213	−0.071	−0.212	−0.318	−0.145
	−0.021	−0.03	−0.031	−0.035	−0.037	−0.032	−0.028
Grammar/Word Study/Vocab.	−0.048	−0.075	−0.024	−0.004	−0.011	0.112	−0.068
	−0.023	−0.034	−0.036	−0.039	−0.042	−0.037	−0.032

instruction result from the fact that most secondary ELA teachers studied literature during college and are thus more confident and competent with content related to literature rather than to writing. English majors may be more familiar and hence more comfortable discussing theme or character in a novel than they are explaining the intricacies of persuasive rhetoric.

There were, however, several instructional practices that were stronger during writing, including strategy use and instruction and modeling. Indeed, other broad survey research (Applebee & Langer, 2011) indicates the teachers use a great deal of modeling during writing instruction. This makes conceptual sense, as writing provides the opportunity to generate a concrete model or exemplar (student work, published pieces, or teacher's own writing). Moreover, professional development around the teaching of writing advocates the modeling of writing strategies, such as brainstorming, organizing, revising (Atwell, 1987; Calkins, 1986) and using model texts. Unfortunately, based on our prior research and these findings from the MET data, these affordances of writing instruction seem to be accompanied by other instructional challenges, including managing students and maximizing use of instructional time.

Student Characteristics as Context for Instructional Quality

Students are clearly one of the most important factors related to teaching. The particular composition of students in a classroom may affect how teachers teach and what students learn. A number of scholars have advocated for tailoring one's instructional approach to the specific needs and characteristics of students, including advocates of culturally relevant or culturally responsive teaching that "scaffold[s], or build bridges, to facilitate learning" (Ladson-Billings, 1995, p. 481). Lisa Delpit (1988) argued for the importance of explicit instruction in literacy classrooms with high percentages of minority students to help mitigate differences in background knowledge. This type of explicit instruction does not assume shared tacit background knowledge but makes explicit the various strategies needed to achieve instructional goals. Morrison, Robbins, and Rose (2008) emphasized the importance of providing instructional modeling for minority students.

Students' linguistic diversity is another increasingly important factor in instruction. One in nine students in the United States is labeled an "English language learner" (ELL), and two states in the MET study—North Carolina and Tennessee—have seen some of the largest increases in ELL population over the past two decades (Goldenberg, 2008). Although much of the research on ELLs in inconclusive, two major reviews of the research have provided information regarding effective practices, including cooperative learning (students working interdependently on group instructional tasks) and allowing students time for meaningful discussions (Goldenberg, 2008).

In addition to tailoring instruction to students from various ethnic and linguistic backgrounds, educators are increasingly called upon to differentiate their instruction for students with special needs (Tomlinson, 1999). Such differentiation may involve modifying the reading level of a text, presenting information in multiple formats, or allowing various methods for assessing student learning. Those designated as "special education" students are very diverse, with learning needs that may range from developmental delays to Asperger's syndrome; because of this, no one method will suffice for all students. However, meta-analyses of research have found that a combination of direct instruction and explicit strategy instruction yields the best results for students with special needs (Swanson, 2001).

Although conceptually distinct, direct instruction and strategy instruction contain many overlapping instructional practices: clear instructional explanations containing multiple and varied examples, step-by-step progression through subtopics, and modeling of procedures, processes, or skills. We might, therefore, expect that the PLATO practices of modeling, and strategy use and instruction would be used more frequently in classrooms with a high percentage of students with special needs.

To look at the associations between the composition of students in a classroom and PLATO scores, we disaggregated the MET data by student characteristics and examined variations in the quality of instruction using classroom-level percentages of student characteristics.[3] To determine whether teachers' instructional practices, as measured by PLATO, differ depending on the makeup of students in the classroom, we first created two groups of classes based on the percentage of students from a specific demographic group. We then compared the average instructional practice scores across these different groups of classrooms.

Across the entire MET sample, there are sizable populations of students from different ethnic groups and a range of socioeconomic status (SES) (Kane & Staiger, 2012). Table 10.7 shows the breakdown of demographics across the sample.

However, there is substantial variability of student populations within districts. For example, some districts have very few students who are ELLs, while

TABLE 10.7. **Student Demographics Across MET Sample**

Student Characteristics	Percentage
Hispanic	31
Black/American Indian	33
White/Asian	34
Gifted	11
Male	50
SPED	8
ELL	13
Subsidized Lunch	56

other districts have sizeable ELL populations. To account for the variation in student demographics by district, a classroom was designated as having a "high proportion" of a specific student population if the percentage of students from a particular student demographic was larger than the district average of that group. Likewise, a classroom was designated as being a "low proportion" class if it contained less than the district average of that particular demographic. For example, a "high proportion" ELL classroom means that the classroom contains a higher percentage of ELL students than that district's average.

Once classrooms were designated as "high proportion" or "low proportion," we computed the PLATO element averages for each group and tested the statistical significance of the differences between those averages using t-tests. We also computed an effect size to measure the magnitude of the difference between the two groups, independent of sample size.

Next, we explore how classroom practices differ depending on the composition of students in the class. We look at four different student demographics: race, income, English language learner status, and special education classification. Table 10.8 illustrates the breakdown of PLATO scores in MET

TABLE 10.8. **Average PLATO Scores for Black/Hispanic/American Indian**

Instructional Practices	High Proportion (N = 761)		Low Proportion (N = 543)		Effect Size
	Mean	SD	Mean	SD	
Modeling	1.51	0.51	1.53	0.53	−0.05
Strategy Use and Instruction	1.77	0.53	1.76	0.56	0.01
Intellectual Challenge	2.30	0.44	2.29	0.47	0.01
Classroom Discourse	2.21	0.48***	2.30	0.49	−0.19
Time Management	3.49	0.58	3.53	0.56	−0.06
Behavior Management	3.67	0.52**	3.75	0.45	−0.16
PLATO Average	2.49	0.35*	2.53	0.34	−0.11

classrooms that contain higher or lower proportions than the district average of each student demographic. We find evidence suggesting that scores on some PLATO teaching practices differ systematically by the composition of students in a classroom.

The first set of findings in Table 10.8 relates to racial composition. In this analysis, students who identified as being Black, American Indian, or Hispanic were grouped into one category, and students who identified as white or Asian were grouped into another category. (Kane & Staiger [2012] use a similar approach to student demographic data in the MET report.) We then looked at how instructional practices differed depending on the proportion of each category of students in the class. Classroom discourse, in particular, is lower in classes with more students who identify as

Black/Hispanic/American Indian. This means that classrooms that have more minority students than the district average have fewer opportunities to engage in ELA-related discussion with their classmates or teacher. On average, the difference is almost two-tenths of a standard deviation, which is among the biggest instructional differentials we find in the student demographic analysis. Behavior management is also statistically significantly lower in classes with higher-than-average proportion of non-Asian minority students.

Our next analysis explores the relationship between PLATO practices and classrooms with varying proportions of students qualifying for free and reduced-price lunch.[4] This analysis (Table 10.9) shows that instruction itself, as measured by PLATO, looks remarkably similar across classrooms with students from different socioeconomic groups. Behavior management is the only statistically significant difference for higher-than-average percentages of students qualifying for subsidized lunch than for their wealthier peers. Since the behavior management protocol asks for a mix of environmental information

TABLE 10.9. Average PLATO Scores for Subsidized Lunch

Instructional Practices	High Proportion (N = 566)		Low Proportion (N = 507)		Effect Size
	Mean	SD	Mean	SD	
Modeling	1.52	0.50	1.55	0.56	−0.06
Strategy Use and Instruction	1.73	0.52	1.78	0.58	−0.08
Intellectual Challenge	2.28	0.45	2.28	0.46	0.00
Classroom Discourse	2.21	0.48	2.25	0.49	−0.08
Time Management	3.50	0.57	3.51	0.58	−0.02
Behavior Management	3.68	0.52*	3.75	0.45	−0.14
PLATO Average	2.49	0.34	2.52	0.35	−0.09

(e.g., orderliness of classroom) along with teacher-centered behavior (e.g., consistency of consequences), it is difficult to say whether the variability in behavior is a product of the teacher's expectations, the behavior of the students, or the culture and expectations of the school. Regardless, it is heartening that so little variability exists between comparatively high-proportion and low-proportion socioeconomic classrooms in the sample.

Next, we analyze instruction for classrooms with higher-than-average and lower-than-average proportions of English language learners (Table 10.10). Here, we see a distinct pattern. Where instructional differences exist—specifically in the elements of time management and modeling—it is higher in classrooms with more ELLs. This means that classrooms with high proportions of English learners spend more time on task than do classrooms with a low proportion of ELLs.

TABLE 10.10. Average PLATO Scores for English Language Learners

Instructional Practices	High Proportion (*N* = 479)		Low Proportion (*N* = 825)		Effect Size
	Mean	SD	Mean	SD	
Modeling	1.55	0.54*	1.50	0.50	0.11
Strategy Use and Instruction	1.79	0.54	1.75	0.54	0.08
Intellectual Challenge	2.31	0.45	2.28	0.46	0.06
Classroom Discourse	2.23	0.46	2.25	0.50	−0.04
Time Management	3.55	0.54~	3.48	0.58	0.11
Behavior Management	3.73	0.44	3.70	0.52	0.06
PLATO Average	2.53	0.33~	2.49	0.35	0.10

It also means that teachers are more likely to model, to visibly or audibly enact a skill, process, or strategy that is central to a student task, for classes that have a higher-than-district-average proportion of ELLs.

Finally, we analyze instructional quality in classrooms with relatively high or low percentage of students who are designated to receive special education services (Table 10.11). We see the largest differences in instruction for this student demographic. The results show that there are statistically significant differences in five of the six PLATOPrime practices. These PLATO practices are scored higher in classrooms that contain more special education students than the district average. The relationship is strongest for the instructional scaffolding factor, which contains the elements of modeling and strategy use and instruction. The effect sizes are 0.22 and 0.24, respectively, indicating that

TABLE 10.11. Average PLATO Scores for Special Education Students

Instructional Practices	High Proportion ($N = 488$)		Low Proportion ($N = 816$)		Effect Size
	Mean	SD	Mean	SD	
Modeling	1.59	0.54***	1.48	0.49	0.22
Strategy Use and Instruction	1.85	0.55***	1.72	0.53	0.24
Intellectual Challenge	2.34	0.45**	2.27	0.45	0.18
Classroom Discourse	2.28	0.47*	2.23	0.50	0.12
Time Management	3.56	0.56**	3.47	0.57	0.15
Behavior Management	3.71	0.50	3.71	0.49	0.00
PLATO Average	2.55	0.35***	2.48	0.34	0.22

teachers in classes with higher-than-district-average number of special education students scored almost a quarter of a standard deviation higher than teachers in classes with relatively fewer special education students.

This analysis provides some evidence that systematic differences in instruction do exist, depending on classroom student demographics; however, they are not always the differences that we would have anticipated. We do not see evidence in this sample that teachers are increasing their instructional scaffolding in classrooms with relatively high percentages of racial minorities or low-SES students, although the literature suggests such practices can be helpful in supporting student learning. Unfortunately, classrooms with relatively high percentages of racial minority students also experience fewer opportunities to engage in ELA-related talk with their teachers and peers. Teachers do appear to be answering the call to scaffold instruction for special education students. In fact, instructional practices appear uniformly higher for classrooms with relatively more special education students. However, there may be other factors, including class size or differential teacher preparation for special education, that help explain these differences in instructional practice.

CONCLUSIONS AND RECOMMENDATIONS FOR PRACTITIONERS

Teacher evaluation is about more than making personnel decisions, important as those are in any educational system. Ideally, any system of teacher evaluation should also play a significant role in the improvement of instruction at both the individual and organizational levels. Part of the value of observation protocols is that they provide districts and schools with a snapshot of instruction—by teacher, by school, and across the district. Such snapshots could provide diagnostic information to help districts make strategic decisions about where to target resources, such as curriculum or professional development, to help improve instructional quality and, ultimately, student learning. The data in this chapter provide such a snapshot of what ELA teaching looks like in the six MET districts through the eyes of PLATO and suggest areas that might be strengthened.

Our analysis suggests that it would make sense for districts to target resources toward the improvement of middle school instruction in ELA, given the steady downward trend in instructional quality by grade level. This finding may reflect the fact that, over the past few decades, more resources have been targeted to the improvement of elementary literacy, through programs such as Reading First, or perhaps that elementary teachers receive stronger preparation in literacy than do middle school teachers. Regardless of cause, the MET data suggest middle school students may be short-changed by instruction that provides less intellectual challenge and fewer opportunities for high-quality classroom discussion, even as students approach the higher demands of high school.

Most observation protocols do not collect information about the content of the lesson being taught in a systematic way. However, collecting data that includes the content of observed lessons, as well as instructional practices, can help districts make more targeted decisions about how to allocate scarce resources around specific content domains. Coding for content is relatively easy, and it generally requires little extra time for observers. Our analysis suggests that instructional quality, as measured by PLATO, varies significantly by content domain. Based on these data from MET, districts could consider increasing instructional support around the teaching of writing to make lessons more intellectually challenging, to help teachers engage students in conversations about their writing, and to use time efficiently and effectively. Writing lessons were, however, significantly more likely to include modeling and strategy use and instruction. Thus, teaching of reading would seem to benefit from support around how to model or provide strategy use and instruction.

This variation of instructional quality by content domain also reinforces the importance of capturing multiple lessons for any system of teacher evaluation. If observers happen to observe on a day when grammar is being taught, for example, teachers' scores may be lower than if observers had observed a reading lesson instead. While it is important to know that teachers vary in the quality of the lessons by content domain, it is even more important that evaluations accurately represent the average quality of a teacher's practice and are not biased by the particular lesson that was observed. Thus, purposive sampling across content domains in language arts might be an important evaluation strategy for districts wanting a more representative portrait of a teacher's practice.

Understanding more about how teaching may vary according to the students in the class is also an important part of developing a fair and reliable system for evaluation and feedback. While most value-added models control for student demographics, statistical control does not equate with understanding how student demographics affect teaching and learning. It is important to continue to analyze how instruction might vary according to the composition of students in the classroom. Given students with different prior achievement and needs, teachers are expected to differentiate instruction based on these needs. Understanding more about which practices support the learning of English language learners, for example, is a critical part of improving outcomes for all students.

Evaluation systems also make transparent what an organization values. Every measure of teaching has an implicit theory of instruction and desired educational outcomes. No observation instrument is neutral; in the very act of selecting which features of instruction to observe, developers make explicit their implicit theories of instruction. In choosing observation protocols, policymakers must be clear about the kind of teaching and learning they value and choose measures that reflect those values.

Teaching is complex and, like any complex practice, it resists simple measures. In developing a system of teacher evaluation, classroom observation protocols represent one component that can provide diagnostic feedback to teachers, school leaders, and district administrators. Using these data to understand how instructional quality might vary by content domain, by grade level, or by student demographics provides districts with a deeper understanding of how best to use scarce resources to improve the quality of instruction for all students, which is the aim of any high-quality system.

NOTES

1. For the MET study, we used a checklist to capture the extent to which there were errors in the representation of ELA content during observed lessons.

2. A correlation matrix of the content domains is located in Table 10.A.3 of the Appendix.

3. One district did not report the percentage of students receiving free and reduced-priced lunch, an indicator of poverty; that district is omitted from the subsidized lunch analysis.

4. The groups are correlated at .36. The correlation matrix of all student demographic categories can be found in the Appendix.

REFERENCES AND ADDITIONAL RESOURCES

Applebee, A. N., & Langer, J. A. (2011). A snapshot of writing instruction in middle schools and high schools. *English Journal, 100*(6), 14–27.

Atwell, N. (1987). *In the middle: Writing, reading, and learning with adolescents.* Portsmouth, NH: Heinemann.

Beck, I. L., & McKeown, M. G. (2002). Questioning the author: Making sense of social studies. *Educational Leadership, 30*, 44–47.

Calkins, L. (1986). *The art of teaching writing.* Portsmouth, NH: Heinemann.

Delpit, L. (1988). The silenced dialogue: Power and pedagogy in educating other peoples' children. *Harvard Educational Review, 58*(3), 280–298.

Denham, C., & Lieberman, A. (Eds.). (1980). *Time to learn.* Washington, DC: U.S. Dept. of Education, National Institute of Education, Program on Teaching and Learning.

Goldenberg, C. (2008). Teaching English language learners: What the research does—and does not—say. *American Educator, 33*(2), 8–44.

Graham, S. (2006). Strategy instruction and the teaching of writing: A meta-analysis. In C. A. MacArthur, S. Graham, & J. Fitzgerald (Eds.), *Handbook of writing research.* New York: Guilford.

Grossman, P., Loeb, S., Cohen, J., & Wyckoff, J. (2013). Measure for measure: The relationship between measures of instructional practice in middle school English Language Arts and teachers' value-added scores. *American Journal of Education, 119*(3), 445–470.

Grossman, P., Greenberg, S., Hammerness, K., Cohen, J., Alston, C., & Brown, M. (2009). *Development of the Protocol for Language Arts Teaching Observation (PLATO).* Paper presented at the annual meeting of the American Educational Research Association, San Diego, CA.

Heath, S. B. (1983). *Ways with words: Language, life, and work in communities and classrooms.* New York: Cambridge University Press.

Hillocks, G. (2000). *Teaching writing as reflective process.* New York: Teachers College Press.

Kane, T. J. & Staiger, D. O. (2012). *Gathering feedback for teaching: Combining high-quality observations with student surveys and achievement gains.* Seattle, WA: Bill & Melinda Gates Foundation.

Ladson-Billings, G. (1995). Toward a theory of culturally relevant pedagogy. *American Educational Research Journal, 32*(3), 465–491.

Lassen, S. R., Steele, M. M., & Sailor, W. (2006). The relationship between school-wide positive behavior support to academic achievement in an urban middle school. *Psychology in the Schools, 43*(6), 701–12.

Morrison, K. A., Robbins, H. H., & Rose, D. G. (2008). Operationalizing culturally relevant pedagogy: A synthesis of classroom-based research. *Equity & Excellence in Education, 41*(4), 433–452.

Nystrand, M. (1997). *Opening dialogue: Understanding the dynamics of language and learning in the English classroom.* New York: Teachers College Press.

Rowan, B., Correnti, R., & Miller, R. J. (2002). What large-scale, survey research tells us about teacher effects on student achievement: Insights from the "Prospects" study of elementary schools. *Teachers College Record, 104*, 1525–1567.

Rumberger, R. W., & Palardy, G. J. (2005). Does segregation still matter? The impact of student composition on academic achievement in high school. *Teachers College Record, 107*(9), 1999–2045.

Schwab, J. J. (1978). Education and the structure of the disciplines. In I. Westbury & N. J. Wilkof (Eds.), *Science, curriculum and liberal education* (pp. 229–272). Chicago, IL: University of Chicago Press.

Snow, C., & Biancarosa, G. (2003). *Adolescent literacy development among English language learners.* New York: The Carnegie Corporation of New York

Sperling, M., & Freedman, S. W. (2001). Research on writing. In V. Richardson (Ed.), *Handbook of research on teaching* (4th ed.). Washington, DC: American Educational Research Association.

Swanson, H. L. (2001). Searching for the best model for instructing students with learning disabilities. *Focus on Exceptional Children*, *34*(2), 1–15.

Taylor, B. M., Pearson, D. P., Peterson, D. S., & Rodriguez, M. C. (2005). The CIERA School Change Framework: An evidence-based approach to professional development and school reading improvement. *Reading Research Quarterly, 40*(1), 40–69.

Tomlinson, C. A. (1999). *The differentiated classroom: Responding to the needs of all learners.* Alexandria, VA: Association for Supervision and Curriculum Development.

Warren, J. S., Edmonson, H. M., Griggs, P., Lassen, S. R., McCart, A., Turnbull, A., et al. (2003). Urban applications of school-wide positive behavior support: Critical issues and lessons learned. *Journal of Positive Behavior Interventions, 5*, 80–91.

APPENDIX

TABLE 10.A.1. **PLATO Scores by Grade Level**

Grade	Mean	SD
4	2.663	0.271
5	2.667	0.269
6	2.458	0.333
7	2.322	0.345
8	2.326	0.355
Across Grades	2.4872	0.3146

Note: We are continuing to investigate features of the ninth grade sample and consider those findings preliminary.

TABLE 10.A.2. Average PLATO Raw Scores in Different Kinds of Lessons

	Plato Average	Disciplinary Demand Factor		Instructional Scaffolding Factor		Classroom Environment Factor	
		Classroom Discourse Average	Intellectual Challenge Average	Modeling Average	Strategy Use and Instruction Average	Time Mgmt Average	Behavior Mgmt Average
Reading and Writing Instruction	2.36	2.13	2.15	1.42	1.58	3.26	3.6
Grammar/Word Study/ Vocabulary	2.51	2.32	2.3	1.49	1.78	3.46	3.68
Reading Only	2.55	2.34	2.38	1.49	1.79	3.57	3.74
Writing Only	2.59	2.17	2.35	1.81	1.92	3.59	3.68

TABLE 10.A.3. Correlation Matrix of Content Domains

	Reading	Writing	Literature	Speaking and Listening	Word Study	Grammar	Research
Reading	1						
Writing	−0.498	1					
Literature	−0.001	−0.229	1				
Speaking and Listening	−0.192	0.028	−0.015	1			
Word Study	0.041	−0.058	−0.032	0.034	1		
Grammar	−0.278	0.025	−0.116	−0.065	0.137	1	
Research	−0.022	−0.022	−0.092	−0.036	−0.006	0.013	1

TABLE 10.A.4. Correlation Matrix of Student Demographics

	Special Education	English Language Learners	Subsidized Lunch	Black/Hispanic/ American Indian
Special Education	1			
English Language Learners	0.19	1		
Subsidized Lunch	0.20	0.46	1	
Black/Hispanic/ American Indian	−0.03	0.28	0.36	1

TABLE 10.A.5. Alternate Correlation Matrix of Student Demographics

| Grade | PLATO Average | Disciplinary Demand | | Instructional Scaffolding | | Classroom Environment | |
		Intellectual Challenge	Classroom Discourse	Modeling	Strategy Use and Instruction	Behavior Management	Time Management
4	2.67	2.40	2.35	1.74	1.99	3.82	3.69
5	2.67	2.41	2.40	1.70	1.97	3.83	3.73
6	2.46***	2.25***	2.23***	1.42***	1.69***	3.71**	3.45***
7	2.32***	2.13***	2.07***	1.31***	1.57***	3.57***	3.27***
8	2.33***	2.21***	2.11***	1.32***	1.49***	3.55***	3.29***

CHAPTER

How Working Conditions Predict Teaching Quality and Student Outcomes

RONALD F. FERGUSON WITH ERIC HIRSCH

ABSTRACT

This chapter tests a series of hypotheses concerning how working conditions for teachers influence professional learning, teacher expectations, teaching quality, and student outcomes. The findings identify mechanisms inside the "black box" of schooling that help to explain why some schools operate more effectively than others to produce high-quality teaching and learning. *Teaching enablers* that make good teaching more possible—especially school-level conduct management and effective professional development—play central roles. The chapter distinguishes four types of teachers who differ in their expectations for students and in the intensity of their participation with colleagues in professional learning. It identifies implications of the findings for all levels of educational leadership.

INTRODUCTION

This chapter presents new evidence on the conditions under which "good teaching is both possible and likely." It tests hypotheses along a logic chain that begins with school-level working conditions at one end, through teacher beliefs and professional behaviors that predict teaching quality and student engagement and, ultimately, student learning outcomes at the other end. Data come from the Bill & Melinda Gates Foundation Measures of Effective Teaching (MET) project and cover fourth through eighth graders in reading and math. MET included a tailored version of the Teacher Working Conditions (TWC) survey that the second author oversees in his role as chief external affairs officer at the New Teacher Center. Because TWC data were not analyzed for MET reports, this chapter is the first study to employ MET teachers' responses to the TWC survey. Student perceptions of teaching quality, happiness in class, effort in class, and whether the teacher inspires an interest in college come from the MET version of the Tripod survey, for which the first author is the developer. Value-added scores in the chapter combine results from state accountability tests, the Balanced Assessment in Math, and the Stanford 9 (an English language arts exam). It is rare to have such a rich mix of data—including metrics for working conditions, teacher quality, classroom conditions, and achievement—matched at the teacher level. With these data, the authors test a combination of hypotheses not feasible in previous studies.

"If public education is to attract, sustain, and retain able teachers— individuals whose students succeed year after year—then all schools must become places where good teaching is both possible and likely."
—Susan Moore Johnson, 2006, p. 17.

Nonetheless, we emphasize at the outset that the chapter cannot prove causation for the patterns that it documents. To show causation in a definitive way would require methodology and data not available for this study. Instead, the goal for the chapter is to identify potentially important patterns that seem likely to be causal and to suggest how, in the absence of more definitive evidence, those patterns might inform the judgment of officials in real school systems struggling to improve leadership, teaching, and learning. Empirical findings first address between-school and then within-school differences in instructional effectiveness. The chapter ends with a summary of key findings and associated Implications for policy and practice.

BASIC FRAMEWORKS

The chapter develops around two primary frameworks. Figure 11.1 summarizes the first. It concerns the logic chain connecting *base working conditions*, at the beginning of the chain, with *student outcomes* at the end of it.

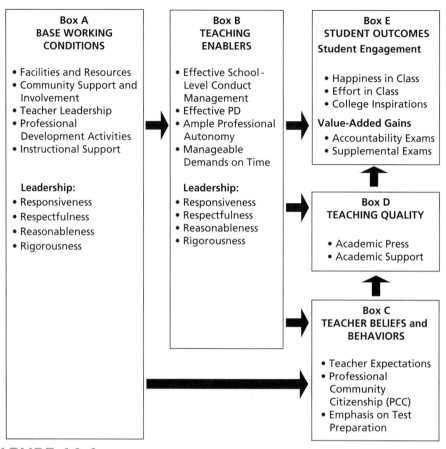

FIGURE 11.1. *Reasoning from Basic Working Conditions to Student Outcomes*

The framework is the conceptual structure for the authors' analysis of why some schools achieve better student outcomes than others do. The second framework is a four-way classification of teachers. It rates teachers above or below average along two dimensions. One concerns *teacher expectations* for students, and the other concerns *professional community citizenship*. The four-way typology helps organize the analysis of why some teachers in any given school produce better student outcomes than their colleagues do.

From Working Conditions to Student Outcomes

Figure 11.1 shows the logic chain linking *base working conditions* with *student outcomes*. Our theory is that the more powerful the connections indicated by arrows on the figure, the greater will be the impact of teacher working conditions on student outcomes. Metrics that capture the *base working conditions* in Box A and the *teaching enablers* in Box B are all considered working conditions in the TWC survey. However, we maintain that the *teaching enablers* are logically more proximate to teaching than the *base working conditions* are. In other words, *teaching enablers* affect classroom practices more strongly because they more directly affect the teacher's ability and willingness to do the job with skill and enthusiasm.

Next, we hypothesize that the indices in Box C are influenced by both *base working conditions* and *teaching enablers*. Box C pertains to three issues. The first is *teacher expectations* for student effort and performance; second is *professional community citizenship;* and the third is the level of *emphasis on test preparation*. We hypothesize that enhanced *base working conditions* and *teaching enablers* will raise *teacher expectations* and increase *professional community citizenship*. However, we remain agnostic about the expected direction of any impacts on *emphasis on test preparation*.

We hypothesize that *teaching enablers*, *teacher expectations*, *professional community citizenship*, and *emphasis on test preparation* affect the *teaching quality* measures in Box D. Box D uses the Tripod 7Cs framework to distinguish *academic support* (where teachers care, confer, captivate, clarify, and consolidate) from *academic press* (where teachers challenge students and control classrooms in order to achieve rigor, respect, order, and persistently on-task behaviors). Finally, Box E comprises *student engagement* (including *effort, happiness*, and *college inspiration*) and *value-added achievement gains*.

We use the logic chain from Boxes A through E in Figure 11.1 to organize our analysis of between-school differences. Tables showing results from the multiple regressions that the chapter discusses appear in the Appendix.

Defining Teacher Prototypes

An analysis of within-school variation toward the end of the chapter distinguishes four types of teachers, depending on their expectations and professional community behaviors. Specifically, when teachers rate above the MET-sample mean on *teacher expectations* for students, we call them *believers*. Otherwise, we call them *agnostics*. When they rate at or above the MET-sample mean for *professional community citizenship*, we call them *active*. Otherwise, they are *isolated*. Hence, the typology is

- Isolated Agnostic

- Active Agnostic

- Isolated Believer

- Active Believer

Every teacher in the data fits one of these types. Table 11.1 shows response patterns for the TWC survey items that define them. The chapter explores how the teacher types differ from one another in teaching quality, student engagement, and value added. In addition, we examine differences between the types in how their perspectives on *teaching enablers* and *school leadership* predict their effectiveness on featured dimensions of performance.

PREVIOUS STUDIES

In the past, empirical studies of working conditions in education have focused primarily on predicting teacher turnover. Authors have examined how strongly salaries, principal leadership, and other conditions affect teachers' decisions to change jobs. Compared to the number of turnover studies, research on the ways that working conditions at one end of a causal chain affect student achievement at the other end is quite rare. Moreover, unlike the present study, which uses student value added at the teacher level, past studies have been restricted to whole-school achievement measures and have only rarely used controls for past test performance. Consequently, they have focused on

TABLE 11.1. Row Percentages for the Teacher Expectations and Professional Community Citizenship Items Used to Define Teacher Types

Response Options	Strongly Disagree	Disagree	Don't Know	Agree	Strongly Agree	Total
Teacher Expectations Items						
A. "I believe almost every student has the potential to do well on a particular assignment."						
Isolated Agnostic	1.7	11.7	0.7	79.0	6.9	100
Active Agnostic	0.7	7.4	0.4	84.8	6.7	100
Isolated Believer	0.0	0.0	0.0	33.5	66.5	100
Active Believer	0.0	0.0	0.0	24.6	75.4	100
B. "I require students in my class to work hard."						
Isolated Agnostic	1.0	2.1	1.4	62.5	33.1	100
Active Agnostic	0.8	1.9	0.4	62.2	34.8	100
Isolated Believer	0.0	0.0	0.0	6.4	93.6	100
Active Believer	0.0	0.0	0.0	2.7	97.3	100
C. "I believe that what I teach will make a difference in my students' lives."						
Isolated Agnostic	2.1	3.8	1.4	83.3	9.6	100
Active Agnostic	0.7	1.1	0.7	90.3	7.1	100
Isolated Believer	0.0	0.0	0.0	8.5	91.5	100
Active Believer	0.0	0.0	0.0	5.2	94.8	100
Professional Community Citizenship Items						
D. "It is easy for other teachers in this school to know what students learned in my class."						
Isolated Agnostic	5.1	35.8	1.0	53.9	4.1	100
Active Agnostic	0.0	1.1	0.0	71.5	27.4	100
Isolated Believer	7.3	29.4	0.0	54.6	8.8	100
Active Believer	0.3	2.2	0.0	34.5	63.0	100

(continued)

(Table 11.1 continued)

Response Options	Strongly Disagree	Disagree	Don't Know	Agree	Strongly Agree	Total
E. "I collaborate with other teachers to achieve consistency in how we assess student work."						
Isolated Agnostic	2.4	37.2	15.0	45.1	0.3	100
Active Agnostic	0.0	0.0	0.4	84.5	15.1	100
Isolated Believer	4.8	36.9	10.9	45.9	1.5	100
Active Believer	0.0	0.7	1.4	50.6	47.4	100
F. "I have detailed knowledge of the content covered and instructional methods used by other teachers at this school."						
Isolated Agnostic	6.5	66.8	3.4	22.3	1.0	100
Active Agnostic	0.0	3.0	0.4	81.2	15.5	100
Isolated Believer	12.7	66.2	2.7	16.6	1.8	100
Active Believer	0.2	9.8	0.5	47.5	42.1	100

Note: Isolated Agnostic (N = 291); Active Agnostic (N = 269); Isolated Believer (N = 331); Active Believer (N = 593).

predicting differences between schools, not between teachers. The present examines both between-school and between-teacher differences in student achievement using achievement gains, not levels as dependent variables.

Past Research on Working Conditions and Value Added

We are aware of only one study that examines a broad range of working conditions as statistical predictors of student achievement gains (as opposed to levels). In that study, Johnson, Kraft, and Papay (2011) use the MassTells survey—a Massachusetts version of the New Teacher Center survey—to predict between-school differences in achievement growth in Massachusetts. Their growth measure is a school-average student growth percentile (SGP), which is favored by the Massachusetts Department of Elementary and Secondary Education (DESE). The SGP and the types of value-added measures that this and other studies use are intended to capture how much students learn over defined time periods, not simply how much they know at any point in time.

Instead of growth or value-added measures, the dependent variables in other recent studies have been achievement levels. Even with adjustments for socio-economic background differences, failing to account for previous achievement levels makes it likely that the achievements these studies are predicting include what students have learned over longer time periods. Hence, between-school differences in the achievement measures reflect more than just teaching and learning over the past year. For example, Ladd (2009) uses a two-stage procedure in which the dependent variable for the second stage is a "school fixed effect" generated from a first-stage regression that predicts achievement controlling for student background measures. There is no measure of previous achievement in the analysis. Similarly, Hirsch and Emerick (2006) use school proficiency rates as dependent variables. Both the Ladd and Hirsch and Emerick studies find evidence that working conditions, including facilities and material resource conditions, help to predict achievement.

In contrast, facilities and material resource conditions were not among the statistically significant predictors of achievement in the Johnson, Kraft, and Papay study. Instead, the most predictive working conditions were indices representing the social conditions of the school as a workplace. The authors describe them as providing a "context in which teachers can work" (related to the *teaching enablers* in the present study). To avoid multicollinearity between working conditions, Johnson, Kraft, and Papay ran separate regressions for each working condition to predict school average SGP measures for reading and math. They controlled for school-average student and teacher demographics, school type, and district fixed effects. The strongest individual predictor of SGP was community support, followed by principal leadership, school culture, and relationships among teachers as professional colleagues. Note that Johnson, Kraft, and Papay did not have a measure for how well the school manages student conduct, which we show below is strongly predicted by the community support measure and correlated with school demographic composition.

Past Research Related to Figure 11.1

Influenced by the findings summarized above, as well as by the discussion of "internal states" representing "teachers' feelings and knowledge" that most directly affect instruction in Leithwood and McAdie (2007), we hypothesize that some working conditions are more directly enabling of teaching than others and should have more direct impacts on the ways that teachers do their jobs. Indeed, some working conditions may be inputs for other working conditions. Accordingly, as explained above, we distinguish *base working conditions* from *teaching enablers*.

Note that *school leadership* appears as both a *base working condition* and a *teaching enabler*, because there are reasons to expect that it matters in multiple ways. Empirical evidence that leadership can affect achievement outcomes is growing. Branch, Hanushek, and Rivkin (2013) report, "Our results indicate that highly effective principals raise the achievement of a typical student in their schools by between two and seven months of learning in a single school year" (p. 63) compared to average principals. Similarly, after more than a decade of tracking schools in Chicago, Bryk (2010) writes, "Put simply, whether classroom learning proceeds depends in large measure on how the school as a social context supports teaching and sustains student engagement" (p. 24); he makes it clear that leadership is a key ingredient to making this happen.

Concerning school leadership, Robinson, Lloyd, and Rowe (2008) have conducted what is probably the most thorough and rigorous meta-analysis. Their focus is on ways that school leadership affects student outcomes. Following an extensive international search, they identified twenty-seven published, peer-reviewed studies (eighteen were from the United States) that linked leadership with student outcomes. Twenty-two examined only academic outcomes, and several used growth measures. The authors found that the strongest predictors of achievement were not the leadership practices that aimed to inspire teachers. Instead, similar to Bryk's statement, the strongest predictors of achievement were practices focused explicitly and actively on improving the quality of instruction. Robinson, Lloyd, and Rowe found that practices focused on improving instruction had achievement impacts three to four times as large as practices targeting teachers' attitudes.

This does not mean that attitudes are unimportant. Indeed, it may be that a focus on making instruction highly effective is a better way to improve teachers' attitudes than targeting attitudes directly; in that case, the resulting change in attitudes may provide an additional boost. Initially, it may even help to drive *some* people's attitudes to be worse, by pressing them to alter their practices in particular ways against their wishes, before they believe that the changes will make a positive difference. More positive attitudes might develop later, as an outcome of success at what they initially resisted. For example, see discussions of the Great Expectations program in Ferguson (2003) and

Brockton High School in Ferguson, Hackman, Hanna, and Ballantine (2010). Indeed, Johnson (2006) reminds us that "this emerging line of research [on working conditions] does not assume that the characteristics of teachers are fixed or static. It indicates, rather, that they are malleable and dynamic within a rich, professional context that encourages learning and growth" (p. 2).

Finally, recall that Box C includes the teachers' *emphasis on test preparation*. This is an appropriate topic for us to consider in this chapter, because of concerns among practitioners and researchers alike about negative impacts of explicit preparation for accountability exams (Koretz, 2008).

MEASURES AND DATA SOURCES

As indicated above, all of the data come from the MET project. However, within the MET project, data come from multiple sources. The teacher survey is an adapted version of the New Teacher Center Working Conditions (TWC) survey; the student survey draws from the Tripod Project for School Improvement; and school districts provided data from their state accountability exams and student demographic records. In addition, the MET project administered the Basic Assessment in Math (BAM) and the Stanford 9 (SAT 9) for English language arts. These achievement tests were used in the classrooms of participating teachers in order to test whether findings for accountability exams also applied to exams not used for accountability. In addition, the BAM and SAT 9 are considered more rigorous than most state exams, and there was an interest in learning whether results are different when the tests are more demanding. Unless otherwise specified, each metric in the chapter is scaled to have a mean of 0 and standard deviation of 1, defined on the teacher-level distribution.

Metrics for Base Working Conditions (Box A)

The MET version of the TWC covers eight whole-school constructs. They address much of what Johnson (2006) and Leithwood and McAdie (2007) characterize as important features of teacher work environments. Box A includes six of the eight constructs (the other two appear in the following section for Box B). Cronbach alpha reliabilities for distinguishing between MET teachers are the following:

1. Facilities and Resources (alpha = 0.87)

2. Community Support and Involvement (alpha = 0.90)

3. Opportunities for Teacher Leadership (alpha = 0.93)

4. School Leadership (original alpha = 0.96; modified, see the four Rs that follow)

5. Professional Development (original alpha = 0.93; modified version, alpha = 0.93)

6. Instructional Supports (original alpha = 0.81; modified version, alpha = 0.76)

The TWC survey uses multiple items for each of these constructs to ask teachers about the school as a whole. For the eight indices, respectively, the intraclass correlations indicating what proportion of the variation is between schools are

▪ Time Management, 0.178

▪ Facilities and Resources, 0.242

▪ Community Support, 0.400

▪ Student Conduct Management, 0.344

▪ Teacher Leadership, 0.276

▪ School Leadership, 0.241

▪ Professional Development, 0.157

▪ Instructional Support, 0.125

In preparation for the MET project, Swanlund (2011) conducted a psychometric evaluation of the TWC instrument. He proposed refinements to the way that items were grouped into the eight domains. Our analysis uses the first five indices in the forms that Swanlund proposed and the other three in modified forms, as explained below.

School leadership is a category that we modified. We conducted a factor analysis on the items and found four dimensions (four Rs) that we represent here as distinct indices. These are *responsiveness, respectfulness, reasonableness*, and *rigorousness* (i.e., leader emphasis on rigorous instruction). Our analysis treats each as a separate measure.

Metrics for Teaching Enablers (Box B)

Four concepts are in Box B. Each is something that, at least in theory, enables teachers to do their jobs effectively. Introduced initially in the context of Figure 11.1, *teaching enablers* pertain to whether demands on teachers' time are excessive or manageable (*manageable demands on time*); whether school-level mechanisms for managing student behavior are effective (*school-level conduct management*); whether school-level professional development activities effectively enhance teachers' skills (*effective PD*); and whether teachers have sufficient autonomy to make instructional decisions (*professional autonomy*). Indices for *manageable demands on time* (alpha = 0.82) and *school-level conduct management* (alpha = 0.88) are used in the forms that Swanlund proposed.

Our index for *effective PD* was formed by transferring four items from the indices that Swanlund proposed for *professional development* and *instructional supports*. Most of the items in the *professional development* index that Swanlund proposed concerned the substance and procedures of professional learning activities. They include the use of data to drive professional development offerings, differentiation of professional development to meet different teachers' needs, and whether professional development is evaluated. Items that Swanlund suggested for the *instructional supports* index differ conceptually from those in the *professional development* index, only insofar as they concern professional support activities and norms outside of more formal professional development programming. For example, they concern whether assessment data are available in time to be useful to teachers, whether teachers work routinely in professional learning communities to develop and align instructional practices, and whether teachers are encouraged to try new approaches.

While most items in the *professional development* and *instructional support* indices pertain to activities, resources, and procedures, four do not. Instead, these four ask directly about actual effectiveness—not just ways that procedures are aligned with best practices. These items ask whether all of the professional development procedures aimed at promoting quality teaching *actually improve teaching*. We removed these four items from the *professional development* and *instructional support* indices and used them to compose our *effective PD* index.

In addition, one item in the *instructional support* category pertains to whether teachers have professional autonomy in their classrooms. Specifically, "Teachers have autonomy to make decisions about instructional delivery (i.e., pacing, materials, and pedagogy)." Since the possible loss of teacher autonomy has sometimes been a theme in resistance to the standards movement, we chose to move this item from *instructional support* and treat it separately as the *professional autonomy* measure among the four *teaching enablers*.

Metrics for Teacher Expectations and Engagement (Box C)

The MET version of the TWC survey includes a collection of items to elicit teachers' beliefs about their own, their students,' and their colleagues' abilities and behaviors. In addition, there are items asking teachers about participation with peers in professional learning and emphasis on preparing students for test questions like the ones on state exams. We introduced the *teacher expectations* and *professional community citizenship* items above while defining the four teacher types (Table 11.1).

The test preparation variable in the analysis asks about agreement with the following statement: "I have my students review test preparation questions like those on this state's required test(s)." Test preparation warrants attention in the analysis because of a widely shared concern that it tends to narrow the curriculum and undermine the external validity of test results. Including it here allows us to estimate its impact on key outcomes.

Metrics for Teacher Quality (Box D)

Student perceptions of instruction are measured using the Tripod 7Cs framework. MET data are from the 2009–2010 school year. Each component in the framework represents a distinct concept associated with effective teaching and is measured using a multi-item index. Like the value-added measures, 7Cs components have been adjusted by the MET research team to remove variation due to student background differences and classroom composition. The 7Cs components are

- *Care:* e.g., "My teacher makes me feel that s/he really cares about me."

- *Confer:* e.g., "My teacher respects my ideas and suggestions."

- *Captivate:* e.g., "I like the ways we learn in this class."

- *Consolidate:* e.g., "My teacher takes time to summarize what we learn each day."

- *Clarify:* e.g., "My teacher explains difficult things clearly."

- *Challenge:* e.g., for effort: "My teacher accepts nothing less than our full effort;" for rigor: "My teacher wants us to use our thinking skills, not just memorize things."

- *Control:* e.g., "Our class stays busy and doesn't waste time."

MET findings provide validation for the use of the 7Cs components as teaching quality variables in the present chapter. (See Kane, McCaffrey, & Staiger, 2010, 2012.)

While MET used all of the 7Cs in a single composite index, we in this chapter unbundle the set. (Also see Ferguson with Danielson, Chapter 4 in this volume.) We combine *Challenge* and *Control* into an index of *academic press*, while grouping the other five—*Care, Confer, Captivate, Clarify*, and *Consolidate*—to form a measure of *academic support*.

Metrics for Student Outcomes (Box E)

We use the variables in Boxes A through D to predict two general categories of student outcomes in Box E. One is *student engagement* and the other is *value added*.

Engagement The MET survey included measures of whether students were happy to be in the class, whether they pushed themselves hard to do their best, and whether their teacher in the surveyed class made them feel inspired to go to college. We examine degrees to which each of the three is predicted by prior variables in the logic chain.

Value Added As indicated above, MET used four different tests: each state's standardized English language arts (ELA) test; each state's standardized math test; the Balanced Assessment of Math (BAM); and the Stanford 9 (SAT). In our initial work for this chapter, we began by analyzing each of the tests separately. However, we did not find consistent and statistically significant differences distinguishing the different tests, subjects, or grade levels. So in order to simplify the analysis and presentation, we form a single composite from the two available scores for each subject: the state ELA score and the SAT 9 for English and the state math score with the BAM for math. All scores were originally standardized to have a mean of 0 and a standard deviation of 1 at the student level within grade, year, and district. Because this chapter concerns differences between teachers, the value-added measure that we use is re-standardized to have a mean of 0 and a standard deviation of 1 at the teacher level across the MET sample.

The findings reported below cover grades 4 through 8. Like the value-added measures, all student survey variables are net of variation due to measured student demographic differences and have been standardized to have a mean of 0 and standard deviation of 1 at the teacher level (after initially being standardized by grade level within each home district). Further, because our initial analyses of between-school differences for the 203 schools lacked sufficient statistical power to identify clear grade or subject differences in main effects, the findings here are for all grades and subjects pooled, with appropriate grade level and subject indicator variables to allow for differences in intercepts by level and subject.

PREDICTING BETWEEN-SCHOOL DIFFERENCES

Our aim is to develop a storyline following the outline presented in Figure 11.1 and the four-way typology of teachers presented above. We focus on between-school variation through most of the analysis and within-school variation at the end. To follow the storyline, it will help to be aware that two *teaching enablers*—specifically, *school-level conduct management* and *effective PD*—tend to play the most important roles as predictors of between-school variation in the other variables that we examine.

Base Working Conditions That Predict Teaching Enablers

To examine the relationship between *base working conditions* and *teaching enablers*, we conducted a multivariate statistical analysis taking each of the *teaching enablers* in turn as the variable to be predicted, and all of the *base working conditions* as predictors (Table 11.A.1 in the Appendix). We generated results using only between-school variation because at this point we are interested in understanding what distinguishes schools from one another.

For each *teaching enabler*, the following lists the *base working conditions* that our analysis finds to be positive and statistically significant predictors:

Manageable Time Demands (R-Sq. 0.59)

- Facilities and Resources

- Leadership Responsiveness

School-Level Conduct Management (R-Sq. 0.76)

- Facilities and Resources

- Community Support

- Leadership Responsiveness

- Leadership Respectfulness

Teacher Autonomy (R-Sq. 0.46)

- Teacher Leadership

- Instructional Supports

Effective Professional Development (R-Sq. 0.82)

- Professional Development (e.g., principles and practices)

- Instructional Supports (e.g., principles and practices)

Among all of the *base working conditions*, only *leadership reasonableness* and *leadership rigorousness* were not positive and statistically significant predictors for at least one of the *teaching enablers* in our multivariate analysis.

Generally, it is encouraging that the patterns are so logical. Compared to other schools, those rated higher on *facilities and resources* can probably afford to place fewer time demands on their teachers. These findings indicate that leaders whom teachers rate high on responsiveness run their schools in ways that make teachers feel that time demands are reasonable. Also quite logical is that conduct management is perceived to be better in schools with particular types of climates: those in which there are more community support, better facilities, and resources and leaders who are responsive and respectful.

Teachers perceive greater autonomy in schools in which they play more active roles as leaders and, where informal instructional supports are more plentiful. Recall that TWC *professional development* and *instructional support* indices assign higher values for compliance with principles and practices that contemporary experts tend to recommend. While certainly expected, it is important to confirm that teachers in schools where professional learning activities use state-of-the-art principles and practices report more frequently that professional development is truly effective.

Bottom line: the general hypothesis that the *base working conditions* in Box A of Figure 11.1 should predict the *teaching enablers* in Box B is affirmed. All four *teaching enablers* are predicted by variables that school leaders can target for improvement with the aim of enabling teachers to do their jobs more effectively.

How Teaching Enablers Predict Teacher Expectations and Professional Community Citizenship

Continuing through Figure 11.1, here we will examine how *base working conditions* and *teaching enablers* predict *teacher expectations* and *professional community citizenship*—in other words, we examine how Boxes A and B in Figure 11.1 predict Box C. Again, we use only between-school variation in order to understand between-school differences.

Teacher Expectations The *teacher expectations* index in this study is the average of three items (shown on Table 11.1). The first pertains to whether students have the ability to do well on assignments; the second to whether lessons will make a difference in students' lives; and the third to whether the teacher pushes students to work hard. To study the index, our between-school regressions include *base working conditions* and the *teaching enablers* as predictors (Table 11.A.2 in the Appendix). In addition, in this section we address whether components of the *teacher expectations* index are predicted by the racial or income composition student body.

We find that the only variables that helps in predicting between-school differences in *teacher expectations* are *effective PD* from the *teacher enablers* category and *professional development* from the *base working conditions* category. *Effective PD* predicts higher *teacher expectations* with or without *professional development* in the equation. However, counter to what we expected, the *professional development* variable has a negative sign when *effective PD* is held constant and a near 0 coefficient when *effective PD* is absent from the equation. We believe this is due to reverse causation rather than colinearity. Specifically, if administrators perceive that their teachers have low expectations for students, they may respond by placing greater emphasis on formal professional development. In any case, the most important conclusion here is that schools rated higher on *effective PD* tend also to rate higher on *teacher expectations* for students. It is important to understand that this finding pertains to professional development *effectiveness*, not necessarily its other qualities, such as alignment with particular principles or practices.

It seems quite natural at this point to divert the discussion and ask whether *teacher expectations* might be predicted more by student characteristics, especially race, than by working conditions. The question is interesting enough to consider separately for each item in the *teacher expectations* index. At first, we control for grade level, subject, race, percent free or reduced-price lunch eligibility, and the percentage of male students. We find that *teacher expectations* are higher for one of the three measures—whether the teacher believes that the students can do well on their assignments—when there is a higher percentage of white students (or a lower percentage of black and Hispanic students). However, a single control variable—*community supports*—is sufficient to render the effect very small and statistically insignificant (Table 11.A.3 in the Appendix). This suggests, as Johnson, Kraft, and Papay (2011) conclude, that between-school differences in what appear to be race-based teacher perspectives may instead reflect race-correlated community conditions. Bottom line: our results do not support a strong role for race in predicting between-school differences in *teacher expectations*. Instead, our findings suggest that the strongest predictor of between-school differences in *teacher expectations* is *effective PD*.

Professional Community Citizenship In contrast to *teacher expectations*, we find that four of the constructs in the *base working conditions* category are positive and statistically significant predictors of *professional community citizenship* at the 0.05 level or better when we leave *teaching enablers* out of the equation (Table 11.A.2). The four are *community supports*, *professional development, instructional supports*, and *leadership reasonableness*. When we add *teaching enablers* to the equation predicting *professional community citizenship*, estimated coefficients for *community supports* and *professional development* drop modestly below conventional levels of statistical significance. Despite this impact of their inclusion in the analysis, none of the *teaching enablers* is *at all* statistically significant as a predictor of *professional community citizenship*. (The findings also indicate that, other things equal, schools with better facilities and more resources have somewhat lower levels of PCC. Why this might be so is unclear.)

To reflect further on the strongest and most positive predictors of why some schools achieve higher levels of *professional community citizenship* than others, consider that the items in the *leadership reasonableness* index are

- The procedures for teacher evaluation are consistent.

- Teacher performance is assessed objectively.

- Teachers receive feedback that can help them improve teaching.

    Similarly, items from the *instructional supports* index include

- State assessment data are available in time to impact instructional practices.

- Teachers use assessment data to inform their instruction.

■ Teachers work in professional learning communities to develop and align instructional practices.

■ Teachers are encouraged to try new things to improve instruction.

Note that these are distinctly different criteria from those captured by our *teaching enablers*. The latter focuses more directly on factors associated with whether teachers will think effective teaching is feasible.

Hence, it appears that *professional community citizenship* is not primarily the result of teachers feeling that the job of teaching is doable. Instead, we find that *professional community citizenship* is higher in schools in which teachers feel supported by leaders who are both reasonable and focused on helping teachers improve—leaders who support the work by which professional learning activities *might ultimately* become effective.

Finally, the other metric in Box C of Figure 11.1 is *emphasis on test preparation*. Only *leadership reasonableness* is a statistically significant predictor at the 0.05 level or better. Higher ratings on *leadership reasonableness* predict more test preparation.

Predicting Teaching Quality

Figure 11.1 suggests that the *teaching enablers* in Box B and the *teacher beliefs and behaviors* in Box C predict *teaching quality* in Box D. As introduced earlier, our measures of *teaching quality* come from the Tripod 7Cs framework and distinguish *academic press* (a composite of *Control* and *Challenge*) from *academic support* (a composite of *Care, Confer, Captivate, Clarify*, and *Consolidate*).

Do Teaching Enablers Predict Teaching Quality? We find that all four *teaching enablers—effective school-level conduct management, effective PD, professional autonomy*, and *manageable demands on time*—have positive signs as predictors of both *support* and *press* (Table 11.A.4). However, only *manageable time demands* is significant at the 0.05 level for both *support* and *press*. Perhaps teachers who are not stressed by time demands are willing and able to deliver more effective instruction. *Teacher autonomy* also predicts both domains of *teaching quality*, but only at the 0.10 significance level.

The largest and most important estimates of how *teaching enablers* influence *teaching quality* are for *school-level conduct management* and *effective PD* as predictors of *academic press*. (Neither of these two predictors reaches the 0.05 significance level for *academic support*.) Imagine schools that do a great job of managing student conduct and, in addition, provide truly effective professional learning experiences for teachers. These are the schools in which students rate teachers higher on *academic press*. Teachers in such schools are more prone to *Challenge* their students to work hard (*press for effort*) and think hard (*press for rigor*) in classrooms that are under *Control*—orderly, respectful, and on task. How students rate these same teachers on *academic support* may depend on teachers' own satisfaction—in particular, their perspectives on *manageable time demands* and perhaps also *autonomy*.

Do Teacher Beliefs and Behaviors Predict Teaching Quality? To consider *teacher beliefs and behaviors* as predictors of teaching quality, we use the four teacher types defined earlier. Recall that they blend the *teacher expectations* and *professional community citizenship* variables. *Active believers* are treated as the base group for comparison. The finding is that, compared to having higher percentages of *active believers*, students rate the teaching staff lower on both *academic support* and *academic press* when more of their teachers are *isolated agnostics*. While the estimates are not highly precise—only the finding for *academic support* is significant at the 0.05 level—they are surprisingly large. Shifting a school from all *active believers* to all *isolated agnostics* is predicted to reduce *press* by 0.34 standard deviations and *support* by 0.45 standard deviations.

Do Perceptions of School Leadership Predict Teaching Quality? Recall from earlier that *leadership respectfulness* was a negative predictor (Table 11.A.1) for *effective PD*, holding constant the other *base working conditions*. Now we find that *leadership respectfulness* is also a negative predictor of *teacher quality* measures (Table 11.A.4). Specifically, holding constant the other *base working conditions*, *leadership respectfulness* is a negative predictor of between-school differences for both *academic support* and *academic press*. An interpretation for both findings is that, when holding constant other things that matter and increasing *only leadership respectfulness*, the effect under some circumstances may be to lower the sense of urgency that people feel to work hard and to improve.

Leadership rigorousness is the other leadership variable with a negative and statistically significant predicted effect on between-school differences in teaching quality, other things equal. In this case, however, the finding applies mainly to *academic press*, not *support*. *Academic press* is composed of two components, *Control* and *Challenge*. Initially, we suspected that the negative relationship of *leadership rigorousness* to *academic press* in the multivariate equations might reflect between-school differences in standards for rigor. However, when we analyzed *Control* and *Challenge* separately, we discovered that the negative finding for *leadership rigorousness* was mainly as a predictor of *Control*. Further, the *rigorousness* index has two items. When we took it apart, we discovered that the effect was operating mainly through the item: *"Teachers are held to high professional standards for delivering instruction."* As we conducted additional analyses an interesting possibility emerged. Specifically, it could be that increasing pressure on teachers to deliver rigorous instruction might create problems with classroom management for teachers and students lacking sufficient skill or supports to respond to such demands in more constructive ways.

To summarize our findings on predictors of teaching quality, between-school differences in how students rate teaching are predicted by all four types of *teaching enablers*. Furthermore, there are clear differences in what predicts *academic support* versus *academic press*. Teacher responses for *school-level conduct management* and *effective PD* are much stronger predictors of student perceptions of *academic press* than is *academic support*. At the same time, *manageable time demands* are equally effective at predicting *academic support* and *academic press*, but with coefficients only about half as large as those for *school-level conduct management* and *effective PD* when they predict *academic press*. All in all, an important bottom line is that teachers' responses to the TWC survey on items concerning *teaching enablers*, *teacher expectations*, and *professional community citizenship* predict their students' responses to Tripod survey items concerning teaching quality.

Predicting Student Outcomes

Up to this point in the chapter, we have empirically examined the logic chain from *base working conditions* to *teaching enablers*, from *teaching enablers* to *teacher beliefs and behaviors*, and from *teacher beliefs and behaviors* to *teaching quality*. We now complete the chain by considering between-school differences in *student outcomes*.

Predicting Value Added Value added and achievement growth measures are becoming the most common focus of contemporary school accountability metrics. If we consider only *base working conditions* as predictors, the one statistically significant predictor of between-school differences in value added is *professional development*. But when we add *teaching enablers* to the analysis, the coefficient on *professional development* drops from 0.25 to 0.067 and becomes statistically insignificant (Table 11.A.5). It appears that professional development norms and procedures affect *value-added gains* by enhancing *teaching enablers*. Among the four teaching enablers in the analysis, only *manageable time demands* is not a statistically significant predictor of value added (although the statistical significance drops when *teaching quality* is added to the equation).

The most important *teaching enabler* for predicting between-school differences in value added is *school-level conduct management*. In the most complete specification, after all of the *teacher beliefs and behaviors* and *teaching quality* measures are added to the equation, the only two positive and statistically significant predictors of value added are *school-level conduct management* and *academic press*.

There are two negative predictors. For the four teacher types, schools with higher percentages of *active agnostic* teachers have lower average value added (with *active believer* as the base comparison category [Table 11.A.6]). In fact, other things equal, our estimates indicate that adding *active agnostics* is worse than adding *inactive agnostics* insofar as school-level value added is concerned. Perhaps *active agnostics* are intellectually contagious—spreading their agnostic beliefs, while *isolated agnostics* would keep to themselves. Indeed, negative peer influence among teachers is a genuine concern for some of the educators with whom we have worked.

Emphasis on test preparation is another negative predictor. One interpretation is that targeted preparation for state exams is a bad investment of time. Alternatively, this may be an instance of reverse causation; perhaps administrators press teachers to spend more time on test preparation at schools where performance is likely to be low and where, without explicit preparation, it would be even lower.

In any case, taking these results at face value, we venture a summary statement. Specifically, schools that achieve greater value added tend to have

- More effective ways than other schools of maintaining order (i.e., the *Control* component of *academic press* from student surveys and *school-level conduct management* from teacher surveys);

- A propensity to insist that students persist in the face of difficulty and strive to think rigorously (i.e., the *Challenge* component of *academic press*);

- Less time than other schools on practicing for standardized tests; and

- A higher percentage of *active believer* teachers (especially versus *active agnostics*).

It is worth noting that, after *academic press* is accounted for, *academic support* adds no additional explanatory power to the prediction of between-school differences in value added. See Ferguson with Danielson, Chapter 4 in this volume, for related findings.

Predicting Student Engagement

Before interpreting the results for value added to mean that *academic press* is much more important than *academic support* for predicting between-school differences, consider how strongly *academic support* predicts selected student engagement outcomes: *happiness in class, effort in class*, and *college inspiration*. Figure 11.2 graphs the coefficients, based on Tables 11.A.6, 11.A.7, and 11.A.8. For happiness, effort, and inspiration, *academic support* is a stronger predictor of between-school differences than *academic press*. Indeed, for both *happiness in class* and *college inspiration*, the coefficient

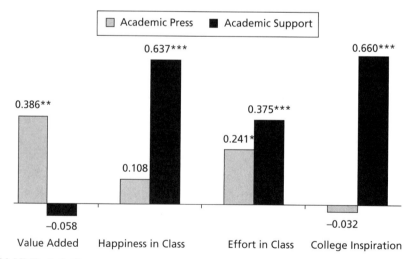

FIGURE 11.2. *Multiple Regression Coefficients on Academic Press and Academic Support for Between-School Differences in Student Outcomes and Engagement*

Note: Statistical significance: +=.10; *=.05; **=.01; ***=.001.

estimates for *academic press* are very small and completely insignificant. For *effort in class*, *academic press* is a statistically significant predictor, but its estimated impact is smaller than for *academic support* and not nearly as statistically significant.

To this point in the chapter, we have focused on predicting between-school differences. We have confirmed that *teaching enablers* are predicted by *base working conditions* and that *teaching enablers*, in turn, predict *teacher beliefs and behaviors* and *teaching quality*. We have found that variables from all of these categories contribute either directly or indirectly to predicting why some schools achieve greater value-added test score gains and more *student engagement*.

PREDICTING WITHIN-SCHOOL DIFFERENCES IN TEACHING QUALITY AND STUDENT OUTCOMES

Our findings above indicate that the most important indicators for distinguishing why some schools achieve better teaching, learning, and student engagement than others are two *teaching enablers*—specifically, *school-level conduct management* and *effective PD*. But do the same indicators predict differences from one teacher to another within a school? and Are there within-school differences in how teachers experience or perceive these enablers—specifically, differences reflected in responses to the TWC survey? If so, do such differences predict teacher-to-teacher differences in what students report about classrooms and the value added that they achieve on standardized exams?

To answer such questions, we examine ways that teachers' reports on *school-level conduct management, effective PD*, and *school leadership* predict within-school differences in their students' *effort in class, happiness in class, college inspiration*, and *value-added outcomes*, as well as perceptions of *academic support* and *academic press*. We test for whether coefficient patterns differ by whether teachers are *isolated agnostics, active agnostics, isolated believers*, or *active believers*. All multiple regressions performed in this part of the chapter included a separate intercept term for each school. Thereby, the variation under consideration comes only from within schools and pertains only to comparisons between same-school teachers.

Average Differences by Teacher Type To begin, Figure 11.3 shows average differences between types of teachers, holding constant beliefs about *teaching enablers* and *school leadership* (Table 11.A.9). Consistent with much

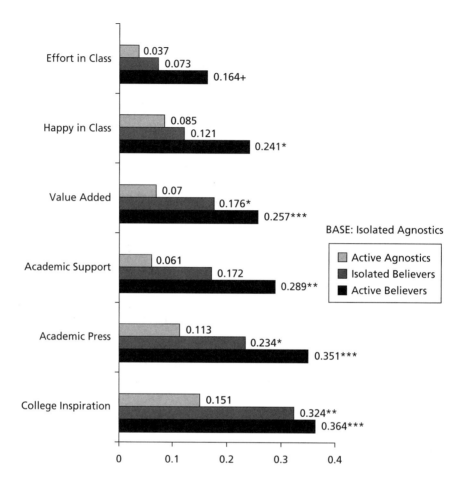

FIGURE 11.3. *Student Outcomes, Value Added, and Student Perceptions of Quality by Teacher Type Compared with "Isolated Agnostics" as the Base Category*

Note: Statistical significance: +=.10; *=.05; **=.01; ***=.001. Coefficients from Table 11.A.9 std. dev. units.

conventional wisdom, our estimates indicate that teachers with high expectations who participate actively as members of their schools' professional communities (i.e., *active believers*) are more effective along every dimension shown, especially compared to teachers with below-average expectations and professional community citizenship (i.e., *isolated agnostics*). The figure shows that average outcomes and teacher quality perceptions among students of *active believers* consistently exceed those among students of *isolated agnostics*. The differences range from a low of 0.153 standard deviations for *effort in class* to 0.34 for *academic press* and 0.35 for the degree to which the teacher generates *college inspiration*. Indeed, for each predicted variable on Figure 11.3, there is stepwise improvement as we move from *isolated agnostics*, to *active agnostics*, to *isolated believers*, to *active believers*.

How Teaching Enablers Predict Within-School Differences in Teaching Quality and Student Outcomes Figures 11.4 show predictions (simulations) based on multiple regression coefficients from Table 11.A.9. The labels TEQ1 through TEQ4 in the figure stand for "Teaching Enablers Quartile" for Quartiles 1 through 4 of a composite *teaching enablers* index that equally weights *school-level conduct management* and *effective PD*. Recall that the *teaching enablers* in this context are the teacher's own perspectives from the TWC survey. Quartiles of this composite are defined on the full data set of all MET teachers who responded to the TWC survey.

The essentially flat lines for *active believers* indicate no clear relationship between student perceptions or value-added outcomes and teachers' perceptions of *teaching enablers*. If anything, there appears to be a slightly negative pattern in which *active believers* who rate *teaching enablers lower* tend to have *better* student outcomes; five of the six lines for *active believers* slope slightly downward. The reason is unclear, but it may be that *active believers* who rate *teaching enablers* lower tend to have more exacting standards in their teaching and also in the way that they rate the school. This interpretation is very tentative, and none of the negative slopes is statistically significant. Clearly, however, the general pattern for *active believers* indicates that they seldom allow their opinions about *teaching enablers* to affect how well they serve their students.

The same is not true for other teacher types. The effectiveness of "middle-category" teachers (i.e., the *active agnostics* and *isolated believers*) appears most sensitive to *teaching enablers*. Compared to *active believers* and *isolated agnostics*, Figure 11.4 indicates that we should expect *isolated believers* and *active agnostics* to improve their instructional practices the most in response to building-level improvements to conduct management and professional supports. Indeed, there tends to be less difference in student outcomes and engagement achieved by the four teacher types among those who rate *teaching enablers* at the TEQ4 level—in other words, when they rate both *school-level conduct management* and *effective PD* in the top quartile.

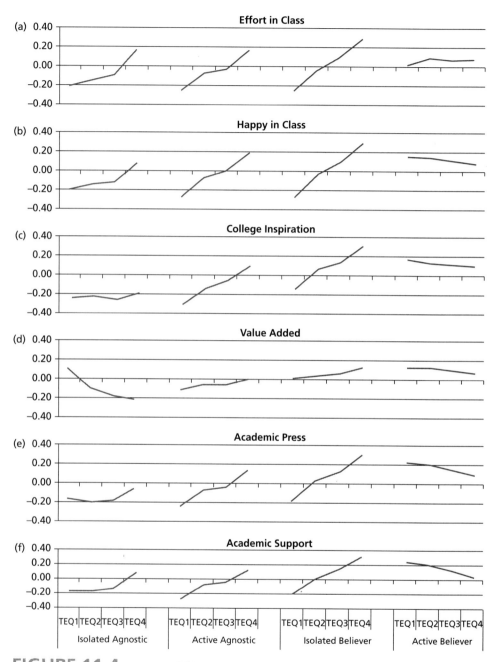

FIGURE 11.4. *How Within-School Differences in Perceptions of Teaching Enablers Predict Teaching Quality and Student Outcomes, by Teacher Type*

Distinct Patterns for Isolated Agnostics The estimated effects of *teaching enablers* for *isolated agnostics* are generally positive, but they are almost always smaller than for *active agnostics* and *isolated believers* teachers. The exceptions to this pattern—the places where effects appear larger for isolated agnostics than for middle-category teachers—are interesting to consider.

First, the estimated effects of *school-level conduct management* on student *happiness in class, academic press*, and *academic support* (Table 11.A.9) are greater for isolated agnostics than for other teacher types. It makes sense that *school-level conduct management* might have the greatest effect on classroom-level effectiveness among teachers who are both *isolated* (tending not to interact much with colleagues) and *agnostic* in their expectations for students. These are the teachers who might naturally experience the most difficulty managing students on their own, without support.

Second, and perhaps most interesting, *isolated agnostics* who give lower ratings to their school leaders tend to produce higher instead of lower value added (Table 11.A.6, Column 4). This relationship between lower ratings for *school leadership* and higher value added (or conversely, higher ratings for *school leadership* and lower value added) is why we see a negative slope in the value-added simulation for isolated agnostics of Figure 11.4. Perhaps *isolated agnostics* assign lower *school leadership* ratings to the supervisors who press them hardest (and most successfully!) to improve their students' performance. Whatever the explanation, it is interesting that value added is the only one among the six metrics covered in Figure 11.4 that shows this curious pattern.

KEY FINDINGS AND THEIR IMPLICATIONS

The following comprise important albeit common-sense implications of the findings in this chapter. They fit well with existing conventional wisdom, while potentially strengthening it.

1. We find that schools with more community support achieve more effective conduct management, which, in turn, predicts higher value-added learning gains. **Implication:** Cultivate community support for the school, with an emphasis on strengthening ties with families.

2. There is evidence that, when teachers regard professional development and instructional support activities as meeting high standards, they are

more likely to regard them as truly effective at enhancing instructional skills. When more of a school's teachers regard professional learning activities as truly effective, they tend to have higher expectations for students. In addition, their students rate them higher on *academic press* (which predicts achievement gains) and report feeling more inspired to attend college. **Implication:** Build state-of-the-art principles and practices into professional development and instructional support activities.

3. State-of-the-art design does not guarantee effectiveness. Be aware that teachers may not regard professional learning activities as effective at building their skills, even if they regard those activities as state-of-the-art. Actual effectiveness matters. Evidence in the chapter indicates that professional learning activities are unlikely to improve teaching and learning for students if those activities are not truly effective at enhancing professional knowledge and skill. **Implication:** Monitor and seek continually to improve the effectiveness of professional development and instructional support activities.

4. We, as well as Ferguson and Danielson (Chapter 4 in this volume), find that value-added achievement gains are predicted by *academic press* more than by *academic support*. Consequently, some might be tempted to focus instructional improvement on *press* while neglecting *support*. We find that, compared to *academic press*, *academic support* is a stronger predictor of *happiness in class*, *effort in class*, and whether the teacher provides *college inspiration*. Hence, equipping teachers with skills to provide *support* may be as important as preparing them to deliver *press*. Recall the chapter's finding that teacher perceptions of *effective PD* predict higher levels of *academic press*, but not of *academic support*. Perhaps there is less urgency in professional learning when focused on *academic support*—i.e., *Care, Confer, Captivate, Clarify*, and *Consolidate*—than when focused on Challenge and Control, the components of *academic press*. **Implication:** Professional supports that aim to enable good teaching should entail skill building targeted to both *academic press* and *academic support*, not one or the other.

5. Evidence indicates that schools achieve higher levels of *professional community citizenship* when teachers perceive that their leaders are reasonable and when instructional supports encourage collaboration. This applies *even if professional learning activities are not yet truly effective.* If school

leaders are fair, supportive, and consistent in dealing with teachers, there is a chance that professional learning activities might attract and sustain sufficient participation to achieve their potential. Otherwise, lack of participation by teachers who feel disgruntled or indifferent may undermine school-wide progress. **Implication:** Monitor and cultivate norms by which school leaders are fair, supportive, and consistent in dealing with teachers.

6. Excessively respectful leaders may fail to provide the sense of urgency necessary to motivate high performance. Conversely, leaders who press too hard can cause dysfunctional responses to the stress that they impose. There are indications that pressure to perform—for example, heavy demands for rigor in classroom instruction—can prompt behavior problems in classrooms lacking capacity to respond constructively to the demands. At the same time, other things equal, we find that teachers who perceive school leaders as *more* respectful tend to be rated by their students as *lower* on both *academic support* and *academic press*. **Implication:** Supervise teachers in ways that balance serious press to perform with respectful personal support.

7. Evidence shows that *active believer* teachers generate higher value-added achievement gains and greater student engagement than their same-school colleagues. **Implication:** Take special steps to identify, cultivate, and retain *active believer* teachers and create opportunities for their beliefs and behaviors to influence other teachers. School leaders should seek ways to help teachers believe that their students are able, that the curriculum is important to students' lives, and that students will respond when pressed to work harder and smarter. They should also strive to create and encourage participation in strong, instructionally focused, and student-centric professional communities.

8. We find that *isolated agnostics* tend to be the lowest rated teachers in the school by their students. In addition, they tend to produce the lowest value added under conditions when they are the *most* satisfied (instead of the *least* satisfied) with school leadership. **Implication:** Make special efforts to identify *isolated agnostics* and provide them with both support and press to improve. School leaders should find ways to engage *isolated agnostics* more actively in collaborative forms of professional work and learning and give them honest feedback on their performance, even if doing so requires difficult conversations that risk diminishing job satisfaction.

CONCLUSION

Data from the MET project make it possible to answer questions with large data sets that have been out of reach to researchers until now. We have been confined when using large data sets to treat schools mostly as black boxes in which teacher experience, class sizes, funding, student characteristics, and a short list of other measurable quantities predicted outcomes. Generally, we had no measures of what students and teachers were actually doing to produce those outcomes. Furthermore, the range of outcomes measured was narrow. Genuine value-added measures were rare, and we seldom had any measures of student engagement. Times are changing.

Our analysis of teacher working conditions, especially *teaching enablers*, points to some quite plausible ways that educational leaders can go about improving school outcomes. Our findings indicate that *community supports* from parents and others can help foster the types of *school-level conduct management* that enables classroom teachers to do their work effectively. In addition, our estimates suggest that *effective professional development* can help raise *teacher expectations* and that well-designed *instructional supports* can increase *professional community citizenship*, thereby increasing the share of their teachers who are *active believers*.

Active believers are defined as teachers who expect more of students and participate more actively with colleagues as professional citizens concerned about improving teaching and learning. Our analysis indicates that *active believer* teachers deliver more *academic support* and impose more *academic press* than their same-school colleagues do. Comparing schools to one another, as well as comparing teachers, we find that a high level of *academic press* from teachers predicts greater value-added achievement gains for students, but not *happiness in class* or *college inspiration*. Conversely, high levels of *academic support* predict more *happiness in class* and greater *college inspiration*, but not value-added achievement gains. Both *academic support* and *academic press* predict *effort in class*. Hence, a quite coherent story has emerged, albeit with some interesting nuance.

A number of states and districts have begun using data from the TWC and Tripod surveys to take the pulse of their schools and set priorities for support and accountability. Some are further ahead than others in organizing to use the data effectively, but capacity is growing. As understanding grows and communication becomes better framed and delivered, deliberations can be enhanced at a number of levels—among school board members, central office staffs, school-level administrators, and others—expanding the number of places where, as Susan Moore Johnson says, "good teaching is both possible and likely."

REFERENCES AND ADDITIONAL RESOURCES

Berry, B., Smylie, M., & Fuller, E. (2008, November). *Understanding teacher working conditions: A review and look to the future.* Carrboro, NC: Report from the Center for Teaching Quality.

Branch, G. F., Hanushek, E. A., & Rivkin, S. G. (2013, Winter). School leaders matter. *Education Next*, pp. 63–69.

Borko, H. (2004). Professional development and teacher learning: Mapping the terrain. *Educational Researcher, 33*, 3–15.

Brown-Sims, M., & Menon, R. (2011, January). *Working conditions and their impact on teacher retention and student achievement: Literature review.* Washington, DC: Learning Point Associates, American Institutes for Research.

Bryk, A. A. (2010, April). Organizing schools for improvement. *Phi Delta Kappan.*

Ferguson, R. F. (2003, July). Teacher perceptions and expectations and the black-white test score gap. *Urban Education, 38*(4).

Ferguson, R. F., Hackman, S., Hanna, R., & Ballantine, A. (2010, June). *How high schools become exemplary.* A report from the Achievement Gap Initiative at Harvard University. www.agi .harvard.edu

Hanushek, E. A., & Rivkin, S. G. (2007, Spring). Pay, working conditions, and teacher quality. *The Future of Children, 17*, pp. 69–86.

Hirsch, E., & Emerick, E. (with Church, K., & Fuller, E). (2006). *Teaching and learning conditions are critical to the success of students and the retention of teachers.* Hillsborough, NC: Center for Teacher Quality. www.teachingquality.org/legacy/twcccsd2006.pdf

Ingersoll, R. M., & Smith, T. M. (2003). The wrong solution to the teacher shortage. *Educational Leadership, 60*, pp. 30–33.

Johnson, S. M. (2006, July). *The workplace matters: Teacher quality, retention, and effectiveness.* Best Practices Working Paper. Washington, DC: National Education Association.

Johnson, S. M., Kraft, M. A., & Papay, J. P. (2011, June 29). *How context matters in high-need schools: The effects of teachers' working conditions on their professional satisfaction and their students' achievement.* Cambridge, MA: Project on the Next Generation of Teachers, Harvard Graduate School of Education.

Kane, T. J., McCaffrey, D. F., & Staiger, D. O. (2010). *Learning about teaching: Initial findings from the Measures of Effective Teaching Project.* Seattle, WA: Bill & Melinda Gates Foundation.

Kane, T. J., McCaffrey, D. F., & Staiger, D. O. (2012). *Gathering feedback for teaching: Combining high-quality observations with student surveys and achievement gains.* Seattle, WA: Bill & Melinda Gates Foundation.

Koretz, D. M. (2008). *Measuring up: What educational testing really tells us.* Cambridge, MA: Harvard University Press.

Ladd, H. (2009, December). *Teachers' perceptions of their working conditions: How predictive of policy-relevant outcomes?* Washington, DC: National Center for Analysis of Longitudinal Data in Education Research, Working Paper 33.

Lee, V. E., Dedrick, R. F., & Smith, J. B. (1991, July). The effect of the social organization of schools on teachers' efficacy and satisfaction. *Sociology of Education, 64,* 190–208.

Lee, V. E., Smith, J. B., Perry, T. E., & Smylie, M. A. (1999, October). *Social support, academic press and student achievement.* Report of the Chicago Annenberg Research Project, Chicago Consortium for School Research.

Leithweed, K., & McAdie, P. (2007). Teacher working conditions that matter. *Education Canada,* pp. 42–45.

Robinson, V. M. J., Lloyd, C. A., & Rowe, K. J. (2008). The impact of leadership on student outcomes: An analysis of the differential effects of leadership types. *Educational Administration Quarterly, 44*(5), 635–674.

Swanlund, A. (2011, January). *Identifying working conditions that enhance teacher effectiveness: The psychometric evaluation of the Teacher Working Conditions Survey.* Washington, DC: Learning Point Associates (of American Institutes for Research), report commissioned to develop the MET version of the New Teacher Center Working Conditions Survey.

Wilson, S. M., & Berne, J. (1999). Teacher learning and the acquisition of professional knowledge: An examination of research on contemporary professional development. *Review of Research in Education, 24,* 173–209.

Yoon, K. S., Duncan, T., Wen-Yu Lee, S., Scarloss, B., & Shapley, K. L. (2007). *Reviewing the evidence on how teacher professional development affects student achievement.* Issues & Answers Report, REL No. 033. Washington, DC: U.S. Department of Education, Institute of Education Sciences, National Center for Education Evaluation and Regional Assistance, Regional Educational Laboratory Southwest.

APPENDIX

TABLE 11.A.1. **Multiple Regressions Predicting Between-School Differences in Teaching Enablers (from Box B) Using Base Working Conditions, Including Leadership Indices (from Box A from Figure 11.1)**

	Time Demands	Conduct Management	Teacher Autonomy	Effective PD
Column	1	2	3	5
Facilities and Resources	0.256***	0.136*	−0.214**	−0.106*
Community Support	0.046	0.224***	−0.048	−0.023
Teacher Leadership	0.088	−0.215*	0.586***	0.044
Professional Development	−0.027	−0.109	0.097	0.749***
Instructional Supports	0.108	0.141+	0.241**	0.177***
Responsiveness	0.307**	0.243**	−0.061	0.083
Respectfulness	0.156	0.501***	0.064	−0.165**
Reasonableness	−0.001	−0.068	0.071	0.086
Rigorousness	−0.114	0.123+	−0.262**	0.048
Student Race White	0.09	0.126	−0.008	0.07
Free and Reduced Lunch	0.262*	−0.079	−0.066	0.075
Level and Subject Indicators	Yes	Yes	Yes	Yes
Constant	−0.148	0.157	0.386*	0.047
R-Square Between	0.585	0.762	0.458	0.82
N Teachers	1426	1397	1421	1426
N Schools	203	203	203	203

Note: Significance indicators: +=.10; *=.05; **=.01; ***=.001.

TABLE 11.A.2. Multiple Regressions Predicting Between-School Differences in Teacher Expectations, Professional Engagement with School-Level Colleagues, and Emphasis on Test Preparation

Column	Teacher Expectations	Prof. Community Citizenship	Emphasis on Test Prep.	Teacher Expectations	Prof. Community Citizenship	Emphasis on Test Prep.
	1	2	3	4	5	6
Box A: Base Working Conditions						
Facilities and Resources	−0.042	−0.155*	−0.102	0.019	−0.186*	−0.115
Community Supports	0.148+	0.153*	0.056	0.152+	0.14+	0.092
Teacher Leadership	−0.002	0.025	0.108	0.007	0.061	0.142
Professional Development	−0.122	0.193*	−0.019	−0.363*	0.135	0.034
Instructional Supports	0.158	0.261**	0.123	0.116	0.241*	0.189+
Student Race: White	0.102	−0.18	−0.138	0.08	−0.197	−0.113
Free and Reduced Lunch	0.194	−0.081	0.045	0.205	−0.114	0.021
Leadership						
Responsiveness	0.047	−0.03	−0.095	0.038	−0.08	−0.052

	(1)	(2)	(3)	(4)	(5)	(6)
Respectfulness	-0.075	-0.025	-0.154	-0.02	-0.04	-0.062
Reasonableness	0.132	0.192*	0.294**	0.105	0.19*	0.294**
Rigorousness	0.082	0.012	0.018	0.044	-0.002	0.02

Box B: Teaching Enablers

	(1)	(2)	(3)	(4)	(5)	(6)
Manageable Time Demands				-0.113	0.086	0.018
Conduct Management				0.043	0.038	-0.199+
Teacher Autonomy				-0.012	-0.059	-0.127
Effective PD				0.325*	0.097	-0.08
Level and Subject Indicators	Yes	Yes	Yes	Yes	Yes	Yes
Constant	-0.128	0.09	-0.188	-0.151	0.117	-0.103
R-Square	0.163	0.498	0.144	0.195	0.506	0.17
N Teachers	1392	1392	1384	1392	1392	1384
N Schools	203	203	203	203	203	203

Note: Significance indicators: += .10; * = .05; ** = .01; *** = .001.

TABLE 11.A.3. Multiple Regressions Using Student Characteristics and Community Supports to Predict Between-School Differences in Teacher Expectations on the Three Items in the Teacher Expectations Index

Column	On Assignments		Hard Work Required		Improve Student Lives	
	1	2	3	4	5	6
Community Supports		0.209**		0.223***		0.236***
Hispanic Students	−0.423+	−0.166	−0.01	0.263	−0.308	−0.018
Black Students	−0.309*	−0.092	−0.061	0.172	−0.188	0.059
Free and Reduced Lunch	0.042	0.17	−0.178	−0.043	0.033	0.177
Males	1.147+	1.157+	0.872	0.88	−0.016	−0.04
Level and Subject Indicators	Yes	Yes	Yes	Yes	Yes	Yes
Constant	−0.466	−0.829*	−0.007	−0.268	0.338	0.025
R-Square Between	0.064	0.111	0.084	0.145	0.042	0.112
N Teachers	1423	1423	1419	1419	1425	1425
N Schools	203	203	203	203	203	203

Note: Statistical significance: +=.10; *=.05; **=.01; ***=.001.

TABLE 11.A.4. Between-School Multiple Regression Predictions of Academic Support (Care, Confer, Clarify, Captivate, and Consolidate) and Academic Press (Challenge and Control)

Column	Press	Support	Press	Support	Press	Support
	1	2	3	4	5	6
Box C: Teaching Beliefs and Behaviors						
Active Believers					Base	Base
Isolated Believers					−0.034	−0.199
Active Agnostics					0.013	−0.011
Isolated Agnostics					−0.336	−0.447*
Emphasis on Test Prep					−0.014	0.009
Box B: Teaching Enablers						
Manageable Time Demands			0.170*	0.177*	0.163*	0.161*
School-Level Conduct Mgmt			0.276**	0.146	0.293**	0.168+
Teacher Autonomy			0.124+	0.112	0.124+	0.121+
Effective PD			0.296*	0.092	0.286*	0.089
Box A: Base Working Conditions						
Facilities and Resources	0.043	0.105	0.017	0.072	0.015	0.081
Community Support	0.006	−0.017	−0.061	−0.052	−0.078	−0.073

(continued)

(Table 11.A.4 continued)

Column	Press 1	Support 2	Press 3	Support 4	Press 5	Support 6
Teacher Leadership	0.075	0.073	0.047	0.036	0.038	0.022
Professional Development	0.099	0.149	−0.114	0.077	−0.097	0.078
Instructional Supports	0.059	0.059	−0.066	−0.020	−0.072	−0.042
Responsiveness	0.072	0.062	−0.070	−0.037	−0.067	−0.034
Respectfulness	−0.164	−0.187+	−0.290*	−0.285*	−0.300**	−0.296*
Reasonableness	0.054	−0.008	0.037	−0.014	0.018	−0.051
Rigorousness	−0.181*	−0.108	−0.186*	−0.085	−0.191*	−0.091
Constant Level and Subject Indicators	Yes	Yes	Yes	Yes	Yes	Yes
R-Square	0.063	0.084	0.172	0.140	0.187	0.167
N Teachers	1337	1337	1337	1337	1337	1337
N Schools	203	203	203	203	203	203

Note: Statistical significance: += .10; * = .05; ** = .01; *** = .001.

TABLE 11.A.5. Multiple Regressions Predicting Between-School Differences in Value Added

	1	2	3	4
Box D: Teaching Quality				
Academic Press				0.386**
Academic Support				−0.058
Box C: Teaching Beliefs and Behaviors				
Active Believer			Base	Base
Isolated Believer			−0.225	−0.224
Active Agnostic			−0.477+	−0.483*
Isolated Agnostic			−0.027	0.076
Emphasis on Test Prep.			−0.211**	−0.205**
Box B: Teaching Enablers				
Manageable Time Demands		−0.017	−0.006	−0.059
School-Level Conduct Management		0.433***	0.377***	0.274*
Teacher Autonomy		0.180*	0.147+	0.106
Effective PD		0.267+	0.210	0.105

(continued)

(Table 11.A.5 continued)

Box A: Base Working Conditions

	1	2	3	4
Facilities and Resources	0.001	0.011	0.019	0.018
Community Supports	0.086	−0.023	−0.009	0.017
Teacher Leadership	−0.145	−0.167	−0.156	−0.17
Professional Development	0.258*	0.067	0.11	0.152
Instructional Supports	−0.038	−0.154	−0.118	−0.092
Responsiveness	0.045	−0.059	−0.072	−0.048
Respectfulness	0.062	−0.107	−0.114	−0.015
Reasonableness	−0.072	−0.088	−0.026	−0.036
Rigorousness	−0.095	−0.13	−0.156	−0.087
Constant and Level and Subject Indicators	Yes	Yes	Yes	Yes
R-Square Between	0.058	0.166	0.210	0.279
N Teachers	1337	1337	1337	1337
N Schools	203	203	203	203

Note: Statistical significance: +=.10; *=.05; **=.01; ***=.001.

TABLE 11.A.6. Multiple Regressions Predicting Between School Differences in Happiness in Class

	1	2	3	4
Box D: Teaching Quality				
Academic Press				0.108
Academic Support				0.637***
Box C: Teaching Beliefs and Behaviors				
Active Believer			Base	Base
Isolated Believer			−0.297	−0.166
Active Agnostic			−0.236	−0.230
Isolated Agnostic			−0.393+	−0.072
Emphasis on Test Prep.			0.043	0.039
Box B: Teaching Enablers				
Manageable Time Demands		0.091	0.079	−0.041
School-Level Conduct Management		0.249**	0.266**	0.128*
Teacher Autonomy		0.196**	0.212**	0.121*
Effective PD		0.018	0.006	−0.082

(continued)

(Table 11.A.6 continued)

Box A: Base Working Conditions

	1	2	3	4
Facilities and Resources	0.066	0.051	0.073	0.020
Community Supports	−0.037	−0.099	−0.118+	−0.063
Teacher Leadership	0.093	0.038	0.022	0.004
Professional Development	0.155	0.129	0.138	0.099
Instructional Supports	−0.033	−0.112	−0.151	−0.117+
Leadership Responsiveness	0.085	0.005	0.002	0.031
Leadership Respectfulness	−0.110	−0.255*	−0.257*	−0.037
Leadership Reasonableness	0.034	0.029	−0.012	0.018
Leadership Rigorousness	−0.169*	−0.146+	−0.158+	−0.079
Constant and Level and Subject Indicators	Yes	Yes	Yes	Yes
R-Square Between	0.086	0.167	0.195	0.635
N Teachers	1337	1337	1337	1337
N Schools	203	203	203	203

Note: Statistical significance: +=.10; *=.05; **=.01; ***=.001.

TABLE 11.A.7. Multiple Regressions Predicting Between-School Differences in Effort in Class

	1	2	3	4
Box D: Teaching Quality				
Academic Press				0.241*
Academic Support				0.375***
Box C: Teaching Beliefs and Behaviors				
Active Believer			Base	Base
Isolated Believer			−0.123	−0.040
Active Agnostic			−0.104	−0.103
Isolated Agnostic			−0.537*	−0.289
Emphasis on Test Prep.			0.006	0.006
Box B: Teaching Enablers				
Manageable Time Demands		0.144+	0.132+	0.033
School-Level Conduct Management		0.075	0.104	−0.030
Teacher Autonomy		0.088	0.094	0.018
Effective PD		0.207	0.187	0.084

(continued)

(Table 11.A.7 continued)

Box A: Base Working Conditions

	1	2	3	4
Facilities and Resources	−0.009	−0.019	−0.014	−0.048
Community Supports	−0.015	−0.031	−0.060	−0.014
Teacher Leadership	−0.020	−0.064	−0.081	−0.098
Professional Development	0.214*	0.053	0.083	0.077
Instructional Supports	0.024	−0.056	−0.079	−0.046
Leadership Responsiveness	0.083	0.006	0.007	0.036
Leadership Respectfulness	−0.080	−0.115	−0.126	0.057
Leadership Reasonableness	0.040	0.023	−0.015	0.000
Leadership Rigorousness	−0.117	−0.100	−0.112	−0.031
Constant and Level and Subject Indicators	Yes	Yes	Yes	Yes
R-Square Between	0.073	0.114	0.149	0.415
N Teachers	1337	1337	1337	1337
N Schools	203	203	203	203

Note: Statistical significance: +=.10; *=.05; **=.01; ***=.001.

TABLE 11.A.8. Multiple Regressions Predicting Between-School Differences in College Inspiration

	1	2	3	4
Box D: Teaching Quality				
Academic Press				−0.032
Academic Support				0.660***
Box C: Teaching Beliefs and Behaviors				
Active Believer				
Isolated Believer			−0.196	−0.065
Active Agnostic			0.096	0.103
Isolated Agnostic			−0.458*	−0.174
Emphasis on Test Prep.			−0.012	−0.018
Box B: Teaching Enablers				
Manageable Time Demands		−0.004	−0.023	−0.124*
School-Level Conduct Management		0.158+	0.179+	0.077
Teacher Autonomy		−0.006	0.001	−0.075
Effective PD		0.279*	0.282*	0.233*

(continued)

(Table 11.A.8 continued)

Box A: Base Working Conditions

	1	2	3	4
Facilities and Resources	0.041	0.048	0.053	0.000
Community Supports	0.068	0.029	0.010	0.055
Teacher Leadership	0.149	0.170	0.157	0.143
Professional Development	0.221*	0.030	0.020	-0.034
Instructional Supports	-0.093	-0.151	-0.164+	-0.139+
Leadership Responsiveness	0.122	0.065	0.071	0.091
Leadership Respectfulness	-0.325**	-0.355**	-0.369**	-0.184+
Leadership Reasonableness	-0.066	-0.080	-0.114	-0.080
Leadership Rigorousness	-0.140	-0.180*	-0.183*	-0.129+
Constant and Level and Subject Indicators	Yes	Yes	Yes	Yes
R-Square Between	0.118	0.151	0.181	0.497
N Teachers	1337	1337	1337	1337
N Schools	203	203	203	203

Note: Statistical significance: +=.10; *=.05; **=.01; ***=.001.

TABLE 11.A.9. Multiple Regression Results Predicting Within-School Differences in Student Outcomes for Four Types of Teachers

Column	Happy in Class	Effort in Class	College Inspiration	Value Added	Academic Press	Academic Support
	1	2	3	4	5	6
Isolated Agnostic (IA)	Base	Base	Base	Base	Base	Base
Active Agnostic (AA)	0.085	0.037	0.151	0.070	0.113	0.061
Isolated Believer (IB)	0.121	0.073	0.324**	0.176*	0.234*	0.172
Active Believer (AB)	0.241**	0.164+	0.364***	0.257***	0.351***	0.289**
Base for Effective PD	0.008	−0.030	−0.059	−0.034	−0.044	−0.037
Eff PD Interaction, IA	0.017	0.136	0.146	0.057	0.083	0.072
Eff PD Interaction, AA & IB	0.102	0.182*	0.216*	0.076	0.207*	0.175*
Base for Conduct Mgmt	−0.064	−0.002	0.017	−0.048	−0.067	−0.074
Cond Mgmt Interaction, IA	0.270*	0.072	0.010	0.022	0.178	0.222+
Cond Mgmt Interaction, AA & IB	0.224**	0.160+	0.086	0.126+	0.180*	0.166*

(continued)

(Table 11.A.9 continued)

Column	Happy in Class	Effort in Class	College Inspiration	Value Added	Academic Press	Academic Support
	1	2	3	4	5	6
Base for Leadership	0.026	0.067	0.008	0.060	0.057	0.035
Ldrshp Interaction, IA	−0.156	−0.079	−0.140	−0.268*	−0.162	−0.126
Ldrshp Interaction, AA & AB	−0.045	−0.138	−0.067	−0.113	−0.096	−0.029
Level and Subject Indicators	Yes	Yes	Yes	Yes	Yes	Yes
Constant	−0.038	0.104	−0.299*	−0.141	−0.102	0.007
R-Square Within	0.033	0.032	0.044	0.022	0.037	0.037
Number of Cases	1352	1352	1352	1399	1352	1352

Note: Statistical significance: +=.10; *=.05; **=.01; ***=.001.

SECTION

3

THE PROPERTIES OF EVALUATION SYSTEMS

Issues of Quality,
Underlying Frameworks,
and Design Decisions

CHAPTER

12

Evaluating Efforts to Minimize Rater Bias in Scoring Classroom Observations

YOON SOO PARK, JING CHEN, AND STEVEN L. HOLTZMAN

ABSTRACT

Prior research has shown that rater bias can threaten the accuracy of scores assigned by trained observers. This study examines whether the implementation of a rigorous scoring system to train, certify, and monitor raters contributed to minimizing rater bias among observers in the Measures of Effective Teaching (MET) study. Rater bias associated with characteristics of observers, teachers, and classroom settings were investigated using four MET observation instruments—(1) Classroom Assessment Scoring System, (2) Framework for Teaching, (3) Mathematical Quality of Instruction, and (4) Protocol for Language Arts Teaching Observation—based on video-recorded observations of classroom teaching. Results, which indicated minimal bias associated with characteristics of rater, teacher, and classroom settings, may support the effectiveness of the scoring processes developed and implemented by the MET study. As a policy implication for the field, the use of a scoring system that provides bias training and conducts ongoing monitoring of rater performance is recommended. These findings provide new and important understanding of practices for training and monitoring raters that can help to minimize possible bias associated with raters.

INTRODUCTION

When using a rubric to observe classrooms, trained observers must be cognizant of *rater bias*—personal preferences, viewpoints, or interpretations of the instrument that are external to the scoring rubric (Hoyt, 2000; Myford & Wolfe, 2003; Rudner, 1992). Rater bias can influence a rater's judgment and can lead to systematic errors in scoring, threatening the accuracy of scores assigned. For example, a rater may systematically assign higher scores based on familiarity of the classroom setting or characteristics of the teacher, which would threaten the interpretation and credibility of the performance category indicated by the scoring rubric.

In the Measures of Effective Teaching (MET; Bill & Melinda Gates Foundation, 2012) study, a rigorous scoring system was implemented that included a systematic process in the selection, training of bias awareness, and monitoring of the quality of scores assigned by raters. Although best practices in scoring performance-based assessments were considered in the development of the MET scoring system, it was unclear whether such efforts helped to minimize preexisting rater bias, as observers can be subject to various factors that can influence their scoring behavior. Given overwhelming evidence in the literature that raises concerns about features of the observers, teachers, and classroom settings that may bias raters (e.g., Bejar, 2012; Coffman, 1971), it becomes necessary to investigate the value of developing and applying resources to monitor raters. The scoring protocol developed for the MET project included the following components: (1) high-quality rater training, (2) demonstration of raters' ability to assign accurate scores prior to operational scoring, and (3) continued monitoring of scoring performance. In practice, scoring programs in local districts may lack rigor in one or more of the above components in terms of training and monitoring raters for classroom observation. Verifying whether practices undertaken by the MET study to train and monitor raters resulted in improving the accuracy of scores can have powerful implications for states, school districts, and local agencies that are developing scoring systems for evaluating effective teachers.

To date, no studies have examined the effect of applying rigorous scoring systems for minimizing rater bias to large-scale scoring of classroom observations. As with any scoring procedure, scores assigned by raters must be invariant of construct-irrelevant factors; in other words, scores must be reliable and valid, regardless of characteristics of raters, teachers, and their classroom settings. Because scoring of classroom observations can be influenced by subjective factors, it is of interest to identify how an individual rater's leniency or strictness influences overall agreement with other raters and to detect evidence of bias in rater scoring. Given that scores assigned by raters are used in high-stakes settings to evaluate teaching performance and to direct substantial resources in providing teacher feedback, the significance of minimizing rater bias is particularly important.

In this chapter, we evaluate the effectiveness of efforts to minimize bias in the MET study. Identifying sources of rater bias addresses whether features of the observers (raters) and the observed teachers and classroom settings relate to scoring accuracy. This chapter is divided into four sections. The first section is a literature review. The second section provides an overview of the process involved in selecting, training, and monitoring raters for the MET study. The third section conducts a comprehensive analysis to determine whether practices of the MET study succeeded in minimizing rater bias and has three subsections: examining (1) how rater characteristics (e.g., professional background, compliance with training/scoring protocol, and attention to detail) affect scoring accuracy, (2) whether raters exercise differential levels of severity in scoring certain types of teachers or classroom settings, and (3) the interactions of rater characteristics and teacher/classroom characteristics. The final section provides implications and best practices for implementing a scoring system for classroom observation.

Four MET scoring instruments were used: (1) Classroom Assessment Scoring System (CLASS), (2) Framework for Teaching (FfT), (3) Mathematical Quality of Instruction (MQI), and (4) Protocol for Language Arts Teaching Observation (PLATO). Details of each scoring rubric can be found in the MET research report (Bill & Melinda Gates Foundation, 2012). Both CLASS and FfT measure general qualities of effective classroom instruction, whereas MQI and PLATO are content-specific observation instruments for mathematics and English language arts, respectively. This chapter presents an examination of rater effects on measuring classroom teaching and their implication for scoring observations. It aims to contribute to a better understanding of scoring classroom observations and issues that emerge in practice.

WHAT THE RESEARCH ON RATER BIAS SAYS

The research literature is divided into three areas: studies of rater bias, studies of rater background, and studies of differential rater functioning.

Studies of Rater Bias

The examination of rater bias addresses features of the observers (raters) and the observed (teachers and classroom setting) as they relate to scoring accuracy. Previous studies in educational and psychological measurement have examined these issues within the context of essay scoring or assessment of speaking ability (Ling, Mollaun, & Chen, 2011; Park & DeCarlo, 2011; Xi & Mollaun, 2009). In the medical literature, observation has been used to assess the performance of doctors being trained to diagnose patients (Colliver & Williams, 1993; van der Vleuten & Swanson, 1990). The main concern in the use of raters to assess performance is the large variability in scores. For example, in a classic study by Diederich, French, and Carlton (1961) in which three hundred essays were judged by fifty-three raters on a nine-point scale, it was found that 94 percent of the essays received at least seven different scores. Researchers have found differences in rater severity to be a factor that leads to differences in scores assigned (Shohamy, Gordon, & Kraemer, 1992), where some raters are more stringent or lenient than other raters. Other studies have attributed differences in raters to scoring precision—how well raters are able to discriminate differences between categories of the scoring rubric (DeCarlo, 2005); when raters have lower scoring precision, they cannot discriminate differences between a high or a low score, and this can obscure the true meaning of their scores.

Studies that have noted differences in rater characteristics have called for developing rigid protocols within scoring systems to train and monitor rater performance (Congdon & McQueen, 2000). These studies have implications for rater training and measurement of performance-based tasks and behaviors. However, to date, there has not been a study that investigated these characteristics for observations of teaching effectiveness with the scoring rigor used in the MET study. To improve consistency and minimize rating errors, the literature asserts that raters need to (1) be familiar with the measures they are using, (2) understand the sequence of operation, and (3) be trained on how they should interpret the scoring rubric (Coffman, 1971). There are several examples of classic studies that support the effectiveness of these strategies. For example, in a study by Latham, Wexley, and Purcell (1975), employment interviewers were trained to reduce rater effects, and the training used by Pulakos (1986), which focused on the type, interpretation, and usage of data, yielded greater inter-rater reliability. Furthermore, Shohamy, Gordon, and Kraemer (1992) found that the overall reliability coefficients were higher for trained raters than for untrained raters, whereas the background of the raters did not affect their reliability. Although rater training may help to alleviate rater differences to a degree, studies have shown that completely overcoming them is difficult (Hoskens & Wilson, 2001; Wilson & Case, 2000).

Studies of Rater Background

Beyond examining scoring characteristics of raters with respect to severity and scoring precision, a number of studies have investigated how raters' background may impact their scoring performance. Most of these studies were conducted in the context of language tests, such as those for writing or speaking (e.g., Brown, 1991; Hamp-Lyons, 2003, Hinkel, 1994; Pula & Huot, 1993; Schoonen, Vergeer, & Eiting, 1997; Weigle, 2002; Xi & Mollaun, 2009). These studies provide no consensus on how rater backgrounds impact their scoring performance. For instance, some researchers (e.g., Johnson & Lim, 2009; Myford, Marr, & Linacre, 1996) found no strong, consistent correlation between raters' native language background and measures of their performance in scoring oral and written responses. However, other studies (Brown, 1995; Eckes, 2008) found that raters' background variables, such as native linguistic background, partially accounted for some scoring differences. In Carey, Mannell, and Dunn (2011), familiarity in accented speaking of English was examined, where a significant proportion of non-native-speaker raters scored candidates from their home country higher than candidates who were not from their home country. Little research has been conducted on the effect of raters' professional background on their video scoring performance.

Studies of Differential Rater Functioning

Compared to studies on rater background, few studies have examined differential rater functioning, which can occur when a rater exercises differential scoring behavior, such as severity toward a specific gender or ethnicity (Engelhard, 2007; Tamanini, 2008). In a study conducted by Chase (1986), the impact of interaction between student gender, race, expectations of the reader, and quality of penmanship was examined to assess its effects on raters' perception of essays. Using essays of two different qualities of penmanship, eighty-three in-service teachers who varied in ethnicity and gender scored packets of essays that contained records and pictures of the students, in order to investigate the expectations of the raters. Using an analysis of variance model, the authors found that the interactions had a significant effect on the score. In studies of medical training, the interaction between the gender of the patient and the doctor has been examined. The results were mixed regarding significance of the interaction effect (Colliver, Vu, Marcy, Travis, & Robbs, 1993; Furman, Colliver, & Galofre, 1993; Stillman, Regan, Swanson, & Haley, 1992).

The findings from these studies on raters place emphasis on the need to train and monitor raters. This same principle can be applied for scoring classroom observations, which this chapter investigates. Although the context of assessment content may differ between previous studies on essay scoring and teaching effectiveness, scoring of performance is based on raters who may be subject to bias; in fact, measuring of teaching quality may be subject to an even greater array of factors contributing to bias because scoring is based on observations that not only involve teachers, but also involve various characteristics of classroom settings. For these reasons, prior research on rater bias translates into measurement of teaching effectiveness, where characteristics of teachers and classrooms may present areas of training and monitoring of scores assigned by raters.

SELECTION, TRAINING, AND MONITORING OF MET STUDY RATERS

The scoring protocol of the MET study was designed and implemented by the Educational Testing Service (ETS). The general process involved in the scoring protocol included (1) recruiting raters; (2) training; (3) administering a certification test; (4) recalibration; and (5) monitoring of rater performance through reviews of validation cases, remediation, and feedback. Raters assigned scores based on observations using a prerecorded video of a classroom. A detailed review of the process used by the MET study is described in the MET research report (Bill & Melinda Gates Foundation, 2012) and policy brief (Joe, Tocci, Holtzman, & Williams, 2013).

Rater Recruitment and Training

ETS began rater recruitment for the MET study in September of 2010. Each scoring instrument (CLASS, FfT, MQI, and PLATO) required different qualifications for raters. Most raters recruited were either current or former teachers or graduate students in education. Some subject-specific instruments required experience in mathematics or English language arts. Ultimately, ETS selected a workforce of raters, who were subsequently required to take up to thirty hours of online training and pass a four-hour certification test. Of those who took the certification test, the average pass rate was 77 percent across all of the instruments. As a result, approximately nine hundred trained and certified raters participated in the operational scoring.

Training consisted of instruction on the specific instrument the rater would be using to score, software training for the scoring platform, and bias awareness training. For some instruments, raters were trained separately on multiple groups of scales (dimensions or scoring domains) and had to pass multiple certification tests before scoring.

Bias awareness training was conducted online at the individual pace of the raters. This training introduced raters to the notion that everyone has hidden biases and personal preferences. These biases and personal preferences are often developed over one's lifetime. The training was designed to help raters gain a better understanding of their biases and provide them with strategies to reduce the influence of bias on their scoring. The bias awareness training instructed raters on how to identify biases and personal preferences and how to distinguish them from evidence. The training also included several activities. One activity was a word association activity modeled after the Implicit Attitudes Tests. During this exercise, words were flashed across the screen. Raters were instructed to write the first thoughts that came to mind when they saw each word. Afterward, raters were encouraged to reflect on these thoughts and note anything that might indicate a bias. A similar association exercise using video clips was also included in the training. These activities were intended to help raters uncover preexisting and hidden biases.

Raters were encouraged to identify individual factors and triggers that could contribute to bias in their own scoring based on the word association and video-based activities. Several examples of known bias factors in classroom observation were provided to model the type of trigger list they were expected to develop. These bias factors included teacher's physical characteristics, student-specific factors such as school uniforms, and classroom-specific factors such as the way a classroom is organized. Raters were asked to reference and update the trigger list throughout the scoring period to help them monitor the effects of their biases on scores.

Certification Tests

Each scoring instrument of the MET study had a separate certification test. The format of certification tests varied by instrument in terms of the number of videos, the length of videos, and the number of scoring dimensions being tested. Regardless of the certification test format, at least ten scores were collected from each potential rater to resolve concerns relating to the reliability of his or her performance due to insufficient number of items scored. The number of videos also took into account the representativeness of different types of videos that raters might potentially watch, which ensured content- and grade-level representation in the certification test.

Prior to allowing raters to observe and score videos of classroom teaching, raters were required to complete several steps. These included meeting hiring qualifications, successfully completing training, and passing the certification test within two attempts. The enforcement of these criteria, especially the cutscore for passing certification, affected the pool of available raters for scoring. Raising standards in the certification test through higher cutscores would have resulted in a smaller pool of raters, whereas lowering the standards would have resulted in a larger pool. As such, the cutscore was adjusted to allow selection of the highest-scoring raters, taking as many as needed who could successfully score and receive remediation when necessary.

Calibration Test and Validation Cases

To further monitor the performance of raters who passed the certification test, calibration tests and validation cases were developed to ensure ongoing rater quality. Prior to each scoring shift, raters were required to pass a calibration test within two attempts. Raters who did not meet the passing standard for calibration were prevented from scoring during a given shift. As part of monitoring, validation cases with known, master-coded "true" scores were randomly dispersed throughout the scoring session, to allow scoring leaders and analysts to examine the quality of rater performance during operational scoring.

The protocols built into the scoring system of the MET study allowed for the collection of measures of rater performance through multiple indicators of their observation ability. Previous research has shown that having mechanisms in place to conduct real-time monitoring of raters (Myford, 2012) can increase the validity of scores.

METHODS USED TO ANALYZE THE EXTENT OF RATER BIAS IN THE MET STUDY

Data used for the analysis of rater bias were collected from the MET classroom observations. ETS collected background data from each rater, which included gender, age, race/ethnicity, teaching experience, educational background, and perceptions and experience about the training and the observation instruments. Data were also collected from all participating districts about the teachers and classrooms in each of the videos scored. Additionally, a voluntary survey was sent to all raters, following the completion of the MET study (details of the survey items are presented in Appendix A; this survey was not directly part of the MET study). In order to measure raters' ability to follow directions, a nine-question assessment was administered using items from the Chernyshenko Conscientiousness Scales (Hill & Roberts, 2011). To determine raters' attention to detail, each rater answered eighteen questions from the Behavioral Indicators of Conscientiousness (Jackson, Wood, Bogg, Walton, Harms, & Roberts, 2010). Cronbach's alpha for the ability to follow directions and the attention to detail measures was .75 and .89, respectively. Items from the attention to detail and the ability to follow directions scales are presented in Appendix B.

Rater Characteristics

The relationship between rater performance (scoring accuracy) and rater characteristics was examined using correlations, analysis of variance (ANOVA), and multivariate analysis of variance (MANOVA). The dependent variables were measures of scoring accuracy using the following indicators: (1) certification test score, (2) average calibration test score, and (3) accuracy of scores on validation videos. The independent variables were rater characteristics, such as gender, age, race/ethnicity, teaching experience, educational background, and perception and experience about the training and the observation instruments, as well as scores on the rater's ability to follow directions and the attention to detail measures. Correlations between each independent variable and the dependent variables were examined to assess whether there were associations between rater characteristics and scoring accuracy. Each indicator of rater accuracy was used separately as the dependent variable in an ANOVA; the three indicators were used together as dependent variables in the MANOVA. Each rater characteristic was used as the independent variable in both ANOVA and MANOVA. The analyses based on correlations, ANOVA, and MANOVA were replicated for each scoring instrument: CLASS, FfT, and PLATO. MQI was not included in the analysis of rater characteristics, as it differed from other instruments in how certification and calibration test scores were calculated. The combined analyses based on correlations, ANOVA, and

MANOVA provided information on the univariate and multivariate associations between the rater characteristics (independent variables) and measures of scoring accuracy (dependent variables).

Teacher and Classroom Characteristics

Across all instruments, each classroom was observed and scored by a primary rater, and a subset of the classrooms (about 5 percent) was re-scored by a secondary rater. Consistency (agreement) in scores between the primary and secondary raters was used as a proxy for scoring accuracy. Double-scored data were used to derive agreement measures—exact or exact-plus-adjacent agreement—between the primary and secondary raters based on the number of scoring categories by which they differed. Exact agreement refers to exact match in scores between raters; exact-plus-adjacent agreement is the proportion of scores that are 1 point above or below the score of another rater. However, a limitation to this approach is the lack of consideration for agreement that can occur by chance. For example, in a rating task scored on a 1 to 4 scale, the probability of exact agreement by chance between two raters is 25 percent. Given that agreement can result from chance, researchers have also used the kappa statistic (Cohen, 1960); this statistic takes into account agreement that can occur by chance. The weighted kappa penalizes larger discrepancies between raters more than smaller discrepancies do (Cohen, 1968; Schaeffer, Briel, & Fowles, 2001). For linearly weighted kappa, the penalty is the absolute difference in the ratings, while the penalty is the squared difference in the ratings for quadratically weighted kappa.

Differences between primary and secondary rater scores were dichotomized to align the analysis to operational methods used during ongoing monitoring of raters. In other words, how well the primary and secondary raters agreed was converted into a binary indicator of *agreed* and *not agreed*. Throughout the MET study, raters were evaluated based on how well they agreed with predetermined "true" scores (determined through consensus by expert master scorers) or how well they agreed with another secondary rater scoring the same video. As such, a focus of this chapter is to provide information on whether specific factors of teachers and classroom settings were associated with exact and exact-plus-adjacent agreement.

To calculate measures of agreement (exact and exact-plus-adjacent agreement), scores from primary and secondary raters were used. The four scoring instruments used in this study (CLASS, FfT, MQI, and PLATO) have multiple dimensions. CLASS has twelve dimensions; FfT has eight dimensions; MQI has six dimensions; and PLATO has six dimensions. This study made an assumption that scores from a particular dimension were independent of scores from different dimensions for the same observed classroom. This assumption was based on operational use in the field that treats each dimension as independent. Given this assumption, scores assigned from the same rater across multiple dimensions of the same classroom were aggregated for analysis. In other words, for CLASS, which requires each rater to assign twelve scores per each classroom observed (one score for each dimension, for a total of twelve dimensions), this led to twelve different scores that were compared to twelve other scores assigned by a different (secondary) rater. These aggregated data were used to calculate measures of agreement, kappa, weighted kappa (linear and quadratic), correlations, and mean squared difference scores for each scoring instrument.

Using the aggregated data that treats dimension scores independently, measures of agreement were correlated with teacher characteristics (gender, race/ethnicity, years of experience, and educational level) and classroom characteristics (proportion of racial composition, gifted, gender, specialized, English language learner [ELL], free lunch, and age). Logistic regression was used to examine the effects of teacher/classroom characteristics on rater agreement for all four instruments. In the logistic regression, the dependent variables were the dichotomous indicator of exact agreement (1 = exact agreement between primary and secondary raters, 0 = any difference between primary and secondary raters) and exact-plus-adjacent agreement (1 = exact or adjacent agreement, 0 = discrepant). The independent variables were teacher characteristics and classroom characteristics. The use of logistic regression allows an examination of whether characteristics of teacher and classroom settings affected the odds of exact or exact-plus-adjacent agreement between primary and secondary raters. Given that operational methods used in districts rely on exact and exact-plus-adjacent agreement measures, results from the logistic regression would be meaningful for users of the instrument. The analysis based on aggregated data (measures of agreement, correlations, and logistic regression) does not consider the possibility that the distribution of agreement may not be the same for all dimensions and that the disagreements in the dimensions may be dependent. However, this method was selected to examine whether characteristics of the teacher and classroom settings were associated with the scoring instrument as a whole.

Interaction Between Rater and Teacher/Classroom Characteristics

Correlations and logistic regression were used to investigate the interaction between the rater and teacher/classroom characteristics for all four instruments, similar to the approach used in the analysis of teacher/classroom characteristics.

HOW RATER CHARACTERISTICS AFFECTED SCORING ACCURACY

This section presents results on whether the scoring protocol used by the MET study contributed to minimizing rater bias associated with rater characteristics. This section is divided into three subsections. In the first subsection, results of rater bias associated with raters' background and experience are presented. In the second subsection, raters' perceptions of the instrument and training experience are presented. Finally, in the third subsection, raters' ability to follow direction and attention to detail are presented.

Raters' Backgrounds and Experience

Data from a subset of raters with complete information on rater background and experience were used for this subsection (579 raters; CLASS = 354, FfT = 149, PLATO = 76) to examine whether their scoring accuracy (certification test score, average calibration test score, and accuracy of scores on validation videos) was associated with rater background variables (i.e., raters' gender, ethnicity, highest degree, teaching experience, and the number of years of teaching; see Table 12.A.1 in Appendix A for categories in each background variable). Results based on correlations and ANOVA indicated no significant influence of rater background variables on each indicator of scoring accuracy. To study the influence of rater background variables on three indicators of scoring accuracy simultaneously, MANOVA was used. Results based on the MANOVA also indicated no significant influence of rater background variables on rater accuracy measured by all three scoring accuracy indicators (see Table 12.C.1 in Appendix C for p values associated with each scoring instrument).

Rater Perception and Training Experience of the Observational Instruments

Rater characteristics also included information collected through a voluntary survey (not directly part of the MET study) on rater perception and experience about the training and the observation instrument (Table 12.A.2 lists all the questions in the survey and the choices that raters could select for each question; see Appendix A). For example, the first question was "Were you familiar with the instrument prior to the MET project?" Raters were required to select *yes* or *no*. The survey also included statements, such as "I was confident in my ability to score after the online training program," that required raters to indicate the level of their agreement on a 5-point scale ranging from 0 (strongly disagree) to 4 (strongly agree). In addition, raters were required to indicate the level of importance of each training component on a scale ranging from 1 (not important) to 4 (very important). For most of the questions in the survey, the level of rater agreement was not significantly correlated with any indicator of raters' scoring accuracy. To examine whether any survey variables were related to the overall scoring accuracy, MANOVA was conducted using all three indicators of scoring accuracy as dependent variables (univariate analyses based on correlation and ANOVA preceded the MANOVA, which found no significant results).

In general, results from MANOVA did not provide significant evidence that variables collected in the rater survey were associated with scoring accuracy (certification test score, average calibration test score, and accuracy of scores on validation videos) across all instruments (see Table 12.C.2 in Appendix C). For the CLASS instrument, the MANOVA showed the following: raters who were familiar with the CLASS instrument prior to the MET project performed better in their scoring than raters who were not familiar with the instrument; raters who indicated that they examined and reflected on their own teaching practices as a result of scoring videos for the MET project performed better in scoring; and raters who indicated that the CLASS instrument could be used as a professional development tool to support or improve teaching and learning performed better in scoring. However, the first finding was based on a very small sample of raters ($n = 5$) who indicated that they were familiar with the instrument; this finding needs to be further tested. The second and third findings relate to raters' behavior or opinion after scoring, and these were not useful in evaluating their scoring. In summary, data collected from the rater survey did not suggest any strong influence from raters' perception and experience of training and the observation instrument on scoring.

Raters' Ability to Follow Direction and Attention to Detail

Table 12.1 presents correlations between raters' attention to detail and ability to follow directions (measured by a voluntary assessment) and raters' certification, calibration, and validation scores.

TABLE 12.1. **Pearson Correlations Between Raters' Attention to Detail and Ability to Follow Directions and Certification, Calibration, and Validation Scores**

Instrument	Variable	Certification	Calibration	Validation
CLASS	Attention to detail	.05	.06	.16
	Ability to follow directions	.03	.07	.05
FfT	Attention to detail	−.07	.28	.06
	Ability to follow directions	.11	.09	.00
PLATO	Attention to detail	−.04	−.05	−.14
	Ability to follow directions	.09	−.10	−.02
Total	Attention to detail	.01	.10	.09
	Ability to follow directions	.02	−.02	.05

Note: Correlations should be not be considered as meaningfully different from 0 or indicate direction of relationship, as most estimates are small (including negative correlations). CLASS = Classroom Assessment Scoring System; FfT = Framework for Teaching; PLATO = Protocol for Language Arts Teaching Observation.

Although correlations were small, scores for the attention to detail scale had marginally higher correlation with the CLASS (validation $r = .16$) and FfT (calibration $r = .28$) instruments. However, based on the size of the correlations, it is difficult to assess whether the magnitude of association has meaningful implications for raters. As such, correlations presented in Table 12.1 should not be interpreted as having meaningful effect sizes that are different from 0 or indicate direction of relationship (for negative correlations). Moreover, multivariate linear regression analysis did not present any meaningful and significant results pertaining to these measures.

HOW TEACHER CHARACTERISTICS AND CLASSROOM SETTINGS AFFECTED SCORING ACCURACY

To examine whether characteristics of teachers and classroom settings affected raters, analyses were restricted to double-scored video clips from actual observations of classrooms (rather than the certification, calibration, and validation data used for studying rater characteristics above). Table 12.2 shows descriptive statistics and agreement statistics for the double-scored data.

As illustrated in Table 12.2, the observation instruments differed in the number of video clips observed, raters, scoring categories, and measures

TABLE 12.2. **Descriptive Statistics and Agreement Statistics for the Double-Scored Data**

	Observation Instrument			
	CLASS	FfT	MQI	PLATO
Number of video clips observed	1,221	690	320	347
Number of raters	344	147	74	77
Number of dimensions	12	8	6	6
Scoring categories	7	4	2 or 3	4
% Agreement: Exact	34%	57%	76%	59%
% Agreement: Exact or adjacent	77%	97%	99%	92%
% Agreement: Discrepant	23%	3%	1%	8%
Mean squared difference	1.68	0.52	0.27	0.73
Correlation	.69	.36	.52	.72
Kappa	.21	.24	.51	.45
Kappa (linear weighted)	.49	.29	.51	.60
Kappa (quadratic weighted)	.69	.36	.52	.72

Note: Results are based on summary across all dimensions/domains observed in the instrument to facilitate interpretation of results. Agreement statistics (exact, adjacent, and discrepant) need to be viewed with respect to the number of scoring categories used. For MQI, different dimensions within the instruments have different numbers of scoring categories. Instruments also have different numbers of dimensions measured, as shown. Both MQI and PLATO also have scores for different video segments (MQI = 4 segments and a global score; PLATO = 2 segments). CLASS = Classroom Assessment Scoring System; FfT = Framework for Teaching; MQI = Mathematical Quality of Instruction; PLATO = Protocol for Language Arts Teaching Observation.

of rater agreement. Using the double-scored data, difference scores were derived and dichotomized based on exact agreement (1 = exact agreement; 0 = other) and exact-or-adjacent agreement (1 = exact-or-adjacent agreement; 0 = discrepant). Values for kappa, linear weighted kappa, and quadratic weighted kappa, all of which account for chance agreement, are presented in Table 12.2. Correlations between the primary and the secondary rater and mean squared difference are also presented to supplement the comparison of results. Given differences in the number of scoring categories for each instrument, agreement statistics (exact, adjacent, and discrepant) need to be considered accordingly. For example, CLASS has seven scoring categories, while FfT has four scoring categories; comparing differences in exact agreement and quadratically weighted kappa provide a rationale for presenting different measures of agreement.

The agreement statistics in Table 12.2 show that the percentage of exact or adjacent agreement is over 75 percent for all scoring instruments. However, when chance agreement is taken into account, the kappa values are .21, .24, .51, and .45 for CLASS, FfT, MQI, and PLATO, respectively. Moreover, using the quadratically weighted kappa, which has weights that are proportional to the square of the number of categories by which the ratings differ, the agreement relative to chance becomes .69, .36, .52, and .72, for CLASS, FfT, MQI, and PLATO, respectively. This indicates that both FfT and MQI have low agreement relative to chance. The reason for the low agreement was the lack of variation in the end categories. For the FfT, it was found that more than 92 percent of scores from operational scoring (not calibration or validation cases) were in the middle categories (2 and 3 on a 4-point scale), with less than 3 percent of scores assigned as 4. For the MQI, nearly 98 percent of scores were assigned as 1 and 2 on a 3-point scale. This lack of variation in scores may have contributed to the low kappa statistics for FfT and MQI.

Results from Table 12.3 indicate that the largest correlation between characteristics of teacher/classroom settings and measures of agreement was .06. Positive correlations indicate greater agreement; however, the magnitudes of correlations were too small (all less than ± .07) to give sufficient meaning to the relative strength of these associations. These results indicate that there were weak associations between characteristics of teacher/classroom settings and measures of agreement at the univariate level. In other words, a simple pairwise comparison between characteristics of the teacher/classroom and the degree of how well the primary and secondary raters agreed did not

TABLE 12.3. Point-Biserial Correlations of Exact and Exact-Plus-Adjacent Agreement with Classroom Settings and Teacher Characteristics

Classroom and teacher characteristics	CLASS		FfT		MQI		PLATO	
	Exact only	With adjacent	Exact only	With adjacent	Exact only	With adjacent	Exact only	With adjacent
Classroom								
% Hispanic	.01	.00	.03	.03	.01	.00	−.03	.02
% Black/Native American	−.02	.00	−.01	.02	.01	.02	.01	.01
% White/Asian	.02	.01	−.02	−.04	−.01	−.02	.01	−.03
% Gifted	.02	.00	−.01	−.02	.01	−.02	.01	−.02
% Male	.01	.01	−.02	−.01	.01	.02	−.02	−.02
% Special education	.00	.01	.00	.00	.00	.01	−.01	.03
% ELL	.00	.00	.00	.00	.00	.02	−.02	.02
% Age	−.02	−.03	−.01	−.01	−.01	.01	.01	−.01
% Student lunch	−.01	−.01	.02	.02	.00	−.01	−.04	.03

(continued)

(Table 12.3 continued)

Classroom and teacher characteristics	CLASS		FfT		MQI		PLATO	
	Exact only	With adjacent	Exact only	With adjacent	Exact only	With adjacent	Exact only	With adjacent
Teacher								
Male	-.01	.00	-.03	-.01	.03	.02	-.02	.01
White	.00	-.03	.00	.03	.01	.00	-.01	-.03
Black	-.02	.01	.00	.01	.01	.01	.01	.03
Hispanic	.02	.03	-.01	-.06	-.04	-.03	.01	.01
District experience	.00	-.03	.02	-.03	.01	-.01	-.01	-.03
Advanced degree	.01	.01	.00	.04	.02	.00	.04	.05

Note: Correlations should be not be considered as meaningfully different from 0 or indicate direction of relationship, as most estimates are small (including negative correlations). CLASS = Classroom Assessment Scoring System; FfT = Framework for Teaching; MQI = Mathematical Quality of Instruction; PLATO = Protocol for Language Arts Teaching Observation; ELL = English language learner.

indicate bias. This is evident by the correlation estimates that are all close to 0 for all comparisons presented in Table 12.3.

Controlling for simultaneous effects, a multiple logistic regression was conducted, with dichotomous measures of agreement as the dependent variable (exact or exact-plus-adjacent). In logistic regression, a coefficient greater than 0 indicates greater log odds of agreement in the logit scale; a logit is defined as $\ln[(p/1-p)]$, where p is the probability of exact or exact-plus-adjacent agreement.

For CLASS, FfT, and MQI, when there was a large percentage of either Hispanic, Black/Native American, or White/Asian students in the classroom, rater agreement was significantly greater than it was for heterogeneous classrooms, as indicated by log odds greater than 0 (see Table 12.C.3 in Appendix C). However, the significance of the odds ratios diminished when teacher and classroom characteristics were examined using both exact and adjacent agreement measures. Further analysis related to this particular finding may be needed in a subsequent study using more heterogeneous populations in order to derive generalizable implications on how racial composition in classrooms may affect rater agreement.

In general, as shown through correlations and also based on multiple logistic regression, results indicate no significant and meaningful association between characteristics of teacher/classroom settings and measures of agreement. However, it is noted that the measures of agreement for FfT and MQI are low relative to chance (based on low quadratically weighted kappa). In other words, although we found no meaningful bias associated with characteristics of teacher/classroom settings, we also found measures of agreement to be low for FfT and MQI. It may be difficult to detect bias when agreement is low, but this may not always be true. Because of this, the finding needs to be examined further, as it is not clear whether teacher and classroom characteristics were associated with measures of agreement for FfT and MQI.

HOW INTERACTIONS BETWEEN RATER AND CLASSROOM/TEACHER CHARACTERISTICS AFFECTED SCORING ACCURACY

Interactions between rater and classroom/teacher characteristics were examined with correlations and logistic regression using the double-scored data. Correlations were calculated between interaction terms as independent variables and dichotomized measures of agreement (exact or exact-plus-adjacent agreement) as dependent variables; logistic regression was used to examine whether the interactions between characteristics of teacher/classroom settings and raters were associated with measures of agreement. However, there were no significant effects for any combination of interactions; in other words, there was no evidence of bias associated with irrelevant factors observed in the video and the background characteristic of the rater. Results from examining interactions between rater and classroom/teacher characteristics indicate that these effects were either too insignificant or too weak (logistic regression coefficient representing log odds close to 0) to establish any meaningful interpretations that improve scoring accuracy. Although there seemed to be no meaningful association between interactions of characteristics between teacher/classroom settings and raters on measures of agreement, given the low measures of agreement for FfT and MQI relative to chance (based on quadratically weighted kappa), further examination may be needed.

BEST PRACTICES FOR IMPLEMENTING A SCORING SYSTEM FOR CLASSROOM OBSERVATION

Investigating rater bias has particular value, because classroom observations can be influenced by various subjective factors. Given that scores assigned by raters can have significant impact on teacher evaluation, paying attention to rater bias becomes important and necessary. To minimize rater bias, the MET study implemented a rigorous scoring process that involved training and monitoring of rater performance.

Examining characteristics of raters, teachers, and classroom settings in the MET data provided limited evidence to suggest significant and meaningful bias that raters had on scoring quality. Furthermore, in general, the group-level behaviors of raters were relatively invariant of construct-irrelevant factors.

Among rater characteristics, background variables such as gender, race/ethnicity, experience, and educational level did not have significant influence on scoring accuracy. Factors such as self-reported levels of familiarity, clarity, or understanding of the instruments also did not generate any meaningful effects on scoring accuracy. Attention to detail and raters' ability to follow directions were not found to be relevant in affecting scoring accuracy. For classroom settings and teacher characteristics, most factors had weak correlations with rater agreement. Finally, there was no conclusive evidence to support meaningful effects of interactions between rater and classroom/ teacher characteristics.

The following policy recommendations for states, school districts, and local agencies can be made.

Develop a Scoring Protocol That Trains and Monitors Rater Performance

The MET study implemented a scoring system that outlined specific requirements for raters through the hiring, training, certification, and recalibration stages; there were efforts to provide ongoing feedback and remediation for raters who did not perform well for calibration and validation cases, relative to other raters. These ongoing efforts to track rater performance cannot be ignored and should, in fact, be emphasized with greater significance. Given the evidence in the literature on differences in rater behavior that are reflected in variability of scoring, the bias training and scoring protocol developed by ETS may have significantly contributed to minimizing rater effects.

Implement Ongoing Statistical Monitoring of Raters

Although this study found very little evidence of rater bias, ongoing statistical monitoring of raters should be conducted. The procedures for such statistical monitoring can follow the methods outlined in this chapter.

Conducting statistical monitoring of rater performance requires agencies that collect scores from classroom observations to have a scoring system that provides readily accessible data for routine and operational analysis. This means that a protocol for routine monitoring of raters should be implemented that outlines the type of analysis to be executed and the personnel to conduct such statistical work. Operational methods for monitoring raters can include examining measures of agreement with expert observers and from double-scored classrooms. Although ongoing monitoring of raters is necessary, some analyses require larger sample sizes. A technical advisory panel is also recommended that can review and provide advice regarding the patterns or trends in rater performance, including identification of analyses that can be conducted frequently and studies that can occur as periodic checks on rater accuracy, following industry standards in testing.

Provide Individual Feedback and Remediation for Raters

Although most factors associated with classroom and teacher characteristics were not significant, identifying specific raters who are not accurate observers requires the use of systems to monitor raters. The MET study used calibration scores, validation cases, and double scoring of data as sources for identifying raters who need remediation. When such raters can be identified, diagnostic information and feedback can be provided to improve training.

In summary, this chapter provides basic principles that districts should consider implementing in the development of their scoring systems. However, these guidelines do not necessarily indicate that the exact procedures implemented in the MET study (e.g., thirty-four hours of training and certification testing) should be followed. The most important points to consider are that raters should be provided with high-quality training and should demonstrate their ability to score accurately prior to scoring when the stakes are high. Moreover, scores assigned by trained raters should be monitored on a regular and frequent basis. Given varying degrees of resource constraints and feasibility concerns, districts should prioritize and weigh various consequences of implementing each decision.

CONCLUSION

Scoring classroom observations requires that reliable and valid scores be assigned by raters, before such ratings should have meaningful implications for teacher evaluation. Scores assigned by raters have multiple uses in the observation of teacher performance, as they are used not only to provide feedback to the teacher in terms of professional development, but also for evaluation purposes in conjunction with student achievement. Given the increasing use of classroom observations, the stakes associated with these scores can become greater over time. However, raters observing classrooms can be subject to various forms of bias. This chapter describes the process implemented by the MET project to minimize such bias from an operational perspective.

Although guidelines and best practices for scoring classroom observations have not been thoroughly discussed within professional organizations for educational measurement, the testing standards currently used in other test formats should equally be applied (American Educational Research Association, American Psychological Association, & National Council on Measurement in Education, 1999). These standards used in the testing and in the educational measurement industry will need to be emphasized as scores assigned to classroom observation become increasingly valuable.

Results from this study add new insights into the growing measurement literature on scoring of observations and provide new and important understanding of issues that emerge in identifying rater bias and improving rater training. In fact, best practices used for scoring performance assessments in other contexts, such as essay scoring or assessment of speaking ability, were suggestive to be effective guidelines for minimizing rater bias. Examples of these guidelines include establishing mechanisms for training and monitoring raters that have consequences for rater performance through the administration of certification and calibration tests. The use of validation cases also allows real-time monitoring of rater performance through their scoring activity.

It is noted here that this study did not implement an experimental design, where data from raters who had not gone through bias training, raters who were not monitored, or raters who had not been calibrated were compared with raters described in this chapter who did receive training, monitoring, and calibration tests. However, the observation system and protocol, as a whole, produced favorable results. If a district desires to replicate those results, then it may need to implement the mechanisms employed in the MET study, as described in this chapter. It is still unclear what effects failure to implement these scoring protocols would have on the accuracy of scores assigned by raters. It is also noted that methods of analysis used in this study were used for the purposes described in this chapter, and they were not employed during the MET study.

Although the features described in this study were implemented with a video-based scoring platform, it is still necessary to evaluate the best manner to implement such practices in live scoring through direct observation or for small districts. Additional studies that replicate these procedures should be conducted to confirm these findings. Continued studies on the topic of rater bias can improve our understanding of how raters observe effective teaching in classrooms.

REFERENCES AND ADDITIONAL RESOURCES

American Educational Research Association, American Psychological Association, & National Council on Measurement in Education. (1999). *Standards for educational and psychological testing.* Washington, DC: American Educational Research Association.

Bejar, I. (2012). Rater cognition: Implications for validity. *Educational Measurement: Issues and Practice, 31*(3), 2–9.

Bill & Melinda Gates Foundation, Measures of Effective Teaching (MET). (2012). *Gathering feedback for teaching: Combining high-quality observations with student surveys and achievement gains.* Seattle, WA: Author.

Brown, A. (1995). The effect of rater variables in the development of an occupation-specific language performance test. *Language Testing, 12,* 1–15.

Brown, J. D. (1991). Do English and ESL faculties rate writing samples differently? *TESOL Quarterly, 25,* 587–603.

Carey, M. D., Mannell, R. H., & Dunn, P. K. (2011). Does a rater's familiarity with a candidate's pronunciation affect the rating in oral proficiency interviews? *Language Testing, 28,* 201–219.

Chase, C. I. (1986). Essay test scoring: Interaction of relevant variables. *Journal of Educational Measurement, 23,* 33–41.

Coffman, W. E. (1971). Essay examinations. In R. L. Thorndike (Ed.), *Educational measurement* (2nd ed., pp. 271–302). Washington, DC: American Council on Education.

Cohen, J. A. (1960). Coefficient of agreement for nominal scales. *Educational and Psychological Measurement, 20,* 37–46.

Cohen, J. A. (1968). Weighted kappa: Nominal scale agreement with provision for scaled disagreement or partial credit. *Psychological Bulletin, 70,* 213–220.

Colliver, J. A., Vu, N. V., Marcy, M. L., Travis, T. A., & Robbs, R. S. (1993). The effects of examinee and standardized-patient gender and their interaction on standardized-patient ratings of interpersonal and communication skills. *Academic Medicine, 68*(2), 153–157.

Colliver, J. A., & Williams, R. G. (1993). Technical issues: Test application. *Academic Medicine, 68*(6), 454–463.

Congdon, P. J., & McQueen, J. (2000). The stability of rater severity in large-scale assessment programs. *Journal of Educational Measurement, 37,* 163–178.

DeCarlo, L. T. (2005). A model of rater behavior in essay grading based on signal detection theory. *Journal of Educational Measurement, 42*(1), 53–76.

Diederich, P. B., French, J. W., & Carlton, S. T. (1961). *Factors in judgments of writing ability* (Research Bulletin No. RB-61-15). Princeton, NJ: Educational Testing Service.

Eckes, T. (2008). Rater types in writing performance assessments: A classification approach to rater variability. *Language Testing, 25*(2), 155–185.

Engelhard, G. (2007). Differential rater functioning. *Rasch Measurement Transactions, 21*(3), 1124.

Furman, G., Colliver, J. A., & Galofre, A. (1993). Effects of student gender and standardized-patient gender in a single case using a male and a female standardized patient. *Academic Medicine, 68,* 301–303.

Hamp-Lyons, L. (2003). Writing teachers as assessors of writing. In B. Kroll (Ed.), *Exploring the dynamics of second language writing* (pp. 162–189). Cambridge, UK: Cambridge University Press.

Hill, P. L., & Roberts, B. W. (2011). The role of adherence in the relationship between conscientiousness and perceived health. *Health Psychology, 30,* 797–804.

Hinkel, E. (1994). Native and nonnative speakers' pragmatic interpretations of English texts. *TESOL Quarterly, 28,* 353–376.

Hoskens, M., & Wilson, M. (2001). Real-time feedback on rater drift in constructed-response items: An example from the Golden State Examination. *Journal of Educational Measurement, 38*(2), 121–145.

Hoyt, W. T. (2000). Rater bias in psychological research: When is it a problem and what can we do about it? *Psychological Methods, 5*(1), 64–86.

Jackson, J. J., Wood, D., Bogg, T., Walton, K. E., Harms, P. D., & Roberts, B. W. (2010). What do conscientious people do? Development and validation of the behavioral indicators of conscientiousness (BIC). *Journal of Research in Personality, 44,* 501–511.

Joe, J. N., Tocci, C. M., Holtzman, S. L., & Williams, J. C. (2013). *Foundations of observation: Considerations for developing a classroom observation system that helps districts achieve consistent and accurate scores.* MET Project Policy and Practice Brief. Seattle, WA: Bill & Melinda Gates Foundation.

Johnson, J. S., & Lim, G. S. (2009). The influence of rater language background on writing performance assessment. *Language Testing, 26*(4), 485–505.

Latham, G. P., Wexley, K. N., & Purcell, E. D. (1975). Training managers to minimize rating errors in the observation of behavior. *Journal of Applied Psychology, 60,* 550.

Ling, G., Mollaun, P., & Chen, L. (2011). *An investigation of factors that contribute to speaking responses with human rating disagreement.* Unpublished manuscript.

Myford, C. (2012). Rater cognition research: Some possible directions for the future. *Educational Measurement: Issues and Practice, 31*(3), 48–49.

Myford, C. M., Marr, D. B., & Linacre, J. M. (1996). *Reader calibration and its potential role in equating for the Test of Written English* (TOEFL Research Report No. 52). Princeton, NJ: Educational Testing Service.

Myford, C. M., & Wolfe, E. W. (2003). Detecting and measuring rater effects using many-facet Rasch measurement: Part I. *Journal of Applied Measurement, 4,* 386–422.

Park, Y. S., & DeCarlo, L. T. (2011, April). *Effects on classification accuracy under rater drift via latent class signal detection theory and item response theory.* Paper presented at the Annual Meeting of the American Education Research Association, New Orleans, LA.

Pula, J. J., & Huot, B. A. (1993). A model of background influences on holistic raters. In M. M. Williamson & B. A. Huot (Eds.), *Validating holistic scoring for writing assessment: Theoretical and empirical foundations* (pp. 237–265). Cresskill, NJ: Hampton Press.

Pulakos, E. D. (1986). The development of training programs to increase accuracy of different rating forms. *Organizational Behavior and Human Decision Processes, 37,* 76–91.

Rudner, L. M. (1992). Reducing errors due to the use of judges. *Practical Assessment, Research & Evaluation, 3*(3). Retrieved from http://pareonline.net/getvn.asp?v=3&n=3

Schaeffer, G. A., Briel, J. B., & Fowles, M. E. (2001). *Psychometric evaluation of the new GRE writing assessment* (Research Report No. RR-01-18). Princeton, NJ: Educational Testing Service.

Schoonen, R., Vergeer, M., & Eiting, M. (1997). The assessment of writing ability: Expert readers versus lay readers. *Language Testing, 14,* 157–184.

Shohamy, E., Gordon, C. M., & Kraemer, R. (1992). The effects of raters' background and training on the reliability of direct writing tests. *The Modern Language Journal, 76,* 27–33.

Stillman, P. L., Regan, M. B., Swanson, D. B., & Haley, H. A. (1992). Gender differences in clinical skills as measured by an examination using standardized patients. In I. Hart, R. M. Harden, & J. Des Marchais (Eds.), *Current developments in assessing clinical competence* (pp. 390–395). Montreal, Canada: Can-Heal.

Tamanini, K. B. (2008). *Evaluating differential rater functioning in performance ratings: Using a goal-based approach* (Unpublished doctoral dissertation). Ohio University, Athens, OH.

van der Vleuten, C. P., & Swanson, D. B. (1990). Assessment of clinical skills with standardized patients: State of the art. *Teaching and Learning in Medicine, 2*(2), 58–76.

Weigle, S. C. (2002). *Assessing writing.* Cambridge, UK: Cambridge University Press.

Wilson, M., & Case, H. (2000). An examination of variation in rater severity over time: A study in rater drift. In M. Wilson & G. Engelhard (Eds.), *Objective measurement: Theory into practice* (Vol. V, pp. 113–133). Stamford, CT: Ablex.

Xi, X., & Mollaun, P. (2009). *How do raters from India perform in scoring the TOEFL iBT® speaking section and what kind of training helps?* (TOEFL iBT Research Series No. 11). Princeton, NJ: Educational Testing Service.

APPENDIX A

TABLE 12.A.1. **Rater Background Variables**

Background Variables	Classifications of Each Variable
Gender	Not disclosed Male Female
Race/ethnicity	Not disclosed Caucasian African American Native Hawaiian or Other Pacific Islander Hispanic/Latino Asian American Indian or Alaskan Native
Please indicate your experience as a full-time classroom teacher in a K–12 setting.	No response I have never been a full-time teacher in a K–12 setting I was formerly a full-time teacher in a K–12 setting I am currently a full-time teacher in a K–12 setting
For how many years have you been a full-time classroom teacher?	No response 0 years 1 to 2 years 3 to 5 years 6 to 10 years More than 10 years
Highest degree	No degree Bachelor Master Doctor

TABLE 12.A.2.   **Questions Included in the Rater Survey**

Rater Survey Variables	Response Categories
Were you familiar with the instrument prior to the MET project?	No Yes
I was confident in my ability to score after the online training program. The rubrics were clear and helped me to discriminate among the different score levels. The benchmarks and rangefinders were useful tools for understanding how to assign scores. The instrument measures some of the essential elements for effectively teaching. I examined and reflected on my own teaching practices as a result of scoring videos for the MET project. The instrument could be used as a professional development tool to support or improve teaching and learning. The instrument is a fair and valid teaching observation tool.	0 = Strongly disagree 1 = Disagree 2 = Neutral 3 = Agree 4 = Strongly agree
The usefulness of each training component: Overview of the instrument and the components within each cluster Benchmark video clips Rangefinder video clips Review practice segments Practice scoring for all elements before certification If applicable, scoring leader training	1 = Not important 2 = Moderately important 3 = Important 4 = Very important

APPENDIX B

TABLE 12.B.1. Ability to Follow Directions: Items from the Chernyshenko Conscientiousness Scale

Item	Response Categories
Even if I knew how to get around the rules without breaking them, I would not do it.	1 = Disagree strongly
I have the highest respect for authorities and assist them whenever I can.	2 = Disagree somewhat
	3 = Agree somewhat
	4 = Agree strongly
People respect authority more than they should. [reversed]	
I behave properly.	
I support long-established rules and traditions.	
People who resist authority should be severely punished.	
In my opinion, all laws should be strictly enforced.	
In my opinion, censorship slows down progress. [reversed]	
When working with others, I am the one who makes sure that rules are observed.	

TABLE 12.B.2. Attention to Detail: Items from the Behavioral Indicators of Conscientiousness

Item	Response Categories
Make an itinerary.	1 = Never performed the behavior
Keep my desk or work area clean.	2 = Perform the behavior infrequently
Used a planner to schedule the day's events.	3 = Perform the behavior occasionally
Make a grocery list before going to the store.	4 = Perform the behavior somewhat often
File papers in a desk drawer.	5 = Perform the behavior quite often
Organize my closet.	
Use a calendar or date book to plan my activities.	
Label drawers in my office.	
Use a file system for important papers.	
Write in a date book.	
Make lists.	
Complete the projects I start.	
Organize books by height, author, or genre.	
Cross off items from my to-do list.	
Organize work files and materials in a systematic manner.	
Alphabetize or organize recipes.	
File financial documents.	
Set a timeline for getting a project done.	

APPENDIX C

TABLE 12.C.1. Test of Difference Between Background Variables on Scoring Accuracy: MANOVA Results (*p* values)

Scoring Instrument	Number of Raters	MANOVA *p* values					
		Gender	Ethnicity	Teaching Experience	Years of Teaching	Highest Degree
CLASS	354	.812	.102	.566	.784	.073
FfT	149	.814	.835	.567	.418	.515
PLATO	76	.589	.564	.811	.654	.939
Total	579	.814	.445	.788	.519	.226

Note: Values represent *p* values. All factors were nonsignificant. The dependent variables are certification test score, average calibration test score, and accuracy of scores on validation videos. CLASS = Classroom Assessment Scoring System; FfT = Framework for Teaching; PLATO = Protocol for Language Arts Teaching Observation.

TABLE 12.C.2. Test of Difference Between Survey Variables on Scoring Accuracy: MANOVA Results (*p* values)

Survey Questions	CLASS (*n* = 174)	FfT (*n* = 75)	PLATO (*n* = 45)
Previous familiarity with the instrument	.006**	.943	NA
Confident in own ability to score after training	.208	.737	.586
The rubrics were clear	.447	.933	.966
The benchmarks and rangefinders were useful	.182	.914	.648
The instrument measures essential elements for effectively teaching	.773	.803	.975
I reflected on my own teaching practices after MET scoring	.016*	.694	.267
The instrument can be used as a professional development tool	.013*	.661	.968
The instrument is fair and valid	.180	.763	.203
The usefulness of the overview of the instrument and the components	.958	.365	.465
The usefulness of the benchmark video clips	.098	.515	.329
The usefulness of the rangefinder video clips	NA	.708	.877
The usefulness of reviewing practice segments	NA	.465	.725
The usefulness of practice scoring for all elements before certification	.661	.936	.702
The usefulness of scoring leader training (if applicable)	.287	.146	.859

Note: Values with NA indicate questions not included in the rater survey of a particular instrument. Details of the questions and response categories are presented in Table 12.A.2 of Appendix A. Sample size of raters was limited to respondents (raters) that provided responses for the voluntary survey. The dependent variables are certification test scores, average calibration test scores, and accuracy of scores on validation videos. CLASS = Classroom Assessment Scoring System; FfT = Framework for Teaching; PLATO = Protocol for Language Arts Teaching Observation.

*p < .05; **p < .01.

TABLE 12.C.3. Coefficients from Multiple Logistic Regression: Exact Agreement with Classroom Settings and Teacher Characteristics

Classroom and Teacher Characteristics	CLASS		FfT		MQI		PLATO	
Classroom								
% Hispanic	0.44	(0.19)*	0.72	(0.27)**	0.61	(0.25)*	−0.05	(0.32)
% Black/Native Am.	0.51	(0.24)*	0.93	(0.36)**	0.60	(0.31)*	−0.17	(0.39)
% White/Asian	0.46	(0.22)*	0.76	(0.33)*	0.61	(0.31)*	−0.09	(0.36)
% Gifted	0.06	(0.04)	−0.04	(0.06)	0.02	(0.06)	0.02	(0.04)
% Male	0.04	(0.03)	0.00	(0.04)	0.04	(0.04)	−0.07	(0.04)
% Special ed.	−0.03	(0.03)	−0.04	(0.05)	−0.03	(0.04)	0.03	(0.04)
% ELL	−0.01	(0.04)	−0.20	(0.07)**	−0.07	(0.08)	−0.10	(0.06)
% Age	−0.05	(0.03)	0.07	(0.05)	−0.13	(0.04)**	0.03	(0.04)
% Student lunch	−0.04	(0.04)	0.17	(0.07)*	0.00	(0.07)	−0.09	(0.05)

(continued)

(*Table 12.C.3 continued*)

Classroom and Teacher

Characteristics	CLASS		FfT		MQI		PLATO	
Teacher								
Male	0.02	(0.03)	−0.06	(0.04)	0.22	(0.05)***	0.01	(0.05)
White	−0.14	(0.11)	0.21	(0.26)	−0.12	(0.16)	0.02	(0.15)
Black	−0.18	(0.10)	0.14	(0.25)	−0.08	(0.16)	0.13	(0.15)
Hispanic	−0.06	(0.05)	0.02	(0.12)	−0.16	(0.09)	0.05	(0.07)
District experience	0.00	(0.03)	0.02	(0.04)	0.00	(0.05)	−0.03	(0.05)
Advanced degree	0.03	(0.03)	0.00	(0.05)	0.07	(0.05)	0.03	(0.04)

Note: Values represent coefficients from the logistic regression. Coefficients represent log odds (i.e., log [$p/1-p$]), where p is probability of exact agreement. Coefficient values greater than 0 indicate greater log odds of agreement; a value below 0 indicates greater log odds of disagreement. Values in parenthesis are standard errors. The standard errors do not take into account the dependence between scores from different dimensions of the same video observed; they are treated as independent for these results. An analysis that considers dependency between different dimensions of the same video will lead to an increase in the standard errors (current values of standard errors may be underestimated). CLASS = Classroom Assessment Scoring System; FfT = Framework for Teaching; MQI = Mathematical Quality of Instruction; PLATO = Protocol for Language Arts Teaching Observation; ELL = English language learner.

*$p < .05$; **$p < .01$; ***$p < .001$.

CHAPTER

Scoring Design Decisions

Reliability and the Length and Focus of Classroom Observations

JILLIAM N. JOE, CATHERINE A. McCLELLAN, AND STEVEN L. HOLTZMAN

ABSTRACT

The field knows very little about the empirical and cognitive tradeoffs between "short" and "full" observations, or between observation instruments that require observers to attend to all observable teaching traits versus protocols that require them to attend to a few complementary traits at a time. Knowing how these variables impact the accuracy and reliability of observations can help practitioners make better resource and design decisions, and support high-quality observations. The purpose of this chapter is to present two studies that address scoring design decisions associated with observation length and observation instrument structure. MET project data were used in both studies. In Study 1, the amount of time that is necessary to observe and score classroom teaching practice was examined. The results indicate that a score based on the first thirty minutes of the lesson has a strong relationship with and is a good predictor of the full lesson score when using CLASS, FfT, MQI, PLATO, and QST instruments. Next, in Study 2, differences in inter-rater reliability when the observation instrument requires the observer to focus on a select group of traits during a thirty-minute observation, and when an observer scores all traits on the instrument, were examined. The findings suggest that inter-rater reliability is higher when observers focus on a smaller set of complementary traits during a thirty-minute observation than when they use the full instrument. The chapter concludes with some discussion on how these results may be applied in practice.

INTRODUCTION

The use of classroom observations for high-stakes teacher evaluation requires scoring designs that produce reliable and accurate scores and scoring designs (procedures) that are effective, efficient, and sustainable. To achieve this, the design of scoring procedures must account for a variety of factors: to include the number of lessons to observe, observer training content and mode, ongoing monitoring and support activities, and when and where the observations should be conducted (live or video). In addition to these logistical constraints, the question of how to manage the cognitive complexity of the observation task must also be considered. It was discovered early into the design of the MET scoring that balancing these factors to achieve acceptable inter-rater reliability, efficiency, and sustainability was going to be no easy task, even with more than twenty years of collective staff experience in scoring large-scale performance assessments as a reference.

Cognitive Load in Observation

A certain amount of information processing is required for any complex task. Different tasks demand different degrees of cognitive effort. Classroom observation, for example, places a variety of demands on the observer, including aural and visual information processing, decision making, and switching between external and internal foci (e.g., viewing, gathering evidence, sorting evidence, and consulting the scoring rubric). In addition to the cognitive load inherent to the observation task itself, cognitive load can be introduced variably by the classroom environment—a factor over which an observer has little control. Cognitive load can also be introduced systematically through the scoring procedures.

Scoring Rubric One obvious source of cognitive load in the scoring procedures is the observation instrument and its scoring rubric (Jerald, 2012). The observation instrument defines the domains (overarching areas of teaching practice) and dimensions (specific traits that exemplify each domain) of classroom teaching practice. The instrument's rubric defines the judgment criteria and rating scale along which the dimensions are to be measured. Specifically, within each score level of the rating scale are descriptions of the characteristics of typical teaching at that level. These levels are distinct and mutually exclusive. In the context of classroom observation, instruments comprise varying numbers of dimensions and score points depending on their focus. For example, one end of the spectrum is the version of Charlotte Danielson's Framework for Teaching (FfT) instrument used for the MET project. The FfT comprises four domains of teaching practice, two of which are used for classroom observation: The Classroom Environment and Instruction. Within each of the observation domains are four dimensions of classroom teaching practice, eight dimensions to be assessed in total. The dimensions are measured along a four-point rating scale. Characteristics of teaching practice at each level of the scale are described. In addition, there are three to nine behavioral cues, "indicators," that are indicative of practice at that level. On the other end of the spectrum is the MET version of the Classroom Assessment Scoring System (CLASS)—also a content-neutral instrument—that comprises three domains and twelve dimensions. The dimensions are measured along a seven-point scale. Similar to the FfT, there is a higher-order description of teaching practice at each level, followed by a series of behavioral cues or indicators. In both cases, the observer is tasked with internalizing all of these dimensions and their definitions to some degree to facilitate evidence collection during the observation. One could argue that the amount of detail included in both of these rubrics should, in theory, improve inter-rater reliability. It is unclear whether such complexity negates this effect.

The extent to which an observer can gather evidence for and reliably score the number of dimensions on the rubric within a relatively small window of time in the lesson should be examined during instrument development. Consider that a rubric with several criteria for evaluation that must be assessed simultaneously can increase the cognitive load placed on observers. When cognitive load is a non-negligible factor in scoring, inter-rater reliability suffers (Arter & McTighe, 2001). This is because there is a finite amount of cognitive space available in the human brain for such functions (Hunt & Ellis, 2004). Pressed beyond their information-processing capacity, observers provide scores that are less accurate and are influenced by individual biases and professional preferences. In other words, if the construct being observed necessitates the use of a lengthy or complex scoring rubric, for example, a rubric that contains multiple dimensions of teaching practice, the complexity of that task can erode the quality of scoring. The scoring process must be designed in such a way as to minimize cognitive load and its impact on inter-rater reliability.

Recent research has shown that observation scores generally exhibit lower than expected inter-rater reliability, compared to traditional performance assessments and commonly accepted standards (Cash, Hamre, Pianta, & Myers, 2012; Graham, Milanowski, & Miller, 2012; Hill, Charalambous, & Kraft, 2012). This suggests that there are aspects of the classroom observation system, including cognitive load and time demands that interact with observers in ways that the field has yet to fully understand, control, and standardize.

Time on Task Time demands placed on the observers (principals, department chairs, coaches, and others) also present a significant challenge to the efficiency and effectiveness of scoring in classroom observation systems, particularly when there are few observers, many teachers, and multiple observations per teacher to complete (Hill, Charalambous, & Kraft, 2012). The amount of time spent on task has also been found, in the context of a speaking assessment, to have an adverse effect on the quality of scoring for extended periods of time (Ling, Mollaun, & Xi, 2009). In this case, as raters become fatigued, scoring accuracy declines. The longer the rater spends on a single task, the more quality performance wanes. Limiting the amount of consecutive scoring time and providing multiple opportunities to recalibrate (stop scoring and refresh one's knowledge of the specifics of the scoring rubric) during the scoring session are some solutions large-scale assessments have implemented to mitigate the influence of time on scoring quality.

Classroom observations are inherently more complex than speaking assessments. Greater efficiency and consistency can be obtained by reducing the time observers are required to spend on an observation and by focusing their attention on a subset of classroom teaching practice attributes as a means to reduce cognitive load associated with the observation task. Having multiple observers assigned to a lesson would allow for each observer to specialize in different dimensions of the rubric, which is the approach applied in the MET scoring. In practice, what this might mean is that observers with content expertise could specialize in the aspects of the rubric that required examination of content accuracy and delivery. Other observers could then focus on the content-neutral dimensions of practice, such as behavior management and classroom climate. Again, the purpose of limiting the amount of information the observer must manage cognitively is to improve the quality of the observation and its scores.

Scoring Designs

A scoring design is a comprehensive plan for the systematic collection of performance-assessment scores. It details the conditions in which lessons (in the present context) are to be scored and how the scoring should be conducted, and tries to account for the conditions that might lead to excessive cognitive load on observers. Specifying the scoring design is an important step in the implementation of the classroom observation system. Careful attention to it will help to ensure reliability and comparability of scores from lesson to lesson and teacher to teacher. The scoring design for classroom observation can include, but is not limited to, the assignment of lessons to observers (which teachers' lessons will be scored by which raters), as well as the quality controls for scoring (e.g., percent double-scored, percent validity responses,[1] and percent back-scoring[2]).

The scoring design is intended to promote efficiency and quality in the observation system. When the scoring design imposes conditions that are not optimal for observers and do not facilitate efficiency, even highly trained observers will make inaccurate judgments. In typical large-scale video scoring, such as the MET project, several principles are adopted to ensure the effectiveness of the scoring designs implemented:

- Raters work fixed shifts scheduled by staff responsible for managing scheduling and logistics

- Raters work in teams under the supervision of a scoring leader

- All raters within a team are using the same rubric

- Raters score prerecorded video

- Raters may not score teachers who are known to them personally

- Raters are expected to have no other obligations during their shifts

- Raters score in software systems that support use of quality control measures, such as those mentioned earlier.

Shifting from the more controlled environment of scoring videos of classroom practice to live observations means that some of the conditions listed in the previous paragraph are applicable, but that some are not. For example, if there is more than one observer in a school, each of them should be using the same observation instrument to measure teaching practice, as was the case with the MET scoring. Standardization is paramount. Further, in practice, some instruments require that scores be assigned after fixed periods of observed time in live classrooms, as was the case with the MET scoring. Aside from these two conditions, none of the other conditions previously mentioned describes the reality of classroom teaching practice observation in schools. Nonetheless, there are useful lessons from the highly structured MET scoring to guide live observation, which will be explored further in the chapter.

MET Scoring Design

The MET project was designed to measure teaching effectiveness through a multi-measure approach. Student achievement, classroom observation, and student survey data were gathered to improve the reliability of the teaching effectiveness measure. This section describes the scoring design and processes used to support high-quality standardized scoring for the classroom observation data collection. CLASS and FfT were the two content-neutral instruments used in the MET project, as described earlier. Mathematical Quality of Instruction (MQI), Protocol for Language Arts Teaching Observations (PLATO), and Quality Science Teaching (QST) were the three content-specific instruments used. A brief description of these instruments is given below.

MQI comprises six dimensions. Five dimensions are scored along a 3-point rating scale. The sixth dimension is scored along a dichotomous (yes or no) rating scale. For two of the dimensions, Classroom Work Connected to Mathematics and Explicitness and Thoroughness, the raters had to keep in mind that only one could apply, depending on the content of the lesson and the grade level. In addition to assigning segment scores, raters were required to assign a holistic score for each dimension as well as an overall MQI score that was based on all segments of video viewed and a lesson-based guess at Math Knowledge for Teaching (MKT). PLATO comprises seven dimensions of teaching practice. All dimensions are scored along a 4-point rating scale. In addition, raters were required to assign a dichotomous (yes or no) rating to items related to the content domain (seven elements) and activity structure (eight elements). QST comprises five domains and twelve dimensions. All dimensions are scored along a 7-point rating scale.

Prior to the scoring that was conducted for the MET main study, a set of videos was "master coded" to identify exemplar videos—videos with "correct" scores that are clear representations of teaching practice within a dimension and score level. These exemplars were then used to train, certify, calibrate, and monitor observers. Master coding requires that highly trained experts review a set of videos intensely. This process provides not only correct scores for each segment in the video from beginning to end, but also time-stamped indications of the location on the video of all evidence that influenced the assignment of each segment score. The videos used for master coding were selected to represent a wide variety of teacher performance across all dimensions of teaching practice and span all of the score points within each dimension of each instrument.

Master coding was completed separately for each of the five observation instruments used in the MET project. The master coding process varied somewhat by instrument but followed a basic process. Master coders were grouped in pairs, and the pairs scored a subset of the videos selected for master coding. Each member of the pair independently scored each lesson in the timeframes specified by the instrument developer. In accordance with the instruments' design, CLASS, FfT, PLATO, and QST videos were master coded in fifteen-minute segments. MQI videos were master coded in 7.5-minute segments.

After pairs of master coders individually assigned their initial scores, the master coders met to compare their evidence and scores and discussed and reconciled evidence and scores that disagreed. If any scores could not be easily reconciled, the video was scored by a third master coder; then all three master coders had a reconciliation session.

Phases of MET Scoring

MET scoring was conducted in two phases. As will be explained in more detail, the dimensions of each instrument's rubric were divided into two non-overlapping groups in the Phase 1 study. The dimensions were divided in this way based on the rationale that scoring reliability would be higher if individual observers focused on a few dimensions during the observation rather than on the full set. In addition, the timeframe for viewing each lesson differed from traditional whole-lesson observations. Observation times were typically thirty minutes (more discussion of time segments is provided later in the chapter when special Study 1 is discussed). The Phase 1 study included FfT, MQI, and PLATO. Videos were not scored using the CLASS or QST observation protocol in Phase 1.

In the Phase 2 study of the MET project, the scoring design was modified to ensure the scoring was completed well in advance of project reporting deadlines. Each observer used the full rubric (all dimensions) for each of the observation instruments. Phase 2 scoring included all five instruments: FfT, MQI, PLATO, QST, and CLASS. Viewing timeframes changed slightly for FfT, MQI, and PLATO from the timeframes that were used in the Phase 1 study. It is important to note that the scoring design for both Phase 1 and Phase 2 also included elements such as daily calibration of observers prior to scoring, random assignment of videos to raters based on an observer's eligibility,[3] and back-scoring by scoring leaders. The design also specified that a small percentage of the videos raters scored were to be used for validation purposes. Videos that had been given correct scores during the master coding process were seeded into the set of videos distributed to each rater. The validation videos enabled scoring leadership to monitor scoring accuracy of an individual rater or group of raters during a scoring shift. Because of the differences in the two scoring designs, videos scored in Phase 1 were re-scored in Phase 2 scoring.

MET Phase 1 For the Phase 1 study of the MET project, research was conducted for each instrument to identify the "ideal" amount of time needed for observation. The goal of this was to limit the amount of time observers were required to watch each video, while still yielding high-quality scores that agreed with the scores that would be assigned from scoring after watching the entire video. First, the frequency distributions of master-coded evidence collected over the length of the lesson for roughly fifty videos were examined. Then, for each dimension, content experts identified the points along the timeline of the lessons for which there was a "critical mass" of evidence. If a teacher were going to exhibit a particular behavior related to the dimension, it would most likely happen within these time points. The frequency distributions for FfT dimension 2a (Creating an Environment of Respect and Rapport) and 2b (Using Questioning and Discussion Techniques) are illustrated in Figure 13.1 and Figure 13.2. Along the x-axis of these graphs is the number of minutes in the lesson. Along the y-axis is the frequency of master-coder comments for that dimension. The number of videos is also plotted against the number of minutes in the lesson (green line). There were very few master-coded videos that went beyond sixty minutes. As shown in these graphs, the preponderance

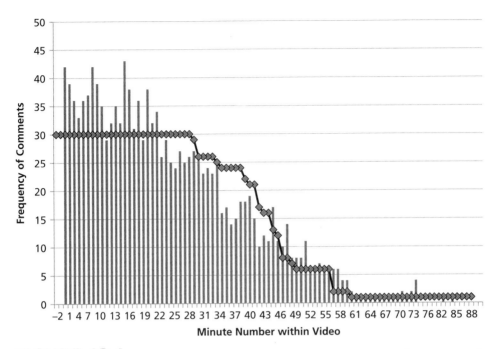

FIGURE 13.1. *FfT Dimension 2a, Creating an Environment of Respect and Rapport*

of evidence for both of these dimensions generally occurred during the first twelve minutes of the lesson and between minutes twenty-five and thirty-five.

Next, the content experts grouped dimensions based on the similarity of time spans when maximal evidence was available. They also considered the amount of cognitive demand the combination of dimensions would place on an observer and placed dimensions with similar time spans in a group that balanced cognitive load.

Small-scale tryouts were conducted to determine the extent to which scores from the reduced timeframe and grouped dimensions yielded results that were comparable to master codes. Instrument developers used the findings to establish the viewing timeframe applied in the MET Phase 1 study. Once the groups of dimensions and timeframes were set, raters were randomly assigned to train, certify, calibrate, and score one of the groups of dimensions. Figure 13.3 summarizes the process just described.

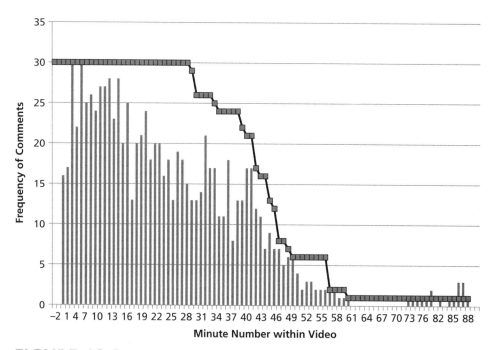

FIGURE 13.2. *FfT Dimension 3b, Using Questioning and Discussion Techniques*

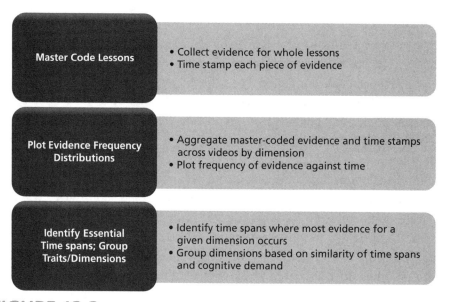

FIGURE 13.3. *A Summary of the Process*

Based on the process described in Figure 13.3, the scoring of the MQI videos was done on the first four 7.5-minute segments for each video. A score was assigned to each of the four segments. The segments were scored on three of the six MQI dimensions by one group of observers; the other group evaluated three dimensions as well. The scoring of all videos for PLATO was done on the first two fifteen-minute segments. A score was assigned to each of the two segments. The segments were scored on four of the eight PLATO dimensions by one group of observers; the other group scored the remaining four dimensions. The scoring of all videos for FfT was more nuanced. For the first group of dimensions (comprised of two of the eight FfT scales), scoring was done on a combination of the first twelve minutes plus the segment of the video from minutes twenty-five to thirty-five. A combination of the first fifteen minutes plus the segment from minutes thirty to thirty-five was used for a second group of dimensions comprised of three of the eight FfT dimensions. A combination of the segment from minutes five to fifteen and a segment from minutes twenty-five to thirty-five was used for a third group, comprised of the remaining three FfT dimensions.

MET Phase 2 The second phase marked the point in the MET project where the scoring design was changed. Each observer used the full rubric for each of the observation instruments. Due to this difference in scoring design, all videos from Phase 1 were re-scored in Phase 2 using the revised procedures.

The Phase 2 scoring of all videos for CLASS was done on the first two fifteen-minute segments, each of which was scored on all twelve dimensions of the instrument. QST was only scored in Phase 2. The scoring of the QST laboratory videos was done on up to four fifteen-minute segments. All of the QST laboratory dimensions were coded for all segments. Scoring for dimensions of teaching practice in the non-laboratory setting was done on the first two fifteen-minute segments. Also, the dimensions were divided into two groups with four dimensions in two groups. Scoring for MQI was done on the first four 7.5-minute segments. The scoring for PLATO was done on the first two 15-minute segments of a video. Also, Activity Structure was excluded from the scoring rubric during this phase of the scoring. Finally, the scoring of the FfT videos was done on a combination of the segment of the video from minutes zero to fifteen and the segment from minutes twenty-five to thirty-five. This was slightly different from the timeframe used in Phase 1.

Differences between Phase 1 and Phase 2 timing designs for all of the instruments are summarized in Table 13.1.

Given the limitations of the small-scale tryouts explained above, it was important for us to continue exploring the idea that a short observation could

TABLE 13.1. Summary of MET Phase 1 and Phase 2 Scoring Designs

	Phase 1	Phase 2
MQI	First four 7.5-minute segments:	First four 7.5-minute segments All dimensions
	Group 1: Errors and Imprecision Classroom Work Connected to Mathematics Explicitness and Thoroughness	
	Based on all segments: Holistic Errors and Imprecision Holistic Classroom Work Connected to Mathematics Holistic Explicitness and Thoroughness Overall MQI Overall MKT	
	Group 2: Student Participation in Meaning- Making and Reasoning Richness Working with Students and Mathematics	

	Based on all segments:
	Holistic Student Participation in
	    Meaning-Making and Reasoning
	Holistic Richness
	Holistic Working with Students and
	    Mathematics
	Overall MQI
	Overall MKT	

	Phase 1	**Phase 2**
PLATO	First two 15-minute segments	First two 15-minute segments All dimensions except Activity Structure
	Group 1: Intellectual Challenge Classroom Discourse Behavior Management Representations of Content Content Domain (seven elements) Activity Structure (five elements)	
	Group 2: Modeling Strategy Use and Instruction Time Management Representations of Content Activity Structure (three elements)	

FfT	*Group 1* (minutes 0–12 and 25–35):
	Creating an Environment of Respect
	  and Rapport
	Using Questioning and Discussion
	  Techniques
		Minutes 0–15 and 25–35
		All dimensions

	Group 2 (minutes 0–15 and 30–35[4]): Establishing a Culture for Learning Managing Classroom Procedures Communicating with Students	
	Group 3 (minutes 5–15 and 25–35): Managing Student Behavior Engaging Students in Learning Using Assessment in Instruction	
CLASS	N/A	First two 15-minute segments All dimensions

(continued)

(Table 13.1 continued)

	Phase 1	Phase 2
QST	N/A	*Group 1* (First two 15-minute segments): Sets the Context and Focuses Learning on Key Science Concepts Uses Representations Demonstrates Content Knowledge Provides Feedback for Learning *Group 2* (First two 15-minute segments): Promotes Students' Interest and Motivation to Learn Science Assigns Tasks to Promote Learning and Addresses the Task Demands Uses Modes of Teaching Science Concepts Elicits Evidence of Students' Knowledge and Conceptual Understanding *Group 3* (First four 15-minute segments): Initiates the Investigation Provides Guidelines for Conducting the Investigation and Gathering Data Guides Analysis and Interpretation of Data Elicits Evidence of Students' Knowledge and Conceptual Understanding

produce a score similar to the score for a longer observation. In addition, the small-scale tryouts were limited in helping us to assess the differences in inter-rater reliability between a scoring model that used a few dimensions of the rubric versus a model that used the full rubric for a thirty-minute observation. Concerns about how long classroom observations can reasonably be and how much of the rubric one observer can reliably manage during the observation period were addressed through two special studies conducted separately from the main MET project.

SPECIAL STUDIES

Two special studies were performed by reanalyzing data collected during the scoring that occurred during the main MET study (described above). Both studies can be viewed as attempts to limit the load on the cognitive capacity of the raters, by shortening time viewed (to reduce fatigue) and/or by reducing the number of aspects of the domain of teaching practice to which the rater was required to attend (to reduce cognitive load).

Study 1 examined the issue of optimizing observers' time by viewing and scoring only part of each video. Scores from master coding were used to investigate several possible strategies for optimizing the observers' time by limiting which parts of videos. Study 2 focused on limiting the cognitive load on observers by requiring them to score only a subset of the dimensions on each rubric. Study 2 compared inter-rater reliability from the MET Phase 1 scoring (for which individual observers used a subset of the dimensions) to inter-rater reliability from Phase 2 scoring (for which observers were required to attend to all of the rubric's dimensions).

Study 1: Optimizing Observers' Time on Task

The purpose of Study 1 was to examine what part-whole relationships can be determined among time-segment scores—the part being scores from individual time segments (e.g., zero to fifteen minutes) and the whole being scores aggregated across all of the time segments. The study was also designed to investigate whether scores from a particular time segment are more strongly related to the aggregate score than to any other segment. CLASS, MQI, PLATO, and QST master-coded data were used for this analysis. For CLASS, fifty videos were master-coded. These videos were scored for the entire class session length in fifteen-minute segments on all twelve dimensions. MQI also had fifty master-coded videos that were coded in 7.5-minute segments for the full length of the class session; individual master-coder ratings as well as a single consensus master code was used for each segment. There were fifty-one master-coded QST classroom videos; including a small set of laboratory videos (laboratory videos comprised only 18 percent of the QST). The small sample and possible non representativeness may limit the utility and stability of any analyses of the QST lab video scores.

Study 1 Procedures The analytic approach was straightforward. In each case, the scores assigned to each segment of the video on each dimension were correlated with the overall mean score on the video across all segments. There is a part-whole dependency in this approach, of course. In a part-whole dependency, the strength of the relationship between two variables is inflated when one variable is a "part" of or highly dependent on the other. In addition to the part-whole dependency, it is worth noting that individual master coders did see the entire video that they scored. It may be that, beyond the statistical dependency, there is also a cognitive tendency to "agree with oneself" (the halo effect). In this context, a halo effect would result in a tendency to assign similar scores across segments to the same teacher within a lesson. Both of these factors may contribute to inflated correlation values.

Study 1 Results Across all the instruments, generally, the relationship between each segment and the total score is quite high. For three of the instruments—CLASS, FfT, and QST—the relationship tended to be strongest in segment 2 (running from minute fifteen to minute thirty) and segment 3 (from minute thirty to minute forty-five). These results are presented in Figures 13.4, 13.5, and 13.6. The correlation values were often above 0.8 for either segment 2 or 3 individually. Recall that the square of the correlation is the proportion of variance accounted for the relationship. So a correlation of 0.8 indicates that the scores on one fifteen-minute segment accounts for about 65 percent of the variability of the scores based on watching the entire video.

For CLASS (Figure 13.4), for example, segment 2 had a correlation value of 0.9 with the whole-lesson score Analysis and Problem Solving. The correlation between segment 2 score and whole-lesson score was lower ($r = 0.8$)

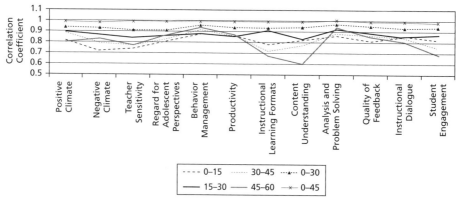

FIGURE 13.4. *CLASS Dimensions Part-Whole Correlations*

for Content Understanding. The combination of segments 1 and 2 produced a correlation with total score over 0.9 for most dimensions on these instruments. These strong relationships suggest that scores, from the middle of the lesson in particular, are an excellent predictor of the overall score for the lesson. A score based on a combination of the first thirty minutes of the lesson is also a good predictor of the score for the overall lesson. For CLASS, FfT, and QST, scoring only part of the video (especially from the middle of the lesson)

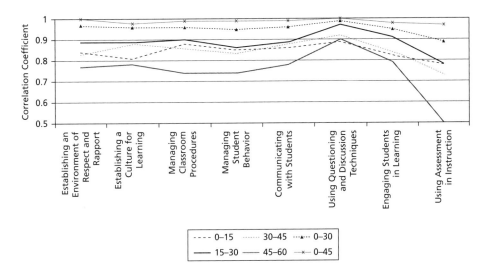

FIGURE 13.5. *FfT Dimensions Part-Whole Correlations*

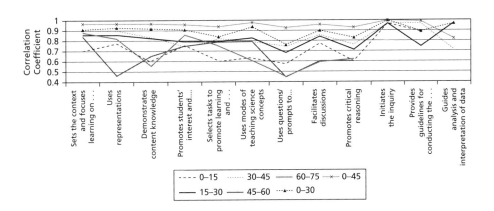

FIGURE 13.6. *QST Dimensions Part-Whole Correlations*

may serve as an adequate approximation to the score from the full video. This is discussed below.

For PLATO, the pattern was a little more nuanced (Figure 13.7). Segment 2 was a good predictor (correlation > 0.8) for some (e.g., Intellectual Challenge, Modeling, and Strategy Use), but not all dimensions (e.g., Guided Practice and Classroom Discourse). No single segment was consistently a strong predictor of total scores by itself, and a combination of segments 1, 2, 3, and 4 (whole sixty-minute lesson) was required to be a strong predictor of total score. Although a score based on the combination of segments 1 and 2 was not as strong a predictor as the segment 1, 2, 3, and 4 combination (whole sixty-minute lesson), it was a fairly good predictor of the total score.

MQI produced a somewhat different pattern of results (Figure 13.8). Bear in mind that MQI segments were scored in 7.5 minute segments. MQI segments 1 and 2 would be equivalent to segment 1 for all other instruments. The correlation values (segment scores with overall video scores) were reasonably high, but lower than those observed on the other instruments. This may be related to the fact that the dimensions on MQI have only two or three score levels; CLASS has seven levels, PLATO four levels, and QST four levels. Also, MQI scores tended to have relatively small variability. The scoring in relatively short (compared to other instruments) 7.5-minute segments may also be a factor in the lower correlation values. There was no clear pattern of

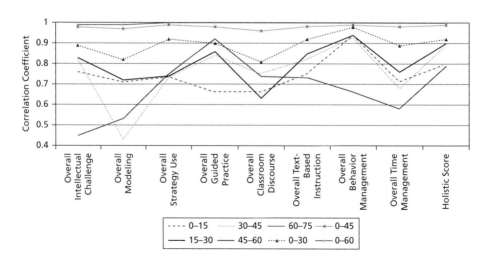

FIGURE 13.7. *PLATO Dimensions Part-Whole Correlations*

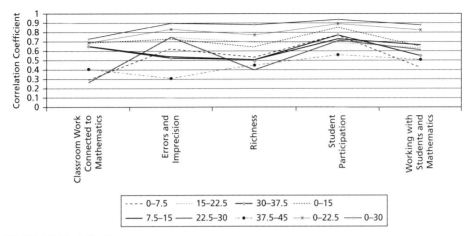

FIGURE 13.8. *MQI Dimensions Part-Whole Correlations*

one segment being more strongly correlated than the others with the overall score. The correlation between segments 1, 2, 3, and 4 (roughly equivalent to time for segments 1 and 2 for the other tools) produce correlations of around 0.7 or better.

Study 2: Limiting Cognitive Load

Our second study examines inter-rater reliability for the different scoring designs. Inter-rater reliability from the MET Phase 1 study was compared to inter-rater reliability from the MET Phase 2 study. As noted above, Phase 1 scoring procedures limited the cognitive demand on observers by requiring them to conduct observations with a small set of dimensions. Different groups of observers were assigned to different subsets or groups of dimensions. While a given lesson was to receive a score for each of the dimensions, the scores were provided by multiple observers; each specialized in scoring a subset of those dimensions. Inter-rater reliability was expected to be higher under Phase 1 scoring procedures than under Phase 2 scoring procedures (scoring with a full set of dimensions). Because CLASS and QST were not scored in Phase 1, Study 2 only examines FfT, MQI, and PLATO.

As described previously, a single observer contributed primary[5] scores for a small set of an instrument's dimensions in Phase 1. In Phase 2, a single observer contributed primary scores for the full set of dimensions for a given video segment. All lessons were scored based on approximately thirty minutes of viewing time in Phase 1 and between twenty-two and thirty minutes of viewing time in Phase 2. It is important to note that the data used in the analysis did not permit us to test the effect of the change in the number of dimensions an observer used independent of the effect of the change in the duration of viewing time.

Study 2 Procedures FfT, MQI, and PLATO scores were used in this analysis (N = 1,563, N = 735, and N = 631, respectively). Recall that CLASS and QST were not scored in the MET Phase 1 study. As was discussed above, all the videos scored in Phase 1 were re-scored in Phase 2 to allow researchers to measure the effect of the scoring design change. In preparation for Phase 2 scoring, Phase 1 observers were required to train and certify on the dimensions to which they had not been previously assigned. Newly recruited observers trained and certified on all of the dimensions as well. Because of random assignment of video segments to observers, it cannot be assumed that the same group of observers who contributed to the Phase 1 scores for these videos also contributed to the Phase 2 scores. The composition of the pool of observers, and hence, the observers who contributed to the re-scores, changed for several reasons: (1) additional newly recruited observers, (2) the loss of a number of Phase 1 observers who failed to certify on the "new" dimensions, and (3) normal attrition. Despite the changes in the pool, we argue that the observation abilities of the observers did not change, because the standards for certification and calibration did not change between the two phases of scoring.

Within each phase, a subset of the scores was randomly selected to be scored by a second observer. Table 13.2 shows the percentage for double-scores for each instrument and phase. Note that Explicitness and Thoroughness (MQI) was only applicable in a small subset of lessons, which explains the low percentage of double-scored responses.

It should be noted that, in Phase 1, multiple observers assigned scores to a specific lesson, while in Phase 2 a single observer assigned scores to all of the dimensions in an instrument. The assignment of re-scores in each phase reflected that phase's design. Because re-scores are only computed within, not across, phases, this difference does not confound the comparisons performed in Study 2.

Study 2 Results A measure of inter-rater reliability was estimated using an approach proposed by Livingston (2004; see Appendix for the formula). The statistic captures the amount of "noise" associated with a scoring process in

TABLE 13.2. **Percentage of Double-Scored Responses in MET Phase 1 and Phase 2 Scoring**

	Phase 1	Phase 2
FfT	30% to 43%	12%
MQI	4% to 65%[a]	1% to 10%
PLATO	25% to 27%	5%

Note: Ranges represent the percentage of double-scored segments across dimensions.

[a]Explicitness and Thoroughness was only applicable in a small subset of lessons.

which responses are randomly assigned to observers and a subset of those responses is randomly selected to receive a second score. In the scoring process applied to the phases of the MET scoring, lessons were randomly assigned to observers, and there was a percentage of double scores. Values of Livingston's coefficient can range from 0 to 1. The closer the coefficient is to 0, the more unreliable the scoring process. A single coefficient is reported for each instrument; variance among observers was aggregated across dimensions. Applying Livingston's method of estimating scoring reliability allows the use of all available score data rather than a data set limited to double-scored segments—as would have been the case had other classical methods, such as raw agreement, kappa, or Generalizability Theory, been used. As mentioned, the objective of this study is to examine the difference in inter-rater reliability between Phase 1 and Phase 2 scoring designs. To this end, Fisher's z-transformation was applied as a variance stabilizing measure, and t-tests were used to test the significance of the differences between Phase 1 and Phase 2 scoring reliability coefficients.

Standard error of scoring (SES) is also examined. SES is the inverse of the reliability coefficient; the closer SES is to 0, the more reliable the process. SES captures the variation in scores error due to scoring error.

As shown in Table 13.3, inter-rater reliability ranged from 0.70 to 0.78 for MET Phase 1 across instruments. In contrast, MET Phase 2 inter-rater reliability was somewhat lower, and ranged from 0.66 to 0.70 across instruments. The differences from Phase 1 to Phase 2 are significant. However, note that the difference in the SES between FfT Phase 1 and Phase 2 scores is quite small ($\Delta = 0.02$). Nevertheless, the difference in inter-rater reliability suggests

TABLE 13.3. FfT, MQI, and PLATO Phase 1 and Phase 2 Inter-Rater Reliability

| | Phase 1 | | Phase 2 | | Difference Test of Scoring Reliability Coefficients | |
	Inter-rater reliability	SES	Inter-rater reliability	SES	z	ρ
FfT	0.70	1.42	0.66	1.40	2.08	<.05
MQI	0.78	0.75	0.70	0.82	3.41	<.01
PLATO	0.77	1.20	0.69	1.40	3.06	<.01

that the change in scoring designs between Phase 1 and Phase 2 influenced the reliability of scoring. Similarly, for content-specific instruments it appears that scoring with fewer dimensions promoted higher inter-rater reliability than scoring with the full set of dimensions. The change in SES between Phase 1 and Phase 2 for MQI ($\Delta = 0.07$) and PLATO ($\Delta = 0.20$) was considerably larger than for FfT.

APPLICATIONS TO PRACTICE

The two special studies presented in this chapter were conducted to examine aspects of classroom observation that impact cognitive complexity, the scoring rubric, and time on task. More specifically, these studies addressed scoring design decisions related to use of the scoring rubric and time on task to explore ways to improve the efficiency and reliability of scoring. To examining efficiency, Study 1 investigated the relationships between scores assigned to short continuous segments of a lesson and a total score based on the average of all segment scores for a lesson. CLASS, FfT, MQI, PLATO, and QST instruments were used. The key question was: Can scoring less than the full lesson yield scores that are similar to scores based on the whole lesson? Part-whole correlations tended to exceed 0.90 when segments 2 and 3 (minutes fifteen to thirty) were combined—indicating that a similar score can be made by watching the middle of a lesson. When segments 1 and 2 were combined, the correlation with scores from the whole lesson exceeded a value of 0.80. This suggests that the first thirty minutes would also be a sufficient predictor of classroom teaching practice for a given lesson.

The MQI was the exception to this finding. There was no clear pattern of one segment having a stronger relationship with the overall score than other segments had. The relationship between segments 1, 2, 3, and 4 (which is roughly equivalent to time for segments 1 and 2 for the other tools) produce correlations values of around 0.7 or better.

Even though the context of this study was video classroom observation, the results are suggestive of a "triage" approach (Hill, Charalambous, & Kraft, 2012) that can be applied to conducting observations in a live setting. In order to limit the amount of time an observer must spend in a classroom, it may be that a short first observation (analogous to screening tests used in medicine) of about thirty minutes in length, completed in the middle segment of the classroom session and focused strongly on scoring only, would be a good start. This observation would not be intended to provide substantial feedback or diagnosis to the teacher. Based on our findings in Study 1, these scores would be expected to be highly related to the overall scores of the entire class session. The preliminary scores could be used as an indication of a pattern of overall strengths and weaknesses that might be anticipated in subsequent, full-evidence observations—intended to diagnose issues and recommend professional development.

If further work supports findings from Study 1 and data from the short observations prove to be strongly predictive of what is seen in the later diagnostic observation, an observation cycle suggests itself:

- A short, scoring-focused observation to glean a pattern, followed by
- A longer, confirmatory diagnostic observation, and
- Treatment of observed weaknesses through professional development or mentoring.

Repeating the cycle after the treatment would provide information on the efficacy of the intervention and allow tracking of changes in patterns over time. This approach could prove very effective while reducing the total time required of the observer.

Study 2 examined differences in inter-rater reliability between the different scoring designs implemented during Phase 1 and Phase 2 of the MET project. The Phase 1 design required raters to score with only a subset of an instrument's dimensions. In contrast, Phase 2 design required raters to score with the full set of dimensions. The observations for both Phase 1 and Phase 2 were roughly thirty minutes long. The results showed that the Phase 1 design promoted higher inter-rater reliability than the Phase 2 design did.

The results of Study 2 lend some support to limiting the number of dimensions an observer uses at any one point in time for content-specific instruments for short observations (roughly thirty minutes of a lesson). Because inter-rater reliability was higher in Phase 1 than for Phase 2 for MQI and PLATO, in particular, one could argue that, for the content-specific instruments, the requirement and use of background knowledge, in addition to managing five or more dimensions in a short observation period, are factors that inhibit observers' ability to score consistently with one another. Although there was a statistically significant difference between the reliability coefficients for FfT (content-neutral instrument), the practical significance may have been marginal. Without the benefit of another content-neutral instrument by which to draw comparisons, we do not know whether reliability did not differ as significantly for FfT because of its nature (content neutrality) or because of the clarity and specificity of the FfT rubric language. Additional research would be helpful in isolating these effects.

While limiting a principal to scoring a few dimensions at a time may be impractical for small schools and school districts, for other, larger districts with multiple observers in a school, it may be beneficial to allow observers to specialize in a subset of dimensions. Under this scoring design, the administrator could focus on more content-neutral or less content-specific dimensions of an instrument and an instructional leader or department chair could specialize in the more content-specific dimensions. Implementing such a design would be challenging, particularly for districts that have not adopted video-based observation and when most schools have a single observer. In the absence of video, two observers would be needed for all live classroom observations. Perhaps a blended model of some paired observation and some observations captured by video would help to alleviate the logistical strain of scheduling two observers for live observations.

LIMITATIONS

In Study 1, we found a small tendency for correlations to be higher for segments that were closer together in time than for segments that were farther apart. It is not certain that, if the observers had not seen the first segment before scoring the second and third, the correlation values with the overall scores would remain as high. It is also worth noting that, as the lessons, and hence the videos, were of different lengths, there were fewer videos with segments four, five, or six in the set, so the correlation value becomes unstable for the relationship between the later segments and the overall score due to the very small numbers of cases.

Further, a limitation of the comparison between Phase 1 and Phase 2 inter-rater reliability is the paucity of experimental controls that could be applied. In Study 2, we also do not know how continual practice impacts the quality of scoring over time. Perhaps, as observers become more practiced in their scoring, the amount of cognitive load associated with having to consider multiple dimensions at one time will diminish. We might expect that the more observers internalize a rubric, the more efficient they will become in identifying relevant evidence and applying a score, as models of expert versus novice performance suggest (Beilock & Carr, 2004). Due to these potential confounds, the findings comparing Phase 1 and Phase 2 are suggestive, but not definitive.

CONCLUSION

Our two studies utilized scoring data that were collected as an adjunct to the main MET study. Study 1 established that shorter observations can yield scores that are highly predictive of scores based on a whole-lesson observation. Based on this result, and provided the strength of the relationship holds across each of the dimensions in an instrument, live classroom observers can target that period of a lesson for shorter observations, maximizing the value of the time spent in an observation and reducing the substantial staff-time resources needed when operationalizing new teaching observation systems in the field.

It is important to note that our findings do not support the inference that one short observation is the *only* observation that should be made in an academic year. It was not within the scope of this chapter to determine how many occasions (lessons) of short observations were required to produce a reliable measure of a classroom teacher's practice. The reader is referred to "Ensuring Fair and Reliable Measures of Effective Teaching" (Bill & Melinda Gates Foundation, 2013) for a discussion of the number of lessons needed for a reliable measure of classroom teaching practice. In addition, our Study 2 findings established that short observations with a small set of dimensions can produce more reliable scores than can observation with the full set of dimensions, particularly for content-specific instruments. These results may support an observation system that would allow multiple observers to focus their cognitive resources on a few dimensions at a time during a short observation.

Clearly, there are differences between the scoring designs implemented in the MET study and the designs for live scoring that will most likely be implemented in practice. MET scoring was conducted in a highly monitored and controlled online environment using videotaped lessons. The amount of real-time monitoring that can occur in live classroom observation is limited, because the lessons are not videotaped and the scoring conditions are less controlled. In addition, scoring was the only job many of the raters who participated in the MET study had. This clearly is not the case for the principals who will have to manage observations, along with their other administrative tasks. Nevertheless, the research presented in this chapter represents a systematic and research-based effort to inform decisions about the design and execution of observation systems and scoring—an approach that can be modeled in practice.

NOTES

1. "Validity responses" here refers to videos scored by a rater who is unaware that the response has previously been scored by an expert rater or master coder. Agreement of the rater-assigned score with the validity score is a measure of scoring accuracy.

2. "Back scoring" here refers to the leader of a team of raters re-scoring a video after the rater scores it in order to evaluate agreement. Disagreement with the team leader's score may trigger an intervention, such as a resolution call, increased monitoring, retraining, or suspension from scoring.

3. Raters were ineligible to score a particular video if the teacher represented a district in which the rater currently or previously taught. Raters were also ineligible to provide a second score to a video selected for double-scoring.

4. FfT content experts explained that the thirty- to thirty-five-minute footage was selected not only because there was a frequency of behaviors relevant to the dimensions in Group 2, but also because it was the segment in which those behaviors were confirmatory of what happened in the first fifteen minutes of the lesson, which would lead to the score remaining the same. However, if the behaviors were so significantly different from what happened in the first fifteen minutes, there would be a change in the score. The time from thirty to thirty-five minutes is often when an observer can gather evidence that indicates whether

the implementation of established classroom procedures has been successful. Further, that timeframe allows the observer to assess whether students are "getting it," that is, comprehending what has been communicated to them (Communicating with Students)? Are they delving in and exploring important content and taking responsibility for their own learning because that is the culture that has been established (Establishing a Culture for Learning)? Do the procedures continue to function smoothly, especially if there are shifts in the organization of the task as far as groupings, materials, and so forth (Managing Classroom Procedures)?

5. First scores were categorized as "primary," and second scores for the double-scored sample were categorized as "secondary." When the term "score" is used alone, the primary score is being referred to.

REFERENCES AND ADDITIONAL RESOURCES

Arter, J., & McTighe, J. (2001). *Scoring rubrics in the classroom: Using performance criteria for assessing and improving student performance.* Thousand Oaks, CA: Corwin Press.

Beilock, S. L., & Carr, T. H. (2004). From novice to expert performance: Attention, memory, and the control of complex sensorimotor skills. In A. M. Williams, N. J. Hodges, M. A. Scott, & M.L.J. Court (Eds.), *Skill acquisition in sport: Research, theory and practice* (pp. 309–328). New York: Routledge.

Bill & Melinda Gates Foundation. (2013). Ensuring fair and reliable measures of effective teaching: Culminating findings from the MET project's three-year study. Retrieved from www.metproject .org/downloads/MET_Ensuring_Fair_and_Reliable_Measures_Practitioner_Brief.pdf

Cash, A. H., Hamre, B. K., Pianta, R. C., & Myers, S. S. (2012). Rater calibration when observational assessment occurs at large scale: degree of calibration and characteristics of raters associated with calibration. *Early Childhood Research Quarterly, 27,* 529–542.

Crocker, L. M., & Algina, J. (1986). *Introduction to classical and modern test theory.* New York: Holt, Rinehart, and Winston.

Fleiss, J. L. (1981). *Statistical methods for rates and proportions* (2nd ed.). Hoboken, NJ: John Wiley & Sons.

Graham, M., Milanowski, A., & Miller, J. (2012). Measuring and promoting inter-rater agreement of teacher and principal performance ratings. Retrieved from http://cecr.ed.gov/pdfs/Inter_Rater .pdf.

Hartmann, D. P. (1977). Considerations in the choice of interobserver reliability measures. *Journal of Applied Behavior Analysis, 10,* 103–116.

Hill, H. C., Charalambous, C. Y., & Kraft, M. A. (2012). When rater reliability is not enough: teacher observation systems and a case for the Generalizability Study. *Educational Researcher, 41*(2), 56–64.

Hunt, R. R., & Ellis, H. C. (2004). *Fundamentals of cognitive psychology* (7th ed.). New York: McGraw-Hill.

Jerald, C. (2012). Ensuring accurate feedback from observations. Retrieved from https://docs .gatesfoundation.org/Documents/ensuring-accuracy-wp.pdf.

Landis, J. R., & Koch, G. G. (1977). A one way components of variance model for categorical data. *Biometrics, 33,* 671–679.

Ling, G., Mollaun, P., & Xi, X. (2009, February). *A study of raters' scoring accuracy and consistency across time during the scoring shift.* Presented at the ETS Human Constructed Response Scoring Initiative Seminar. Princeton, NJ.

Livingston, S. A. (2004). An interesting problem in the estimation of scoring reliability. *Journal of Educational and Behavioral Statistics, 29*(3), 333–341.

Stemler, S. E. (2004). A comparison of consensus, consistency, and measurement approaches to estimating inter-rater reliability. *Practical Assessment, Research & Evaluation, 9*(4). Retrieved from http://PAREonline.net/getvn.asp?v=9&n=4

APPENDIX

The inter-rater reliability coefficient is expressed as:

$$estdrel_{all}\left(X_{total}\right) = 1 - \frac{estdVES_{all}(X_{total})}{\text{var}_{all}(X_{total})},$$

where $estVES_{all}(X_{total})$ is the estimated variance of errors of scoring across single- and double-scored video segments across all dimensions and $\text{var}_{all}(X_{total})$ is the sum of observed score variance across single- and double-scored responses.

CHAPTER

14

Assessing Quality Teaching in Science

SUSAN E. SCHULTZ AND RAYMOND L. PECHEONE

ABSTRACT

The Quality Science Teaching (QST) instrument is an evidence-based observation instrument representing the Next Generation Science Standards (NGSS). The original QST measures six domains of science practices; QST-MET, a condensed version of the original instrument, requires raters to gather evidence on biology teachers' instruction from videotaped lessons and use an analytical rubric to rate qualities of effective science teaching practices that promote student learning. This chapter discusses teachers' science instructional practices measured by the QST-MET and evaluates the reliability and validity of the QST-MET instrument. Findings reveal significant gaps in teacher content knowledge and a striking absence of the use of scientific practices in non-lab and lab lessons; teachers' lab scores were significantly lower on average than the non-lab scores. Inter-rater reliability between raters for QST (original) was significantly higher than for QST-MET, possibly due to rater training method (in-person versus online); and factor analysis supports the construct validity of the QST-MET. QST-MET data reveals the need to invest in the systematic collection of high-quality data from multiple measures aligned to the NGSS with targeted support to build teacher capacity to use scientific practices and to support greater student learning.

INTRODUCTION

Despite numerous Science Technology Engineering and Math (STEM) initiatives in the past decade, science instruction has not significantly improved (Dorph, Shields, Tiffany-Morales, Hartry, & McCaffrey, 2011; Martinez, Borko, & Stecher, 2012). The conceptual *Framework for K–12 Science Education* (National Academy of Sciences, 2011) and the recent release of the Next Generation Science Standards (NGSS) focusing on performance-based learning competencies have raised expectations for improving science education. The new standards focus on science teaching practices, crosscutting themes, and high-quality science content. NGSS will require teachers to rethink their instructional strategies to help students master these performance-based learning targets (Windschitl, Thompson, & Braaten, 2012). This blueprint for improving science education provides limited specifics about science teaching practices that promote the greatest impact on student learning (Martinez, Borko, & Stecher, 2012).

For many teachers, integrating major conceptual ideas and providing students with opportunities to engage in scientific practices are challenging without a clear understanding of the teaching practices that are central to student learning. To help students achieve science competency, teachers themselves need to develop proficiency in science content knowledge and science practices (Dorph, Shields, Tiffany-Morales, Hartry, & McCaffrey, 2011; Fulp, 2002; Weiss, 2006).

To support improvements in teacher understanding of science content, instructional practice, and student learning, an evidence-based observation instrument that provides formative and summative feedback to teachers, coupled with targeted professional development, is needed. To test this hypothesis, the Quality Science Teaching (QST) observation instrument was designed by Susan Schultz and colleagues at the Stanford Center for Assessment, Learning, and Equity (SCALE) to assess quality science instruction representing the full continuum of teaching performance. The QST used in the Measure of Effective Teaching (MET) project requires raters to gather evidence on biology teachers' instruction from videotaped lessons and use an analytical rubric to rate qualities of effective science teaching practices that promote student learning.

RESEARCH QUESTIONS

This section identifies the four research questions addressed in the chapter.

1. What are the features of QST, and how was the QST-MET instrument adapted for the MET study? We describe the key domains and indicators of QST and why we think these indicators represent quality science teaching. We also discuss what we learned from examining some initial MET biology lesson videos and how the instrument was condensed into QST-MET.

2. What did we learn about teachers' science instructional practices using the QST-MET? To evaluate the effectiveness of teachers' biology instruction, we present the distribution of teachers' scores for each indicator of QST-MET. The intent of the instrument is to identify teachers' strengths as well as areas for improvement on each indicator. Our goal is for this information to help teachers strengthen their teaching of science in alignment to the NGSS. We also compare the teachers' quality of instruction during lab and non-lab lessons to determine whether teachers' scores differed based on the type of lesson. This could have important implications for a teacher evaluation process.

3. What did we learn about the reliability of QST and QST-MET to evaluate teachers' science practices? We examine the QST to determine whether the QST instrument can reliably detect and distinguish between teachers' science practices. In other words, it is important to determine whether different raters using QST and QST-MET can consistently assign scores for teachers' science practices based on the rubric. We analyzed differences in the scoring agreement between raters scoring the same video (i.e., inter-rater reliability) based on two different training processes (in-person versus online). Understanding the benefits and challenges of different types of training methods and which technique results in the highest agreement between raters is an important factor to consider when using this instrument in the future.

4. What did we learn about the validity of the QST-MET instrument? We report whether QST-MET was actually measuring the indicators we were trying to measure (i.e., construct validity) and whether the grouping of the indicators into three clusters made sense (i.e., factor analysis). We

share what we learned about the instrument in terms of its sensitivity to student characteristics (gender, ethnicity, socioeconomic status, and English language proficiency). We also explore the relationships between the indicators in QST-MET and the Tripod survey that reports data related to students' perception of their teachers.

METHODS AND RESULTS

In this section of the chapter, we present the methods and results for each of the research questions.

Description of QST and QST-MET

To address the first research question, we describe the features of the original QST and what we learned from our initial analysis of fifty MET videos. We also explain how we modified the instrument into QST-MET based on our initial analysis.

Features of Quality Science Teaching (QST) QST consists of six key domains of science teaching that include a total of eighteen indicators of quality science instruction. Each QST indicator uses quality descriptions of a specific science practice that ranges from providing little to no evidence (score of 1) to providing consistently strong evidence (score of 4) in terms of the specific quality of science practice being evaluated (see Appendix A: Quality Science Teaching QST Rubric).

The QST Observation Instrument domains are listed below.

1. *Assessing Teacher's Content Knowledge and Pedagogy* examines the extent and quality with which the teacher sets the learning context, uses representations, and accurately conveys scientific knowledge.

2. *Engaging Students in Learning Science* focuses on the ways in which the teacher explicitly promotes student interest in the biology lesson, which elicits student motivation to engage in the academic work of the day. It also examines whether the teacher selects a rich and intellectually challenging science task or topic, and how the teacher specifically addresses the academic challenges it presents for students. This domain also examines how the teacher employs different instructional strategies to ensure

participation by all students, and to promote teacher-to-student and student-to-student interactions.

3. *Facilitating Scientific Discourse and Reasoning* centers on the quality of and extent to which the teacher uses questions to initiate and conduct classroom discourse and the teacher's ability to appropriately facilitate discussions that promote critical reasoning by students.

4. *Promoting Laboratory-Based Inquiry* examines how the teacher initiates inquiry, provides guidelines for conducting investigation, and guides students in the analysis and interpretation of data.

5. *Providing Opportunities for the Application of Science* focuses on the teacher's ability to initiate a task that requires students to apply scientific concepts to solve a problem or to address a societal issue. The teacher engages students in research and guides them through the analytical process to understand the implications of the issue.

6. *Monitoring Student Learning* captures the teacher's ability to gather evidence of student knowledge and conceptual understanding throughout a lesson, to provide specific feedback to students, and to give opportunities for students to reflect on their own learning.

The selection of the domains and indicators was informed by and aligned with the *National Science Education Standards* (NRC, 1996), *Inquiry and the National Science Education Standards* (NRC, 2000), *What Teachers Should Know and Be Able to Do* (NBPTS, 2002), and *Taking Science to School: Learning and Teaching Science in Grades K–8* (NRC, 2007). Key authors Helen Quinn and Jonathan Osborne of the 2011 Framework for K–12 Science Education were members of the QST advisory committee. As a result, there are clear overlaps between QST indicators and the science practices included in the Next Generation Science Standards (NGSS). A Delphi study (Kloser, in review) confirms that the QST domains are highly aligned to essential science teaching practices.

Modification of Quality Science Teaching for the MET Study (QST-MET) A condensed version of the original QST, called QST-MET, was used in year two of the MET study. The primary reason for condensing the original QST instrument was to reduce the cognitive demands placed upon the raters. It was agreed that scoring eighteen indicators for multiple segments of 1,087 valid videos would be too demanding on the raters and could lead to increased levels of unreliability.

To make an informed decision about how to condense the instrument, we convened a group of expert high school biology teachers and conducted a two-day in-person training to teach them about the QST instrument and how to accurately score videos of biology instruction using QST. The group of teacher raters scored videos for fifty MET biology lessons.

After analyzing the scoring of the fifty videos, we learned that there was very little variability in the range of scores for Facilitating Scientific Discourse and Reasoning (Domain 3). In the videos, we observed teachers:

1. Asking very factual or procedural questions requiring a single correct response.

2. Asking a question, receiving a response from one or two students, indicating whether the answer was correct or not, and then moving on to the next question. This pattern is referred to as initiate, respond, and evaluate (IRE).

3. Providing very limited opportunities for students to respond to higher-order thinking prompts or stimuli. On the few occasions we did observe teachers asking students to respond to higher-order prompts, students were not asked to provide evidence or explain their responses.

When examining the QST rubric for this specific domain (see Appendix A: QST Domain 3), the observed teachers' behaviors consistently scored in the lowest category, which explains the lack of variability in the scores for this domain. These are significant findings and highlight the need for teachers to learn and receive coaching on how to become more effective at facilitating science discussions. Science discussion should provide opportunities for multiple students to share ideas with evidence and explanation, while allowing other students to question the findings and offer alternative explanations. These learning experiences will help students improve their argumentative skills, apply their content knowledge, and learn to effectively communicate their ideas and findings. Scientists engage in these essential practices, and they are emphasized in the NGSS.

Of even greater concern, we did not observe any lessons in which teachers made explicit connection to the application of science or asked students to use their content knowledge to apply it to a science topic or issue during a lesson.

Therefore, we were unable to gather any data for Providing Opportunities for the Application of Science (Domain 5) in the fifty videos.

We think both of these constructs (Domains 3 and 5) are vital to developing critical thinking and scientifically literate citizens. We are concerned that we did not observe any teachers providing students with opportunities to apply science to what they were learning and observed very limited examples of teachers engaging students in discussions with other students using evidence and argumentative skills to express their ideas. This is a significant finding in itself—that students are not being provided with opportunities to engage in meaningful scientific discourse or to understand the application of science in their everyday world.

We continue to think that gathering additional evidence for Domains 3 and 5 in the QST-MET instrument would highlight the need for significant improvement in these areas and provide an important contribution to help districts identify professional development needs for developing more effective science teachers. However, for practical reasons, the MET project leaders decided to remove these two domains, as it is impossible to calculate the validity of a domain when there is very limited or no data available.

Features of QST-MET The QST-MET official version consisted of three domains or clusters, with a total of twelve indicators (see Table 14.1 and the complete QST-MET rubric in Appendix B). We refer to these as clusters because they include indicators from four of the original QST domains (Domains 1, 2, 4, and 6). Each cluster contains four different indicators that are grouped together to measure a specific aspect of effective biology teaching. To reduce cognitive demands, each QST-MET rater completed the online training for only one specific cluster (Cluster 1, 2, or 3) so that they were only responsible for scoring four indicators while observing the videos.

Teachers' Science Instructional Practices

Our second research question focuses on what we learned about teachers' science instructional practices using the QST-MET. To answer this question, we present some information about the sample of teachers and the quantity of science teaching videos provided for the study. We explain how raters were trained and certified to score videos using QST-MET. We also share our findings on the distribution of teachers' scores and provide an explanation of the scores for each QST-MET indicator.

TABLE 14.1.   QST-MET Clusters and Indicators

Cluster	Indicator
Cluster 1: Assessing Teacher's Knowledge and Pedagogy	
This cluster focuses on how the teacher uses content knowledge of the discipline and pedagogical expertise to enhance students' learning.	Sets the context and focuses learning on key science concepts
	Uses representations
	Demonstrates content knowledge
	Provides feedback for learning
Cluster 2: Engaging Students in Science Learning	
This cluster examines how the teacher engages students' interaction with biological concepts, provides scaffolding to support the learning process, and monitors students' learning.	Promotes students' interest in and motivation to learn science
	Assigns tasks to promote learning and addresses the task demands
	Uses modes of teaching science concepts
	Elicits evidence of students' knowledge and conceptual understanding
Cluster 3: Promoting Laboratory-Based Inquiry	
This cluster explores how the teacher promotes inquiry-based learning and provides students with opportunities to deepen their understanding of a biological concept, conduct an investigation, analyze data, and monitor their own learning.	Initiates the investigation
	Provides guidelines for conducting the investigation and gathering data
	Guides analysis and interpretation of data
	Elicits evidence of students' knowledge and conceptual understanding

Teachers   A total of 236 biology teachers submitted videos for the MET study. Some of the demographic data were missing in the information submitted by teachers, but based on 203 responses, there were 59 males and 144 females. The ethnic breakdown of this sample included 129 Caucasian, 43 black, 11 Hispanic, and 19 other. Teachers (n = 176) responding to the survey questions had taught an average of 9.63 years (s.d. = 8.60). Figure 14.1 indicates that most of the teachers had fewer than ten years of teaching experience, with the highest concentration of teachers having fewer than five years of experience.

Teaching Video Sample The QST-MET study design required each teacher to videotape four lessons for each year of the study. Teachers were asked to provide at least one lab lesson as one of the four lessons each year, resulting in a total of two lab and six non-lab lessons. The number of videos provided by each teacher varied across teachers, which impacted the amount of data available for analysis. The average number of videos submitted per teacher was 4.61. A subset of 149 teachers provided valid videos for both academic years. Of those, only twenty-five teachers had at least three videos scored in both years for Cluster 1: Assessing Teacher's Knowledge and Pedagogy; nineteen teachers had at least three videos scored in both years for Cluster 2: Engaging Students in Science Learning; and forty-eight teachers had at least one video scored in both years for Cluster 3: Promoting Laboratory-Based Inquiry. These numbers reflect the attrition in sample size due to missing data.

Rater Training, Certification, and Scoring Fifty-nine raters were recruited, hired, and certified by the Educational Testing Service (ETS) to score videos using QST-MET. ETS randomly assigned each rater to Cluster 1, 2, or 3 in

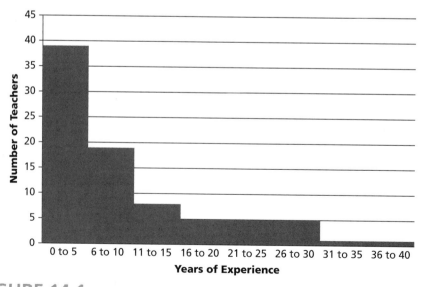

FIGURE 14.1. *Number of Teachers by Years of Teaching Experience*

an effort to improve reliability and to reduce the cognitive load on any one rater. Raters were hired from across the United States, so it was not realistic to provide an in-person scoring training. We worked in collaboration with Teachscape to create an online scoring training and certification process. The online training program was developed for each of the three QST-MET clusters. For each cluster, we used the same materials and video clips in order to standardize the training experience and provide a comparable user experience.

Each online training segment introduced the rater to one indicator at a time. For each of the four indicators, the raters viewed numerous video segments, cited the evidence they used to assign a score, and indicated the score. If the rater's score agreed with the score provided by the expert team, the rater received immediate feedback and was shown the evidence provided by the expert team. If the rater had a different score, he or she was prompted to review the segment and assign another score. After assigning a second score, the rater was provided with the score and evidence from the SCALE expert team.

Once a rater went through the entire online scoring training, he or she was advanced to the certification process. In the certification process, the rater viewed a fifteen-minute video segment and assigned a score for all four indicators. Those scores were compared to the scores provided by the SCALE expert team. If 80 percent of the scores were in exact agreement, with no more than 20 percent being adjacent scores, then the person was certified and was designated as "ready to score" QST-MET videos for a specific cluster (1, 2, or 3). If the rater did not pass certification, he or she contacted the scoring leader for that cluster for an interactive session. The scoring leader discussed the rater performance to deepen rater understanding of the scoring protocol. After the interactive session, the rater attempted to certify on a second video clip. Any rater not passing the second certification process was not advanced to the scoring program.

The ETS calibration process is highly rigorous. Raters who advanced to the "ready to score" category had to calibrate on a different sample video each time they entered the scoring system in order to qualify to score. Raters were given two chances to calibrate; if they failed to calibrate, they were no longer eligible to score QST-MET videos.

When raters scored non-lab videos, they examined fifteen minutes of video, assigned scores between 1 and 4 based on the observed evidence in the video, and submitted scores. Then the raters repeated the process with the next fifteen-minute segment. For the lab videos, the raters followed the same procedures with two important exceptions. Raters for the lab videos scored up to four fifteen-minute segments and assigned a score of 0 to 4 based on the descriptions in the rubric. The lab indicators were time-dependent, which means there were some indicators one would not expect to see in every segment of a lab lesson. For example, one would not expect to see the analysis of data at the beginning of an investigation, so the raters scoring this cluster had to be able to assign a "0" score when a specific behavior was not observed.

Teachers' Scores For each QST-MET cluster, we present the distribution of teacher scores and provide a discussion of the key findings for the indicators within each cluster. Figure 14.2 shows the distribution of teachers' scores for Cluster 1: Assessing Teacher's Knowledge and Pedagogy.

When analyzing the bars on the figure, it is apparent that very few of the teachers earned the top scoring level (4) for this cluster, indicating that behaviors associated with expert teaching were rarely observed. See Appendix B: QST-MET Rubric for Cluster 1: Assessing Teacher's Knowledge and Pedagogy for the specific qualities raters were looking for when scoring the videos.

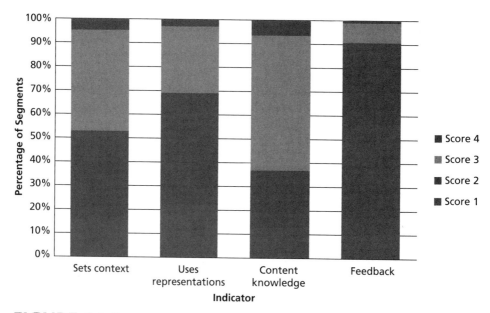

FIGURE 14.2. *Distribution of Scores by Score Value for Cluster 1 Indicators*

Note: The bottom bar in each case indicates a score of 1, the lowest score possible. The top bars represents a score of 4, the highest score possible.

Sets the context indicator. In 15 percent of the teaching segments, the teachers did not set any context for the lesson and did not provide any objectives. Thirty-three percent of the total teaching segments observed received a score of 2, indicating that teachers provided either a general context or vague objectives for the lesson. Both of these findings are particularly problematic. It is important for students to clearly understand the specific objectives for a lesson because it provides a framework for them to learn new information. When teachers provide a context that students can relate to or that builds on students' prior learning or life experiences, it increases students' engagement in the learning and helps them make connections, resulting in improved learning. Approximately 48 percent of the observed segments indicate that teachers provided students with a clear context and specific objectives and referred back to the objectives throughout the lesson.

Uses representations indicator. The data reveals that only 2 percent of the video segments revealed teachers who used multiple, different types of representations providing the most number of students with opportunities to clarify and distinguish between key biological concepts. Twenty-eight percent of the segments showed evidence of teachers using multiple, similar types of representations to enhance students' understanding of the biological concepts. The remaining 70 percent of the segments revealed that teachers either did not use any representations (23 percent) or used very general representations that in some cases limited students' ability to distinguish between concepts (47 percent). These findings raise serious concerns for teachers as well as administrators that less than one-third of the segments showed teachers effectively using representations to help students see models or concrete examples of biological concepts.

Demonstrates content knowledge indicator. In approximately 37 percent of the segments, the raters observed teachers making numerous content errors that were either significant (13 percent) or minor (24 percent), but that were not corrected by the teacher during the segment. In 57 percent of the segments, teachers were observed making minor content errors, but they did correct the error before the end of the segment. Only 6 percent of the segments observed showed no teacher content errors. In summary, we found some level of teacher content error in 96 percent of the teaching segments in the MET project.

Provides feedback indicator. One percent of the segments observed teachers providing specific, constructive, and detailed feedback to students with explicit suggestions for how to improve their learning. In an additional

8 percent of the segments, raters assigned scores of 3, indicating teachers provided students with more general feedback, including strengths and targeted areas for improving learning. In another 34 percent of the segments, teachers provided students with general feedback, primarily on the strengths of their performance, but not on how to improve their learning. The remaining 57 percent of the segments observed teachers saying things like "Good job," "You rock," or "Way to go," instead of specifically giving students feedback that would help them improve their learning and/or performance. Nonspecific feedback provides students with little or no useful information on how to improve their learning. Students need to know teachers' expectations and to receive constructive, specific feedback so they can master a particular skill or meet an objective. If teachers consistently give students specific feedback on both their strengths and areas for improvement, students will eventually be able to monitor their own performance and/or knowledge and become independent learners.

Figure 14.3 shows the distribution of teachers' scores for Cluster 2: Engaging Students in Science Learning. For each indicator in this cluster, we observe low percentages of top scores consistent with the indicators in Cluster 1. See Appendix B: QST-MET Rubric for Cluster 2: Engaging

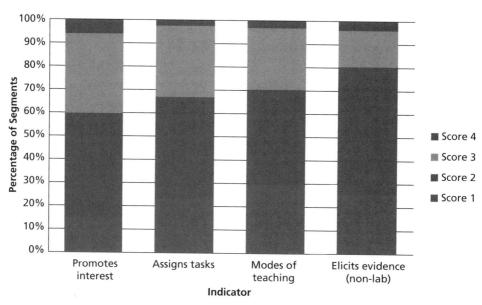

FIGURE 14.3. *Distribution of Scores by Score Value for Cluster 2 Indicators*

Student in Science Learning to see the specific qualities the raters were looking for when scoring the videos.

Promotes interest and motivation indicator. This indicator focuses on whether the teacher makes connections between what he or she is trying to teach and students' life experiences or prior learning, with the goal of promoting students' interest and motivation for learning. In 60 percent of the scored segments, teachers either did not make any connections (15 percent) or presented students with very superficial or surface level connections (45 percent). In 34 percent of the segments, teachers made explicit and meaningful connections between new content and students' life experiences *or* prior learning. In the remaining 6 percent of segments, teachers made explicit and meaningful content connections to both students' life experiences and prior learning.

There are clear advantages to helping students make connections between things they have already learned and new knowledge. Effective teachers, as well as content experts, formulate a mental model of how different concepts are related, and when learning something "new," they think about organized ways to incorporate the new concepts or information into their existing structure. Effective teachers are transparent with students about relationships between concepts and explicitly help students understand how the new content is related to their prior knowledge. These teachers also know students will learn more if they see connections between content learned in school and their life experiences.

Assigns tasks indicator. When observing a lesson, it is important to think about the academic rigor of the task and how the teacher makes the information available or accessible to all students in the class. The data indicates that 67 percent of the segments reveal teachers assigned tasks that either did not contain science content (23 percent) or that were scientific in nature but not academically challenging for the students (44 percent). Thirty-one percent of the segments indicate that tasks were intellectually challenging and the teachers provided scaffolding that helped many students access the material. In 2 percent of the segments, teachers assigned rich and challenging tasks that appeared challenging for all students and provided ways for students to access the material without taking away the complexity of the task. We are cautious when reporting these results, because raters found this indicator difficult to score, as they did not have any context about the students or any rationale from the teacher about the selection of the task. Although cautious about these findings, we are compelled to highlight the importance of maximizing instructional time by selecting tasks that connect to the science concepts being taught and that provide students with some intellectual rigor.

Uses modes of teaching indicator. Engaging students in the learning process helps to reinforce key science concepts and enables students to be active learners. This indicator examines whether the teacher uses different types of teaching modes and if these different strategies result in higher levels of student engagement. The findings indicate that 2 percent of the teaching segments showed teachers incorporating a number of different teaching modes into their instruction, which resulted in a high level of engagement from most of the students. In an additional 28 percent of the segments, teachers used multiple modes of teaching strategies, but a limited number of students engaged in the learning. In the remaining segments (70 percent), teachers primarily lectured and provided few to no opportunities for students to ask questions or to respond to teacher-generated questions. In a few extreme cases, all of a teacher's non-lab videos showed him or her lecturing, posing questions, and answering his or her own questions without pausing for any student response. There is definitely a place for direct instruction within science lessons, but there must be opportunities for students to engage with the material, share ideas about the content, and be active learners.

Elicits evidence (non-lab) indicator. The goal of this indicator is to better understand how teachers are monitoring students' learning progress and to determine whether teachers focus on content knowledge or conceptual understanding or both. The raters did not observe teachers monitoring any type of students' learning in 25 percent of the teaching segments. The vast majority of segments (55 percent) found a strong emphasis on monitoring content knowledge by primarily asking questions resulting in one right answer. In the remaining 20 percent of the teaching segments, teachers used a variety of techniques to monitor students' content knowledge and conceptual understanding. Some teachers asked "How" and "Why" questions where students had to share their conceptual thinking. Other teachers arranged students into small learning groups where students "taught" each other while the teacher walked around monitoring students' ability to demonstrate knowledge as well as conceptual understanding.

Figure 14.4 shows the distribution of teachers' scores for Cluster 3: Promoting Laboratory-Based Inquiry. See Appendix B: QST-MET Rubric for Cluster 3: Promoting Laboratory-Based Inquiry for the specific qualities the raters were looking for when scoring the videos. We observed no or

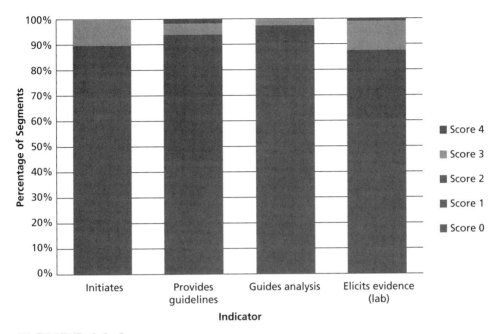

FIGURE 14.4. *Distribution of Scores by Score Value for Cluster 3 Indicators*

Note: The gray bar at the bottom of each column indicates a score of 0, the lowest score possible. The top bars represent a score of 4, the highest score possible.

very small percentages of top scores in each indicator for this cluster. Another unique feature of this cluster is that raters could assign a "0" score, which indicated that the specific behavior would not be expected to be observed in that segment of the lesson. For the lab lessons, raters reviewed and scored four fifteen-minute segments for a total of one hour of instruction, instead of the half-hour time allotted to non-lab lessons.

Initiates the lab indicator. This indicator measures whether teachers make connections to science content when introducing the lab. We focused on this aspect of lab instruction because students frequently are unable to explain why they are conducting a lab or how the lab is connected to what they are learning. This indicator had one of the largest percentages of "0" scores (72 percent). This is an expected result, as teachers typically introduce the lab in the first fifteen minutes of the lesson and we would not expect them to re-introduce the lab unless there was a problem with student understanding. In the remaining 28 percent of the segments, teachers either did not make any connections (8 percent), made superficial or vague references to the content (9 percent), or made meaningful content connections (11 percent) when introducing the lab. It is important to note that none of the lab lessons provided students with an opportunity to make connections between the content and the investigation.

Provides guidelines for the investigation indicator. In 27 percent of the segments, raters assigned a score of "0," indicating teachers would not be expected to discuss the guidelines or procedures for the lab in that segment of any lab lesson. Raters observed teachers providing highly prescribed lab procedures to the students in 67 percent of the segments. Four percent of the segments, teachers allowed students some choice in the samples tested or in designing some portion of the lab. In only a few classrooms (2 percent of segments) did teachers introduce a topic or research questions and ask students to design and conduct the investigation. In light of the emphasis on students' designing investigations and engaging in innovative science practices in the NGSS, we are concerned about the high level of prescribed lab procedures observed in the MET study.

Guides analysis of the data indicator. Raters assigned a "0" score for this indicator in 72 percent of the segments, which is expected since the discussion and analysis of the data would normally occur at the end of the lesson. In 18 percent of the segments, teachers did not conduct any discussion or analysis of the data during the observed lesson. Teachers led students through a discussion of the data and explained the "expected" results in 7 percent of the segments. Teachers guided students in the analysis of the data and students demonstrated their ability to find patterns or to provide an explanation of the data in only 3 percent of the teaching segments.

Elicits evidence (lab) indicator. This indicator is found in Cluster 2: Engaging Students in Science Learning and in Cluster 3: Promoting Laboratory-Based Inquiry. In 23 percent of the segments, raters assigned a score of "0," indicating teachers would not be expected to monitor student learning in that segment of any lab lesson. The raters expected but did not observe teachers monitoring any type of students' learning in 37 percent of the teaching segments. Over one-fourth of the segments (27 percent) found a strong emphasis on monitoring content knowledge by primarily asking questions resulting in one right answer. In the remaining 13 percent of the segments, teachers used a variety of techniques to monitor students' content knowledge and conceptual understanding.

Comparing Lab and Non-Lab Lessons Using teacher scores, we examined whether we could detect a relationship between teachers' scores in lab versus non-lab lessons. We know there are different pedagogical strategies being observed in these different types of lessons. We would expect the lesson structure for non-lab lessons (Clusters 1 and 2) to be very similar, whereas the types of teaching strategies in a lab lesson (Cluster 3) are quite different. Based on differences in lesson structures, we would predict that it would be difficult to generalize teachers' effectiveness across different types of science lessons. In other words, being an effective science teacher in non-lab lessons does not necessarily mean the teacher will be effective in lab lessons.

The data shown in Figure 14.5 demonstrates a significant but low correlation (0.304, $p < 0.01$) between teachers' scores on lab and non-lab lessons. Close examination of the data reveals that teachers' lab scores were significantly lower, on average, than their non-lab scores. The significant but low correlation supports our prediction that many of the teaching strategies incorporated in the lab and non-lab lesson types are different.

Reliability of QST and QST-MET

The third research question examines what we learned about the reliability of QST and QST-MET to evaluate teachers' science practices. To verify the findings of the distribution of teachers' scores, it is necessary to know whether different raters viewing the same video consistently assigned the same scores (i.e., inter-rater reliability). We also compare the inter-rater reliability of QST-MET and QST.

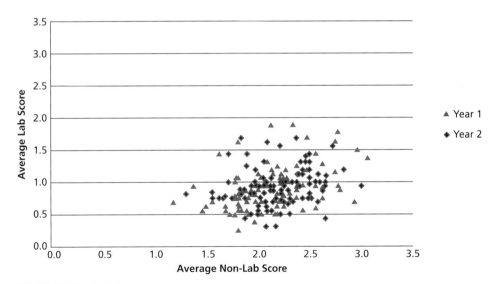

FIGURE 14.5. *Teacher Non-Lab to Lab Score Comparison*

Reliability of QST-MET We present reliability data for QST-MET with some caution, as we had a limited number of valid videos that were double-scored for each cluster (Cluster 1 = forty-one videos, Cluster 2 = forty videos, and Cluster 3 = thirteen videos). In addition to the limited number of double-scored videos, the distribution of scores for each indicator was skewed toward the lower levels on the rubric. For the non-lab lessons, at least 25 percent of the scores are at the lowest level (1), while less than 6 percent of the scores were at the highest level (4). The problem is even more pronounced for the lab lessons; almost 50 percent of the scores were at the "0" level, and only 1 percent of the scores were at the highest level (4). The Cohen's kappa statistic was used to assess inter-rater reliability.

Table 14.2 reveals moderate to low levels of reliability for exact matches between raters who participated in the online training for QST-MET. The overall inter-rater reliability for Cluster 1: Assessing Teacher's Knowledge and Pedagogy is 0.477; Cluster 2: Engaging Students in Science Learning is 0.360; and Cluster 3: Promoting Laboratory-Based Inquiry is 0.787. The results indicate that the reliability for the lab indicators (Cluster 3) is considerably higher than the reliability of the non-lab indicators (Clusters 1 and 2).

A close examination of the lab indicators reveals that two of the indicators, Initiates the Inquiry (0.959) and Provides Guidelines for Conducting the Experiment and Gathering Data (0.821), had the highest inter-rater reliability, whereas the remaining indicators, Guides Analysis and Interpretation of Data (0.410) and Elicits Evidence of Students' Knowledge (0.521), had considerably lower reliabilities.

Inter-Rater Agreement of QST-MET Although the reliabilities for QST-MET are relatively low, when we examined the percentages of exact matches by indicator, we saw a range of 34 percent to 90 percent, with the lowest value for the Assigns Tasks to Promote Learning (ATPLATD) indicator. If we expand the level of agreement to include exact matches and adjacent scores (i.e., +/− 1), we find that the inter-rater agreements by indicator range between 88 percent and 100 percent (see Table 14.3).

Reliability of QST The breakdown of inter-rater reliability by domain and indicator for the original QST are presented in Table 14.4. Examining the inter-rater reliability at the domain and indicator level revealed that the original QST raters had high levels of inter-rater reliability when raters independently scored video segments after the in-person training. The overall inter-rater reliability between scorers was 90 percent, which represents a high level of reliability considering that

TABLE 14.2. Inter-Rater Reliability of QST-MET by Cluster and Indicator

Cluster and Indicator	Inter-Rater Reliability
Cluster 1: Assessing Teacher's Knowledge and Pedagogy	0.477
Sets context and focuses on learning	0.407
Uses representations	0.353
Demonstrates content knowledge	0.330
Provides feedback for learning	0.252
Cluster 2: Engaging Students in Science Learning?	0.360
Promotes students' interest and motivation	0.465
Assigns tasks to promote learning	0.248
Uses modes of teaching science concepts	0.361
Elicits evidence of students' knowledge	0.350
Cluster 3: Promoting Laboratory-Based Inquiry	0.787
Initiates the inquiry	0.959
Provides guidelines for conducting the experiment and gathering data	0.821
Guides analysis and interpretation of data	0.410
Elicits evidence of students' knowledge	0.521

Note: For the weighted Cohen's kappa statistics, the weights were approximately 0, 0.1, 0.4, and 1 for the non-lab clusters. The weights were 0, 0.06, 0.25, 0.56, and 1 for the lab videos.

TABLE 14.3. Inter-Rater Agreement for QST-MET by Cluster and Indicator

Cluster and Indicator	Total Number of Segments	Exact Matches		Raters Differ by One Category		Raters Differ by Two Categories		Raters Differ by Three Categories	
		N	%	N	%	N	%	N	%
Cluster 1: Assessing Teacher's Knowledge and Pedagogy									
Sets context	82	37	45%	38	46%	7	9%	0	0%
Representations	82	39	48%	38	46%	5	6%	0	0%
Content knowledge	82	44	54%	30	37%	7	9%	1	1%
Feedback	82	43	52%	34	41%	4	5%	1	1%
Cluster 2: Engaging Students in Science Learning									
Promotes interest	80	43	54%	32	40%	5	6%	0	0%
Assigns tasks	80	27	34%	47	59%	6	8%	0	0%
Modes of teaching	80	33	41%	40	50%	7	9%	0	0%
Elicits evidence (non-lab)	80	44	55%	26	33%	8	10%	2	3%
Cluster 3: Promoting Laboratory-Based Inquiry									
Initiates	52	47	90%	5	10%	0	0%	0	0%
Provides guidelines	52	38	73%	11	21%	3	6%	0	0%
Guides analysis	52	38	73%	10	19%	3	6%	1	2%
Elicits evidence (lab)	52	25	46%	23	44%	2	4%	2	4%

raters were scoring eighteen different indicators for each fifteen-minute video segment, with videos ranging from forty-five to ninety minutes in total length.

All the QST domains, except one, had an inter-rater reliability greater than 0.750. As previously mentioned, raters found no evidence of Domain 5: Providing Opportunities for the Application of Science. As these behaviors were not observed in any of the videos, the raters all assigned "0" scores. Likewise, for Domain 4, there was no evidence found by the raters for Guides Analysis and Interpretation of Data, so the raters all assigned "0" scores, resulting in a high inter-rater reliability not observed from the online raters. This is particularly disturbing given the emphasis on this dimension of science investigation by NSF and represented in the science standards. The lowest level of inter-rater reliability (0.548) was the indicator in Domain 2 focusing on the types of assignments selected by the teacher to promote learning (i.e., whether the tasks were challenging for the students) and how the teacher helped students access the material.

Comparing Reliability Between QST and QST-MET Comparing Tables 14.2 and 14.4, we found significant differences between the inter-rater reliability of the raters scoring the original QST and those raters scoring the QST-MET. The findings indicate a wide discrepancy between the inter-rater reliability of raters trained in person as compared to the online program. The breakdown of inter-rater reliability for QST by domain and indicator presented in Table 14.4 reveals that all of the domains, except one, had an inter-rater reliability greater than 0.750. In contrast, the inter-rater reliability of the raters trained online for the QST-MET rubric reveals that the two non-lab clusters (Assessing Teacher's Knowledge and Pedagogy and Engaging Students in Science Learning) were 0.477 and 0.360, whereas the lab cluster (Promoting Laboratory-Based Inquiry) was 0.787. There was more consistency in inter-rater reliability between QST-MET Cluster 3 and the original QST.

Validity of QST-MET

To address the fourth question, we share what we learned about the validity of QST-MET. Since QST and QST-MET were not piloted prior to their use in the MET project, we needed to examine the validity of the QST-MET instrument. Validity provides an indication of whether an instrument is actually measuring what the developer intended it to measure. We tested whether the indicators assigned to the three different clusters would actually hold together as three separate groups when conducting a factor analysis.

TABLE 14.4. Inter-Rater Reliability for QST by Domain and Indicator

Domain and Indicator	Inter-Rater Reliability
1. Assessing Teacher's Content Knowledge	0.793
Sets context and focuses on learning	0.843
Uses representations	0.72
Demonstrates content knowledge	0.763
2. Engaging Students in Science Learning	0.754
Promotes students' interest and motivation	0.778
Assigns tasks to promote learning	0.548
Uses modes of teaching science concepts	0.811
3. Facilitating Scientific Discourse and Reasoning	0.862
Initiates and facilitates discussion	0.953
Uses questions to promote discourse	0.867
Promotes critical reasoning	0.794
4. Promoting Laboratory-Based Inquiry	0.989
Initiates the inquiry	1
Provides guidelines for conducting the experiment	1
Guides analysis and interpretation of data	Not applicable[a]
5. Providing Opportunities for the Application of Science	Not applicable[a]
Initiates investigation of science issue or application	Not applicable[a]

Provides opportunities for students to demonstrate research skills	Not applicable[a]
Guides analysis and societal implications	Not applicable[a]
6. Monitoring Student Learning	0.864
Elicits evidence of students' knowledge and conceptual understanding	0.706
Provides students with feedback	0.797
Provides students with opportunities to summarize and reflect	0.92

Note: For the weighted Cohen's kappa statistics, the weights were approximately 0, 0.1, 0.4, and 1 for the non-lab clusters. The weights were 0, 0.06, 0.25, 0.56, and 1 for the lab videos.

[a]All scores were 0.

Factor Analysis The factor analysis shows whether the twelve indicators in QST-MET actually group together as a cluster, indicating that they measure similar types of information. This is referred to as "construct validity." We expected the factor analysis to break the QST-MET indicators into at least two distinct groups, because there are distinct differences in teaching behaviors between lab and non-lab lessons. We ran a factor analysis using a Varimax rotation. Table 14.5 confirms that the indicators within QST-MET initially split into two distinct groups: the first group representing the eight indicators observed in non-lab lessons and the second group showing the four lab lesson indicators.

The first column of numbers shows the first eight indicators are "loading" into this factor, which means these indicators are measuring similar things and belong to the same construct (specifically, they represent teaching behaviors observed in a non-lab lesson). The next column shows a similar "loading" pattern for the last four variables, indicating they belong to the same construct measuring lab teaching behaviors. All of the QST-MET indicators reveal factor loadings greater than 0.7, which is quite high, except Guides Analysis (0.622). The communality of each indicator is listed in the third column and

TABLE 14.5. Factor Analysis of QST-MET Indicators

Indicator	Non-Lab	Lab	Communality
Sets context	**0.797**	−0.011	0.635
Representations	**0.747**	0.027	0.559
Content knowledge	**0.765**	−0.065	0.589
Feedback	**0.726**	−0.060	0.530
Promotes interest	**0.804**	0.129	0.663
Assigns tasks	**0.790**	0.122	0.638
Modes of teaching	**0.809**	0.075	0.661
Elicits evidence (non-lab)	**0.787**	0.067	0.624
Initiates	0.103	**0.746**	0.567
Provides guidelines	0.013	**0.845**	0.715
Guides analysis	−0.060	**0.622**	0.391
Elicits evidence (lab)	0.103	**0.926**	0.868

indicates the amount of variation in the indicator. Values over 0.50 are generally considered acceptable. All of the communality values for this factor analysis are greater than 0.50 except the lab indicator, Guides Analysis (0.391). Recall that the QST-MET clusters were designed to capture different aspects of science teaching behaviors, specifically Cluster 1: Assessing Teacher's Knowledge and Pedagogy and Cluster 2: Engaging Students in Science Learning. To determine whether there were differences between the non-lab indicators, we ran a second factor analysis to generate a three-factor solution. (In this analysis, we included a factor whose Eigenvalue was 0.969 instead of the more traditional value of greater than 1.)

Table 14.6 reveals the indicators loaded into three distinct factors that align with the QST-MET clusters. In the second factor analysis, all of the QST-MET indicators reveal factor loadings greater than 0.7, except for Feedback (0.616) and Guides Analysis (0.648). All of the communality values for this factor analysis are greater than 0.50 except the lab indicator, Guides Analysis (0.462).

TABLE 14.6. **Factor Analysis of QST-MET Indicators, Forced Three-Factor Solution**

Indicator	Engaging Students in Science Learning	Assessing Teacher's Knowledge and Pedagogy	Promoting Laboratory-Based Inquiry	Communality
Sets context	.293	**.848**	.034	0.807
Content knowledge	.255	**.842**	−.017	0.775
Uses representation	.316	**.752**	.063	0.670
Feedback	.416	**.616**	−.043	0.554
Promotes interest	**.773**	.354	.097	0.732
Modes of teaching	**.792**	.342	.041	0.745
Assigns tasks	**.803**	.301	.084	0.743
Elicits evidence (non-lab)	**.838**	.260	.022	0.771
Guides analysis	−.177	.101	**.648**	0.462
Initiates	.132	.012	**.741**	0.567
Elicits evidence (lab)	.147	−.002	**.920**	0.868
Provides guidelines	.088	−.072	**.838**	0.715

Sources of Bias To examine possible sources of bias, we looked for any relationships between teacher performance (i.e., scores) and the following classroom demographic characteristics: ethnicity, gender, English language proficiency, and free or reduced lunch. Table 14.7 indicates that teacher performances on QST-MET were free of bias, with two specific exceptions. In Year 2, we found significant but low-level correlations between teachers' scores in Cluster 1 and the ethnicity category "Other" (0.199), and between teachers' scores in Cluster 3 and the ethnicity category "Caucasian" (0.203).

Relationship Between QST-MET and Tripod Survey Another way to examine the validity of QST-MET is to compare the findings from the same sample with another well-established instrument. We explored the relationship between QST-MET and a survey developed by the Tripod Project for School Improvement. The Tripod survey asks students their level of agreement with a series of statements related to different aspects of classroom climate and instruction. These statements are organized into seven categories: Care (encouragement and support), Control (culture of cooperation and peer support), Clarify (success seems feasible), Challenge (press for effort, perseverance, and rigor), Captivate (learning seems interesting and relevant), Confer (students sense their ideas are respected), and Consolidate (ideas are connected and integrated). Table 14.8 shows the correlation between the QST-MET indicators and the Tripod categories. The sample included 206 matched pairs.

We ran correlations between the Tripod categories and the QST-MET indicators. We found a generally positive significant correlation between the non-lab indicators (Clusters 1 and 2) of QST-MET and Tripod, ranging from 0.138 to 0.25. The positive correlations are quite low, indicating that the two measures assessed somewhat different dimensions of teachers' competence. One Tripod category, Control, revealed particularly weak relationships with all of the QST-MET indicators. The Control category is related to a culture of cooperation and peer support. This finding is not surprising, because each of the QST-MET indicators focus on the teacher (e.g., the teacher's demonstration of content knowledge, ability to set the context, use of representations, etc.), while the Control category in the Tripod instruments assesses teachers' capacity to establish a culture of cooperation and peer support.

In contrast, the QST-MET lab indicators indicate almost no correlation with the Tripod categories. We found only two occasions in which the Tripod categories showed any significant correlations with the QST-MET lab

TABLE 14.7. Correlations Between QST-MET Clusters and Demographic Categories

Demographic Categories		Cluster 1: Assessing Teacher's Knowledge and Pedagogy		Cluster 2: Engaging Students in Science Learning		Cluster 3: Promoting Laboratory-Based Inquiry	
		Pearson correlation	p	Pearson correlation	p	Pearson correlation	p
Caucasian	Year 1	−0.106	0.085	−0.003	0.965	−0.016	0.885
	Year 2	0.103	0.207	0.039	0.639	0.203*	0.039
Black	Year 1	0.032	0.607	0.036	0.57	0.025	0.819
	Year 2	−0.154	0.057	−0.093	0.255	−0.133	0.175
Hispanic	Year 1	0.016	0.789	−0.108	0.09	−0.113	0.297
	Year 2	0.057	0.482	0.023	0.781	−0.034	0.731
Asian	Year 1	0.063	0.301	0.076	0.237	0.141	0.193
	Year 2	0	0.999	0.133	0.107	0.051	0.609
Other	Year 1	0.099	0.106	0.044	0.488	−0.157	0.147
	Year 2	0.199*	0.015	−0.049	0.555	−0.055	0.584
Gender	Year 1	−0.007	0.911	−0.031	0.628	−0.161	0.137
	Year 2	0.069	0.393	−0.102	0.213	−0.106	0.281
Reduced lunch	Year 1	0.123	0.057	0.082	0.225	0.045	0.693
	Year 2	0.019	0.83	0.024	0.789	−0.097	0.376
English language learner	Year 1	0.036	0.56	0.02	0.755	−0.023	0.831
	Year 2	−0.009	0.91	0.015	0.857	−0.073	0.459

Note: * = $p < 0.05$.

TABLE 14.8. Correlations Between QST-MET Indicators and Tripod Categories

Cluster and Indicator	Tripod Categories						
	Consolidate	Confer	Captivate	Challenge	Control	Clarify	Care
Cluster 1: Assessing Teacher's Knowledge and Pedagogy							
Sets context							
Pearson correlation	.204**	.215**	.180**	.227**	.169*	.203**	.262*
p	0.00	0.00	0.01	0.00	0.01	0.00	0.00
Using representations							
Pearson correlation	.162*	.149*	.204**	.180**	.155*	.180**	.212*
p	0.02	0.03	0.00	0.01	0.03	0.01	0.00
Content knowledge							
Pearson correlation	.235**	.220**	.237**	.262**	.190**	.248**	.241*
p	0.00	0.00	0.00	0.00	0.01	0.00	0.00
Feedback							
Pearson correlation	.235**	.244**	.191**	.285**	0.08	.207**	.250*
p	0.00	0.00	0.01	0.00	0.23	0.00	0.00

Cluster 2: Engaging Students in Science Learning

Promotes interest							
Pearson correlation	0.04	0.13	0.09	0.12	0.13	0.11	0.13
p	0.54	0.06	0.22	0.09	0.06	0.12	0.07
Assigns tasks							
Pearson correlation	0.14	.172*	0.12	.195**	0.06	0.10	.178*
p	0.05	0.01	0.08	0.00	0.37	0.14	0.01
Modes of teaching							
Pearson correlation	.184**	.225**	.180**	.244**	0.12	.154*	.205**
p	0.01	0.00	0.01	0.00	0.08	0.03	0.00
Elicits evidence (non-lab)							
Pearson correlation	.205**	.261**	.230**	.271**	0.14	.222**	.265**
p	0.00	0.00	0.00	0.00	0.05	0.00	0.00

(continued)

(Table 14.8 continued)

	Tripod Categories						
Cluster and Indicator	Consolidate	Confer	Captivate	Challenge	Control	Clarify	Care
Cluster 3: Promoting Laboratory-Based Inquiry							
Initiates							
Pearson correlation	−0.01	0.00	0.00	0.10	.148*	0.00	−0.02
p	0.85	0.98	0.96	0.17	0.03	0.98	0.82
Provides guidelines							
Pearson correlation	−0.12	−0.10	−0.11	−0.04	−0.04	−.138*	−0.07
p	0.08	0.15	0.12	0.61	0.61	0.05	0.34
Guides analysis							
Pearson correlation	−0.04	0.01	0.03	−0.01	0.01	0.00	0.04
p	0.52	0.91	0.63	0.88	0.93	0.97	0.53
Elicits evidence (lab)							
Pearson correlation	−0.06	−0.04	−0.05	0.05	0.03	−0.05	−0.01
p	0.37	0.55	0.52	0.48	0.62	0.45	0.86

Note: $* = p < 0.05$, $** = p < 0.01$.

indicators (Cluster 3: Control and Clarify). The lab indicators measure very specific science teaching behaviors not captured in the Tripod categories.

DISCUSSION

In this section, we focus on what we learned about teachers' content knowledge and science instructional practices. We discuss the differences in reliability of QST and QST-MET and propose some additional studies to compare the effects of in-person and online training. We also report on the validity of QST-MET.

Teachers' Science Instructional Practices

The majority of the science teaching observed in the MET study videos represent a very traditional view of teaching, and there will have to be significant shifts in instructional practices to be more in alignment with the new science standards (NGSS). The distribution of teachers' scores reveals some significant gaps in teachers' content knowledge and pedagogical skills.

When examining teachers' content knowledge, we found teacher content errors in 96 percent of the teaching segments. This finding should cause serious alarm within the science education community. If the MET study teachers are representative of teachers across the country, we need to take some immediate action to support deepening teachers' content knowledge. For example, we should ensure teachers are credentialed in the subjects they are teaching, provide safe atmospheres in which it is the norm for teachers to work with lead teachers to improve their content knowledge, and provide additional learning opportunities for teachers to strengthen their content knowledge when specific gaps are identified.

QST-MET detected significant gaps in teachers' pedagogical practices in more than half of the teaching segments (see Figures 14.2, 14.3, and 14.4). Teachers either did not exhibit the specific teaching behavior or made general statements resulting in more student confusion. Raters' scores indicate that the following pedagogical practices were *not* observed and indicate the frequency as a percentage of the total teaching segments: (1) setting clear objectives for the lesson (48 percent); (2) using representations such as examples, analogies, or models to help students learn new science concepts (70 percent); (3) providing feedback on students' performance or learning (57 percent); (4) promoting interest in the lesson by making connections to students' previous experiences or prior learning (60 percent); (5) assigning tasks that were scientific and intellectually challenging to the students (67 percent); (6) using multiple modes of teaching (29 percent); and (7) monitoring students' conceptual understanding (80 percent). These results indicate teachers need additional support in developing these pedagogical strategies and comfort level in increasing student engagement within their lessons to empower students to be more independent learners.

If the findings from the analysis of teachers' scores in the MET project are reflective of science instruction across the country, it indicates a significant gap in teacher content knowledge and pedagogy, suggesting the need for professional development during which teachers can observe lead teachers model these strategies, as well as the need for opportunities to practice these strategies.

We also found that lab and non-lab instruction differ in important ways that must be accounted for in classroom observations. Teachers' lab scores were significantly lower on average than their non-lab scores. The significant but low correlation supports our prediction that many of the teaching strategies incorporated in the lab and non-lab lesson types are different. This finding reveals the importance of observing both non-lab and lab lessons when measuring science teachers' effectiveness. In other words, teachers' proficiency in one type of lesson (i.e., non-lab) does not guarantee proficiency in the other type of lesson (i.e., lab), as these lessons are measuring different aspects of science teaching.

We plan to conduct future studies to see whether we can replicate these same results or find higher correlations between lab and non-lab lessons when working with teachers who embrace science practices aligned with the new NGSS (i.e., focus on student engagement, support student learning through hands-on inquiry experiences, provide students with opportunities to analyze data and to construct scientific arguments to communicate their learning). We did not see teachers using strong science practices in the videos for the MET project.

Reliability of QST-MET

The findings reveal moderate to low levels of inter-rater reliability between raters who participated in the online training for QST-MET (see Table 14.2). The results indicate that the reliability for the lab indicators (Cluster 3 = 0.787) is considerably higher than the reliability of the non-lab indicators (Cluster 1 = 0.477 and Cluster 2 = 0.360). Raters could assign a "0" score if the indicator was not observed, because we did not expect all the indicators to be evident within each segment of a lab lesson given the time-dependent nature of the indicator. The lab cluster had a large number of "0" scores, and this might contribute to the higher levels of reliability.

A close examination of the lab indicators reveals that two of the indicators, Initiates the Inquiry (0.959) and Provides Guidelines for Conducting and Gathering Data (0.821), had the highest inter-rater reliability, whereas the remaining indicators, Guides Analysis and Interpretation of Data (0.410) and Elicits Evidence of Student's Knowledge (0.521), had considerably lower reliabilities. Raters were able to accurately identify teachers introducing the lab or giving procedural directions, but it was more difficult for them to identify teachers guiding the analysis or interpretation of data. The low reliability of Guides Analysis and Interpretation of Data suggests that we need to re-examine the quality descriptions for this indicator, as well as strengthen the training videos and/or evidence for this indicator.

Since the reliabilities were relatively low, we examined the inter-rater agreement between raters for QST-MET. When we examined the percentages of exact matches by indicator, we saw a range of 34 percent to 90 percent. The other observation instruments in the MET project used an expanded level of agreement to include exact matches and adjacent scores (i.e., +/− 1). When we reanalyzed the agreement to include exact matches and adjacent scores, QST-MET's inter-rater agreements by indicator ranged between 88 percent and 100 percent (see Table 14.3). These are very acceptable ranges, especially for a new instrument.

Reliability of QST

The overall inter-rater reliability between raters for QST was 90 percent (see Table 14.4). This represents a high level of reliability, considering the raters were scoring eighteen different indicators for each fifteen-minute video segment for the entire video, which ranged from forty-five to ninety minutes. The inter-rater reliabilities for five of the six domains of QST ranged between 0.754 and 0.989. No inter-rater reliability was assigned for Domain 5: Providing Opportunities for the Application of Science, because there was no evidence of this type of teaching behavior in the initial fifty MET videos. The raters assigned "0" scores to each of the indicators within this domain, so we listed it as not applicable. The lowest level of inter-rater reliability (0.548) was the indicator Assigns Tasks to Promote Learning, focusing on the types of assignments selected by the teacher to promote learning (i.e., whether the tasks were challenging for the students) and how the teacher helped students access the material. In retrospect, it makes sense that raters would have difficulty making these judgments without any contextual information about the students.

Comparing Reliabilities Between QST and QST-MET

We found significant differences between the inter-rater reliability of the raters scoring QST-MET (see Table 14.2) and those raters scoring the original QST (see Table 14.4). Since the QST-MET was a condensed version of the original QST, we do not think the differences in inter-rater reliability are attributed to the different versions of the instrument. More likely, the differences appear to be related to the training design (in-person versus online training).

The findings indicate a wide discrepancy between the inter-rater reliability of raters trained in person as compared to the online program. The breakdown of inter-rater reliability for QST by domain and indicator presented in Table 14.4 reveals that all of the domains, except one, had an inter-rater reliability greater than 0.750. In contrast, the inter-rater reliability of the raters trained online for the QST-MET presented in Table 14.2 shows that the two non-lab clusters (Assessing Teacher's Knowledge and Pedagogy and Engaging Students in Science Learning) were 0.477 and 0.360, whereas the lab cluster (Promoting Laboratory-Based Inquiry) was 0.787. There was more consistency in inter-rater reliability between QST-MET Cluster 3 and the original QST.

In addition to QST-MET being piloted for the first time, we used an untested online training program to prepare raters to score the MET biology videos. Based on our inconsistent findings, we plan to revisit the training design, materials, and video segments used in the online training. The wide discrepancy between the inter-rater reliabilities for the in-person training and the online training warrants a future comparison study to evaluate these two training methods. At this point, we hypothesize that the raters in the in-person training had more opportunities than the raters in the online program for discussion, to ask questions, to discuss evidence, and to clarify the differences in score levels.

We understand the need for being able to conduct large-scale training programs, so we need to think about ways to incorporate chat rooms or phone call sessions during the online trainings to enable raters to discuss scoring issues during the training process. This could be an important direction for future study.

Validity of QST-MET

The result of the factor analysis supports the construct validity of the QST-MET clusters. Both factor analyses clearly separate the non-lab and lab lessons. These findings support the hypothesis that QST-MET indicators for lab and non-lab constructs contain significantly different teaching strategies (see Table 14.5). For example, the lab indicators focus on the key components teachers need to use when facilitating a laboratory-based inquiry, such as introducing the investigation, providing guidelines for conducting the lab, and guiding students through the analysis and interpretation of data. In contrast, the non-lab constructs Assessing Teacher's Knowledge and Pedagogy and Engaging Students in Science Learning focus on two different aspects of effective teaching, namely teachers' mastery of content knowledge and how teachers engage students in the learning process. The second factor analysis (see Table 14.6) revealed three clearly delineated factors separating the twelve indicators into factors directly aligned with the three QST-MET clusters. Again, this finding supports the construct validity of the QST-MET clusters and indicates that differences between the two non-lab clusters were detected.

To further test construct validity, we ran correlations between the QST-MET indicators and the Tripod categories (see Table 14.8). The comparison of Tripod and QST-MET provided two different ways to evaluate teacher effectiveness. For non-lab lessons, there were significant but low correlations with all of the non-discipline-specific Tripod survey categories. There appears to be overlap between the two instruments, but they are not measuring the same constructs. We would not expect these two instruments to be highly correlated because the QST-MET is focused on discipline-specific indicators and the two tools are using different modes to gather data (i.e., survey versus observational tool). The fact that we do see a significant but low correlation indicates there is something in common with the type of information captured by the Tripod and QST-MET. We conclude that the two instruments are detecting some common understandings of effective teaching; however, the QST-MET is measuring different dimensions of specific teaching behaviors within a discipline. Overall, these results lead to the conclusion that both instruments provide different and useful information to judge teacher quality. Therefore, a teacher evaluation system would be strengthened by including both measures.

We also examined any possible sources of bias in QST-MET (see Table 14.7). In the Year 2 data, we found significant but low-level correlations between teachers' scores in Cluster 1 and the ethnicity category "Other" (0.199), and between teachers' scores in Cluster 3 and the ethnicity category "Caucasian" (0.203). However, these correlations were not consistent both years, suggesting that these findings might be an artifact of differences in the classroom makeup (student diversity) from year to year, instead of systematic difference in QST-MET performance due to possible bias. In future applications of the QST-MET, we will continually examine outcomes to improve the QST-MET and to minimize any sources of possible bias.

POLICY IMPLICATIONS

The QST-MET is in many ways unique in the MET study; it is the one observational instrument that was built from scratch. The conceptualization of the assessment, design, and development was based on a vision of science teaching focusing on student-centered teaching and learning guided by numerous national science frameworks and, more recently, Next Generation Science Standards (NGSS).

The NGSS and elements of the Common Core State Standards (CCSS) were designed to create a national dialogue and consensus around a collective and common vision of effective science teaching and learning. These standards are designed to provide guidance for understanding how students learn, what should be taught, and the teaching skills necessary to support meaningful student achievement.

Examination of the QST-MET data highlights the wide gap in teacher knowledge, pedagogy, and scientific practices needed to support the vision of the NGSS standards. The QST-MET study revealed significant gaps in teacher content knowledge and a striking absence of the use of scientific practices in non-lab and lab lessons. It is clear from the QST-MET data that districts need to invest in the systematic collection of high-quality data from multiple measures aligned to the NGSS standards. To achieve these goals, targeted coaching, collaboration, and feedback must be incorporated into all levels of the system to build the capacity of teachers to use scientific practices and to support greater student learning. High-quality assessments will not change system practices alone. We need to move beyond a singular focus on the assessment instrument and to construct a system of assessments and supports that can provide the foundation for systemic change. Following are three key points that could possibly impact science teaching in the future.

Establishing a Clear Vision for Assessment

Step 1 is for schools and districts to come to consensus about the science knowledge, skills, dispositions, and behaviors that can most impact student learning. Clear standards, coupled with teacher support to implement the standards in the classroom, set the foundation for fostering changes in instructional practice. Setting clear expectations benefits the entire school system by creating a shared understanding and a common language of instruction that guides teacher conversations around teaching and learning. Additionally, clear expectations enable administrators and teachers to set priorities and broker support to build student and teacher capacity in relationship to standards. Looking forward, we see the NGSS standards focusing on scientific processes as one powerful conception for defining effective teaching in science.

High-Quality Science Teaching Requires Multiple Measures

Multiple observations are needed because teaching over the course of a year is influenced by lesson content, diversity of the classroom, and student progress. Building a high-quality observation system requires ongoing training and certification of observers to ensure rater consistency over time. Training of observers is not enough; a high-quality observation system must be able to identify specific information to help teachers improve their practice. All administrators should receive training and support in using effective methods both to provide feedback to teachers and to recommend high-leverage strategies to improve teaching and learning.

While observations are essential, a high-quality evaluation system includes other essential measures of teacher effectiveness. The MET study provides a number of key metrics that should be considered in a multiple measure assessment system, including student surveys to assess the instructional environment, content tests of teacher knowledge, and estimates of student learning gains on standardized tests. The takeaway from the MET studies is to design a system of teacher assessment that includes multiple measures in order to obtain a balanced, fair, and comprehensive picture of teacher competence. Information from a multiple-measure evaluation system should be used to inform decisions at all levels of the system (classroom, school, and district).

Focus on Continuous Improvement

The evaluation of teaching must go beyond simply sorting teachers by their level of effectiveness from low to high. The system of assessments should be a catalyst for the school and district to invest in continuous improvement of teaching and learning. At the core of improvement is the ability of observers (e.g., peer and administrators) to provide high-quality feedback to teachers about their teaching practice. Administrators should draw on proven protocols and tools to help ensure that they provide quality feedback to teachers. New evaluation systems can help teachers use data from the assessment system to rethink and redesign their approaches to teacher support and learning. Consideration should be given to more personalized and collaborative systems of support. Teachers need time to obtain images of effective teaching, possibly through peer visitations to classrooms, access to video libraries (e.g., Teaching Channel Videos, Annenberg Science Teaching Videos, TIMMS videos, and others), and teacher collaboration and discussion of student work.

CONCLUSION

In summary, the QST-MET is only one part of a comprehensive multiple-measure teacher evaluation system. In the design of a teaching and learning system of evaluation, the use of a reliable and valid evaluation instrument (QST-MET) and procedures is necessary, but not sufficient. We must also consider the development of the system in light of the state policy systems in which teachers are held accountable, as well as the school-based conditions that must be in place to support and drive continuous learning and improvement. Finally, consideration of the needs of the students the teacher serves and the creation of a valid and appropriate assessment of learning for all students (including students with special learning needs and new English language learners) must be addressed to support the development of a fair and balanced system of teacher evaluation that is designed to meet the needs of all students.

REFERENCES AND ADDITIONAL RESOURCES

Dorph, R., Shields, P., Tiffany-Morales, J., Hartry, A., & McCaffrey, T. (2011). *High hopes—few opportunities: The status of elementary science education in California.* Sacramento, CA: The Center for the Future of Teaching and Learning at WestEd.

Fulp, S. L. (2002). *2000 National survey of science and mathematics education: Status of elementary science teaching.* Chapel Hill, NC: Horizon Research.

Kloser, M. (in review). Determining a core set of science teaching practices: A Delphi expert panel approach.

Martinez, J. F., Borko, H., & Stecher, B. M. (2012). Measuring instructional practice in science using classroom artifacts: Lessons learned from two validation studies. *Journal of Research in Science Teaching, 49*(1), 38–67.

National Academy of Sciences. (2011). *A framework for K–12 science standards: Practices, cross-cutting concepts, and core ideas—report brief.* Washington, D.C. Retrieved from http://www7. nationalacademies.org/bose/Standards_Framework_Homepage.html

National Board for Professional Teaching Standards. (2002). *What teachers should know and be able to do.* Arlington, VA: Author.

National Research Council. (1996). *National Science Education Standards.* Washington, DC: The National Academies Press.

National Research Council. (2000). *Inquiry and the National Science Education Standards: A guide for teaching and learning.* Washington, DC: The National Academies Press.

National Research Council. (2007). *Taking science to school: Learning and teaching science in grades K–12.* Washington, DC: The National Academies Press.

Weiss, I. R. (2006). *Research on professional development for science teachers.* Paper presented at the Astronomical Society of the Pacific, Baltimore, MD.

Weiss, I. R., Pasley, J. D., Smith, P. S., Banilower, E. R., & Heck, D. J. (2003). *Looking inside the classroom: A study of K–12 mathematics and science education in the United States.* Chapel Hill, NC: Horizon Research, Inc.

Windschitl, M., Thompson, J., & Braaten, M. (2012). Proposing a core set of instructional practices and tools for teachers of science. *Science Education, 96*(5), 878–903.

APPENDIX A: QUALITY SCIENCE TEACHING (QST) RUBRIC

Domain 1: Assessing Teacher's Content Knowledge and Pedagogy

Indicators	1 Provides little or no evidence	2 Provides limited evidence	3 Provides clear evidence	4 Provides consistently strong evidence
I.1. Sets the context and focuses learning on key science concepts	The teacher does *not* set the context for the lesson AND does *not* provide objectives/goals OR focuses on loosely connected biological facts and definitions.	The teacher sets the context for the lesson in general terms and provides vague objectives/goals OR occasionally focuses on relevant biological concepts.	The teacher sets the context for the lesson in clear terms and provides clear objectives/goals OR focuses primarily on relevant biological concepts.	The teacher explicitly sets the context for the lesson in clear and specific terms and provides clear and worthwhile objectives/goals OR continually promotes scientific thinking and coherent conceptual understanding.
I.2. Uses representations Representations include examples, analogies, models, simulations	The teacher does *not* use representations OR uses representation(s) that lead students to misunderstand or misinterpret key biological concepts.	The teacher uses representation(s) that are general in nature OR that *may limit the* students' ability to understand or distinguish among related biological concepts.	The teacher uses multiple representations that are similar in nature and enhance students' ability to understand or distinguish among related biological concepts.	The teacher uses multiple representations that are different but related, enabling students to understand and distinguish among key biological concepts and ways of thinking/doing biology.
I.3. Demonstrates content knowledge	The teacher makes significant and/or numerous inaccuracies about main biological concepts and processes OR the teacher does *not* recognize or does *not* address students' preconceptions.	The teacher makes minor OR occasional inaccuracies but does *not* immediately correct the error about the main biological concepts and processes OR the teacher recognizes students' preconception and indicates the student is incorrect.	The teacher makes minor OR occasional inaccuracies AND immediately corrects the error related to biological concepts and processes OR the teacher recognizes and corrects students' preconceptions continuing with the planned lesson.	The teacher makes no observed inaccuracies related to biological concepts and processes AND the teacher recognizes and utilizes students' preconceptions as an entry point for students to engage with key biological concepts.

Domain 2: Engaging Students in Science Learning

Indicators	1 Provides little or no evidence	2 Provides limited evidence	3 Provides clear evidence	4 Provides consistently strong evidence
II.1. Promotes students' interest and motivation to learn science	The teacher makes inappropriate or no connections between the lesson and students' experiences or to previous class learning.	The teacher makes superficial connections between the lesson and students' experiences or to previous class learning.	The teacher makes explicit connections between the lesson and students' experiences or to previous class learning.	The teacher makes explicit and meaningful connections between the lesson and students' experiences or to previous class learning.
II.2. Assigns tasks to promote learning and addresses the demands of the task for all students	The teacher does not assign tasks or assigns tasks that are non-scientific and do *not* promote student learning. AND The teacher does *not* address the demands of the tasks (cognitive and linguistic) making them accessible to few or no students.	The teacher assigns scientific tasks that are *not* intellectually challenging for most of the students. OR The teacher addresses the demands of the tasks (cognitive and linguistic), superficially making them accessible to a limited number of students.	The teacher assigns scientific tasks that are intellectually challenging for most of the students. AND The teacher addresses the demands of the tasks (cognitive and linguistic) making them accessible to the majority of the students in class.	The teacher assigns scientific tasks that are rich and intellectually challenging for all students. AND The teacher effectively addresses the demands of the tasks (cognitive and linguistic), making them accessible and challenging to most students.
II.3. Uses modes of teaching science concepts Modes include lectures, modeling, guided practice, etc.	The teacher primarily uses one mode of teaching, resulting in little or no student engagement with biological concepts.	The teacher uses several similar modes of teaching, resulting in limited student engagement with biological concepts.	The teacher uses several similar modes of teaching, resulting in the majority of students engaging with biological concepts.	The teacher uses multiple, different modes of teaching, resulting in most students engaging with biological concepts.

(continued)

Domain 3: Facilitating Scientific Reasoning and Discourse

Indicators	1 Provides little or no evidence	2 Provides limited evidence	3 Provides clear evidence	4 Provides consistently strong evidence
III.1. Uses questions/ prompts to promote discourse	The teacher uses mostly factual and/or procedural-based questions/ prompts that *elicit* no response or a single correct response.	The teacher uses mostly factual and/or procedural based questions/prompts that *elicit* a range of student responses and/or positions.	The teacher uses mostly open-ended questions/prompts that *elicit* a range of student responses and/or positions.	The teacher uses mostly higher-order, analytical thinking questions/ prompts that *elicit* a wide range of student responses and/or positions.
III.2. Initiates and facilitates discussions	The teacher does not initiate a science discussion. OR The teacher initiates a verbal exchange, but it results in little or no science discourse (primarily IRE).	The teacher initiates a general science discussion and takes a dominating role that elicits significant teacher to students science discourse (not IRE) and/or limited student to student science discourse.	The teacher initiates a meaningful science discussion and takes a dominate role in orchestrating opportunities, which result in student to student exchanges of ideas, explanations, and opinions.	The teacher initiates a meaningful science discussion and takes a supporting role that facilitates students sharing ideas, explanations, and opinions with evidence directly with peers.
III.3. Promotes critical reasoning	The teacher does *not* provide students with critical thinking prompt/ stimulus.	The teacher provides students with a critical thinking prompt/ stimulus but does *not* ask students to demonstrate scientific argumentation skills.	The teacher provides students with a critical thinking prompt/stimulus resulting in students' demonstrating limited scientific argumentation skills.	The teacher provides students with a critical thinking prompt/stimulus, resulting in students' demonstrating a wide range of scientific argumentation skills.

Domain 4: Promoting Laboratory-Based Inquiry

Indicators	1 Provides little or no evidence	2 Provides limited evidence	3 Provides clear evidence	4 Provides consistently strong evidence
IV.1. Initiates the inquiry	The teacher initiates a lab activity or experiment but does *not* make connections between the investigation and science content.	The teacher initiates a lab activity or experiment and makes ambiguous or partial connections between the investigation and relevant science content.	The teacher initiates a lab activity or experiment and makes meaningful connections between the investigation and relevant science content.	The teacher initiates a lab by presenting a content-related problem. Students formulate testable questions to investigate and are able to make connections to the relevant science content.
IV.2. Provides guidelines for conducting the experiment and gathering data	The teacher provides students with a pre-scribed lab procedure, but students do *not* produce a product except answering questions.	The teacher provides students with a pre-scribed lab procedure, and students produce product(s) as a result of the investigation, such as drawings, models, data tables, graphs, etc.	The teacher provides students with a lab plan but with options for different aspects of the investigation such as generating hypothesis, developing procedures, gathering data, AND/OR testing samples, etc.	The teacher provides students with technical guidance, and students design and conduct the entire investigation including hypothesis, procedures, data tables/graphs, AND analysis.
IV.3. Guides analysis and interpretation of data	The teacher does *not* ask students to present or summarize their data, and there is no analysis of data.	The teacher asks students to present their data and leads students to articulate the "expected" interpretations.	The teacher gathers students' data and walks them through the analysis. Students demonstrate the ability to find patterns AND/OR provide explanations of the data.	The teacher guides students in *how to* analyze and find patterns in the data. Students articulate evidence-based explanations of the data.

(continued)

Domain 5: Providing Opportunities for the Application of Science

Indicators	1 Provides little or no evidence	2 Provides limited evidence	3 Provides clear evidence	4 Provides consistently strong evidence
V.1. Initiates investigation of science-related issue or application	The teacher presents an issue or science application but does not make the connections between the topic and the intended content clear to the students.	The teacher presents an issue or science application and makes connections between the topic and the intended content.	The teacher presents a content-related issue and engages students in sharing their current knowledge and opinions about that issue.	The teacher presents a content-related issue and uses it as a springboard for engaging students in examining the relationship between science concepts, the application of science, and the implications for society.
V.2. Provides opportunities for students to demonstrate research skills	The teacher provides students with a narrow set of reading resources about the issue.	The teacher provides students with a balanced set of resources about the issue, offering contrasting information on the issue.	The teacher provides "starters" and asks students to research and analyze relevant resources and examine the merit of the information they find.	The teacher asks students to research and analyze relevant resources, and students evaluate the credibility of the information they find.
V.3. Guides analysis and societal implications	The teacher does *not* ask students to present or summarize their information, and there is no analysis of the societal implications of the issue.	The teacher asks students to present their data and leads the class to articulate the "expected" societal implications.	The teacher gathers class data, walks students through the analysis, and students demonstrate ability to identify key societal implications of the issue.	The teacher guides students in *how to* analyze and find patterns in the information, and students articulate the evidence-based societal implications of the issue.

Domain 6: Monitoring Student Learning

Indicators	1 Provides little or no evidence	2 Provides limited evidence	3 Provides clear evidence	4 Provides consistently strong evidence
VI.1. Elicits evidence of students' knowledge and understanding	The teacher does *not* elicit evidence of student knowledge or understanding.	The teacher primarily elicits evidence of student knowledge.	The teacher occasionally elicits evidence of student knowledge AND conceptual understanding.	The teacher systematically and consistently elicits evidence of student knowledge AND conceptual understanding.
VI.2. Provides students with feedback	The teacher provides no or nonspecific feedback to students/class.	The teacher provides specific feedback to students/class that focuses on the general strengths of the work OR how to improve learning.	The teacher provides specific feedback to students/class that focuses on the general strengths of the work AND how to improve their learning.	The teacher provides constructive, specific, detailed feedback to students/class AND includes explicit suggestions on how to improve their learning.
VI.3. Provides opportunities to summarize/reflect on learning	The teacher does *not* summarize the key points within the learning segment AND does *not* provide students with opportunities to summarize or reflect on their learning.	The teacher summarizes the key points within the learning segment BUT does *not* provide students with opportunities to summarize or reflect on their learning.	The teacher summarizes the key points within the learning segment AND provides students with opportunities to summarize or reflect on their learning.	The teacher asks students to summarize or reflect on the key points of the learning segment.

APPENDIX B: QST-MET RUBRIC

Cluster 1: Assessing Teacher's Knowledge and Pedagogy

Indicators	1 Provides little or no evidence	2 Provides limited evidence	3 Provides clear evidence	4 Provides consistently strong evidence
1. Sets the context and focuses learning on key science concepts	The teacher does *not* set the context for the lesson AND does *not* provide objectives/goals OR focuses on loosely connected biological facts and definitions.	The teacher sets the context for the lesson in general terms and provides vague objectives/goals OR occasionally focuses on relevant biological concepts.	The teacher sets the context for the lesson in clear terms and provides clear objectives/goals OR focuses learning primarily on relevant biological concepts.	The teacher explicitly sets the context for the lesson in clear and specific terms and provides clear and worthwhile objectives/goals, AND continually promotes scientific thinking and coherent conceptual understanding.
2. Uses representations. Representations include examples, analogies, models, simulations	The teacher does *not* use representations OR uses representation(s) that lead students to misunderstand or misinterpret key biological concepts.	The teacher uses representation(s) that are general in nature OR that may limit the students' ability to understand or distinguish among related biological concepts.	The teacher uses multiple representations that are similar in nature and enhance students' ability to understand or distinguish among related biological concepts.	The teacher uses multiple representations that are different but related, enabling students to understand and distinguish among key biological concepts and ways of thinking/doing biology.
3. Demonstrates content knowledge	The teacher makes significant and/or numerous inaccuracies about main biological concepts and processes OR the teacher does *not* recognize or does *not* address students' preconceptions.	The teacher makes minor OR occasional inaccuracies but does *not* immediately correct the error about the main biological concepts and processes, OR the teacher recognizes students' preconception and indicates the student is incorrect.	The teacher makes minor OR occasional inaccuracies AND immediately corrects the error related to biological concepts and processes, OR the teacher recognizes and corrects students' preconceptions continuing with the planned lesson.	The teacher makes no observed inaccuracies related to biological concepts and processes, AND the teacher recognizes and utilizes students' preconceptions as an entry point for students to engage with key biological concepts.
4. Provides students with feedback	The teacher provides no or nonspecific feedback to students/ class.	The teacher provides specific feedback to students/class that focuses on the general strengths of the work OR how to improve learning	The teacher provides specific feedback to students/class that focuses on the general strengths of the work AND how to improve their learning	The teacher provides constructive, specific, detailed feedback to students/class AND includes explicit suggestions on how to improve their learning.

Cluster 2: Engaging Students in Science Learning

Indicators	1 Provides little or no evidence	2 Provides limited evidence	3 Provides clear evidence	4 Provides consistently strong evidence
1. Promotes students' interest and motivation to learn science	The teacher makes inappropriate or no connections between the lesson and students' experiences or to previous class learning.	The teacher makes superficial connections between the lesson and students' experiences or to previous class learning.	The teacher makes explicit connections between the lesson and students' experiences or to previous class learning.	The teacher makes explicit and meaningful connections between the lesson and students' experiences or to previous class learning.
2. Assigns tasks to promote learning and addresses the demands of the task for all students	The teacher does not assign tasks or assigns tasks that are nonscientific and do not promote student learning. AND The teacher does *not* address the demands of the tasks (cognitive and linguistic), making them accessible to few or no students.	The teacher assigns scientific tasks that are *not* intellectually challenging for most of the students. OR The teacher addresses the demands of the tasks (cognitive and linguistic), superficially making them accessible to a limited number of students.	The teacher assigns scientific tasks that are intellectually challenging for most of the students. AND The teacher addresses the demands of the tasks (cognitive and linguistic), making them accessible to the majority of the students in class.	The teacher assigns scientific tasks that are rich and intellectually challenging for all students. AND The teacher effectively addresses the demands of the tasks (cognitive and linguistic) making them accessible and challenging to most students.
3. Uses modes of teaching science concepts	The teacher primarily uses one mode of teaching, resulting in little or no student engagement with biological concepts.	The teacher uses several similar modes of teaching, resulting in limited student engagement with biological concepts.	The teacher uses several similar modes of teaching resulting in the majority of students engaging with biological concepts.	The teacher uses multiple, different modes of teaching, resulting in most students engaging with biological concepts.
4. Elicits evidence of students' knowledge and understanding	The teacher does not elicit evidence of student knowledge or understanding,	The teacher primarily elicits evidence of student knowledge.	The teacher occasionally elicits evidence of student knowledge AND conceptual understanding.	The teacher systematically and consistently elicits evidence of student knowledge AND conceptual understanding.

(continued)

Cluster 3: Promoting Laboratory-Based Inquiry

Indicators	1 Provides little or no evidence	2 Provides limited evidence	3 Provides clear evidence	4 Provides consistently strong evidence
1. Initiates the inquiry	The teacher initiates a lab activity or experiment but does *not* make connections between the investigation and science content.	The teacher initiates a lab activity or experiment and makes ambiguous or partial connections between the investigation and relevant science content.	The teacher initiates a lab activity or experiment and makes meaningful connections between the investigation and relevant science content.	The teacher initiates a lab by presenting a content-related problem. Students formulate testable questions to investigate and are able to make connections to the relevant science content.
2. Provides guidelines for conducting the experiment and gathering data	The teacher provides students with a prescribed lab procedure, but students do *not* produce a product except answering questions.	The teacher provides students with a prescribed lab procedure and students produce product(s) as a result of the investigation, such as drawings, models, data tables, graphs, etc.	The teacher provides students with a lab plan, but with options for different aspects of the investigation such as generating hypotheses, developing procedures, gathering data, AND/OR testing samples, etc.	The teacher provides students with technical guidance, and students design and conduct the entire investigation, including hypothesis, procedures, data tables/graphs, AND analysis.
3. Guides analysis and interpretation of data	The teacher does *not* ask students to present or summarize their data, and there is no analysis of data.	The teacher asks students to present their data and leads students to articulate the "expected" interpretations.	The teacher gathers students' data and walks them through the analysis. Students demonstrate the ability to find patterns AND/OR provide explanations of the data.	The teacher guides students in *how to* analyze and find patterns in the data. Students articulate evidence-based explanations of the data.
4. Elicits evidence of students' knowledge and understanding	The teacher does not elicit evidence of student knowledge or understanding.	The teacher primarily elicits evidence of student knowledge.	The teacher occasionally elicits evidence of student knowledge AND conceptual understanding.	The teacher systematically and consistently elicits evidence of student knowledge AND conceptual understanding.

CHAPTER

15

Evidence on the Validity of Content Knowledge for Teaching Assessments

DREW H. GITOMER, GEOFFREY PHELPS, BARBARA H. WEREN,
HEATHER HOWELL, AND ANDREW J. CROFT

ABSTRACT

This chapter describes a research and development effort around Content Knowledge for Teaching (CKT) assessments in mathematics and English language arts (ELA) for the Measures of Effective Teaching (MET) project. CKT represents content knowledge that is used in carrying out tasks of teaching, including anticipating student challenges, evaluating student ideas, providing helpful explanations, creating and adapting resources, developing activities, and selecting instructional resources. We first developed a generalizable framework to support the design of CKT assessments within and across domains. From this, five assessments (in mathematics, grades 4–5, grades 6–8, and ninth grade algebra; in ELA, grades 4–6 and 7–9) were developed, piloted, and administered to teachers participating in the MET study. Development of each item included creating a detailed rationale that described the knowledge and reasoning called for, along with justifications for all answer options.

We then developed and evaluated several key components of a validity argument for these assessments. The assessments were able to reliably differentiate teachers in terms of their CKT. Scores were broadly distributed across the scale, and there was a substantial, but partial, correlation of ELA and mathematics scores for those elementary teachers who took both assessments. We then reported on a study of a select sample of MET teachers who had scored in either the 2nd or 4th quartile on the elementary assessments. These teachers

(continued)

(continued)

were interviewed one year later and asked to reason through a subset of test questions. We found substantial evidence that observed reasoning patterns for both correct and incorrect responses were consistent with the anticipated reasoning built into the design of the assessment items. These various analyses provide consistent evidence that the MET assessments can support valid inferences about teachers' CKT. Further work is needed to understand exactly how CKT is called on in the regular execution of instruction.

INTRODUCTION

Content knowledge is a long-established basic prerequisite for teaching a subject, and it is an essential requirement for teacher certification (Mitchell, Robinson, Plake, & Knowles, 2001). States typically establish minimum coursework requirements for licensure and almost uniformly mandate passing a test of content knowledge. Such requirements are also used to satisfy the Highly Qualified Teacher provision of the Elementary and Secondary Education Act (Higher Education Act of 1998, 1998; Hill, 2007).

However, does knowing a body of content mean that one is able to teach that content? The idea that teachers need to understand and use content in ways particular to teaching is captured in arguments developed by Lee Shulman, who conceptualized *pedagogical content knowledge* (PCK), as comprising "the most useful forms of representation of those ideas, the most powerful analogies, illustrations, examples, explanations, and demonstrations—in a word, the ways of representing and formulating the subject that make it comprehensible to others. . . . Pedagogical content knowledge also includes an understanding of what makes the learning of specific topics easy or difficult: the conceptions and preconceptions that students of different ages and backgrounds bring with them to the learning of those most frequently taught topics and lessons" (Shulman, 1986, p. 9).

The notion of PCK has contributed to interest in research focused on the central role of content in teaching and has provided a way to conceptualize teaching as professional work with its own unique knowledge base (Ball, Thames, & Phelps, 2008, p. 392). Across domains, many attempts have been made to define PCK (e.g., Abell, 2007; Baxter & Lederman, 1999; Magnusson, Krajcik, & Borko, 1999; Niess, 2005; Van Driel, Verloop, & De Vos, 1998), reflecting the widespread adoption of the term. As interest in PCK has grown, the ideas have been applied in very broad ways, and in some cases have even expanded to include everything a teacher could know and do to teach a subject (Ball et al., 2008).

Recently Ball and colleagues sought to clarify what constitutes content knowledge specific to teaching and put forth the concept of *content knowledge for teaching* (CKT). Their CKT model articulates distinctions among the types of content knowledge used in teaching a subject, including both the shared or common types of content knowledge used in many professions and activities and the content knowledge that is needed for teaching, including PCK. Their model defines CKT as knowledge that directly links the work of teaching and the content knowledge that is required to do that work (Ball et al., 2008, p. 395).

Assessments, primarily in mathematics, have been developed in order to measure the construct of CKT (Buschang, Chung, Delacruz, & Baker, 2012; Hill, Schilling, & Ball, 2004; Kersting, 2008; Krauss et al., 2008). There has also been preliminary work in reading (Carlisle, Correnti, Phelps, & Zeng, 2009; Kucan, Hapgood, & Palincsar, 2011; Phelps & Schilling, 2004). Development efforts have been accompanied by validation studies, which have begun to establish the extent to which test scores are related to professional knowledge (Hill, Dean, & Goffney, 2007; Krauss, Baumert, & Blum, 2008; Phelps, 2009) and to test relationships to valued outcomes such as instruction and student learning (Baumert et al., 2010; Hill et al., 2008; Hill, Rowan, & Ball, 2005; Hill, Umland, Litke, & Kapitula, 2012; Kersting, Givvin, Sotelo, & Stigler, 2010; Kersting, Givvin, Thompson, Santagata, & Stigler, 2012). Initial results are promising, but such studies are often limited in scale and to particular grade levels.

In this chapter we report on advances made in the design and validation of measures of CKT for both mathematics and English language arts (ELA) that were developed for the Measures of Effective Teaching (MET) project to assess one component of teaching quality. Given the conceptualization of CKT, we hypothesize that this knowledge is most likely to contribute to teaching effectiveness when teachers are engaged in content-related teaching practices (e.g., interpreting student errors, selecting appropriate representations for instruction, or eliciting student thinking).

Because such practices are common to all teaching, we present a generalizable design process that should be useful to others measuring CKT by focusing on practices that are common to most teaching contexts at an abstract level but become specialized within specific domains. To date, no such design specifications for CKT assessments exist.

We then explore a set of validity issues. We examine the extent to which the assessments are reliable measures of CKT and are able to distinguish CKT among teachers. We are also interested in the extent to which performance on particular items is associated with the grade levels taught by teachers. We also probe the content specificity of CKT by comparing assessment results in mathematics and ELA for teachers who teach both subjects in self-contained classrooms. Finally, we examine the extent to which assessment results are associated with the way that individuals reason about these assessment tasks.

We begin with a description of the design framework that supported the development of the CKT assessments in both mathematics and English language arts. Next, we explain how the assessments were developed and describe the actual assessment questions and types of knowledge and reasoning these questions were designed to measure. We then present evidence to support the initial stages of a validity argument (Kane, 1992, 2006) that CKT assessments are measuring the knowledge they are designed to assess and that the scores support valid inferences about teachers' CKT. We conclude the chapter by discussing the viability of the CKT assessment design framework for guiding future assessment development and the potential of assessments of CKT for teacher professional development, teaching licensure and certification, and teaching quality evaluation.

A DESIGN FRAMEWORK FOR CKT ASSESSMENTS

We define CKT as the content reasoning and knowledge used to recognize, understand, and respond to the range of content problems encountered in teaching practice. Obviously, this conception involves teachers' interactions with students around the content and learning activities that occur within the classroom. However, it also includes the many content practices that occur outside of the classroom as teachers plan how to teach a topic, make sense of student work products to decide what to do next, share teaching approaches with colleagues, design lessons or curriculum materials, interpret standards, and much more. These core practices, or *tasks of teaching*, are the organizing foundation for the CKT assessment design framework. Many tasks of teaching are common across subject areas and grade levels and, thus, provide a common structure to describe CKT generally. This common structure, in turn, provides a basis for elaborating the variable enactments of these tasks in specific subject areas and for particular curricular content and grade levels.

The tasks of teaching are not fully exclusive of one another. In many cases, the work of teaching includes multiple tasks, or a single task might potentially be described in more than one way. For example, a piece of student work completed in class might first be evaluated by the teacher, then become an example that is evaluated and selected because it highlights a particular point that the teacher wishes to emphasize. Larger tasks of teaching not represented here may be made up of smaller tasks of teaching. Responding to students requires a teacher to evaluate what the student has said and done, choose an appropriate response, and then deliver that response. While teaching often involves the coordination of multiple tasks of teaching, individual assessment questions typically focus on just one or two tasks in order to more directly assess teacher knowledge. Selected examples that illustrate the task of teaching framework are presented in Table 15.1.

Tasks of teaching are intended to make sense to teachers, teacher educators, administrators, and policymakers. For these reasons, the design framework provides a natural and easily transferable conceptual basis for what teachers need to know and learn in order to teach a subject. Scores on the assessments should be easy to interpret, with lower scores indicating gaps in relevant content that teachers need to study and master.

THE STRUCTURE OF MET CKT ASSESSMENTS

The CKT design framework was used to guide item development for the MET assessments. A team of researchers from Educational Testing Service (ETS)[1] and the University of Michigan developed assessments for teachers of students in grades 4 through 9 in mathematics and English language arts. A first question was to decide how to align particular test forms with the grade levels that teachers taught. Forms were developed to reflect patterns in school organization, in the nature of content focus for different grade levels, and, as much as possible, to align with the content focus and grade range of the observational instruments developed for the MET study. Thus,

TABLE 15.1. Tasks of Teaching Requiring CKT

Task of Teaching	Mathematics Examples	ELA Examples
1. Anticipating student challenges, misconceptions, partial misconceptions, alternate conceptions, strengths, interests, capabilities, and background knowledge	Anticipating student challenges in reasoning about and doing mathematics due to the interplay of content demands and students' understanding Anticipating likely misconceptions, partial conceptions, and alternate conceptions about particular mathematics content and practices	Anticipating the impact of limited English language proficiency on students' comprehension of text and speech and on their written and spoken expression Anticipating how students' background knowledge, life experiences, and cultural background can interact with new ELA concepts, texts, resources, and processes
2. Evaluating student ideas evident in work, talk, actions, and interactions	Evaluating student work, talk, or actions in order to identify conceptions in mathematics, including incorrect or partial conceptions Evaluating non-standard responses for evidence of mathematical understanding and in terms of efficiency, validity, and generalizability	Evaluating student work, talk, and actions for evidence of strengths and weaknesses in reading, writing, speaking, and listening Evaluating discussion among groups of students for evidence of understanding ELA concepts, texts, and processes
3. Explaining concepts, procedures, representations, models, examples, definitions, and hypotheses	Explaining mathematical concepts, or why a mathematical idea is "true" Interpreting a particular representation in multiple ways to further understanding	Explaining literary or language concepts, using definitions, examples, and analogies when appropriate Explaining processes of reading, including why certain processes are appropriate for particular texts and/or tasks

Task of Teaching	Mathematics Examples	ELA Examples
4. Creating and adapting resources for instruction (examples, models, representations, explanations, definitions, hypotheses, procedures)	Creating and adapting examples that support particular mathematical strategies or to address particular student questions, misconceptions, or challenges with content Adapting student-generated conjectures to support instructional purposes	Creating and adapting examples or model texts to introduce a concept or to demonstrate a literary technique or a reading, writing, or speaking strategy Creating and adapting analogies to support student understanding of ELA concepts, texts, and processes
5. Evaluating and selecting resources for instruction (examples, models, representations, explanations, definitions, hypotheses, procedures)	Evaluating and selecting representations or models that support multiple interpretations Evaluating and selecting explanations of mathematical concepts for potential to support mathematical learning or in terms of validity, generalizability, or explanatory power	Evaluating and selecting examples to develop understanding of a concept, literary technique, or literacy strategy, or to address particular student questions, misconceptions, or challenges with content Evaluating and selecting procedures for writing or working with text
6. Developing questions, activities, tasks, and problems to elicit student thinking	Creating or adapting questions, activities, tasks, or problems that demonstrate desired mathematical characteristics Creating or adapting classes of problems that address the same mathematical concept or that systematically vary in difficulty and complexity	Creating or adapting prompts or questions with the potential to elicit productive student writing Developing questions, activities, or tasks to elicit evidence that students have a particular literary understanding or skill

(*continued*)

(Table 15.1 continued)

Task of Teaching	Mathematics Examples	ELA Examples
7. Evaluating and selecting student tasks (questions, problems) to elicit student thinking	Evaluating and selecting questions, activities, or tasks to elicit evidence that students have a particular mathematical understanding or skill Evaluating and selecting problems that support particular mathematical strategies and practices	Evaluating and selecting questions, activities, or tasks to elicit discussion about a specific text or literary concept Evaluating and selecting questions, activities, or tasks to support the development of a particular literary understanding or skill
8. Doing the work of the student curriculum	Doing the work that will be demanded of the students as part of the intended curriculum	Doing the work that will be demanded of the students as part of the intended curriculum

for mathematics, three forms were developed: grades 4 and 5, grades 6 to 8, and ninth grade algebra.[2] For ELA, two forms were developed: grades 4 to 6 and grades 7 to 9.

Given that the MET sample drew from districts across the United States, we could make no assumptions about particular curricula. Nor could we assume that content coverage would be similar within grades, either within or across districts, or even within schools. Because of this variability and also because teachers often need to teach concepts that are associated with curricular goals in prior or subsequent grades, we adopted a strategy of developing a relatively small number of assessments that aligned with the content demand within a range of grade levels.

Test Design

The assessments were designed to meet a set of constraints. Each assessment task had to have clear target goals and scoring rules that led to clear interpretations. Selected-response items needed to have an unambiguous key (the correct answer), and there had to be clear rules for interpreting and assigning scores to constructed-response items. The assessments were also designed to be completed within approximately one hour so as not to be too burdensome to MET teachers. Thus, in order to have sufficient numbers of items to achieve reasonable test reliability, we had to include predominantly selected-response items. We did anticipate that reliabilities would not be as high as conventional teacher certification tests, which typically take two hours to complete, simply because of the limited number of questions administered.

We modeled many of the questions using item formats that had been used in previous work at the University of Michigan (Hill et al., 2004; Phelps & Schilling, 2004), including single-selection multiple choice, in which the single best answer is chosen from among the four answer choices given; "table sets," in which a common stimulus is presented along with a set of items that each includes two answer choices; and short constructed-response formats.

For clarity, in all subsequent descriptions of the assessments and in the discussion of the data analyses, each *response* to a selected-response question will be referred to as an *item*. Therefore, a *single-selection multiple-choice question* corresponds to a *single item*, but a *table question* corresponds to *several items*, one for each row in the table. Each table question in the MET teacher knowledge assessments corresponds to three to six items.

Even though the response format is limited to a single choice, selected-response items can elicit complex forms of reasoning. Indeed, for each item we developed a Task Design Rationale (TDR) that hypothesized the reasoning process a teacher would need to use to arrive at the correct answer. We also designed item distractors (incorrect choices) to be plausible responses representing possibilities that could arise in classroom teaching. In the TDRs we explained the logic of the incorrect or incomplete reasoning that might lead a participant to select a distractor. An example of a TDR for a multiple-choice selected-response item is presented in Exhibit 15.1.

The Ms. Hupman example in Exhibit 15.1 is representative of CKT items in several ways. The work the test-taker must do to answer is a task of teaching that a teacher would do in the course of his or her daily work. The item is situated in a teaching context, in which the test-taker is required to consider content from the perspective of the teacher. In this case, considering what it means for a classroom task to be *useful* requires an orientation toward seeing mathematics problems as tools that teachers use to reveal student thinking. As is the case with many CKT items, answering correctly requires activating and

EXHIBIT 15.1. Task Design Rationale (TDR) Example for a Selected-Response Item

The relevant task of teaching is Evaluating and selecting questions, activities, or tasks to elicit evidence that students have a particular mathematical understanding or skill.

> Ms. Hupman is teaching an introductory lesson on exponents. She wants to give her students a quick problem at the end of class to check their proficiency in evaluating simple exponential expressions. Of the following expressions, which would be least useful in assessing student proficiency in evaluating simple exponential expressions?
>
> A. 3^3
>
> B. 2^3
>
> C. 2^2
>
> D. All of these are equally useful in assessing student proficiency in evaluating simple exponential expressions.

Task Design Rationale: This item asks for the least useful of a set of problems for assessment purposes, but without specifying what the criteria for *usefulness* should be. In order to answer correctly, the test-taker must understand that

- a *useful* problem for assessing students is one that reveals to the teacher whether or not the students have understood

- a common mistake students make in evaluating exponential expressions is multiplying the base by the exponent

- there are other less common errors students make, which include reversing the base and the exponent or substituting other operations, for example, adding the base and exponent

Test-takers might be familiar with these errors from prior experience or might be able to imagine plausible ways in which a student could approach the problems incorrectly. A useful problem for assessment would be one that would alert the teacher if a student uses any one of these incorrect methods. A less useful assessment problem would be one that the student could coincidentally answer correctly using one of these erroneous methods, masking the underlying misconception from the teacher.

Option A: If 3^3 is evaluated incorrectly by multiplying base times exponent, the result is $3 \times 3 = 9$, which is a different answer from the correct answer ($3 \times 3 \times 3 = 27$), so the teacher would know that an error has been made.

If evaluated incorrectly by reversing the exponent and the base, the result would be 27, which is the same as the correct answer, so the teacher might not know that an error has been made. If evaluated incorrectly by adding the base and exponent, the result would be 6, which is different from the correct answer, so the teacher would know that an error has been made.

The most common mistake is revealed by this problem, but one other possible mistake is not, so this problem is only somewhat useful in revealing student errors.

Option B: If 2^3 is evaluated incorrectly by multiplying base and exponent, the result is $2 \times 3 = 6$, which is different from the correct answer ($2 \times 2 \times 2 = 8$), so the teacher would know that an error has been made.

If evaluated incorrectly by reversing the exponent and base, the result would be 9, which is also different from the correct answer and would reveal the error. If evaluated incorrectly by adding the base and exponent, the result would be 5, which is again different from the correct answer.

This is a useful assessment problem that reveals several common errors.

Option C: If 2^2 is evaluated incorrectly by multiplying base and exponent, the result is $2 \times 2 = 4$, which is the same as the correct answer ($2 \times 2 = 4$), and would mask the mistake from the teacher.

If evaluated incorrectly by reversing the exponent and base, the answer would be 4, which is the same as the correct answer, and likewise would mask the mistake. If evaluated incorrectly by adding the base and exponent, the answer would still be 4 and the teacher would not know an error had been made. This assessment problem hides several common errors from the teacher by allowing the student to arrive at a correct answer using incorrect reasoning, and it is less useful than the other options.

Option D: Because Option C is clearly less useful than A or B, Option D is ruled out.

deploying content knowledge that differs from more conventional knowledge of mathematics. In this case, there is a difference between simply being able to do the content problems (i.e., being able to evaluate an expression like 2^3) and the content knowledge used in imagining incorrect mathematical procedures and how those procedures would play out in the evaluation of particular problems. Like other CKT items, the Ms. Hupman item is designed, even in a short selected-response format, to elicit reasoning that draws on multiple types of knowledge from the test-taker.

Exhibit 15.2 is an example of a table set question in which the same problem context sets the stage for a series of items that require the test-taker to select one of two options.

Finally, we present an example of a constructed-response item in Exhibit 15.3. In this problem, the teacher must generate three fractions that will satisfy the presented problem.

EXHIBIT15.2. **Sample English Language Arts (ELA) Table Question**

Ms. Rice begins a unit on memoir writing by reading a passage from a literary model. She then asks students to complete a warm-up activity to help them generate ideas for their own writing.

For each assignment, indicate whether or not it will help students focus their brainstorming on generating a memoir.

	Will help focus brainstorming	Will not help focus brainstorming
(A) Write a poem about the ways you have changed, using the form "I used to be . . . but now I am. . . ."		
(B) Write a sequence of sentences describing some of your experiences, beginning each sentence with the phrase "I remember. . . ."		
(C) Write a few adjectives that describe your personality.		
(D) Write down some of your favorite foods and describe what you like about them.		

Correct answers are Will, Will, Will not, Will not. The relevant task of teaching is evaluating and selecting questions to elicit productive student writing.

EXHIBIT15.3. **Sample Math Constructed-Response Problem**

Ms. Franco was assessing students' work on comparing fractions. She assigned the following problem:

Put the following fractions in increasing order and explain your reasoning.

$$\frac{4}{7}, \frac{5}{8}, \frac{2}{5}$$

She noticed that Zachary got a correct answer with incorrect reasoning. He explained that $\frac{2}{5} < \frac{4}{7} < \frac{5}{8}$, because $2 < 4 < 5$ and $5 < 7 < 8$.

To help Zachary understand that his reasoning is incorrect, Ms. Franco wants to give a similar problem using 3 different fractions. She wants to include fractions with 3 different numerators and 3 different denominators that, using Zachary's reasoning, would lead to ordering the fractions incorrectly, from greatest to least instead of least to greatest. List 3 such fractions in the boxes below in any order.

The correct answers include any set of fractions in which the magnitude of the fractions is in increasing order while the magnitude of the numerators and/or denominators does not increase. The relevant tasks of teaching are Developing questions, activities, tasks, and problems to elicit student thinking; and Creating or adapting problems that support particular mathematical strategies and practices.

A pool of more than 200 items was developed across the five measures. We piloted the items and conducted cognitive interviews with teachers to elicit their thinking. Psychometric analyses of the pilot data, along with findings from the cognitive interviews and comments from the external reviewers, were used to select and revise the items for inclusion in final versions of the CKT assessments.

THE MET CKT ASSESSMENTS

Administration and Scoring of MET CKT Assessments

The administered forms are summarized in Table 15.2. For each form we report the total number of selected-response and constructed-response items. Table 15.2 also includes data on excluded items and reliability (Cronbach's raw alpha), to be discussed subsequently.

Sample Teachers in the six MET districts could complete assessments online at any time during the administration period. The assessment for teachers of mathematics in grades 4 and 5 was administered in the fall of 2010, and the

TABLE 15.2. **Summary of Question Types, Item Exclusion, and Assessment Reliability**

Assessment Form	Total Selected-Response (SR) Items	SR Items Excluded	SR Item Reliability	Total Constructed-Response Items	Final Reliability
Mathematics 4–5	38	0	0.74	2	0.76
Mathematics 6–8	46	0	0.82	2	0.83
Algebra I	37	2	0.77	0	0.77
ELA 4–6	51	5	0.71	2	0.74
ELA 7–9	48	3	0.66	2	0.69

other four assessments were administered in early 2011. Table 15.3 reports the number of assessments administered and those that were included in scoring.

Overall, approximately 9 percent of assessments were excluded from the analysis based on evidence that these cases were sufficiently problematic that they cast doubt on the validity of the scores. These cases were not included in item analyses and were not individually scored. The largest proportion of excluded cases was due to compelling evidence that two or more teachers collaborated in ways that rendered it impossible to attribute the scores to a particular individual. We excluded additional cases for other reasons that also created concern about "good faith effort," including patterns of responses and response times. Exclusion rates were highest for the elementary assessments.

Item-Level Analyses For each item, we calculated percent of responses correct (i.e., p-plus value) and biserial correlations as measures of item performance. We investigated the impact on the reliability of each assessment when excluding items with poor discrimination, as measured by item biserial correlations (i.e., the relationship between respondents' performance on one item and performance on the entire assessment). First, items, including table items, with negative biserial correlations were excluded. Second, items were eliminated

TABLE 15.3. **Content Knowledge for Teaching (CKT) Assessments Administered and Scored in the MET Study**

Assessment Form	Administered	Excluded	Final Scored Sample	% Scored
Mathematics 4–5	465	68	397	85
Mathematics 6–8	398	25	373	94
Algebra I	148	5	143	97
ELA 4–6	635	80	555	87
ELA 7–9	434	16	418	96
Total	2,080	194	1,886	91

one at a time, starting with the item with the lowest biserial correlation. If the assessment reliability (measured by Cronbach's raw alpha) increased by 0.01 or greater when an item was excluded, then that item was removed from the subsequent score computations and the process was repeated. If the alpha did not increase by 0.01 or more from the previous value following the exclusion of an item, then that item was not removed from the subsequent calculations and the process of excluding items from that assessment was concluded. The number of excluded items by form is reported in Table 15.2.

Scoring of Assessments Each multiple-choice item was given equal weight and counted as 1 point because each requires a single selected response. Analyses indicated that items within table sets could be treated as independent items for scoring purposes. Therefore, we gave all table-item responses the same weight as the multiple-choice item responses. Taking the item in Exhibit 15.2 as an example, a test-taker who answered all four rows correctly was credited with four items correct.

To complete the analysis of the assessments of teacher knowledge, we calculated scores for constructed-response items. For each item, we defined a set of concepts or propositions that represented a correct and complete response to the prompt. We then developed a set of scoring rules that matched the presence of some subset of concepts with a score on the item. Scorers evaluated whether each of the key concepts was present in the response. Inter-rater reliability (quadratic weighted kappa) of human scorers averaged 0.86 for the mathematics assessments and 0.77 for the ELA assessments. Because of the significantly greater effort needed to respond to the constructed-response items, we triple-weighted each of the constructed-response items. However, our analyses indicated that using different weights for the constructed-response items had no meaningful impact on any of the study findings.

Findings from the MET Assessments

This study investigated several validity issues associated with CKT scores. Are these scores sufficiently reliable so as to support meaningful distinctions among teachers across the entire scale? Do teachers who teach different grade levels, and who may have different content-related backgrounds, respond differently to the same CKT items? Is there evidence that assessments in different subjects are measuring different domains of knowledge?

To what extent do scores reflect reliable differences between individuals in their performance on the CKT assessments? The CKT assessments were developed to evaluate differences in teacher knowledge. In this section, we examine how scores are distributed across the sample of teachers in the study. Because different assessment forms included different numbers of items, we transformed all scores to percent correct. Figure 15.1 includes score distribution data for each of the assessments. Across all assessments there was a substantial spread in scores. The range of scores on the ELA assessments was somewhat smaller than for mathematics.

Specific items varied substantially in their difficulty. Averaged across assessment forms, the most difficult items were answered correctly by fewer than 20 percent of teachers. A relatively small number of items were answered correctly by virtually all candidates, and these were always table items in which there was a binary choice.

We then investigated the reliabilities of these scores. Table 15.2 reports two sets of reliabilities (Cronbach's raw alpha), the first based only on the selected-response items and the second also including the constructed-response items.

These reliabilities are less than those associated with traditional tests of teacher knowledge, which have been reported to be in the range of 0.80 to 0.90 (Mitchell, Robinson, Plake, & Knowles, 2001). However, those tests

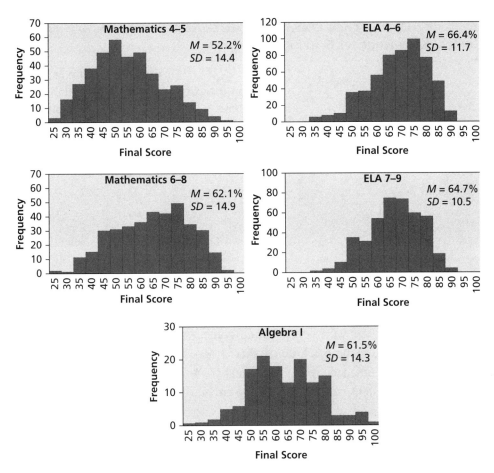

FIGURE 15.1. *Final Score Distributions on CKT Assessments (Percent Correct)*

are expected to be completed in two hours, twice as long as the time designated for the CKT assessments. If the CKT assessments were two hours long, the expected reliabilities, assuming twice as many questions and using the Spearman-Brown prophecy formula, would range from 0.82 to 0.91. These estimated reliabilities of the CKT assessments are comparable in terms of their internal consistency to other measures of teacher knowledge. As with the traditional assessments, reliabilities for the mathematics assessments are somewhat higher than for ELA assessments.

Is there a relationship between how individuals who teach students at different grade levels perform on common subsets of CKT items? Teachers at different grade levels have varying experience in teaching particular concepts. It is

TABLE 15.4. **Comparison of Percent Correct on Common Subsets of Content Knowledge for Teaching (CKT) Items**

Assessment Forms	Items Shared Across Forms	Percentage of Items With Average Scores Higher on Higher-Grade Form
Mathematics 4–5 and Mathematics 6–8	9	100%
Mathematics 6–8 and Algebra I	12	92%
ELA 4–6 and ELA 7–9	19	79%

also true that teachers in middle school are more likely than elementary teachers to major in the content area that they are teaching (Gitomer, 2007). Thus, we explored whether there were consistent differences in performance between these two groups on the same CKT items shared across tests taken by lower-grade and higher-grade teachers (e.g., Mathematics 4–5 versus Mathematics 6–8). We found a consistent pattern, in which a greater percentage of teachers at the higher-grade levels answered common items correctly, compared with teachers at the lower-grade levels. This discrepancy in group performance was greater for mathematics items than for English language arts items (see Table 15.4).

Is there a relationship between elementary teachers' scores across the mathematics and ELA CKT assessments? Stodolsky (1988) demonstrated that elementary teachers employ different instructional practices when they teach different content. For a variety of reasons, including the characteristics of individual teachers and generalized understanding of tasks of teaching, we might expect to see a reasonable correlation between assessments in ELA and in mathematics. However, if the correlation were unitary, we might question whether we were assessing a generalized trait rather than content-specific knowledge.

We compared the 271 teachers who had valid scores for both elementary assessments and found a significant positive correlation between performance on both assessments ($r = 0.49$, $p < .01$), plotted in Figure 15.2.

Are elementary teachers ranked differently depending on which assessment they took? Table 15.5 presents the quartile classification for teachers who took

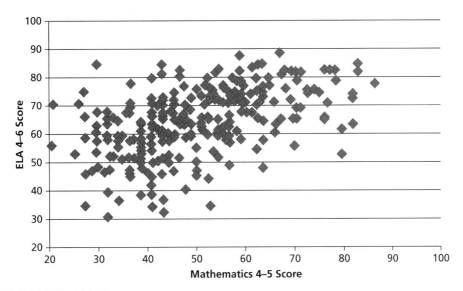

FIGURE 15.2. *Correlation Between Elementary-Level Assessment Scores*

TABLE 15.5. **Elementary Assessment Score Quartile Cross-Tabulation**

Math Scale Score Quartiles	ELA Scale Score Quartiles				
	1	2	3	4	Total
1	51	17	14	3	85
2	18	23	16	8	65
3	8	16	25	16	65
4	5	12	14	25	56
Total	82	68	69	52	271

both assessments. While teachers who did relatively well on one assessment tended to do relatively well on the other assessment, a substantial number of teachers were relatively strong on one test and relatively weak on the other. For example, of the 85 teachers in the lowest mathematics quartile, 17 (20 percent) had ELA CKT scores in the upper two quartiles.

These data suggest that CKT is not simply measuring some general ability. Based on the reliabilities of each of the assessments, if the tests were measuring the same constructs, we would expect a correlation of approximately 0.74 between the two tests, using the formula $\sqrt{r_1 \cdot r_2}$. Given the observed reliabilities of each assessment, the fact that many teachers would be classified differently further supports the idea that CKT is not simply measuring a general skill.

Summary of Assessment Evidence

The evidence from the MET administrations provides support for the validity of the CKT assessments. Items were built on a developing theory of CKT and supported by a design framework for CKT items. Scores were distributed across the scale in ways that suggest substantial individual differences in performance, and the measures were reasonably reliable, particularly in light of the relatively short length of each test's administration. Questionable items that did not meet quality control standards were identified and removed from scoring, eliminating at least one potential source of error and/or bias.

TEACHER REASONING ON CKT TASKS

To better understand the actual knowledge and reasoning used by teachers as they answer the MET items, we conducted a separate study in which we asked a group of teachers selected from the MET sample to describe their thinking as they worked through a subset of MET items. We used the data from this study to investigate three fundamental validity issues.

The first is simply whether we are measuring what we intend to measure. Do test-takers demonstrate correct knowledge and reasoning when selecting the correct answer and also demonstrate incorrect knowledge and reasoning when selecting one of the incorrect answers? The validity claims about what these assessments measure are undermined to the extent that test-takers provide defensible reasoning to support one of the incorrect responses or when certain features of items, such as reading load or a lack of critical information, lead participants to not engage with the item task or response choices as intended.

A second validity issue concerns the design of the assessment tasks and the potential introduction of construct-irrelevant sources of variance. Are the assessment tasks perceived by teachers to legitimately capture problems that arise in practice? Is there anything that suggests that teachers may not understand what the question is asking (independent of whether they are able to answer the question) or may be distracted by some feature of the assessment item that confuses them in ways that were not intended by the design?

A third validity issue addresses the relationship between how teachers reason through individual items and their overall scores on the CKT assessment. To the extent that such relationships exist, this provides evidence that the scores from the assessments are supporting valid inferences about the CKT held by teachers.

Study Design

Sample The study was conducted approximately one year after the CKT testing was completed with teachers who had taken the elementary versions (grades 4 and 5 for mathematics and grades 4 to 6 for ELA) of the CKT assessments. Thirty teachers were interviewed in ELA and 31 in mathematics, with 18 participating in both interviews. Half of the teachers were recruited from the second quartile and half from the fourth (highest) quartile on the given MET assessment. We did not select individuals from the first quartile because their accuracy was at close to chance levels, suggesting that participants may have guessed at answers.[3]

Procedure For mathematics and ELA, a ten-question subset (including table sets with multiple items) of each MET CKT form was selected such that there was a reasonable distribution of difficulty, content coverage, and question type. Abbreviated forms containing these items were then mailed to the participating teachers. Each teacher worked through the ten questions independently and, within two days, participated in a phone interview with a member of the research team, during which they were asked a set of questions that explored their reasoning and perceptions about the assessment questions. The full set of questions was discussed in all but three of the mathematics interviews. In those three interviews there was not sufficient time to discuss the last few questions. Because one of these questions was a table set with five rows, this resulted in a total of eleven missing responses across all the collected data.

The unit of analysis was one person's response to one item, where each multiple-choice item, constructed-response item, and table row was considered a single item. This yielded a total of 640 data points (21 items × 31 teachers minus the 11 missing data points) in mathematics and 540 (18 items × 30 teachers) in ELA for all analyses involving item responses. For analyses of interview questions where an entire table is considered as a whole (e.g., whether the question felt authentic), there was a total of 303 data points in mathematics and 300 in ELA.

Data were transcribed, cleaned, and uploaded into the Dedoose qualitative software for coding purposes. Coding was done by two groups from the research team, one with ELA content and teaching expertise, the other with mathematics content and teaching expertise. Approximately one-third of responses were double- or group-coded to maintain consistency of coding over time.

Coding Teacher Reasoning

To provide a context for understanding the results presented in this section, we provide in this section examples that illustrate our coding rules and decisions.

Teacher reasoning was coded as *conforming* or *not conforming* to the TDR, where conforming to the TDR indicates that the teacher has engaged with the item as designed and reasoned in a way that demonstrated CKT. Using the TDR, the coding system specified the essential information required for the response to count as conforming. For example, for the Ms. Hupman item presented in Exhibit 15.1, a response was coded as conforming if the test-taker selected 2^2 *and* also indicated that a student would provide a seemingly correct answer by using either a correct or an incorrect process to evaluate 2^2.

Conforming responses characteristically showed evidence that the test-taker had understood the task of teaching, often explicitly relating it to the idea that the purpose of such an assessment problem is for the teacher to know what the student understands. For example, one teacher stated:

> **Teacher (T):** *She wants her students to show their proficiency in evaluating an exponential expression. I think that, and which is least useful. I think the common mistake that a student would make in this is multiplying the whole number by the exponent so option three, two times two is four and two squared is the same thing, also four. So giving students that problem doesn't give you clarity as to whether they understand exponents or if they're still confusing them with multiplying the whole number by the exponent directly.*

Responses often indicated that the teacher was familiar with the common student error of multiplying base and exponent.

> **T:** *It's a very common misconception of what to do with the exponent, and what that exponent means.*

> **Interviewer (I):** *Can you say a little more about the common misconception?*

T: *Sure, a common misconception would just be to see the number and then to see the exponent and to multiply the two.*

However, it was not necessary for the teacher to report familiarity with an error in order for the response to conform. The TDR allows for variation in how a test-taker might understand the item, including the possibility of figuring out what a plausible student error is, even when unfamiliar with the error.

T: *So then, in option two, two to the third power, two times two is four times two is eight. They couldn't just multiply the two times the three. I would have imagined some students would make that mistake. In option three, the two squared would be just two times two. So they could use that exponent as a factor instead and get the same answer.*

Most non-conforming responses were ones in which teachers answered incorrectly by not connecting the mathematical content to the task of teaching. In the response below, the teacher decided that all the problems are equally useful because they are all basic and represent content you would want to teach to students. The response takes into account the given context, that the teacher is teaching an introductory unit on exponents, but fails to take into account the purpose of an assessment problem.

T: *Well, I picked . . . I mean, sorry to generalize all of them, but I mean the lady is teaching them how to evaluate very simple exponential expressions, and I feel like all of these are pretty basic. I mean, if I was going to teach exponents, these are probably three problems that I would choose to use because, . . . especially option three, because . . . I mean two times two is a very basic fact that the kids have learned and I would probably use option two to say, "Okay, let's see two to the third power, see how easy it is. All you're adding is another two to it." And then say . . . well. . . Because a lot of kids will say, "Well, can you do this with every number?" Well, of course you can. So then I would say option three, well three to the third power would be three times three times three. So I feel like I would use all of these, to be honest.*

The same teacher goes on to summarize her sense of the teacher's purpose as represented in the item and clearly states that the purpose of such a strategy is to understand whether the students learned.

T: *I feel like she wanted to give a quick problem at the end of class to check their proficiency, and I think that's good. That's like an exit ticket type of strategy to see if they learned anything today and any of these options, all three of them. She could write all of them on the board.*

What the teacher does not seem to understand in this case is how a specific problem can serve to reveal or conceal student misunderstandings from the teacher because of the ways in which students tend to misunderstand exponents. It is as though her view of assessment assumes a student who understands will answer any problem right, and one who doesn't will answer any problem wrong. She is not able to take into account the specific ways in which students might misunderstand. For her, the selection of an assessment problem really is more about tracking mastery than about understanding student thinking.

Similarly, other responses also focused on the perceived need for "quick" assessment problems and concluded that any of these problems would do because they can all be computed quickly. Such responses show that the test-taker was attentive to the given context, but failed to connect with the idea that assessment problems are really about student thinking.

Another way in which responses failed to conform was by the teacher not understanding what kinds of errors students make. The teacher below focused on the size of the numbers, concluding that, because both 2 and 3 are small numbers, students would have equal difficulty with them.

T: *Well, I just looked at those numbers, and you know they're pretty small numbers, and I just said, well, three time three times three and I just kept on going to the next one.*

I: *And then for option two what was your thinking on that one?*

T: *Same thing, I just looked at this because that number was a two right there and then two times two times two.*

I: *And for option three?*

T: *Same, two squared is just two squared is two squared equals four, yeah.*

I: *Can you just walk me through how this, how options one, two, and three, looking through them helped you to select option four?*

T: *Yeah, the reason being that just because the numbers, the whole numbers were low, because they're just doing simple you know one, two, three, that's the only reason why I chose option four.*

I: *Because, I'm sorry you said all of the numbers were . . .*

T: *Yeah, well, just relatively small numbers.*

While it is true that a student might make arithmetic errors in working by hand with large numbers, this would not represent a conceptual misunderstanding of exponents, and it is far more common that students first learning this content struggle with the meaning of the operation than with the size of the numbers. Even if this teacher understood that an assessment problem should reveal common student misconceptions, he was simply unfamiliar with student thinking about exponents so was unable to take into account how students might answer these problems incorrectly.

Also worth noting in the Ms. Hupman item responses is that none were coded as non-conforming due to incorrect content alone, and only one was coded as demonstrating any incorrect content knowledge at all. While this pattern does not generalize to all CKT items, it does illustrate clearly how such an item measures more than simply the associated student-level content knowledge. Even if a teacher is quite able to evaluate exponential expressions, this is not sufficient to determine which problems will elicit student thinking in appropriate ways. And even if the content represented is relatively easy, solving the CKT item can be difficult. Most people can evaluate the exponential expressions without difficulty. In the MET administration, only 39 percent of elementary teachers and 58 percent of middle school teachers answered this item correctly, and most of those who answered incorrectly chose "equally useful" as an answer, just as the teachers in the cognitive interviews did.

Summary Findings of Cognitive Interviews

Coding results were aggregated over teachers for each item and summarized over all items. While there are interesting patterns of results for each item, only the aggregated data across items and teachers are reported in this analysis. All data are reported by subject area.

To what extent was the answer key defensible? To what extent did the knowledge and reasoning elicited by the CKT item reflect the TDR? For each participant who gave a correct answer we looked to see whether the reasoning conformed to the TDR, and for each participant who gave an incorrect answer we looked to see whether the reasoning did not conform to the TDR.

The vast majority of responses, 89 percent in mathematics and 91 percent in ELA, showed the pattern we would expect. Correct answers corresponded to conforming reasoning, and incorrect responses corresponded to non-conforming reasoning. Of the 455 correct responses in the mathematics interviews, 385 (85 percent) conformed. Of the 399 correct responses in ELA, 348 (87 percent) were conforming. By definition, all incorrect responses did not conform (185 and 141 incorrect responses, respectively).

We found no systematic evidence of problems with the keying of items. Reported confusion about the questions was relatively infrequent as well. Teachers reported being confused for construct-irrelevant reasons in fewer than 5 percent of item responses in mathematics and fewer than 11 percent of item responses in ELA, indicating limited evidence that construct-irrelevant factors affected participant reasoning. Of course, what the reporting of construct-irrelevant factors means is itself unclear. Such reporting may also reflect an inability to focus on the construct-relevant features of the problem and may not be an indictment of the questions themselves.

To what extent did the items remind teachers of an authentic problem that would be encountered in real teaching? The vast majority of responses across all items confirmed that the teaching problems represented in the CKT assessments were familiar to teachers. Indeed, 97 percent of responses in mathematics and 96 percent of those in ELA indicated that the items reminded the teachers of something they experienced in their teaching or that the items included problems they expected other teachers might encounter. Such strong face validity can reduce construct-irrelevant variance that may result from test-takers feeling that test questions are irrelevant to them and also provide support for the theoretical basis for the CKT items.

To what extent were teachers' scores on the MET CKT assessment related to the quality of the reasoning they demonstrated as they solved these items? We examined the extent to which the nature of reasoning on particular items was associated with how well the teachers performed when they took the assessments the prior year. For Mathematics 4–5, the correlation between total assessment scores and interview item scores for all participants ($n = 397$) is $r = 0.88$, $p < .01$. For ELA 4–6, ($n = 555$), it is $r = 0.78$, $p < .01$, indicating that the reliability of the two versions of the measure is strong.

Figures 15.3 and 15.4 illustrate the degree to which the quartile groupings on the CKT assessment differ when taking into account the entire test or only considering the subset of items used in the interviews. In each plot, the boxes represent scores from the 25th to 75th percentiles, and the horizontal line within boxes represents the median percent correct. The lines extending from the boxes represent the full range of scores and show there is minimal overlap among the quartile groups. Taken together, these analyses

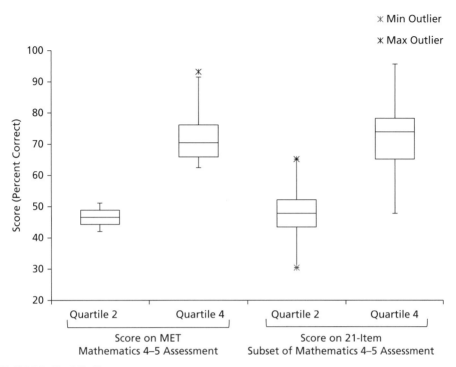

FIGURE 15.3. *Scores on MET Mathematics Assessment Compared to Scores on Subset of Items Used in Interviews*

support the argument that the items selected for the interviews are representative of the full set of items on the MET test forms and that the quality of reasoning demonstrated in the interviews is highly related to the MET CKT scores.

We then examined the quality of item reasoning by quartile group. For both mathematics and ELA, there is substantial variation across items in the extent to which assessment scores are related to quality of reasoning. In mathematics, group differences are highly significant, χ^2 (1, N = 640) = 80.97, $p < .01$, and the association between MET quartile and aligning justification is strong. Teachers who score better on the MET elementary mathematics tests are much more likely to engage in reasoning that conforms to the TDR. For ELA, group differences are significant, but much less consistent, χ^2 (1, N = 540) = 3.91, $p < .05$. Teachers who score better on the MET elementary ELA tests are somewhat more likely to engage in reasoning that conforms to the TDR (see Table 15.6).

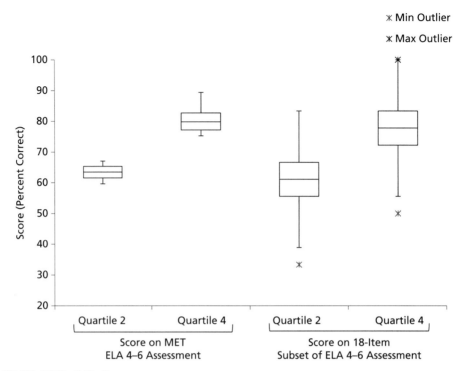

FIGURE 15.4. *Scores on MET ELA Assessment Compared to Scores on Subset of Items Used in Interviews*

TABLE 15.6. **Conformity to TDR by MET Quartile Group**

	Conforms (%)	Does Not Conform (%)
Mathematics Responses (n = 640)		
Quartile 2	141 (43)	186 (57)
Quartile 4	244 (78)	69 (22)
ELA Responses (n = 540)		
Quartile 2	163 (60)	107 (40)
Quartile 4	185 (69)	85 (31)

Summary of Interview Evidence

Interviews of MET teachers provide substantial support for the claims that items are correctly keyed, that they measure the intended knowledge and reasoning, and that they function as designed to elicit CKT. Items are sensitive to significant differences in the quality of reasoning that teachers bring to particular problems. Teachers confirmed that the items are representative of real teaching problems that they and their colleagues face, and there is little indication that item performance might be subject to construct-irrelevant sources of variance. Thus, there is strong evidence that a correct answer on these items is associated with reasoning that is consistent with the task rationale.

We also found support for the claim that CKT scores are an indication of more effective CKT reasoning. This was particularly true in mathematics, where the relationship between performance on the interviews and scores on the MET CKT assessment is strong. The relationship for ELA is significant, but not as consistent.

DISCUSSION

Contributions to the Development of CKT Assessments

The work described in this chapter makes several key contributions to efforts to systematically develop rigorous assessments of CKT. We have presented a framework for the design of CKT assessments organized around the fundamental aspects of the instructional work of teaching that is common across content areas and also for content-specific tasks of teaching. This framework was used to guide the design of assessments and assessment tasks within the content areas that were tested in the MET study. Our goal was to develop a generative framework to be used to move forward into new content domains by supporting the specification of tasks of teaching that are relevant to content-specific assessments. This framework represents a step forward from approaches that have grown out of the relatively *ad hoc* identification of interesting contexts and problems, as identified within a single subject. The presence of a framework provides, first, a set of theoretical claims about the nature of the construct that can then be evaluated through a range of validity studies. Second, the framework provides a language and set of targets not only for assessment developers, but also for the professional development of teachers.

A second contribution has been the first large-scale application of CKT to the domain of English language arts. Differences between ELA and mathematics presented unique challenges to the design of the corresponding tasks of teaching and assessments. The ELA domain does not lend itself to determinations of correctness in the same way that mathematics does. Rather, teaching ELA and, consequently, the CKT assessments for ELA, depend in part on expert judgments and wisdom of practice to determine best instructional responses to a particular situation. Using content knowledge in ELA teaching may involve consideration of how students' particular backgrounds and interests shape their interactions with particular tasks, or it may involve consideration of the literacy or instructional purposes for a task. Inherently, deciding whether a student's solution to a mathematical expression is correct is qualitatively different from judging whether an opening to a short story should be judged as trite for a given student or in a particular context.

Despite these challenges, we successfully developed assessments that were comparable in their measurement quality to existing tests of teacher knowledge. While the reliability coefficients were lower for the CKT tests, they were half the length of knowledge tests in current use. Had the tests been equivalent lengths, the reliabilities would have been comparable to the more traditional knowledge tests, such as those from the Praxis Series™. CKT tests for ELA were less reliable than those for mathematics, a finding that is also true for traditional content tests for teachers (Educational Testing Service, 2010, p. 58), likely indicating domain difference rather than an inherent shortcoming of the CKT measures.

The tests were able to discriminate reliably among teachers, and there were substantial differences in individual performance. For elementary teachers who took both tests, those who did better on one test tended to do better on the other, but the assessments were also picking up subject-specific knowledge. Many teachers performed differently on the two assessments. Teachers who taught higher-grade levels and likely had more substantial training in specific content areas tended to do better on items that were common across assessments.

The CKT items in both mathematics and ELA had score distributions that are in keeping with expected values for teacher knowledge assessments. This is an initial, but very important, type of validity evidence. That items fit to a scale score provides evidence that they are defensibly scored. In addition, that these items formed a scale score that has acceptable levels of reliability is evidence that we are controlling sources of error in the measure and generalizing to a potentially larger set of items that goes beyond the particular items used in these assessments. The evidence from these interviews provided strong support, at least for the subset of items included in the cognitive interviews, for the claim that the response choices performed as intended.

We also drew on data from the teacher interviews to examine the extent to which the item tasks elicited the knowledge and reasoning expected in the domain of content knowledge for teaching. The results confirmed the intended design. We found substantial support that the items were measuring what we had intended and that the correctness of a response was very strongly related to the quality of reasoning and knowledge that teachers used in reasoning through the response. We also found a very strong correlation between the quality of reasoning through these items and overall test scores for mathematics. We found a significant but weaker relationship for ELA. These results, taken together, support the argument that differences in test scores are related to the underlying knowledge and reasoning that defines CKT.

Next Steps Toward Improving the Understanding of CKT Assessment Validity

As a dynamic process, other steps can be taken to investigate and strengthen the validity argument for these measures. A next step would be to submit both the design framework and the assessments themselves to independent expert review. While the overall development effort involved multiple individuals and many internal reviews, it is important to include judgments from expert individuals who have not been involved with the process to date. Independent expert review can be used to evaluate the task of teaching framework, the appropriateness of scoring rules, and the overall structure of the assessments to provide backing for the claim that the tested tasks of teaching are representative of the larger framework.

The second important validation direction is to investigate the CKT assessment scores related to other measures of interest. Two classes of measures that have been the focus of the MET study are those based on student achievement and those based on classroom observation. We made the decision to focus on the relationship with other classes of measures in subsequent publications to give that work the treatment it deserves. However, we take this opportunity to begin to lay out the validity argument for these inferences.

The primary issue to consider in such an analysis is how, why, and to what degree two measures should be related. In terms of classroom observation, there is very limited theoretical and empirical work that explores how CKT is related to classroom interactions. A few studies in mathematics (Baumert et al., 2010;

Hill et al., 2008) begin to make the argument, but neither used large-scale observation instruments of the type used in MET. Even the version of the Mathematical Quality of Instruction (MQI) protocol used in the Hill study is substantially different from the observation protocol used in MET.

Nevertheless, it would be reasonable to expect some relationship between measures of CKT and those dimensions of classroom observation most directly associated with teachers' use of content knowledge. There is no reason to expect that many of the other facets of instruction measured by these protocols would be related to CKT at all. Thus, we would expect any correlational analyses to show stronger correlations of CKT with content-related dimensions of the respective protocols than with those that are not grounded in content.

However, to the extent that the observed lessons, in MET, do not provide opportunity for exercise of many of the tasks of teaching described in the framework, correlations may be weak overall. For example, if the majority of teachers are not asking questions that elicit student thinking, providing feedback, or asking students to engage in substantial reasoning, then we would not expect to see strong relationships because of the restricted range of the criterion measure. Indeed, in MET, scores were lowest on many of the content-related measures across protocols. Thus, the knowledge being assessed by the CKT assessments may not be used very much in routine classroom practice. Such practice may be due to decisions of the teacher or may be the result of constraints (real or imagined) imposed by the curriculum and district/school policy. Thus, although we expect some relationship between CKT and classroom observations, they should not be uniform and are unlikely to be very strong.

Additionally, we do not have a clear understanding of what kind of instruction is producing gains associated with value-added estimates. Absolute gains on annual achievement tests are typically quite modest. Student gains by middle school are about 0.25 of a standard deviation of the previous year test scores (Bloom, Hill, Black, & Lipsey, 2008). If students are, in effect, answering only a very few items correctly on an annual basis, what is it that they are learning? If, for example, teachers can achieve gains in low-performing mathematics students by using drill-and-practice techniques, then CKT might not be related at all to the observed gains.

The argument would be much more compelling if it were clear that students who gain the most are actually improving their understanding in ways that would demand more substantive content-focused instruction and, therefore, CKT. Although, as noted in other chapters in this volume, the MET project showed a minimal overall relationship between CKT and value-added (VAM) scores, this may reflect a legitimate disconnect between what accounts for higher VAM scores in MET classrooms and what CKT is measuring.

Given current limitations in theory, available measures, and the sophistication of study design and modeling techniques, we are cautious about including as part of the validity argument claims that CKT scores will necessarily be strongly related either to measures of instruction or to student outcomes. Even the MET study, which is unparalleled in scope and sophistication, relies on models that omit many critical variables that would be needed in order to provide adequate backing for warrants that would support or refute a validity argument. Before such efforts can be undertaken, much more needs to be understood about the limitations of current theory, models, and measures to guard against unwarranted conclusions about test validity. For example, in new work to explore these issues, we are pursuing the question of how content knowledge for teaching in a very bounded content area is enacted in the teaching of that content and reflected by tightly aligned measures of student learning in that content area. With such a targeted design, we hope to be able to make a tighter theoretical connection between CKT and teaching quality.

Policy Implications

At this point, the policy implications for the development of CKT assessments are speculative. There is reasonably strong evidence that the assessments are capturing information about teacher knowledge that is grounded in teaching practice. However, as noted above, we must have a better understanding of how teacher knowledge, classroom practice, and student learning are related. Before concluding that CKT ought to be included in the evaluation of teachers, stronger theoretical and empirical support is required.

We have only just begun to explore the range of uses that might be appropriate for tests of CKT. The study reported in this chapter focused on practicing teachers with a general emphasis on assessing teaching quality. However, CKT assessments could also be a powerful tool for use in initial certification, and even to support teacher education or professional development.

In other work, we are investigating performance on these assessments for individuals in teacher education programs. Of interest is how individuals who have not yet spent much, if any, time in classroom practice perform on these measures. This work provides us with information about the relationships of

CKT to conventional measures of teacher content knowledge in mathematics and ELA, something we were unable to do in MET. Initial findings from the study of prospective teachers suggest that content knowledge is a necessary but insufficient prerequisite for CKT. Having content knowledge is necessary to do well on the CKT assessments, but there are individuals with content knowledge who also do relatively poorly on the assessments. Further, we find that teacher education students almost uniformly perceive the assessments to be measuring important things for them to learn and that engaging with the items is a productive use of time. However, they also report that not all teacher preparation programs develop the kind of knowledge and skills that are valued in these assessments. These initial findings support the promise of the CKT measures for guiding teacher education, and for use in certification assessment.

Taking this work, as well as research upon which this study has built, there is sufficient validity evidence to warrant further studies to investigate the development and use of CKT assessments in a variety of professional contexts, including teacher preparation. A series of carefully carried out interventions that attempt to develop CKT in targeted areas and examine effects on practice and student learning can provide important insight into the utility of this construct and associated assessments for improving practice.

NOTES

1. When the project started, Drew Gitomer was a researcher at ETS. He later moved to Rutgers University during the project.

2. Although algebra is often taught prior to ninth grade, the MET project focused on algebra teaching only in ninth grade.

3. In order to recruit an adequate sample, two individuals who had scores at the high end of the first quartile were included.

REFERENCES AND ADDITIONAL RESOURCES

Abell, S. K. (2007). Research on science teacher knowledge. In S. K. Abell & N. G. Lederman (Eds.), *Handbook of research on science education* (pp. 1105–1149). Mahwah, NJ: Lawrence Erlbaum Associates.

Ball, D. L., Thames, M. H., & Phelps, G. (2008). Content knowledge for teaching: What makes it special? *Journal of Teacher Education, 59*(5), 389–407. doi: 10.1177/0022487108324554

Baumert, J., Kunter, M., Blum, W., Brunner, M., Voss, T., Jordan, A., . . . Tsai, Y.-M. (2010). Teachers' mathematical knowledge, cognitive activation in the classroom, and student progress. *American Educational Research Journal, 47*(1), 133–180. doi: 10.3102/0002831209345157

Baxter, J., & Lederman, N. (1999). Assessment and measurement of pedagogical content knowledge. In J. Gess-Newsome & N. G. Lederman (Eds.), *Examining pedagogical content knowledge, 6,* 147–161. Netherlands: Kluwer Academic Publishers. doi: 10.1007/0-306-47217-1_6

Bloom, H. S., Hill, C. J., Black, A. R., & Lipsey, M. W. (2008). *Performance trajectories and performance gaps as achievement effect-size benchmarks for educational interventions* (MDRC Working Paper on Research Methodology). New York, NY: MDRC. Retrieved from http://www.mdrc.org/sites/default/files/full_473.pdf

Buschang, R. E., Chung, G. K., Delacruz, G. C., & Baker, E. L. (2012). Validating measures of algebra teacher subject matter knowledge and pedagogical content knowledge. *Educational Assessment, 17*(1), 1–21. doi: 10.1080/10627197.2012.697847

Carlisle, J. F., Correnti, R., Phelps, G., & Zeng, J. (2009). Exploration of the contribution of teachers' knowledge about reading to their students' improvement in reading. *Reading and Writing, 22*(4), 457–486. doi: 10.1007/s11145-009-9165-y

Educational Testing Service. (2010). *Praxis™ technical manual.* Princeton, NJ: Educational Testing Service.

Gitomer, D. H. (2007). *Teacher quality in a changing policy landscape: Improvements in the teacher pool.* (Policy Information Report). Princeton, NJ: Educational Testing Service.

Higher Education Act of 1998, Pub. L. No. 105-244, § 112, Stat. 1581 (1998).

Hill, H. C. (2007). Mathematical knowledge of middle school teachers: Implications for the No Child Left Behind Policy Initiative. *Educational Evaluation and Policy Analysis, 29*(2), 95–114. doi: 10.3102/0162373707301711

Hill, H. C., Blunk, M. L., Charalambous, C. Y., Lewis, J. M., Phelps, G. C., Sleep, L., & Ball, D. L. (2008). Mathematical knowledge for teaching and the mathematical quality of instruction: An exploratory study. *Cognition and Instruction, 26,* 430–511. doi: 10.1080/07370000802177235

Hill, H. C., Dean, C., & Goffney, I. M. (2007). Assessing elemental and structural validity: Data from teachers, non-teachers, and mathematicians. *Measurement, 5*(2–3), 81–92. doi: 10.1080/15366360701486999

Hill, H. C., Rowan, B., & Ball, D. L. (2005). Effects of teachers' mathematical knowledge for teaching on student achievement. *American Educational Research Journal, 42*(2), 371–406. doi: 10.3102/00028312042002371

Hill, H. C., Schilling, S., & Ball, D. L. (2004). Developing measures of teachers' mathematics knowledge for teaching. *The Elementary School Journal, 105*(1), 11–30. doi: 10.1086/428763

Hill, H. C., Umland, K., Litke, E., & Kapitula, L. R. (2012). Teacher quality and quality teaching: Examining the relationship of a teacher assessment to practice. *American Journal of Education, 118*(4), 489–519. doi: 10.1086/666380

Kane, M. T. (1992). An argument-based approach to validity. *Psychological Bulletin, 112*(3), 527–535. doi: 10.1037/0033-2909.112.3.527

Kane, M. T. (2006). Validation. In R. L. Brennan (Ed.), *Educational measurement* (4th ed., pp. 17–64). New York, NY: Praeger.

Kersting, N. B. (2008). Using video clips of mathematics classroom instruction as item prompts to measure teachers' knowledge of teaching mathematics. *Educational and Psychological Measurement, 68*(5), 845–861. doi: 10.1177/0013164407313369

Kersting, N. B., Givvin, K. B., Sotelo, F. L., & Stigler, J. W. (2010). Teachers' analyses of classroom video predict student learning of mathematics: Further explorations of a novel measure of teacher knowledge. *Journal of Teacher Education, 61*(1–2), 172–181. doi: 10.1177/0022487109347875

Kersting, N. B., Givvin, K. B., Thompson, B. J., Santagata, R., & Stigler, J. W. (2012). Measuring usable knowledge: Teachers' analyses of mathematics classroom videos predict teaching quality and student learning. *American Educational Research Journal, 49*(3), 568–589. doi: 10.3102/0002831212437853

Krauss, S., Baumert, J., & Blum, W. (2008). Secondary mathematics teachers' pedagogical content knowledge and content knowledge: Validation of the COACTIV constructs. *ZDM, The International Journal on Mathematics Education 40*(5), 873–892. doi: 10.1007/s11858-008-0141-9

Krauss, S., Brunner, M., Kunter, M., Baumert, J., Blum, W., Neubrand, M., & Jordan, A. (2008). Pedagogical content knowledge and content knowledge of secondary mathematics teachers. *Journal of Educational Psychology, 100*(3), 716–725. doi: 10.1037/0022-0663.100.3.716

Kucan, L., Hapgood, S., & Palincsar, A. S. (2011). Teachers' specialized knowledge for supporting student comprehension in text-based discussions. *The Elementary School Journal, 112*(1), 61–82. doi: http://dx.doi.org/10.1086/660689

Magnusson, S., Krajcik, J., & Borko, H. (1999). Nature, sources, and development of pedagogical content knowledge for science teaching. In J. Gess-Newsome & N. G. Lederman (Eds.), *Examining pedagogical content knowledge: The construct and its implications for science education* (Vol. 6, pp. 95–132). Netherlands: Kluwer Academic Publishers. doi: 10.1007/0-306-47217-1

Mitchell, K. J., Robinson, D. Z., Plake, B. S., & Knowles, K. T. (Eds.). (2001). *Testing teacher candidates: The role of licensure tests in improving teacher quality.* Washington, DC: National Academies Press.

Niess, M. L. (2005). Preparing teachers to teach science and mathematics with technology: Developing a technology pedagogical content knowledge. *Teaching and Teacher Education, 21*(5), 509–523. doi: http://dx.doi.org/10.1016/j.tate.2005.03.006

Phelps, G. (2009). Just knowing how to read isn't enough! Assessing knowledge for teaching reading. *Educational Assessment, Evaluation and Accountability, 21*(2), 137–154. doi: 10.1007/s11092-009-9070-6

Phelps, G., & Schilling, S. (2004). Developing measures of content knowledge for teaching reading. *The Elementary School Journal, 105*(1), 31–48. doi: 10.1086/428764

Shulman, L. S. (1986). Those who understand: Knowledge growth in teaching. *Educational Researcher, 15*(2), 4–14. doi: 10.3102/0013189X015002004.

Stodolsky, S. S. (1988). *The subject matters: Classroom activity in math and social studies.* Chicago, IL: University of Chicago Press.

Van Driel, J. H., Verloop, N., & De Vos, W. (1998). Developing science teachers' pedagogical content knowledge. *Journal of Research in Science Teaching, 35*(6), 673–695. doi: 10.1002/(SICI)1098-2736

CHAPTER

16

Optimizing Resources to Maximize Student Gains

CATHERINE A. McCLELLAN, JOHN R. DONOGHUE, AND ROBERT PIANTA

ABSTRACT

In this study, data were simulated to investigate the effects on student learning of two interventions: professional development (PD) and student-teacher assignment. The assumptions made as the basis of the simulation, and the research from which they were drawn, are described in detail. The professional development intervention was structured based on a fixed budget, so that the number of teachers receiving the PD was limited by the cost of the PD and the financial resources available. Teachers with the greatest need, as indicated by the smallest academic gains in their classes, were chosen for the PD intervention when costs limited the number of teachers to whom it could be offered. The assignment intervention was designed using either random assignment or the best alignment of students and teacher on content knowledge, on instructional and learning styles, or both. Results for all conditions are measured as the percentage of possible instructional units delivered; the number of students with no academic gain; the number of students with the maximum possible academic gain; and the number of students who complete the course with full knowledge of the course contents. With two exceptions, all conditions produced similar results. The best results were observed when students and teachers were matched on content knowledge or on instructional and learning styles.

INTRODUCTION

Education decision-makers at all levels struggle with allocating limited resources to maximize the effectiveness of teacher evaluation systems. A teacher evaluation system serves two primary related purposes: (1) to improve teacher skills and student academic outcomes and (2) to inform human resource decisions such as retention and rewards. The present study focuses on resource allocation in service of the first goal, that is, it simulates the consequences of different approaches to improving classroom skills and student achievement— either through assignment of teachers or through enrolling teachers in professional development. Presumably, district leaders could choose to improve teacher and student performance by assigning certain teachers to certain groups of students, based on profiles of their characteristics, in an effort to achieve a good match between teacher and learner; alternatively, districts could invest in professional development of teachers as a means to improve performance.

This study attempts to provide some direction on optimizing choices when investing resources based on currently available research findings. The study is a simulation, so the data are not "real" in the sense of being collected directly from teachers and students, but the designs are based on data from the Measures of Effective Teaching study (2012), among others. The work investigates the impact of different decisions about how teachers are assigned to professional development and how effective it is, given a fixed budget of resources. Although the results are not drawn from experiments in classrooms, nonetheless, they can provide insights and ideas for decision making in one aspect of complex and heavily constrained education systems. The primary research questions investigate the impact of different decisions about the distribution and intensity of teacher professional development, given a fixed budget of resources, and what combination of interventions leads to the maximum gains in student performances. Because the data are simulated, as with any simulation, a set of assumptions is necessary to build the data sets. Various aspects of the design are described in detail in the "Design of Data used in this Study" section, so that the basis for the conclusions and inferences are clear. We recognize at the outset that the data, simulations, and results are based on a set of assumptions about teachers and learners and measuring their performance; it is certainly possible to make other sets of assumptions. The ones here were selected based on data from existing research or widespread beliefs about the US educational system.

In order to make the simulation approximate the real world, both the assumptions and data structure needed are quite complex. The results of the instruction under different assumptions about the two "interventions" being simulated—professional development and student-teacher assignment—are described in the Interventions section. Interpretation of the results and possible inferences and actions that might follow are provided in the "The Impact of PD section," along with some thoughts on the broader value of work of this type. *It is important to remember that this study is a simulation and that, in the context of actual schools and districts, actual results may vary.* We advance this work not only for the possible interest in the results obtained for professional development or student-teacher assignment as interventions, but also for the broader purpose of demonstrating that challenging problems in education may benefit from the use of simulation in order to more fully examine tradeoffs and expected benefits to be obtained from various decisions. It is our impression that the MET study data set offers district leaders an unprecedented opportunity for such activities.

CONCEPTUAL FRAMEWORK

The statistician George Box once wrote that "Essentially, all models are wrong, but some are useful." We believe that simulations and models such as the one presented here can be useful. They allow education researchers and theoreticians to examine a variety of assumptions with a quick feedback loop. If the results conform to expectations, there is some evidence that the ideas the model is based on are at least internally consistent. If the results depart from the expectations, it presents a constructive opportunity. It may be that the assumptions have to be reconsidered, or the unexpected result may provide an insight suggesting a new line empirical investigation. In this section we outline the conceptual and empirical bases for choosing between teacher professional development or student-teacher assignment as a means to improve teacher and student performance.

Teacher Professional Development as an Intervention to Improve Performance

Recent federal policies, such as Race to the Top, that fund measuring and improving teaching performance have increased demand for teaching effectiveness that is linked with gains in student achievement. Traditionally, professional development (PD) programs have been used as a mechanism for improving the quality of classroom instruction and student achievement (Yoon, Duncan, Lee, Scarloss, & Shapley, 2007). However, there has been a lack of well-conducted studies that provide empirical evidence on effect sizes of PD programs that measure their impact on student achievement.

Characteristics of effective PD programs include coherence, active participation, and a focus on content knowledge and classroom practice. The No Child Left Behind Act of 2001 (2002) mandates teachers to receive high-quality PD that accompanies the following criteria:

- Is sustained, intensive, and content focused (effects on classroom instruction and teacher performance)

- Aligns with state academic content standards, student achievement standards, and assessments

- Improves teachers' knowledge of subjects they teach

- Advances teachers' understanding of effective instructional strategies based on scientific research

- Is regularly evaluated for effects on teacher effectiveness and student achievement

Despite these guidelines, there has been criticism surrounding the effectiveness of PD programs; studies have found that PD programs based on single-shot, one-day workshops are often superficial and incoherent (Ball & Cohen, 1999; Pianta, 2011; Wilson & Berne, 1999). Yoon and others (2007) examined 1,300 studies that have addressed the effect of PD on student achievement. However, only nine of those studies met the authors' qualifications for scientific evidence. More recently, Blank (2009) conducted a meta-analytic study that examined the same question of PD effects on student achievement and was only able to identify sixteen qualified studies from a total of seventy-four more narrowly focused studies.

Importantly, most models of effective PD programs that affect student achievement follow the logic model illustrated in Figure 16.1 (Blank, 2009; Yoon and others, 2007). In this model of the hypothesized chain of PD influence, the effect of PD intervention on student achievement is mediated by teacher knowledge and skills and practices of classroom teaching; if one link is weak or missing, then increased student learning may not occur.

FIGURE 16.1. *Effect of Professional Development on Student Achievement*

Note: Figure modified from Yoon, Duncan, Lee, Scarloss, and Shapley, 2007.

Other frameworks such as Pianta (2011) and Allen, Pianta, Gregory, Mikami, and Lun (2011) characterize the mediators in Figure 16.1 as "teacher-student interactions." In either case, PD is presumed to have its effect on student achievement because it changes teachers' knowledge or skill (or interactions), which in turn changes student learning.

The following study designs have been identified in evaluating PD effects on teachers and students:

- *Randomized controlled trials (RCT):* Participants are randomly assigned to different experimental groups (control versus treatment).

- *Quasi-experimental design (QED):* Designs do not require random assignment of participants; however, groups are matched or assumed to be equivalent prior to PD intervention.

Most studies that failed to be included in Yoon and others' 2007 meta-analyses had problems with study design. Most studies using QED had problems in establishing equivalence between treatment and control groups at baseline. Furthermore, most studies did not take into consideration the clustering effect of students[1] who are nested within teachers or classrooms. In attempting to summarize effect sizes across studies, the quality of empirical evidence is of critical concern. So even though most studies consistently show that PD programs enhance teacher knowledge and skills, a poorly designed evaluation creates challenges in estimating proper effect sizes and attributing the causal influence to teacher PD. In general, most studies have examined PD in the context of workshops, not studying the effects on classroom observations or teacher skills or reporting pre- and post-intervention scores of student achievement. Studies have ranged widely in specific analytic technique used. Summarizing across these varied analytic techniques is challenging.

Main Findings from Teacher PD Studies The central finding in Yoon and others (2007) is that teachers who receive substantial PD (average of forty-nine hours) can improve student achievement, based on studies completed in elementary school settings. The average increase in student achievement across science, mathematics, and reading/ELA was 0.54 standard deviation units or about 21 percentile points. This is an unusually large effect size and not typical of findings in other studies, which raises questions at the outset. To follow up on Yoon and others (2007), Blank (2009) conducted a meta-analysis that examined PD effect sizes on student achievement, focusing on mathematics and science across grade levels. This report identified sixteen studies and 104 effect sizes, with results ranging across elementary, middle, and high schools. The results in Blank (2009) indicate smaller average effect sizes than those reported in Yoon and others (2007) but nonetheless suggest that there is some validity for the chain in the PD logic model that links PD inputs to effects on teacher or student performance. Tables 16.A.1 to 16.A.4 in the Appendix provide details of the studies and effect sizes from Yoon and others (2007) and the Blank (2009) report.

Observation of teaching practice based on highly structured protocols is a relatively recent approach to assessing teacher performance, and it can be the basis of PD recommendations. The Measures of Effective Teaching (MET) study (2012) did not use an RCT design and did not provide any feedback or PD to teachers based on the observations but was an early large-scale use of complex observation rubrics. The effect sizes for the association between teacher practices and student learning (one of the links in the chain in the PD logic model) seen in MET were small, based on observations of different sections taught by the same teacher or in different years. The maximum reported value was for the UTOP observation instrument, with an estimated effect size of 0.11 or about a 4 percentile point difference in student learning as a consequence of teacher practice. In a different set of studies examining impacts of a PD model, a series of papers examined impacts of MyTeachingPartner coaching (which gives teachers feedback on the basis of observations using the CLASS observation instrument) and reported significant gains in student achievement. More detailed data from these sources is provided in Tables 16.A.5 and 16.A.6 in the Appendix. As these sources indicate, PD effects on teacher and student performance vary widely.

Variability of Impact of PD Just as a medical treatment might affect individuals differently, professional development is unlikely to have a uniform effect on all people who receive it. Literature from a wide variety of professions, including teaching (Borko, 2004; Richter, Kunter, Klusmann, Lüdtke, & Baumert, 2011), medicine (Grimshaw, Shirran, Thomas, Mowatt, Fraser, Bero, Grilli, Harvey, Oxman, & O'Brien, 2001), nursing (Estabrooks, Thompson, Lovely, & Hofmeyer, 2006), and social services (Chagnon, Pouliot, Malo, Gervais, & Pigeon, 2010) finds that organizational characteristics, as well as individual characteristics such as personal attitudes and career stage, can influence the effectiveness of training, just as the mode or intensity of the training might. Even though it may not be feasible to customize training to each individual, it is important to consider that not every teacher will gain the same benefits from a specific professional development effort. In order to maximize benefits overall, the differential effects of an intervention on different teachers must be factored in.

Teachers' level of proficiency at pre-test on the skill that is the focus of PD can have considerable influence on the effects of that PD on performance. For example, it is possible that teachers who were selected for PD because they demonstrate superior performance in the behavior of interest (e.g., student questioning) on a pre-intervention test may have *lower* scores on a post-test of skill, simply due to the statistical phenomenon of regression toward the mean (Galton, 1886). This well-established idea implies that, with imperfect measurement of a trait, a person with an extreme (high or low) score is predicted to have score closer to the mean at a second measurement, simply due to measurement error. It is less probable that someone with superior performance will learn new skills from training, because he or she already has that knowledge. If a highly skilled candidate achieves a notably high score at pre-test on the instrument used to measure that skill, there is no room for the score to improve due to a ceiling effect, but there is room for the score to decrease. Similarly, it is possible that those people with the greatest room for improvement in performance will see the greatest benefits of training, because they are being provided with information that they are currently lacking.

Other factors may also come into play. For example, Chagnon and others (2010) found that personal attitudes play a role in the likelihood of uptake of professional development information. A person with poor performance may have a negative attitude toward professional development activities and be less likely to absorb information or respond to training. In such a case, professional development training might not be beneficial, because a teacher is resistant to the change that is required for improvement. Of course, there are many other reasons influencing why individual teachers may improve, or not change, or have performance degrade, after or because of training. In short, for all PD studies, those with estimates of significant impacts and those that show no impact, variability in treatment effects are often masked by averaging across individuals, and interpretation of effect sizes (and further research) can benefit from further, more comprehensive, considerations.

How we used the size and effects of PD in this study. The purpose of reviewing these studies was to describe some of the overall issues in the field of research on teacher professional development and to generate some broad estimates of the size(s) of the impact(s) of PD to be used in the simulation. Unfortunately, the research literature does not provide definitive guidance on the impact of professional development on teacher skills or on student achievement. Nonetheless, we can draw on the PD literature more generally to construct a band of likely effect sizes, given the range described in the limited PD literature that meets acceptable standards for causal inference. The effect sizes chosen for use in this study represent increases in teacher performance comparable to effect sizes of 0.01, 0.05, 0.10, and 0.50, values within the range seen in the studies reviewed and among the more common values observed.

Costs Associated with Teacher Professional Development

The costs of teacher professional development are not trivial and provide a context for interpreting estimates of the impacts derived from the simulations to be presented in this chapter. Clearly, costs must be weighed by district decision-makers in relation to expected outcomes. Odden, Archibald, Fermanich, and Gallagher (2002), Archibald, Coggshall, Croft, and Goe (2011), and Rice (2001) provide frameworks for calculating the cost for PD. According to these reports, most previous calculations of PD costs may be flawed because they based their estimates on different frameworks that led to under- or over-estimating PD costs. Inclusion of relevant factors in previous reports of PD costs changed the estimates. A summary of costs using the Odden, Archibald, Fermanich, and Gallagher (2002) framework estimates between $2,000 and $7,000 is spent annually per teacher on in-service training. Odden, Goetz, and Picus (2008) provide an example using the 2002 framework and report expenses of $100 per student, assuming instructional coaches for every two hundred students, ten days of professional learning time, expenses associated with trainers, conferences, and travel. Using the

2002 framework, PD costs associated with the CLASS-MTP program have been reported (see, for example, Allen, Pianta, Gregory, Mikami, & Lun, 2011; Pianta, 2011):

- About twenty hours of in-service training, spread across thirteen months

- Approximately $3,700 per teacher for the full cost of teacher-consultants and video equipment

Assuming that each instructor teaches five or more courses with twenty to twenty-five students, costs can be assumed to be under $40 per student for this particular PD approach. This is one example of a cost estimate for a professional development approach that has been proven effective. Unfortunately, there are very few estimates attached to most professional development models and, for the most part, a good deal of existing professional development cost is very difficult to estimate, because costs are embedded in district operations and not easily separable.

How we used the costs of PD in this study. In the present study, we considered costs of the intervention alternatives of professional development for teachers and student-teacher assignments. The study design assumes a simulated "school district" in which one hundred teachers work, each teaching twenty-five students. If we assume this district has a teacher PD budget selected based on the Odden, Archibald, Fermanich, and Gallagher (2002) estimate of approximately $40 per student, then $100,000 would be the total cost "spent" on professional development for teachers.

Assignment of Students to Classrooms and Teachers

A second way to possibly improve teacher and student performance is to consider the assignment of students to teachers as one variable that districts or schools could manipulate more systematically to improve teacher-student match. Presumably, there may be profiles of teachers based on certain skill sets that match better (or worse) to certain student profiles, and optimizing the fit between these profiles may be a key way to improve outcomes for all. There may be good pedagogical and logistical reasons for placing certain students together (or apart), but the result can be that classrooms within a school can have large variations in their demographic profiles (Baker, Barton, Darling-Hammond, Haertel, Ladd, Linn, Ravitch, Rothstein, Shavelson, & Sheperd, 2010). This variation can be consequential for student achievement.

There is evidence to suggest, in general, that teachers are more effective in classrooms with more students with a higher socioeconomic status, who are Asian, or whose parents are better educated, and are less effective with more students with limited English proficiency (LEP), even after controlling for factors like previous test scores and relevant student demographics (Newton, Darling-Hammond, Haertel, & Thomas, 2010). Other studies have found that grouping students by ability (also referred to as "tracking") generally is beneficial to stronger students and, conversely, detrimental to weaker students (Barker Lunn & Ferri, 1970, cited in Eder, 1981). This may be because, in a class of weaker students, teachers spend more time on behavior management; in a class of stronger students, there are fewer disruptions of instruction (Eder, 1981).

Adding more complexity to this issue of student-teacher match is evidence to suggest that more effective teachers tend to be placed with more advantaged, higher-performing students, both within and across schools (Clotfelder, Ladd, & Vigdor, 2006). Others have suggested that classes of stronger students are used as a reward to teachers (Sieber, 1982). Conversely, principals may assign classes of students who are lower performing or have behavioral issues to teachers who are perceived as weak, perhaps with the intent of trying to get the teacher to leave the school. Freeman, Scafidi, and Sjoquist (2002) found that teachers are more likely to transfer schools or quit teaching altogether if they have been most recently assigned low-income or low-performing students. Thus, although not exploited systematically, there is reason to believe that better alignment between student and teacher profiles could lead to measurable improvements in outcomes for both groups. Of course, there are considerable challenges in identifying the relevant (and causally influential) teacher and student characteristics from which to draw these profiles, in identifying the decision trees and cutpoints on these characteristics that will drive student assignment to teachers, and assuring all stakeholders that this type of assignment scheme will be in their best interest. Nonetheless this is a relatively inexpensive (compared to most PD) intervention, assuming it has expected benefits.

How we used assignment of students in this study. Assignment of students to teachers and classrooms is one of the factors we elected to manipulate as an experimental condition. Students are assigned to teachers randomly or based on the best fit between their content knowledge, between their instructional and learning styles, or both. Importantly, relative to teacher professional development, assignment of students to teachers does not, on the surface, appear to result in additional marginal costs. This may not be the case, as district leaders and decision-makers will undoubtedly have to address planning needs and the concerns of parents and staff, and there may be costs related to procedures and decision-supports. Thus, although we posit assignment of students to teachers as a potential "lower cost" alternative to PD, it may be the case that we are underestimating real costs.

Design of Data Used in This Study

The data design for this study is quite complex, although simpler than the reality observed in schools. In order to simulate the data for the analyses, we specify: (a) the exact variables that will be the focus of the analyses and that will have to be created for simulation and (b) the distribution of those variables as we consider how they would occur in school systems. These specifications will be defined as the variables are introduced. The descriptions of the variables will be separated into the parameters defining three main areas that are the focus of the simulation: (1) the content that is the focus of instruction, (2) the teachers, and (3) the students.

Simulating the Content of Instruction as a Variable

Here, we use the term "course" to define the content assigned to be taught in a single academic year. For an elementary teacher, this typically would be one grade-level sequence of content in each academic area (such as English Language Arts, Science, Math, Social Studies, and Arts). For middle school and high school teachers, this may be one content sequence or multiple sequences within one academic area (such as courses in Algebra 1, Geometry, and Trigonometry assigned to a single mathematics teacher, or courses in Physical Science and Biology assigned to a science teacher). This study assumes that whatever a teacher is assigned to teach within the academic year is that teacher's "course." Because we need to measure completion of the course content, a course is designated to begin at 0.0 and end at 1.0 on an arbitrary scale for this study. This scale can be seen as approximating the proportion of the course material that the student successfully learns in one academic year.

Simulating Teacher Content Knowledge and Practice Expertise

Teachers in this study are defined as having two distinct dimensions of performance. One is content knowledge; the other is practice expertise. These terms are defined only loosely herein, as the focus of this study is not on the specifics of these definitions. Other chapters in the present volume attend very closely to these two features of teachers' professional performance, their conceptualization, measurement, and impacts on student learning. We readily admit the complexity of these features of teaching performance; however, in this chapter we make a number of assumptions regarding these complex variables in order to conduct the intended simulation.

- Teachers' content knowledge is defined as the range of academic content over which each individual teacher is competent to provide instruction. This feature of performance is often captured in state regulations related to certification.

- Instructional practice is defined as a set of approaches and behaviors most typical of the teachers' delivery of lessons when providing instruction.

Note that the definition of "teacher content knowledge" does not include the full range of content that the teacher knows or understands but is limited to the content span in which he or she is assumed to be most proficient. By this definition, two teachers may have the same academic background but have quite different teaching content spans. Both may know the same subject—say mathematics—and know it equally well, but one may prefer or be assigned to teach the fundamentals of arithmetic operations and the other may prefer or be assigned to teach calculus.

Similarly, "instructional practice" does not include all of the teaching style and instructional techniques that the teacher is familiar with but instead refers to the set of techniques the teacher prefers and is assumed to be most confident and effective in using. To continue with our example from the preceding paragraph, the two math teachers may both prefer to place students in small groups, or one may prefer to lecture and one may prefer to assign ability-level pairs for activities. Any instructional practice preference can occur in combination with any teaching content span.

Specifications for teacher content knowledge. Teachers were modeled as having three features of content knowledge and expertise: a location, a width, and a height. These variables define teachers' status with regard to their knowledge and comfort level teaching the content they were assigned, their capability of teaching that content, and their degree of effectiveness. These variables were defined as occurring on the same scale as courses (described above), although the teacher content knowledge values may fall below 0.0 and above 1.0.

That is, teachers could vary on the extent to which they had the requisite knowledge to teach a particular content area; even when they had knowledge, they may prefer to not teach that area. Teacher content location was drawn from a mixture of two statistical distributions.[1] It was assumed that 90 percent of the teachers were located between 0.25 and 0.75 on content, intentionally placing most teachers near the middle (0.50) of the course content they were assigned. That is, we assumed most teachers had solid levels of knowledge and comfort with the content they were teaching. The other 10 percent of teachers were chosen so that it was quite likely some teachers with extreme content locations occurred in the sample. Again, these are assumptions. The teacher content location values were designed so that the large majority of teachers were well-matched to the course they were assigned to teach, with a few who were not. In this design, the mismatched teachers would prefer and be more effective teaching different content rather than what they were assigned.

All teacher content width values were drawn from a single distribution.[2] The content width values were chosen so that most teachers had a content width close to 1.0, implying that the teachers were capable of teaching all content in the course. The teacher's content was assigned a height to permit indication of partial instructional effectiveness. A height of 1.0 indicates a span of content where the teacher is completely effective in teaching; less than 1.0 indicates less than full instructional effectiveness, so students will learn part, but not all, of that content; and 0.0 indicates no effectiveness in teaching that content—students learn nothing from a teacher with this content height.

Combining all of these ideas (content location, width, and height or, correspondingly, teachers' knowledge/comfort, expertise, and effectiveness), teaching content is envisioned mathematically as a plateau. This plateau has a height at the maximum value of 1.0 throughout the content width assigned to the teacher. Because teaching content is conceived as having a preference component, it does not disappear abruptly at the edge of the plateau. Instead, it decays down to 0 across an additional span (half of teacher's content width) at each end. The shape of a teacher's content span is that of an isosceles trapezoid, as shown in Figure 16.2, with the teacher content in blue and the course location shown on the horizontal axis in green. This teacher is optimally matched to this course assignment, since he has a content location of 0.5 (the center of the course content) and has a content width of 1.0. In this case, his content span runs from 0.0 to 1.0, exactly the course location and width. This teacher would be partly effective

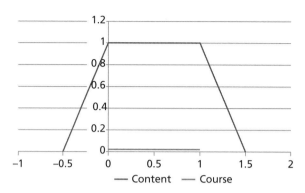

FIGURE 16.2. *Example: Teacher Content Location 0.5, Content Width 1.0*

in teaching some content just before or after the content in this course, as shown by the slanting lines going down from the maximally effective level. The farther away from the course content we move, the less effective this particular teacher is, until, at locations −0.5 and 1.5 and beyond, where his content height is 0, he is completely ineffective.

Again, although mathematically complex and based on several assumptions, the prior discussion is one way of defining and operationalizing one feature of teachers that has been shown to be important for student achievement—their knowledge and expertise in the content domains they are assigned to teach.

Simulating Teacher Instructional Practice

Teachers also were modeled as having a location, width, and height on the dimension of instructional practice. Again, the approach we used was intended to model teachers' status with respect to at least three aspects of instructional practice that could be operationalized and defined. As with content, we assumed teacher practice locations were drawn from a normal distribution,[3] selected based on a theory that many teachers prefer similar instructional practice styles. Teachers tend to be drawn from a pool of successful students—those who enjoyed an academic environment and who thrived there. Students with uncommon learning styles may find traditional academic settings uncomfortable and perhaps be less drawn to teaching as a career. This set of assumptions leads logically to a somewhat clustered set of instructional practices, represented by the bell-shaped curve used.

Instructional practice width was drawn from a distribution chosen with the student learning styles (described below) in mind, so that 95 percent of the teachers have a practice width of 2.5 or greater and the median of the distribution is approximately 4.1. In other words, we conceptualize and operationalize the nature and breadth of the distribution of teachers' instructional practices as, in part, mapping to the characteristics of students they teach. The width distribution was selected so that a teacher whose practice span is maximally wide would be able to encompass "all" modes of teaching practice. Such a teacher can be effective with all students, regardless of the students' individual learning preferences. For any given practice width, it is assumed the teacher is effective and, like the teaching content dimension, is assigned a height of 1.0 in that range. Unlike teaching content, teaching practice is designed so that teachers do not have a zone in which their instructional practice is partly effective—it is fully effective or it is ineffective. Thus, the shape of an individual teacher's practice span is rectangular (the sides are vertical).

Simulating Student Content Knowledge and Preferences

We conceptualize characteristics of students in terms of two dimensions related to their learning performance that parallel those of the teachers: content and instructional preference. Again, these terms are defined only loosely here, as it is not the purpose of this data-modeling study to refine the definitions of these constructs.

- Student content is the combination of prior academic knowledge and a receptive attitude that permits a student to engage in the learning of new content.

- Student instructional preference is the pedagogical and interpersonal styles, practices, and techniques the student prefers and from which he or she learns most effectively.

Each of these two student characteristics is modeled only in terms of location for the sake of (relative) design simplicity. A given student's value for student content is drawn from a normal distribution.[4] In this case, we use a very narrow and peaked distribution because we assume that nearly all students are located quite close to the new academic material at the beginning of instruction; that is, they are all relatively bunched in terms of preparation for that course or content. Similar to the teachers, the result is that the majority of students are well-matched to the course they are assigned. A student with a negative content location value is assumed to be less prepared to learn the material in the course than one located at 0.0 or above. A student with a 0.0 or positive content location value is assumed to be prepared to engage with and learn the material. Students with a location value greater than 1.0 were located "above" the course material and might not benefit much from instruction in that course because they already knew the content. Given the very narrow distribution used, it was unlikely that a student with such a large positive value would appear in the data set.

A number of investigations (e.g., Pashler, McDaniel, Rohrer, & Bjork, 2008) have discounted theories that argue that optimal learning occurs when there is matching of instructional and learning styles. As we have conceptualized and use the student instructional preference dimension here, we do not focus on a particular individual "learning style" *per se* but explicitly include in the model the fact that it is a combination of instructional methods, techniques, practices, and interpersonal mannerisms under which a particular student produces the greatest academic gains.

Student instructional preference was drawn from a uniform distribution that had no ordering; the distribution was intended only to separate students under the assumption that each had different preferences. In such a distribution, students were evenly distributed across all possible preferences, in contrast with the teacher practice locations, which were clumped around the center value. This difference was intentional, reflecting the hypothesis that teachers tend to be clustered around a particular set of preferences reflected in their instructional practices, but students represent a broader span of receptive learning preferences.

The interaction of the student content and instructional preference locations places each student on a two-dimensional plane, marked by an X in Figure 16.3. As expected, the students are clustered near 0 on the content dimension, all falling within 0.3 units of the center, and much more dispersed on the instructional preference dimension, with some values beyond ±2 units.

Simulating the Combination(s) of Student and Teacher Characteristics

Up to this point, we have described our approach to conceptualizing and operationalizing features of students and teachers relevant for producing learning and some of the assumptions on which these variables are simulated. Now we combine student and teacher characteristics more formally. We do this for the two key aspects of content and instruction; that is, we assume that learning occurs as a function of some degree of alignment between teacher and student with regard to content and to instruction. We describe below the variability

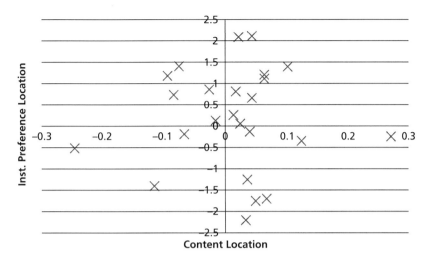

FIGURE 16.3. *Locations on Content and Instructional Preference for a Sample Class of Twenty-Five Students*

in this feature of alignment with respect to combining student and teacher on content and instructional features.

Content. In order for a teacher to be effective at providing instruction to a student, the teacher and student must be located close to each other on content at the beginning of the academic year; visually, the student must fall under the teacher's content "plateau," as shown in Figure 16.2. In this study, each teacher was assigned twenty-five students, and each student had an individual content location. Some examples of teachers and classes of students, plotted to show the relationship between them on the content dimension, are shown in Figures 16.4a through 16.4d.

Of the examples in Figure 16.4, those in Figures 16.4a and 16.4d were the most typical. Here, the teacher is modeled as (shown in the blue line) completely effective with regard to aspects of content (described earlier) throughout the course, as in Figure 16.4d, or nearly so, as in Figure 16.4a. The teacher in Figure 16.4a was not completely effective in the initial ~10 percent of the course content but was no less than 80 percent effective, even in that range. For example, it could be the case that a teacher might assume that students remember more than they actually do about material from a previous course and not be thorough in covering it at the beginning of a course. Because most students would have learned the material the previous year, the limited instruction on this material is still largely effective. In Figure 16.4d

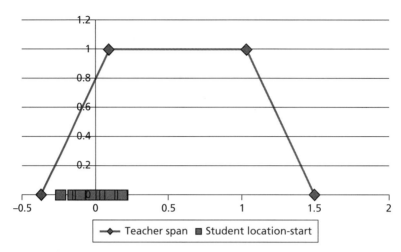

FIGURE 16.4a. *Example of Content Data Structure: Teacher and Class of Students, Position 0.56, Width 0.929*

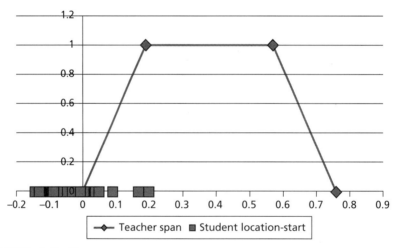

FIGURE 16.4b. *Example of Content Data Structure: Teacher and Class of Students, Position 0.38, Width 0.379*

the students (shown as the red squares) were tightly clustered around the beginning point of the course content, falling within the content span where the teacher was completely effective (where the line is horizontal at height 1.00)—all of these students will learn from this teacher. In Figure 16.4a, although the students were also clustered around the beginning point of the course content, the teacher's content status meant that this teacher would

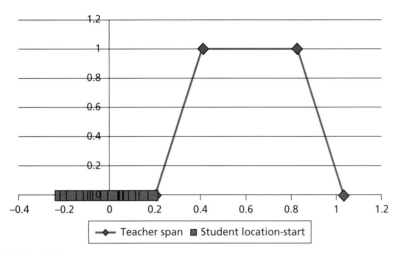

FIGURE 16.4c. *Example of Content Data Structure: Teacher and Class of Students, Position 0.62, Width 0.415*

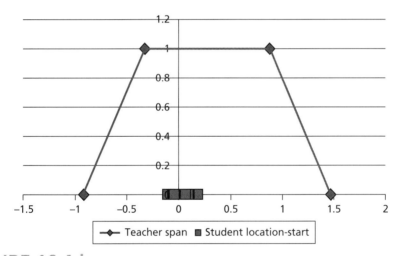

FIGURE 16.4d. *Example of Content Data Structure: Teacher and Class of Students, Position 0.27, Width 1.194*

be only partly effective teaching the students who begin the course below a location of about 0.2. This can be seen by the sloped line above the squares representing those student locations. The farther below 0.0 a student's initial location was, the less effective the teacher in Figure 16.4a was for that student. From locations of about 0.2 and greater, the teacher's content line was horizontal at height 1.0, indicting complete effectiveness for those students.

The teacher in Figure 16.4b had a reasonable content location for the course but had an unusually narrow content width. As a result, this teacher was completely effective in instruction for only about 40 percent of the course content, partly effective for about 40 percent, and completely ineffective for the final 20 percent. This teacher also was not well-matched to the students, as about half of the class of students fell below the teacher's lower bound of content efficacy at about 0.0. The poor match of the teacher to the course and to this class of students meant that the students who started the class located below 0.0 would not learn anything from this teacher. The teacher in Figure 16.4c was a poor match to the course in both location (he or she was somewhat high) and width—quite narrow. The teacher also was a poor match for the class, despite the students being reasonably placed in the course based on their content location near 0.0. None of the students in the class fell within the teacher's content span, and none of these students would learn from this teacher. Such a teacher might incorrectly assume that material intended to be taught at the beginning of this course already was learned by the students in a previous course, thus beginning instruction in the current course above the content location of all of the students in the class. If the teacher proceeds to move to more complex topics, and the students all lack the requisite knowledge to enter into the instruction being provided, the students will not learn.

Teacher Instructional Practice and Student Preference Interactions In order for a teacher to be effective providing instruction to a student, in addition to matching well on content, the student and teacher must also match on their instructional practice preferences. By that we mean that the teacher must teach in a manner that allows the student to engage with content and gain academically. Similar to content, the teacher and student must be located close to each other. Some examples of teacher instructional practice and student instructional preferences are shown in Figure 16.5a through 16.5d. Given the distributions from which values were selected for this study, a typical teacher's practice status would encompass 40 to 50 percent of the students in a class. This may seem overly harsh in terms of assuming that any given teacher's instruction is effective for only about half the students in the class, but this is not inconsistent with conventional assumptions that most instruction is geared toward the middle of the classroom distribution.

The teacher in Figure 16.5a was located close to the center of the instructional practice continuum but had a very narrow width of applicability.

Twenty-three of the twenty-five students in the class had a receptive learning preference outside of this teacher's expressed instructional practice span, meaning this teacher's instructional methods were ineffective with 92 percent of this class! Obviously, this is a very bad match of teacher and students. The teacher in Figure 16.5b had a fairly broad width of instructional practice, and her location is comparatively high on the continuum. Because the student locations were uniformly distributed, the teacher location had limited impact on the proportion of the class within the teacher's instructional practice span. In this case, twelve of the twenty-five students in the class—about half—were within her instructional practice span. The teacher in Figure 16.5c was similar, although located at the other end of the practice continuum. This teacher was located at a relatively low value on the scale and had a larger width than the teacher in Figure 16.5b. This combination of teacher practice location and width encompassed nineteen of the twenty-five students—all but six—assigned to this class. The teacher in Figure 16.5d had an unusually large instructional practice width: more than 5.5, meaning we assume her approach to instruction to be widely effective, matching the instructional practice preferences for 84 percent of the students in this class. In this respect she is not far from being a "super-teacher" on the practice dimension, able to encompass *all* students' instructional preferences.

Combining teacher content and instructional practice with student content and instructional preference. The preceding sections have considered how teachers and students interact along either of two single dimensions of the data design—either content or instructional practice. In the final step of modeling, we considered all relevant features of students and teachers as they combine to produce learning. We do not go into detail on the modeling of these combinations but describe below some of the situations that the final model encompasses in order to illustrate its applicability to a broad set of configurations of alignment of teacher and student characteristics. Figure 16.6 presents an example of how the content and instruction aspects combine to create a plateau of teacher effectiveness.

For example, a teacher could be completely effective through most of a course (located between 0.0 and 1.0 in terms of content), with some small loss of effectiveness at the very end of the course content. Assuming that students are well-placed into the course, this teacher can be very effective for students through nearly all of the content. Because we have assumed that students are uniformly distributed, this teacher should be effective with about

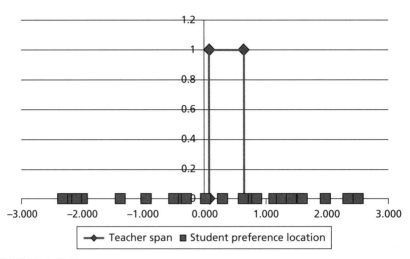

FIGURE 16.5a. *Examples of Instructional Practice Data Structure: Teacher and Class of Students, Location 0.366, Width 0.570*

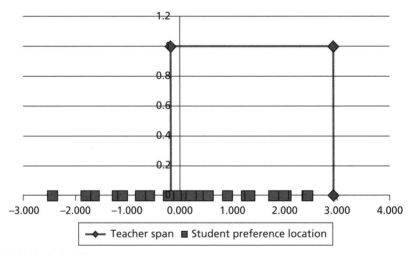

FIGURE 16.5b. *Examples of Instructional Practice Data Structure: Teacher and Class of Students, Location 1.3878, Width 3.100*

54 percent of a randomly chosen class of students. That means he or she will be effective with thirteen or fourteen students from a class of twenty-five in providing instructional practice that meets the learning preference of the students. The other eleven or twelve students, despite the teacher's broad content efficacy, will not learn from this teacher because their practice locations do not overlap. Thus, we include in the model the possibility that a student

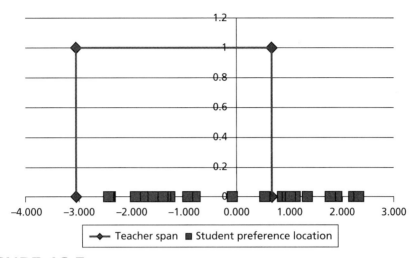

FIGURE 16.5c. *Examples of Instructional Practice Data Structure: Teacher and Class of Students, Location -1.1775, Width 3.720*

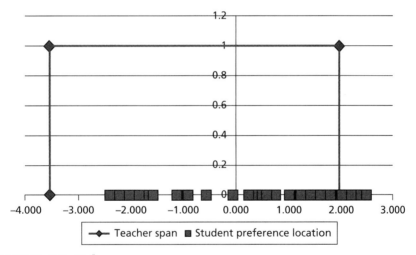

FIGURE 16.5d. *Examples of Instructional Practice Data Structure: Teacher and Class of Students, Location -0.7952, Width 5.5126*

may align well on content with his or her teacher but may not align on instructional features, so the model indicates that he or she will not learn course material from this teacher. Note that the mismatch can occur on content or instruction and can occur because of either teacher or student being above or below the other with respect to these features.

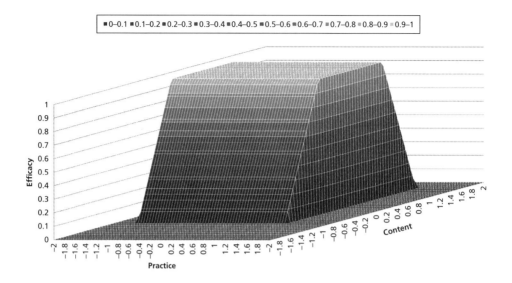

FIGURE 16.6. *Teacher Content by Practice "Plateau"*

STUDENT ACHIEVEMENT GAINS DURING A COURSE

For the sake of analysis, we define the ideal amount of academic progress as the change from location 0.0 to 1.0 of the course content. That is, we assume ideal learning in a specific course of content to go from no knowledge in that course content to complete knowledge of that specific course content. Of course, the learning of the vast majority of students falls somewhere between those two endpoints of the distribution. Moreover, the amount of academic gain that a student achieved in this study design is delimited by a set of constraints and interactions. As described above, the student must be located within the teacher's content and instructional practice span in order to make gains. If a student is outside of *either* the teacher's content span or the teacher's practice span, the student will make no instructional gain. Importantly, for the purposes of the simulation, additional constraints are imposed on how much gain students may achieve during the course:

- We assume no student in the course will end the year with a content value greater than 1.0. Students cannot progress beyond the "end" of the course content.

- Because of the constraint above, no student in the course will end the year with a gain larger than 1.0. Students cannot learn "more" content than the unit taught in the course.

These boundaries do not necessarily represent what occurs in real classrooms. Students do make more than a single year's academic progress when taught by excellent teachers, and students can learn more content than that which "belongs" in the course when opportunities offer; however, these more complex situations are not modeled here. The simulation constraints also imply that

- A student entering a course behind in terms of content can gain a full unit of instruction but cannot "make up ground" to end the course at a content value of 1.0. Such a student cannot reach the end-of-course content location, as that would imply a gain of more than one unit. This student can have a gain up to and including 1.0 unit of instruction.

- A student entering a course ahead in terms of content cannot gain a full unit of instruction but can reach content location 1.0. This student can have a final content value as high as 1.0 but cannot have an academic gain of one full unit, as that would imply a final content location above location 1.0.

How Much Do Students Learn in a Year of Instruction?

Given all of the above assumptions and the definitions and operationalization of student and teacher characteristics, we combined these features into a model that calculated student learning (ranging from 0.0 to 1.0) based on combinations of student and teacher characteristics drawn from the distributions of each feature. This enabled us to simulate student learning during a year of instruction. We then simulated learning under various conditions: PD that changed the teachers' efficacy in instruction; PD that changed teacher content knowledge; and assignment of students to teachers. In order to know how much of a difference any of these interventions made, we had to know what happened when no interventions were in place—the baseline case. That reference data set is described as follows:

- There was a simulated "school district."

- In this district, one hundred teachers were employed, with content and practice parameters as described in the previous section.

- Each teacher had a class of twenty-five students, each student with content and instructional preference parameters as described in the previous section.

- Each teacher taught a course intended to provide one unit of instruction to each student during an academic year.

To establish the properties of the baseline data set, the following question was posed: Given the basic conditions, what were the student results after an academic year of instruction? Specifically:

- What were the mean and distribution of student instructional gains at the end of the academic year?

- What proportion of students had no instructional gain at the end of the academic year?

- What proportion of students had a full unit of instructional gain at the end of the academic year?

As a point of reference, under this design, with one hundred teachers providing one academic year's worth of instruction to twenty-five students each, the optimal outcome would be a total increase of 2,500 units of student instruction, or one full unit per student.

The baseline data set is the result of taking students and teacher with parameters from the distributions described above, randomly assigning twenty-five students to each class, and assigning a teacher randomly to each of the classes. These teachers instructed the students during an academic year, in which these teachers received no professional development that altered the teacher content and practice parameters as drawn initially. We recognize that random assignment of classes to teachers and students to classes does not occur, but in the simulated case we assume this to take place. Under these assumptions, how do the students do after the academic year is over?

Figure 16.7 shows the pattern of initial and final locations for the baseline condition. Under the assumptions above and in prior sections, the simulation models that a substantial number of students do not move from their initial value (have a change of size 0); in fact, 810 of the 2,500, or about one-third of the students, receive no benefit from instruction under this model (see Figure 16.8). Of those 810 students who had no academic content gain, two received no instruction through a content mismatch with the teacher and 808 received no instruction through a practice mismatch. Of the 2,500 possible total instructional units that could have been delivered, only 1,237.7 or about 49.5 percent were actually achieved.

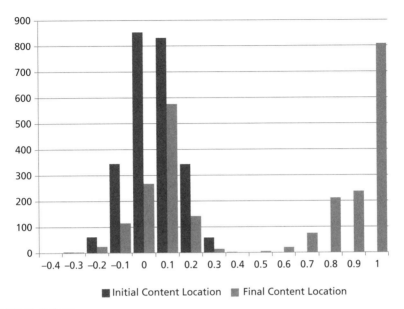

FIGURE 16.7.   *Initial and Final Locations of Students in the Baseline Condition*

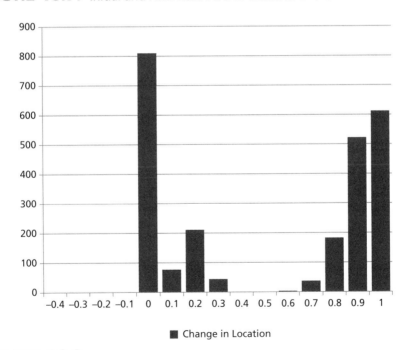

FIGURE 16.8.   *Numbers of Students with Various Amount of Change (Baseline Condition)*

Simulating the Impact on Student Learning of Teacher PD and Student-Teacher Assignment Interventions

The first set of research questions contrast the baseline data set as described above with one incorporating interventions for each of the two teacher dimensions: content or practice. A second set of questions examined impacts of student-teacher assignments. For simplicity of interpretation, in the set focused on PD, we held the initial teachers and student assignments constant. That is, we essentially modeled the intervention under the same set of *a priori* circumstances described above for the baseline condition. In one set of teachers and students, there is no intervention (the baseline set of results above); in the other, an intervention (content- or practice-focused) is applied at the beginning of the school year before instruction occurs. The goal of choosing this set of circumstances is to make the outcome comparison as simple as possible: any effects were the result of the *intervention only*. The teachers and the students are exactly the same; the only difference is the PD intervention happening or not.

PD Interventions

We modeled gains from PD by increasing the teacher's width on the dimension of the intervention (content or practice) by an amount shown in Table 16.1. The values chosen represent gains in performance comparable to effect sizes of 0.01, 0.05, 0.10, and 0.50. These effect sizes fall within the range seen in the literature on teacher professional development. Three groups of interventions are shown in Table 16.1. In the first, the intervention is on one dimension—either content or practice. The intervention is not targeted in terms of which type of intervention (content or practice) would most benefit the teacher; every teacher received the same PD. In the second group, teachers were sent to PD on each dimension independently but were sent to both. This is the reason the cost per teacher is double the cost from the first group, since all teachers were treated twice, with both a content and a practice intervention. In the third group, teachers received treatment on only one dimension, as in the first group, but in this case, the PD *was targeted*—selected for each teacher so as to create the maximum improvement in student outcomes for that individual teacher.

The interventions were framed within a fixed PD budget for the district in which these one hundred teachers work. A budget was selected based on the Odden, Archibald, Fermanich, and Gallagher (2002) estimate of approximately

TABLE 16.1.   PD Intervention Descriptions

Single Dimension—Untargeted				
Cost per Teacher	**Performance (Width) Gain**	**N Teachers Treated**	**Intervention Cost**	**Remaining PD Budget**
$250.00	1%	100	$25,000.00	$75,000.00
$1,000.00	5%	100	$100,000.00	$0
$2,000.00	10%	50	$100,000.00	$0
$10,000.00	50%	10	$100,000.00	$0
Both Dimensions—Untargeted				
$500.00	1%	100	$50,000.00	$50,000.00
$2,000.00	5%	50	$100,000.00	$0
$4,000.00	10%	25	$100,000.00	$0
$20,000.00	50%	5	$100,000.00	$0
Single Dimension—Targeted				
$250.00	1%	100	$25,000.00	$75,000.00
$1,000.00	5%	100	$100,000.00	$0
$2,000.00	10%	50	$100,000.00	$0
$10,000.00	50%	10	$100,000.00	$0

$40 per student, resulting in a district PD budget of $100,000. This total cost will be used as the maximum "spent" on professional development for teachers and impacts the number of teachers who can be provided with the PD services. The impact of the PD on the teachers was varied directly with the cost of the intervention; more expensive PD had a more positive impact.

Teacher-Student Assignment Interventions

In addition to the PD interventions, student assignment to teachers also was examined as an intervention. Research done as part of the MET study has shown that, as done currently, student assignment does not bias estimates of teacher results (Mihaly, McCaffrey, Staiger, & Lockwood, 2013). In other words, the specific students assigned to a teacher do not strongly influence the instructional efficacy of the teacher as measured with these value-added models. In this study, we took a different approach and considered ways that students might be assigned to teachers so that the educational outcomes *would be* different.

Two dimensions of student assignment were used in this design: student grouping into classes and teacher assignment to the classes of students. Students can be grouped by content location, by instructional preference, or by both. Teachers can be assigned to the classes of students randomly or by best match to class characteristics (either ignoring the second dimension when students are grouped by a single dimension or matching on both dimensions).

The questions to be answered in this work are

- Which of the interventions produced the greatest gain in overall instructional units taught across all students?

- Which of the interventions resulted in the greatest reduction in individual students with no instructional gain above the baseline data set?

- Which of the interventions resulted in the greatest increase in individual students with a full unit of instructional gain?

- Which of the interventions resulted in the greatest increase in individual students with a final content location at 1.0, the upper boundary of the course?

THE IMPACT OF PD: CONTENT

How much improvement was realized when content professional development interventions are provided to the teachers? In this design, the interventions were provided to all teachers if the PD budget allowed. In cases for which the budget limited the number of teachers who could be treated, the teachers with the smallest average academic gain for their classes were selected for the intervention. Again, this is an unrealistic "best case," as it assumes perfect knowledge of what would happen.

In order to make the changes across the intervention conditions more visible, the results of all four levels of PD will be presented together. One metric, shown in Figure 16.9, is the percentage of the total academic units (2,500) delivered by the system after the intervention was applied. The bars represent the conditions of no PD intervention; a 1 percent intervention for all teachers; a 5 percent intervention for all teachers; a 10 percent intervention for half of the teachers; and a 50 percent intervention for 10 percent of the teachers. There is little variation in the outcomes across interventions using this metric.

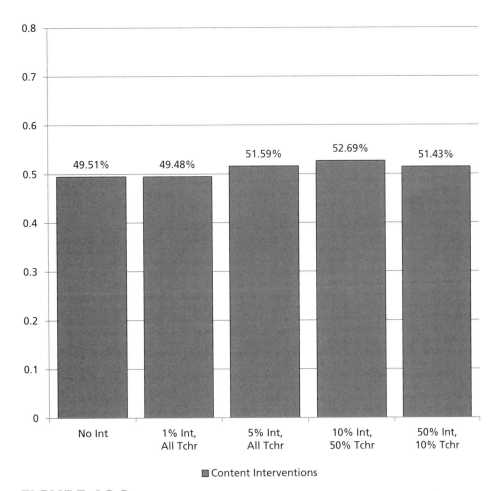

FIGURE 16.9. *Impact of Content Interventions as a Percentage of Instructional Units Delivered*

The other metric is the number of students who

■ Have a gain of 0 units, a number to be minimized

■ Have a gain of 1 unit, a number to be maximized

■ End the academic year at the upper bound of the course content (location 1.0), also a number to be maximized

These measures are shown in Figure 16.10, with the intervention categories the same as in Figure 16.9. The number of students with no gain varies between 808 and 810, effectively the same. The number of students with a gain of 1 unit and the number of students who end the course at location 1.0 vary somewhat more, with ranges from 612 and 783, and 808 to 920, respectively. The 5 percent content intervention for all teachers produces the best effect across all of these metrics. In short, very little academic gain was demonstrated as a result of content-focused PD, and the conditions optimizing this level of gain involved a modestly potent content-focused intervention delivered to all teachers.

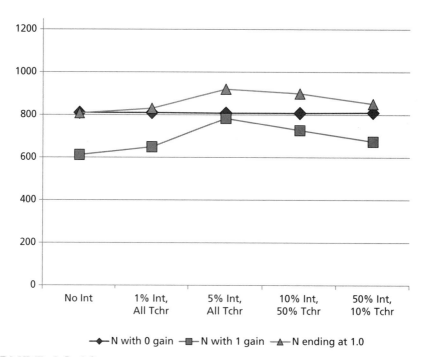

FIGURE 16.10. *Impact of Content Interventions as Numbers of Students in Specific Final States*

THE IMPACT OF PD: INSTRUCTIONAL PRACTICE

How much improvement was realized when instructional practice PD interventions were provided to the teachers? As was the case for content PD, the interventions were provided to all teachers in the sample if the PD budget allowed. For cases in which the budget limited the number of teachers who could be treated, the teachers with the smallest average academic gain for their classes were selected. As was the case with the content interventions, in Figure 16.11 it is clear that there is little variation in the outcomes.

The other metrics are shown in Figure 16.12. The number of students with no gain varies between 746 and 810, somewhat more variable than for the content intervention. The number of students with a gain of 1 unit and the

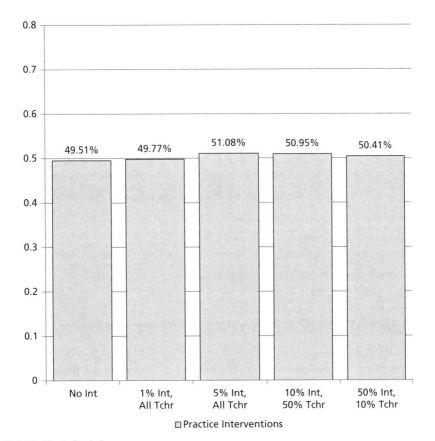

FIGURE 16.11. *Impact of Instructional Practice Interventions as Percentage of Instructional Units Delivered*

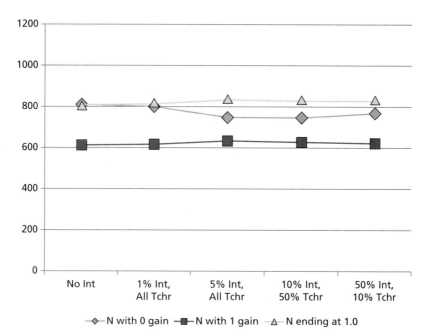

FIGURE 16.12. *Impact of Instructional Practice Interventions as Numbers of Students in Specific Final States*

number of students who end the course at location 1.0 both vary trivially, with ranges from 612 and 633 and 808 to 833, respectively. The 5 percent and 10 percent content interventions produce very similar results and the best effect across all of these metrics, suggesting again that a modestly potent professional development approach focused on instructional practice delivered to all teachers is likely to have the greatest effect on student learning, although the effect was small overall.

The Impact of PD Focused on Both Content and Practice

How much improvement was realized when content *and* instructional practice PD interventions were provided to the teachers? Because all treated teachers received both types of intervention, the cost of the PD doubled and the number of treated teachers was reduced commensurately. For cases in which the budget limited the number of treated teachers, those with the smallest average academic gain for their classes were selected. As can be seen in Figure 16.13, there is little variation in the outcomes.

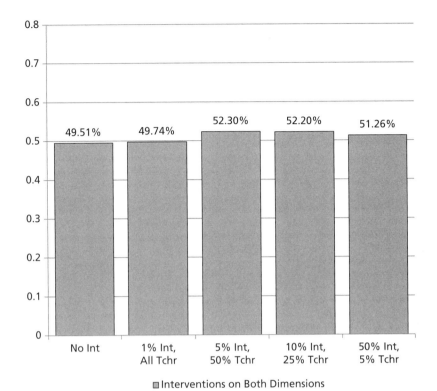

FIGURE 16.13. *Impact of Both Content and Instructional Practice Interventions as Percentage of Instructional Units Delivered*

As displayed in Figure 16.14, the number of students with no gain varies between 768 and 810. The number of student with a gain of 1 varies between 612 and 690. The number of students who end the course at location 1.0 ranges from 808 to 871. The 5 percent intervention on both dimensions produces the best results across all metrics for reasons similar to those noted above.

Impact of PD That Targets Teacher Needs

Having low-performing teachers attend professional development on both content and teaching practice dimensions assures that, whatever the teacher's limitation, one of the interventions should address it. However, from a time and cost perspective, it is inefficient, as teachers may be attending PD that is irrelevant to their weaknesses—indeed, teachers may be treated on a dimension on which they are quite effective. Instead of sending all low-performing

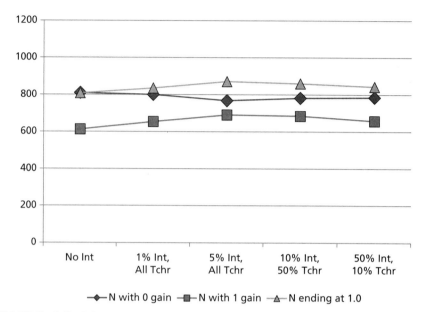

FIGURE 16.14. *Impact of Both Content and Instructional Practice Interventions as Numbers of Students in Specific Final States*

teachers to both interventions, it would be more efficient to send teachers to only the interventions that deliver the most improvement in student outcomes. Although in reality it might be difficult to diagnose the best possible intervention, in a simulation such as this one, it is quite simple.

To create this data set, the results from the content interventions and the instructional practice interventions were examined independently for each level of intervention. The intervention that produced the largest mean gain in student final content location was selected as the best choice for that teacher at that level of intervention. The interventions chosen were a mix of content and instructional practice, as shown in Table 16.2.

The results of the targeted intervention are shown in Figure 16.15. This approach did result in an improvement over untargeted intervention—but not by much. The best overall system delivery remained at just over 50 percent.

The other metrics are shown in Figure 16.16. The results approximate a combination of the best results of the previous conditions. The number of students with no gain is smallest (754), the number with a gain of 1 (740) is largest, and the number of students who end the academic year at content location 1.0 (912) are the largest of all of the conditions in the study, all in

TABLE 16.2. **Targeted Interventions by Dimension and Level**

Intervention Level	N Teachers: Content Intervention	N Teachers: Instructional Practice Intervention	N Teachers: No Intervention
No Intervention	0	0	100
1% Impact	78	22	0
5% Impact	57	43	0
10% Impact	25	25	50
50% Impact	8	2	90

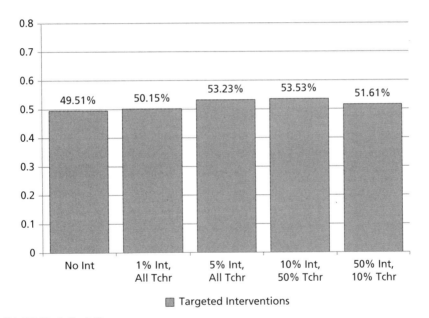

Targeted Interventions

FIGURE 16.15. *Impact of Targeted Interventions as Percentage of Instructional Units Delivered*

the 5 percent intervention condition. In short, the simulation model suggests that optimal, albeit modest overall, results on student achievement for teacher professional development are obtained when PD is tailored to the needs (e.g. relative weaknesses) of each teacher.

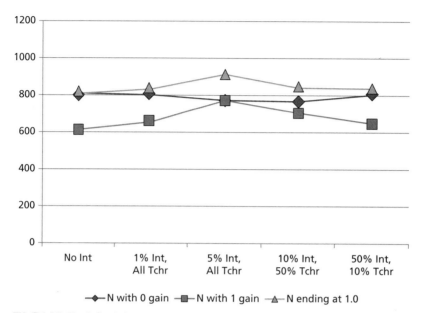

FIGURE 16.16. *Impact of Targeted Interventions as Numbers of Students in Specific Final States*

The Impact of Student Grouping and Teacher Assignment

In addition to interventions that altered the content or practice of the teachers, we included another approach: we took the same sample of one hundred teachers and 2,500 students, and defined the "intervention" as a careful analysis of each teacher's content status as well as practice status. Each student also had his or her content and instructional preference pinpointed on those distributions. Using this information, students could be placed into relatively homogeneous groups based on similarity in content location, similarity in instructional preference, or similarity in both. Teachers could be assigned to the classes of students so assembled randomly or by the best match of teacher and student characteristics. The conditions evaluated are listed in Table 16.3.

Some studies (for example, Clotfelder, Ladd, & Vigdor, 2006 and Sieber, 1982) indicate that teacher assignments to high- or low-performing classes are made for reasons that include seniority, reward or punishment, and motivation to depart from employment. We modeled these conditions as approximating random assignment of teachers to classes where the students have been

TABLE 16.3. Assignment Intervention Conditions

Condition	Students Grouped by	Teacher Assigned Using
Random (Baseline)	Random	Random
St-Content	Content location	Random
St-Inst Preference	Instructional preference location	Random
St-Both	Both content and instructional preference location	Random
T&S Content	Content location	Best match on content
T&S Practice	Instructional preference location	Best match on instructional practice
T&S Both	Both content and instructional preference location	Best match on content and instructional practice

grouped by one or both of the dimensions modeled. Results for the assignment conditions are presented in Figures 16.17 and 16.18.

The data in the first bar are the same "no intervention" data as in previous figures, here labeled "random" to reflect the description of the other conditions in this section. Figure 16.17 shows more variability than seen in any previous set of conditions. The condition under which students were sorted on content location and had a teacher randomly assigned showed slightly better performance than most, at almost 53 percent. The condition under which students were sorted on instructional preferences and had a teacher randomly assigned showed the worst performance seen so far, at near 46 percent. But all conditions in which the students were grouped and then had a teacher randomly assigned achieved results that were similar to the baseline and all other intervention conditions—about 50 percent of the 2,500 instructional units the system could potentially deliver.

The conditions under which the students were grouped and the teachers were matched to their class's characteristics delivered the best results of all conditions examined. Sorting students and matching a teacher to them on

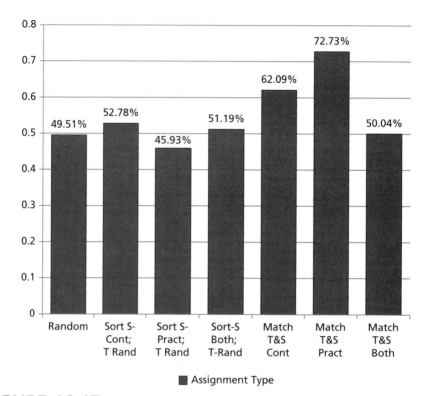

FIGURE 16.17. *Impact of Student Grouping and Teacher Assignment as a Percentage of Instructional Units Delivered*

content resulted in delivery of just over 62 percent of the possible instruction. Sorting students and matching a teacher to them on instructional practice and preferences did even better, with almost 73 percent.

Figure 16.18 and Table 16.4 present results for student status after instruction. The data from the conditions under which the students are grouped and the teachers assigned randomly were relatively similar to the previous PD intervention conditions. The condition under which the students are grouped by instructional preference and the teachers assigned to classes randomly performed the worst on these metrics.

The data from the conditions in which the students were grouped on a dimension and the teachers matched to classes on that dimension performed notably differently. Grouping students on content location and matching a teacher on content lowered the number of students with no gain somewhat, but the number of students with a full unit of academic gain and those who

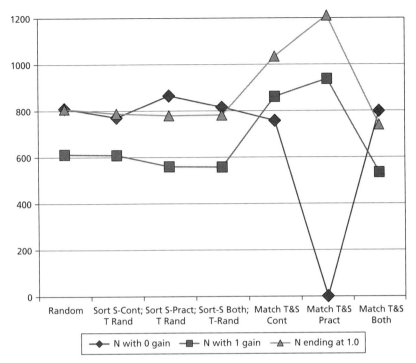

FIGURE 16.18. *Impact of Student Grouping and Teacher Assignment as Numbers of Students in Specific Final States*

concluded the academic year at the end of the course content increased substantially above random assignment of both students and teachers, by about 250 students, or 10 percent of the total sample.

Grouping students on instructional preference and matching the teacher with instructional practices to their preferences had an even more dramatic impact. The number of students with a full unit of academic gain was about three hundred more than the random assignment, and the number of students who concluded the academic year at the end of the course content location was about four hundred more. The most impressive change was the drop in the number of students with no academic gain—from more than eight hundred students in the random-assignment condition to just one student when instructional preferences and practices were matched. Clearly, the most powerful impact on student learning was produced by focusing on aligning teachers' instructional practice styles with students' preference for engagement. In a sense, this "intervention" condition recognizes the powerful impact of

TABLE 16.4. Numbers of Students in End-of-Year Categories

Condition	Students with No Academic Gain*	Students with 1 Unit Academic Gain**	Students Ending the Academic Year at Content Location 1.0**
Random (Baseline)	810	612	808
St-Content	771	609	788
St-Inst Preference	866	560	780
St-Both	816	558	782
T&S Content	758	862	1035
T&S Practice	1	938	1211
T&S Both	799	534	740

Note: *The fewer students with no gain, the better.

** The more students with a 1 unit of gain and who end the year at the end of the course content, the better.

processes related to instructional practices and student engagement but also attempts to more systematically exploit natural variation in students and in teachers so that the preferences of both are better aligned, not through PD, but through matching and assignment.

The design in which the fewest students had either a 1 unit gain or ended the year at the end of the course content was the condition under which teachers and students were matched on *both* content and instructional practice/preferences. Attempting to optimize everything resulted in definitely non-optimal results! It may be that, when students are clustered using a combination of content location and instructional preference location, the classes formed are heterogeneous enough that no single teacher was effective across that spread. As a result, some students in nearly every class receive no instruction. This paralleled the outcome of randomly assigning students and teachers to classes, despite the effort involved in creating classes with students as similar as possible.

What Did We Learn?

If one accepts the assumptions and premises of the data models presented in this chapter, the conclusion is fairly clear. Focusing time and effort on professional development for teachers is substantially less effective in increasing student achievement than thoughtfully grouping students within classes and then assigning the best-matched teachers to instruct them. Of course, in practice this would be predicated on having good, aligned measures of the relevant dimensions of teachers and students. The simulation also suggests that it is likely that targeting professional development to fill in gaps—so that all students received instruction from a teacher with both content and instructional practices that were well-aligned to the needs and preferences of the class—would continue to make things better. Nonetheless, the big initial gain is to be had from putting the right teams of teachers and students together, which we suggest is also a somewhat less expensive approach than offering PD to all teachers. Importantly, if only one dimension can be matched between students and teachers, then matching on instructional practice provides more gain in outcomes than matching on content. Again, good measures of teachers' instructional practice will be important for this type of approach to be useful and effective.

It is important to note that the definitions of the two dimensions used in these data, content and instructional practice, were fairly arbitrary. The statistical distributions underlying the samples selected were chosen so that the teachers were mostly well-placed in content, with sufficient span to teach the course as assigned. Most teachers had a fairly broad set of instructional practices at their command, and they were somewhat clustered in their location on this dimension. Most students were located close to the beginning of the course but uniformly distributed across instructional preferences. All of these decisions were made thoughtfully, in order to align with a particular set of beliefs about American education. A different model could lead to quite different results and any of a number of alternatives is possible.

The goal of this data design and analysis was not to assert that it perfectly replicates the very complex reality of teaching and learning as it occurs in schools; obviously, it does not. The data model, as complex as it is, is nowhere near as intricate as the reality of education. The intent of the study was to

1. Create a set of reasonable assumptions.

2. Describe them so that they are explicit.

3. Follow the data analytically through an "academic year" under some specific conditions.

4. See which produced the best outcomes in "student learning."

Of these steps, the second is perhaps the most important. All the assumptions that underlie the data structures in this work are made manifest. If disagreements arise about the choices made, the model can be modified and data can be generated based on the new assumption(s). One obvious benefit is that simulation-based experiments of this sort are cheaper and less difficult than working with real humans. Given careful modeling and strong assumptions, many theories can be tried and results considered before live tryouts, with their demands on people, time, money, and facilities, are implemented.

We believe that work such as that presented here targets thinking and theorizing at a level of granularity that is different from a large amount of educational research. At the micro level, a good deal of educational research focuses on the interactions of small numbers of teachers and students. At the opposite end of the spectrum, macro-level studies using econometric and/or value-added models target very high levels of abstraction. The type of simulation-based modeling presented in this chapter sits in between and invites another level of discussion. This type of work is valuable if it leads to fruitful discussions of the assumptions made and what might happen if they were modified. Our intent was to provide a mechanism for making assumptions manifest and the consequences of the assumptions direct and, in so doing, to help clarify disagreements and sharpen the discussion. We invite readers—scholars, practitioners, decision-makers—to consider this approach for their work.

NOTES

1. "Clustering" occurs when subjects are more similar to one another than subjects randomly sampled from a population. For example, students from a single classroom share common experiences. Failure of data analysis procedures to properly account for clustering can yield substantially biased estimates and incorrect statements about which effects are statistically significant.

2. Ninety percent of the teachers are drawn from a *Beta* (2, 2) distribution, re-scaled so that the endpoints are at 0.25 and 0.75. The remaining 10 percent are drawn from a *U* (–0.75, 1.75), assuring a strong probability of some teachers with extreme content locations in the sample. All teacher content width values are drawn from a *Beta* (24, 8) re-scaled so that the endpoints are at 0.25 and 1.25. All teacher content width values are drawn from a *Beta* (24, 8) re-scaled so that the endpoints are at 0.25 and 1.25. The distributions from which the values for these parameters were drawn are illustrated in Figure 16.19. The content location distribution for

90 percent of the teachers is shown in the solid dark line, the content location distribution for the remaining 10 percent of the teachers is the dashed medium line, and the content width distribution for all teachers is the light dotted line.

3. Teacher practice location is drawn from an $N(0, 1)$ distribution. Teacher practice width is drawn from a *Beta* (8, 12) distribution re-scaled to fall between 0.25 and 10. These distributions are illustrated in Figure 16.20; the location is shown in the solid dark line and the width is in the lighter dotted line.

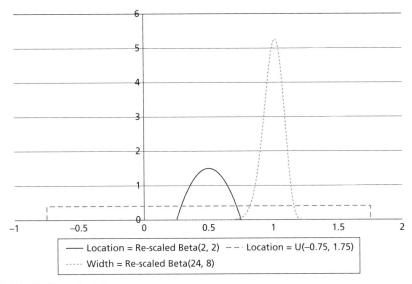

FIGURE 16.19. *Teacher Content Location Distributions*

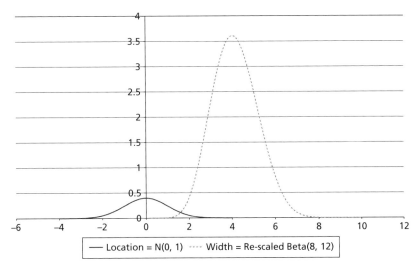

FIGURE 16.20. *Teacher Practice Location and Width Distributions*

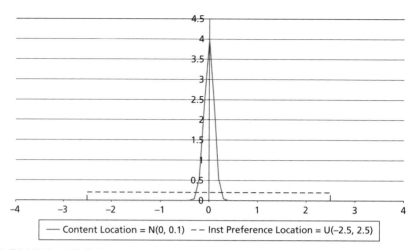

FIGURE 16.21. *Student Content Location and Instructional Preference Distributions*

4. Student content location is drawn from a $N(0, 0.1)$ distribution, shown in the solid line in Figure 16.21. Student instructional preference is drawn from a $U(-2.5, 2.5)$ distribution, shown in the darker dashed line in the figure.

REFERENCES AND ADDITIONAL RESOURCES

Allen, J. P., Pianta, R. C., Gregory, A., Mikami, A. Y., & Lun, J. (2011). An interaction-based approach to enhancing secondary school instruction and student achievement. *Science, 333,* 1034–1036.

Allen, J. P., Gregory, A., Mikami, A., Lun, J., Hamre, B., & Pianta, R. C. (in press). Observations of effective teaching in secondary school classrooms: Predicting student achievement with the CLASS-S. *Journal of School Psychology.*

Archibald, S., Coggshall, J. G., Croft, A., & Goe, L. (2011, February). *High-quality professional development for all teachers: Effectively allocating resources.* (Research and Policy Brief). Washington, DC: National Comprehensive Center for Teacher Quality.

Baker, E. L., Barton, P. E., Darling-Hammond, L., Haertel, E., Ladd, H. F., Linn, R. L., Ravitch, D., Rothstein, R., Shavelson, R., & Sheperd, L. A. (2010). *Problems with the use of student test scores to evaluate teachers.* EPI Policy Paper #278. Washington, DC: EPI.

Barker Lunn, J. C., & Ferri, E. (1970). *Streaming in the primary school: A longitudinal study of children in streamed and non-streamed junior schools.* Slough, Bucks: National Foundation for Educational Research in England and Wales.

Ball, D. L., & Cohen, D. K. (1999). Developing practices, developing practitioners: Toward a practice-based theory of professional development. In G. Sykes & L. Darling-Hammonds (Eds.), *Teaching as the learning profession: Handbook of policy and practice* (pp. 30–32). San Francisco, CA: Jossey-Bass.

Blank, R. K. (2009, June). *Effects of teacher professional development on gains in student achievement: How meta-analysis provides scientific evidence useful to education leaders.* Washington, DC: Council of Chief State School Officers.

Borko, H. (2004). Professional development and teacher learning: mapping the terrain. *Educational Researcher, 33*(8), 3–15.

Carpenter, T., Fennema, E., Peterson, P., Chiang, C., & Loef, M. (1989). Using knowledge of children's mathematics thinking in classroom teaching: An experimental study. *American Educational Research Journal, 26*(4), 499–531.

Chagnon, F., Pouliot, L., Malo, C., Gervais, M-J., & Pigeon, M. E. (2010). Comparison of determinants of research knowledge utilization in the field of child and family social services. *Implementation Science, 5*, 41. http://www.implementationscience.com/content/5/1/41

Clotfelter, C. T., Ladd, H. F., & Vigdor, J. L. (2006). Teacher-student matching and the Assessment of Teacher Effectiveness. *Journal of Human Resources, 41* (4). 778–820.

Dickson, T. K. (2002). *Assessing the effect of inquiry-based professional development on science achievement tests scores.* (doctoral dissertation, University of North Texas). (UMI No. 3076239).

Eder, D. (1981). Ability grouping as self-fulfilling prophecy: A micro-analysis of teacher-student interaction. *Sociology of Education, 54*(3): 151–162.

Estabrooks, C. A., Thompson, D. S., Lovely, J. J., & Hofmeyer, A. (2006). A guide to knowledge translation theory. *Journal of Continuing Education in the Health Professions, 26*(1), 25–36.

Freeman, C., Scafidi, B., & Sjoquist, D. L. (2002). *Racial segregation in Georgia public schools, 1994–2001: Trends, causes, and impact on teacher quality.* Paper presented at Resegregation of Southern Schools? A crucial moment in the history (and the future) of public schooling in America. University of North Carolina at Chapel Hill.

French, J. W. (1955). *The coachability of the SAT in public schools* (ETS RB 55-26). Princeton, NJ: Educational Testing Service.

Galton, F. (1886). Regression towards mediocrity in hereditary stature. *The Journal of the Anthropological Institute of Great Britain and Ireland, 15*, 246–263.

Grimshaw, J. M., Shirran, L., Thomas, R., Mowatt, G., Fraser, C., Bero, L., Grilli, R., Harvey, E., Oxman, A., & O'Brien, M. A. (2001). Changing provider behavior: an overview of systematic review of interventions. *Medical Care, 39*(8 Suppl. 2), 112–145.

Heller, J. I., Curtis, D. A., Rabe-Hesketh, S., Clarke, C., & Verbencoeur, C. J. (2007, August 29). The effects of "Math Pathways and Pitfalls" on students' mathematics achievement. National Science Foundation final report. (ERIC Document Reproduction Service No. ED498258).

Jagielski, D. A. (1991). *An analysis of student achievement in mathematics as a result of direct and indirect staff development efforts focused on the problem-solving standard of the National Council of Teachers of Mathematics.* (doctoral dissertation, Loyola University of Chicago).

Lane, M. L. (2003). *The effects of staff development on student achievement.* (doctoral dissertation, University of Denver).

Mashburn, A. J., Pianta, R. C., Hamre, B. K., Barbarin, O. A., Bryant, D., Burchinal, M., Early, D. M., & Howes, C. (2008). Measuring of classroom quality in prekindergarten and children's development of academic language and social skills. *Child Development, 79*(3), 732–749.

Measures of Effective Teaching (MET). (2012). *Gathering feedback for teaching: Combining high-quality observations with student surveys and achievement gains.* Seattle, WA: Bill & Melinda Gates Foundation.

META Associates. (2006, March). *Northeast Front Range math/science partnership (MSP) to increase teacher competence in content.* Year 2 evaluation report: January 1, 2005–December 31, 2005. Golden, CO: Author.

META Associates. (2007, March). *Northeast Front Range math/science partnership (MSP) to increase teacher competence in content.* Final evaluation report: January 1, 2004–December 31, 2006. Golden, CO: Author.

Meyer, S. J., & Sutton, J. T. (2006, October). *Linking teacher characteristics to student mathematics outcomes: Preliminary evidence of impact on teachers and students after participation in the first year of the Math in the Middle Institute Partnership.* Paper presented at the MSP Evaluation Summit II, Minneapolis, MN.

Mihaly, K., McCaffrey, D., Staiger, D., & Lockwood, J. (2013). *A composite estimator of effective teaching.* (Technical Report). Seattle, WA: Bill & Melinda Gates Foundation, Measures of Effective Teaching Project.

Newton, X., Darling-Hammond, L., Haertel, E., & Thomas, E. (2010). Value-added modeling of teacher effectiveness: An exploration of stability across models and contexts. *Educational Policy Analysis Archives, 18* (23).

Niess, M. L. (2005). *Oregon ESEA Title IIB MSP: Central Oregon consortium.* Report to the U.S. Department of Education, Mathematics and Science Partnerships. Corvallis, OR: Department of Science & Mathematics Education, Oregon State University.

No Child Left Behind Act of 2001. 107 P. L. 110. 115 Stat. 1425. 2002 Enacted H.R. 1(2002).

Odden, A., Archibald, S., Fermanich, M., & Gallagher, H. A. (2002). A cost framework for professional development. *Journal of Education Finance, 28*(1), 51–74.

Odden, A., Goetz, M., & Picus, L. O. (2008). Using available evidence to estimate the cost of educational adequacy. *Education Finance and Policy, 3*(3), 374–397.

Palmer, E. A., & Nelson, R. W. (2006, September). *Researchers in every classroom.* (Evaluation report, 2005–2006). Barnes, WI: ASPEN Associates.

Pashler, H., McDaniel, M., Rohrer, D., & Bjork R. (2008, December). Learning styles: Concepts and evidence. *Psychological Science in the Public Interest, 9,* 105–119.

Pianta, R. C. (2011, November). *Teaching children well: New evidence-based approaches to teacher professional development and training.* Washington, DC: Center for American Progress.

Rice, J. K. (2001). *Cost framework for teacher preparation and professional development.* Washington, DC: The Finance Project.

Richter, D., Kunter, M., Klusmann, U., Lüdtke, O., & Baumert, J. (2011). Professional development across the teaching career: Teachers' uptake of formal and informal learning opportunities. *Teaching and Teacher Education, 27*(1), 116–126.

Rubin, R. L., & Norman, J. T. (1992). Systematic modeling versus the learning cycle: Comparative effects of integrated science process skill achievement. *Journal of Research in Science Teaching, 29,* 715–727.

Saxe, G. B., Gearhart, M., & Nasir, N. S. (2001). Enhancing students' understanding of mathematics: A study of three contrasting approaches to professional support. *Journal of Mathematics Teacher Education, 4,* 55–79.

Scott, L. M. (2005). The effects of science teacher professional development on achievement of third-grade students in an urban school district. *Dissertation Abstracts International, 66*(04), 1268A. (UMI No. 3171980).

Sieber, R. T. (1982). The politics of middle class success in an inner-city public school. *Boston University Journal of Education, 30*(1): 30–47.

Siegle, D., & McCoach, D. (2007). Increasing student mathematics self-efficacy through teacher training. *The Journal of Secondary Gifted Education, 18*(2), 278–331.

Snippe, J. (1992, July). *Effects of instructional supervision on pupils' achievement.* Paper presented at the annual meeting of the American Educational Research Association, San Francisco, CA.

Supovitz, J. (2012, April). *The linking study—First year results: A report of the first year effects of an experimental study of the impact of feedback to teachers on teaching and learning.* Paper presented at AERA, Vancouver, BC.

Walsh-Cavazos, S. (1994). A study of the effects of a mathematics staff development module on teachers' and students' achievement. *Dissertation Abstracts International, 56*(01), 165A. (UMI No. 9517241).

Wilson, S. M. & Berne, J. (1999). Teacher learning and the acquisition of professional knowledge: An examination of research on contemporary professional development. *Review of Research in Education, 24*, 173–209.

Yoon, K. S., Duncan, T., Lee, S., W.-Y., Scarloss, B., & Shapley, K. (2007). *Reviewing the evidence on how teacher professional development affects student achievement.* (Issues & Answers Report, REL 2007-No. 033). Washington, DC: U.S. Department of Education, Institute of Educational Sciences, National Center for Education Evaluation and Regional Assistance, Regional Educational Laboratory Southwest.

APPENDIX: DETAILS ON TEACHER PROFESSIONAL DEVELOPMENT STUDIES

TABLE 16.A.1. Summary of Effect Sizes from Yoon and Others (2007) Report: PD Effect on Student Achievement

Subject Area	Number of Effect Sizes	Mean		Minimum		Maximum	
		Effect size	Percentile points	Effect size	Percentile points	Effect size	Percentile points
Science	2 (1 QED, 1 RCT)	0.51	19%	0.39	15%	0.63	23%
Mathematics	6 (2 QED, 4 RCT)	0.57	22%	−0.53	−20%	2.39	49%
Reading and ELA	12 (1 QED, 11 RCT)	0.53	20%	0.00	0%	1.11	37%
Overall	20 (3 QED, 16 RCT)	0.54	21%	0.00	0%	2.39	49%

TABLE 16.A.2. Summary of Effect Sizes from Blank (2009): PD Effect on Student Achievement

Subject	Study Design	Pre-Post Comparison		Post-Only Comparison	
		Effect size (SE)	# Effects	Effect size (SE)	# Effects
Mathematics	Mean	0.21 (0.08)	21	0.13 (0.03)	68
	RCT	0.27 (0.13)	5	0.26 (0.05)	35
	QED	0.17 (0.08)	16	0.04 (0.04)	33
Science	Mean	0.05 (0.08)	10	0.18 (0.24)	7
	RCT	0.13 (0.20)	4	−0.15 (0.28)	4
	QED	−0.02 (0.05)	6	0.63 (0.16)	3

Note: Summarized from Blank (2009).

TABLE 16.A.3. Summary of Effect Sizes by Grade Level in Mathematics: PD Effect on Student Achievement

Subject	Grade Level	Pre-Post Comparison		Post-Only Comparison	
		Effect size (SE)	# Effects	Effect size (SE)	# Effects
Mathematics	Elementary	0.32 (0.08)	15	0.27 (0.07)	30
	Middle	0.01 (0.08)	6	0.03 (0.04)	17
	High			0.11 (0.05)	21

TABLE 16.A.4. Description, Duration, Component, and Effect Size by Study in Blank (2009)

Study (N = 16)	PD	Treatment (Total) Sample Size	Hours	Months	Component	Effect Size
Carpenter & others, 1989 (RCT)	Cognitively guided instruction (CGI)	20 (40) teachers; 20 (40) students	80	4.5	Summer institute, coursework, in-service activity, study group, self-directed	0.11 to 0.69 (7 effects)
Dickson, 2002 (QED)	Inquiry institute science	4 (8) teachers; 86 (165) students	24	8	In-service, activity internship	0.10 to 0.43 (2 effects)
Heller & others, 2007 (RCT)	Mathematics pathways and pitfalls (MPP)	48 teachers; 936 (1,971) students	10	8	Summer institute, in-service activity, internship	0.27 to 0.76 (6 effects)
Jagielski, 1991 (QED)	Mathematics curriculum improvement project	43 (70) teachers; 63 (70) students	36	8	In-service activity, conference, study group	−0.42 to 0.78 (20 effects)
Lane, 2003 (QED)	Problem solving and reasoning math	12 (22) teachers; 245 (490) students	17	8	In-service activity, study group	0.08 to 0.13 (2 effects)
META Associates, 2006 (QED)	Northeast front range math/science partnership (MSP)	19 (34) teachers; 495 (767) students	120	7.5	Summer institute, in-service activity, coaching, mentoring	−1.52 to 0.22 (6 effects)
META Associates, 2007 (QED)	Northeast front range math/science partnership (MSP)	17 (40) teachers; 1,099 (2,256) students	120	7.5	Summer institute, in-service activity, coaching, mentoring	−0.19 to 0.11 (2 effects)
Meyer & Sutton, 2006 (QED)	Math in the middle institute partnership	31 (155) teachers; (7813) students	540	16	Summer institute, in-service activity courses	−0.10 to 0.13 (10 effects)

Study	Program	Sample size		Duration	Activities	Effect size range
Niess, 2005 (RCT)	High desert MSP math teaching	24 (42) teachers; 310 (985) students	304	8	Summer institute, in-service activity	−0.14 to 0.37 (4 effects)
Palmer & Nelson, 2006 (QED)	REC lesson study science	16 (43) teachers; 396 (792) students	60	8	Summer institute, study group	−0.21 to 0.11 (5 effects)
Rubin & Norman, 1992 (RCT)	Systematic modeling strategy science teaching	7 (16) teachers; 108 (324) students	30	3	Courses, in-service activity, mentoring	−0.36 to 0.64 (8 effects)
Saxe, Gearhart, & Nasir, 2001 (QED)	Integrating mathematics assessment (IMA) or collegial support (SUPP)	17 (6) teachers; 17 (23) students	41	8	Summer institute, in-service activity, study group, mentoring, internship	−1.55 to 2.54 (6 effects)
Scott, 2005 (QED)	TEAMS professional development model	3 (6) teachers; 66 (100) students	168	8	In-service activity, summer institute, conference, study group, coaching, mentoring	0.20 to 0.54 (2 effects)
Siegle & McCoach, 2007 (RCT)	Self-efficacy teaching strategies and implementation math	7 (15) teachers; 430 (872) students	2	1 day	In-service activity, coaching	0.20 to 0.22 (2 effects)
Snippe, 1992 (RCT)	National research center for career and technical education (NRCCTE) model	87 (198) teachers; 114 (274) students	14	3 days	In-service activity, study group	−0.43 to 0.79 (21 effects)
Walsh-Cavazos, 1994 (QED)	Probability, statistics, and graphing (PSG) module	4 (6) teachers; 78 (111) students	12	3 days	In-service activity	0.26 to 0.56 (2 effects)

Note: Summarized from Blank (2009). For "treatment sample size," values in parentheses represent all teachers or all students.

TABLE 16.A.5. Difference Between Top and Bottom Quartiles, Math and ELA Gains in Prior Year and in Another Section

Instrument	Mathematics		ELA	
	Students in prior year	Another section	Students in prior year	Another section
CLASS	0.08	0.10	0.03	0.01
FfT	0.06	0.07	0.03	0.02
UTOP	0.11	0.07		
MQI	0.05	0.05		
PLATO			0.01	0.04

Note: Results based on MET (2012, pp. 42–48). Data from 1,333 teachers (7,491 lessons of video) and over 44,500 students in grades 4 to 8.

TABLE 16.A.6. Summary of Effect Sizes in CLASS-MTP Studies: PD Effect on Student Achievement

Study	Setting	Design	Treatment (total) sample size	Effect sizes	Percentile points
Mashburn & others, 2008	PreK	QED	(671) teachers; (2,439) students	0.12 to 0.38	5 to 15
Allen & others, in press	Secondary	QED	Not available (currently in press; results based on description of findings in Pianta, 2011)	0.67	25
Allen & others, 2011	Secondary	RCT	39 (78) teachers; (2237) students	0.22	9
Supovitz, 2012*	Elementary	RCT	21 (50) teachers; (775) students	0.02	1

Note: *Supovitz (2012) did not use the CLASS-MTP program. They used their own observation instrument with external experts rating videos. "Treatment (total) sample size" values in parenthesis represent total sample size reported when available.

CONCLUSION

Measuring Effective Teaching—The Future Starts Now

ROBERT PIANTA AND KERRI A. KERR

As states seek to implement education reforms, assessment and evaluation of teacher performance as a vehicle for driving continued growth and improvement is top of mind for school district superintendents, school principals, teachers, union leaders, and state or federal policymakers. There is no shortage of debate and opinion on the challenges and promises of teacher performance evaluation, with interests weighing in on all sides—unions seeking protection of members from undue harm; reformers advancing a good argument for the need to use metrics as levers for workforce development and improvement; teachers pressing for fair and reliable systems and meaningful feedback and support; and parents and members of the public wanting better schools for all students. Education leaders are stuck in the middle of this swirling debate, needing to act now to set and implement new policies and protocols. Layered onto this focus on assessment for practicing teachers is the massive need, and increased attention to, competency-driven assessment and improvement of teacher-preparation programs. Accountability, evidence of impact, and data-driven decision making are guiding forces in the efforts to improve both current teachers' practice and teacher-preparation programs. In the end, assessment of teacher performance—whether it is classroom practice or student learning—has become the new normal.

EVIDENCE

In this context in which assessment plays such a prominent role, both for purposes of evaluation and, more important, for purposes of improvement, it is tremendously important that evidence guide the development of assessments along with their uses. Unfortunately, there is precious little precedent for the effective use of real performance assessment of teachers, with aligned and high-quality support and development efforts, in K–12 settings or in teacher

583

preparation. The well-documented shortcomings of the most common methods practiced for decades, such as principal drive-by observations and ratings, hiring interviews and selection procedures, and tenure reviews, all lead to the same set of related conclusions. Namely, nearly every person "passes" whatever "test" he or she faces; the "tests" themselves do not discriminate good from poor performers, and there is virtually no connection between these "tests" and student achievement, professional development, or incentives to improve. Similarly, teacher education program faculty and administrators must make decisions about (1) whom to admit, (2) how to assess their teacher candidates' progress toward becoming effective teachers, and (3) whom to recommend for state licensure as teachers. The quality of data for informing these decisions is determined, in part, by the uses to which those data are to be put. Data used to help faculty and program leaders take steps to improve a program (i.e., formative evaluation) have different standards for technical quality than the data used to determine whether a program should continue.

In fact, teacher performance assessment and its uses, as typically practiced in the field or in teacher preparation, until very recently was a non-system, characterized by a lot of moving parts of dubious value—with very little connection among them. With Race to the Top (RTTT) funding, a number of states developed systems to tie data on teacher education graduates to data on K–12 student learning. Many also developed multi-method approaches for measuring teachers' performance, including data from classroom observation, state standardized tests, and student surveys, among others. This activity, collectively characterized as the first wave of teacher performance assessment, is now well under way. Moreover, most states are now in the process of implementing the Common Core State Standards to ensure that preK–12 students graduate from high school ready for college and careers. States are implementing plans to assess the attainment of higher-order learning, and most states are in the process of implementing new standards for evaluating teachers and teacher preparation programs in light of these new standards. Thus, there has been a tremendous amount of activity in the broad domain of teacher performance assessment; however, it remains the case that teacher performance assessment is in an emergent, nascent state, with much work to be done.

Missing from the first wave of assessment and uses has been a strong evidence base for the assessments themselves, and for their various applications. One could argue that the considerable level of activity in this area has resulted in a lot of data, yet too little actionable information leading to real improvements for teachers or for students. In fact, done poorly, even the recent wave of new, "enhanced" teacher performance assessment systems could end up preserving a status quo of perfunctory measurement and improvement activities—a waste of precious time and energy that, most important, does a disservice to the teaching professionals seeking quality feedback and opportunities for professional growth and to the students relying on them for high-quality instruction. As policy trends and requirements have forced systems to rethink and redesign their evaluation systems, the need for high-quality and data-driven evidence to guide and drive improvements in these development plans creates a sizable risk that the new systems may not make the significant improvements from the status quo that are needed.

One of the reasons for the lack of evidence broadly supporting the need for better assessments, or more specifically pointing to high-quality assessment methods, appropriate uses, or professional development and training models based on assessment, is a larger lack of capacity in the field pertaining to the scientific study of effective teaching. There are big and meaningful questions driving teacher performance assessment: What methods can be used to select or hire an effective teacher? What data are useful sources of feedback for teacher improvement? What experiences in preparation or professional development cause teachers' performance to improve? Too often, the research base that might contribute to addressing these questions has been fragmented (e.g., focused on only one assessment or method), small scale (a single district or teacher preparation program, or sample of convenience), or based on weak-inference designs or instrumentation that does not scale well.

As is attested to by the various chapters in this volume, perhaps one of the greatest contributions of the MET project was its creation of a research infrastructure and database that addresses nearly every one of these weaknesses. In so doing, MET created an infrastructure for enabling the accumulation of evidence around the questions that are driving teacher performance assessment. The chapters in this volume are strategic and systematic exploitations of the MET database in the service of producing evidence to inform questions of importance to the field.

A CLUSTER OF PROMISING PERFORMANCE ASSESSMENTS

At the core of nearly every proposal and early-stage rollout of next-generation teacher performance evaluation in districts and states are combinations of a suite of indicators of effectiveness, the most common being (1) student achievement in state standards tests or other assessments, (2) an observational measure of teachers' classroom practices, and (3) student surveys. These are the cornerstones of the new wave of teacher evaluation. In method and message, each in its own way is at the core of any definition of "effective teaching" and what most teachers would identify as a marker of their professional contributions to student learning.

The chapters in this volume approached the measurement of effective teaching with the premise that the purpose of performance assessment is improvement, and not high-stakes evaluation. That is, we are interested in describing the uses of assessment data for teachers, instructional support personnel, building and district leaders, relevant policymakers, and state regulators for two key purposes: first, to inform the effective uses of assessments to drive feedback, support, and other professional development activities intended to improve teacher practice and student achievement and, second, to guide decision making regarding the components of preparation programs that contribute to teacher effectiveness, distinguishing them from those that do not, focusing attention on increasing the impact and intensity of productive preparation experiences. This frame for the use of evidence on teacher effectiveness contrasts with high-stakes evaluation, in which evidence would be used to sanction people, schools, or preparation programs.

A systematic approach to gathering, analyzing, and using assessment data should start with clear statements of what is to be measured and why; what data are to be collected and how they are to be analyzed; how decisions are to be made on the basis of the data; and how the intended and unintended consequences of the assessment activities will be evaluated. An important facet of the assessment design is the explicit alignment of the evaluations' overall goals with what is actually measured and how inferences are drawn from the data and actions taken. Thus, not only is the utility of evidence related to effective teaching predicated on measures, but it is even more dependent on the questions framed, alignment of those questions to data sources, and the quality of analysis—examining the evidence for and against certain conclusions. Importantly, for chapters in the present volume, questions drove the analysis, and results were vetted not only against standards for evidence but also by groups of contributors and editors.

Thus, in the context of important, field-generated questions about teacher performance, it is sensible that students' achievement gains, students' direct reports of their classroom experiences, and observations of teachers' classroom behavior would be components of a teacher's evaluation. Yet, like most initiatives in education reform, each of these indicators and its measurement is subject to implementation and policy challenges that, if not surfaced early and solved fairly, could hinder its intended value for both informing evaluation scores and also ultimately driving performance improvement to the benefit of teachers and students. For school and district leaders feeling pressure to make personnel decisions based on any one or combination of these indicators, these implementation challenges lead to tremendous uncertainty, even as the pace of implementation and resulting expectations for use of the new systems' emerging data continue to increase.

For the most part, the first generation of research on teacher effectiveness and its measurement informed debates on the relative merits of markers such as credentials or qualifications, experience, and the lack of utility of nearly every performance assessment currently in use. In the recent past, this second generation of assessment research shows the promising properties of value-added indicators, observations, and student surveys, although rarely have these indicators been used in the same study, with large and diverse groups of teachers, and with attention to use at scale. Although this new wave of studies has been important in laying a foundation for inquiry into teacher effects, most fail to articulate specific processes or instructional practices that may lead to student learning and other positive classroom and student outcomes, thereby failing to take into account and place value on both the statistical and diagnostic merits of various measures.

For example, although statistically strong, the value-added approach, when used alone, provides virtually no guidance to the development of ways to produce good teaching, and therefore is weak as a diagnostic and support tool. Thus, although promising, past research on teacher-effectiveness measures failed to provide guidance to the field that is both technically strong *and* practical in nature.

THE PRESENT VOLUME: MET BUILDS CAPACITY FOR EVIDENCE IN APPLIED DECISION MAKING

The MET project sought to move the field forward by providing an evidence base from which to build more effective and rigorous teacher evaluation and support systems, while also tending to the practical questions of implementation of import to education leaders and policymakers. MET findings to date paint a picture supporting the use of multiple measures for assessing teacher effectiveness. While student achievement scores continue to be a strong predictor of a teacher's performance with other students, other indicators, such as classroom observation scores and student survey results, also provide reliable data. When measures are combined, predictive power and reliability improve, as do practitioners' ability to use results to drive feedback and improvement conversations with teachers. Other findings point to the importance of the type of student assessment used when measuring student gains, and to a number of technical results pertaining to properties of observation and training protocols that maximize reliability.

Legislation at the federal, state, and local levels increasingly promotes the formation of teacher evaluation systems that can provide a well-rounded appraisal of a teacher's instruction, including both observational measures of the quality of instruction and quantifiable impacts on students' learning. An effective evaluation and feedback system should provide the basis for making decisions about facets of human capital development, such as professional development or merit pay.

In creating comprehensive evaluation systems, school districts are tasked with building fair *and* rigorous systems, often from the ground up, that incorporate multiple measures—often in varying combinations and weights. District leaders face numerous decisions in this work, including determining which of many protocols to use, how best to determine whether their measures of choice correspond to broader aims to improve student learning, how to determine trigger points for certain contingencies (e.g., supplementary professional development or merit pay), and which of the myriad professional development programs to utilize, among other decisions.

Education decision-makers face a host of complex challenges and trade-offs. Too often, they have little or no evidence upon which to base decisions of great consequence—either at the level of individuals (e.g., should a particular teacher be hired or tenured, or enrolled in specific professional development?) or in the aggregate (e.g., in what ways do varying categories of performance relate to resources available for improvement?). It is in this domain of applied decision making based on evidence that MET promises to have perhaps its greatest influence. As illustrated in the chapters in this volume, this influence is not through a set of prescriptions for policy and practice, but rather as a resource for the field that enables the scientific study of effective teaching and its correlates: examples of which abound in the present volume—simulations of decision-making contingencies; linkages between school working conditions and teacher performance; and the role of content or grade level or assessment method on estimates of teacher performance. These are critical issues faced by nearly every school district or state decision-maker in the country. Heretofore, there was no way of investigating these questions in a timely manner to provide guidance on trade-offs, risks, or promises. For the first time, with MET, qualified researchers working for or with districts can access a database and subject it to the questions they face every day. High-stakes decisions can at least be simulated, and perhaps improved, by low-stakes analysis.

The present volume extends and enriches the information available from MET's existing reports by fully utilizing this rich data source and shifting to focus more squarely on questions of interest to practitioners and decision-makers in the field. It is intended to have widespread interest and applicability, relevant to district and state decision-makers and those in charge of large scale implementation of teacher evaluation systems. In so doing, the volume fills a very large void in the current spectrum of decision making and evidence in teacher performance assessment—a data-driven, research-grounded response to issues of pressing importance to practitioners.

Just as no single assessment adequately captures all of a teacher's performance or value, no single chapter in this volume captures the complexity of performance assessment and its application to decision making in the field. No doubt readers will want to investigate and explore the chapters with direct relevance to problems they themselves face. But perhaps the real value of this volume, and the MET project's data going forward, is as a set of existence proofs demonstrating that questions of relevance to decision-makers in the field can actually be addressed with contemporary data collected with rigor at scale. And they provide leverage on challenges that to this point have seemed insurmountable: How can someone measure, even quantify, something as important and complex as teaching? And, if we could measure teaching, what would be the consequences for teachers, children, and schools of varying approaches to measurement? Going forward, the work presented in this volume can serve as a set of templates for investigation of the rich questions pressing on the field.

Leaders facing challenging, complex, high-stakes decisions can use these chapters or, better yet, partner with others to conduct analyses better aligned to the specific questions and decisions they face. No longer a data-collection enterprise, MET is now a laboratory for districts and states to simulate the consequences of decision making. In a very unique way, MET contributes to the scientific basis for making applied decisions in education, in much the same way as major scientific studies in other areas such as health care, for example, guide decisions about nutrition, exercise, or disease prevention. Perhaps most important, the chapters in this volume, and the MET project at large, serve as exemplars to secure the study of teaching as a focus of scientific study, a legacy that can foster advances for what might be the most critical and important resource in public education—our nation's teachers.

AUTHOR INDEX

SUBJECT INDEX

Page references followed by *fig* indicate an illustrated figure; followed by *t* indicate a table.